Gail Wagner, HT
776-9125

Advanced Abnormal Child Psychology

Advanced Abnormal Child Psychology

Edited by

Michel Hersen
Nova Southeastern University
Robert T. Ammerman
Western Pennsylvania School for Blind Children

LAWRENCE ERLBAUM ASSOCIATES, PUBLISHERS
1995   **Hillsdale, New Jersey**   **Hove, UK**

Lawrence Erlbaum Associates, Inc., Publishers
365 Broadway
Hillsdale, New Jersey 07642

Cover design by Mairav Salomon-Dekel

Library of Congress Cataloging-in-Publication Data

Advanced abnormal child psychology / edited by Michel Hersen, Robert
T. Ammerman.
    p. cm.
  ISBN 0-8058-1203-2 (cloth : acid-free paper). — ISBN
0-8058-1204-0 (paper : acid-free paper)
  1. Child psychopathology. 2. Child psychiatry. I. Hersen,
Michel.   II. Ammerman, Robert T.
RJ499.A327 1995
618.92′89 — dc20   94-6098
                                                CIP

Printed in the United States of America
10 9 8 7 6 5 4 3 2 1

To Vicki, Jonathan, and Nathaniel
—*Michel Hersen*

To Ruth and Linwood Benner, Sr.
—*Robert T. Ammerman*

Contents

Preface

There was a time when abnormal child psychology was the stepchild of abnormal psychology, with perhaps one or two chapters in an entire advanced textbook devoted to issues concerning children. Given the explosive amount of new material in child psychology in general since the 1980s, the stepchild status obviously is no longer the case. Indeed, many new journals devoted to abnormal child psychology have made their appearance on library bookshelves. Although several advanced textbooks on abnormal child psychology have also been published over the years, none, in our opinion, has had sufficient breadth to show the advanced undergraduate and beginning graduate student in the field the extent of our existing knowledge base. It is to this end that we undertook the task of assembling the present text, integrating both empirical and clinical issues. Indeed, throughout we have endeavored to maintain the spirit of empiricism that fortunately now pervades the field.

Advanced Abnormal Child Psychology is divided into three parts, each preceded by a unifying editorial introduction. Part I (General Issues) contains the requisite material to enable the student to have a firm grounding so that the subsequent information presented in parts II and III is more meaningful. Chapter 1 (Historical Overview) reviews the historical developments, essentially documenting both the neglect and abuse that children suffered at the hands of society, well into the 20th century. Chapter 2 (Diagnosis and Classification) reviews the salient issues relating to classification and diagnosis of childhood disorders, including new developments in *DSM–IV*. Chapter 3 (Epidemiologic Considerations) familiarizes the student with epidemiologic principles. Chapter 4 (Development and Psychopathology) underscores how developmental psychopathology provides a theoretical framework that can guide research and clinical efforts. Chapter 5 (Psychophysiological Determinants) looks at psychophysiological determinants of behavior, with special attention focused on childhood autism, Attention Deficit Disorder, and Antisocial/Conduct Disorder. Chapter 6 (Familial Determinants) carefully looks at the evidence detailing familial factors that are contributory to child psychopathology. Finally, chapter 7 (Research Strategies in Child Psychopathology) reviews the theoretical, methodological, and practical considerations involved in determining the course a researcher will take when investigating a problem in child psychopathology.

Part II (Assessment and Treatment), often given short shrift in textbooks, is thoroughly discussed from an empirical perspective and appears early in the book. Chapter 8 (Intellectual and Cognitive Assessment), with a particular emphasis on traditional intelligence tests, provides an in-depth coverage of test development, administration, and interpretation of results. Chapter 9 (Behavioral Assessment) contrasts the philosophical and procedural differences between behavioral and other forms of psychological assessment. Chapter 10 (Behavioral Treatment) reviews the most commonly used behavioral techniques. Multiple case examples are provided to illustrate how behavioral treatments are implemented. Chapter 11 (Pharmacological Treatment) examines specific psychiatric disorders in which pharmacotherapy shows promise, including conduct disorders, depression, and developmental disorders. The final chapter in part II (chapter 12, Community and Prevention) reviews various types of preventive interventions, concluding with an illustration of prevention principles involving Conduct Disorder and major depression.

Part III (Description of the Disorders) has 10 chapters with an identical organizational structure, including treatment for the specific disorders and numerous case examples. Such case illustrations should appeal to the student and make the material much more salient. Listed below is the specific format for each chapter in part III:

1. Clinical Descriptions
2. Causes of the Disorder(s)
3. Course of the Disorder(s)
4. Familial Contributions
5. Psychophysiological and Genetic Influences
6. Current Treatments (with Case Illustrations)
7. Summary

In light of the wealth of information that now abounds in the field of abnormal child psychology, we opted to have respective experts in the area contribute to the effort. We thank our eminent contributors and colleagues for sharing with us and subsequent readers their views on what has been accomplished and where the field is going. Next, we thank Burt G. Boulton, Ann Huber, Angela Dodson, and Christine Ryan for their technical contributions to the book. Finally, but hardly least of all, we thank Larry Erlbaum and Hollis Heimbouch for their encouragement and good cheer in spite of some of the inevitable delays encountered when bringing to fruition a multi-authored textbook.

Michel Hersen
Robert T. Ammerman

Part I

General Issues

When compared with the rest of abnormal psychology, the history of abnormal child psychology is relatively brief. Indeed, the major findings in the field can only be traced to the last three to four decades. And within that time span, the most exciting developments have taken place in the past 20 years. Although abnormal child psychology is a relatively new subdiscipline, it already has had numerous influences that include developmental psychology, epidemiology, psychophysiology, genetics, psychopathology, and the data-based approaches to assessment, diagnosis, and treatment. Overall, the influences have been of an empirical nature. In a very short time, the exponential growth of this subdiscipline has made the area complex. Given the extent of such complexity, we believe that the student requires a firm grounding in the basics before he or she can have a full understanding of the nuances of psychopathology and its treatment interventions.

In this part of the text, we provide the reader with an overview of advanced abnormal child psychology, outlining the contributions from a variety of directions. First, in chapter 1, Brad Donohue, Michel Hersen, and Robert T. Ammerman review the historical developments, essentially documenting both the neglect and abuse that children suffered at the hands of society, well into the 20th century. The authors describe historical antecedents that led to the discipline of child psychology, consider the status of contemporary psychotherapies, review the short history of child psychopharmacology, and look at the progression of behavioral classification and diagnostic classification.

In chapter 2, Irwin D. Waldman and Scott O. Lilienfeld review the salient issues relating to classification and diagnosis of childhood disorders, including new developments in DSM-IV. Criticisms of the psychiatric diagnostic scheme are considered, but the authors document the improvements in reliability and validity of DSM-III and DSM-III-R. Also discussed are the relations among diagnostic entities and the best methods for evaluating categorization of children at the empirical level.

In chapter 3, Gale A. Richardson, Peggy McGaughey, and Nancy L. Day familiarize the student with epidemiologic principles. Classic studies in the field are reviewed. Critical issues in child psychiatric epidemiology are addressed, such as comorbidity (i.e., multiple diagnoses), definitions of psychopathology, developmental issues, and use of multiple informants to reach diagnostic conclusions.

In chapter 4, Shelley Ross and Kay D. Jennings provide an overview of development and psychopathology. The authors underscore how developmental psychopathology provides a theoretical framework that can guide research and clinical efforts. Throughout this chapter the importance of defining normal and abnormal behavior from an age perspective, adaptation and maladaptation, and continuity and discontinuity is emphasized.

In chapter 5, Rafael Klorman looks at psychophysiological determinants of behavior, with special attention focused on childhood autism, attention deficit disorder, and antisocial/conduct disorder. Autonomic measures most frequently studied have been heart rate and skin conductance (referred to as GSR). Researchers have studied autonomic reactivity in order to classify subjects on a continuum (e.g., sleep/drowsiness to alertness/excitement). Also, studies have examined moment-to-moment reaction of subjects to specific stimuli, looking at the emotional significance of such stimuli. The author brings the reader's attention to the exciting developments in the field, such as the recent finding showing that antisocial subjects may display heightened information processing.

In chapter 6, David Reitman and Alan M. Gross carefully look at the evidence detailing familial factors that are contributory to child psychopathology. In so doing they dispel myths about the field and point out the myriad of factors that directly or indirectly influence family management. Included are various forms of adult psychopathology, alcohol and drug abuse, divorce, and extrafamilial stressors. Given the age of the child, his or her vulnerability to such stressors will differ. The authors underscore how in the future additional studies will be required to disentangle parental factors and child characteristics that produce psychopathology.

Finally, in chapter 7, Eric J. Mash and Gloria L. Krahn review the theoretical, methodological, and practical considerations involved in determining the course a researcher will take when investigating a problem in child psychopathology. The research endeavor has been likened to a process that follows a number of stages. Included are considerations of sampling, design selection, measurement, and data analysis, in addition to pragmatic concerns. Research areas most often studied involve the determinants of childhood disorders, risk and protective factors, and treatment and prevention.

Chapter 1

Historical Overview

Brad Donohue
Michel Hersen
Nova Southeastern University

Robert T. Ammerman
Western Pennsylvania School for Blind Children

The study of abnormal child psychology is of recent origin. Historically children have been treated as miniature adults, with few, if any, legal rights to protect themselves from unfair labor practices, neglect, and physical abuse. Throughout much of history, children have been regarded solely for their economic worth and family servitude. In fact, it was not until the 1800s that children with handicaps or deformities were no longer publicly scorned or rejected as "useless burdens" to society. Several historical events have brought about better treatment for children, including writings of great philosophers, success of early hospitals that stressed "humane" treatment, legislation protecting children's rights, emergence of child guidance clinics, scientific study of child development, and empirical evaluation of child psychotherapies.

Our introductory chapter (a) examines the long historical neglect of children in many societies, (b) discusses major historical antecedents that have led to the science of child psychology, (c) briefly examines the etiology and current status of major contemporary psychotherapies, (d) reviews the brief history of child psychopharmacology, and (e) examines the progression of behavioral classification and diagnostic categorizing with children.

HISTORY OF THE TREATMENT OF CHILDREN

Ancient Greece

In ancient Greece, physical strength and intelligence were highly esteemed. The great philosophers Plato and Aristotle encouraged proper childhood education and practical experiences for attainment of maturity and success in later vocation. These philosophers helped to create a *zeitgeist* that stressed education, athletics, and skills training for the brightest boys in Greece. Girls in this society assumed the primary role of childbearers. However, children with mental or physical handicaps were publicly scorned by society. Less frequently, children with mental retardation and psychopathology were put to death in a practice called *infanticide* or abandonment to rid the parents and state of the economic burden.

Roman Empire

Similar to the ancient Greek society, children in the Roman empire who were regarded with value to the family were educated in art, poetry, and encouraged to participate in sporting events. However, whereas in the Greek society the child's destiny was largely determined by the father and the state, during the Roman Empire the father had full control over the fate of his children. Decisions as to whether the child would be sold as a slave, abandoned, or slain depended on his or her value to the family. Children with disabilities and deformities were disdained by society, as they brought about embarrassment and shame to the family.

Middle Ages (500–1300)

The importance of development and education for children was overlooked during the Middle Ages, even for those with great promise. Whereas the brightest children were taught to embellish their talents in earlier Greek and Roman societies, during the Middle Ages even the most talented children were neglected. There were no special children's games or literature (Aries, 1962). Paintings of children during these times depicted them in adult clothing with adult mannerisms.

Lack of concern for childhood development and education was consistent with the pervasive neglect and physical abuse of this era. Children were legally sold into slavery before the age of 7, and severe beatings were commonly accepted. Many children served their life in a monastery or convent in order to better the soul of their parents. To improve economic stability in the family, children often started their vocational career at age 6 and worked up to 14 hours a day. Some children entered into marriage contracts at 12 years of age to ensure their continued economic worth.

Aries (1962) speculated that parents purposely did not become attached to their children because of a high child mortality rate at that time. During this time in history, children had 3 to 1 odds of reaching the age of 5 (Kessen, 1965). High mortality rates were most likely due to long hours in poor working conditions. Epidemics, malnutrition, and childhood disease were additional contributors to the high child mortality rate. Although the Catholic Church considered the practice of infanticide a sin (Aries, 1962), the number of unwanted, illegitimate, or female children who were killed was high during the Middle Ages (holmes & Morrison, 1979).

During the Spanish Inquisition, the Catholic Church believed that bizarre behavior was the result of Satanic possession and evil spirits. Calvin and Luther condemned the mentally retarded as "filled with Satan." Children evincing psychopathology were easy targets for ridicule and harsh treatment. Ways of cleansing children of evil spirits included rejection, humiliation, and imprisonment. Parents often reported their children to public officials in order to avoid their own condemnation, even though they knew that this would likely result in their children being tortured or burned at the stake.

The Renaissance (1300–1600)

Historically the Renaissance was a period of scientific and societal enlightenment. For children, however, such enlightenment was minimal and slow to develop. It was not until the Renaissance that problems common to children were comprehensively addressed in the literature. Thomas Phaire's *The Boke of Chyldren* was written in 1545 and was the first publication to address pediatric problems, such as nocturnal enuresis and nightmares. It is interesting to note that this "treatment" book was published during a time in which widespread neglect and abuse of children would indicate that adults were not concerned with such child anguish. The motivation, however, was probably borne of the idea that child psychopathology was a nuisance to the parent, rather than the idea of helping the child per se. Nevertheless, it does demonstrate that during the Renaissance child psychopathology became a concern.

Treatment of children during the Renaissance initially was largely as it had been in the Middle Ages. Continuing until the 1600s, child psychopathology was believed to be the result of demonic possession. Physical punishment was still widely used by both the poor and the rich. For example, Louis XIII was whipped throughout his childhood to the extent that he experienced nightmares about these beatings throughout his adulthood (deMause, 1974). However, some worthy changes did occur during this time period. Infanticide was rebuked and replaced with the then acceptable practice of abandonment of the child to an orphanage or the Church. Although this practice appears more merciful than infanticide, most abandoned children died before reaching puberty in the orphanage. Unabandoned children did not fare much better, with mortality rates indicating that one of every three children born during this time did not live to adulthood. Parent–child attachment was further removed with the employment of wet nurses to relieve wealthy mothers of many of their parental duties. In fact, as few as 3% of the infants born in Paris in the 1600s were nursed by their own mothers (deMause, 1974).

By the late 1600s, however, it became customary for European parents to show affection and play with their children, particularly in the case of those who were affluent. Although such play was more an amusement for parents, it nevertheless led to greater attachment and the more benign treatment of children in Europe.

Colonial America (1600–1700)

Whereas Europe at this time began to promote nurturant treatment, colonial America continued to treat children abusively. Children were treated and appraised as economic pawns. During colonial expansion of America, children were often imprisoned, punished, or killed if they refused to be transported from England to the New World, where they were to be exploited for their labor. Once in the New World, these children, many under the age of 6, were forced to work on farms and shops. Young girls sometimes under 12 years old, known as "tobacco brides," were sent to the American settlers to reduce discontent. Laws were established to give fathers total control of the welfare of their children. For example, the 1654 Stubborn Child Law allowed a parent to put "stubborn" children to death for noncompliance. Public health officials today have estimated that in colonial America, as many as two thirds of children died before they were 4 years old (Duffy, 1976). Deaths were due to the harsh conditions of the

New World (e.g., disease, starvation, "toughening" infants with icy baths, severe beatings).

Europe and America (1700–1900)

Conditions for children began to improve in the 1700s. However, high morbidity rates and poor treatment were still common among children, particularly with the poor. In the 18th century, children born in London had only a 50% chance of reaching their fifth birthday. Poor children typically worked in factories as cheap labor to help their families survive. Although many were opposed, a bill was submitted that prohibited children from the ages of 9 to 13 to work more than 48 hours a week and also prohibited children 13 to 18 years old from working more than 68 hours per week. As judged by the standards of today, this bill appears harsh. However, it was a substantial improvement at that time.

In the late 1600s and 1700s, there was a resurgence of the organic disease model that was combined with humane treatment of the mentally ill. The writings of Locke and Rousseau helped to create this resurgence. Both Locke and Rousseau maintained detailed records of the development of their own children. These published findings helped to create public concern about child development and education. Locke theorized (*tabula rasa*, or blank slate) that adulthood is a product of the learning that occurs during childhood. Consistent with this theory, Locke encouraged use of toys and pictures to stimulate physical and intellectual growth during childhood. Jean Jacques Rousseau, like Locke, believed that a healthy learning environment during childhood was important for normal development. The writings of Locke and Rousseau brought about public desire to educate children and paved the way for compulsory education and humane treatments for children.

In 1792, Pinel's unchaining of the mentally ill at the Bicêtre Hospital in Paris reflected the prevailing societal attitude towards the mentally ill of the time. Pinel believed that cruel treatments (e.g., dunking in water and bloodletting) exacerbated mental illness. He attributed mental illnesses to organic factors that could be ameliorated with humane treatments that stressed kindness. His belief was supported when the patients of the Bicêtre Hospital demonstrated consistent behavioral improvements after he instructed the staff to unchain and subsequently treat them with benevolence.

Independent of Pinel, William Tuke established the York Retreat to care for the mentally ill in England at about the same time. York purposely called his facility a "retreat" because he wanted to avoid the stigma associated with the traditional terminology "asylum." The York Retreat involved a family-like setting in which mentally ill persons could live, exercise, and work in a therapeutic environment.

During the early 1800s, American advocates of moral treatment established several facilities resembling the York Retreat. However, persons receiving these treatments were generally affluent adults. The poor were unaware and unable to afford such treatment facilities. In addition, children were rarely considered for mental health care at these more costly facilities and, as a result, were restricted to the more crude "traditional" treatments.

Benjamin Rush, the first American psychiatrist, used Tuke's and Pinel's model of humane treatment at the Pennsylvania Hospital. While at the Pennsylvania Hospital, Rush became one of the first persons to study children. He suggested that children were less likely than adults to suffer from mental illness because their brains were too unstable to retain whatever mental phenomena caused insanity. During his studies, Rush became the first person to describe cholera symptoms in infants.

Other developments in the medical field created an environment conducive to change for the betterment of child welfare in the late 1800s. Hospital-based interventions for children's medical and psychological conditions were implemented for the first time. Charles Caldwell wrote the first medical degree dissertation on pediatrics. The first medical textbooks specializing in child psychopathology were published in Germany, France, and Britain.

The combined efforts of Rousseau, Locke, Pinel, Rush, and Tuke led to the belief that sensory stimulation, or lack of stimulation, during childhood was a primary determinant of later development. For the first time "psychological" factors were promoted as a means of beneficially affecting the mentally ill. This concept was different from the previous belief that behavioral problems were caused by chronic organic factors that were untreatable psychologically.

After viewing "insane" children in cages and cellars during the mid 1800s, Dorothea Dix formerly requested the state legislature to increase federal funding to treatment centers that supported moral treatment of children. Her efforts resulted in establishment of approximately 30 new mental hospitals that emphasized moral treatment with the mentally ill. However, these facilities soon became overcrowded due to insufficient governmental funding, and moral treatment subsequently was often neglected (Achenbach, 1974).

Compulsory Education

During the late 1800's, the first precision studies of the child-study movement were performed. G. Stanley Hall was the originator of the child study movement and is responsible for establishment of the Illinois Society of Child Study. He studied motor and emotional development of children by devising the "baby bibliography." His work consisted of sending questionnaires to parents, teachers, mental health professionals, and children about various areas of child development (e.g., fears, dreams, motor functioning) in order to obtain normative data. In doing so, he was the first person to use developmental norms that allowed comparisons between normal and abnormal child developmental abilities. He also encouraged others to monitor development of children and consider the stages of development when interacting with children. Hall founded the first scholarly journal devoted to pediatric development, entitled *Pedagogical Seminary*. After performing much of his research on child developmental stages, he wrote a two-volume text entitled *Adolescence: Its Psychology and Its Relations to Physiology, Anthropology, Sociology, Sex, Crime, Religion and Education* (Hall, 1904) as a further attempt to understand the tasks, transitions, and experiences encountered by children of this age range. This was the first written document to define "adolescence" as a unique stage of development.

The child study movement facilitated growth of compulsory education. Public schools in the United States were rich in ethnic and cultural diversity during the late 1800s to early 1900s. As a result of such diversity, the public school system took on the role of teaching English and social standards to thousands of immigrant children. An increase in student enrollment restricted the time that public school teachers were available to assist students with learning disabilities. In order to serve this population, further educational alternative programs were established to accommodate children who were not able to adapt to regular school programs (e.g., special classes, ungraded programs, tutorial sessions, truancy classes). Many of these programs were implemented into special schools offering training to employees and volunteer public education teachers in the late 1800s. Nearly 200 cities instituted special schools to educate difficult pupils at the turn of the century. The poor and ethnic minorities were disproportionately represented in these alternative schools, and issues related to labeling and discrimination were noted in the literature of the times. By the early 1930s, many colleges included departments for special education, and some states required certification to teach special education to children with intellectual, behavioral, or physical disabilities.

At about the same time that special education was being established for children with learning difficulties, Edouard Seguin began to treat the mentally retarded in the world renowned Bicêtre Hospital. His work resulted in the study of education with the mentally retarded. Seguin's "physiological method" consisted of stimulating the central nervous system while teaching various visual and motor activities. Shortly after Seguin, schools for mentally retarded individuals were established throughout Europe and America. Unfortunately, lack of effective treatments resulted in the pessimistic attitude that most children with retardation would have to remain in custodial care for the rest of their lives.

Early 1900s

In 1905, Herbart was one of the first to introduce the idea that children pass through distinct stages of development. The idea of developmental stages was bolstered by Binet's concept of "mental age," which was defined as the highest age level at which a child could perform adequately. Although Galton was the first to systematically study human intelligence, Albert Binet performed the first measurements of intelligence with children. With increased emphasis on educating children, the French Ministry of Education in the late 1800s requested that Binet attempt to develop an examination that could predict school performance. In response to this request, Binet developed a test that consisted of a collection of verbal and motor tasks that assessed "intelligence." Based on responses of dozens of children, he devised an objective and standardized way to detect deviance from normal intellectual functioning. In 1916, this test was adapted by Lewis Terman of Stanford University for use with American children. The Stanford–Binet Scale was one of the first standardized instruments to compare each child's performance with standardized norms at different age ranges. Terman divided the test score (mental age) by the chronological age to yield the child's intelligence quotient or IQ. Development of this test assisted with identification of learning problems in school. The Stanford–Binet also facilitated the large-scale requirement of education for all children not demonstrating intellectual disabilities. The discriminative ability of the Stanford–Binet test influenced several scientists in the 1920s to begin longitudinal studies, using large numbers of children to produce standard norms on physical, intellectual, emotional, and behavioral characteristics.

Starting in the late 1800s, political organizations that promoted the welfare of children first began to appear. These organizations helped to facilitate federal funding to treatment centers that demonstrated moral treatment of child psychopathology. In addition, these organizations created public sentiment that influenced establishment of child protection laws. In 1870, the American Society for the Prevention of Cruelty of Animals brought a case of child abuse to court for the first time, claiming that the child had the same rights as other animals (Brown, Rox, & Hubbard, 1974). The Society for the Prevention of Cruelty to Children was founded in the late 1800s in England and the United States. Establishment of this organization was largely a result of high rates of child mortality due to child abuse at this time. Public responsibility for delinquent children was expedited with correctional institutions in America, such as the Board of Charities and Corrections in Massachusetts. In 1909, President Theodore Roosevelt organized the first White House Conference on Children. His political reform movement condemned various cruelties perpetrated by adults in society (e.g., that children should be removed from their home solely on the basis of their family's poverty). Federal support was provided for implementation of the Children's Bureau in 1912 to protect rights and welfare of children and to provide aid to dependent children. Volunteer services, such as the Child Welfare League of America, were also formed about this time. Federally funded child development institutes in the United States were initiated after the Iowa Child Welfare Research Station was founded in 1916. These child development institutes were established in Ohio, New York, Connecticut, Minnesota, and California to study the cognitive and behavioral development of children.

In 1922, the National Committee of Mental Hygiene helped to promote the idea that childhood difficulties led to later mental illness. Adolph Meyer, a psychiatrist and member of the National Committee on Mental Hygiene, promoted the consideration of child psychopathology and requested that psychiatrists be placed in the school system to work with teachers to prevent problems that would interfere with school performance.

After the Wages and Hours Bill was passed in 1938, children under 16 years of age were no longer allowed to work in hazardous occupations. Child protection laws have continued into the latter 20th century.

The Juvenile Justice Delinquency Prevention Act implemented in 1974 was the catalyst for community-based diversion programs. With this act, federal funding was made available to deinstitutionalize juvenile status offenders. The goal of the act was to place juvenile offenders in community-based services to remove the stigma of court records, prevent association with other more chronic offenders, and promote rehabilitation.

In 1975, the Education for All Handicapped Children Act (Public Law 94–142) guaranteed the right of public education for all handicapped children. This law stated that if a state is to receive federal funds supporting special education, all handicapped children between the ages of 3 and 21 must have the provision of free education.

Child Guidance Clinics

Treatment centers began to emerge for children in the early 1900s. The early clinics focused on educational problems, social dysfunction, and behavioral disorders. The first psychology clinic was established in 1896 at the University of Pennsylvania by Lightner Witmer. This was the initial clinic to primarily assess, treat, and study childhood difficulties relevant to school performance, such as stuttering, spelling, and intellectual difficulties. Target populations were mentally retarded individuals, gifted children with speech impediments, and those requiring vocational adjustment. Empirically derived interventions were educational, directive, and based on principles of perception and learning. The success of the early psychology clinics in America helped to create emergence of the child guidance clinics, which aimed at rehabilitation rather than punishment.

In 1908, Clifford Beers wrote *A Mind that Found Itself*. This autobiography described the harsh treatment he had received while he was a patient in a psychiatric hospital. His book focused attention on the inhumane treatment of psychiatric patients who were hospitalized in mental asylums. Public compassion for the mentally ill resulting from publication of this book helped Clifford Beers, Adolph Meyer, and others to establish the National Committee for Mental Hygiene in 1909. This organization educated the public about mental illness, so there was early identification of problems in addition to improved treatment conditions in psychiatric hopitals. The committee supported research surveys on children's mental health. After reviewing the research, this organization concluded (a) that children experienced many more psychological problems than previously thought, (b) that mental health services for children were totally inadequate, and (c) that behavioral disorders for children were not hopeless (Rie, 1971).

The mental hygiene movement paved the way for child guidance clinics. Child guidance clinics were largely the result of the efforts of William Healy. In 1909, William Healy established the Juvenile Psychopathic Institute, which primarily focused on the etiology, prevention, and treatment of court-referred juvenile delinquents as an aid to the Cook County courts. Healy and his wife, Augusta Bronner, later developed the Judge Baker Guidance Center in Boston, which followed the same model. Healy emphasized the social-affective aspects of development and was largely responsible for the beginning of the child guidance movement.

The purpose of these clinics was to diagnose and provide treatment recommendations for children who were referred by the juvenile court system. Early child guidance clinics were criticized by analytic theorists because of the inability of the psychoeducational focus to cope with internalized neurotic problems of children. In response to this criticism, psychiatrists were incorporated into teams consisting of psychologists and social workers. The psychiatrist directed the team and attempted to modify basic underlying pathological personality structures by gaining insight and understanding. The psychologist performed psychological testing, and the social worker performed assessments with parents and provided guidance for the youths. This "holy trinity" emphasized the role of individual traits and social influences on behavior.

The Commonwealth Fund Report of 1921 provided governmental funding for the development of child guidance clinics across the country. Child guidance clinics were established in many teaching hospitals and laboratories. Referrals to these clinics typically came from juvenile courts, but family and school referrals were also made. The court system sent most juvenile offenders to state outpatient clinics. Court recommendations sometimes included referrals to child youth organizations, such as the YMCA. These organizations were established to provide juveniles with prosocial activities to reduce delinquency rates that had been exacerbated with increased urbanization.

The burden of increased caseloads and limited funding for child guidance clinics contributed to advocation of education as a means to promote better mental health in America. Mental health professionals from child guidance clinics helped to teach parents, teachers, court workers, and social workers in mental health hygiene. By 1932, there were over 200 clinics in America.

The earliest investigative studies of child psychotherapy effectiveness were performed at the child guidance clinics during the 1930s and 1940s. Such investigations revealed that some 70% to 80% of children evaluated demonstrated significant improvement. But these investigations were based exclusively on therapists' judgments of improvement and, of course, lacked controlled comparison conditions.

Currently, most child guidance clinics have been incorporated into broad based mental health centers. In addition to these centers there has been a dramatic increase in the number of programs offering training in clinical child psychology. From the mid-1970s to the early 1980s, there has been an increase from 12 programs to 36 "formal" and 29 "informal" programs. This trend has continued into the 1990s but at a slower rate (Shirk & Phillips, 1991; Tuma, 1990).

CURRENT CHILD PSYCHOTHERAPIES

Psychoanalytic Therapies for Children

In 1915, Hermine von Hug-Hellmuth modified adult psychoanalysis for use with children employing drawings and play techniques. Approximately 10 years later, publication of Anna Freud and Melanie Klein's work established child psychoanalysis as a discipline. Child psychoanalysis was easily adopted by most psychiatrists working in America's child guidance clinics. Differences in basic analytic concepts led to more specialized methods (e.g., child psychoanalysis proper, expressive child psychotherapy, supportive psychotherapy, and expressive–supportive psychotherapy). Common to most psychoanalytic therapies for children is the attempt to bring unconscious conflicts into conscious awareness through art and play. With play therapy, the therapist attempts to establish an alliance with the child through use of toys and games. In this manner, the unthreatened child feels comfortable expressing feelings without criticism and purportedly learns to manage feelings and develop adaptive abilities, while experiencing self-acceptance. Dynamically oriented child psychotherapists typically perform therapy in "play therapy rooms," but sessions are less frequent than with adult counterparts. With greater understanding of child development, the analytic psychotherapies were applied to a wider variety of disorders. From the mid-1950s to the mid-1960s, psychodynamically oriented psychotherapies were considered to be the only accepted strategies in residential settings. However, in general, the nondirective therapies appear to be less successful than their behavioral counterparts (Gelfand, Jenson, & Drew, 1982). Indeed, the behavioral strategies, as a consequence of empirical support, are now routinely applied in clinical settings (Kendall, 1991; Kratochwill & Morris, 1991).

Behavioral Psychotherapies for Children

Lightner Witmer's emphasis on observed behavior as opposed to inferred internal phenomena paved the way for the empirical evaluation of child psychotherapies. John Watson's conditioning and deconditioning of simple fears in young children in the

1920s frequently is considered to be the beginning of the behavioral movement. Other studies, such as Mowrer and Mowrer's investigation with childhood nighttime enuresis, using the "bell-and-pad" technique, brought increased attention to the efficacy of behavioral procedures. However, the established influence of the psychoanalytic theories overshadowed the reports that appeared from the 1920s to the 1950s on the laboratory-derived principles of behavior.

B. F. Skinner's *Science of Human Behavior* in 1953 was the first text to describe the possible application of empirically derived theories of learning to social issues and human psychology. Based on the fundamentals of Skinner's laboratory studies, Sidney Bijou and his associates (Baer, Wolf, and Risley) at the University of Washington used operant programs in the late 1950s to early 1960s to improve social skills and academic performance with handicapped children. Other behaviorists, such as Ivar Lovaas and Nathan Azrin, employed operant conditioning techniques with autistic and mentally retarded populations in the 1960s. Studies in the 1960s began to demonstrate successful outcome using behavioral techniques with disorders that appeared to be untreatable with standard approaches (e.g., severe vomiting, physical self-abuse). Less severe problems in children were also effectively treated with behavioral interventions, including bedtime crying, inappropriate classroom behavior, and thumb sucking. With the increased study and application of behavioral techniques, behavior therapy journals began to appear in the 1960s and 1970s: *Behavior Research and Therapy* in 1963, *Journal of Applied Behavior Analysis* in 1968, *Behavior Therapy* in 1970, *Journal of Behavior Therapy and Experimental Psychiatry* in 1970, *Behavior Modification* in 1976, and *Child Behavior Therapy* in 1979.

During the 1950s to 1960s, clinics and educational settings applying behavioral psychotherapy demonstrated remarkable therapeutic gains. However, follow up, evaluation of concurrent behaviors, and generalization of results were lacking. Very few controlled outcome studies with sophisticated experimental designs were extant. In addition, behavioral therapists largely ignored modeling, cognitive, and developmental factors. By the 1970s, however, behavioral scientists began to pay more attention to these issues. Behavioral therapies in the 1970s began to incorporate cognitive techniques to successfully facilitate internal control in children and improve behavioral outcome in disorders, such as social withdrawal, aggression, learning disabilities, and hyperactivity. In addition, behavior therapy has become much more cognizant of modeling influences (Bandura, 1986) and developmental factors (Forehand & Wierson, 1993). Since the mid-1980s, behavioral techniques have been applied to the entire spectrum of childhood disorders and continue to be used extensively today.

PSYCHOPHARMACOLOGY WITH CHILDREN

Although adult psychopharmacological research has become widespread in the last 20 years, psychopharmacological research with children has lagged behind on a comparative basis. This is due to several factors, including the unique biologic system of the developing child, the relatively few diagnoses that are only specific to children, the inability of children to articulate evaluative comments related to drug response, and the reluctance of some human research committees to permit pharmacological study of minors.

Children absorb, metabolize, and eliminate drugs at different rates, thereby resulting in distinct reactions to psychotropic medications at various age levels. Prepubescent children have efficient livers that allow them to metabolize drugs rapidly. After puberty drug metabolism decelerates. These changing rates of metabolism make it difficult to prescribe psychotropic medications in a standardized manner. Reports of children who had died subsequent to tricyclic antidepressant medication treatments underscore the care and sensitivity clinical researchers must exercise when treating children with psychopharmacologic drugs (Biederman, 1991).

Stimulants

Drug therapy for the treatment of child psychopathology was almost exclusively nonexistent prior to the 1930s. Benzedrine, a stimulant, was the first drug that was systematically studied with children. In a pioneering study, Bradley (1937) demonstrated effectiveness of benzedrine for the improvement of school performance with children living in the first group home in America: the Emma Pendleton Bradley Home. Effectiveness of benzedrine was substantiated when later studies found that this drug improved verbal intelligence scores for adolescents at the New Jersey State Home for Boys. Although benzedrine continued to be used widely throughout the 1940s in facilities such as Bellevue Hospital in New York, it was gradually replaced with other stimulants (e.g., dextroamphetamine) because of their equally efficacious results at reportedly lower doses. Methylphenidate (Ritalin) was synthesized in 1954 and quickly became one of the most frequently prescribed drugs for children in the 1950s and 1960s.

Stimulant medications have continued to maintain their popularity with psychiatrists today. Stimulant medications are currently the most frequently prescribed psychotropic drugs in child psychiatry, with more than 6% of elementary aged children receiving these medications (Wilens & Biederman, 1992). They are favored by practitioners because they are among the safest and most efficacious medications for the management of childhood psychiatric disorders, particularly Attention-Deficit Hyperactivity Disorder (Gadow, 1992). Approximately 70% to 80% of all children respond favorably to stimulant medication. However, efficacy of stimulants may be short-lived, as their long-term success is not supported in the literature (Greenhill, 1992).

Major Tranquilizers (Neuroleptics)

Major tranquilizers (e.g., chlorpromazine), also known as antipsychotic agents, are the treatment of choice for active psychotic states. Other neuroleptics (e.g., haloperidol) have been used to treat motor and vocal tics. Psychotropic medications were first investigated in the 1950s, but were reported to have mixed results with children and thus were not widely accepted at this time. Major tranquilizers including the piperazines (e.g., trifluoperazine, fluphenazine, and prochlorperazine), and the piperidine compounds (e.g., thioridazine, thiothixene, and haloperidol) began to be researched in the mid-1960s to early 1970s with children.

Recent studies investigating major tranquilizers with children have demonstrated improvements in hyperactivity, learning ability, and aggression. However, adverse side effects resulting from neuroleptic medications (e.g., dyskinesias, sedation, dystonias, and Parkinsonian symptoms) suggest that these medications should only be used in the most severe cases. It is interesting to note that side effects caused by psychopharmacological drugs with children were first reported during the 1960s. However, recent studies of toxicity have added little to what was originally determined from earlier studies (Gadow, 1992).

Antidepressants

Antidepressant medications (e.g., imipramine, desipramine) were also introduced for use in the 1960s to treat a variety of disorders. Early studies with imipramine (Tofranil) and amitripyline (Elavil) were encouraging. However, recent studies using controlled double-blind procedures have found antidepressants to be no more effective than placebo for depressed adolescents and prepubertal children (see reviews by Gadow, 1992; Ryan, 1992). Of the few controlled studies that have evaluated use of tricyclic antidepressants with children, the number of subjects has been minimal and the results mixed, suggesting that efficacy of the tricyclic antidepressants remains to be demonstrated. Such discouraging lack of confirming data has encouraged study of other medications for childhood depression, including lithium augmentation and monoamine oxidase (MAO) inhibitors. However, efficacy of these medications for use with children is uncertain at this time.

The first text on pediatric psychopharmacology (Werry, 1978) and the inauguration of the *Journal of Child and Adolescent Psychopharmacology* reflect the increased attention to biological aspects of child psychiatry in the literature. Presently, there is a trend to evaluate use of medications in a more methodologically sound manner and as a conjoint therapy to facilitate behavioral therapies (Dupaul & Barkley, 1993). The complementary effects of behavior therapy and psychopharmacology have also been acknowledged in the literature (Hersen, 1985). However, dose-response issues are still largely unanswered, thus making it somewhat difficult to evaluate the synergistic effects of behavior therapy and pharmacotherapy.

DIAGNOSTIC AND CLASSIFICATION SYSTEMS WITH CHILDREN

Prior to the 20th Century

With the vast number of psychotherapists believing in different fundamental principles, it is essential that a commonly espoused diagnostic system define psychological disorders in terms of age-specific symptoms. Interestingly, however, it was not until the 20th century that children and adolescents were included in standard classification systems of mental illness.

The first classification system to differentiate mental disorders was devised by Hippocrates over 2,000 years ago. He divided mental disorders into acute disturbances with and without fever, chronic disturbances without fever (melancholia), hysteria, and scythian disease (transvestism). Most likely due to disinterest with the welfare of the mentally ill, classification systems were crude, overly broad, and not widely used until the 19th century. Emil Kraepelin created an interest in classification in the mid-1800s with the publication of numerous texts that described case histories using objective behavioral observations of various mental disorders. Kraepelin theorized that mental disorders could be categorized according to behavioral patterns, precipitating circumstances, course, and outcome. His textbooks often contained tables of contents that were organized into discrete mental disorders. In 1899, Kraepelin published *Psychiatrie*. This text included 16 major categories of mental disorders and was the most comprehensive classification system of mental disease up to that time.

The first classification system of mental disorders used in America was the U.S. Census of 1840, which contained one psychological classification entitled *Emotional Disorders*. Forty years later, the U.S. Census revised this classification to include 7 categories of "Mental Disorder," none of which was specific to children.

Twentieth Century

In 1917, the newly established American Psychiatric Association proposed its first psychiatric classification system, modeled after Kraepelin's 1899 classification system. A revision to this system, the *Standard Classified Nomenclature of Diseases*, was proposed in 1933 (American Psychiatric Association). However, leading psychoanalytically oriented psychiatrists of that time considered this system to be inferior to Kraepelin's established system, and as a result, this classification system was not widely accepted.

During World War II, the army, navy, and Veterans Administration were each using their own classification system for mental illness. Many psychological disturbances that were suffered by World War II veterans were not included in these systems. In an attempt to better understand these disorders, psychiatry and medicine developed closer links with one another. This then created a need to have psychiatric nomenclature more clearly tied to medical terminology in order to facilitate communication across disciplines. In order to satisfy practitioners and provide a standardized method of statistically coding psychiatric cases, members of the American Psychiatric Association's Committee of Nomenclature and Statistics established the first *Diagnostic and Statistical Manual of Mental Disorders* (*DSM-I*; American Psychiatric Association, 1952). This was the first manual of mental disorders to contain a glossary of descriptions of the diagnostic categories. Childhood disorders were represented with a single classification designated as Transient Situational Personality Disorders. This novel classification included adjustment reactions of infancy, childhood, and adolescence that were thought to be an acute symptom response capable of remitting when stress in the environment diminished. Childhood adjustment reactions were divided into three categories that identified habit disturbances (e.g., thumb sucking, enuresis, masturbation, tantrums, etc.), conduct disturbances (e.g., truancy, stealing, destructiveness, cruelty, sexual offenses, use of alcohol, etc.), and neurotic traits (e.g., tics, phobias, overactivity, somnambulism, stammering, etc.). Psychotic reactions in children, including primary autism, were classified as "Schizophrenic reaction, childhood type." Of all the categories in the DSM-I, only the Schizoid Personality category described the progression of pathology from childhood to adulthood: "As children, they are usually quiet, shy, obedient, sensitive and retiring. At puberty, they frequently become more withdrawn, then manifesting the aggregate of personality traits known as introversion, namely, quietness, seclusiveness, "shut-in-ness" and unsociability, often with eccentricity" (American Psychiatric Association, 1952, p. 35). Supplementary terms specific to childhood were also coded in this manual but were not described (e.g., enuresis, feeding problems in children, tantrums, and thumb sucking).

In 1966, the Group for Advancement of Psychiatry, primarily as a result of the absence of child psychopathology classification, developed its own nomenclature in its attempt to be systematic. However, this system relied primarily on clinical judgment and did not have an empirical base. Thus, it suffered from the same flaws as *DSM–I* (American Psychiatric Association, 1952). Nonetheless, this system did underscore the importance of developing a viable classificatory system for children and adolescents.

In 1968, the *Diagnostic and Statistical Manual of Mental Disorders Second Edition* (*DSM–II*; American Psychiatric Association, 1968) was published as a revision of the *DSM–I* in order to modify descriptions of many disorders, reorganize nomenclature, and encourage recording multiple psychiatric diagnoses. Two main categories were included in this manual for use with children. The first category, Transient Situational Disturbances, was generally the same as it had been in the *DSM–I*, as it included adjustment reactions of infancy, childhood, and adolescence. A new category, Behavior Disorders of Childhood and Adolescence, described childhood disorders that were "more stable, internalized, and resistant to treatment than transient situational disturbances, but less so than psychoses, neuroses, and personality disorders" (American Psychiatric Association, 1968). The childhood disorders within this classification included various "reactions of childhood or adolescence" (e.g., hyperkinetic, overanxious, runaway, unsocialized aggressive, withdrawing, and group delinquent).

In 1980, the *Diagnostic and Statistical Manual of Mental Disorders Third Edition* (*DSM–III*; American Psychiatric Association, 1980) replaced *DSM–II* as an attempt to provide more objective criteria to assist with categorization. More than 4 times as many categories specific for use with children were contained in the *DSM–III*. New developments of the *DSM–III* included requirement of a specific number of pathological characteristics to receive a diagnosis, duration of disturbance, and exclusion of related psychological disturbances. The *DSM–III* relied less on psychoanalytic terms than did earlier versions and emphasized observable behavior. A multiaxial classification system allowed children to be assessed with several distinct dimensions for the first time (e.g., physical conditions, global functioning).

Many researchers were dissatisfied with the reliability and validity of numerous *DSM–III* subtypes of childhood disorders. In 1987, the *DSM–III* was revised in an effort to accommodate new information adduced from contemporary diagnostic studies. The *DSM–III–R* and *DSM–IV* (American Psychiatric Association, 1987, 1994) are much more sensitive to child psychopathology than their predecessors. Axis IV incorporates psychosocial stressors and environmental problems for children and adolescents (e.g., rejecting and harsh parents). A new section entitled "Disorders Usually First Diagnosed in Infancy, Childhood, or Adolescence" includes greater detail of common disorders found within these age ranges (e.g., mental retardation, pervasive developmental disorders, learning disorders, disruptive behavior disorders, anxiety disorders, gender identity disorders, elimination disorders, etc.). Advances in the objective study of the personality disorders resulted in the empirically justified inclusion of personality disorders in adolescents. With the exception of occasional features that apply specifically to infants, children, and adolescents, the "essential" features of the Mood Disorders and Schizophrenia categories are considered to be the same in children and adults in the *DSM–III–R* and *DSM–IV*.

Behàvioral Classification

Historically, diagnostic categories for children have evolved from clinical observation. Using this clinical approach to classification, those familiar with child psychopathology classify behavior problems according to a consensus of experiential, rather than empirical, validation. Starting in the mid-1900s, however, there has been increased emphasis on use of sophisticated statistical techniques to determine behavioral correlates, thus forming empirically derived syndromes of deviant behaviors that may then be coded into a classification system. Hewitt and Jenkins (1946) performed the first systematic investigation of children using statistical techniques to isolate interrelated patterns of childhood behavioral problems. These investigators examined intercorrelations of 45 behaviors from the records of 500 children admitted to a child guidance clinic in Chicago. From their visual inspection of the intercorrelations, three syndromes were found to exist among the behavioral traits (e.g., unsocialized aggressive, socialized delinquent, and overinhibited).

Peterson (1961) performed one of the first studies with factor analysis (a statistical procedure that isolates clusters of behaviors that are interrelated) to classify childhood behavior problems. These investigators examined the records of over 400 children that were treated in a child guidance clinic. The most frequently occurring problems were incorporated into a checklist of 58 items descriptive of deviant behavior. This checklist was then given to 831 grammar school children. A factor analysis was able to classify the problem behaviors of these children into either "conduct" (aggressive) or "personality" (withdrawal) categories.

Since Peterson's (1961) investigation, there have been dozens of factor analytic studies that have attempted to construct a behavioral taxonomy for disorders of childhood and adolescence. In a review of the behavioral taxonomy literature, Quay (1986) found only a few behavioral classifications that cluster together. A dimension most reasonably labeled Undersocialized Aggressive Conduct Disorder (e.g., aggressive, disruptive, noncompliant) was found in over 30% of the 61 studies reviewed. Anxiety-Withdrawal-Dysphoria Disorder (anxious, shy, sad, hypersensitive) was found to be the second most frequently appearing behavioral cluster of problem behaviors. Immaturity, Attention Deficit Disorder (e.g., poor concentration, daydreaming, distractible) involves problems of concentration, including both hyper- and hypoactivity. A pattern labeled Socialized Conduct Disorder (e.g., having "bad" companions, truancy, stealing in company of others) has emerged less frequently.

SUMMARY

The scientific study of psychopathology in children has emerged relatively recently after centuries of child neglect and maltreatment. Prior to the 1800s, indifference to high rates of child mortality due to physical abuse, long hours of employment in poor working conditions, and malnutrition was reflected in the laws that overlooked the welfare of children. In fact, until the 1600s, it was legal to publicly scorn, torture, and kill mentally ill children due to their increased "burden" to society. The harsh treatment of children generally improved in the 1900s due to child protection laws that were encouraged by the mental hygiene and child guidance movements.

As recently as 1982, only one of every nine mental health dollars was spent on services for children and adolescents despite their representation of almost 50% of the population. Child psychological, psychopharmacological, and diagnostic research is largely a 20th century phenomenon. Prevention and treatment of child psychopathology have until recently been an extrapolation of adult psychopathology, and the field indeed is still in its very early stages.

REFERENCES

Achenbach, T. M. (1974). *Developmental psychopathology*. New York: Ronald Press.

American Psychiatric Association. (1933). Notes and comment: Revised classified nomenclature of mental disorders. *American Journal of Psychiatry, 90*, 1369–1379.

American Psychiatric Association. (1952). *Diagnostic and statistical manual of mental disorders* (1st ed.). Washington, DC: Author.

American Psychiatric Association (1968). *Diagnostic and statistical manual of mental disorders* (2nd ed.). Washington, DC: Author.

American Psychiatric Association. (1980). *Diagnostic and statistical manual of mental disorders* (3rd ed.). Washington, DC: Author.

American Psychiatric Association. (1987). *Diagnostic and statistical manual of mental disorders* (3rd rev. ed.). Washington, DC: Author.

American Psychiatric Association (1994). *Diagnostic and statistical manual of mental disorders* (4th ed.). Washington, DC: Author.

Aries, P. (1962). *Centuries of childhood*. New York: Springer.

Bandura, A. (1986). *Social foundations of thought and action: A social cognitive theory*. Engelwood Cliffs, NJ: Prentice-Hall.

Beers, C. (1908). *A mind that found itself*. New York: Longmans, Green.

Biederman, J. (1991). Sudden death in children treated with a tricyclic antidepressant. *Journal of the American Academy of Child and Adolescent Psychiatry, 30*, 495–498.

Bradley, C. (1937). The behavior of children receiving Benzedrine. *American Journal of Psychiatry, 94*, 577–585.

Brown, R. H., Rox, E. S., & Hubbard, E. L. (1974). Medical and legal aspects of the battered child syndrome. *Chicago-Kent Law Review, 50*, 45–84.

deMause, L. (1974). The evolution of childhood. In L. deMause (Ed.), *The history of childhood* (pp. 1–74). New York: Harper & Row.

Duffy, J. C. (1976). "Special article" in honor of the bicentennial year, 1776–1976. *Child Psychiatry and Human Development, 6*, 189–197.

Dupaul, G. J., & Barkley, R. A. (1993). Behavioral contributions to pharmacotherapy: The utility of behavioral methodology in medication treatment of children with attention deficit hyperactivity disorder. *Behavior Therapy, 24*, 117–141.

Forehand, R., & Wierson, M. (1993). The role of developmental factors in planning behavioral interventions for children: Disruptive behavior as an example. *Behavior Therapy, 24*, 117–141.

Gadow, K. D. (1992). Pediatric psychopharmacotherapy: A review of recent research. *Journal of Child Psychology and Pediatric Psychiatry, 33*, 153–195.

Gelfand, D. M., Jenson, W. R., & Drew, C. J. (1982). *Understanding child behavior disorders*. New York: Wiley.

Greenhill, L. L. (1992). Pharmacologic treatment of Attention Deficit Hyperactivity Disorder. *Psychiatric Clinics of North America, 15*, 1–27.

Group for Advancement of Psychiatry, Committee on Child Psychiatry. (1966). *Psychopathological disorders in childhood. Theoretical considerations and a proposed classification* (Vol. 6, Rep. No. 62). New York: Author.

Hall, G. S. (1904). Adolescence: Its psychology and its relations to physiology, anthropology, sociology, sex, crime, religion, and education (Vols. 1–2). New York: Appleton

Hersen, M. (Ed.). (1985). *Pharmacological and behavioral treatment: An integrative approach*. New York: Wiley.

Hewitt, L. E., Jenkins, R. L. (1946). *Fundamental patterns of maladjustment, the dynamics of their origin*. Springfield: State of Illinois.

Holmes, D. L., & Morrison, F. J. (1979). *The child: An introduction to developmental psychology*. Monterey, CA: Brooks/Cole.

Kendall, P. C. (Ed.). (1991). *Child and adolescent therapy: Cognitive behavioral procedures*. New York: Guilford.

Kessen, W. (1965). *The child*. New York: Wiley.

Kraeprlin, E. (1893). *Psychiatrie* (4th ed.). Leipzig: Meiner.

Kratochwill, T. R., & Morris, R. J. (1991). *The practice of child therapy* (2nd ed.). Elmsford, NY: Pergamon.

Peterson, D. R. (1961). Behavior problems of middle childhood. *Journal of Clinical Psychology, 25,* 205–209.

Phaire, T. (1545). The boke of children.

Quay, H. C. (1986). Classification. In H. C. Quay & J. S. Werry (Eds.), *Psychopathological disorders of childhood* (pp. 1–34).

New York: Wiley. Rie, H. E. (1971). *Perspectives in child development*. Chicago: Aldine-Atherton.

Ryan, N. D. (1992). The pharmacologic treatment of child and adolescent depression. *Psychiatric Clinics of North America, 15,* 29–40.

Shirk, S. R., & Phillips, J. S. (1991). Child therapy training: Closing gaps with research and practice. *Journal of Consulting and Clinical Psychology, 59,* 766–776.

Skinner, B. F. (1953). *Science and human behavior*. New York: Macmillan.

Tuma, J. (1990). Mental health services to children: State of the art. In P. Magreb & P. Wohlford (Eds.), *Improving psychological services for children and adolescents with severe mental disorders: Clinical training in psychology* (pp. 51–55). Washington, DC: American Psychological Association.

Werry, J. S. (Ed.). 1978. *Pediatric psychopharmacology: The use of behavior modifying drugs in children*. New York: Brunner/Mazel.

Wilens, T. E., & Biederman, J. (1992). The stimulants. *Psychiatric Clinics of North America, 15,* 191–222.

Chapter 2

Diagnosis
and Classification

Irwin D. Waldman
Scott O. Lilienfeld
Emory University

Why should psychologists classify and diagnose psychiatric syndromes, including those that originate in childhood? In our opinion, this is perhaps the single most important question in the field of abnormal child psychology; nevertheless, in our experience, it is rarely addressed adequately in either courses on childhood disorders or in textbooks dealing with this topic. Consequently, in this chapter we focus primarily on two central issues: (a) the classification of childhood psychiatric syndromes, and (b) the diagnosis of these syndromes.

By *classification*, we mean a system for delineating the major categories or dimensions of syndromes, as well as the boundaries and interrelations among these categories or dimensions. In contrast, by *diagnosis* we mean the process of assigning individuals to the categories generated by a classification system. With rare exceptions that will not be discussed here, a syndrome can be defined as a set of signs and symptoms that covary (i.e., intercorrelate) across individuals. In turn, signs are features that are observable by others (e.g., a sad face), whereas symptoms are features that can be reported only by the individuals themselves (e.g., sad feelings).

In this chapter, we place particular emphasis on the raison d'être of psychiatric classification and diagnosis and underscore our major points with examples drawn from the abnormal child psychology literature. The format of the chapter is as follows. A number of questions typical of those asked by advanced undergraduate or beginning graduate students in abnormal child psychology classes are posed, followed by responses to each question with reference to the literature on the classification and diagnosis of childhood (and in some cases, adult) psychiatric syndromes.

GENERAL ISSUES IN THE CLASSIFICATION AND DIAGNOSIS
OF CHILDHOOD SYNDROMES

Can Psychologists Accurately Distinguish Mentally Ill
From Normal Individuals?

Yes. Although this question typically has been raised in the context of adult psychiatric syndromes, it has implications for childhood psychiatric syndromes as well. The study most often cited as evidence for the claim that mental health professionals cannot distinguish the mentally ill from the nonmentally ill is that of Rosenhan (1973), who reported that eight "pseudopatients" (i.e., normal individuals who feign mental illness) gained admission to a number of mental hospitals simply by informing the admitting officers that they had been hearing voices saying "empty," "hollow," and "thud." According to Rosenhan, all of the pseudopatients behaved normally during their hospitalization and were recognized as imposters by most of the patients. Nevertheless, most of these pseudopatients apparently went undetected by the psychiatric staff and consequently were not discharged until several weeks following their admission. Finally, in virtually all cases, the pseudopatients were discharged with diagnoses of "schizophrenia in remission," apparently corroborating Rosenhan's claim that mental health professionals cannot distinguish mentally ill from normal individuals.

In a trenchant critique of Rosenhan's study, Spitzer (1975) pointed out that the psychiatrists' use of the phrase "in remission" indicates that they recognized that the pseudopatients no longer exhibited abnormal behavior, belying Rosenhan's assertion that mental health professionals cannot distinguish abnormality from normality. Moreover, in a survey of several psychiatric hospitals, Spitzer found that the diagnosis of "schizophrenia in remission" was made extremely rarely, suggesting that the psychiatrists who made this diagnosis recognized that the pseudopatients were markedly different from most individuals who initially present with signs and symptoms typical of schizophrenia. Finally, Spitzer noted that Rosenhan presented little or no evidence that the psychiatric staff considered the pseudopatients' behavior in the hospital to be abnormal. Thus, Rosenhan's central arguments do not withstand close scrutiny.

Can Psychologists Reliably Diagnose Psychiatric Syndromes,
Including Those Originating in Childhood?

In general, the answer is yes. Reliability, as traditionally defined, refers to the consistency or replicability of a measure. A reliable measure of a psychiatric syndrome assesses this syndrome consistently, that is, with a minimal degree of measurement error. Although a number of types of reliability are applicable to measures of psychiatric syndromes, including test–retest reliability and internal consistency, the type of reliability most relevant to our discussion is *interrater reliability*, the degree to which different raters (e.g., two psychologists) concur on the diagnosis of a set of individuals.

Although psychiatric syndromes have often been criticized for exhibiting low interrater reliability (e.g., Eysenck, Wakefield, & Friedman, 1983), the *Diagnostic and Statistical Manual of Mental Disorders, Third Edition* (*DSM–III*; American Psychiatric Association, 1980) and its two revisions (*DSM–III–R*, American Psychiatric

Association, 1987; *DSM–IV*, American Psychiatric Association, 1993) have provided clinicians with a powerful tool for augmenting the interrater reliability of both childhood and adult syndromes. Unlike the previous two editions of the *DSM*, which contained only global descriptions of psychiatric syndromes, *DSM–III*, *DSM–III–R*, and *DSM–IV* contain clearly delineated diagnostic criteria, including explicit inclusion and exclusion criteria and objective scoring algorithms, to enhance interrater agreement. For the diagnosis of Attention-Deficit/Hyperactivity Disorder (ADHD), for example, *DSM–III–R* mandates that the child (a) possess 8 or more of 14 symptoms for at least 6 months, (b) have an onset of these signs prior to age 7 (an inclusion criterion), and (c) not meet criteria for a pervasive developmental disorder, such as autistic disorder (an exclusion criterion).

Indeed, a number of researchers have reported that the *DSM–III* and *DSM–III–R* criteria for a number of childhood syndromes, as assessed by structured or semistructured interviews such as the Diagnostic Interview for Children and Adolescents (DICA; Reich, Herjanic, Welner, & Gandhy, 1982) and the NIMH Diagnostic Interview Schedule for Children (DISC; Costello, Edelbrock, Duncan, & Kalas, 1984) exhibit moderately to very high levels of inter-rater agreement. The levels of agreement tend to be somewhat higher for "externalizing" (i.e., disruptive; American Psychiatric Association, 1987) syndromes, such as Conduct Disorder (CD) and ADHD, than for "internalizing" syndromes, such as depression and Separation Anxiety Disorder (SAD, Welner, Reich, Herjanic, Jung, & Amado, 1987), probably because the former syndromes are characterized by diagnostic indicators that are more salient and readily agreed on by observers. In addition, it is worth noting that the reliabilities of most major psychiatric syndromes are comparable to those of many medical conditions (Spitzer, 1975), a point that critics of traditional psychiatric diagnosis frequently neglect to mention. It should be borne in mind, however, that adequate reliability is generally a necessary, but not sufficient, condition for adequate *validity*. We shall return to the concept of validity shortly.

Isn't Psychiatric Classification Simply a Matter of "Pigeonholing"? Why Can't We Simply Design Treatments Based on Each Person's Unique Characteristics?

Because it is rarely this simple. If each individual were regarded as entirely unique, research on both the treatment and etiology of psychiatric syndromes would essentially be impossible to conduct. As a consequence, we would often have little or no guidance regarding how to proceed in the treatment of a given individual. Personality psychologists frequently distinguish between *nomothetic* and *idiographic* approaches to assessment. In the nomothetic approach, the psychologist attempts to delineate general principles that apply across many or all individuals. Classification schemes are inherently nomothetic, because they presume the existence of broad commonalities across individuals who possess similar signs and symptoms. In the idiographic approach, the psychologist eschews general principles and instead attempts to understand the unique configuration of characteristics within a single individual. Although both nomothetic and idiographic approaches are useful for certain purposes, purely idiographic approaches are limited in that they do not permit generalizations to be made across individuals.

For example, imagine that a child exhibits profound sadness, loss of interest in almost all activities, irritability, sleep and appetite difficulties, feelings of worthlessness, suicidal ideation, and fatigue. A psychiatrist might prescribe tricyclic antidepressants in order to remedy these signs and symptoms. But how did the psychiatrist know to do this? The psychiatrist knew this from previous research on the pharmacological treatment of both childhood and adult major depressions. Note, however, that such research would not have been possible without the diagnostic category of major depression and that the very existence of this category is premised on a nomothetic assumption. Similarly, research on potential etiological factors in childhood depression, such as the role of neurotransmitter abnormalities or psychosocial stressors, would essentially be impossible without the existence of this diagnostic category. Thus, a valid classification system is a prerequisite for meaningful research on both treatment and etiology and, in many cases, for the proper treatment of a given individual.

In practice, of course, all clinicians recognize that each individual is different and typically tailor their interventions around the unique characteristics of each patient. The existence of broad similarities among individuals in no way implies the absence of important differences among these individuals. Thus, nomothetic and idiographic approaches to diagnostic assessment are not incompatible and often work hand-in-hand.

Are Diagnostic Labels Useful? Put a Somewhat Different Way, Do These Labels Provide Diagnosticians With Information Over and Above the Labels Themselves?

In many cases, yes, although the jury still appears to be out for a number of childhood syndromes, such as developmental arithmetic disorder (American Psychiatric Association, 1987). For a diagnostic label to be useful, it must convey information that is not directly derivable from the label itself. Otherwise, a label simply becomes a tautological summary term for the characteristics subsumed by this label, as a number of critics of psychiatric labels have justifiably pointed out. Although one of the functions of psychiatric diagnosis is the facilitation of communication among professionals, a valid diagnostic label must do more than describe what is already known about an individual; it must inform about what is unknown.

It is clear that, for a number of childhood psychiatric syndromes, labels do indeed provide diagnosticians with additional important information. For instance, if a child is correctly given a diagnosis of ADHD, we know that the child exhibits severe problems in domains such as inattention, overactivity, and impulsivity, which are the central features of this syndrome. Nevertheless, we also know a great deal more. We know, for example, that this child has an increased likelihood of:

1. concurrent syndromes such as conduct disorder (Lilienfeld & Waldman, 1990),
2. a family history of antisocial personality and somatization disorders (e.g., Lahey et al., 1988),
3. poor passive avoidance learning (i.e., difficulty learning to inhibit responses that lead to punishment; Freeman, 1978) and other abnormalities on laboratory tasks,
4. psychophysiological abnormalities such as diminished skin conductance levels (Satterfield, 1978),
5. developing antisocial behaviors in later life, and
6. responding positively to stimulant medications.

Thus, the diagnosis of ADHD is useful and possesses least some degree of *construct validity*. It is to the concept of construct validity that we now turn.

ISSUES IN THE CLASSIFICATION OF CHILDHOOD SYNDROMES

What Is the Best Approach for Studying Psychiatric Classification?

In our view, the principle of construct validation provides a useful unifying framework for approaching the study of psychiatric classification. In their classic article, Cronbach and Meehl (1955) first introduced this principle and explicated its relevance to psychological tests. Validity, as traditionally defined, refers to the extent to which a test assesses what it is purported to measure. According to Cronbach and Meehl, construct validity is the type of validity appropriate when evaluating the extent to which a test successfully assesses a *construct*, that is, a hypothesized characteristic of individuals that cannot be directly observed. Intelligence, extraversion, and artistic ability are all constructs, because they must be inferred by the assessor. Similarly, all or virtually all childhood psychiatric syndromes can be viewed as constructs, because they refer implicitly to latent entities that are not observable. The diagnosis of SAD, for example, implies the existence of a construct—excessive separation anxiety—that must be inferred by the diagnostician. The diagnostic criteria for SAD, including "persistent avoidance of being alone" and "persistent reluctance or refusal to go to school" (American Psychiatric Association, 1987, p. 61), can be thought of as manifest, although fallible, indicators of this latent condition.

Construct validation proceeds in a deductive fashion, much like the process of testing scientific theories (Cronbach & Meehl, 1955). First, one explicates a "nomological network," or interconnected system of laws, in which the construct is embedded. This network consists of interconnections (a) between the construct and other constructs, (b) between the construct and its manifest indicators, and (c) among manifest indicators. By incorporating manifest indicators into the nomological network, the researcher generates a set of falsifiable predictions derived from the construct.

According to Cronbach and Meehl, all other types of validity, such as content, convergent, discriminant, and predictive validity, are subsumed by construct validity whenever one is attempting to validate a measure of a construct. If, for example, one is validating a measure of extraversion, evidence that this measure (a) adequately samples the psychological domains relevant to extraversion (content validity), (b) correlates positively with established measures of extraversion (convergent validity), (c) correlates negligibly with measures of constructs presumed to be unrelated to extraversion, such as neuroticism (discriminant validity), and (d) predicts future "extraverted" behaviors in the real world (predictive validity) would provide support for the construct validity of this measure. The key point is that any evidence consistent with the assertion that a measure assesses the construct in question is evidence for that measure's construct validity.

The establishment of the validity of a diagnostic category can be likened to the process of construct validation (Morey, 1991). A psychiatric diagnosis can be likened to a test, and the criteria comprising this diagnosis can be likened to items on a test.

Thus, in validating a diagnostic category, one attempts to accumulate the same sorts of evidence that would be relevant for the validation of a psychological measure.

Robins and Guze (1970) outlined an approach to establishing the validity of psychiatric diagnoses, although they did not explicitly discuss the relation of their approach to construct validation. According to Robins and Guze, a valid diagnostic label accomplishes several major things in addition to describing the clinical picture of the syndrome itself. Specifically, it provides information concerning diagnosed individuals' (a) performance on laboratory tests and psychometric measures, (b) natural history (i.e., course and outcome), and (c) family history of psychiatric syndromes, as well as with information concerning (d) the differentiation of the diagnosis from other syndromes. In addition, although not discussed by Robins and Guze, a valid diagnosis also ideally informs us about diagnosed individuals' (e) response to treatment. Each of these five sources of information can be viewed as evidence for the construct validity of a psychiatric syndrome.

An example of a simplified nomological network for ADHD appears in Fig. 2.1. As seen in this diagram, ADHD is hypothesized to overlap with CD, to predict a

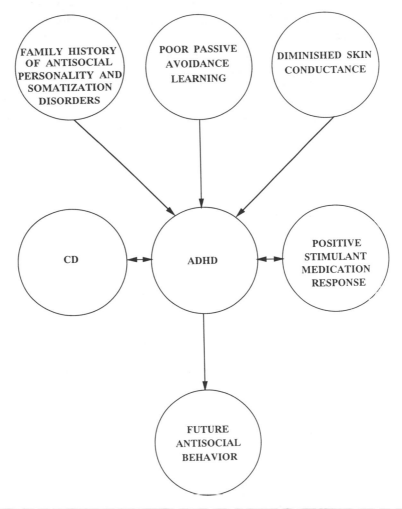

FIG. 2.1.   A simplified nomological network for ADHD.

positive response to stimulant medication, and to be related to poor passive avoidance learning and diminished skin conductance on laboratory measures. In addition, individuals with ADHD are hypothesized to be more likely to have a family history of antisocial personality and somatization disorders and to be at greater risk for engaging in future antisocial acts. As noted earlier, the diagnosis of ADHD possesses at least some degree of construct validity, because it satisfies most or all of the Robins and Guze criteria. It also should be noted that ADHD is thus *defined* in some important sense via its relations with other constructs represented in the nomological network. A *constitutive definition* is the definition of a construct in terms of its relations with other constructs (Cook & Campbell, 1979). This is in contrast to an *operational definition*, in which ADHD would be defined strictly and exclusively by the specific criteria used to make the diagnosis.

As alluded to earlier, reliability is a prerequisite for construct validity but does not ensure it. Some authors (e.g., Faust & Miner, 1986; Valliant, 1984) have contended that *DSM-III* and *DSM-III-R* emphasized reliability at the expense of construct validity. High interrater reliability often was the decisive factor in the selection of diagnostic criteria for disorders in *DSM-III* and *DSM-III-R*. Partly in response to the perceived overemphasis on reliability in *DSM-III* and *DSM-III-R,* greater emphasis was placed on construct validity in selecting diagnostic criteria for the childhood disorders in *DSM-IV*. For ADHD and CD, for example, the diagnostic criteria in *DSM-IV* were chosen partly on the basis of maximizing relations with indicators of impairment, such as poor peer relations (Waldman & Lahey, 1994).

How Can We Know Which and How Many Diagnostic Entities Exist?
How Can We Tell Whether These Entities Are Categorical or Dimensional?

One way to assess construct validity, whether of a test or a diagnostic entity, is by examining its convergent and discriminant validity, as mentioned earlier. Another way that is particularly applicable to diagnostic entities is to examine their internal and external validity (Skinner, 1981). Internal validation refers to the testing of hypotheses regarding a diagnostic entity's internal structure. These hypotheses concern issues such as whether the diagnostic entity is categorical or dimensional, how many categories or dimensions underlie the indicators pertaining to the syndrome, and what the boundaries and relations are among different underlying dimensions or categories. A categorical entity is one in which individuals differ in kind, whereas a dimensional entity is one in which individuals differ in degree only. In contrast, external validation involves examining the relations of these underlying categories or dimensions with important "external" correlates of syndromes such as course and outcome, treatment response, family history, and laboratory tests and psychometric measures. Hence, external validation subsumes convergent and discriminant validation and is quite similar to Robins and Guze's approach for establishing the validity of psychiatric diagnoses. In our opinion, at least some strong attempts ideally should be made at discerning the internal underlying structure of syndromes prior to examining them in terms of course and outcome, treatment response, family history, and laboratory measures. The use of internal and external validation to establish the construct validity of diagnostic entities should be an *iterative process*, that is, each approach to validation should successively inform and refine the other.

A first set of questions regarding the internal validity of a diagnostic entity concerns which and how many diagnostic entities exist and whether these are categorical or dimensional in nature. How does a psychopathology researcher go about answering these questions? One common approach is to use *exploratory* (i.e., inductive) statistical techniques that use correlations among indicators to make inferences regarding the number and composition of underlying diagnostic entities. Exploratory factor analysis (Loehlin, 1992) is such an approach for inferring underlying dimensions, whereas cluster analysis (Meehl & Golden, 1982) is such an approach for inferring underlying categories. Despite the empiricist appeal of these statistical procedures in "letting nature reveal itself," they have a number of limitations. Perhaps the most significant of these is that the results of these procedures can be somewhat arbitrary (i.e., the classes or dimensions derived from these procedures may not really exist in nature) and may be affected by factors extraneous to the questions at hand. In addition, these procedures are better suited to *hypothesis generation* than to *hypothesis testing*. We believe that *confirmatory* (i.e., deductive) procedures tend to be better suited for addressing questions of internal validity, as they allow psychopathology researchers to test specific hypotheses regarding the number and composition of underlying diagnostic entities. Confirmatory factor analysis (Loehlin, 1992) is such an approach for testing hypotheses regarding the number and composition of underlying dimensions, whereas taxometric (Meehl & Golden, 1982), admixture (Grove & Andreasen, 1986), and latent class analyses (Grove & Andreasen, 1986; Meehl & Golden, 1982) are appropriate for testing hypotheses regarding the number and composition of underlying categories. In general, exploratory approaches are preferable when one's understanding of a diagnostic entity is in a relatively primitive stage of development, whereas confirmatory approaches are preferable when one has sufficient understanding of a diagnostic entity to generate testable hypotheses.

An example may clarify how these procedures can be used. Imagine an investigator who wishes to test the *DSM–IV* characterization of ADHD as a syndrome consisting of two *dimensions*, inattention and hyperactivity-impulsivity (American Psychiatric Association, 1993). This investigator may seek to test his or her hypothesis by "putting it into competition" with several alternative hypotheses. These competing alternatives might include (a) testing for the presence of a single category underlying the indicators of ADHD using taxometric, admixture, or latent class analyses, (b) given the failure of alternative hypothesis A, testing for the presence of a single dimension underlying the indicators of ADHD using confirmatory factor analysis, and (c) given the failure of alternative hypothesis B, testing for the presence of two dimensions underlying the indicators of ADHD using confirmatory factor analysis and examining whether these dimensions are correlated or uncorrelated. Testing a sequence of alternative hypotheses, specified *before* the analyses are conducted, permits much stronger conclusions to be made regarding the internal, underlying structure of diagnostic entities than do the exploratory strategies more commonly used in classification research.

Figure 2.2 illustrate such a comparison. A single, general dimension underlying the ADHD criteria appears on the right-hand side of the diagram, and the two dimensions of hyperactivity-impulsivity and inattention appear on the left-hand side. This figure also suggests the possibility that both a general dimension and the two specific dimensions all underlie ADHD criteria.

A related question may arise at this point, namely, *how do psychopathology researchers know which hypotheses about classification to test?* Good hypotheses regarding the underlying structure of diagnostic entities do not simply come out of thin

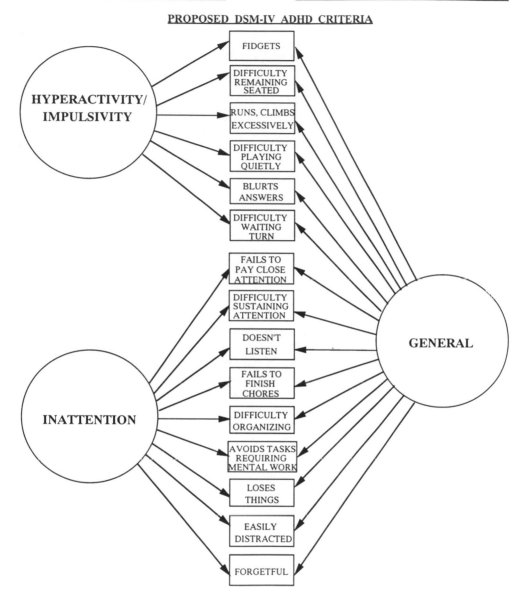

MODEL 1: TWO SPECIFIC DIMENSIONS   **MODEL 2: ONE GENERAL DIMENSION**

PROPOSED DSM-IV ADHD CRITERIA

HYPERACTIVITY/
IMPULSIVITY

FIDGETS

DIFFICULTY
REMAINING
SEATED

RUNS, CLIMBS
EXCESSIVELY

DIFFICULTY
PLAYING
QUIETLY

BLURTS
ANSWERS

DIFFICULTY
WAITING
TURN

FAILS TO
PAY CLOSE
ATTENTION

DIFFICULTY
SUSTAINING
ATTENTION

DOESN'T
LISTEN

GENERAL

FAILS TO
FINISH
CHORES

DIFFICULTY
ORGANIZING

AVOIDS TASKS
REQUIRING
MENTAL WORK

LOSES
THINGS

INATTENTION

EASILY
DISTRACTED

FORGETFUL

FIG. 2.2.   Two models for the underlying structure of ADHD.

air (Thank goodness!). It is common for a considerable amount of exploratory research to precede such confirmatory analyses. Such exploratory work may include clinical impressions of only a few cases with similar indicators, preliminary efforts at demonstrating diagnostic group differences on laboratory tests or psychological measures, and investigations of the co-occurrence of indicators in samples of children who are not clinically referred. This work may also include exploratory factor and cluster analytic research. Hence, classification researchers often have ample prior research to guide their development of alternative classification models to be tested using confirmatory approaches. Ideally, this research process is continuous and evolutionary in nature.

How Can We Know the Boundaries or Correlations Are Among Different Syndromes? What Does It Mean if Syndromes Are Correlated in the Population?

Fortunately, all of the confirmatory techniques mentioned previously allow the classification researcher to estimate the correlations or boundaries among different underlying diagnostic entities. In confirmatory factor analysis, estimates of the correlations among underlying dimensions are provided, whereas in the case of taxometric, admixture, or latent class analyses, estimates of the overlap or discriminability among underlying categories are provided. In addition, in many of these procedures, researchers may test hypotheses regarding not only the number and composition of underlying dimensions or categories but also the degree to which these dimensions are correlated or to which these categories are distinguishable.

Often a researcher finds that two (or more) syndromes are correlated to a substantial degree. A substantial correlation between two diagnostic entities may indicate, among other things, that they have common causes, that the appearance of a given syndrome may be similar to another at a particular point in its development or course, that they are distinct at the underlying level but share certain surface indicators, or that they are really minor variations on a single diagnostic entity and are thus currently misclassified. Thus, such a correlation indicates that further research is necessary to discriminate among these possibilities.

In childhood (and adult) psychopathology research, the term *comorbidity* is frequently used to denote the existence of a correlation between two diagnostic categories. Nevertheless, it should be borne in mind that this term, which derives from the medical epidemiology literature (Feinstein, 1970), refers to correlation among *diseases*. Diseases can be defined as syndromes whose pathology and etiology are relatively well-understood (Kazdin, 1983). Because the pathologies and etiologies of virtually all childhood syndromes are poorly understood, the use of the term *comorbidity* to refer to correlations among them is potentially misleading and generally should be avoided. Our point here is not simply semantic: The reader should resist the temptation to conclude that the correlation between two childhood syndromes necessarily reflects an association between two discrete disease entities. As noted in the previous paragraph, such a correlation is consistent with a number of quite different possibilities.

Which Childhood Syndromes Have Been Identified by Psychopathology Researchers?

Although many fundamental questions remain regarding the classification of childhood disorders, a number of preliminary conclusions may be drawn about the underlying structure of child psychopathology from extant research. For example, it is clear that childhood psychopathology may be broadly differentiated into two domains: externalizing (or undercontrolled) and internalizing (or overcontrolled) problems (Achenbach & Edelbrock, 1978; Achenbach, McConaughy, & Howell, 1987). Externalizing or undercontrolled problems include hyperactivity, impulsivity, distractibility, aggression, delinquency, and antisocial behavior, whereas internalizing or overcontrolled problems include anxiety, depression, social withdrawal, somatic complaints, and inattention-passivity (Achenbach et al., 1987). In an exploratory factor analysis of parents' ratings of behavior problems in over 8,000 6 to 16-year-old Dutch and American children, Achenbach and his colleagues (Achenbach, Conners, Quay, Verhulst, & Howell, 1989) found evidence for several uncorrelated problem dimensions beyond the general externalizing and internalizing dimensions. These specific dimensions included Aggression, Anxiety/Depression, Attention Problems, Delinquency, Somatic Complaints, Withdrawal, and Schizoid. Perhaps most importantly, these dimensions emerged for both males and females and across all ages from 6 to 16 years. The authors also provided evidence for a Socially Inept dimension in boys at all ages, a Meanness dimension in girls at all ages, and a Sex Problems dimension in girls at ages 6 to 11 years (Achenbach et al., 1989).

Beyond this general level of consistency, there are several controversies that have been prominent in child psychopathology research. One of these issues concerns the distinction among various externalizing problems. Historically, there have been two dominant perspective regarding different externalizing problems. One set of researchers (e.g., Quay, 1979; Sandberg, Rutter, & Taylor, 1978) has viewed problems such as inattention, hyperactivity, and aggression as minor variations around a common theme, whereas a second set (Hinshaw, 1987; Loney & Milich, 1982) has viewed these problems as separable yet related domains. Although still a matter of some controversy, the research evidence appears to support the latter view. Exploratory factor analytic studies (e.g., Hinshaw, 1987) have found dimensions of inattention, hyperactivity, and aggression to be separable (but highly correlated), and studies contrasting children who are exclusively inattentive-hyperactive, exclusively aggressive, and both inattentive-hyperactive and aggressive have found such groups to differ on important external variables (e.g., Loney & Milich, 1982).

A similar controversy has arisen in the area of internalizing or overcontrolled problems regarding the distinction between anxiety and depression. *DSM–IV* includes separate diagnoses for Major Depression and Dysthymia and separate diagnoses for several anxiety disorders (e.g., Social Phobia, Panic Disorder, Obsessive-Compulsive Disorder). Nevertheless, several authors have questioned the distinctiveness of anxiety and depression in both adults and children (Brady & Kendall, 1992; Clark & Watson, 1991) and have proposed a mixed anxiety-depression syndrome. Although this issue is far from resolved, the suggestion of such a mixed syndrome appears to have merit based on studies comparing exclusively anxious, exclusively depressed, and mixed anxious-depressed groups on external variables (e.g., Brady & Kendall, 1992).

For both of these controversies, it appears that confirmatory research techniques used in both internal and external validation efforts will be necessary to achieve a full resolution. For example, confirmatory factor analytic techniques may help resolve the presence of general and/or specific factors underlying ratings of problems in hyperactivity, impulsivity, inattention, and aggression/antisocial behavior. It may be the case that both a general externalizing dimension *and* specific problem dimensions underlie ratings of such problems (Waldman, Elder, Voelker, & Sprague, 1993), rather than one or the other being the case. Similarly, confirmatory techniques should be used to examine the unique versus common relations of these dimensions with external validating variables (e.g., family history, course and outcome, treatment response). Needless to say, such analyses must be conducted for anxiety and depression in order to fully understand their distinctiveness.

ISSUES IN THE DIAGNOSIS OF CHILDHOOD SYNDROMES

Once a classification scheme has been decided on, it is appropriate to consider several issues regarding diagnosis. These issues include (a) which indicators are best for diagnosing a particular syndrome, (b) which indicators may aid us in differential diagnosis, and (c) how many indicators are necessary for making a given diagnosis.

How Can We Tell Which Indicators Are Best for Diagnosing a Given Syndrome?

This question is one of *diagnostic efficiency*, which essentially involves determining which indicators will maximize our diagnostic "hits" and which will minimize our diagnostic "misses." Both researchers and clinicians want to know which indicators, when present, most strongly indicate the presence of a syndrome and which indicators, when absent, most strongly indicate the absence of a syndrome. Let us consider for a moment only a single indicator and a single syndrome. When both are present this is known as a *true positive*, and when the indicator is present but the syndrome is not this is known as a *false positive*. Similarly, when an indicator is absent and a syndrome is absent this is known as a *true negative*, and when the indicator is absent but the syndrome is present this is known as a *false negative*.

Several statistical indices have been developed to quantify the diagnostic efficiency of indicators. Among the most useful are *positive predictive power* (PPP) and *negative predictive power* (NPP) (Baldessarini, Finkelstein, & Arana, 1983). An indicator's PPP for a given diagnosis is calculated by dividing the number of true positives by the total number of patients for whom the indicator is present. This index has a certain intuitive appeal, as it represents the proportion of patients who have the indicator who also have the diagnosis. An indicator's NPP for a given diagnosis is calculated by dividing the number of true negatives by the total number of patients for whom the indicator is absent. This index also is intuitively appealing, as it represents the proportion of patients who do not have the indicator who also do not have the diagnosis. These indices are particularly useful aids in the task of diagnosis, for they allow clinicians to make predictive statements regarding the presence or absence of a diagnosis—something they *want* to know—given the presence or absence of an indicator—something they *can* know through clinical interviews, rating scales, or self-report measures. Knowledge of which indicators when present or absent are most predictive of the presence or absence of a syndrome can significantly aid the clinician in diagnostic decision making.

As an example, we recently examined the diagnostic efficiency of the *DSM–III–R* criteria for oppositional defiant disorder (OD) and ADHD (Waldman & Lilienfeld, 1991). We found that the ADHD indicators "physically dangerous," "blurts answers," "difficulty waiting turn," and "often interrupts" were not only good indicators when present of the presence of ADHD (all had PPPs $\geq .81$), but were also all good indicators when absent of the absence of ADHD (all also had NPPs $\geq .84$). Similarly, four of the OD indicators appeared to be good predictors of both the presence and absence of this syndrome. The OD indicators "spiteful," "swears," "angry/resents," and "actively defies" were not only good indicators when present of the presence of OD (all had PPPs $\geq .89$) but were also all good indicators when absent of the absence of OD (all had NPPs $\geq .90$).

Which Indicators Are Best for Differential Diagnosis?

Often the task of the clinician and/or researcher is not to decide whether a *single* syndrome is present, but rather, to decide which among *several* syndromes may be present. This raises the issue of *differential diagnosis*, which involves the use of diagnostic indicators (and possibly other relevant pieces of information) to differentiate among several syndromes, which may in some cases be rather difficult to distinguish from one another. Diagnostic efficiency indices such as PPP and NPP can also be helpful in distinguishing among different syndromes. An indicator that is particularly useful in differential diagnosis is one that shows a high PPP for one syndrome whereas its presence is also highly predictive of the absence of a different syndrome. Put in less technical terms, the presence of such an indicator would strongly suggest the presence of a particular syndrome and the absence of another syndrome.

Unfortunately, such a situation is unlikely to occur for two syndromes that overlap moderately or highly (e.g., OD and ADHD). Hence, a more realistic situation is that a diagnostic indicator may have a high PPP for one syndrome and a high NPP for another syndrome. Again, in less technical terms, this would mean that a diagnostic indicator would be useful in indicating the presence of one syndrome when it is present and the absence of another syndrome when it is absent. For example, ADHD and OD are common childhood syndromes that are characteristically difficult to differentiate from one another. Nonetheless, in our study we found that the ADHD indicator "often interrupts" was not only a good indicator when present of the presence of ADHD but also was a good indicator when absent of the absence of OD (NPP = .93). Similarly, the OD indicator "angry/resents" was not only a good indicator when present of the presence of OD but also was a good indicator when absent of the absence of ADHD (NPP = .81). Future studies of diagnostic utility should focus more on the issue of differential diagnosis and may need to move beyond investigating symptoms and signs as diagnostic indicators. Preliminary studies suggest that laboratory measures of inattention and impulsivity may be useful as differential diagnostic indicators for externalizing disorders such as ADHD and OD (e.g., Halperin et al., 1990; Waldman & Greenberg, 1993).

How Many Indicators Are Necessary for Making a Diagnosis?

Once one has decided which indicators best suggest the presence and absence of a given syndrome or of multiple syndromes, it becomes reasonable to ask *how many* indicators are necessary for making an accurate diagnosis. Several procedures may be used in making this decision. First, one can extend the application of diagnostic efficiency indices for a single indicator to multiple indicators. This would involve maximizing PPP and NPP for a given diagnosis using particular combinations of indicators (e.g., Widiger, Frances, Warner, & Bluhm, 1986). Second, one can examine changes in the relation of the number of indicators present for a syndrome to a relevant external criterion variable. One should observe a meaningful change in the nature of this relation at the optimal cut-off for the number of indicators. For example, in Fig. 2.3, we show two hypothetical relations of the number of CD symptoms to the number of school suspensions. The bold curve suggests that the number of school suspensions is only weakly related to the number of CD indicators until one reaches approximately 7 or 8 indicators, at which point the relation increases substantially. This curve would

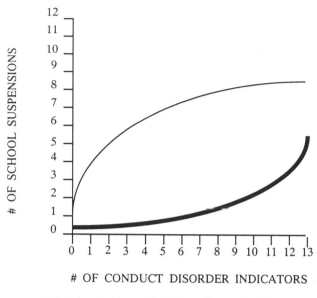

FIG. 2.3.   Two examples of a nonlinear relation.

suggest an optimal cut off of 7 or 8 indicators for making the diagnosis of CD, as it is not until one reaches this high threshold that problems with school suspensions are observed. In contrast, the thin curve suggests a strong relation of the number of CD indicators to the number of school suspensions only at low indicator levels. This curve would suggest an optimal cut off of 3 or 4 indicators for making the diagnosis of CD, as all children who exceed this threshold have problems with school suspensions.

SUMMARY

In this chapter, we reviewed a number of key issues concerning the classification and diagnosis of childhood psychiatric syndromes. We began by addressing a number of frequent criticisms concerning classification and diagnosis and demonstrated that psychiatric classification and diagnosis can be both reliable and valid and are prerequisites for meaningful research on etiology and treatment. We next argued that a construct validation framework is best for guiding research aimed at improving the classification and diagnosis of childhood psychiatric syndromes. Following from this, we generated a number of important questions—as well as tentative answers—that are addressed particularly well within a construct validation framework. Such questions include inquiries regarding the number and type of diagnostic entities (i.e., questions regarding their internal validity), inquiries regarding the boundaries and relations among various diagnostic entities and about their correlations with important external variables (i.e., questions regarding their external validity), and inquiries regarding the best methods for assigning individuals to diagnostic categories (i.e., questions regarding diagnostic efficiency). We believe that such a construct validation framework will aid readers in evaluating the research on childhood psychopathology discussed in subsequent chapters.

REFERENCES

Achenbach, T. M., Conners, C. K., Quay, H. C., Verhulst, F. C., & Howell, C. T. (1989). Replication of empirically derived syndromes as a basis for taxonomy of child/adolescent psychopathology. *Journal of Abnormal Child Psychology, 17*, 299–323.

Achenbach, T. M. & Edelbrock, C. S. (1978). The classification of childhood psychopathology: A review and analysis of empirical efforts. *Psychological Bulletin, 85*, 1275–1301.

Achenbach, T. M., McConaughy, S. H., & Howell, C. T. (1987). Child/adolescent behavioral and emotional problems: Implications of cross-informant correlations for situational specificity. *Psychological Bulletin, 101*, 213–232.

American Psychiatric Association. (1980). *Diagnostic and Statistical Manual of Mental Disorders* (3rd ed.). Washington, DC: Author.

American Psychiatric Association (1987). *Diagnostic and Statistical Manual of Mental Disorders* (3rd rev. ed.). Washington, DC: Author.

American Psychiatric Association. (1993). *DSM-IV draft criteria.* Washington, DC: Author.

Baldessarini, R. J., Finkelstein, S., & Arana, G. (1983). The predictive power of diagnostic tests and the effect of prevalence of illness. *Archives of General Psychiatry, 40*, 569–573.

Brady, E. U., & Kendall, P. C. (1992). Comorbidity of anxiety and depression in children and adolescents. *Psychological Bulletin, 111*, 244–255.

Clark, L. A., & Watson, D. (1991). Tripartite model of anxiety and depression: Psychometric evidence and taxonomic implications. *Journal of Abnormal Psychology, 100*, 316–336.

Cook, T. D., & Campbell, D. T. (1979). *Quasi-experimentation: Design and analysis issues for field settings.* Boston, MA: Houghton Mifflin.

Costello, A. J., Edelbrock, C. S., Duncan, M. K., & Kalas, R. (1984). *Testing of the NIMH Diagnostic Interview Schedule for Children (DISC) in a clinical population* (Contract No. DB-81-0027). Final report to the Center for Epidemiological Studies, National Institute for Mental Health. Pittsburgh: University of Pittsburgh.

Cronbach, L. J., & Meehl, P. E. (1955). Construct validity in psychological tests. *Psychological Bulletin, 52*, 281–302.

Eysenck, H. J., Wakefield, J. C., & Friedman, A. (1983). Diagnosis and clinical assessment: The DSM-III. *Annual Review of Psychology, 34*, 167–193.

Faust, D., & Miner, R. A. (1986). The empiricist and his new clothes: DSM-III in perspective. *American Journal of Psychiatry, 143*, 962–967.

Feinstein, A. R. (1970). The pre-therapeutic classification of co-morbidity in chronic disease. *Journal of Chronic Diseases, 23*, 455–468.

Freeman, R. J. (1978). *The effects of methylphenidate on avoidance learning and risk taking by hyperkinetic children.* Unpublished doctoral dissertation, University of Waterloo, Waterloo, Ontario.

Grove, W. M., & Andreasen, N. C. (1986). Multivariate statistical analysis in psychopathology. In T. Millon & G. L. Klerman (Eds.), *Contemporary directions in psychopathology: Towards the DSM-IV* (pp. 347–362). New York: Guilford.

Halperin, J. M., O'Brien, J. D., Newcorn, J. H., Healey, J. M., Pacualvaca, D. M., Wolf, L. E., & Young, J. G. (1990). Validation of hyperactive, aggressive, and mixed hyperactive/aggressive disorders in children: A research note. *Journal of Child Psychology and Psychiatry and Allied Disciplines, 31*, 455–459.

Hinshaw, S. P. (1987). On the distinction between attentional deficits/hyperactivity and conduct problems/aggression in child psychopathology. *Psychological Bulletin, 101*, 443–463.

Kazdin, A. E. (1983). Psychiatric diagnosis, dimensions of dysfunction, and child behavior therapy. *Behavior Therapy, 14*, 73–99.

Lahey, B. B., Piacentini, J. C., McBurnett, K., Stone, P., Hartdagen, S., & Hynd, G. (1988). Psychopathology in the parents of children with conduct disorder and hyperactivity. *Journal of the American Academy of Child and Adolescent Psychiatry, 27*, 163–170.

Lilienfeld, S. O., & Waldman, I. D. (1990). The relation between childhood attention-deficit hyperactivity disorder and adult antisocial behavior reexamined: The problem of heterogeneity. *Clinical Psychology Review, 10*, 699–725.

Loehlin, J. C. (1992). *Latent variable models* (2nd ed.). Hillsdale, NJ: Lawrence Erlbaum Associates.

Loney, J., & Milich, R. (1982). Hyperactivity, inattention, and aggression in clinical practice. In M. Wolraich & D. Routh (Eds.), *Advances in behavioral pediatrics* (Vol. 2, pp. 113–147). Greenwich, CT: JAI Press.

Meehl, P. E., & Golden, R. R. (1982). Taxometric methods. In P. C. Kendall & J. N. Butcher (Eds.), *Handbook of research methods in clinical psychology* (pp. 127–181). New York: Wiley.

Morey, L. C. (1991). Classification of mental disorder as a collection of hypothetical constructs. *Journal of Abnormal Psychology, 100*, 289–293.

Quay, H. C. (1979). Classification. In H. C. Quay & J. S. Werry (Eds.), *Psychopathological disorders of childhood* (2nd ed., pp. 1–42). New York: Wiley.

Reich, W., Herjanic, B., Welner, Z., & Gandhy, P. R. (1982). Development of a structured interview for children: Agreement on diagnosis comparing parent and child. *Journal of Abnormal Child Psychology, 10*, 325–336.

Robins, E., & Guze, S. B. (1970). Establishment of diagnostic validity in psychiatric illness: Its application to schizophrenia. *American Journal of Psychiatry, 126*, 983–987.

Rosenhan, D. L. (1973). On being sane in insane places. *Science, 179*, 250–258.

Sandberg, S. T., Rutter, M., & Taylor, E. (1978). Hyperkinetic disorder in psychiatric clinic attenders. *Developmental Medicine and Child Neurology, 20*, 279–299.

Satterfield, J. H. (1978). The hyperactive child syndrome: A precursor of adult psychopathy? In R. D. Hare & D. Schalling (Eds.), *Psychopathic behaviour: Approaches to research* (pp. 329–346). Chichester: Wiley.

Skinner, H. A. (1981). Toward the integration of classification theory and methods. *Journal of Abnormal Psychology, 90*, 68–87.

Spitzer, R. L. (1975). On pseudoscience in science, logic in remission, and psychiatric diagnosis: A critique of Rosenhan's "On being sane in insane places." *Journal of Abnormal Psychology, 84*, 442–452.

Valliant, G. (1984). The disadvantages of DSM-III outweigh its advantages. *American Journal of Psychiatry, 141*, 542–545.

Waldman, I. D., Elder, R. W., Voelker, S., & Sprague, D. (1993). *Measurement invariance of the IOWA-Revised Conners scale in clinically-referred and non-referred samples.* Manuscript submitted for publication.

Waldman, I. D., & Greenberg, L. M. (1993). *Inattention and impulsivity discriminate among disruptive behavior disorders.* Manuscript submitted for publication.

Waldman, I. D., & Lahey, B. B. (1994). Design of the DSM-IV Disruptive Behavior Disorder Field Trials. *Child and Adolescent Psychiatric Clinics of North America, 3*, 195–208.

Waldman, I. D., & Lilienfeld, S. O. (1991). Diagnostic efficiency of symptoms for Oppositional Defiant Disorder and Attention-Deficit Hyperactivity Disorder. *Journal of Consulting and Clinical Psychology, 59*, 732–738.

Welner, Z., Reich, W., Herjanic, B., Jung, K. G., & Amado, H. (1987). Reliability, validity, and parent–child agreement studies of the Diagnostic Interview for Children and Adolescents (DICA). *Journal of the American Academy of Child and Adolescent Psychiatry, 26*, 649–653.

Widiger, T. A., Frances, A., Warner, L., & Bluhm, C. (1986). Diagnostic criteria for the Borderline and Schizotypal Personality Disorders. *Journal of Abnormal Psychology, 95*, 43–51.

Chapter 3

Epidemiologic Considerations

Gale A. Richardson
Peggy McGauhey
Nancy L. Day
Western Psychiatric Institute and Clinic

This chapter presents basic epidemiologic principles and methods to provide a framework for understanding current research in the field of abnormal child psychology. The chapter also discusses issues specific to the field of child psychiatric epidemiology. Several classic studies in the field of child psychiatric epidemiology are introduced, and these studies are used to provide examples of the methods and issues presented.

The organization of the chapter is as follows: definition of child psychiatric epidemiology, description of classic studies in child psychiatric epidemiology, and an introduction to epidemiologic methods (sample selection, sampling, study designs, incidence and prevalence, and considering correlates of disorders). Issues in child psychiatric epidemiology, including comorbidity, categorical versus dimensional approaches, use of a developmental perspective, and use of data from multiple informants are also addressed.

DEFINITION

Epidemiology is the study of the patterns of disease in human populations and of the factors that influence these patterns. The focus is on populations rather than on individual cases. In the past, epidemiology dealt with the study of infectious diseases in a population. A single cause model was usually used to explain the presence of a particular disease (Day, 1992; Verhulst & Koot, 1992). The emphasis of epidemiology has gradually shifted to the study of long-term, chronic diseases, including psychiatric disorders. Most chronic diseases, such as psychiatric disorders, are determined by more than one cause (e.g., personal characteristics of the individual and environmental factors) (Verhulst & Koot, 1992).

The first systematic epidemiologic study in the field of child psychiatry was reported by Lapouse and Monk (1958). These investigators studied the frequency of mother-reported problem behaviors in a random, representative sample of 482 6- to 12-year-old-children in Buffalo, New York. The authors found a high frequency of emotional and behavioral problems, particularly among the 6- to 8-year-olds. Common problems included fears and worries, nightmares, overactivity, and temper tantrums. Early studies, such as Lapouse and Monk's, demonstrated the importance of systematic data collection, the need for examining prevalence of psychiatric disorders in children, and the high rate of problems among children.

The goals of child psychiatric epidemiology are to estimate the overall prevalence of childhood disorders and to identify the possible causes and correlates of the disorders (Verhulst & Koot, 1992). These data are necessary to provide appropriate treatment for psychiatrically disordered children, to evaluate mental health services, and to implement preventive measures.

SELECTED CLASSIC STUDIES

Five classic studies have been selected to familiarize the reader with child psychiatric epidemiology. These studies are used to illustrate principles throughout the chapter. The following section briefly summarizes the purpose, study design, and major findings of each study.

The first large-scale child psychiatric epidemiologic study was conducted by Rutter and his colleagues (Rutter, Tizard, & Whitmore, 1970). The Isle of Wight Study examined educational and intellectual disorders in a prospective investigation of the entire population of 3500 9- to 11-year-old children who lived on a semirural island off the coast of England. Children were also evaluated for psychiatric and physical disorders a year after the initial interview and again when they were 14 to 15 years old. The aims of the study were to identify age of onset of psychiatric disorders, examine risk factors associated with disorders, and examine the course of disorders over time. This study had numerous methodologic strengths including: use of multiple data sources (parents, teachers, children, school and medical records), a two-stage research strategy (a screening instrument was used to identify high-risk children who were then followed with more extensive assessment), use of standardized interviews, and use of social impairment as a criterion of severity along with the symptoms of the psychiatric disorder (Rutter, 1989).

Rutter et al. (1970) found that the overall rate of child psychiatric disorders in the 9- to 11-year-olds was 6.8%. However, the rate of specific types of disorders changed with age. For example, depressive disorders were more common at 14 to 15 years than at 10 to 11 years. Psychiatric disorders in adolescence (onset after age 10) had a different set of correlates than those arising in earlier childhood.

Low agreement was found between parent and teacher reports of children's functioning, demonstrating the importance of obtaining information from multiple sources because children act differently in different settings. The Isle of Wight Study was also important in noting the need to consider the overlap in conditions, or *comorbidity*, where more than one disorder is present at a time.

During a 3-year period in the mid-1950's, the Kauai Pregnancy Study (Werner, Bierman, & French, 1971) recruited more than 2,000 pregnant women in Kauai, Hawaii. The purpose of this prospective study was to compare the relative contributions of perinatal stress (medical problems during pregnancy, labor, or delivery) and the characteristics of the family environment to outcomes such as physical, cognitive, and social development of preschool and school-age children. Over 1,000 of the offspring were seen at 2 and 10 years of age for follow-up evaluations. Werner et al. (1971) found that higher levels of perinatal stress were associated with poorer development at 2 years of age. An inadequate environment exacerbated the effects of perinatal stress; that is, the children with high levels of perinatal stress and a poor environment had the worst outcomes. Further, emotionally unsupportive childrearing practices in the home were related to child behavior problems. By 10 years of age, however, the effect of perinatal stress had diminished and the impact of the environment had increased.

The London Epidemiologic Study (Richman, Stevenson, & Graham, 1975) investigated the prevalence of behavior problems among 3-year-old children living in a London borough. A two-stage sampling design was used. A random sample of 705 children was selected and a semistructured screening instrument (the Behavior Screening Questionnaire, BSQ) was used to identify children who were reported by their parents as having behavior problems. The estimated rate of moderate to severe behavior problems in the random sample was 7%; an additional 15% had mild behavior problems. Boys were more likely to be described as being overactive, having more problems with toilet training, and having fewer fears than girls.

Each child identified as having a behavior problem was then matched by sex and social class with a child with no behavior problems to create a behavior problems group and a control group. The two groups of children and their families then received an in-depth interview and developmental assessment. These children were seen again at 4 and 8 years of age. Of the children in the behavior problems group at 3 years of age, 69% and 62% were identified as having behavior problems at 4 and 8 years of age, respectively. This compares with 14% and 22% of the control group that which had behavior problems at 4 and 8 years, respectively (Richman, 1977; Richman, Stevenson, & Graham, 1982). Persistence of behavior problems was associated with maternal depression and poor marital relationships.

Earls (1980) replicated the London Epidemiologic Study (Richman et al., 1975) with a sample of 100 3-year-old children in a rural U.S. community (Martha's Vineyard, Massachusetts). This sample represented 90% of the entire population of 3-year-olds. Interviews were conducted with both parents and play interviews were done with the children. The BSQ from the London study (Richman et al., 1975) was used to identify behavior problems. Earls reported that 11% of the children had behavior problems—a rate similar to that reported by Richman et al. (1975), despite differences in geographic locale and sample size. Common behavior problems included sleep difficulties, fears, and bedwetting. The children were seen again at 6 to 7 years of age, after they began first grade. Twenty-five percent of those children with behavior problems at 3 years were reported by their teachers to have adjustment problems in school (Earls, 1983).

The Ontario Child Health Study (Boyle et al., 1987; Offord et al., 1987) surveyed parents of 2,679 4- to 16-year-old children to determine prevalence of emotional and behavioral disorders among children in Ontario, Canada. Families were randomly sampled from large and small urban areas and rural areas. Parents and teachers completed a behavior problem checklist that asked about conduct disorders (physical violence against people or property), hyperactivity, emotional disorders (anxiety, depression, obsessive-compulsive disorder), and somatization disorders (physical symptoms without organic cause). A subsample of children also received a clinical evaluation by a child psychiatrist. In addition to behavior problems, parents were asked about social and demographic characteristics, family composition, functioning, alcoholism, criminality, stressful life events, social support, and the child's medical history. Nineteen percent of the boys and 17% of the girls had one or more disorders. Conduct disorders and hyperactivity were reported more frequently for boys than for girls. Emotional disorders were more frequent in 12- to 16-year-old girls. In a separate analysis of the 4- and 5-year-olds in the study, predictors of behavior problems included the child's general health, maternal depression, marital status, parent health problems, and number of siblings (Thomas, Byrne, Offord, & Boyle, 1991).

EPIDEMIOLOGIC METHODS

Sample Selection

Research in child psychiatric epidemiology has involved both clinic and community samples (Verhulst & Koot, 1992). *Clinic samples* consist of children who have already been identified as suffering from a disorder and who usually are receiving treatment. Clinic samples differ in demographic characteristics from the general population. In a study of 62 children who were inpatients in a psychiatric hospital, Kazdin, Esveldt-Dawson, Sherick, and Colbus (1985) reported that 82% of the children were males and 82% were white. Clinic samples are also unrepresentative of the general population because of factors associated with referral to treatment, the family's access to health care, and their utilization of health services. Jensen, Bloedau, and Davis (1990) found that family size, marital status, and parental psychopathology were related to utilization of a child psychiatric clinic. An additional limitation of clinic samples is that information about the development of the disorder can only be collected retrospectively because the children have the disorder at the beginning of the study.

Community samples are drawn from a more general population and are not limited to children who have developed a disorder or who are in treatment. Each of the five classic studies was a population-based community investigation. To the extent that the population that is sampled yields a random or representative sample, these studies can be used to generate prevalence rates of disorders in the community. Clinic samples cannot be used for this purpose because the subjects are a select group. For example, Kashani, Orvaschel, Rosenberg, and Reid (1989), in a community sample of 8-, 12-, and 17-year-olds, reported that 3% had a depressive disorder, whereas Kazdin et al. (1985) found a 17.7% rate of depressive disorders in a clinic sample.

Both clinic and community samples can be either descriptive or analytic. When there are few data available on the disorder in the population, *descriptive studies* are undertaken. These studies are hypothesis generating, collecting data on the distribution of psychiatric disorder by age, gender, social class, or geographic variables. These data can then be used to generate specific hypotheses. Once hypotheses are formulated, *analytic studies* test the hypotheses to further the understanding of the causes of the disorder.

Sampling

Although several of the classic studies previously reviewed included an entire population (Earls, 1980; Werner et al., 1971), it is generally not feasible or necessary to enroll the whole population into a study. Rather, a sample of the population is evaluated to generate information about the entire population. The ability to generalize study findings is directly related to the degree to which the sample is representative of the entire population and of other populations to which one might wish to extend the findings. If the sample is derived from a population with special characteristics, generalizability to the entire population will be compromised. For example, clinic samples are already identified with disorders and, therefore, findings will not be comparable to those in the community. However, community samples are not exempt from generalizability problems. Factors, such as urban/rural differences, race, gender, and social class, must be similar to the population to which one wishes to generalize in order for results to be comparable. The study by Earls (1980), which sampled all 3-year-olds on Martha's Vineyard, has been criticized as being unrepresentative of the larger population of 3-year-olds because of the geographic locale and isolated nature of the island.

There are two methods of sampling: *nonprobability* and *probability*. Nonprobability or "convenience" sampling is subject to the most error. An example of nonprobability sampling would be a study conducted in a clinical setting, such as a pediatrician's office. The children in the office who are surveyed differ in important ways from potential subjects who are not seen at the office. For example, factors such as social class, gender, and employment status may be associated with seeking medical care and, therefore, inclusion in the study. Findings from the study would be limited to people who share similar characteristics with the sample.

In contrast, in probability sampling, each subject in the population has a known probability of selection. Sampling is random, such that the selection of one subject is independent of the selection of other subjects. There are several types of probability sampling: simple random, systematic, stratified, cluster, and multistage (Verhulst & Koot, 1992). The London Epidemiologic Study randomly chose one out of every four 3-year-old children who were living in the borough (Richman et al., 1975). Probability sampling enables the investigator to make inferences from the sample to the population from which it was drawn and maintains the representativeness of the sample.

Study Designs

There are several major study designs used in epidemiology. *Cross-sectional study designs* are also referred to as prevalence studies or surveys (Verhulst & Koot, 1992). The relationship between risk factors and disorders is assessed at a single point in time. Most community surveys are cross-sectional designs. For example, the Lapouse and Monk (1958) study was a cross-sectional study as was the initial phase of the Earls (1980) study on Martha's Vineyard. The cross-sectional design allows the study of variations between individuals but not within individuals over time. Cross-sectional designs allow the researcher to discuss age differences but do not allow an interpretation of changes which occur as an individual ages. Although useful for prevalence information and planning of treatment services, the cross-sectional design cannot determine timing or sequence of the relationship between risk factors and onset of the disorder. A longitudinal study design is needed to begin to understand cause and effect relationships.

Longitudinal or prospective study designs allow the investigation of changes over time within individuals, of the developmental course of a disorder, and of factors that influence this course (Verhulst & Koot, 1992). Longitudinal research is critical in the study of child psychiatric disorders in order to understand which disorders do and do not persist over time, to assess effectiveness of treatment, and to understand causes of a disorder (Verhulst & Koot, 1991).

A specific type of longitudinal design is a *cohort study* in which a group (cohort) is identified based on exposure to hypothesized risk factors and followed prospectively over time to determine which subjects subsequently develop the disorder of interest. Etiology is studied by comparing incidence of the disorder in relation to the risk factors. The Kauai Pregnancy Study (Werner et al., 1971) investigated the relative effects of perinatal stress and quality of the home environment on short- and long-term development by using a longitudinal design. Rutter (1989) noted that longitudinal studies of family breakup show that it was family disorganization and disagreement that preceded the breakup, rather than the event of the breakup itself, that were associated with child behavior problems. Findings such as these are only possible with a longitudinal design.

Case-control or retrospective studies define the study population by presence (cases) or absence (controls) of a disorder. The investigator then studies the presence and nature of risk factors in each group through collection of retrospective data. For example, in the Isle of Wight Study, from the total sample of 3,500 children, 110 children were identified as having a psychiatric disorder (cases) (Rutter et al., 1970). The characteristics of the cases were then compared with those of the controls. More children in the disordered group than in the nondisordered group came from homes characterized by parental separation, divorce, or death.

Incidence and Prevalence

Epidemiologic studies quantify occurrence of a disorder by deriving incidence and prevalence rates. *Incidence* is the number of new cases of a disorder within a population in a defined period of time. Only prospective studies can yield true incidence rates because the population is disease-free at the start of the study. The development of cases makes it possible to study the relationship between the risk factors and the occurrence of the psychiatric disorder.

The *prevalence* rate is the number of cases that exist at a given point in time (point prevalence) or over a specified period of time (period prevalence). Both the Richman et al. (1975) study and the Earls (1980) study determined prevalence of behavior problems among 3-year-old children. Offord et al. (1987) reported that the 6-month prevalence of one or more disorders was 18% in a group of 4- to 16-year-olds.

Several measures of association are derived using these rates. The *relative risk* (RR) is the incidence of the disorder in the exposed group compared with the incidence among those who are not exposed. RR can only be calculated from prospective data. Another statistic, the *odds ratio* (OR), has been developed to estimate the relative risk in cross-sectional study designs. Both the RR and OR are interpreted similarly. An exposure is associated with an increased risk if the ratio is greater than one and with a decreased risk if the ratio is less than one. Garrison, Earls, and Kindlon (1984) investigated the relationship between the mother's rating of the child's temperament at 3 years and the child's adjustment problems in first grade. An OR of 3.5 for school maladjustment was found for children whose mothers rated them as persistent or oppositional compared with children who were not rated as persistent. That is, persistent/oppositional children were more than three times as likely to have adjustment problems in school as children who were not persistent/oppositional.

Correlates of Disorders

Because psychiatric disorders are usually determined by many factors, epidemiologic studies must examine numerous risk factors. Costello (1989b) summarized some of the demographic correlates associated with child psychiatric disorders. Younger children were generally less likely than older children to have a disorder. Girls were more likely to have emotional, or internalizing, disorders, whereas boys were more likely to have behavioral, or externalizing, disorders. Children from lower social class families were more likely than children from higher social class families to have emotional and behavioral disorders. Other correlates of child psychiatric disorders included cognitive ability, self-esteem, family functioning, and parental psychopathology (Costello, 1989b). In order to understand the effect of any separate risk factor, it is necessary to consider other correlates of the disorder. For example, a researcher may be interested in whether children from single-parent families develop more behavior problems than those from two-parent families. If the investigator fails to consider the difference in income levels between one- and two-parent families, an effect on behavior problems may be misattributed to family structure rather than to income level.

ISSUES IN CHILD PSYCHIATRIC EPIDEMIOLOGY

In addition to decisions about sampling techniques and study design, a researcher interested in psychiatric disorders must define the disorder. How to define a *case*, that is, how to accurately discriminate between normality and pathology, is an issue that is still unresolved in psychiatric epidemiology. The definition of a case can differ across assessment techniques, clinicians, institutions, disciplines, and cultures.

In child psychiatric epidemiology, defining a case is made even more difficult because of the following issues: comorbidity, recognition of the dimensional nature of child psychopathology, need for a developmental approach, and lack of a consistent method to incorporate and synthesize data from multiple informants (Verhulst & Koot, 1992). Each of these challenges is discussed.

Comorbidity

One consideration in defining a case concerns *comorbidity*, the presence of more than one disorder. Several epidemiologic studies have reported a high level of comorbidity. The Isle of Wight studies found that depressive symptoms were common in many other disorders, especially conduct disorders (Rutter, 1989). Bird et al. (1988) reported that 54% of children with attention deficit disorder also had conduct disorder. Poorer long-term outcomes may be more strongly related to the combination of disorders, such as hyperactivity and aggression (Rutter, 1988). These findings highlight a need for more systematic study of patterns of comorbidity in child psychiatry.

Categorical Versus Dimensional Approaches

Two approaches in psychiatric epidemiology represent divergent views of psychiatric disorders. In the *categorical approach*, cases are based on separate, distinct, and definable disorders. The categorical approach generally represents the biomedical view. The past decade in psychiatric epidemiology has been characterized by the development of a formal taxonomic system, the *Diagnostic and Statiscal Manual of Mental Disorders DSM–III–R* (American Psychiatric Association, 1987) and the *DSM–IV* (American Psychiatric Association, 1993) which has explicit criteria to operationalize disorders, as well as by the creation of structured interviews for detecting psychiatric disorders in the community (Brandenburg, Friedman, & Silver, 1990). The Diagnostic Interview Schedule for Children (DISC) and the children's version of the Schedule for Affective Disorders and Schizophrenia (Kiddie-SADS) are examples of instruments scored to derive *DSM–III* diagnoses.

The DISC (Costello, Edelbrock, Dulcan, Kalas, & Klaric, 1984) is a highly structured interview developed for use in epidemiologic surveys with 6- to 18-year-olds. Because of its structure, less training and clinical judgment is required, and it can be administered by lay interviewers. The DISC covers a broad range of child behavior and symptoms in both the home and school. Symptom scores correspond to diagnostic constructs such as attention deficit disorder, conduct disorder, and depression. The DISC has parallel forms for parent and child.

The Kiddie-SADS (Puig-Antich & Chambers, 1978) is a semistructured interview for 6- to 17-year-olds. The less structured format requires the clinical judgment of a trained interviewer. Both parent and child are interviewed and discrepancies in their reports are resolved by the interviewer. The symptoms of various disorders, such as depression, schizophrenia, attention deficit disorder, conduct disorder, and substance use are evaluated.

By contrast to the categorical approach, the *dimensional approach* views mental health and illness on a continuum and is more consistent with a psychosocial view. Psychopathology is seen as a greater or lesser degree of normality rather than as a separate disorder (Edelbrock & Costello, 1988). Important information about the degree of impairment can be lost if disorders are characterized as present versus absent. In addition, for some disorders, such as behavior problems, there is evidence that there is a continuous distribution of problem severity rather than a clear cut presence or absence of problems (Edelbrock & Costello, 1988). Empirically derived symptom rating scales measure gradients of disorders rather than providing diagnoses. The most widely used dimensional assessment is the Child Behavior Checklist.

The Child Behavior Checklist (CBCL) was developed for children 4 to 18 years of age (Achenbach, 1991). Recently, a version has been developed for use with 2- to 3-year-old children (Achenbach, 1992). The instrument is designed to describe behavior symptoms rather than to provide a diagnosis of a disorder. The CBCL has undergone extensive psychometric testing with national normative samples and clinical samples. The constructs and symptom scores have been statistically derived. Eight syndromes, such as attention problems, aggressive behavior, and delinquent behavior, are normed separately by sex within age groups. Parent, teacher, and youth self-report versions are available. The CBCL is widely used in epidemiologic studies of the prevalence of behavior problems (Bird et al., 1988; Verhulst, Koot, & Berden, 1990).

Developmental Approach

Epidemiologists have begun to incorporate a *developmental framework*, which is crucial to the study of abnormal child development. This view argues that deviant behavior must be determined in the context of the child's developmental level, because some behaviors are normal or abnormal, depending on the child's age. The definition of psychopathology is based on an understanding of normal development in normal environments (Masten & Braswell, 1991). For example, if a child is referred to a clinic because he or she is afraid of a monster under his or her bed, it is important to know that fears of ghosts and monsters are common in kindergartners but not in sixth graders (Bauer, 1976). Rutter (1988) described a developmental perspective as a consideration of age with respect to the prevalence, onset, remission, developmental appropriateness, and continuity or discontinuity of a disorder across the life span.

An example of incorporating a developmental perspective is the Isle of Wight Study. The longitudinal design allowed the description of disorders according to age of onset. Different disorders were common at different ages. Depression was more common in teenagers than preadolescents (Rutter, 1989). In another longitudinal study, Loeber et al. (1993) studied 500 boys in each of the first, fourth, and seventh grades and followed them every 6 months. These investigators showed that there was a development or unfolding of problem behaviors that progressed from minor problem behaviors, such as stubbornness, to severe delinquency. In order to more fully understand the course and causes of a disorder, it is necessary to be aware of developmental issues.

Multiple Informants

Traditionally, only parents reported on a child's problems, but there has been an increasing recognition of the usefulness of multiple informants, each of whom contributes unique information about the child's behavior (Loeber, Green, & Lahey, 1990). Accurately defining whether a child has a disorder is a complex issue in child psychiatric epidemiology because of the necessity of obtaining data from multiple sources, such as parents, teachers, and the child, to evaluate the child's functioning in different settings. However, it is important to collect data from these multiple sources for two reasons. First, child behavior and adjustment problems may be situation specific. Second, different reporters may observe different behaviors. Costello (1989a) reported that relying on parental reports of problems would have resulted in the misdiagnosis of 50% of the children who had a disorder; relying on the child's reports would have resulted in an equally high rate of misdiagnosis.

Loeber, Green, Lahey, and Stouthamer-Loeber (1989) interviewed a clinic sample of 7- to 13-year-olds boys, their parents, and teachers. They found the highest agreement between informants for oppositional behaviors and conduct disorders and the lowest agreement for hyperactivity/inattention disorders. The children reported the least amount of hyperactive symptoms for themselves the reports of their compared with parents and teachers. Teachers generally are better reporters of hyperactive/inattention disorders, parents are better reporters of oppositional behaviors, and children are better reporters of behaviors such as worrying, anxiety, and depressive symptoms (Loeber et al., 1990). Thus, each informant has unique data to contribute about the child's functioning.

There are several approaches that can be used to integrate data from multiple sources (Verhulst & Koot, 1992). A child can be defined as having a disorder if at least one informant reports symptoms. A more stringent definition is to require that more than one informant report that the child exhibits symptoms in order for him or her to be defined as having a disorder. A third approach is to determine an optimal informant; that is, information from one informant is used for certain symptoms and from another informant for other symptoms. The Utility of using data from multiple informants to define pervasive and situation-specific disorders was demonstrated by Rutter (1989). The approach carried out to integrate data from multiple informants depends on the nature of the research question.

SUMMARY

This chapter has introduced the reader to child psychiatric epidemiology by describing classic studies in the field and by outlining basic epidemiologic methods. Important issues that must be considered in child psychiatric research, such as comorbidity, approaches to defining psychopathology, use of a developmental perspective, and multiple informants, were also addressed. Child psychiatric epidemiology incorporates numerous research questions that have major implications for clinicians and policy makers. The field has evolved from describing prevalence of psychopathology to developing and applying diagnostic and conceptual frameworks. However, continued attention should be accorded to developing standardized, reliable assessment tools for defining disorders, using appropriate study designs for investigating causes of disorders, and developing methods to integrate data from multiple informants (Verhulst & Koot, 1992).

REFERENCES

Achenbach, T. M. (1991). *Manual for the child behavior checklist/4–18 and 1991 profile*. Burlington: University of Vermont Department of Psychiatry.

Achenbach, T. M. (1991). *Manual for the child behavior checklist/2–3 and 1992 profile*. Burlington: University of Vermont Department of Psychiatry.

American Psychiatric Association. (1987). *Diagnostic and statistical manual of mental disorders* (3rd rev. ed.) Washington, DC: Author.

American Psychiatric Association. (1993). *DSM–IV draft criteria*. Washington, DC: Author.

Bauer, D. H. (1976). An exploratory study of developmental changes in children's fears. *Journal of Child Psychology and Psychiatry, 17*, 69–74.

Bird, H. R., Canino, G., Rubio-Stipec, M., Gould, M. S., Ribera, J., Sesman, M., Woodbury, M., Huertas-Goldman, S., Pagan, A., Sanchez-Lacay, A., & Moscoso, M. (1988). Estimates of the prevalence of childhood maladjustment in a community survey in Puerto Rico. *Archives of General Psychiatry, 45*, 1120–1126.

Boyle, M. H., Offord, D. R., Hofmann, H. G., Catlin, G. P., Byles, J. A., Cadman, D. T., Crawford, J. W., Links, P. S., Rae-Grant, N. I., & Szatmari, P. (1987). Ontario Child Health Study. I. Methodology. *Archives of General Psychiatry, 44*, 826–831.

Brandenburg, N. A., Friedman, R. M., & Silver, S. E. (1990). The epidemiology of childhood psychiatric disorders: Prevalence findings from recent studies. *Journal of the American Academy of Child and Adolescent Psychiatry, 29*, 76–83.

Costello, A. J., Edelbrock, C. S., Dulcan, M. K., Kalas, R., & Klaric, S. H. (1984). *Development and testing of the NIMH Diagnostic Interview Schedule for Children in a clinic population: Final report.* Rockville, MD: National Institute of Mental Health.

Costello, E. J. (1989a). Child psychiatric disorders and their correlates: A primary care pediatric sample. *Journal of the American Academy of Child and Adolescent Psychiatry, 28,* 851–855.

Costello, E. J. (1989b). Developments in child psychiatric epidemiology. *Journal of the American Academy of Child and Adolescent Psychiatry, 28,* 836–841.

Day, N. L. (1992). Epidemiology. In L. K. Hsu & M. Hersen (Eds.), *Research in psychiatry: Issues, strategies, and methods* (pp. 293–308). New York: Plenum.

Earls, F. J. (1980). Prevalence of behavior problems in 3-year-old children. *Archives of General Psychiatry, 37,* 1153–1157.

Earls, F. J. (1983). An epidemiological approach to the study of behavior problems in very young children. In S. B. Guze, F. J. Earls, & J. E. Barrett (Eds.), *Childhood psychopathology and development* (pp. 1–15). New York: Raven.

Edelbrock, C., & Costello, A. J. (1988). Convergence between statistically derived behavior problem syndromes and child psychiatric diagnoses. *Journal of Abnormal Child Psychology, 16,* 219–231.

Garrison, W., Earls, F., & Kindlon, D. (1984). Temperament characteristics in the third year of life and behavioral adjustment at school entry. *Journal of Clinical Child Psychology, 13,* 298–303.

Jensen, P. S., Bloedau, L., & Davis, H. (1990). Children at risk: II. Risk factors and clinic utilization. *Journal of the American Academy of Child and Adolescent Psychiatry, 29,* 804–812.

Kashani, J. H., Orvaschel, H., Rosenberg, T. K., & Reid, J. C. (1989). Psychopathology in a community sample of children and adolescents: A developmental perspective. *Journal of the American Academy of Child and Adolescent Psychiatry, 28,* 701–706.

Kazdin, A. E., Esveldt-Dawson, K., Sherick, R. B., & Colbus, D. (1985). Assessment of overt behavior and childhood depression among psychiatrically disturbed children. *Journal of Consulting and Clinical Psychology, 53,* 201–210.

Lapouse, R., & Monk, M. A. (1958). An epidemiologic study of behavior characteristics in children. *American Journal of Public Health, 48,* 1134–1144.

Loeber, R., Green, S. M., & Lahey, B. B. (1990). Mental health professionals' perception of the utility of children, mothers, and teachers as informants on childhood psychopathology. *Journal of Clinical Child Psychology, 19,* 136–143.

Loeber, R., Green, S. M., Lahey, B. B., & Stouthamer-Loeber, M. (1989). Optimal informants on childhood disruptive behaviors. *Development and Psychopathology, 1,* 317–337.

Loeber, R., Wung, P., Keenan, K., Giroux, B., Stouthamer-Loeber, M., Van Kammen, W. B., & Maughan, B. (1993). Developmental pathways in disruptive child behavior. *Development and Psychopathology, 5,* 103–133.

Masten, A. S., & Braswell L. (1991). Developmental psychopathology: An integrative framework. In P. R. Martin (Ed.), *Handbook of behavior therapy and psychological science: An integrative approach* (pp. 35–56). New York: Pergamon.

Offord, D. R., Boyle, M. H., Szatmari, P., Rae-Grant, N. I., Links, P. S., Cadman, D. T., Byles, J. A., Crawford, J. W., Blum, H. M., Byrne, C., Thomas, H., & Woodward, C. A. (1987). Ontario Child Health Study: II. Six-month prevalence of disorder and rates of service utilization. *Archives of General Psychiatry, 44,* 832–836.

Puig-Antich, J., & Chambers, W. (1978). *The schedule for affective disorders and schizophrenia for school-aged children.* New York: New York State Psychiatric Institute.

Richman, N. (1977). Short-term outcome of behaviour problems in three year old children. In P. J. Graham (Ed.), *Epidemiological approaches in child psychiatry* (pp.165– 179). New York: Academic Press.

Richman, N., Stevenson, J. E., & Graham, P. J. (1975). Prevalence of behaviour problems in 3-year-old children: An epidemiological study in a London Borough. *Journal of Child Psychology and Psychiatry, 16,* 277–287.

Richman, N., Stevenson, J. E., & Graham, P. J. (1982). *Pre-school to school: A behavioral study.* New York: Academic Press.

Rutter, M. (1988). Epidemiological approaches to developmental psychopathology. *Archives of General Psychiatry, 45,* 486–495.

Rutter, M. (1989). Isle of Wight revisited: Twenty-five years of child psychiatric epidemiology. *Journal of the American Academy of Child and Adolescent Psychiatry, 28,* 633–653.

Rutter, M., Tizard, J., & Whitmore, K. (Eds.). (1970). *Education, health, & behaviour*. London: Longman. (Reprinted 1981, Melbourne: Krieger.)

Thomas, B. H., Byrne, C., Offord, D. R., & Boyle, M. H. (1991). Prevalence of behavioral symptoms and the relationship of child, parent, and family variables in 4- and 5-year-olds: Results from the Ontario Child Health Study. *Journal of Developmental and Behavioral Pediatrics, 12*, 177–184.

Verhulst, F. C., & Koot, H. M. (1991). Longitudinal research in child and adolescent psychiatry. *Journal of the American Academy of Child and Adolescent Psychiatry, 30*, 361–368.

Verhulst, F. C., & Koot, H. M. (1992). *Child psychiatric epidemiology: Concepts, methods, and findings*. Newbury Park, CA: Sage.

Verhulst, F. C., Koot, H. M., & Berden, G. F. (1990). Four-year follow-up of an epidemiological sample. *Journal of the American Academy of Child and Adolescent Psychiatry, 29*, 440–448.

Werner, E. E., Bierman, J. M., & French, F. E. (1971). *The children of Kauai: A longitudinal study from the prenatal period to age ten*. Honolulu: University of Hawaii Press.

Chapter 4

Development and Psychopathology

Shelley Ross
Western Psychiatric Institute and Clinic

Kay D. Jennings
University of Pittsburgh

Developmental psychopathology is the "study of the origins and course of individual patterns of behavioral maladaptation" (Sroufe & Rutter, 1984, p. 14). Each part of this definition is significant and has multiple implications. First, developmental psychopathology stresses the factors leading to the development, onset, and course of maladaptive behavior. Second, it typically focuses on individual rather than group differences. Third, behavioral maladaptation, rather than diagnosis or classification, is emphasized. In addition, developmental psychopathology focuses on adaptive behavior as well as maladaptive behavior. In this chapter, we further define developmental psychopathology and describe how it is different from other related fields. We discuss how a developmental approach enhances our understanding of psychopathology and give illustrations from both research and clinical domains.

Developmental psychopathology was clearly defined as a distinct and separate field in 1984, when a special issue of *Child Development* was devoted to theoretical and research papers on the topic. By that time, it had become clear that many researchers were studying the development of psychopathology in young children in longitudinal research projects. Considerable resources were being devoted to the task of identifying protective and risk factors for psychopathology in young children from developmental perspectives (Cicchetti, 1989). Stress, vulnerability, coping, and resilience were central themes in many research programs (Garmezy & Masten, 1986). Although the studies were similar in many respects, the researchers approached their questions from varying (e.g., developmental, clinical, and medical/psychiatric) perspectives.

WHAT IS "PSYCHOPATHOLOGY" IN "DEVELOPMENTAL PSYCHOPATHOLOGY"?

Cowan (1988) stated, "Developmental psychopathology shifts our focus from the endless and perhaps fruitless debate about what psychopathology is, to how dysfunction emerges and is transformed over time" (p. 6). Nonetheless, developmental psychology must pursue the task of developing a working definition of what is maladaptive.

Garber (1984) discussed three definitions of psychopathological disorders. First, they can be viewed as deviations from age-appropriate norms (e.g., a 4-year-old child who has never had a temper tantrum). Second, they can be exaggerations of normal developmental trends (e.g., being rebellious as an adolescent). Third, they can be behaviors that interfere with normal developmental processes (e.g., extreme aggressiveness that interferes with the development of friendships). As Garber noted, all of these definitions assume some knowledge of the range of normal, adaptive development. In addition, because current diagnostic systems depend heavily on syndromes, that is, the co-occurrence of maladaptive behaviors, in defining pathology, behaviors that seem to indicate pathology should not be viewed in isolation. As with adults, few individual behaviors in children indicate pathology; rather, we rely on clusters of behaviors to determine most childhood disorders (Cicchetti, 1987; Rutter, 1988).

Another complexity is that both adaptive and maladaptive behaviors vary in intensity and frequency over time. All children have "good days" and "bad days" with respect to their behavior (Kazdin, 1989). Clinical psychologists are often subject to the consequences of this normal variation: Emergency appointments from worried parents are canceled because the child's behavior has returned to baseline (what is typical for that child). Both intensity (also known as "severity") and frequency can indicate maladaptive behavior. For example, a child who has a temper tantrum every 10 minutes is demonstrating a frequency-based problem, whereas a child who viciously hurls himself around during a temper tantrum may have an intensity-based problem. The intensity and frequency of behavior (rather than the type of behavior) often determine whether behavior is viewed as a deviation from age-appropriate norms by both parents and professionals. The chronicity of behavior is an important component of its frequency. For example, depressed children may be referred for psychological evaluation not only because of frequent and intense depressed mood but also because the depression is chronic.

All behavior must be viewed with the child's age in mind. For many behaviors there are "interaction effects" (age × severity/chronicity) that influence how we define what is adaptive or maladaptive. In an interaction effect, a given intensity of behavior is interpreted differently depending upon the age of the child (in other words, the behavior and the age interact). For example, frequent, chronic nighttime enuresis would be considered a problem behavior (and may prompt a clinical referral) in a 6-year-old child but not a 2-year-old child. Infrequent nighttime bedwetting would probably be overlooked in the older child (see Fig. 4.1). These interaction effects contribute substantially to the complexity of the field.

Psychopathological behavior can also be an exaggeration of normal developmental trends. Thus, negative attitudes and "acting out" are typical of most adolescents, but delinquency is viewed as pathological.

Finally, behavior can be considered pathologic because it interferes with normal developmental processes. For example, extreme shyness in young children may inhibit the development of peer relations and independence from parents.

It is important to remember that maladaptive behaviors are still *adaptations* to stressors or circumstances. They are maladaptive, in part, because they will likely lead to further developmental outcomes that are nonoptimal and/or to a narrowing of

Referral

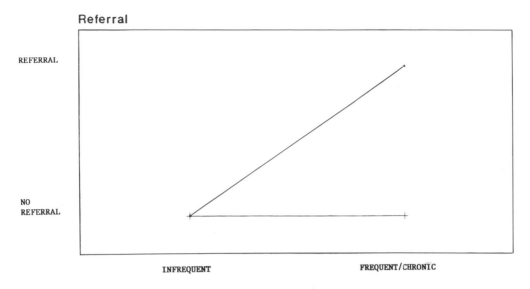

FIG. 4.1. Frequency of nocturnal enuresis. ■ = 6-year-old. | = 2-year-old.

choice points for adaptive development later on (Sroufe, 1989). Avoidance of social interaction is a good example of this point. Fraiberg (1982), in a compelling article on pathological defenses in infancy, explained how avoidance of the caregiver (which may occur as early as 3 months of age) may result from past experiences of parental deprivation or threat. Avoidance, a maladaptive behavior, is a defense against the "painful affects" (i.e., anxiety) associated with experiencing extreme negative parenting behavior and "signifies that the baby has associated the figure of his mother with a threat to his functioning" (p. 622). Avoidance is adaptive in that it enables the child to avoid repeated bouts of the unbearable anxiety associated with seeking comfort and being rejected. Avoidance is also maladaptive in that it prevents corrective experiences and clearly signals a failure to develop trust and a secure attachment relationship. Main and Goldwyn (1984) also described avoidance from a similar perspective.

WHAT IS "DEVELOPMENTAL" IN "DEVELOPMENTAL PSYCHOPATHOLOGY"?

In normally developing children, the specific behaviors that indicate adaptive functioning change with age. For example, with peers the competent 2-year-old silently offers a toy, the 5-year-old suggests a game of hide-and-seek, and the 10-year-old expresses concern when a peer falls down. Thus, within normal development, there are differentiations and transformations of behavior that are adaptive and expectable. The same is true for maladaptive behaviors. Clearly, stability in development does not imply that individual behaviors will be exhibited in the same manner over time but rather that adaptive or nonadaptive patterns of behavior are predictive of similar patterns later in life. Sroufe and Rutter (1984) summarized, "Individual functioning is coherent across periods of discontinuous growth and despite fundamental transformations in manifest behavior" (p. 21). For example, social competence tends to be modestly stable over time and clearly is manifest by different behaviors at different times, such as sharing, altruism, cooperation, assertiveness, conscientiousness, responsibility, and independence (Radke-Yarrow, Zahn-Waxler, & Chapman, 1983). We expect a 3-year-old to be learning to share and a 10-year-old to be learning a broad range of assertiveness skills.

Most models of development include multiple branching points ("trees") and assume that pathways may lead to a variety of outcomes. Pathways may become quite divergent from the normative (i.e., most frequent) paths but then may converge again. Different pathways may also lead to the same outcome. The main task for researchers is to better understand precursors, outcomes, and pathways that connect them (Sroufe & Jacobvitz, 1989). In addition to defining related patterns of adaptation within a domain across ages, we must learn how the "trees" fit together across domains. Important domains of development include the regulation of physiological arousal, motor functioning and ambulation, attachment and social relations, individuation and sense of self, exploration and mastery, peer relations and academic achievement, and gender identity and sexuality. Clearly, some of these domains are more salient at some ages than at others, and many are dependent on competencies developed at earlier stages (Cicchetti, Toth, Bush, & Gillespie, 1988). For example, sexuality is most salient in adolescence, but its development is related to the resolution of gender-identity issues in early childhood.

From this perspective, Sroufe (1989) identified five global questions to be addressed by the field of developmental psychopathology:

1. Which pathways will lead to similar outcomes?
2. What are the variations in outcome associated with a given pathway?
3. What factors determine the choice of a given pathway?
4. What factors determine whether a child continues on the path initially chosen, or is deflected off that path?
5. When do pathways become fixed, in the sense that deviation from the existing path becomes significantly less likely?

In Fig. 4.2, the broken, horizontal lines represent continuity in the type of adaptation expressed. This has been the most typical pattern to be studied. The solid, diagonal lines represent discontinuity and have received less attention.

Obviously there are many factors that determine both the initial path chosen and the later course; two broad categories of factors are genetic/biological determinants and environmental influences. Sroufe (1989, 1991) and Rutter and Quinton (1984) discussed an important third factor: *preceding development.* An individual's past experiences shape his or her personality and his or her environment and constrain the availability and type of future choices he or she can make. They also shape the way in which future experiences are interpreted by the individual. Thus, maladaptive behavior does not spring directly from past experience but rather is influenced both by past factors and present circumstances. For example, shyness and social awkwardness may have significant effects on later experiences. An unassertive and sensitive child may find that over time his or her set of friends has diminished. The child may become increasingly involved with academics or a favored hobby. This in turn influences the environment of the child and his or her opportunities for socialization experiences, such as team sports and dating. Peer relations may become further strained as others tease or reject the child. The child may come to interpret minor social rebuff in a very

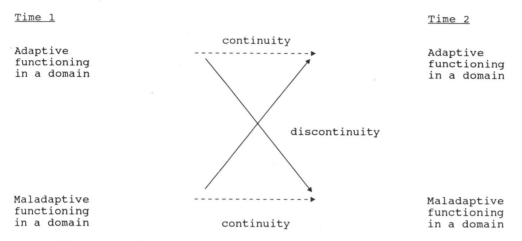

FIG. 4.2.   Possible developmental pathways for adaptive and nonadaptive functioning.

negative light because of his or her lack of experience. For example, the child may be fatalistic about relationships because he or she has never had a relationship that foundered but recovered.

In addition to examining developmental paths and transformations in psychopathology, the field of *developmental* psychopathology also examines other ways in which psychopathology may be affected by age or developmental stage. As Rutter (1989) pointed out, the meaning and expression of behavior varies with the age of the child. First, there may be age-related constraints on the expression of a behavior, especially in young children. For example, it is believed that children under 7 years of age (McConville, Boag, & Purohit, 1973) cannot develop feelings of guilt and worthlessness as a component of depression. (Indeed, until recently, it was held that children cannot experience clinical depression until adequate superego functioning had developed.) Second, behaviors vary as a function of context. For example, children in compromised environments may not have an opportunity to express motivation deficits until they are in school. Third, even when context is constrained, the meaning of behavior varies with age. Separation anxiety represents quite different phenomena in toddlers and adolescents. Finally, some behaviors that superficially appear different may represent the same underlying phenomenon. For example, although avoidant and resistant attachment relationships are manifest in different behaviors and are believed to be the results of different dyadic processes, they both place the child at risk for the development of nonoptimal social behaviors with peers and others and represent insecure attachment patterns (Ainsworth, Blehar, Waters, & Wall, 1978; Matas, Arend, & Sroufe, 1978; Sroufe, Egeland, & Kreutzer, 1990; Sroufe, Fox, & Pancake, 1983; Waters, Wippman, & Sroufe, 1979).

HOW DOES DEVELOPMENTAL PSYCHOPATHOLOGY DIFFER FROM RELATED FIELDS?

Because developmental psychopathology evolved from the combination of many fields, it offers unique approaches to understanding psychopathology (Sroufe & Rutter, 1984). Table 4.1 depicts similarities and differences among the related disciplines.

TABLE 4.1
Areas of Interest for Developmental Psychopathology and Related Fields

	Development		Focus		
Discipline	normal	abnormal	adult	child	diagnosis & treatment
developmental psychopathology	X	X	X	X	(X)
clinical child psychology	X	X		X	X
abnormal psychology		X	X	X	X
developmental psychology	X	(X)	X	X	

As Table 4.1 depicts, developmental psychopathology differs from clinical child psychology in two ways. First, developmental psychopathology focuses on pathways to adult outcomes. Second, developmental psychopathology has only a secondary interest in diagnosis and treatment. In contrast with abnormal psychology, developmental psychopathology focuses on normal development as well as abnormal development. Last, developmental psychopathology is more concerned with abnormal development, diagnosis, and treatment (although the last two are secondary) than is developmental psychology.

HOW DOES DEVELOPMENTAL PSYCHOPATHOLOGY LINK PATTERNS OF ADAPTATION AND MALADAPTATION OVER TIME?

The contribution of developmental psychopathology to understanding continuity and discontinuity is best illustrated with two examples. The first example is taken from the work of Alan Sroufe and his colleagues at the University of Minnesota. They conducted a longitudinal study of high-risk children (from families in poverty), with an emphasis on attachment and the development of social relations (Arend, Gove & Sroufe, 1979; Matas et al., 1978; Sroufe et al., 1983, 1990; Waters et al., 1979.) Sroufe and colleagues demonstrated that there is continuity in children's adaptation to salient developmental issues over time. Infants with secure attachments to their mothers were more autonomous in solving problems as toddlers. Links to preschool behaviors were also observed, although the behaviors were dissimilar. For example, children who had exhibited an anxious attachment in infancy were more dependent on their preschool teachers. They demonstrated dependency by having more contacts with teachers, seeking nurturance and physical contact, and needing more guidance and discipline. Children with a history of secure attachment relationships functioned better in a peer group, and they were less often victims and initiators of peer conflict. Teachers judged secure children to have higher self-esteem and ego resilience. In a general sense one could describe the secure children as flexible, emotionally engaged, and good utilizers of resources.

In a follow-up study when the children were 10-11 years old, Sroufe found that children with a history of secure attachments demonstrated better ego-resiliency, emotional health, social competence and self-confidence. They had resolved dependency issues in more healthy ways. They were less often isolated, less passive in response to aggression, and expressed more positive emotion than children with a history of anxious attachment.

Sroufe's research indicates the underlying coherence of adaptation despite profound developmental changes in the expression of specific behaviors. One reason that it is very difficult to predict specific behaviors across development is that children adapt to their environments (schools, homes, and neighborhoods) and these environments are also changing (Sroufe, 1983).

Grossman and Grossman (1991) also conducted longitudinal studies linking attachment security to later functioning. Children with a secure attachment relationship to their mother at 1 year of age demonstrated higher quality play as 5-year-olds. They also showed better conflict management with peers and superior ego-control and ego-resilience than children who had been anxiously attached. At 6 years of age, children who had been classified as secure were able to verbalize anxious or sad feelings during a projective separation anxiety test. They were also able to find good solutions to the separation problem and suggested that they could gain support from other people. Children who had been anxiously attached denied feelings, were pessimistic about the solution to the problem, or they emphasized abandonment. Their solutions were unrealistic and suggested a failure to cope with feelings.

At 10 years of age, children who had been securely attached continued to deal with stressful situations by acknowledging negative feelings and using relationship-oriented solutions. Peer relations were clearly related to attachment security (using both children's and parents' reports). Secure children had good friends who were trustworthy and reliable. Children who had been anxiously attached more often reported being excluded, teased, or taken advantage of by other children. In addition, although they claimed to have friends, they were unable to name them.

Clearly, both Sroufe's work and the work of the Grossmans indicate the richness of theory-driven models (like attachment theory) to make predictions about functioning in numerous domains. This is due, in part, to the fact that attachment theory addresses the underlying processes that drive development. The findings from both studies are consistent with Bowlby's (1969) theory proposing that the effects of attachment experiences move to a cognitive level of representation ("working models") and that it is these working models that so pervasively influence functioning. The ability to predict behavior over time comes not from stability in specific behaviors but from the underlying processes (the formation and use of working models) that drive behavior.

A second example more illustrative of discontinuity comes from research following the relatively recent (1970s) acknowledgment of depression as a disorder that can occur in childhood. The current guidelines (*DSM–IV*) for the diagnosis of depression in adults require the presence of depressed mood or anhedonia and a number of vegetative and cognitive symptoms (sleep disturbance, appetite disturbance, fatigue, psychomotor agitation or retardation, loss of interest, difficulty concentrating, guilt, and suicidal thoughts or behaviors). However, there are no specific guidelines for adapting these criteria to children. Some of these behaviors may not be symptomatic of depression in children, and the significance of a particular depressive behavior probably varies with age (Digdon & Gotlib, 1985). In addition, the base rates of the behavior in the normal population must be considered. For example, it may be particularly difficult to distinguish hyperkinesis in children from psychomotor agitation, and the base rate of hyperkinesis is quite high. Because decreased appetite is a common (and fluctuating) occurrence in children, it may be difficult to determine whether or not it is a symptom of depression (Digdon & Gotlib, 1985). Typically, in diagnosing disorders in children, one also has to rely more on reports from others (e.g., parents, teachers) than one would in diagnosing adults, and therefore one is susceptible to biases inherent in other's reports.

Another problem contributing to the difficulty in identifying depression in children is that children can find it difficult to distinguish sadness from anger and accurately express their feelings. It is also difficult for children to reflect on their own thoughts and feelings (metacognitive ability). Because children tend to express more positive affect than adults, depressed mood in children may be more evident as a state of neutral or unchanging affect rather than sadness per se. There are also developmental changes in how children describe their experience of depression. Children 6 to 8 years of age report sadness and helplessness, whereas children 8 to 11 years of age report feeling unloved and unworthy, and 12 to 13-year-old children are more likely than younger children to report feeling guilty (McConville et al., 1973). The question of whether these data reflect changes in children's actual experience of depression or in their report of depression remains unanswered.

According to Rutter (1986), we must determine how and why the manifestations of depression vary with age. A second goal is to determine how the development of cognitive abilities influences the experience and expression of depression. Because there is evidence that the onset and course of depression is influenced by stressful life circumstances, we also need to investigate the role of these factors in childhood depression. Again, what we know about normal development is important: When compared to adults, children are less aware of the enduring nature of their circumstances.

SUMMARY

In the area of developmental psychopathology, researchers are attempting to define normal and abnormal behavior, adaptation and maladaptation, and continuity and discontinuity. The tasks are enormous and require both theoretical and methodological advances. However, developmental psychopathology provides an important theoretical framework that directs both research and clinical efforts. Future directions include (a) continued study of normal development, from both a group perspective that describes typical behaviors at different ages and from an individual perspective that describes links across domains of functioning in one person, (b) further definition and identification of maladaptive development and refinement of classification systems, and (c) understanding developmental transformation, vulnerability, and resilience across the life span.

REFERENCES

Ainsworth, M. D. S., Blehar, M. C., Waters, E., & Wall, S. (1978). *Patterns of attachment*. Hillsdale, NJ: Lawrence Erlbaum Associates.

Arend, R., Gove, F., & Sroufe, L. A. (1979). Continuity of individual adaptation from infancy to kindergarten: A predictive study of ego-resiliency and curiosity in preschoolers. *Child Development, 50*, 950–959.

Bowlby, J. (1969). *Attachment and loss (Vol. 1). Attachment*. New York: Basic.

Cicchetti, D. (1987). Developmental psychopathology in infancy: Illustration from the study of maltreated youngsters. *Journal of Consulting and Clinical Psychology, 55*, 837–845.

Cicchetti, D. (1989). Developmental psychopathology: Some thoughts on its evolution. *Development and Psychopathology, 1*, 1–4.

Cicchetti, D., Toth, S. L., Bush, M. A., & Gillespie, J. F. (1988). Stage-salient issues: A transactional model of intervention. In E. D. Nannis & P. A. Cowan (Eds.), *New directions for child development; No. 39. Developmental psychopathology and its treatment* (pp. 123–145). San Francisco: Jossey-Bass.

Cowan, P. A. (1988) Developmental psychopathology: A nine-cell map of the territory. In E. D. Nannis & P. A. Cowan (Eds.), *New directions for child development; No. 39. Developmental psychopathology and its treatment* (pp. 5–29). San Francisco: Jossey-Bass.

Digdon, N., & Gotlib, I. H. (1985). Developmental considerations in the study of childhood depression. *Developmental Review, 5*, 162–199.

Fraiberg, S. (1982). Pathological defenses in infancy. *Psychoanalytic Quarterly, 11*, 612–635.

Garber, J. (1984). Classification of childhood psychopathology: A developmental perspective. *Child Development, 55*, 30–48.

Garmezy, N., & Masten, A. S. (1986). Stress, competence, and resilience: Common frontiers for therapist and psychopathologist. *Behavior Therapy, 17*, 500–521.

Grossman, K. E., & Grossman, K. (1991). Attachment quality as an organizer of emotional and behavioral responses in a longitudinal perspective. In C. M. Parkes, J. Stevenson-Hinde, & P. Marris (Eds.), *Attachment across the life cycle* (pp. 93–114). London: Tavistock/Routledge.

Kazdin, A. E. (1989). Developmental psychopathology. Current research, issues, and directions. *American Psychologist, 44*, 180–187.

Main, M., & Goldwyn, R. (1984). Predicting rejection of her infant from mother's representation of her own experience: Implications for the abused-abusing intergenerational cycle. *Child Abuse and Neglect, 8*, 203–217.

Matas, L., Arend, R. A., & Sroufe, L. A. (1978). Continuity of adaptation in the second year: The relationship between quality of attachment and later competence. *Child Development, 49*, 547–556.

McConville, B. J., Boag, L. C., & Purohit, A. P. (1973). Three types of childhood depression. *Canadian Psychiatric Association Journal, 18*, 133–138.

Radke-Yarrow, M., Zahn-Waxler, C., & Chapman, M. (1983). Children's prosocial dispositions and behavior. In P. H. Mussen (Ed.), *Handbook of child psychology, Vol. 4. Socialization, personality, and social development* (pp. 469–546). New York: Wiley.

Rutter, M. (1986). Child psychiatry: The interface between clinical and developmental research. *Psychological Medicine, 16*, 151–169.

Rutter, M. (1988). Epidemiological approaches to developmental psychopathology. *Archives of General Psychiatry, 45*, 486–495.

Rutter, M. (1989). Age as an ambiguous variable in developmental research: Some epidemiological considerations from developmental psychopathology. *International Journal of Behavioral Development, 12*, 1–34.

Rutter, M., & Quinton, D. (1984). Parental psychiatric disorder: Effects on children. *Psychological Medicine, 14*, 853–880.

Sroufe, L. A. (1983). Infant–caregiver attachment and patterns of adaptation and competence. In M. Perlmutter (Ed.), *Minnesota symposia in child psychology: Vol. 16* (pp. 41–91). Hillsdale, NJ: Lawrence Erlbaum Associates.

Sroufe, L. A. (1989). Pathways to adaptation and maladaptation: Psychopathology as developmental deviation. In D. Cicchetti (Ed.), *The emergence of a discipline: Rochester symposium on developmental psychopathology: Vol. 1* (pp. 13–40). Hillsdale, NJ: Lawrence Erlbaum Associates.

Sroufe, L. A. (1991). Considering normal and abnormal together: The essence of developmental psychopathology. *Development and Psychopathology, 2*, 335–347.

Sroufe, L. A., Egeland, B., & Kreutzer, T. (1990). The fate of early experience following developmental change: Longitudinal approaches to individual adaptation in childhood. *Child Development, 61*, 1363–1373.

Sroufe, L. A., Fox, N. E., & Pancake, V. R. (1983). Attachment and dependency in developmental perspective. *Child Development, 54*, 1615–1627.

Sroufe, L. A., & Jacobvitz, D. (1989). Diverging pathways, developmental transformations, multiple etiologies and the problem of continuity in development. *Human Development, 32*, 196–203.

Sroufe, L. A., & Rutter, M. (1984). The domain of developmental psychopathology. *Child Development, 55*, 17–29.

Waters, E., Wippman, J., & Sroufe, L. A. (1979). Attachment, positive affect, and competence in the peer group: Two studies in construct validation. *Child Development, 50*, 821–829.

Chapter 5

Psychophysiological Determinants

Rafael Klorman
University of Rochester

There is probably little argument that disturbances of emotions, arousal dysfunction, and cognitive processes are relevant to the study of psychopathology. Both normal and abnormal aspects of these processes have been investigated by means of physiological methods for nearly half a century. Because the formal study of developmental psychopathology has lagged behind work on disorders of adult life, the corresponding psychophysiological literature on children is also more limited. This chapter deals with three disorders that have been examined relatively extensively: childhood autism, attention deficit disorder, and antisocial/conduct disorder. This review is selective with respect to both topics and findings.

Some Background

Because the methods used in the research reviewed here are probably unfamiliar to many readers, some background information is presented in this section and throughout the chapter. For a thorough treatment of this methodology, readers should consult standard texts (e.g., Coles, Donchin, & Porges, 1986), Martin & Venables, 1980). Most studies discussed in this chapter use measures involving autonomic or brain electrical activity. These measures have been used to investigate abnormalities of arousal or responsiveness to stimulation.

The *autonomic* measures studied most often are heart rate and skin conductance (also known as GSR or electrodermal activity). Electrodermal measures are viewed as reflecting the activity of sweat glands, which are solely innervated by the sympathetic branch of the autonomic nervous system (Fowles, 1993). Heart rate is affected by the balance between the sympathetic and parasympathetic branches of the autonomic nervous system.

Investigators have been interested in using autonomic activity to classify subjects on a continuum from sleep/drowsiness through alertness to excitement. These aspects of autonomic arousal are usually investigated with tonic measures, that is, those based on periods of several minutes. Comparable measures reflecting arousal of the central nervous system can be derived from the *electroencephalogram* (EEG), the voltages recorded from electrodes attached to the scalp. The frequency of the EEG yields information concerning arousal: Slow waves reflect low levels of arousal whereas fast activity reflects alertness or hyperarousal.

Another focus of research has been on subject's phasic, moment-by-moment reactions to discrete stimuli with emotional significance or those relevant to a task administered to a subject. Generally, the investigator is interested in the magnitude of reactions (e.g., increases in skin conductance or slowing of heart rate) over a period of seconds that is evoked by a particular type of stimulation.

A conceptually related methodology involves *event-related potentials* (ERPs), which are superimposed on the EEG. A discrete stimulus, such as a sound or light, evokes characteristic patterns of voltage changes that may be studied by averaging these responses over several trials. The early (< 100 milliseconds) peaks and valleys of ERPs are obligatory responses to stimulation and reflect sensory processes (e.g., reactions to loudness, brightness, touch). Later ERP components (e.g., $\geq$ 300 milliseconds) tend to be elicited by cognitive aspects of stimulation, such as the designation of a tone stimulus as a target in a task. These cognitive components of ERPs have been examined in an effort to assess abnormalities in attention.

AUTISM

Psychophysiological techniques have been used to increase our understanding of autism. Clearly, these patients are especially handicapped in terms of their language skills, so that conventional methods for assessing cognitive functioning may present difficulties. Therefore, noninvasive tools, such as psychophysiological approaches, appear especially suitable for this population. Although the research in this area varies with respect to whether autonomic responses or ERPs were investigated, most studies focus on the extent to which autistic patients are sensitive to changes in external events.

Autonomic Reactivity in Autistic Children

Reactions to Repeated Stimulation.   The Australian investigators Angela James and Robert Barry (Barry & James, 1988, James & Barry, 1984) have reported abnormal autonomic reactivity in autism. Their basic findings are illustrated in Fig. 5.1. Normal and mentally retarded children displayed the expected orderly decrease in the amplitude of skin conductance responses over five repetitions of visual (squares of two sizes) and auditory stimuli (tones of two loudnesses). This pattern of response diminution with stimulus repetition is a fundamental characteristic of normal orienting responses, that is, autonomic reactions to novel stimulation. In contrast, autistic children's electrodermal responses failed to diminish with stimulus repetition, a result suggesting that they did not detect the familiarity of the repeated stimuli. In fact, the autistic patients had abnormally large skin conductance responses throughout stimulation. A similar lack of amplitude diminution with repetition as obtained for the respiratory pause and

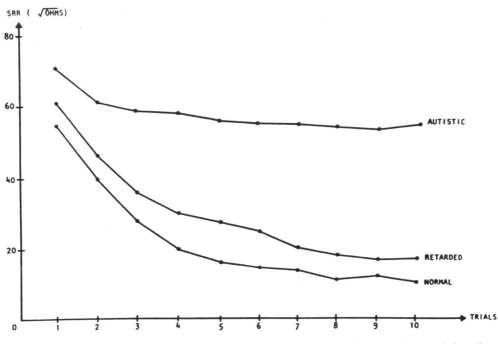

SRR ($\sqrt{\text{OHMS}}$)

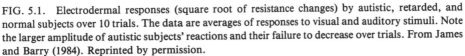

FIG. 5.1. Electrodermal responses (square root of resistance changes) by autistic, retarded, and normal subjects over 10 trials. The data are averages of responses to visual and auditory stimuli. Note the larger amplitude of autistic subjects' reactions and their failure to decrease over trials. From James and Barry (1984). Reprinted by permission.

heart rate deceleration elicited by the same stimuli (James & Barry, 1984). Autistic subjects were not totally insensitive to external stimulation, because their autonomic reactions, like those of the control groups, were increased by the intensity of the stimuli (i.e., size of the squares and loudness of the tones). Thus, the investigators viewed their findings as suggesting a specific defect in the registration of reduced novelty. The fact that this orienting disturbance was absent in mentally retarded subjects implies that it is specific to autism and not secondary to the lower intelligence of the autistic sample.

It is likely that the previous results reflect, at least in part, the effects of abnormal arousal. As the authors noted, their autistic subjects were probably more severely disturbed than those in other investigations, to the extent that the experimenters had to physically restrain their hands to achieve satisfactory recordings. Thus, in comparison to the normal and retarded subjects, the autistic children may have experienced anxiety and heightened arousal, two conditions that may militate against decrement in autonomic responses. Nevertheless, the consistency of Barry and James' findings across their studies and their use of large sample sizes are impressive.

Unfortunately, other investigators have not confirmed James and Barry's (1988) finding of autonomic hyperresponsivity in autistic youngsters. For instance, there have been reports that autistic children have abnormally *small* skin conductance responses to visual patterns (van Engeland, Roelofs, Verbaten, & Slangen, 1991), as well as tones or lights (Bernal & Miller, 1970). There have also been findings of skin conductance responses of *normal* amplitude following tones (Palkowitz & Wiesenfeld, 1980; Stevens & Gruzelier, 1984). Most importantly, none of these investigators replicated Barry and

James' (1988) report that the orienting responses of autistic patients failed to diminish with stimulus repetition.

Responses to Change in Stimulation.   Additional evidence bearing on possible deficits in processing novelty was reported by van Engeland et al. (1991). Their nonretarded autistic adolescent subjects, in comparison to normal and psychiatric controls, were electrodermally underresponsive to an unexpected change in the position of a visual pattern presented repeatedly on a screen. This report was especially noteworthy, because van Engeland et al. (1991) demonstrated that autistic and control groups were comparable in the extent to which they followed the change in location of the pattern with their eyes. The investigators concluded that autistic patients may have deficits in arousal or in cognitive evaluations of change in the visual field.

Unfortunately, van Engeland et al.'s (1991) finding of reduced sensitivity to stimulus novelty in the skin conductance responses of autistic subjects was not obtained in an earlier investigation by Bernal and Miller (1970). These experimenters found no differences between autistic and normal children's electrodermal reactions when the pitch of a tone or the intensity of a light was changed unexpectedly in the middle of a series. It is possible that the type of stimulus change (spatial position vs. pitch or brightness) may account for the difference between the two investigations. Alternatively, it is conceivable that the discrepancy in findings is due to the greater clinical severity and younger age of Bernal and Miller's (1970) subjects. Additional research is needed to resolve these discrepancies.

Comment.   Clearly, there is inconsistent support for hyperresponsiveness and lack of response decrement with stimulus repetition in the electrodermal responses of autistic children. In fact, the majority of studies report hyporesponsiveness. There is also contradictory evidence concerning autistic children's sensitivity to changes in stimulation. Perhaps heterogeneity in the age and severity of the autistic samples or stimulus characteristics may play a role in these discrepancies among studies.

Arousal.   There is some evidence that, consistent with clinical impression, autistic children are autonomically hyperaroused. Abnormally elevated skin conductance levels (Palkowitz & Wiesenfeld, 1980; Stevens & Gruzelier, 1984), heart rate (including sustained tachycardia), and blood pressure have been reported (Cohen & Johnson, 1977; James & Barry, 1984; Kootz & Cohen, 1981; Lake, Ziegler, & Murphy, 1977). However, elevated cardiovascular arousal was sometimes found, not only in the autistic samples, but also among nonautistic children with other disorders (Cohen & Johnson, 1977; James & Barry, 1984). Moreover, other studies detected normal heart rate (Graveling & Brooke, 1978; Hutt, Forrest, & Richer, 1975; MacCulloch & Williams, 1971; Miller & Bernal, 1971; Palkowitz & Wiesenfeld, 1980), skin conductance level, and pupil diameter (van Engeland et al., 1991). Even when autistic patients were found to be sympathetically overaroused, as noted in the original reports, it cannot be established whether these findings are representative of the patients' normal physiological levels or whether they reflect reactions to the stress of being tested. The occasional reports that nonautistic psychiatric comparison groups were similarly overaroused suggest that these evaluations are nonspecifically stressful for psychiatric patients as opposed to normal children. This impression is strengthened by the fact that investigators reporting acclimatization sessions for autistic patients before the actual test found normal heart rates (Bernal & Miller, 1970; Palkowitz & Wiesenfeld, 1980) or decreasing heart rates with repeated testing (Kootz, Marimelli, & Cohen, 1982). As suggested previously, it is difficult to sort out the generality of overarousal findings in autism because of the heterogeneity in clinical severity and age of the samples studied.

A possible explanation for the findings on arousal in autism is suggested by the fact that three investigations that detected normal heart rates in autistic children also found greater variability of cardiac rate (Graveling & Brooke, 1978; Hutt et al., 1975; MacCulloch & Williams, 1971). One interpretation of these results is that the range of heart rate in autistic patients includes abnormally fast as well as slow activity. Thus, it is conceivable that arousing test environments or relatively brief measurement periods would potentiate elevated pulse rates in autism. These sources of variance would need to be controlled in order to settle the question of arousal abnormalities in autism.

Event-Related Potentials in Autism

Oddball Task and Associated Endogenous Components.   Several studies have used ERPs to ask parallel questions to those investigated by means of autonomic measures. These studies have employed the "oddball" task, which typically involved a series of trials in which three stimuli were presented in unpredictable order over several trials. One of these stimuli (frequent or standard) appeared approximately 80% of the time, whereas the other two stimuli were displayed more rarely (e.g., only 10% of the trials each). Subjects were directed to count or press a button when detecting one of the infrequent stimuli (e.g., the target). The other infrequent stimulus is referred to as the novel. The stimuli in this task usually evoke ERPs with at least two components of interest. P3b, as shown in Fig. 5.2, has a positive voltage and reaches maximal amplitude at posterior scalp sites around 300–500 msec after the stimulus is presented. Another important component is Nc, a negative voltage with maximal amplitude at the front of the scalp (See Fig. 5.2). Both Nc and P3b have larger amplitude in response to novel and target stimuli. Several studies have focused on these ERP components in order to study cognitive abnormalities in autism.

Studies of ERPs in the Oddball Task.   In a representative study, Dawson, Finley, Phillips, Galpert, and Lewy (1988) used an oddball task involving frequent clicks and infrequent presentations of the sound *Da* and a piano chord. Subjects were required to raise their hand after hearing *Da*, the target stimulus. In comparison to age-matched normals, autistic adolescents had smaller amplitude of P3b for targets. Moreover, the autistic patients lacked the normal pattern of larger P3b amplitudes to targets than to novels. These abnormalities were not an artifact of poorer performance by the autistic sample, because this pattern was present even among those autistic patients with nearly perfect performance. The ERP results suggest, therefore, that autistic patients did not discriminate to the same extent as normals between the target's linguistic cues and the less experimentally relevant chord stimuli.

Studies by Courchesne's Group.   A similar study by Courchesne, Lincoln, Kilman, and Galambos (1985) investigated P3b abnormalities in autism to both visual and auditory stimuli. Their auditory oddball task consisted of a frequent phonetic stimulus (*me*), an infrequent phonetic target (*you*), and novel acoustic patterns. In turn, their visual task included frequent presentations of the letter *B*, the letter *A* as a

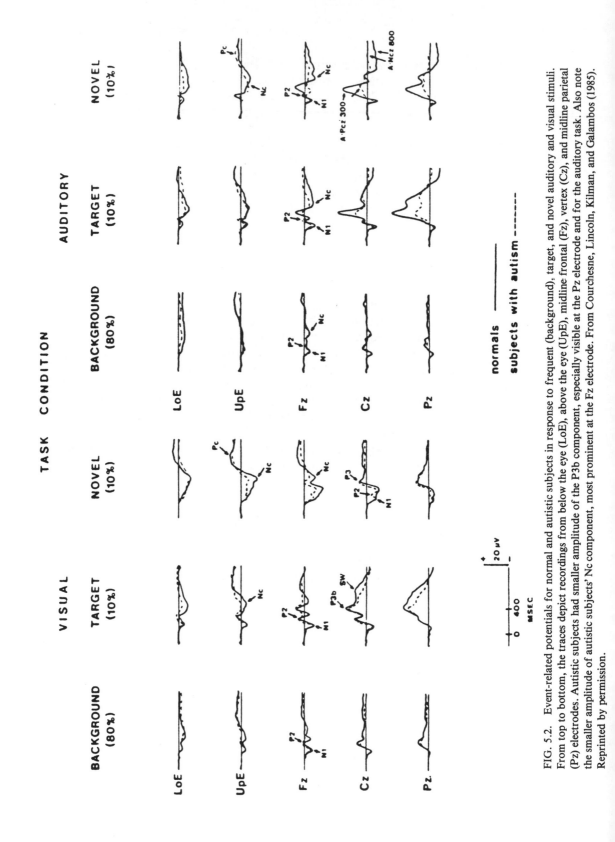

FIG. 5.2. Event-related potentials for normal and autistic subjects in response to frequent (background), target, and novel auditory and visual stimuli. From top to bottom, the traces depict recordings from below the eye (LoE), above the eye (UpE), midline frontal (Fz), vertex (Cz), and midline parietal (Pz) electrodes. Autistic subjects had smaller amplitude of the P3b component, especially visible at the Pz electrode and for the auditory task. Also note the smaller amplitude of autistic subjects' Nc component, most prominent at the Fz electrode. From Courchesne, Lincoln, Kilman, and Galambos (1985). Reprinted by permission.

64

target, and unrecognizable visual patterns as novels. Both oddball series were presented under instructions to (a) merely attend or (b) press a button to the designated target. Figure 5.2, shows that, similar to Dawson et al. (1988), the nonretarded autistic adolescents exhibited abnormally small P3b amplitudes to both targets and novels. Because the reduction of P3b amplitude in autism reached significance for only acoustic stimuli, it might be tempting to conclude that autistic patients have a specific abnormality in processing significant auditory (semantic) versus visual stimuli. However, there were deviant aspects of the visual ERPs of the autistic patients as well. Specifically, as seen in Fig. 5.2, the novelty-sensitive Nc component to visual target and novel stimuli was smaller for autistic than normal patients.

There is yet another result suggesting that the autistic subjects' ERP abnormalities reflect modality-nonspecific, cognitive aspects of processing. Unlike their normal peers, the autistic adolescents lacked larger P3b amplitudes to the letter *A* and the *You* sounds when they required a button press as opposed to the condition of passive stimulation. These findings are remarkable, because autistic and normal subjects were comparably accurate at detecting targets, although autistic children more slowly. Thus, despite behavioral evidence that autistic subjects' attention was appropriately mobilized by the task, their ERPs point to "a *limited* or *selective* capacity to orient to novel information [an ability] critical to cognitive development" (Courchesne et al., 1985, p. 69). Yet, as noted by the investigators, the ERPs of autistic patients were not totally impervious to novelty. Specifically, several components, including P3b, distinguished between novels or targets, on the one hand, and frequent or nontarget stimuli on the other. Clearly, the abnormalities of autistic children in this task are not easily summarized by a single, overarching cognitive disability.

These questions were examined further in a subsequent investigation (Courchesne, Lincoln, Yeung-Courchesne, Elmasian, & Grillon, 1989). Nonretarded autistic subjects ($M = 19.7$ years) were compared with normal subjects ($M = 16.9$ years), and patients with receptive developmental dysphasia ($M = 15.3$). The dysphasic group represents a clinical entity with a different disorder of language development and without the social abnormalities of autism. Once again, the oddball tasks involved either auditory or visual stimuli. Besides the modality of stimulation, the experiment manipulated the nature of the discrimination required. In one condition, the target was defined, separately for each modality, as the less frequent of two stimuli. In another condition, a single stimulus was presented (tone or colored square) at constant intervals, and subjects pressed a button on those trials when the stimulus was omitted.

Accuracy and reaction time of the three groups was comparable, so that ERP differences could not be attributed to discrepancies in subjects' performance. In fact, the autistic patients were uniformly, but nonsignificantly, faster than the other samples. Consistent with previous studies, for both types of targets (infrequent stimulus or skipped nontarget) and modalities (auditory and visual), autistic subjects had smaller P3b amplitude than normal or dysphasic individuals. Once again, these differences were greater and more statistically significant for the auditory than for the visual task.

Summary of Courchesne's ERP Studies.   These studies by Courchesne's group evoked abnormally small P3b amplitude in autistic subjects whether the discriminations required were sensory (pitch/color) or linguistic (*you* vs. *me* or *A* vs. *B*). Especially interesting were the abnormalities detected in response to the *omission* of an expected stimulus, because such an event evokes only cognitive, but not sensory, reactions. This deficit was originally identified in autistic children by Novick, Vaughan, Kurtzberg, and Simson (1980).

Also consistent with Courchesne et al.'s (1985) study, autistic patients displayed abnormally small amplitude of the Nc component in comparison to normal and dysphasic subjects. In fact, across all target events, this component had a positive, rather than negative, polarity among autistic patients.

In combination, the results, once again, present a paradox. Although the task performance of autistic and normal subjects was comparable (in fact, autistic patients were marginally faster), the cognitive ERPs of autistic subjects reflect underresponsiveness to target and novel events. The authors suggested that the autistic patients may have used aberrant physiologicalis processes or strategies to detect target events. Further explication of these findings may be useful in increasing understanding of cognitive deficits in autism.

ERP Abnormalities in Response to Visual Stimuli.   The preceding studies by Courchesne and colleagues revealed stronger P3b abnormalities for the auditory than the visual modality. This finding has not always been obtained in previous research (e.g., Novick, Kurtzberg, & Vaughan, 1979), but its replication might suggest a connection with the speech disorders characterizing autism. Thus, great interest attaches to a study of visual ERPs in autism reported by Verbaten, Roelofs, van Engeland, Kenemans, and Slangen (1991). The investigators compared nonretarded autistic children ($M = 9.7$ years) with age-matched samples of normal children as well as externalizing (conduct disorder) and internalizing (anxiety diagnoses) patients. The autistic patients did not differ from the normal or other clinical groups in their ERPs on the first presentation of visual pattern or in the expected decrease in ERP amplitude with repeated presentation of this stimulus. These findings suggest normal detection of novel visual stimulation by autistic children. However, when the location of the visual pattern on the screen was changed unpredictably after 18 presentations in the same position, only normal subjects reacted with increased amplitude of the Nc component. Notably, the experimenters verified that this difference was not attributable to the length of time that the subjects fixated the stimuli. Thus, the finding is consistent with Courchesne et al.'s (1985, 1989) reports but is qualified by two observations. First, lack of Nc increase following the unexpected change in location was not specific to autism, as internalizing and externalizing patients exhibited the same abnormality. Second, the difference between normal and pathologic groups emerged only among subjects who saw a complex pattern and not those who viewed a simple pattern.

Verbaten et al. (1991) also administered a visual oddball task. The normative pattern of larger amplitude of P3b for targets than for nontargets was found for normals, internalizing patients, and those autistic children with normal performance. However, this pattern was absent among those autistic children with highly erroneous counts of the target and externalizing subjects (who had normal performance). Notably, Verbaten et al. (1991) studied relatively young autistic patients, such that their task proved very difficult for many of them. Thus, the ERP deviance identified was neither specific to autism nor general across all levels of performance ability in the autistic group.

Selective Attention.   Ciesielski, Courchesne, and Elmasian (1990) utilized ERPs to determine whether nonretarded autistic young adults are deficient in selective attention. Selective attention involves focusing more on stimuli central to a task than on task-irrelevant ones. In this experiment, subjects were asked to press a button when viewing a rare green flash as opposed to a more frequent red flash; at the same time, they were asked to ignore frequent and rare tones of different pitches. (In another condition, subjects responded to rare tones, while ignoring the light flashes.) Selective attention was quantified by comparing the ERP evoked by the frequent tone when it was relevant (the target was a rare tone) to the condition when tones were not relevant. (A similar procedure was performed for the visual responses.) As shown in Fig. 5.3, and as expected, normals displayed more negative ERPs for relevant stimuli. (This response is usually termed Nd [negative difference response] or processing negativity, and its derivation is described in Fig. 5.3) Significantly, normals exhibited Nd waves of greater amplitude than autistic patients for both tones and lights, but these differences were more pronounced for auditory stimuli. Thus, ERP indications of selective attention were attenuated in the autistic sample.

Notably, smaller amplitude of Nd was found among autistic patients even though these subjects were able to perform the task satisfactorily, albeit worse than controls. Thus, the authors suggested that "abnormalities in the neurophysiological mechanism of selective attention may underlie the cognitive deficits basic to autism" (p. 218). However, the task had limited selective attention requirements, because the interval between successive stimuli (0.5 to 1.5 seconds) was sufficiently long that it was not necessary to ignore irrelevant stimuli in order to attend to the relevant modality. Of course, temporally overlapping stimuli probably would have made the task too difficult.

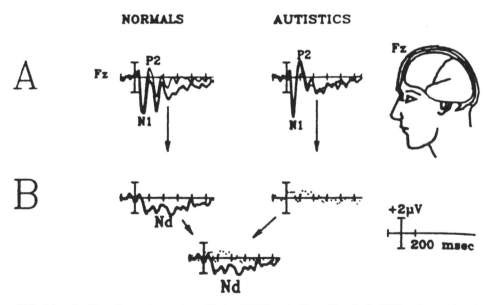

FIG. 5.3.   Auditory focused attention effects—ERPS to Auditory Standards. ERPs of normal and autistic subjects to auditory frequent stimuli (standards) recorded from the midline frontal scalp (Fz). Trace A shows each group's responses to the frequent tones when they were attended (thick lines) and unattended (thin lines). Trace B shows the algebraic difference between the attended and unattended conditions (Nd or processing negativity) for normals (solid thick line) and autistics (dotted line). The lower-most trace superimposes the Nd for normal and autistic subjects. Note the larger amplitude of Nd for normal persons. From Ciesielski, Courchesne, and Elmasian (1990). Reprinted by permission.

Comment. The weight of the evidence involving autonomic and ERP studies point to deficits by autistic patients in the detection of novelty. The ERP studies generally have found that autistic subjects have abnormally small amplitude of P3b and Nc to target and rare novel stimuli, even when their performance is not deficient in comparison to normals. It is impressive that these abnormalities were found in nonretarded autistic persons, so that retardation is excluded as an explanation. Similarly, autistic subjects differed from dysphasic patients, a finding suggesting that these ERP abnormalities are specific to autism. Finally, ERP correlates of selective attention were less pronounced in autistic patients. There is some evidence that the ERP abnormalities concerning novelty as well as selective attention may be more pronounced in response to auditory than visual stimuli, a finding consistent with the linguistic deficits of the autistic disorder.

ATTENTION DEFICIT DISORDER

A burgeoning literature spanning over two decades deals with the psychophysiological study of the Attention Deficit Disorder (ADD) syndrome, now referred to an Attention-Deficit Hyperactivity Disorder. Therefore, this section emphasizes relatively recent work in this area.

Arousal Deficits

In a provocative set of studies, Satterfield and his colleagues (Satterfield, Cantwell, & Satterfield, 1974) challenged the prevalent assumption that ADD children are excessively aroused. They summarized the results of several studies in which they found that ADD children have an excess of slow EEG activity and low skin conductance level, both indications of underarousal. In fact, they reported that ADD patients characterized by physiological underarousal tended to benefit more from stimulant therapy than those with the opposite pattern. In this framework, stimulants were viewed as normalizing ADD children by restoring normal arousal levels. Thus, this position suggested that ADD patients' reaction to stimulant drugs is not paradoxical.

In a later report, Satterfield and his colleagues (Satterfield, Schell, Backs, & Hidaka, 1984) reported on an unusually large sample of ADD children ($N = 138$) and 60 normal boys. They attempted to resolve previous inconsistencies in the literature with regard to abnormalities in EEG arousal among ADD children. Interestingly, their results showed that patients under 7.5 years of age differed from normals in having less EEG activity in the delta, theta, alpha, and beta bands. In contrast, older ADD patients exceeded their normal matches in both alpha and beta activity. Thus, the investigators viewed young ADD patients as having an overaroused central nervous system (diminished activity in the slow frequency bands) and older patients as underaroused. This analysis emphasizes abnormal maturational processes in hyperactive children.

Satterfield, Schell, et al.'s (1984) position is consistent with the findings of other investigators. For instance, Grünewald-Zuberbier, Grünewald, and Rasche (1975) reported that older ADD children ($M = 12.2$) had more EEG activity in the alpha range than non-ADD disturbed children, a finding that they interpreted as evidence of underarousal. In turn, Dykman and colleagues (Dykman, Holcomb, Oglesby, &

Ackerman, 1982) found that both ADD and learning-disordered children had more EEG activity than did normals in the 7 to 10 Hz and 16 to 20 Hz ranges, corresponding to the alpha and beta bands. These two studies involved relatively older ADD patients and are consistent with Satterfield, Schell et al.'s (1984) findings for that age range. On the other hand, at least one study is inconsistent with these trends. Callaway, Halliday, and Naylor (1983) reported that ADD patients 9.6 to 13 years of age obtained *less* activity than normal in the alpha and beta bands.

It is difficult to argue with Satterfield et al.'s (1984) position that age should be considered in evaluating abnormalities of central arousal in ADD. Certainly, their analysis accounts for the data of several studies. However, one methodological difference needs to be considered. In the studies of Dykman et al. (1982), Satterfield, Schell et al. (1984), and Grünewald-Zuberbier (1974), EEG was recorded over relatively long periods (e.g., 45 minutes in Satterfield et al., 1984), whereas the discrepant report by Callaway et al. (1983) was based on an evaluation of 1 minute. It is likely that longer recording sessions may evoke reactions of fatigue or decreased motivation in ADD subjects, factors that may vary with age. Future research should consider this possibility by evaluating EEG frequencies as a function of time in the session.

Autonomic Activity

Although there are several studies of autonomic activity, most of this work is not very recent, and it is summarized relatively briefly. Studies of autonomic arousal have yielded contradictory findings (see Zahn, Abate, Little, & Wender, 1975 for a summary), including reports of normal, excessive, and depressed arousal. As suggested previously, variation in experimental characteristics (e.g., duration) may account for some of these discrepancies.

In contrast, studies of autonomic responsiveness are more consistent. Zahn et al. (1975) reported that ADD children, in comparison to normal peers, exhibited smaller skin conductance responses and attenuated heart rate deceleration to both neutral tones and signals in a reaction time task. The finding that reactions to both nonsignal and significant stimuli were reduced is interpretable as reflecting deficient attentiveness. When ADD patients were tested under clinical doses of stimulant therapy (methylphenidate or amphetamine), heart rate deceleration was increased, but electrodermal responses were reduced in amplitude. At least the cardiac effects are interpretable as reflecting enhanced attentiveness.

In an important study, Zahn, Rapoport, and Thompson (1980) administered a single dose of amphetamine and placebo to both ADD and normal children. The investigators found that, for both groups, amphetamine improved performance, increased heart rate deceleration, and diminished electrodermal reactivity. These results contradict the popular belief that ADD children's reactions to stimulants are paradoxical. Rather, the findings suggest similar benefits for psychomotor performance and associated autonomic changes in both ADD and normal children.

ERP Studies

Nearly all descriptions of ADD emphasize abnormalities in attention or information processing. However, it should be remembered that it is not self-evident that ADD patients have an attentional deficit. In fact, some thoughtful reviewers (e.g., Sergeant,

1988) noted that most of the evidence for this assumption could be interpreted in terms of nonspecific arousal or motivational deficits, as opposed to specific attentional factors. A related question is the extent to which the extensively documented behavioral improvements brought about by stimulant medications involve specific attentional effects. ERP methodology has been used in an effort to clarify this issue.

Selective Attention Deficits in ADD.   Using a selective attention paradigm, Stamm and his colleagues compared two samples of adolescents with a history of ADD and age-matched normals (Loiselle, Stamm, Maitinsky, & Whipple, 1980, Zambelli, Stamm, Maitinsky, & Loiselle, 1977). In a dichotic listening task, subjects received independent sequences of rare and frequent tone pips in each ear. The instructions were to press a button when detecting the rare tone in one ear while ignoring the other ear. (The assignment of the relevant ear was reversed in another part of the task.) Characteristically for ADD patients, these youngsters made more errors and responded more slowly than their normal peers. In addition, the ADD adolescents exhibited an abnormal ERP pattern. Specifically, the normal subjects displayed a larger amplitude of the N1 component for tones presented to the relevant ear than the corresponding stimuli for the irrelevant ear. This classical, early effect of selective attention on N1 was absent among ADD adolescents and children.

A similar question was examined by Satterfield and colleagues (Satterfield, Schell, Nicholas, & Backs, 1988; Satterfield, Schell, & Nicholas, in press). On half the trials, subjects heard a rare loud click or a frequent soft one; on the remainder of the trials, they saw a rare bright light or a dim frequent one. For half of the task, the instructions were to press a button to the rare sound and in the remainder of the test, to respond to the infrequent light. As shown in Fig. 5.4, the click-evoked ERPs of normal controls had larger amplitudes of processing negativity (described in the section on autism). Specifically, normal children's ERPs to the frequent click exhibit a greater negative amplitude when the attention was directed to clicks than when the same click was irrelevant (subjects pressed to lights). Importantly, this evidence of selective attention was lacking in the ERPs of ADD subjects. Similar results were found for the analogous comparisons of responses to the lights (Satterfield et al., in press).

The studies summarized previously suggest that ADD children have abnormally small amplitude of negative ERP components that are sensitive to selective attention. However, there have been somewhat discrepant reports (Callaway et al., 1983; Harter, Anllo-Vento, Wood, & Schroeder, 1988) involving *larger* amplitude of late negative ERP components in ADD samples.

Interestingly, administration of the stimulant methylphenidate increased ADD children's processing negativity to attended versus unattended tones in comparison to their responses under placebo (Klorman, Brumaghim, Salzman, Borgstedt, McBride, & Loeb, 1990). This result supports the conclusion that the stimulant enhanced aspects of selective attention.

Comment.   Research on negative ERP waves sensitive to selective attention, with some discrepant reports, point to smaller amplitudes in ADD children. One study reported reduction of this deficit with stimulant treatment. It is tempting to interpret the results in terms of deficient selective attention. However, as noted in the review of analogous research on autism, most of the research discussed in the present section did not simultaneously present relevant and irrelevant stimuli that competed for subjects'

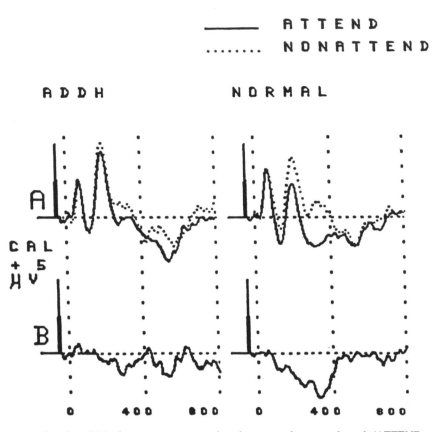

FIG. 5.4.   Panel A: ERPs for nontarget tones when they were relevant to the task (ATTEND, solid line) or not (NONATTEND, dotted line). The data were obtained from Attention-Deficit Hyperactivity Disorder (ADHD) or normal children. Panel B: Nd, that is, difference curves produced by subtracting the ERPs in the Nonattend condition from those in the Attend condition. Note the larger amplitude of the difference response for normal than for ADHD children. From Satterfield, Schell, Nicholas, and Backs (1988). Reprinted by permission.

attention. Such strict paradigms of selective attention are probably too difficult for ADD children. As a result, it is not possible at this point to interpret the results firmly in terms of selective attention.

Studies on P3b in ADD.   As noted in the section on autism, considerable research interest attaches to the P3b component, the amplitude of which has been shown to relate to the degree of capacity allocated to a task and extent of information processed (Johnson, 1988). Intuitively, it would seem that these aspects of attention are impaired in ADD. In fact, there are numerous studies indicating that in comparison to their normal counterparts, ADD children make excessive errors and respond too slowly on the Continuous Performance Test (CPT). Analogously, these deficits in ADD patients' performance are considerably reduced by stimulant treatment. The CPT is similar to an oddball test, except that on each trial one of several letters is presented. One of these letters is designated as a target requiring a button press. Several studies from my laboratory examined the ERPs of ADD and normal children during CPT tests. Characteristically, ADD subjects had worse performance and smaller P3b amplitude than did age-matched controls, and these abnormalities were reduced by stimulant treatment (Klorman, Salzman, Pass, Borgstedt, & Dainer, 1979; Michael, Klorman, Salzman, Borgstedt, & Dainer, 1981).

As illustrated in Fig. 5.5, the abnormal reduction of P3b amplitude and its enlargement by methylphenidate were of comparable magnitude for the target and the nontarget. This aspect of the results argues against interpreting this effect in terms of selective attention. The comparability of findings for targets and nontargets is probably due to the relatively high processing demands imposed by nontargets in this task (e.g., letters) in contrast with the simpler discriminations (e.g., brightness of lights or pitch of tones) required in the typical oddball task. This observation is important in comparing our results to those of other investigators. Thus, other studies also found reduced amplitude of P3b in ADD but only for responses to targets (Holcomb, Ackerman, & Dykman, 1985, 1986; Loiselle et al., 1980; Satterfield et al., 1990). It is likely that the design of these studies minimized the salience of nontargets and, therefore, the relative amplitude of P3b of nontargets in comparison to targets. As result, differences between ADD and normal controls would be more likely for responses to targets. In Holcomb et al.'s study (1985), the discrimination of targets and nontargets was probably maximized by the fact that both were constant over trials. This arrangement contrasted with our use of a variable nontarget (e.g., one of several letters). In Loiselle et al.'s (1980) and Satterfield et al.'s (1990) studies, selective attention instructions probably diverted attention away from nontargets, such that P3b amplitudes were concomitantly minimized.

A notable finding in Holcomb et al.'s (1985) work is illustrated in Fig. 5.6. The abnormally small P3b amplitude was present in patients with ADD with and without hyperactivity as well as in nonhyperactive reading-disordered children. Other studies also have reported abnormally small amplitude of P3b in learning disorder (e.g., Dainer et al., 1981; Taylor & Keenan, 1990). These results suggest that this ERP abnormality is diagnostically nonspecific. In fact, the review of the literature on autism documented similar findings. The clinical characteristics of ADD and reading disorder, on the one hand, and autism on the other are so overwhelmingly different that it is hard to argue that the similarity of P3b findings results from overlap among these disorders. Rather, it is likely that under the conditions of these experiments, similar abnormalities in information processing were elicited from clinically discrepant groups.

Stimulant Effects on P3b in ADD Children.   At this point it is useful to return to the impact of stimulant drugs on the observed ERP abnormalities. Once again, the question investigated is whether the medications known to improve ADD children's behavior also normalize their ERP abnormalities, a finding consistent with a common causal mechanism. In our CPT studies (Klorman et al., 1979; Michael, Klorman, Salzman, Borgstedt, & Dainer, et al., 1981), administration of methylphenidate, as expected, improved ADD patients' performance. In addition, as shown in Fig. 5.5, this stimulant medication increased the amplitude of P3b, comparably so for targets and nontargets. Thus, both performance and P3b were normalized by this medication.

Increase of P3b amplitude by methylphenidate was replicated in several studies. This phenomenon was found regardless of whether ADD children (Michael et al., 1981) and adolescents (Coons, Klorman, & Borgstedt, 1987) were previously treated with stimulants. Thus, the finding is not an artifact of having studied a sample of patients known to respond to the medication, that is, those selected from currently treated

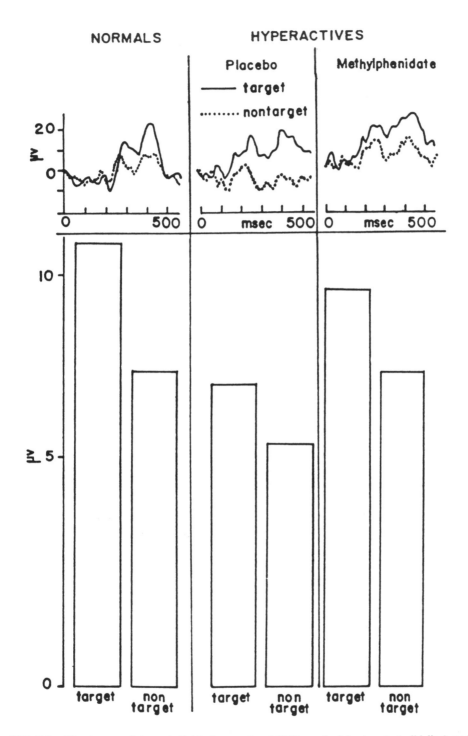

FIG. 5.5. The top panel is an individual example of ERPs evoked by targets (solid line) and nontargets (dotted line) for one normal subject and one ADD patient tested under placebo and methylphenidate. The lower graph displays mean P3b amplitude for the normal sample and for the ADD group under placebo and methylphenidate. From Klorman, Salzman, Pass, Borgstedt, and Dainer (1979). Reprinted by permission.

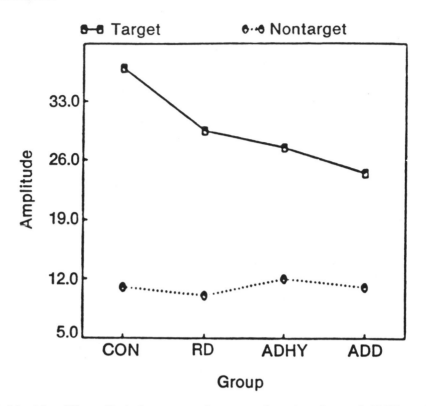

FIG. 5.6.   Mean P3b amplitude for targets and nontargets from normal controls (CON), reading disorder (RD), Attention-Deficit Hyperactivity Disorder (ADHD), and Attention Deficit Disorder (ADD) children. From Holcomb, Ackerman, and Dykman (1985). Reprinted by permission.

patients. Similarly, the result was obtained among children with pervasive ADD (i.e., both at home and school) and those with milder disturbances (Klorman et al., 1988; Klorman, Brumaghim, Fitzpatrick, Borgstedt, & Strauss, 1994; Klorman et al., 1983). Analogously, the stimulant amplified P3b amplitude for ADD children with and without concurrent oppositional/aggressive features (Klorman et al., 1988, 1994). Finally, the same effect was obtained in psychiatrically normal children (Peloquin & Klorman, 1986) and young adults (e.g., Brumaghim, Klorman, Strauss, Lewine, & Goldstein, 1987). Clearly, the generality of the effects of stimulants on P3b and autonomic responses (Zahn et al., 1980) contradict the view that ADD patients' cognitive enhancement by stimulants represents a paradoxical reaction (i.e., one unique to ADD).

Stimulant Effects on Other ERP Components.   Studies by Halliday and associates (Halliday, Callaway, & Rosenthal, 1984, Halliday, Rosenthal, Naylor, & Callaway, 1976) investigated the effects of stimulants in an oddball task involving rare dim lights (targets), frequent bright lights, and frequent tones. Halliday et al. (1976) found that a favorable response to methylphenidate treatment was correlated with an increase by this medication of the amplitude of an ERP component (the peak-to-trough difference between the N1 and P2 waves) to the frequent lights. These results suggest that the ERP may reflect gains in cognitive processing resulting from stimulant therapy and, as a result, have some practical value in predicting response to treatment.

In an effort to replicate some aspects of this study, Klorman et al. (1983) administered a similar task to ADD children under placebo and two doses of methylphenidate (.3 and .6 mg/Kg). Although reaction time was speeded by the stimulant, the drug did not affect the visual ERP component identified by Halliday et al. as sensitive to clinical response to methylphenidate. Rather, the medication had two different effects. First, methylphenidate increased P3b amplitude to nontarget lights. In addition, the stimulant magnified the increase in N1 to nontarget tones when subjects responded to targets (infrequent lights) as opposed to when they received the task in a passive format. Although the tones did not convey any information about the target in this task, they were more salient or meaningful in the active task, so that the stimulant may have amplified this effect.

Comment. Numerous studies report that ADD children have abnormally small amplitude of the P3b component along with concomitant deficits in task performance. Similar to results for autonomic responses, both performance and ERP deficits are reduced by administration of stimulant medication. However, abnormal reduction of P3b amplitude is present in other psychiatric disorders besides ADD. Similarly, amplification of P3b amplitude by stimulants is found in non-ADD populations, including normal children and adults.

Studies on P3b Latency in ADD. The discussion so far has focused on aberrations of P3b amplitude. However, equal interest attaches to the latency of P3b, that is, the timing of its peak amplitude. Extensive research suggests that P3b amplitude reflects the relative timing of stimulus evaluation stages, that is, those preceding the preparation and execution of motor responses. It is, therefore, of significant theoretical interest that ADD patients (with and without hyperactivity) and reading disorder children had slower P3b latency than normal controls in Holcomb et al.'s (1985) visual oddball test.

In a recent study (Klorman, Brumaghim, Fitzpatrick, & Borgstedt, 1992), ADD adolescents were compared with age-matched controls in a memory scanning test. Subjects were asked to memorize lists of 1 to 4 numbers. Subsequently, they were presented one number at a time and required to press with one hand if the number was in the memorized set and a different response if it was not. In comparison to normals, ADD adolescents made more errors to targets and lacked the normative tendency for faster P3b latencies to targets (numbers held in memory) than nontargets. The differentially faster P3b latency to targets is viewed as reflecting the greater ease of identifying a target (a match with a memory template) than a nontarget (a mismatch). Thus, these findings implied that ADD subjects have a deficit in the stage of stimulus identification. The significance of the results, illustrated in Fig.5.7, is that they point to a specific defect of information processing. Thus, the results, along with those of Holcomb et al. (1985), argue against the view that cognitive deficits of ADD subjects are attributable to such nonspecific factors as arousal or motivational variables. On the other hand, abnormally slow P3b latencies were also detected in dyslexic children (Taylor & Keenan, 1990), so that this deficit also is not specific to ADD.

Of equal interest was the finding, illustrated in Fig. 5.7, that treatment with methylphenidate reversed both abnormalities. The drug differentially reduced errors to targets and speeded the latency of P3b to targets. A replication of the study with younger ADD children (Klorman et al., 1994) also found that methylphenidate

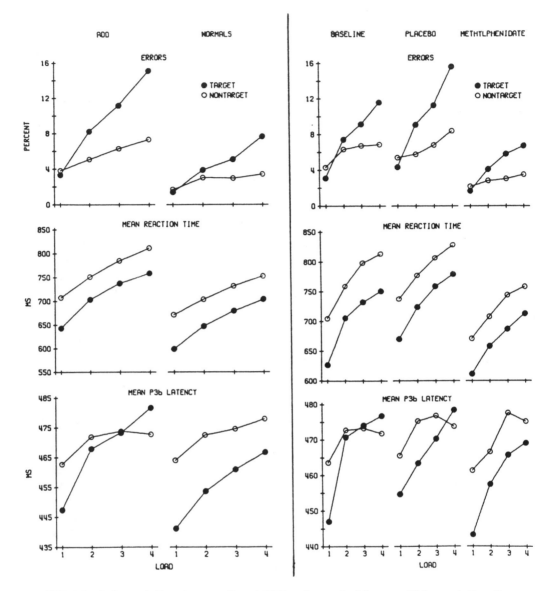

FIG. 5.7. Left panel: Data for unmedicated ADD and normal adolescents. Right panel: Data for ADD adolescents tested in an off-drug baseline session, placebo, and methylphenidate. Top panel: percentage errors; middle panel: mean reaction time; bottom panel: Mean P3b latency. From Klorman, Brumaghim, Fitzpatrick, and Borgstedt (1992). Reprinted by permission.

restored differentially faster P3b latency for targets. The significance of these results is that they point to enhancements of specific aspects of information processing.

Notably, a speeding of P3b in this task by methylphenidate was also found in normal young adults (Brumaghim et al., 1987), suggesting once again that this finding was not diagnostically specific.

Comment. Some studies have reported slower latency of P3b in ADD than normal controls. ADD subjects lacked the normal tendency for faster P3b latency to targets than nontargets, a finding suggesting deficits in stimulus identification. Methylphenidate administration reduced these deficits.

CONDUCT DISORDER

Much research has considered individual differences in psychophysiological responding in individuals with antisocial and conduct disorders. In considering these studies, one should keep in mind the comorbidity of disruptive disorders. It is well established that ADD overlaps significantly with conduct and oppositional disorder. However, most psychophysiological research on ADD samples has not separately examined patients with and without oppositional or conduct disturbances. By the same token, it is likely that a significant proportion of the conduct disorder patients assessed in this research was also comorbid for ADHD, learning disorders, among other disturbances.

Another issue is that much of this work is based on samples identified by criteria related to, but not identical with, the *DSM–III, DSM–III–R,* or *DSM–IV* definitions of conduct disorder. For instance, investigators have studied subjects defined by teacher ratings of antisocial behavior or by legal criteria, like juvenile delinquency. For the sake of simplicity, in the remainder of this section these samples are referred to as antisocial, an admittedly imprecise term.

Autonomic Arousal

As was the case for the disorders examined previously, investigators have assessed abnormalities in physiological arousal among antisocial adolescents. Intuitively, this information seems relevant to theoretically postulated deficits in anxiety for, at least subsets, or criminal persons.

Heart Rate. Several studies related abnormally slow resting heart rate to antisocial tendencies in adolescence. For instance, Raine and Jones (1987) reported that among behaviorally maladjusted children (7 to 15 years old), a low resting heart rate was correlated with high self-ratings of conduct disorder and socialized aggression. Similarly, in a study of psychiatrically unselected adolescent students (14 to 16 years old), Raine and Venables (1984b) obtained an association between slow heart rate with self- and teacher ratings of antisocial behavior. However, this correlation was more pronounced for youngsters from higher than lower social classes.

Along similar lines, Davies and Maliphant (1971) reported that in a sample of British boarding school boys, students classified as "refractory" by their teachers and lower heart rates than those viewed as cooperative. In a parallel study with girls 12 to 13 years old, students classified as refractory also had lower heart rates than their well-behaved peers (Maliphant, Hume, & Furnham, 1990). Especially interesting is an American study of psychiatric inpatients, including 383 boys ($M = 11.8$ years) and 106 girls ($M = 12.5$ years) (Rogeness Cepeda, Macedo, Fischer, & Harris, 1990). The study is unusual because of the large sample and the use of *DSM–III* diagnoses. Conduct Disorder patients of both sexes had lower heart rates than patients with other diagnoses. In fact, for the sample as a whole, Conduct Disorder signs were correlated with low heart rate and low systolic blood pressure. On the other hand, high autonomic arousal (elevated heart rate, systolic and diastolic blood pressure) was correlated with signs of anxiety among male patients. Finally, for both sexes, indications of depression were correlated with high systolic and diastolic blood pressure.

In contrast to the preceding findings, a British study of conduct disorder outpatients did not find abnormally slow heart rate (Garralda, Connell, & Taylor, 1991). However, the authors noted that, in contrast to the preceding studies, their sample was younger ($M = 10$ years old) and combined neurotic and conduct disorders.

In the section on autism, the question arose concerning whether abnormal resting levels of autonomic activity reflect disturbances of arousal as opposed to differences in reactivity to being evaluated. Especially thorough in this respect was the work by Davies and Maliphant (1971), who measured their subjects' heart rates on four different occasions, spread over the course of a school day. This procedure would increase the likelihood that subjects adapt to the stress of being tested. However, unless the finding of lower heart rates in antisocial subjects is based on measurements distributed over the course of several days (e.g., by means of automatic continuous monitoring-equipment), the possibility remains that these results were due to lesser excitement or greater boredom by antisocial adolescents. Conceivably, if controls were assessed without being made anxious, the arousal differences might be reduced.

Another possibility that needs to be controlled is that the lower heart rates of antisocial subjects may be secondary to greater physical fitness. If these alternative explanations could be excluded, results could be attributed to lower autonomic arousal in antisocial adolescents.

Heart Rate Reactivity.   A related question is whether antisocial adolescents have smaller cardiac reactions to stressful stimulation. Evidence of lower responsivity to stress would be especially compatible with the view that these patients are characterized by an anxiety deficit. Interestingly, Davies and Maliphant (1971) found that the refractory boys exhibited smaller heart rate acceleration than did controls during a reaction time test involving threat of shock or loss of monetary rewards. Similarly, Maliphant et al. (1990) reported that refractory girls had lower peak cardiac rates when tested on Raven's mazes test.

There are other studies that obtained discrepant findings, but with considerably less noxious stimuli. Borkovec (1970) found that psychopathic, as opposed to neurotic and normal, juvenile delinquents exhibited nonsignificantly smaller heart reactions to a moderately loud tone. Garralda et al. (1991) did not obtain aberrant heart rate responses in neurotic conduct disordered children's reactions to tones.

In summary, the two studies employing noxious stimuli detected smaller changes in heart rate in antisocial adolescents, a finding compatible with a deficit in anxiety. Admittedly, more extensive research is required before firm conclusions can be drawn.

Electrodermal Activity.   In general, studies of antisocial behavior in children and adolescents have not reported abnormalities in tonic skin conductance level. In contrast, several studies provide evidence of diminished electrodermal responsiveness. Smaller skin conductance responses to a novel tone was detected in psychopathic juvenile delinquents than in their neurotic or normal counterparts (Borkovec, 1970). Similarly, Siddle, Nicol, and Foggitt (1973) found smaller electrodermal responses to a novel tone in incarcerated adolescents judged to be highly antisocial versus juvenile delinquents low in antisociality.

Generally compatible results were found in studies of noncriminal populations.

In the previously cited investigation of 101 unselected school children by Raine and Venables (1984a), ratings of antisocial behavior were associated with a low frequency (rather than small amplitude) of skin conductance responses to stimulation with tones. In turn, Delamater and Lahey (1983) reported a further diagnostic distinction. These authors assessed reactions to tones and a discrimination task in a sample of learning disordered children, half of whom were diagnosed ADD. In general, the most consistent evidence for low electrodermal responsiveness was found in learning disordered children rated high on conduct disorder and low on tension/anxiety. In future research, it would be interesting to replicate these observations in a population not limited to learning disordered children.

Physiological Activity and Subsequent Criminality

Raine, Venables, and Williams (1990a,1990b,1990c) followed up their sample of adolescent students through age 24 and identified 15 who had acquired a criminal record by that age. When originally evaluated in adolescence, those subjects who later became criminals differed from their law-abiding peers by having a slower resting heart rate, nonsignificantly lower skin conductance level, and fewer spontaneous skin conductance responses. Thus, low autonomic arousal predicted criminal status.

Similarly, low resting heart rate and skin conductance level also predicted negative outcomes in a 2-year follow-up of another sample of children and adolescents with disruptive behavior disorders (Kruesi et al., 1992). In combination with previously reviewed evidence of low autonomic arousal in antisocial adolescents, these antero-spective studies support the enduring clinical significance of these abnormalities.

It is significant that evidence for low autonomic arousal is supported by findings of lower cortical arousal in Raine et al.'s (1990b) adolescents who became criminals. Specifically, when evaluated in adolescence, these subjects had more power in the theta (slow) bands of the EEG than did adolescents without a subsequent criminal record. Similar, but nonsignificant findings, were obtained for the delta and alpha bands. Thus, for this sample, there was concordance in autonomic and cortical underarousal for future criminals.

However, a similarly designed study by Satterfield and Schell (1984) yielded generally opposite findings. In their longitudinal study, those ADD children those who did *not* subsequently acquire a criminal record had slower EEG (lower arousal) than ADD patients who became delinquents. In fact, the nondelinquent ADD patients differed from normal controls with respect to EEG frequency and smaller amplitude of the N2 component to clicks. Satterfield and Schell (1984) proposed that ADD children who do not become delinquent probably suffer from a neurological condition, whereas ADD children who become delinquent have a disorder based on adverse environmental conditions.

Clearly, the studies by Raine et al. (1990b) and Satterfield and Schell (1984), respectively, differed in the diagnostic criteria for selecting their samples (unselected adolescents vs. ADD children) and the length of the session in which EEG was recorded (2 minutes vs. 45 minutes). Thus, resolution of the discrepancies between them must await further research.

Another aspect of Raine et al.'s (1990a) follow-up implicated attentional factors in the prediction of future criminality. Specifically, adolescents with a criminal outcome reacted to neutral tones with less frequent electrodermal responses and smaller heart rate responses. This reduced orienting was interpreted as a deficit in the allocation of attentional resources to external stimuli.

Comment. As already noted, the weight of the evidence on adolescents with antisocial tendencies points to abnormally low resting heart rate and autonomic hyporeactivity to stimulation. Several aspects of these findings are compatible with those of research on antisocial adults. Fowles (1993) recently reviewed findings showing that antisocial adults may have abnormally low resting electrodermal arousal. Particularly strong is the evidence that antisocial adults are electrodermally under-responsive to stressful conditions (e.g., threat of shock) or signal stimuli (e.g., reaction time cues). On the other hand, the cardiac reactions (e.g., heart rate acceleration to noxious stimulation) of antisocial persons have been found to be of normal or greater than normal amplitude. Fowles reconciled these findings by suggesting that heart rate reflects the behavioral activation system (rewards or avoidance of punishment) and that skin conductance is related to the behavioral inhibition system (negative affect). In this scheme, the antisocial person has a weak behavioral inhibition system and a dominant behavioral activation system.

The evidence on antisocial children and adolescents is at least partially compatible with Fowles' position. Although there is empirical support for autonomic underarousal in antisocial children, support is most convincing for heart rate whereas in adults it seems more supportive for skin conductance. Similarly, the extensive evidence for underresponsiveness to noxious stimulation among antisocial adults relies on the electrodermal system, whereas in children and adolescents the limited findings are based on cardiac rate.

Despite the apparent discrepancies between the developmental and adult studies of antisocial subjects, a reconciliation is possible. Presumably for ethical reasons, the studies with children generally have not employed truly noxious stimuli like shock and have relied on soft or moderately loud tones. Thus, this aspect of adult antisocial underresponsiveness has not been examined sufficiently in childhood and adolescence. Second, few developmental studies of antisocial tendencies have simultaneously examined heart rate and electrodermal activity, and those that did obtained at least modest associations (Borkovec, 1970; Raine et al., 1990a). Therefore, it has not been possible to determine clearly whether antisocial adolescents exhibit the abnormalities reported for antisocial adults. Third, most of the studies of antisocial adults are based on prisoners, such that the control groups are also composed of prisoners, albeit those deemed not antisocial. In contrast, most of the samples of antisocial children and adolescents studied were not incarcerated. It would be useful for future research to clarify these issues by assessing the relative importance of incarceration, considering cardiac as well as electrodermal activity (as well as other measures discussed later) and evaluating reactions to theoretically important dimensions of stimulation (noxious and signal events).

To the extent that theorists have postulated specific deficits in the experience of anxiety or in the behavioral inhibition system, it would seem especially appropriate for future research to include psychiatric comparison groups. For instance, a neurotic sample would be expected to exhibit directionally opposite autonomic reactions to anxiety signals in comparison to those of antisocial subjects. Attempts in this direction were made by Borkovec (1970) and Garralda et al. (1991), but more work of this sort is needed to determine the specificity of research findings.

Studies Employing ERPs.   Raine and Venables (1987) interpreted the literature on autonomic deviations in antisocial persons in terms of abnormal information processing rather than deficient anxiety. In support of this position is Raine and Venables' (1984a) finding that electrodermal nonresponding was related to schizoid tendencies. In addition, Raine and Venables (1987) pointed to clinical and empirical findings that antisocial adults do not attend to boring tasks but excel in situations they find interesting. Along with this position, these authors reported that antisocial adolescents had *smaller* amplitude of the contingent negative variation (CNV) than did prosocial adolescents. (The CNV is a slow negative potential that develops over the interval [1.5 seconds in this instance] between a warning stimulus and the imperative signal to press a button in a reaction time test. CNV amplitude has been related to cognitive factors like expectancy and attentional capacity.) On the other hand, the antisocial adolescents had *larger* amplitude of the P3b component following the warning tone in the same task. Raine and Venables (1987) regarded the P3b findings as evidence of enhanced information processing in their antisocial subjects.

Additional support for the attentional interpretation came from the finding that the adolescents who later became criminals had smaller autonomic orienting responses when originally assessed (Raine et al., 1990a). In addition, the future criminals exhibited larger amplitude of the N1 component and earlier latencies of P3b to the warning tone in the reaction-time task (Raine et al., 1990c). These results were interpreted, respectively, as indications of deficits in passive attention and enhanced processing speed. Thus, this research again reveals a mixed picture, with both diminished and enhanced attention in the antisocial group. However, the ERP measures sensitive to the original antisocial/prosocial distinction were different from those that discriminated between future criminals and noncriminals.

Generally similar findings to those of Raine et al. (1990c) were obtained by Herning, Hickey, Pickworth, and Jaffe (1989). Herning et al. (1989) found that adolescents with highly delinquent backgrounds, in comparison to peers low in delinquency, had an earlier latency of the N1 component and smaller amplitude of a frontal negative slow wave (following P3b). These differences were detected in response to the target tone in an oddball task performed under noisy conditions. Importantly, the investigators demonstrated that the ERP findings for delinquent adolescents were not dependent on a history of drug use. On the other hand, the ERP components implicated by Herning et al. (1989) were not altogether the same ones identified in Raine et al.'s (1990c) work. However, there were differences in the task (oddball vs. reaction time) and populations (criminal adolescents vs. adolescents with subsequent delinquency) studied.

SUMMARY

Clearly, these provocative findings prompt further consideration of the hypothesis that antisocial adolescents have attentional deficits, that are reflected in autonomic and ERP activity. Especially interesting is the suggestion that, in certain circumstances, antisocial subjects may exhibit enhanced information processing. The challenge for future research is to delineate the specific conditions that elicit deficient and enhanced attentiveness by this population.

Two further cautions are in order for evaluating this research. There is a need for replication, because several findings are based on a single sample (that of Raine et al., 1990a,1990b,1990c). A second issue is that, with the exception of Herning et al. (1989), the possibility of drug use by antisocial subjects has not been systematically evaluated in this research. This possible confounding factor should be considered in future work.

In contrast to research on autism and ADD, ERP work in antisocial disorders of adolescence has been relatively limited. For instance, selective attention paradigms have not been studied. Consistent associations between P3b amplitude and antisocial activity have not been found thus far (Herning et al., 1989; Raine et al., 1990a), although only two of the studies reviewed have searched for them. At the same time, it is important to recall that abnormalities in cognitive ERPs have been identified in other psychiatric groups, such as ADD and autism. Therefore, in order to delineate the specificity of findings, psychiatric comparison groups should be included. Similarly, the significance of results would be maximized if research paradigms are selected on the basis of theoretical relevance.

ACKNOWLEDGMENTS

My work on this chapter was facilitated by NIMH grants MH388118 and MH47333 and NICHD grant HD25802. I am grateful to Joan T. Brumaghim, Christine Carriuolo, Patrica S. Fitzpatrick, Julie Frobel, Seth Pollak, and Serena Rachels for their assistance and advice.

REFERENCES

Barry, R. J., & James, A. L. (1988). Coding of stimulus parameters in autistic, retarded, and normal children: Evidence for a two-factor theory of autism. *International Journal of Psychophysiology*, *6*, 139–149.

Bernal, M. E., & Miller, W. H. (1970). Electrodermal and cardiac responses of schizophrenic children to sensory stimuli. *Psychophysiology*, *2*, 155–168.

Borkovec, T. D. (1970). Autonomic reactivity to sensory stimulation in psychopathic, neurotic, and normal juvenile delinquents. *Journal of Consulting and Clinical Psychology*, *35*, 217–222.

Brumaghim, J. T., Klorman, R., Strauss, J., Lewine, J. D., & Goldstein, M. G. (1987). Does methylphenidate affect information processing? Findings from two studies on performance and P3b latency. *Psychophysiology*, *24*, 361–373.

Callaway, E., Halliday, R., & Naylor, H. (1983). Hyperactive children's event-related potentials fail to support underarousal and maturational-lag theories. *Archives of General Psychiatry*, *40*, 1243–1248.

Ciesielski, K. T., Courchesne, E., & Elmasian, R. (1990). Effects of focused selective attention tasks on event-related potentials in autistic and normal individuals. *Electroencephalography and Clinical Neurophysiology*, *75*, 207–220.

Cohen, D. J., & Johnson, W. T. (1977). Cardiovascular correlates of attention in normal and psychiatrically disturbed children. *Archives of General Psychiatry*, *34*, 561–567.

Coles, M. G. H., Donchin, E., & Porges, S. W. (1986). *Psychophysiology*. New York: Guilford.

Coons, H. W., Klorman, R., & Borgstedt, A. D. (1987). Effects of methylphenidate on adolescents with a childhood history of Attention Deficit Disorder: II. Information Processing. *Journal of the American Academy of Child and Adolescent Psychiatry*, *26*, 368–374.

Courchesne, E., Lincoln, A. J., Kilman, B. A., & Galambos, R. (1985). Event-related brain potential correlates of the processing of novel visual and auditory information in autism. *Journal of Autism and Developmental Disorders*, *15*, 55–76.

Courchesne, E., Lincoln, A. J., Yeung-Courchesne, R., Elmasian, R., & Grillon, C. (1989). Pathophysiologic findings in nonretarded autism and receptive developmental language disorder. *Journal of Autism and Developmental Disorders*, *19*, 1–17.

Dainer, K. B., Klorman, R., Salzman, L. F., Hess, D. W., Davidson, P. W., & Michael, R. L. (1981). Learning-disordered children's evoked potentials during sustained attention. *Journal of Abnormal Child Psychology*, *9*, 79–94.

Davies, J. G. V., & Maliphant, R. (1971). Autonomic responses of male adolescents exhibiting refractory behaviour in school. *Journal of Child Psychology and Psychiatry*, *12*, 115–127.

Dawson, G., Finley, C., Phillips, S., Galpert, L., & Lewy, A. (1988). Reduced P3 amplitude of the event-related brain potential: Its relationship to language ability in autism. *Journal of Autism and Developmental Disorders, 18*, 493–504.

Delamater, A. M., & Lahey, B. B. (1983). Physiological correlates of conduct problems and anxiety in hyperactive and learning-disabled children. *Journal of Abnormal Child Psychology, 11*, 85–100.

Dykman, R. A., Holcomb, P. J., Oglesby, D. M., & Ackerman, P. T. (1982). Electrocortical frequencies in hyperactive, learning-disabled, mixed, and normal children. *Biological Psychiatry, 17*, 675–685.

Fowles, D. C. (1993). Electrodermal activity and antisocial behavior: Empirical findings and theoretical issues. In J. C. Roy, W. Boucsein, D. C. Fowles, & J. H. Gruzelier (Eds.), *Progress in electrodermal research* (pp. 223–237). London: Plenum.

Garralda, M. E., Connell, J., & Taylor, D. C. (1991). Psychophysiological anomalies in children with emotional and conduct disorder. *Psychological Medicine, 21*, 947–957.

Graveling, R. A., & Brooke, J. D. (1978). Hormonal and cardiac response of autistic children to changes in environmental stimulation. *Journal of Autism and Childhood Schizophrenia, 8*, 441–455.

Grünewald-Zuberbier, E., Grünewald, G., & Rasche, A. (1975). Hyperactive behavior and EEG arousal reactions in children. *Electroencephalography and Clinical Neurophysiology, 38*, 149–159.

Halliday, R., Callaway, E., & Rosenthal, J. H. (1984). The visual ERP predicts clinical response to methylphenidate in hyperactive children. *Psychophysiology, 21*, 114–121.

Halliday, R., Rosenthal, J. H., Naylor, H., & Callaway, E. (1976). Averaged evoked potential predictors of clinical improvement in hyperactive children treated with methylphenidate: An initial study and replication. *Psychophysiology, 13*, 429–440.

Harter, M. R., Anllo-Vento, L., Wood, F. B., & Schroeder, M. M. (1988). II. Separate brain potential characteristics in children with reading disability and attention deficit disorder: Color and letter relevance effects. *Brain and Cognition, 7*, 54–86.

Herning, R. I., Hickey, J. E., Pickworth, W. B., & Jaffe, J. H. (1989). Auditory event-related potentials in adolescents at risk for drug abuse. *Biological Psychiatry, 25*, 598–609.

Holcomb, P. J., Ackerman, P. T., & Dykman, R. A. (1985). Cognitive event-related brain potentials in children with attention and reading deficits. *Psychophysiology, 22*, 656–667

Holcomb, P. J., Ackerman, P. T., & Dykman, R. A. (1986). Auditory event-related potentials in attention and reading disabled boys. *International Journal of Psychophysiology, 3*, 263–273.

Hutt, C., Forrest, S. J., & Richer, J. (1975). Cardiac arrhythmia and behaviour in autistic children. *Acta psychiatrica Scandinavica, 51*, 361–372.

James, A. L., & Barry, R. J. (1984). Cardiovascular and electrodermal responses to simple stimuli in autistic, retarded and normal children. *International Journal of Psychophysiology, 1*, 179–193.

Johnson, R. (1988). The amplitude of the P300 component of the event-related potential: Review and synthesis. *Advances in Psychophysiology, 3*, 69–137.

Klorman, R., Brumaghim, J. T., Fitzpatrick, P. A., & Borgstedt, A. D. (1992). Methylphenidate reduces abnormalities of stimulus classification in adolescents with attention deficit disorder. *Journal of Abnormal Psychology, 101*, 130–138.

Klorman, R., Brumaghim, J. T., Fitzpatrick, P. A., Borgstedt, A. D., & Strauss, J. (1994). Clinical and cognitive effects of methylphenidate on attention deficit disorder as a function of aggression/oppositionality and age *Journal of Abnormal Psychology, 103*, 206–221.

Klorman, R., Brumaghim, J. T., Salzman, L. F., Strauss, J., Borgstedt, A. D., McBride, M., & Loeb, S. (1988). Clinical and cognitive effects of methylphenidate on Attention Deficit Disorder with and without aggressive features. *Journal of Abnormal Psychology, 97*, 413–422.

Klorman, R., Brumaghim, J. T., Salzman, L. F., Strauss, J., Borgstedt, A. D., McBride, M. C., & Loeb, S. (1990). Effects of methylphenidate on processing negativities in patients with Attention-Deficit Hyperactivity Disorder. *Psychophysiology, 27*, 328–337.

Klorman, R., Salzman, L. F., Bauer, L. O., Coons, H. W., Borgstedt, A. D., & Halpern, W. I. (1983). Effects of two doses of methylphenidate on cross-situational and borderline hyperactive children's evoked potentials. *Electroencephalography and Clinical Neurophysiology, 56*, 169–185.

Klorman, R., Salzman, L. F., Pass, H. L., Borgstedt, A. D., & Dainer, K. B. (1979). Effects of methylphenidate on hyperactive children's evoked responses during passive and active attention. *Psychophysiology, 16*, 23–29.

Kootz, J. P., & Cohen, D. J. (1981). Modulation of sensory intake in autistic children. *Journal of the American Academy of Child Psychiatry, 20*, 692–701.

Kootz, J. P., Marinelli, B., & Cohen, D. J. (1982). Modulation of response to environmental stimulation in autistic children. *Journal of Autism and Developmental Disorders, 12*, 185–193.

Kruesi, M. J. P., Hibbs, E. D., Zahn, T. P., Keysor, C. S., Hamburger, S. D., Bartko, J. J., & Rapoport, J. L. (1992). A 2-year prospective follow-up study of children and adolescents with disruptive behavior disorders. *Archives of General Psychiatry*, *49*, 429–435.

Lake, C. R., Ziegler, M. G., & Murphy, D. L. (1977). Increased norepinephrine levels and decreased dopamine-b-hydroxylase activity in primary autism. *Archives of General Psychiatry*, *34*, 553–556.

Loiselle, D. L., Stamm, J. S., Maitinsky, S., & Whipple, S. C. (1980). Evoked potential and behavioral signs of attentive dysfunctions in hyperactive boys. *Psychophysiology*, *17*, 193–201.

MacCulloch, M. J., & Williams, C. (1971). On the nature of infantile autism. *Acta psychiatrica Scandinavica*, *47*, 295–314.

Maliphant, R., Hume, F., & Furnham, A. (1990). Autonomic nervous system (ANS) activity, personality characteristics and disruptive behavior in girls. *Journal of Child Psychology and Psychiatry*, *31*, 619–628.

Martin, I., & Venables, P. H. (1980). *Techniques in psychophysiology*. Chichester, England: Wiley.

Michael, R. L., Klorman, R., Salzman, L. F., Borgstedt, A. D., & Dainer, K. B. (1981). Normalizing effects of methylphenidate on hyperactive children's vigilance performance and evoked potentials. *Psychophysiology*, *18*, 665–677.

Miller, W. H., & Bernal, M. E. (1971). Measurement of the cardiac response in schizophrenic and normal children. *Psychophysiology*, *8*, 533–537.

Novick, B., Kurtzberg, D., & Vaughan, H. G. (1979). An electrophysiologic indication of defective information storage in childhood autism. *Psychiatry Research*, *1*, 101–108.

Novick, B., Vaughan, H. G., Kurtzberg, D., & Simson, R. (1980). An electrophysiologic indication of auditory processing defects in autism. *Psychiatry Research*, *3*, 107–114.

Palkowitz, R. J., & Wiesenfeld, A. R. (1980). Differential autonomic responses of autistic and normal children. *Journal of Autism and Developmental Disorders*, *10*, 347–360.

Peloquin, L. J., & Klorman, R. (1986). Effects of methylphenidate on normal children's mood, event-related potentials, and performance in memory scanning and vigilance. *Journal of Abnormal Psychology*, *95*, 88–98.

Raine, A., & Jones, F. (1987). Attention, autonomic arousal, and personality in behaviorally disordered children. *Journal of Abnormal Child Psychology*, *15*, 583–599.

Raine, A., & Venables, P. H. (1984a). Electrodermal nonresponding, antisocial behavior, and schizoid tendencies in adolescents. *Psychophysiology*, *21*, 424–433.

Raine, A., & Venables, P. H. (1984b). Tonic heart rate level, social class and antisocial behaviour in adolescents. *Biological Psychology*, *18*, 123–132.

Raine, A., & Venables, P. H. (1987). Contingent negative variation, P3 evoked potentials, and antisocial behavior. *Psychophysiology*, *24*, 191–199.

Raine, A., & Venables, P. H., & Williams, M. (1990a). Autonomic orienting responses in 15-year old male subjects and criminal behavior at age 24. *American Journal of Psychiatry*, *147*, 933–937.

Raine, A., Venables, P. H., & Williams M. (1990b). Relationships between central and autonomic measures of arousal at age 15 years and criminality at age 24 years. *Archives of General Psychiatry*, *47*, 1003–1007.

Raine, A., Venables, P. H., & Williams (1990c). Relationships between N1, p300, and contingent negative variation recorded at age 15 and criminal behavior at age 24. *Psychophysiology*, *27*, 567–574.

Rogeness, G. A., Cepeda, C., Macedo, C. A., Fischer, C., & Harris, W. R. (1990). Differences in heart rate and blood pressure in children with conduct disorder, major depression, and separation anxiety. *Psychiatry Research*, *33*, 199–206.

Satterfield, J. H., Cantwell, D. P., & Satterfield, B. T. (1974). Pathophysiology of the hyperactive child syndrome. *Archives of General Psychiatry*, *31*, 839–844.

Satterfield, J. H., & Schell, A. M. (1984). Childhood brain function differences in delinquent and non-delinquent hyperactive boys. *Electroencephalography and Clinical Neurophysiology*, *57*, 199–207.

Satterfield, J. H., Schell, A. M., Backs, R. W., & Hidaka, K. C. (1984). A cross-sectional and longitudinal study of age effects of electrophysiological measures in hyperactive and normal children. *Biological Psychiatry*, *19*, 973–990.

Satterfield, J. H., Schell, A. M., & Nicholas, T. (in press). Preferential neural processing of attended stimuli in Attention-Deficit Hyperactivity Disorder and normal boys. *Psychophysiology*.

Satterfield, J. H., Schell, A. M., Nicholas, T. W., & Backs, R. W. (1988). Topographic study of auditory event related potentials in normal boys and in boys with Attention Deficit Disorder with Hyperactivity. *Psychophysiology*, *25*, 591–606.

Sergeant, J. (1988). Functional deficits in attention deficit disorder. In L. M. Bloomingdale (Ed.), *Attention deficit disorder* (Vol. 3, pp. 1–19). Elmsford, NY: Pergamon.

Siddle, D. A. T., Nicol, A. R., & Foggitt, R. H. (1973). Habituation and over-extinction of the GSR component of the orienting response in anti-social adolescents. *British Journal of Social and Clinical Psychology, 12*, 303–308.

Stevens, S., & Gruzelier, J. (1984). Electrodermal activity to auditory stimuli in autistic, retarded, and normal children. *Journal of Autism and Developmental Disorders, 14*, 245–260.

Taylor, M. J., & Keenan, N. K. (1990). Event-related potentials to visual and language stimuli in normal and dyslexic children. *Psychophysiology, 27*, 318–327.

Van Engeland, H., Roelofs, J. W., Verbaten, M. N., & Slangen, J. L. (1991). Abnormal electrodermal reactivity to novel visual stimuli in autistic children. *Psychiatry Research, 38*, 27–38.

Verbaten, M. N., Roelofs, J. W., van Engeland, H., Kenemans, J. K., & Slangen, J. L. (1991). Abnormal visual event-related potentials of autistic children. *Journal of Autism and Developmental Disorders, 21*, 449–470.

Zahn, T. P., Abate, F., Little, B. C., & Wender, P. H. (1975). Minimal brain dysfunction, stimulant drugs, and autonomic nervous system activity. *Archives of General Psychiatry, 32*, 381–387.

Zahn, T. P., Rapoport, J. L., & Thompson, C. L. (1980). Autonomic and behavioral effects of dextroamphetamine and placebo in normal and hyperactive prepubertal boys. *Journal of Abnormal Child Psychology, 8*, 145–160.

Zambelli, A. J., Stamm, J. S., Maitinsky, S., & Loiselle, D. L. (1977). Auditory evoked potentials and selective attention in formerly hyperactive adolescent boys. *American Journal of Psychiatry, 134*, 742–747.

Chapter 6

Familial
Determinants

David Reitman
Alan M. Gross
University of Mississippi

At first blush, the title of this chapter may appear to raise false hopes regarding the current state of knowledge in abnormal child psychology. "Familial Determinants" seems to suggest that social scientists have already identified a cookbook of family factors that reliably lead to psychopathology in children. Although it may be an exaggeration to say that social scientists have discovered the recipe for family factors that may lead to child psychopathology, it is probably safe to say that we can now identify the primary "ingredients." Before identifying these ingredients, a brief review of the historical antecedents of the joint study of family and child psychopathology is conducted. In addition, a few of the obstacles to understanding the influence of families on child psychopathology are reviewed along with a more general discussion of how this influence is believed to be manifested.

HISTORICAL ANTECEDENTS

The scientific study of children and the psychological variables that affect them have only been under scrutiny since about the turn of the 20th century. G. Stanley Hall is generally credited with inspiring interest in child study by sending large numbers of questionnaires to parents, teachers, and children and inquiring about their fears, appetites, emotions, and many other facets of child development. In addition to pioneering the "survey method" of data collection, it may also be said that Hall initiated the scientific study of the child and provided much needed normative data on a wide variety of child behaviors (Knopf, 1984). It is important to note that these norms provided the initial yardstick by which child behavior could be judged "abnormal" and made the study of abnormal child psychology possible.

In 1904, Hall published a landmark book, *Adolescence*, in which he argued that children, and adolescents in particular, required study apart from more general studies of adult behavior. Additionally, the ever popular characterization of adolescence as a time of "storm and stress" originated in this book, though this assertion was later challenged by other researchers. Hall was not alone in beginning to turn psychology's attention to children and childhood. While Hall was researching and writing about children, Sigmund Freud (1959) was beginning to emphasize the importance of childhood experiences and, perhaps more importantly for our purposes, focused the attention of his readers on the psychological significance of early parent–child interaction. In addition, Freud's students, including his daughter Anna, increasingly recognized the importance of the parent–child relationship and social influences on the child. Freud also contended that childhood experiences had important implications for adult dysfunction, lending further status to the study of child psychopathology and raising hopes that intervention could prevent later suffering.

Another important factor in the study of children and their families was the growth of the intellectual testing movement. The debate over whether intelligence was due primarily to "nature or nurture" focused considerable attention on the role parents (and others) played in facilitating learning and ultimately, led to studies in the 1920s that constituted the first comprehensive longitudinal studies of parents and children. These initial projects inspired later studies of parents and their children, which serve as the foundation of the present chapter. A more thorough review of the historical events that led to the study of abnormal child psychology in general is presented in Knopf (1984).

OBSTACLES TO UNDERSTANDING PARENT–CHILD RESEARCH

Though the study of parent–child relations may at times appear fairly straight forward, there exist a multitude of potential obstacles to conducting and interpreting this research. Often, these obstacles result in erroneous or misleading conclusions that oversimplify the nature of parent–child relations and their impact on the psychological development of children.

As a rule, good research begins with definitional consensus. That is, everyone agrees on a definition for the object under study. For example, one of the most important uses of the *Diagnostic and Statistical Manual of Mental Disorders, Fourth Edition*, American Psychiatric Association (1994) is to help clinicians and researchers arrive at definitional consensus regarding the psychological disorders included in the manual. Ultimately, this consensus allows researchers to be more confident regarding the validity of their research findings and the conclusions they draw from their data.

With respect to the family, several questions arise as to definitional consensus. For example, how should the family be defined? A family might be conceived of as a parent–child unit—a dyad or triad. However, other members of the family environment, such as siblings and extended family, might also be considered. Families today may consist of not one but many different structures: nuclear or two parent, single family, foster, and adoptive homes, to name a few. It is possible that the ways in which families influence their children may differ within each type of family and that the importance of some factors, say nurturance or discipline, may vary as well.

One way of reaching definitional consensus is to carefully describe the specific population under study (e.g., single parent—male). Another solution is offered by Radke-Yarrow (1990), who suggested that functional definitions of the family may be more useful than structural classifications (e.g., single vs. two parent). Using the construct of a rearing environment, she proposed that the critical elements of the family in a functional analysis are "(1) providing care and protection of the child, (2) regulating and controlling the child's behavior in line with the needs and requirements from internal and external sources, (3) providing knowledge and skills and understanding the physical and social world, (4) giving affective meaning to interactions and relationships, and (5) facilitating the child's self-understanding" (p. 175). Using these functional criteria, a wider variety of family classifications may be studied with a minimum of confusion. Moreover, the specific factors that make single-parent homes different from two-parent families, for example, may be described in better detail. Consideration of these functional criteria will ultimately allow greater precision in assessing parent–child relations.

Researchers and clinicians sometimes study child and adolescent subjects and their parents without adequately distinguishing between age groups or drawing samples that consist of large or heterogeneous cross sections of children (Reitman, Gross, & Messer, in press). Confusion over the age at which we define an individual as a "child" in child and family research may weaken our assertions about the dynamics of parent–child interaction and may obscure unique aspects of those relations. It is likely that children of different ages interact with their parents in different ways and that these interactions may predict different child outcome. In fact, Collins and Russell (1991) warned against considering parent–child relations "a-developmental" and pointed out that pubertal maturation, for example, may have important effects on family relations.

Another barrier to understanding the significance of parent–child interaction in developing child psychopathology is the difficulty of weighing the relative importance of biological and environmental influences on the child. In most families, children inherit both genes and environments from their parents. Consequently, it is often difficult to determine the extent to which child dysfunction is a product of "nature or nurture." One approach to solving this dilemma is offered by developmental psychologists, or more specifically behavioral geneticists, who capitalize on childrearing environments in which parents and children do not share a common genetic heritage. Examples of such environments are adoptive or foster families. Another approach to determining the contribution of genetic factors are family studies that determine the degree to which family members resemble one another in a given trait, or in many cases, type of psychiatric diagnosis.

Because of limited space and the relatively sparse data available about sibling and extended family factors, we focus primarily on the importance of parent–child interaction. We believe that the focus on parent–child interaction clarifies the relationship of these variables to the development of child psychopathology within families.

A MODEL FOR CONCEPTUALIZING FAMILIAL INTERACTION

Numerous models have been proposed to conceptualize the relationship between parent–child interaction and the development of psychopathology. Among the most useful models to date are those that employ a learning-based approach. However in recent years, researchers and theorists alike have recognized the value of integrating developmental and learning-based approaches to the study of children and their families (Plomin, Nitz, & Rowe, 1990).

Learning-based approaches to the study of parental influences on children have long enjoyed favor among family researchers. The learning-based approach holds that child behavior, be it "normal" or "abnormal," is a product of learned responses to the environment and that the process of learning may be observed. Though behavioral researchers have, on the whole, become more receptive to studying less than fully observable family factors, such as cognitions and affect, the field remains grounded predominantly in direct observation of parent–child interaction, and results are still frequently interpreted in terms of learning theory. Some of the mechanisms proposed have been classical conditioning, operant conditioning, and most recently, modeling.

Classical conditioning in the context of parenting might involve the pairing of strong positive or negative events with parent–child social interaction. As Putallaz and Heflin (1990) suggested, "Children of *warm* positive parents would be expected to develop a generally positive *approach* orientation to social interaction.'(p. 209).

Operant conditioning, on the other hand, involves directly rewarding or punishing of child behavior. For example, a mother's attention to her child's misbehavior might serve as a reinforcer or a consequence that increases the frequency of her child's misbehavior. Conversely, sending the child to bed early following an undesirable response might serve as a punisher but only if it decreased the frequency of the misbehavior. In addition, operant conditioning might also include extinction of child behavior. That is, ignoring the child's previously rewarded misbehavior would result in the behavior's disappearance. Of course, classical and operant conditioning should not be considered mutually exclusive processes. It is likely that most of the time, these processes operate concurrently. For example, parents who use punishment (an operant process) as the exclusive means for disciplining their children may through classical conditioning, come to be regarded negatively and perhaps avoided by their children (Putallaz & Heflin, 1990).

More recently, modeling has been proposed as an important aspect of parent–child interaction and child development. The biggest proponent of this form of learning, also known as observational learning, has been Albert Bandura. In *Social Learning Theory*, Bandura (1977) suggested that this form of learning was fundamental to the learning process as we know it. He commented that "most human behavior is learned observationally through modelling: from observing others one forms an idea of how new behaviors are performed." (p. 22). In the context of parent–child relations this suggests that children may learn a wide variety of behaviors from their parents, including behavioral, emotional, and perhaps cognitive responses. Moreover, research on the influence of models suggests that attributes of parental models, such as being perceived as nurturant and powerful, are most likely to promote imitation of their behavior (Bandura, 1986). Therefore, some parents may ultimately serve as better teachers than others, at least with respect to observational learning.

Developmental approaches also offer several potentially valuable tools for understanding the development of child psychopathology. As noted previously, family, twin, and adoption studies permit greater precision not only in establishing biological contributions to child development but also in isolating important environmental factors. Developmental psychology also offers several other useful tools for the study of parent–child relations. Perhaps the most valuable tool is the longitudinal study. Longitudinal studies, or those studies that sample one group of subjects repeatedly over long periods of time (usually several years), are among the most powerful research tools available to social scientists. The developmental approach also serves to remind us that parent–child interactions are not static but dynamic and multidimensional processes that may alter over time. This approach offers a "wide-angle lens" that nicely complements the sometimes criticized myopic (one-dimensional) view of learning-based or behavioral approaches to family research and theory.

Ultimately, the learning-based and developmental models need not be considered incompatible or mutually exclusive. Indeed, the developmental model has been referred to as a "macroparadigm" capable of accommodating views from many different theoretical orientations. Some prominent developmental psychologists have suggested increased communication between learning-based and developmental approaches to parent–child research. As Plomin et al. (1990) noted, "We need multi-method approaches that consider and compare interviews and questionnaires with self-report, parental ratings, and peer ratings. Additional observational studies are especially needed" (p. 128).

Family Management

Over the years, considerable attention has been paid to the potential familial determinants of child and adolescent psychopathology. Earlier studies suggested specific factors that seem to predict child and adolescent dysfunction, whereas more recent investigations have focused on a constellation of parental attributes that seem to be associated rather reliably with psychopathology in children.

Some of the earliest attempts to study the family and its impact on children stem from investigations of the effects of mother–child separation during World War II. A British psychiatrist, John Bowlby, (1953), observed a wide range of emotional problems in children who were orphaned by the war. In the 1940s, another psychiatrist, Rene Spitz, (1945) studied orphaned children in the United States. Bowlby found that children who did not form long-lasting emotional bonds with their principal caregiver in infancy were likely to evidence emotional distress in adulthood, whereas Spitz concluded that lack of physical contact characteristic of orphanages might have implications for both the physical and emotional well-being of infants. Spitz and Bowlby each concluded that infant–mother interaction must be important to the psychological development of children (and ultimately adults), and their findings stimulated future work in this area.

According to Maccoby and Martin (1983), one of the first researchers to investigate parent–child factors in vivo, was A. L. Baldwin (1955). In addition to confirming the many previous factor analytic findings of a warmth/coldness dimension of parenting, Baldwin (1955) used home observations and parent interviews to identify another parenting dimensions that might be called restrictiveness/permissiveness (he called it democracy/autocracy). Though parent–child relations and their impact on child development have certainly been studied from a wide variety of theoretical orientations, the two-factor (i.e., nurturance [warmth] and restrictiveness [control]) conceptualization of parenting has proven to be highly reliable and especially useful for studying child and adolescent outcome as a function of childrearing orientation (for related terms and sources, see Macoby & Martin, 1983).

Family management refers to the constellation of parent–child interactions that influence children's psychological development. Parenting behaviors associated with family management might include monitoring, discipline practices, and support or encouragement. In light of the significance of the two-factor conceptualization of parenting, it is particularly relevant to focus on those childrearing behaviors which bear on the degree of support or emotional quality of the home environment, as well as the type of discipline and control practices employed by parents.

Parenting Styles

After multitudes of factor analytic studies investigating dimensions of parenting, many investigators sought to describe specific types of parenting behaviors that might be associated with child outcome (e.g., consistent versus inconsistent discipline; Glueck & Glueck, 1950). However, later studies of parenting attempted to link several dimensions of parenting together, integrating these behaviors into a complex or style of childrearing that might be associated with particular kinds of child psychopathology. An example of this approach is a study conducted by Winder and Rau (1962) that found that parental attitudes of ambivalence, punitiveness, and restrictiveness were associated with a subsample of peer nominated deviant boys. Subsequent investigations, such as those undertaken by Baumrind (1967, 1971) and highlighted here, have served to enrich our understanding of parenting and its impact on child behavior.

Baumrind's Parenting Styles

Recognizing the diverse ways in which adult members of the same culture may choose to raise their young, Baumrind (1978) defined parenting style as the overall values, interaction style, and discipline practices that characterize the way in which parents socialize their children.

Baumrind (1967) distinguished three styles of parenting: *authoritarian* style, *authoritative* style, and *permissive* style. Baumrind's formulation of parenting styles has proven to be useful both for describing parent–child relations and predicting general classes of child outcome (Macoby & Martin, 1983). Baumrind (1967) discussed four parental attributes that serve as the basis for parenting style discriminations: *parental control, maturity demands, parent–child communications*, and *nurturance*. McGraw (1987) distinguished among these parental attributes. Parental control refers to the frequency with which parents issue and enforce directives with their children. Maturity demands measures the degree to which parents insist on or encourage independence in their children. Parents scoring high on parent–child communication frequently reason with and listen to their children when discussing discipline and control issues with them. Nurturance refers to features of the parent–child interaction that reflect warmth, love, support, and encouragement.

Specifically, authoritarian parents are defined as being high in control and maturity demands, while being low in both communication and nurturance. For example, authoritarian parents may be unlikely to communicate with children regarding the rationale for their behavior and may be highly restrictive of their children when they are present.

Authoritative parents, while also high in control and maturity demands, are also high in communication and nurturance. In contrast to authoritarian parents, authoritative parents would be much more likely to discuss discipline issues with their children. In addition, these parents would be likely to be perceived as more nurturant than authoritarian parents.

Permissive parents demand little self-control from their children. Dornbusch, Ritter, Leiderman, Roberts, and Fraleigh (1987) suggested that "(P)ermissiveness may refer to a parenting attitude that is essentially neglectful and uncaring, or it may refer to parenting that is caring and concerned but ideologically genuinely permissive" (p. 1247). Consequently, a fourth style, permissive (neglectful), is sometimes described in the literature. Permissive parents may be characterized as diametrically opposed to authoritarian parents with respect to discipline practices.

A multitude of studies illustrate the relationship between parenting style and children's behavior. Baumrind's studies of parental attitudes and behavior have been referred to collectively as representing the "social mold" approach. That is, they conceptualize the child as responding to the unidirectional influence of the parent. Nevertheless, it is important to note that parenting styles and attitudes could also be viewed as resulting from patterns of child behavior (Peterson & Leigh, 1990). Indeed, there is mounting evidence that parenting styles are, to some degree, determined by factors other than parents themselves. For example, Hoffman (1987) investigated cultural differences in childrearing patterns and concluded that the value of children to the parents (e.g., economic, love, solidifying marital bonds, etc.) predicted different parenting practices. Moreover, there is evidence that parents experiment with various parenting styles and behaviors and that their behavior is likely to be, to some degree, shaped by child responses (Rutter, 1985). For example, impulsive children may be more likely to have authoritarian parents because they have become frustrated with the child and more likely to use force. Alternately, impulsive children might be more likely to have permissive parents because they have been "worn out" by the child. Consequently, one must always be alert to possible child influences when interpreting research in the area of parenting styles and childrearing.

Over the last two decades much attention has been paid to the social mold approach adopted by Baumrind and others to identify sets of parenting behaviors and attitudes that impact child development. In one such social mold study, Baumrind (1967) investigated the parenting characteristics associated with three groups of normal children differing in their social and emotional behavior. Results indicated that the most self-reliant, self-controlled, and explorative children had parents who could be characterized as authoritative. Parents of children who could be characterized as relatively discontented, withdrawn, and mistrustful could be described as authoritarian. Finally, parents of the least self-reliant, explorative, and self-controlled children might be referred to as permissive. Interestingly, from a modeling perspective, many similarities between child and parent behavioral and personality characteristics were noted.

Other Parenting Styles Research

Research investigating the impact of parenting styles on child behavior did not cease in the early 1970s. Many researchers have continued to use the framework offered by Baumrind and her colleagues, lending support to her original findings. Again, these results are best conceptualized as falling under the headings of authoritarian, permissive, and authoritative parenting styles.

The authoritarian parenting style has received much attention, perhaps because of the numerous studies which have associated this parenting style with increased incidence of aggression (Macoby & Martin, 1983). In addition to Baumrind's (1967, 1971) studies linking authoritarian parenting to poor behavioral outcomes, more recent investigations have explored authoritarian parenting and its impact on academic achievement. With 7,836 high school students, Dornbusch et al. (1987) used a self-report instrument to sample adolescent ratings of their parents' parenting styles and correlated them with student grades. The results indicated that both authoritarian and permissive styles were associated with poor grades, whereas children of authoritative parents tended to have the highest grades.

Moral development and self-concept have also been studied in relation to authoritarian parenting (Loeb, Horst, & Horton, 1980). For example, a review by Hoffman (1970) indicated that in studies that gave children the opportunity to respond to projective tests, such as story completion, authoritarian parenting styles were most frequently associated with low scores on measures of conscience or moral development. In addition, the investigation conducted by Loeb et al. (1980) suggested that high levels of authoritarian parenting convey to children that they are not to be trusted to complete tasks independently, adversely affecting both their self-esteem and self-competence.

Permissive parenting has also been linked to a number of undesirable outcomes for children. Aggression is suggested as the most significant byproduct of this parenting style (Olweus, 1980). Using a bidirectional model, Olweus (1980) sampled boys' aggressiveness in sixth and ninth grades, as well as collecting maternal ratings of child temperament and maternal attitudes. The results indicated that although permissiveness for aggression tended to be associated with higher levels of aggression, aggressive boys also appeared to generate permissiveness for aggression in their mothers. In addition, Yarrow, Campbell, and Burton (1968) found that aggression in the home was positively correlated with permissive parenting.

Putallaz and Heflin (1990) offered an excellent review of the impact of parenting styles on social competence, with particular emphasis on authoritative control. Specifically, they pointed to the necessity of warmth and control in parent–child relations to insure the development of adequate levels of social competence. They then suggested four possible mechanisms by which parenting styles might facilitate the development of social competence. First, authoritative parents used reinforcement effectively and were consistent in administering discipline. Second, because these parents were nurturant, their disapproval was a more potent punisher to their children. Hence, authoritative parents are more effective shapers of their children's behavior. Third, authoritative parents, by virtue of their nurturance and potency, would be more likely to inspire imitation. Authoritative parents therefore make better models of social competence. Authoritative parents were also more demanding of their children, requiring more autonomous behavior. Finally, authoritative parenting styles tended to inspire more communication than other styles of parenting and consequently, facilitated more socially competent communication in their children.

In summary, the parenting styles research conducted by Baumrind and others employing the social mold model has yielded a great deal of useful information for researchers, clinicians, and the lay public in general. The research to date suggests that successful parents typically use both the "carrot and the stick," that is, they tend to use effective discipline strategies and employ these measures in an environment that is supportive and nurturant. At the same time, other research suggests that child characteristics may alter parenting styles. Therefore, we must temper our assertions about the family dynamics that influence child development with some measure of doubt, at least until more sophisticated research models (e.g., more longitudinal and bidirectional studies) reinforce and confirm these findings.

DIVORCE, DEPRESSION, AND ALCOHOLISM AND DISRUPTED FAMILY MANAGEMENT PRACTICES

As noted previously, several theorists and researchers have speculated about the impact of various family environments on children. For example, many researchers have demonstrated that divorce tends to be associated with child and adolescent dysfunction. However, only rarely have commonalities between seemingly disparate environments been sought, despite repeated observations that these conditions may frequently co-exist (e.g., marital problems–alcoholism or alcoholism–depression). Divorce, depression, and alcoholism have each been studied extensively with respect to their "independent" influence on children. However, divorce, maternal depression, and alcoholism may have a common functional impact on the family that serves to enhance our understanding and appreciation for how they affect child and adolescent development. Rather than each factor independently influencing child behavior, it is possible that each of these factors shares in common a single variable that influences child outcome. At least with respect to divorce, maternal depression, and alcoholism and substance abuse, the disruption of family management practices is suggested as the thread that unites these factors.

Divorce

The impact of divorce on the development of a child or adolescent is perhaps one of the most heavily researched subjects in the family literature. Empirical studies and review articles have distinguished marital conflict and divorce as key, yet distinct, elements in the development of children and adolescents (Atkeson, Forehand, & Rickard, 1982). Currently, more attention is being given to factors associated with divorce (e.g., conflict) than divorce itself.

Though marital turmoil has long been suspected to have a causal role in child and adolescent dysfunction (Framo, 1975), early studies were relatively unsophisticated and contributed to a lack of consensus. Presently, some investigators have concluded that it may be more advantageous to focus on parental conflict than divorce per se (Long, Forehand, Fauber, & Brody, 1987). After level of parental conflict (e.g., intensity) was controlled for, Long et al. (1987) found no differences between adolescents from divorced and nondivorced families on measures of adjustment and independently observed competence. Further, a study conducted by Forehand and McCombs (1989) suggests heated arguments and open conflict within families are actually quite low in absolute terms and that differences in conflict frequency observed between married and divorced couples (divorced couples argued slightly more) was negligible. They hypothesized that parental conflict within divorced families created lasting disruptions in parenting practices that might, in turn, lead to a higher probability of child and adolescent dysfunction.

Divorce is often associated with substantial changes in the environment that may have unspecified consequences for children. Some changes may have a relatively negative timbre, such as decreases in household income, less parental supervision associated with loss of a parent, and change of school and neighborhood (Hetherington, Cox, & Cox, 1982; Stolberg & Anker, 1983). Interestingly, these changes also seem likely to affect the more general class of parental management behaviors, such as, supervision, enforcement of discipline, and ability to provide adequate reinforcement for desirable behavior.

The particular outcomes associated with postdivorce changes for the child or adolescent are likely to be idiosyncratic and relative to the predivorce environment. For example, should the divorce result in a substantial decrease in conflict within the home, the custodial parent may find it easier to monitor and establish house rules than during the conflictual marital period. Hence, the adolescent may evidence improved emotional–behavioral functioning. On the other hand, loss of a parent with whom the child shared a close emotional relationship may result in a worsening of behavior and/or emotional dysfunction. On the whole, girls have been found to be more likely to evidence depressive symptomatology (e.g., withdrawal, anxiety) in response to divorce, whereas boys more commonly exhibit externalizing behaviors such as aggression.

Several factors mediating the outcome of divorce for adolescents have been detailed. In a study that questioned the utility of joint custodial arrangements in promoting healthy child and adolescent development, children who had not had paternal contact within the past 5 years appeared to be functioning better academically and behaviorally than children who had seen their fathers more frequently or recently (Furstenberg, Morgan, & Allison, 1987). They found that the quality of the child's relationship with the custodial mother was a better predictor of postdivorce functioning than noncustodial parental contact. This further suggests that it is the *qualitative* aspects of the parent–child relationship that have the most salience for child outcome. Nevertheless, noncustodial parent–child relations may still be important. Adolescents exposed to interparental conflict and perceiving close relationships with noncustodial fathers evidenced fewer internalizing problems than those with poor relationships (Brody & Forehand, 1990). Moreover, male adolescents who have a good relationship with both parents appear to be "buffered" against negative parental divorce effects (Wierson, Forehand, Fauber, & McCombs, 1989).

There seems to be substantial evidence in the divorce literature that a functional analysis of the divorce environment, which includes a consideration of how divorce affects family management practices, would be valuable in assessing child outcome. Indeed, the available research that has examined the impact of divorce on families and the children in them, has shown both to be adversely affected.

Parental Depression

In a review by Forehand, McCombs, and Brody (1987), it was suggested that "(d)epressive mood states rank foremost among the parental characteristics that have been hypothesized to be associated with children's functioning" (p. 1). Several studies have documented the impact of parental depression on family interaction and many cite the quality of interaction between parents and children as especially significant in influencing parent–child relations (Downey & Coyne, 1990).

There exist a number of studies on the behavior of depressed parents toward their children (Forehand et al., 1987; Radke-Yarrow, 1990). In their review, Forehand et al. (1987) found that clinically depressed parents appear to be less involved with and affectionate toward their children, more guilty and resentful, and have more difficulty in managing and communicating with their children than nondepressed parents. Similarly, a more recent review associates maternal depression with unresponsive, inattentive, intrusive, and inept parenting behavior, as well as fostering negative perceptions of their children (Gelfand & Teti, 1990). A study conducted with a child sample (3 to 8 years old) found depressed mothers to be more critical of their children's behavior than nondepressed mothers, though no significant differences were detected in child behavior (Webster-Stratton & Hammond, 1988). Ostensibly, in cases in which parents evidence depressive disorders, their dysfunction may be so pervasive as to lead to substantial impairment in their ability to function as a parent.

Despite evidence that parental depression has important effects on parent–child interaction, Forehand et al. (1987) suggested that although clinical depression in one or both parents may lead directly to child impairment, a more transactional model is needed to account for the impairment of functioning in children of nonclinically depressed parents. In other words, it may be necessary to appeal to other elements of the home environment (e.g., child behavior, job stress, marital relationship) to account for the relationship of milder forms of parental depression to child or adolescent psychopathology. One such element may be child characteristics. Where externalizing or "acting out" behaviors are considered, child behavioral characteristics have been shown to influence parental depression (Patterson, 1980). Support for this view is provided by a developmentally oriented (e.g., bidirectional/transactional hypotheses) study conducted by Hammen, Burge, and Stansbury (1990) that found that maternal functioning and child characteristics interacted (i.e., child characteristics contribute to maternal functioning), establishing a cycle of negative mutual influence associated with clinical symptomology and dysfunction in children.

The finding that child factors may contribute significantly to subsequent manifestation of disturbance in adolescence and childhood suggests that more within-family studies are needed to ascertain how differences between siblings may result in psychopathology. To the extent that an adolescent may be more capable than a younger child of accessing and soliciting help from external "buffers" such as friends or adults beyond the family unit, Forehand et al. (1987) suggested that siblings should not be assumed to be equally influenced by parental depressive mood.

What are the behavioral correlates of parental depression for children and adolescents? In general, diagnosis of depression in both parents and current maternal depressive symptomology, as opposed to a history of depression, increase the risk for depression and other behavioral disturbances in children and adolescents (Hammen, et al., 1987). In a review and discussion of the rate of psychological disturbance in the children of depressed parents, Miller, Birnbaum, and Durbin (1990) found these children to be at increased risk for psychological symptoms, emotional problems, suicidal behavior, and *DSM-III* diagnosis. The most common diagnoses associated with parental depression were major depression (13.1%) and attention deficit disorder (10.3%). Moreover, girls were more likely than boys to exhibit depressive mood and receive a diagnosis of major depression.

Despite the volumes dedicated to the description of parenting behavior and the behavioral correlates of parental depression, it is estimated that 60% of the children of depressives appear to function normally (Miller et al., 1990). It is apparent that the factors relevant to outcome for children of depressives are multiply determined and complex.

Hops, Sherman, and Biglan (1987) proposed a model based on the "coercive family process" (Patterson, 1982) construct to account for why some adolescents and children fail to exhibit dysfunction where others do. According to their formulation, depressive mood manifested in one or both parents is hypothesized to disrupt normal interactions with their children and ultimately, to lead to affective and/or behavior problems in their offspring. However, the child's response to the mother and the response of other family members to her may contribute to the outcome variation observed for children of depressives. Maternal depressive behavior was hypothesized to be aversive to other family members but functional too, "in that it may (a) reduce the probability of attacks by others, and (b) obtain positive consequences" (p. 187). In addition, the direction of influence is likely to be bidirectional; that is, there is evidence to suggest that a family member's aggressive affect would suppress a mother's dysphoric mood (Hops et al., 1987). At the same time, a mother's dysphoric affect (e.g., withdrawal) may functionally shelter her from overt aggressive behavior (Radke-Yarrow, 1990). Ultimately, it is hypothesized that an interactional style develops based on patterns of aversive interactions, and normal parenting processes may be disrupted. The consensus among investigators involved in maternal depression research seems to suggest that the disruption of family management practices is a likely mechanism for producing child and adolescent dysfunction.

Parental Alcoholism and Substance Abuse

The presence of alcohol or drug abuse in one or both parents has been identified as a significant factor in child and adolescent development, particularly with respect to increased risk for substance abuse (Halebsky, 1987). In their review of the literature, Goodwin and Guze (1989) refer to several studies that found adolescent sons of alcoholics three to four times more likely to be alcoholics than sons of nonalcoholics. However, in another study involving female subjects, the strong relationship between biological parents and their offspring failed to materialize (Goodwin, Schulsinger, Knop, Mednick, & Guze, 1977).

There appears to be a strong genetic contribution to the development of alcoholism in adolescence, at least for males (Jacob, Krahn, Leonard, 1991), yet Niven (1984) indicated that in several family studies, as many as half of the alcoholic subjects did not have an alcoholic parent or other relative. Further, not all offspring of alcoholics become alcoholics themselves. Again, more appears to be involved in alcoholism than genetic influence alone. In addition to increased risk for alcoholism, male adolescent offspring of alcoholics have been shown to experience a higher rate of coping difficulties (Werner, 1986) and conduct disorder (Cadoret, Cain, & Grove, 1979).

Several investigators have studied the influence of parental alcohol abuse on the family environment (Callan & Jackson, 1986; Werner, 1986). Jacob and colleagues (Jacob, Ritchey, Cvitkovic, & Blane, 1981; Jacob & Seilhamer, 1987; Jacob et al., 1991) focused on family interaction and concluded that "the environmental impact of alcoholism is of a current and dynamic nature, rather than reflecting fixed and irreversible effects on the child's level of functioning" (p. 176). A study by Jacob et al.

(1981) illustrates the importance of assessing context and family interaction. In the study, alcoholic and nonalcoholic (father) families were asked to engage in a series of problem-solving tasks in a drinking or no-drinking situation. It was found that an alcoholic father's drinking increased spousal negativity (e.g., criticism, disagree, putdown) toward her children; that is, the impact of the father's drinking was evidenced not between spouses but between mothers and their children in the drinking condition.

Nevertheless, a more recent study by Jacob et al. (1991) did not support the hypothesis that parent alcohol consumption influenced problem-solving behavior. Jacob explained the contrasting results by pointing out differences in the extent to which families in each sample remained intact. According to Jacob, if alcoholics are able to maintain positive affective relationships with their families and utilize effective discipline practices, their children would be expected to function normally. Alcohol then becomes a most salient factor when normal parenting functions are disrupted by abuse. Wolin and Bennet's (1984) work on family rituals supports this view, asserting that disruption (failure to recognize family events such as birthdays and holidays) is associated with adolescent dysfunction. At least for intact families, a general distress factor seems to account for more differences between alcoholic and normal families than alcohol specific effects.

In addition to the alcohol studies, some researchers have considered illicit drug use by parents and its impact on the adolescent. As with alcohol, increased adolescent abuse of marijuana has been associated with parental drug usage (Johnson, Shontz, & Locke, 1984). McDermott's (1984) findings suggest that adolescent perception of parental permissiveness may be a more important variable than parental drug use. Although findings indicated that parents who used drugs were more likely than those who did not to have children who used drugs, they also indicated that regardless of their parents' drug use, adolescents who perceived their parents as more permissive were more likely to use drugs. These results suggest that rules, along with adequate monitoring and enforcement, may have a significant impact on adolescent drug use and abuse. Of course, establishment and maintenance of house rules is a key component of family management practices. A recent longitudinal study suggested that parental modeling and permissiveness were important, but added that parenting style, as measured by warmth and hostility, proved to be the most salient variable influencing adolescent substance abuse (Johnson & Pandina, 1991).

Extrafamilial Stressors

Though not considered a family factor in and of itself, extrafamilial stressors may have a substantial impact on relations within families. The purpose of this section is to outline how some of these stressors may exert their influence on seemingly internal familial relations, which to this point, have been shown to have significant implications for child and adolescent outcome.

The concept of "stressor" has been widely subject to abuse, largely due to a lack of definitional consensus. Still, consideration of extrafamilial stressors does provide a "wide-angle lens" useful for the study of the environmental impact of interpersonal phenomena occurring within the family context. Additionally, the concept of stress permits integration of several disparate approaches to studying adolescent–family relations and reflects the understanding that stressors frequently co-exist (Webster-

Stratton, 1990). In keeping with our emphasis on the study of family interaction and its value as a research tool, these extrafamilial stressors (e.g., unemployment, low socioeconomic status) may be conceptualized as having indirect effects on the adolescent via familial relationships and/or family management practices, as well as direct effects on the youth via economic opportunities, crime rate, and quality of educational support.

In longitudinal studies by Rutter and his colleagues (Rutter, Cox, Tupling, Berger, & Youle, 1975, Rutter & Quinton, 1977), stress, conceptualized as "family adversity," was found to be the key factor in child psychiatric illness in both urban and rural communities. As Bronfenbrenner (1986) explained:

> (W)ith the degree of family adversity controlled, the difference between London and Isle of Wight in rates of child psychiatric illness all but disappeared. The authors interpret this result as indicating that the main adverse effects of city life on children are indirect, resulting from the disruption of the families in which they live. (p. 731)

A substantial proportion of the family stress literature deals with the impact of negative life stress or major stressful life events. In adolescents, drug use and frequency of self-reported antisocial and delinquent behavior has been associated with stressful life events (Vaux & Ruggiero, 1983). Additionally, frequency of negative life events experienced by families has been related to attachment problems (Vaughn, Egeland, Sroufe, & Waters, 1979), harsher discipline, and physical abuse (Gaines, Sandgrund, Green, & Power, 1978). Though much is known about the impact of extrafamilial stressors, much remains to be discovered, as Webster-Stratton (1990) concluded:

> The task for future research in this area is to continue to conceptualize the complex and dynamic relationships between stressors and the family interaction system, as well as to identify those factors that can serve to increase or decrease a maladaptive outcome for the parents and child. For the ultimate challenge is to recognize those families most at risk, those most vulnerable to disruption by life stressors, and to help them develop resources and coping skills that will minimize the disruption. (p. 310)

SUMMARY

Given the decline in the number of traditional nuclear families relative to single-parent and other alternative family environments, a functional analysis of the rearing environment that includes a careful analysis of parent–child interaction would appear to be useful for conceptualizing the psychological development of children and adolescents. With respect to the family environment, disrupted family management practices, such as inept or ineffective discipline, poor or nonexistent monitoring, and negative affective environments appear most reliably associated with adolescent dysfunction.

The roads leading to poor family management are complex and interwoven and it may never be possible to identify all roads leading to child and adolescent dysfunction. Still, substantial progress has been made in describing molar aspects of the family environment. However, more longitudinal investigations are necessary to validate correlational studies and determine whether or not impaired family management processes predate adolescent maladjustment or some other factors within the home (e.g., adolescent characteristics) are implicated. There exists strong support for a transactional model of family interaction and child psychopathology. However, specific circumstances under which this interaction results in an adolescent poorly equipped for life beyond the family system, or alternatively buffers the child or adolescent from serious psychopathology, remain unclear.

As has been shown, a wide variety of factors appear to influence, directly or indirectly, family management. They include: depression (and other forms of adult psychopathology), alcohol and drug abuse, divorce, and extrafamilial stressors. The vast number of elements that may influence family management practices suggests that children and adolescents may be vulnerable to these factors throughout the long course of their development (although perhaps more vulnerable at some times than others). Although correlational studies indicate that a close parent–adolescent relationship is associated with better general adjustment and negatively correlated with adolescent self-report of depression and anxiety (Sarigiani, 1987), it seems difficult to distinguish between the maintenance of "warm" intrafamilial relations and the exercise of effective family management practices. Future research will hopefully address the relationship of these important factors.

Of particular concern for clinicians, researchers, and the public at-large is the role of modeling and long-term outcomes for individuals developing within dysfunctional family environments. The lay, and sometimes professional, observation that our own parenting practices reflect those of our parents seems rather daunting in this instance. Indeed, from a learning perspective adolescents would be likely, via observation and direct experience, to learn a substantial portion of their own parenting behaviors from their parents. Without exposure to positive role models, either through formal education, media, or acquaintances, their parenting behavior and family management practices would be likely to resemble those in which they were raised. Given the powerful influence families appear capable of exerting on their children, even into adolescence, growing evidence that families may be poorly equipped to institute family management practices that will yield healthy and well-adjusted adolescents is disturbing. Failure to address the factors that influence intrafamilial relations and those influences that impinge on the family in the periphery (e.g., poverty, substandard education, and crime) may only exacerbate the problem and lead to future generations poorly equipped for parenting. If continued research supports the supposition that families and family management practices make significant contributions to child and adolescent development, and perhaps, later adult maladjustment, government and social agencies may wish to focus more attention on actively promoting preventative mental health services such as parenting education, community mental health services, and other programs designed to facilitate better family management practices.

Preparation of this chapter was supported in part by NIH Grant DE08641 to Alan M. Gross.

REFERENCES

American Psychiatric Association (1994). *Diagnostic and statistical manual of mental disorders.* (4th ed.). Washington, DC: Author.

Atkeson, B. M., Forehand, R., & Rickard, K. M. (1982). The effects of divorce on children. In B. B. Lahey & A. E. Kazdin (Eds.), *Advances in clinical child psychology* (Vol. 5, pp. 255–281). New York: Plenum.

Baldwin, A. L. (1955). *Behavior and development in childhood*. New York: Dreyden.

Bandura, A. (1977). *Social learning theory*. Englewood Cliffs, NJ: Prentice-Hall.

Bandura, A. (1986). *Social foundations of thought and action: A social cognitive theory*. Englewood Cliffs, NJ: Prentice-Hall.

Baumrind, D. (1967). Child care practices anteceding three patterns of preschool behavior. *Genetic Psychology Monographs, 75*, 43–88.

Baumrind, D. (1971) Current patterns of parental authority. *Developmental Psychology Monograph, 4*, 1–103.

Baumrind, D. (1978). Parental disciplinary patterns. *Youth and Society, 9*, 239–276.

Bowlby, J. (1953). Some pathological processes set in train by early mother–child separation. *Journal of Mental Science, 99*, 265–272.

Brody, G., & Forehand, R. (1990). Interparental conflict, relationship with the noncustodial father, and adolescent post-divorce adjustment. *Journal of Applied Developmental Psychology, 11*, 139–147.

Bronfenbrenner, V. (1986). Ecology of the family as a context for human development: Research perspectives. *Developmental Psychology, 22*, 723–742.

Cadoret, R. J., Cain, C. A., & Grove, W. M. (1979). Development of alcoholism in adoptees raised apart from alcoholic biologic relatives. *Archives of General Psychiatry, 37*, 561–563.

Callan, V. J., & Jackson, D. (1986). Children of alcoholic fathers and recovered alcoholic fathers: Personal and family functioning. *Journal of Studies on Alcohol, 47*, 180–182.

Collins, W. A., & Russell, G. (1991). Mother–child and father–child relationships in middle childhood and adolescence: A developmental analysis. *Developmental Review, 11*, 99–136.

Dornbusch, S. M., Ritter, P. L., Leiderman, P. H., Roberts, D. F., & Fraleigh, M. J. (1987). The relation of parenting style to adolescent school performance. *Child Development, 58*, 1244–1257.

Downey, G., & Coyne, J. C. (1990). Children of depressed parents: An integrative review. *Psychological Bulletin, 108*, 50–76.

Forehand, R., & McCombs, A. (1989). The nature of interparental conflict of married and divorced parents: Implications for young adolescents. *Journal of Abnormal Child Psychology, 17*, 235–249.

Forehand, R., McCombs, A., & Brody, G. H. (1987). The relationship between parental depressive mood states and child functioning. *Advances in Behaviour Research & Therapy, 9*, 1–20.

Framo, J. L. (1975). Personal reflections of a therapist. *Journal of Marriage and Family Counseling, 1*, 15–28.

Freud, S. (1959). *Collected Papers*. New York: Basic Books.

Furstenberg, F. F., Jr., Morgan, S. P., & Allison, P. D. (1987). Parental participation and children's well-being after marital dissolution. *American Sociological Review, 52*, 695–701.

Gaines, R., Sandgrund, A., Green, A. H., & Power, E. (1978). Etiological factors in child maltreatment: A multivariate study of abusing, neglecting, and normal mothers. *Journal of Abnormal Psychology, 87*, 531–540.

Gelfand, D. M., & Teti, D. M. (1990). The effects of maternal depression on children. *Clinical Psychology Review, 10*, 329–353.

Glueck, S., & Glueck, E. (1950). *Unraveling juvenile delinquency*. Cambridge, MA: Harvard University Press.

Goodwin, D. W., & Guze, S. B. (1989). *Psychiatric diagnosis* (4th ed.). New York: Oxford University Press.

Goodwin, D. W., Schulsinger, F., Knop, J., Mednick, S., & Guze, S. B. (1977). Alcoholism and depression in adopted-out daughters of alcoholics. *Archives of General Psychiatry, 34*, 751–755.

Halebsky, M. A. (1987). Adolescent alcohol and substance abuse: Parent and peer effects. *Adolescence, 22*, 961–967.

Hall, G. S. (1904). *Adolescence: Its psychology and its relation to physiology, anthropology, sociology, sex, crime, religion, and education*. New York: Appleton-Century-Crofts.

Hammen, C., Adrian, C., Gordon, D., Burge, D., Jaenicke, C., & Hiroto, D. (1987). Children of depressed mothers: Maternal strain and symptom predictors of dysfunction. *Journal of Abnormal Psychology, 96*, 190–198.

Hammen, C., Burge, D., & Stansbury, K. (1990). Relationship of mother and child variables to child outcomes in a high-risk sample: A causal modeling analysis. *Developmental Psychology, 26*, 24–30.

Hetherington, I. M., Cox, M., & Cox, R. (1982). Effects of divorce on parents and children. In M. E. Lamb (Ed.), *Nontraditional families: Parenting and child development* (pp. 233–288). Hillsdale, NJ: Lawrence Erlbaum Associates.

Hoffman, L. W. (1987). The value of children to parents and child-rearing patterns. *Social Behaviour, 2*, 123–141.

Hoffman, M. L. (1970). Moral Development. In P. H. Mussen (Ed.), *Carmichael's manual of child psychology* (Vol. 2, pp. 261–359). New York: Wiley.

Hops, H., Sherman, L., Biglan, A. (1987). Maternal depression, marital discord, and children's behavior: A developmental perspective. In G. R. Patterson (Ed.), *Depression and aggression in family interaction* (pp. 185–208). Hillsdale, NJ: Lawrence Erlbaum Associates.

Jacob, T., Krahn F. L., & Leonard, K. (1991). Parent-child interactions in families with alcoholic fathers. *Journal of Consulting and Clinical Psychology, 59*, 176–181.

Jacob, T., Ritchey, D., Cvitkovic, J. F., & Blane, H. T. (1981). Communication styles of alcoholic and nonalcoholic families when drinking and not drinking. *Journal of Studies on Alcohol, 42*, 466–482.

Jacob, T., & Seilhamer, R. A. (1987). Alcoholism and family interaction. In T. Jacob (Ed.), *Family interaction and psychopathology* (pp. 613–630). New York: Plenum.

Johnson, G. M., Shontz, F. C., & Locke T. P. (1984). Relationships between adolescent drug abuse and parental drug behavior. *Adolescence, 19*, 295–299.

Johnson, V., & Pandina, R. J. (1991). Effects of the family on adolescent substance use, delinquency, and coping styles. *American Journal of Drug and Alcohol Abuse, 17*, 71–88.

Knopf, I. J. (1984). *Childhood psychopathology: A developmental approach* (2nd Ed.). Englewood Cliffs: Prentice-Hall.

Loeb, R. C., Horst, L., & Horton, P. J. (1980). Family interaction patterns associated with self-esteem in preadolescent girls and boys. *Merrill-Palmer Quarterly, 26*, 203–217.

Long, N., Forehand, R., Fauber, R., & Brody, G. H. (1987). Self-perceived and independently observed competence of young adolescents as a function of parental marital conflict and recent divorce. *Journal of Abnormal Child Psychology, 15*, 15–27.

Macoby, E. E., & Martin, J. A. (1983). Socialization in the context of the family: Parent-child interaction. In E. M. Hetherington (Ed.), *Handbook of child psychology: Vol. 4. Socialization, personality, and social development* (pp. 1–101). New York: Wiley.

McDermott, D. (1984). The relationship of parental drug use and parent's attitude concerning adolescent drug use. *Adolescence, 19*, 89–97.

McGraw, K. O. (1987). *Developmental psychology*. Orlando, FL: Harcourt Brace Jovanovich.

Miller, S. M., Birnbaum, A., & Durbin, D. (1990). Etiologic perspectives on depression in childhood. In M. Lewis & S. M. Miller (Eds.), *Handbook of developmental psychopathology* (pp. 311–325). New York: Plenum.

Niven, R. G. (1984). Alcohol in the family. In L. J. West (Ed.), *Alcoholism and related problems* (pp. 91–109). Englewood Cliffs; NJ: Prentice Hall.

Olweus, D. (1980). Familial and temperamental determinants of aggressive behavior in adolescent boys: A causal analysis. *Developmental Psychology, 16*, 644–660.

Patterson, G. R. (1980). Mothers: The unacknowledged victims. *Monographs of the Society for Research in Child Development, 45*(5), 1–64.

Patterson, G. R. (1982). *Coercive family process*. Eugene, OR: Castalia.

Peterson, G. W., Leigh, G. K. (1990). The family and social competence in adolescence. In T. P. Gullotta, G. R. Adams, & R. Montemayor (Eds.), *Developing Social Competence in Adolescence* (pp. 97–138). London: Sage

Plomin, R., Nitz, K., & Rowe, D. C. (1990). Behavioral genetics and aggressive behavior in childhood. In M. Lewis & S. Miller (Eds.), *Handbook of developmental psychopathology* (pp. 119–133). New York: Plenum.

Putallaz, M., & Heflin, A. H. (1990) Parent-child inter action. In S. R. Asher & J. D. Coie (Eds.), *Peer rejection in childhood* (pp. 189–216). New York: Cambridge.

Radke-Yarrow, M. (1990). Family environments of depressed and well parents and their children: Issues of research methods. In G. R. Patterson (Ed.), *Depression and aggression in family interaction* (pp. 169–184). Hillsdale, NJ: Lawrence Erlbaum Associates.

Reitman, D., Gross, A. M., & Messer, S. C. (in press). Role of family and home environment. In V. B. Van Hasselt & M. Hersen (Eds.), *Handbook of adolescent psychopathology: A guide to diagnosis and treatment*. Lexington, MA: Lexington.

Rutter, M. (1985). Family and school influence on behavioral development. *Journal of Child Psychology and Psychiatry, 26*, 349–368.

Rutter, M., Cox, A., Tupling, C., Berger, M., & Youle, W. (1975). Attachment and adjustment in two geographical areas. I. The prevalence of psychiatric disorder. *British Journal of Psychiatry, 126*, 493–509.

Rutter, M., & Quinton, D. (1977). Psychiatric disorder — Ecological factors and concepts of causation. In H.

McGurk (Ed.), *Ecological factors in human development* (pp. 173–188). Amsterdam: North-Holland.

Sarigiani, P. (1987, April). *Perceived closeness in relationship with father: Links to adjustment and body image in girls*. Paper presented at the biennial meeting of the Society for Research in Child Development, Baltimore, MD.

Spitz, R. A. (1945). Hospitalism: An inquiry into the genesis of psychiatric conditions in early childhood. Part 1. *Psychoanalytic Studies of the Child, 1*, 53–74.

Stolberg, A. L., & Anker, J. M. (1983). Cognitive and behavioral changes in chidlren resulting from parental divorce and consequent environmental changes. *Journal of Divorce, 7*, 23–41.

Vaughn, B. E., Egeland, B. R., Sroufe, L. A., & Waters, E. (1979). Individual differences in infant–mother attachment at twelve and eighteen months: Stability and change in families under stress. *Child Development, 50*, 971–975.

Vaux, A., & Ruggiero, M. (1983). Stressful life change and delinquent behavior. *American Journal of Community Psychology, 11*, 169–183.

Webster-Stratton, C. (1990). Stress: A potential disrupter of parent perceptions and family interactions. *Journal of Clinical Child Psychology, 19*, 302–312.

Webster-Stratton, C. & Hammond, M. (1988). Maternal depression and its relationship to life stress, perceptions of child behavior problems, parenting behaviors, and child conduct problems. *Journal of Abnormal Child Psychology, 16*, 299–315.

Werner, E. E. (1986). Resilient offspring of alcoholics: A longitudinal study from birth to age 18. *Journal of Studies on Alcohol, 47*, 34–40.

Wierson, M., Forehand, R., Fauber, R., & McCombs, A. (1989). Buffering young male adolescents against negative divorce influences: The role of good parent-adolescent relations. *Child Study Journal, 19*, 101–115.

Winder, C. L. & Rau, L. (1962). Parental Attitudes associated with social deviance in preadolescent boys. *Journal of Abnormal and Social Psychology, 64*, 418–424.

Wolin, S. J., & Bennet, L. A. (1984). Family rituals. *Family Process, 23*, 401–420.

Yarrow, M. R., Campbell, J. D., & Burton, R. (1968). *Child-rearing, an inquiry into research and methods*. San Francisco: Jossey-Bass.

Chapter 7

Research Strategies in Child Psychopathology

Eric J. Mash
University of Calgary

Gloria L. Krahn
Oregon Health Sciences University

"My 6-year-old son James still wets the bed one or two nights a week. I think its gotten worse since my husband and I separated three months ago. Is this behavior normal?"

"I just don't understand why my 11-year-old daughter Phyllis is so sad all the time. She's always been a moody child. Is this her personality or is something at home or at school causing her to feel this way?"

"My 9-year-old son Keith is constantly getting into fights with other children. He also has severe tantrums during which he throws and breaks things. My husband thinks he is just a tough kid, but I'm really worried. Will he outgrow this behavior? What can I do about it?"

These are questions that parents frequently ask about their children's problem behaviors; they also exemplify the kinds of questions that research studies in child psychopathology seek to address. Such questions have to do with defining what constitutes normal and abnormal behavior for children of different ages and sexes, identifying the causes and correlates of abnormal child behavior, making predictions about long-term outcomes for varying childhood problems, and developing and evaluating methods for the treatment and/or prevention of abnormal child behavior. When studying childhood disorders, it is crucial that one's choice of research methods and strategies be appropriate to the questions being asked. A research strategy that is effective for answering certain types of questions may prove ineffective for answering other types of questions. In practice, most problems in child psychopathology are best studied through the use of a variety of research methods and strategies. Because there is no one "correct" approach to research in child psychopathology, it is our view that research activities are best conceptualized within a decision-making framework. Such a framework requires an understanding of the theoretical, method-ological, and practical considerations that permit the researcher to make informed decisions about when certain research methods and strategies are appropriate, and when they are not.

This chapter provides an overview of selected research issues and strategies in child psychopathology. We begin with a discussion of the kinds of questions that research studies in child psychopathology typically address. We then consider three fundamental issues in child psychopathology research: the relation between theory and research, the role of developmental factors, and the impact of the child's social context. Next, we examine the process of research and highlight issues that are relevant at various stages of this process. These include general approaches to research, sampling considerations, types of research designs, methods of measurement, and approaches to data analysis. Finally, we consider some of the ethical and pragmatic issues encoun-tered in conducting research with disturbed children and families.

COMMON TYPES OF RESEARCH QUESTIONS

Four common and interrelated types of research questions in the study of child psychopathology are questions about: (a) the nature of childhood disorders, (b) the determinants of childhood disorders, (c) risk and protective factors, and (d) treatment and prevention.

Questions About the Nature of Childhood Disorders

Questions about the nature of childhood disorders are concerned with how disorders are defined and diagnosed, how they are expressed at different ages and in various contexts, constellations and patterning of symptoms, base rates for various problems and competencies, and natural progressions of problems and competencies over time. These kinds of questions are frequently addressed through epidemiological or survey studies of the incidence, prevalence, and co-occurrence of childhood disorders and competencies in the general population of children and in populations of children referred for treatment (Costello, 1989).

In one illustrative large-scale study, Achenbach, Howell, Quay, and Conners (1991) conducted a national survey in the United States with parents of over 5,000 4- to 16-year-old children. Parents of nonreferred and clinic-referred children completed checklists and were interviewed concerning 216 problem child behaviors (e.g., argues, cheats, lonely) and 23 child competencies (e.g., number of friends, social activities, school performance). Important differences in problem patterns were found for children of different ages and sexes. Regional and ethnic differences were minimal, but lower socioeconomic status (SES) children were reported to have more problems and fewer competencies than upper-SES children.

As these and other epidemiological findings indicate, the expression of childhood symptoms and disorders often varies in relation to such variables as: the child's age and sex, the parents' SES (e.g., family income, level of education, and occupational status), ethnicity, geographical region, family size and constellation, and parents' marital and/or mental health status. Consequently, these variables must be assessed and/or controlled for in most studies of child psychopathology. Many of the inconsistent findings in child psychopathology are the direct result of research designs and/or interpretations of findings that have failed to take these important variables into account. For example, it has been reported that physically abused children display more parent-rated problem symptoms than nonabused children. However, this difference is not found when groups of abused and nonabused children are well matched with respect to SES (Wolfe & Mosk, 1983).

Questions About the Determinants of Childhood Disorders

Questions about the determinants of childhood disorders ask how biological, psychological, and environmental processes interact to produce the outcomes that are observed over time. Research into biological determinants has focused on such possible causes of child psychopathology as structural brain damage, brain dysfunction, neurotransmitter imbalances, and genetic influences, whereas environmental models have emphasized the role of environmental toxins, sociocultural contexts, disciplinary practices, early experiences, and family constellations and systems. Questions about the causes of childhood disorders are complicated by the following: (a) what qualifies as a cause varies according to what we are studying and how far back in time we wish to trace a causal chain, and (b) determinants of childhood disorders seldom involve simple one-to-one cause and effect relations.

Childhood disorders are almost always the result of multiple causes. For example, genetic makeup, family history, child temperament, family management processes, and parental personality all are potential contributors to conduct disorders in children. A challenge for research into the determinants of conduct disorders, as well as for research into other childhood problems, is to identify the relative contributions of each of these factors and how they may combine to produce specific outcomes. Because simple cause and effect relations rarely occur in the study of child psychopathology, causes are more appropriately conceptualized as being necessary, sufficient, necessary and sufficient, or contributory factors in the development of childhood disorders (Achenbach, 1982).

Causes of child psychopathology operate at the molecular (e.g., biochemical events, parent–child interaction) and molar (e.g., cultural values) levels. Therefore, one's research methods and strategies depend greatly on the particular determinants and level of influence that one is interested in studying. For example, direct observation and sequential analyses of behavior may be the best methods for capturing the moment-to-moment exchanges that occur during parent–child interactions, whereas questionnaires, interviews, and qualitative analysis may be the more appropriate methods for studying parental beliefs and cultural attitudes about children.

Because the etiologies for most childhood disorders are presently unknown, researchers are frequently interested in identifying characteristics and conditions that are *associated* with a disorder as potential causal factors. For example, the observed association between marital discord and child conduct problems has led to an interest in the possible mechanisms by which marital discord can lead to conduct difficulties (Crockenberg & Covey, 1991). Because the causes of childhood disorders may operate as *direct and/or indirect* influences, marital discord may influence a child directly as a result of his or her exposure to aggression between parents or indirectly when such discord interferes with the parents' ability to provide adequate nurturance and/or consistent discipline. Such findings regarding associated factors raise the important consideration of *directionality* of effects. For example, although marital discord and childhood problems are known to be associated, discord may represent a cause of difficult child behavior, an outcome of difficult child behavior, or as is more commonly the case, both a cause and an outcome (i.e., reciprocal influences). The realities of multiple determinants, associated characteristics, direct and indirect effects and reciprocal influences necessitate that research into the determinants of childhood disorders must rely on design (e.g., longitudinal study) and data analytic strategies (e.g., path analysis) that can distinguish direct and indirect effects, and that can identify, compare, and evaluate alternative pathways and directions of influence.

Illustrative etiologic studies have examined the relationship between parental disciplinary practices and children's antisocial behavior (Patterson, Reid, & Dishion, 1992), the impact of sexual abuse on children (Browne & Finkelhor, 1986), the relationship between quality of early attachments and the later development of behavior problems (Greenberg, Speltz, Deklyen, & Endriga, 1991), the relationship between parental personality disorders and childhood conduct problems (Frick et al., 1992), and the heritability of extreme fearfulness in children (Stevenson, Batten, & Cherner, 1992).

Questions About Risk and Protective Factors

Some research studies seek to identify characteristics, conditions, or circumstances that place a child at-risk for the development of problems. Common *risk* factors that increase the likelihood that some form and degree of disorder will occur include low child intelligence, childhood illnesses, physical or sexual abuse, separations from parents, low maternal education, and parent criminality. Whether or not presence of these or other risk factors will result in emergence of childhood psychopathology is influenced by the number of risk factors present *and* by the presence of *protective* factors. Protective factors are represented by characteristics, conditions, or circumstances that promote or maintain healthy development. Common protective factors include high child intelligence, contact with a supportive and consistent adult, and the availability of social supports.

Research into risk and protective factors often requires that large samples of children be studied and that multiple areas of child functioning (e.g., physical, intellectual, psychosocial) be evaluated over long periods of time. This is necessary because: (a) only a small proportion of children who are at-risk for a problem will actually develop the disorder; (b) the areas of child functioning that will be affected, and how they will be affected, are not known in advance; and (c) the points in development at which a disorder may occur or re-occur are also not known in advance. Sometimes the effects of exposure to a risk factor during infancy or early childhood may not be visible until adolescence or adulthood. The possibility that delayed or *sleeper effects* will occur complicates the study of risk and protective factors, because children must be studied for many years if delayed effects are to be detected.

In an illustrative study of risk and protective factors for child maltreatment (Egeland, 1991), 267 first-time expectant mothers who were assessed to be at-risk for poor quality caregiving were recruited during the last trimester of their pregnancy. The mothers' high-risk status was based on their young age, low education, unplanned pregnancy, and single-parent status. Mothers and children were evaluated at regular intervals from the last trimester of pregnancy through the time that the children were in the sixth grade. Evaluations included information about the children, mothers, mother–child interactions, life circumstances, and stresses. When the children were 2 years of age, approximately 16% of these high-risk mothers exhibited one or more forms of maltreatment (e.g., physical abuse, verbal abuse, psychological unavailability, neglect), a proportion that is considerably higher than the base rate of approximately 3%–5% that would be expected in a community sample of mothers who had not been preselected to be at-risk for maltreatment of their children. The at-risk approach in this investigation also enabled the researchers to identify a comparison group of mothers who were at high-risk for poor caregiving but who did not later maltreat their children. By comparing high-risk families showing positive child rearing outcomes with those showing negative outcomes, possible protective factors could then be identified and used as the basis for designing prevention programs for child maltreatment.

Questions About Treatment and Prevention

Questions about treatment and prevention are concerned with:

1. evaluating the immediate and long-term effects of a variety of psychological, environmental, and biological treatments;
2. comparing the relative effectiveness of differing forms and combinations of treatment;
3. identifying the basic mechanisms to explain why a particular treatment works;
4. understanding the factors that influence the referral and treatment process;
5. understanding how intermediate therapy processes such as client motivation, adherence, parental involvement, or the therapist–client relationship contribute to treatment successes and failures;
6. assessing the acceptability of equivalent forms of treatment for children and significant adults, and
7. evaluating programs designed to reduce the likelihood that children who are at-risk for a disorder will in fact develop the disorder (Kazdin, Bass, Ayers, & Rodgers, 1990).

Kazdin (1988) identified over 200 alternative forms of psychosocial treatment for children and adolescents, the great majority of which have not been evaluated. Although integrative reviews suggest that children who receive psychotherapy are generally better off than children who do not receive psychotherapy (e.g., Weisz, Weiss, Alicke, & Klotz, 1987), there is currently a pressing need for research that evaluates and compares specific types and combinations of child intervention and prevention programs.

Several key issues in treatment outcome research are: (a) identifying the constructs to be used in assessing treatment outcomes, (b) selecting or developing appropriate measures of these constructs, (c) deciding on which informant(s) will be asked to judge treatment outcomes, (d) evaluating the impact of treatment against known age-related improvements in functioning, and (e) specifying the criteria to be used in determining both the short-and long-term impact of treatment. An important distinction to be made in treatment evaluation research relates to the statistical versus clinical significance of change. Although problem children may show statistically significant improvements in their behavior as the result of treatment, their performance may still fall short of normative expectations. For example, Barkley, Guevremont, Anastopolous, and Fletcher (1992) reported that although the behaviors of Attention-Deficit Hyperactivity Disorder (ADHD) adolescents improved following family intervention, only a small proportion of these adolescents were functioning in the normative range. In conducting outcome research, it is important that treatment-related changes be evaluated with respect to their clinical relevance as well as their statistical significance (Jacobson & Truax, 1991).

Illustrative treatment studies have evaluated the impact of child management training for parents of preschool ADHD children (Pisterman et al., 1989), the effects of parent training and problem-solving skill training for the treatment of antisocial behavior (Kazdin, Siegel, & Bass, 1992), and the effectiveness of school-based cognitive–behavioral interventions for aggressive boys (Lochman, 1992). Illustrative prevention studies have evaluated school-based coping and self-esteem building programs for children in alcoholic families (Roosa, Gensheimer, Short, Ayers, & Shell (1989), early interventions to minimize the adverse effects of low birthweight (Rauh, Achenbach, Nurcombe, Howell, & Teti, 1988), and multimodal cognitive–behavioral training to prevent adolescent drug abuse (Botvin, 1990).

FUNDAMENTAL ISSUES IN CHILD PSYCHOPATHOLOGY RESEARCH

Theory and Research

The knowledge base of psychology has traditionally developed through the dynamic dialectic of theory and empiricism leading to new information. Theory, often developed from observations, leads to predictions that are empirically supported or refuted. These empirical findings, in turn, lead to refinement, alteration, or abandonment of the theory. Through theoretical formulations once can integrate related research results and develop meanings that extend beyond the immediate findings. Theory also provides the context to formulate new hypotheses and generalizations. The theoretical model(s) of child development and child psychopathology that the researcher adopts will dictate the variables deemed important to study, the choice of research methods, and the interpretation of research findings.

Several researchers have proposed a hierarchical approach to the conceptualization of child psychopathology (Overton & Horowitz, 1991). From a hierarchical perspective, theory at more general levels can provide an overarching conceptualization of maladaptive behaviors, which can then be examined from a more focused perspective. For example, general theories of development may conceptualize childhood psychopathology in terms of the child's failure to adapt to age-salient developmental tasks. However, more focused theories are then needed to determine the specific adaptations and tasks that are important to study within this general framework.

Achenbach (1990) used the term *macroparadigm* to connote a broad perspective that integrates different approaches around common phenomena and questions. He proposed that the conceptual framework of developmental psychopathology, which considers childhood disorders in the context of maturational and developmental processes, be regarded as a macroparadigm. In contrast, specific theories, such as object relations theory, social learning theory, attachment theory, cognitive-developmental theory, and family systems theory, represent examples of microparadigms under this broader conceptualization. These more focused theories attempt to make immediate empirical reference to the specific domains that they seek to explain (e.g., quality of parent–child relationships, learning of antisocial behavior, social cognition, family processes).

On the other hand, recognizing that broad theories rarely yield testable hypotheses, other researchers have advocated for the development of "minitheories" that are amenable to empirical testing (Kazdin, 1989). Following confirmation of these minitheories, their focus can be expanded and generalized, forming the building blocks for a broader conceptualization of childhood disorders. For example, Gerald Patterson's (1982) "coercion model" proposed a number of family interaction processes to account for the development of antisocial behavior in children. In a series of empirical studies spanning over two decades, Patterson identified specific characteristics and processes that are important in the learning of antisocial behavior (e.g., parental failure to follow through on demands, inadequate monitoring of child behavior) and used these findings to formulate a broader developmental model of how these events unfold over time to produce a variety of antisocial outcomes (Patterson et al., 1992).

Developmental Considerations

Knowledge of normal developmental processes is critical to our general understanding of child psychopathology (see Ross & Jennings, chapter 4, this volume). Moreover, the rapid changes that are known to occur throughout infancy, childhood, and adolescence present unique conceptual, methodological, and pragmatic challenges to research on childhood disorders. Many childhood difficulties, such as fears and oppositionality, are quite common in young children but are known to decrease in magnitude and to change in form over time. The high frequency of occurrence in the general population for many childhood difficulties makes it difficult to determine which of these problems are predictive of later difficulties and which are not.

Many developmental changes are predictable enough by chronological age that normative data from standardized child symptom checklists reveal these patterns of increases and decreases when aggregated across large numbers of children of different ages (Achenbach & Edelbrock, 1981). This type of *normative-developmental* information regarding the base rates of different childhood problems for children of different ages is critical in making judgments about developmental deviation. However, although the timing of developmental changes is related to chronological age, the relationship is not perfect. Although the child's age often provides an adequate marker for developmental stage, some research questions require use of more functional measures of developmental level such as mental age, gestational age, or pubertal maturation.

This issue is especially significant in the study of children with known developmental delays, such as mental retardation or language delay. For these populations, comparisons with mental age or linguistic equivalency may provide a partial but not complete solution to the issue of developmental equivalence (see Stoneman, 1989, for a discussion of mental-age matches). Similarly, in research with prematurely born children, use of chronological versus gestational age matches has been debated. If correction is made to chronological age based on the degree of prematurity, then questions arise as to the length of time that such corrections are to be made and whether age-corrections should be applied uniformly across all domains of functioning. Other studies have found associations between pubertal maturation and parent–child conflict that would not have been revealed had the less discriminating measure of chronological age been used (Steinberg, 1988).

Studies have also shown that the patterning and organization of childhood symptoms and disorders differ as a function of the child's age and developmental stage and, after about age 3, as a function of the sex of the child (Achenbach, 1985). These qualitative developmental changes in the expression and organization of behavioral displays present unique research problems. For example, aggressive behavior that is evident in the kicks and toy-snatches of a preschooler may be manifest as verbally aggressive behavior during childhood or as covert hostility during adolescence. Do these changes reflect developmental symptom substitution (i.e., a specific symptom may disappear and be replaced by another symptom at a different age), or do they represent separate but linked behaviors on a trajectory of aggressive behaviors, with a greater likelihood of the second behavior occurring given the historical presence of the first? The difference in these views stems from differing theoretical assumptions about aggression as a relatively stable personality trait. Because the frequency and form of childhood problems change over time, the ways in which childhood disorders are defined and measured will, of necessity, differ at different ages. As a result, it may be difficult to determine whether observed changes in problem expression over time reflect "true" developmental progressions or whether they are the result of variations in how the problem was defined or measured at different ages (i.e., a result of method variance).

The Social Context of the Child

Theory and research in child psychopathology have emphasized the importance of studying children's behavior and development in relation to the child's social context, typically consisting of the family, school, and peers. Children's dependency on significant adults and the central role that adults play in defining childhood disorders necessitate that the role of social context be considered in conceptualizing research and in deciding how samples of children are recruited, how data are collected, and how findings are interpreted.

Significantly, most children participating in research on emotional or behavioral problems have been referred for treatment by their parents or, in the case of teacher referrals, with the agreement of their parents. Rarely do children refer themselves for treatment. Children referred by adults in different settings may not be comparable with respect to the nature or severity of their problems or with respect to important associated characteristics such as SES. As a result, inconsistent research findings may reflect differences in the referral and selection processes that were used to identify children who participated in the research (Mash & Wolfe, 1991).

The likelihood of parents seeking help for their child is influenced by many factors, including the degree to which the child's behavior is noticeable and bothersome, the parents' own mental health and possible treatment history, the perceived benefits of treatment, and the parents' awareness of and access to resources. Unless precautions are taken, these sources of bias may influence the nature of research samples that are drawn from clinic populations. The reports of parents and teachers may also be biased, for example, in the tendency of parents to see their problem children in a negative light, even when the child's behavior may not warrant such a view. Such biases may reflect a history of conflictual parent–child interaction and/or high levels of parental depression and stress.

The question of who will serve as the respondent in providing research data is an important one, especially in research with older children and adolescents where the child's verbal report becomes increasingly reliable as a source of data. The choice of respondent is a critical decision, because rates of agreement between different informants and across different situations are generally poor to modest (Achenbach, McConaughy, & Howell, 1987). Mothers have been found to report less psychiatric disorder of all types in their children than children self-report, with a higher correspondence between mother and child report when mothers were themselves depressed at the time of reporting (Weissman et al., 1987). Research has also suggested that parents may be more accurate reporters of overt child behavioral difficulties than children, but that children may provide more accurate accounts of their own internal thoughts and feelings. Other studies have found that mothers typically report higher rates of problem child behaviors than fathers.

In an integrative review of a large number of studies in which different informants were used to report on child symptoms, Achenbach et al. (1987) noted average correlations of around .22 between child self-reports of symptoms and the reports of parents, teachers, and mental health workers; average correlations of .60 between similar informants in similar settings (e.g., mothers and fathers, pairs of teachers), and average correlations of .28 between different informants in different settings (e.g., parents and teachers). A recent report by Verhulst and Van der Ende (1992) found levels of agreement (.54) between parents and adolescents that were higher than those previously reported by Achenbach et al. (1987), suggesting that such levels of agreement may be higher for older children and their parents. These and other findings indicate that the magnitude of agreement among informants may depend on the age, sex, and other characteristics of the child, characteristics of the informant, the method of assessment, the setting in which behavior is rated, and the types of problem behaviors being rated. One way of addressing discrepancies in reporting, that avoids searching for a "true" perception, has been a validation approach that seeks to determine whose report is the best predictor of particular outcomes.

The child's social context also serves as an important moderator of behavior. Although some severe forms of child psychopathology may be pervasive across settings (e.g., home, classroom, playground), more typically, the rate and quality of children's behavior will vary from situation to situation. Such variations may reflect the interaction between particular child characteristics and differences in the expectations, demands, and reinforcement contingencies associated with different settings. From a research standpoint, data that are collected in one setting may not be representative of the child's behavior in other settings. For example, a hyperactive child may exhibit few behavioral or attentional difficulties in a nondemanding unstructured situation such as watching television at home. However, the same child may display difficulties in a more demanding situation such as working on a structured academic task in the classroom. Similarly, children who have been physically abused may show high levels of compliant behavior when observed during interactions with their abusive parent. However, these children may show an opposite pattern of noncompliance and aggressive behavior in other situations where their parent is not present. Although the reasons for cross-setting variability in the expression of child psychopathology are numerous and not yet fully understood, the researcher needs to be cognizant of this variability when sampling behavior and when attempting to evaluate the representativeness and generalizability of research findings.

RESEARCH STRATEGIES

Research activities in child psychopathology can be viewed as a multistaged process involving a series of key decisions at various points in this process. The process typically begins with development of hypotheses on the basis of theory and previous findings and then proceeds to deciding on a general approach to research, identifying the population to be studied, developing a plan for sampling from that population, developing a research design and procedures that balance the pragmatics of implementation with the adequacy of the research to address the hypotheses under investigation, selecting or developing data collection measures, gathering and analyzing the data, and interpreting the results in relation to theory and previous findings. The following discussion provides examples of some of the issues that may be encountered at various stages of this research process.

General Approaches to Research

Research varies in the degree to which the study uses an experimental versus correlational approach, employs a longitudinal versus cross-sectional strategy, and whether data are collected prospectively or retrospectively. These alternative, but complementary, approaches offer different advantages and disadvantages. The choice of approach frequently depends on the nature of the population and disorder under investigation, the research questions being addressed, and the availability of resources.

Correlational Versus Experimental Research. The basic distinction between correlational versus experimental research reflects the degree to which the investigator can manipulate the "independent variable" or, alternatively, must rely on examining the covariation of several variables of interest. The greater the degree of control that the researcher has over the independent variable(s), the more the study approximates a true experiment. Conversely, the less control the researcher has in determining who will and will not be exposed to the independent variable(s), the more correlational the research will be. Most variables of interest in child psychopathology can not be manipulated directly (e.g., parenting styles, genetic influences). As a result, much of the research in the field has not been experimental, and correlational approaches have been relied upon extensively. The primary limitations of correlational research are that interpretations of causality are difficult to make because: (a) a correlation between two variables does not imply that one variable causes the other, and (b) the correlation may occur because the two variables are both measures of some other more fundamental variable.

For example, in studying the effects of an independent variable, such as a specific childhood disorder on parenting behavior, research has identified a relationship between child ADHD and high levels of maternal directiveness (Danforth, Barkley, & Stokes, 1991). Because the variables of ADHD and parenting behavior cannot be randomly assigned, these findings are necessarily correlational in nature and do not lend themselves to making a clear causal interpretation. ADHD symptoms such as noncompliance, inattention, and impulsivity may result in the use of greater maternal directiveness. Alternatively, maternal use of high levels of directiveness may provoke noncompliant, inattentive, and impulsive child behaviors. Or, ADHD symptoms and maternal directiveness may both be the result of some other more fundamental variable (e.g., shared genetic dispositions, common environmental stressors). An experimental approach can be used to clarify these correlational findings, for example, by altering the child's behavior via stimulant medication and examining the subsequent effects on maternal behavior. When children with ADHD were given stimulant medication, it was found that improvements in child behavior as a result of stimulant medication led to concomitant reductions in maternal directiveness (Humphries, Kinsbourne, & Swanson, 1978). These experimental findings, support the causal interpretation that higher levels of maternal directiveness are at least in part the result of the ADHD child's difficult-to-manage behaviors.

Longitudinal Versus Cross-Sectional Research. In longitudinal research, the same individuals are studied at different ages/stages of development, whereas in cross-sectional research different individuals are studied at different ages/stages of development. Although cross-sectional research can provide suggestive information concerning developmental changes, definitive answers to questions about continuities and discontinuities in child psychopathology can best be obtained through the use of longitudinal designs.

Longitudinal designs are conducted prospectively, with data collection occurring at specified points in time from the same individuals who were initially selected because of their membership in one or more populations of interest. The prospective longitudinal design allows the researcher to track developmental change within individuals. Because data are collected on the same individuals at Time 1 and Time 2, causal inferences based on temporal ordering can be made. Such inferences of causality cannot be made in cross-sectional designs where different individuals are assessed at the two time points. Longitudinal designs also allow for identification of individual developmental trends that would be masked by aggregating over individuals. The prepubertal growth spurt exemplifies this, where rapid accelerations in growth occurring at different ages across the population are not reflected in growth measures aggregated across adolescents.

Difficulties associated with longitudinal designs are both design related as well as pragmatic. Design difficulties relate to the issues of aging effects, cohort effects, and period effects. Aging effects refer to changes that occur because of aging of the participants, such as increases in physical prowess. Cohort effects refer to influences related to membership in a group of individuals born at one time and experiencing a sequence of events at the same time. Persons who regard themselves as "children of the sixties" reflect self-identified membership in a specific cohort. Period effects refer to influences occurring at particular times historically, such as the economic recession or the increased awareness of child abuse in the 1980s. Longitudinal designs confound aging and period effects whereas cross-sectional designs confound aging and cohort effects (Farrington, 1991). Pragmatic disadvantages of longitudinal designs include the long wait for data, participant attrition, possible changes in diagnostic definitions or measurement instruments, and difficulties in maintaining research funding and resources over many years.

Some of the difficulties associated with longitudinal research can be reduced by using a combined cross-sectional/longitudinal approach in an "accelerated longitudinal design" (Farrington, 1991). With this approach, several cohorts of individuals are followed, each at different but overlapping ages or stages of development. For example, if the hypotheses related to the association between insecure early attachments and subsequent conduct disorder, cohorts of children might be followed from ages 1 to 6, 4 to 10, 8 to 14, and 12 to 18 years. Tracking the same children longitudinally would allow for measurement of aging effects (e.g., the developmental changes that are of interest), whereas use of different samples of children reduces the period effect, and overlap at different ages allows for measurement and control of the cohort effect. This approach assumes that links between early and later events are reflected at intermediate stages. If this assumption is not met, as in the case of delayed effects that only appear at much later ages, the data would fail to reveal these relationships. This shortcoming may be particularly problematic in studies of genetic influences where the effects on some characteristics may become increasingly apparent with age. For example, Scarr and Weinberg (1983), in a study of adopted children, found greater correlations between biological parent's and child's IQ at later ages than at earlier ages. Similarly, certain genetic disorders such as Huntington's Chorea only become evident in early and middle adulthood.

Retrospective Versus Prospective Research.   Research designs may differ with respect to when the sample is identified and when data are collected. Verhulst and Koot (1991) distinguished among three types of designs. In "real-time" prospective designs, the research sample is identified and then followed longitudinally over time, with data collected at specified time intervals. Disadvantages of this design include sample attrition over time and the delay in collecting data that reflect changes over time. In "catch-up" designs, a sample of children is identified from records from an earlier time and then located at a second later time. This design provides for faster data collection, but results can be seriously compromised by the unrepresentativeness of individuals who can be located at the later time.

In "follow-back" or retrospective designs, a sample is identified at the current time and asked for information relating to an earlier time period. For example, a sample of depressed young adults might be asked to provide retrospective ratings and descriptions of their early family experiences. Although data are more immediately available in retrospective studies, they are also highly susceptible to bias and distortion in recall. Moreover, retrospective designs fail to identify individuals who were exposed to certain earlier experiences but do not develop the problem. For example, depressed young adults may report more negative early experiences (e.g., Blatt, Wein, Chevron, & Quinlan, 1979). However, based on this finding, we could *not* conclude that negative early experiences were specific precursors of adult depression, because the retrospective study fails to identify those children whose early experiences were negative but who did not exhibit depression as young adults.

Sampling Considerations

Sample Definition.   A careful definition of the sample of children to be studied is critical if there is to be comparability of findings across studies and clear communication among research investigators. Unfortunately, there has been little consensus on how childhood disorders should be defined, and many studies of childhood disorders have been carried out on poorly defined groups of children given such nonstandardized labels such as "emotionally disturbed" or "clinically maladjusted."

It is especially important that studies that seek to determine the incidence and prevalence of childhood disorders rely on standardized and well-accepted definitions of those disorders. The failure to apply uniform standards in epidemiological research has led to wide differences in estimated base rates for various childhood disorders. For example, estimates of the incidence of Attention-Deficit Hyperactivity Disorder (ADHD) have ranged from 1% to 20% of the general population, depending on such factors as how one defines ADHD, the use or nonuse of exclusionary criteria (e.g., low intelligence), the population studied, the informant (e.g., parent, teacher, physician), and the geographical locale of the survey (Barkley, 1990).

Categorical Diagnosis. Although an extensive discussion of diagnostic issues is beyond the scope of this chapter (for a discussion of diagnosis and classification see Waldman & Lilienfeld, chapter 2, this volume), the quality of any research study in child psychopathology is ultimately dependent on the classification systems that are used to identify the samples of children who participate in the research. The two major approaches that have been used to diagnose mental and emotional disorders in children are represented by the *Diagnostic and Statistical Manual* (*DSM-IV*) of the American Psychiatric Association (1994) and the *International Classification of Diseases* (ICD-9-CM) of the World Health Organization (1992). These diagnostic systems have been criticized for a variety of reasons, including inadequate reliability and validity, implicit assumptions about etiology, subjective nature of the criteria used to derive categories, lack of empirically derived operational criteria for assignment to categories, developmental insensitivity, lack of relevance for treatment, insensitivity to contextual influences, and insufficient attention to childhood disorders. The most recent revisions of both systems reflect a shift to increasingly greater differentiation of categories for children and adolescents and the use of more operationally and behaviorally specified criteria, with correspondingly less reliance on particular theoretical formulations. In addition, there are efforts underway to develop alternative diagnostic schemes that possess greater sensitivity to the specific developmental, familial, and cultural characteristics of infants and toddlers than do the current diagnostic approaches (Greenspan, Harmon, Emde, Sameroff, & Wieder, 1991).

Dimensional Classification. The question has been debated at length as to whether childhood disorders constitute qualitatively distinct categories or extreme points on continuous dimensions that include adaptive, normal behaviors at other points along these dimensions. Psychotic behavior in children may be categorically distinct from nonpsychotic, whereas severe attentional difficulties may differ only in magnitude from attentional functioning that is regarded as normal for age. Both perspectives may have their place, depending on the disorder under consideration. When the disorder is viewed on a continuum, questions arise as to where the cut-points that differentiate normal from abnormal functioning are to be located and how those points are to be established. What magnitude of disorder will lead to a diagnosis for one child, but not for another? Frequently, these decisions are based on statistical departures from the average (e.g., greater than two standard deviations from the mean) or other empirically derived criteria (Achenbach, 1985).

The diagnosis of mental retardation provides an illustration of differences in meaning based on the cut-points chosen. Mental retardation is defined as significantly subaverage general intellectual functioning associated with concurrent impairments in adaptive functioning, and these need to be evident during the individual's first 18 years of life (Grossman, 1983). Prior to 1977, an IQ below 80 met the criterion for subaverage intellectual functioning. In 1977, the American Association on Mental Deficiency changed the cut-point to an IQ of 68, thereby eliminating the largest category, borderline intellectual functioning (IQ = 69–80), from classification as mental retardation.

Comorbidity

The simultaneous occurrence of two or more childhood disorders is far more common than would be predicted from the general population base rates of the individual disorders. For example, for children who are diagnosed as having an Attention-Deficit Hyperactivity Disorder, as many as 50% also have a Conduct Disorder and 20%–25% a specific learning disability (Barkley, 1990). Several possible explanations have been proposed for the observed high rates of comorbidity. These include shared risk factors, assortative mating, and the possibility that one disorder represents an earlier form of, or predisposes the child to, a second disorder (Caron & Rutter, 1991).

Comorbidity has direct implications for the selection of research participants and interpretation of results. Research samples that are drawn from clinic populations will have a disproportionately high rate of comorbidity because referral for treatment is likely to be based on the combined symptomatology of all disorders. To deal with comorbidity in research samples, some researchers may adopt exclusionary criteria in order to select only participants with single "pure" disorders. This strategy may yield small, atypical samples whose findings do not generalize to other populations. On the other hand, the failure to consider comorbidity may result in an interpretation of findings in relation to one disorder, when these findings are more validly attributed to a second disorder or to the combination of disorders. Research strategies that compare children showing single disorders with those showing comorbid disorders are needed to help disentangle the effects of comorbidity.

Setting and Source of Referral for Research

Research samples of problem and nonproblem children have been selected from a variety of settings that include outpatient psychology and psychiatry clinics, schools, pediatric, developmental, and learning disorder clinics, hospitals, daycare centers, social welfare agencies, youth or church groups, and the general community. Effects related to setting are often confounded with those related to referral source, because across settings, referral sources may include parents, teachers, daycare workers, physicians, or mental health personnel. As sufficiently large samples of children with a particular disorder may not be readily available in a single setting, some studies have included samples that consist of children drawn from different settings and referral sources. This procedure will likely contribute to increased sample heterogeneity and subsequently to increased variance in findings. On the other hand, selection of subjects from a single setting may provide potentially unrepresentative findings that are the result of parameters unique to that particular setting.

Samples drawn from different settings and referral sources can be quite different from one another with respect to the nature and severity of the children's problems and with respect to the children's associated behavioral, learning, and developmental characteristics. Samples from different settings may also show systematic differences with respect to important family characteristics and demographics. To illustrate the effects that referral setting and source can have on research findings, in school-identified samples of ADHD children and in samples of ADHD children drawn from learning disorder clinics, ADHD girls have been found to exhibit fewer behavioral and conduct problems than boys and more cognitive and developmental difficulties. However, in psychology and psychiatry clinic samples, where referral is often based on problem severity, differences between ADHD boys and girls have not been found (Barkley, 1990). These and other findings reinforce the importance of carefully examining the ways in which the characteristics of specific settings and referral sources may influence research results, and the need to take this into account when attempting to generalize one's findings to other groups of children.

Sample Size

The question of how large a sample size is needed is an important one in any study of child psychopathology. Too often, sample size has been based on subject availability rather than on logical or statistical criteria. Because many childhood disorders occur infrequently (e.g., Autistic Disorder), many studies have been carried out on very small samples of children. Small sample sizes tend to reduce the likelihood that significant effects will be found, preclude multifactorial analysis of the results, and limit the generalizability of findings.

The concept of statistical power is relevant to any discussion of sample size. The statistical power of a test refers to the probability of detecting a true difference given that certain conditions hold. These conditions include the anticipated effect size, the size of the variance, and the sample size. In general, increasing the sample size increases the power of a test to detect statistically significant differences. Power analyses may be conducted a priori to determine the sample size needed to detect significant effects (see Cohen, 1988, for a discussion of power analysis).

Because a large sample size increases the likelihood of demonstrating statistical significance, studies with very large samples are virtually assured of producing at least some significant findings, even though the magnitude of the effects may be quite small. Consequently, in addition to statistical significance, the researcher is also interested in detecting effect sizes that are large enough to be meaningful. A recent study of the impact of early intervention on children's later intellectual development illustrates this point (Ramey et al., 1992). With an initial sample of almost 1,000 infants and their families, of which one third were randomly assigned to a treatment condition and two thirds to the control condition, the authors predictably obtained statistically significant findings for treatment effects on children's IQ at age 3 years. The authors also reported indices that addressed the clinical significance of their findings including IQ differences between intervention and control groups of 9 points and percentages of children

scoring in the borderline range of intellectual functioning or lower (IQ < 70) of 6.9%
for the intervention group versus 35.5% for the control group.

Sample Attrition

Sample attrition or drop out is a major problem in child psychopathology research,
particularly in longitudinal studies of high-risk populations. Attrition is not a
randomly distributed event, because families who drop out of a research study are
more likely to have particular characteristics (e.g., multiproblem, low SES, single
parent) when compared with those who remain. Sample attrition results in a reduced
sample size, unequal group sizes, and difficulties in generalizing because of a lack of
sample representativeness. For example, a study of high-risk mothers may produce
misleading findings if during the course of the study the most severely impaired
mothers were to drop out, and interpretations were based on those mothers who
remained. Researchers who conduct studies with high-risk populations have devised a
number of methods for keeping families involved in the investigation, including subject
payment, flexible research schedules, and provision of information and services.
Although these procedures are necessary if high-risk samples are to be studied, the
researcher needs to be cognizant of the possibility that such procedures can influence
and distort the data that are obtained.

RESEARCH DESIGNS

Case Studies

The study of child psychopathology through intensive observation and analysis of
individual cases has a long tradition in abnormal child psychology. Itard's description
of Victor, the Wild Boy of Aveyron, Freud's treatment of a phobia in Little Hans, John
Watson's conditioning of a phobic reaction in Albert B, and many other similar case
studies have played an influential role in shaping the way we think about child
psychopathology. Nevertheless, case studies have typically been viewed as unscientific
and flawed because of the uncontrolled methods and selective biases that often
characterize them and the inherent difficulties associated with integrating diverse
observations and generalizing from single cases. Hence, case studies have been viewed
mostly as rich sources of descriptive information that provide a basis for subsequent
hypothesis testing in research with larger samples and using more controlled methods.

On the other hand, it has also been noted that case studies can capture meaningful
life events in specific contexts and can serve the scientific goals of: (a) exploration (i.e.,
revealing rare or previously unrecognized events), (b) description (i.e., formulating
theory and providing ideas for further investigation), and (c) explanation (i.e., via
hypothesis testing) (Mendelson, 1992). There are a number of reasons that systematically conducted case studies are likely to continue to play a useful role in research on
childhood disorders. First, many childhood disorders are rare, making it difficult to
generate large samples of children for research. Second, the analyses of individual cases
may contribute to our understanding of many striking symptoms of childhood
disorders that either occur infrequently (e.g, acts of extreme cruelty) or that are covert
and therefore difficult to observe directly (e.g., stealing). Third, significant childhood

disturbances often develop as the result of naturally occurring extreme events and circumstances (e.g., natural disasters, severe trauma or abuse) that are not easily studied via controlled methods. Improved methods and technologies for data recording and recent advances in qualitative/content analysis have the potential for removing some of the bias that has characterized clinical case studies and for increasing their scientific respectability. Nevertheless, generalization remains a problem as does the time-consuming nature associated with the intensive analyses of single cases.

Single-Case Experimental Designs

Single-case experimental designs have most frequently been used to evaluate the impact of a clinical treatment (e.g, reinforcement, stimulant medication) on problem child behavior. The central features of single-case designs include repeated assessment of behavior over time, the replication of treatment effects within the same subject over time, and the subject serving as his or her own control by experiencing all treatment conditions. There are many different types of single-subject designs, the most common being the ABAB or reversal design, and the multiple baseline design carried out across behaviors, situations, or individuals.

In an ABAB or reversal design, the subject's behavior is monitored repeatedly throughout four successive phases: (a) a baseline phase (A) in which no treatment occurs (b) an intervention phase (B) in which treatment is introduced and behavior is typically observed to change in the desired direction (c) a reversal phase (A) or return to baseline in which the treatment is withdrawn, and (d) a final phase (B) in which treatment is reinstituted. If the treatment was responsible for the observed change during the intervention phase, the behavior should revert to its baseline level during the reversal phase and should again change in the desired direction when the treatment is reinstituted during the final phase.

In a multiple baseline design across *behaviors*, different responses of the same individual are identified and measured over time to provide a baseline against which changes may be evaluated. Each behavior is then successively modified in turn. If each behavior changes *only* when it is specifically treated, the inference of a cause–effect relationship between the treatment and the behavior change is made. Other common varieties of multiple baseline designs involve successive introductions of treatment for the same behavior in the same individual across different *situations* or for the same behavior across several *individuals* in the same situation. The critical feature of the multiple baseline approach is that change must occur only when treatment is instituted and only for the behavior, situation, or individual that is the target of treatment. Concomitant changes must not occur for untreated behaviors, situations, or individuals until the time that each of these are, in turn, targeted for treatment.

There are several advantages and limitations associated with the use of single-case designs. While preserving the personal quality of the case study, these designs: (a) offer some degree of control for potential confounds such as the effects of maturation, history, statistical regression, instrument decay, and reactivity to observation; (b) provide an objective evaluation of treatment for individual cases; (c) permit for the study of rare disorders; and (d) facilitate the development and evaluation of alternative and combined forms of treatment. On the negative side, are the possibility that specific treatments will interact with individual subject characteristics, limited generality of findings, difficulties in interpretation when observed changes are highly variable, subjectivity and inconsistency that is involved when visual inspection is used as the primary basis for evaluating the data, and limitations associated with specific types of case-study designs (e.g., in the ABAB reversal design, in which ethical concerns surround the return to a baseline condition following effective treatment for undesirable or even dangerous behaviors).

Between-Group Comparison Designs

Rather than comparing an individual with his or her own performance under different conditions, many research designs are based on comparisons between a group of individuals assigned to one condition(s) and other groups of individuals assigned to different condition(s). When subjects are randomly assigned to groups and groups are presumed to be equivalent in all other respects, one group typically serves as the experimental group(s) and the other as the control group(s). Any differences observed between groups are then attributed to the experimental condition. More commonly, the nature of the event (e.g., marital discord) or the disorder of interest (e.g., childhood depression) in studies of child psychopathology precludes random assignment to groups. Comparison groups are then selected to provide contrasting information, but with the recognition that the experimental and comparison groups may vary on dimensions other than those of interest to the researcher. The selection of comparison group(s) requires careful attention to specific characteristics of the disorder and the inferences one desires to make. The choice of comparison groups is particularly important if one wishes to make inferences as to the specificity of findings to the particular disorder under consideration.

An example from the literature on social interactions illustrates this point. When compared with children of normal intelligence, children with mental retardation of various etiologies have long been known to show dampened affect or a lack of emotional expressiveness during social interactions with their parents and others (e.g., Cicchetti & Serafica, 1981; Yoder & Feagans, 1988). These differences have led to the interpretation that dampened affect is a specific feature of mental retardation. However, it has also been found that children with physical but not mental delays exhibit dampened affect during social interactions (Wasserman, Shilansky, & Hahn, 1986). These findings with children who are not mentally retarded call into question previous interpretations regarding the specificity and possible cause(s) of this symptom and illustrate the importance of careful selection of comparison groups. One strategy to help address this threat to validity is the use of multiple comparison groups. Each group can provide comparative data on a relevant dimension (e.g., general level of distress). For example, in a study of the parent–adolescent interactions of families with an alcoholic father, Jacob, Krahn, and Leonard (1991) used both nondistressed-and depressed-father families as comparison groups.

Multivariate Approaches

As previously discussed, models of child and family functioning are typically complex, with multiple components and multiple pathways of direct, indirect, and reciprocal influences (Mash & Johnston, 1990; McCubbin & Patterson, 1983; Patterson et al., 1992). Multivariate approaches are needed to test complete or partial versions of these models. In general, multivariate approaches, which include multiple-regression analysis and its many variants (e.g., path analysis), offer several advantages. First, they allow for the simultaneous consideration of multiple variables in combination (i.e., as a system). Multifactorial designs are routinely required to assess the unique effects of salient variables and their interaction effects with other variables. Second, they allow for the simultaneous consideration of multiple outcome measures. In so doing, they identify redundancy or overlapping variance among dependent variables, all of which may be significant because of shared variance with a salient variable; alternatively, they also allow for the potential identification of effects that may only be evident in the combination of dependent variables and not evident in any single variable. Finally, they provide a means for controlling the experiment-wise error rate when using numerous dependent variables.

Multivariate designs are particularly well-suited for testing predictive models of behavior. In a recent examination of behavioral adjustment in children, Abidin, Jenkins, and McGaughey (1992) examined the contribution of family variables measured during the child's first year of life to predict subsequent behavioral adjustment $4\frac{1}{2}$ years later. Hierarchical regression models indicated that 39% of the variance in mother's ratings of the child's behavioral adjustment could be predicted by child gender, family life stress events, child characteristics, and maternal characteristics. No support was evident for models predicting father or teacher ratings of behavioral adjustment.

METHODS OF MEASUREMENT

A variety of measurement methods have been used to assess relevant constructs (e.g., aggression, sociability, temperament, attachment) in child psychopathology (Mash & Terdal, 1988). The most common of these are direct observation, interviews, and questionnaires. As outlined in the comparisons of methods presented in Table 7.1, these methods vary with respect to several important dimensions.

One major distinction relates to who will make inferences about behaviors—the researcher using observational methods or the participant(s) through survey methods. The methods used in child psychopathology research have included unstructured and structured interviews, behavioral checklists and questionnaires, rating scales, self-monitoring procedures, formal tests, psychophysiological recordings, and direct observations of behavior (Messick, 1983). Because data obtained via different methods may vary as a function of the method used (i.e., method variance), researchers frequently must rely on a multimethod approach to define and assess the constructs of interest. Convergent validity is reflected in the extent to which data obtained via different measures of a construct provide similar information.

One's choice of measures in any research study is the result of a decision process based on a number of factors and for which there are no hard and fast rules. In addition to the characteristics of the measure itself (e.g., reliability, validity, complexity, training requirements), other factors that will influence one's choice of measures include:

1. the purpose of the research (e.g., epidemiological, treatment evaluation),
2. the nature of the construct being evaluated (e.g., chronic vs. acute, overt vs. covert),

TABLE 7.1
A Comparison of Three Data-Gathering Methods

	Observation	Interview	Questionnaire
Structure of situation	situation can be structured or naturalistic	semistructured or structured	highly structured
Structure of responses	data to be recorded can be very inclusive to highly selective	opportunity for probes, expansion, and clarification	highly structured, no opportunity for probes or clarification
Resource requirements	extensive time needed for observing and coding observations	considerable time needed for interviewing and coding responses	little experimenter time needed
Sources of bias	does not rely on participants' disclosure, though will be influenced by reactivity	relies on participants' perception and willingness to report; responses may be influenced by interviewer characteristics and mannerisms	relies on participants' perception and willingness to report
Data reduction	what is observed is highly influenced by the observational coding system	requires analysis of narrative responses or recoding into categories	little data reduction needed

3. child characteristics (e.g., age, cognitive level, language skills),
4. family characteristics (e.g., education, SES),
5. research setting characteristics (e.g., home, lab),
6. desired comparability with other research (e.g., use of a new measure vs. an existing one), and
7. characteristics and resources of the researcher (e.g., theoretical preferences, time and personnel).

Observational Methods

Using direct observational methods, the researcher gathers information under conditions that can range from highly structured tasks completed in a clinic or laboratory to unstructured observations in the child's natural environment (Mash, 1991). Tasks assigned to participants for observational data gathering purposes are typically structured to elicit behaviors of particular interest. For example, studies of noncompliance in children frequently employ tasks in which increasing demands are placed on the child by the parent, thereby eliciting multiple instances of the parent issuing commands and the child having the opportunity to demonstrate compliance or noncompliance. Structured laboratory or clinic-based observations are cost effective and offer the advantage of focusing observations on the phenomena of interest. However, questions arise as to whether such observations provide a representative sample of the behaviors of interest.

The ecological validity of observations made in the child's natural environment may be greater than in the clinic or laboratory, but not necessarily so if the degree of intrusiveness associated with observing in the natural environment is also high. Additionally, because observation in the natural environment may require long periods of time to collect a sample of low frequency behaviors that is large enough to analyze statistically, this form of data collection becomes extremely expensive. The settings in which observations are to be conducted in a particular research study depend on a number of factors, many of which are similar to those involved in one's choice of method of measurement.

There are numerous other issues associated with the use of observational methods in research on child psychopathology (see Foster & Cone, 1986, for a comprehensive discussion). These issues relate to: code system characteristics (e.g., number and complexity of categories), characteristics of the behaviors being observed (e.g., rate, complexity), methods for assessing and calculating reliability, observer characteristics, sources of observer and participant bias, reactivity to observation, and summarization and interpretation of observations.

Survey Methods

Survey methods assess the perceptions and opinions of the participants or related others. Questionnaires are popular as an inexpensive means of gathering a defined set of information. Frequently used questionnaires in child psychopathology research include child behavior checklists (completed by the child, parent, or teacher) and measures of personality and affect. The information provided by questionnaires is typically precise but narrow in content. Thus, questionnaires are often used in conjunction with other measures of related variables of interest.

More expensive and time consuming than questionnaires, interviews serve as another survey method. They allow the researcher to listen and adapt to additional insights or directions that the participants' responses may suggest. Interviews can vary widely in structure, both in the nature and phrasing of questions to be asked and the manner in which responses are recorded (verbatim or precoded categories).

Qualitative Data Measurement

Ethnographic or qualitative research methods are intended to provide a holistic view of a situation through inductive and naturalistic inquiry (Patton, 1990). Rather than beginning from already developed coding systems or assessment tools, ethnographic researchers strive to understand the phenomenon from the participant's perspective. Qualitative data are typically collected through observations or open-ended interviewing and are recorded narratively, as case-study notes, for example. The obtained observations and narrative accounts are examined to build general categories and patterns.

Proponents of qualitative research believe that it provides for an intensive and intimate understanding of a situation that is rarely achieved in quantitative research (e.g., Murphy, 1992). The two methods can be used in complementary ways. Common combinations of these methods are to use the qualitative approach to identify salient dimensions that are developed into a theoretical model that can be tested quantitatively or to use qualitative case studies to illuminate the meaning of quantitatively derived findings. Miles and Huberman (1984) provided an excellent and readable account of the collection, reduction, and display of qualitative data and strategies for reaching conclusions. Qualitative data may ultimately be analyzed using quantitative methods if the data have been reduced to numbers, such as through word counts or frequency counts of themes.

DATA ANALYSIS

One's choice of research design and data analytic strategy depends on the hypothesis under investigation and the nature of the data set. Strategies for data analysis are too numerous and varied to be discussed in any great detail here (see Appelbaum & McCall, 1983, for an excellent discussion of design and data analysis issues). However, several analytic approaches that are of particular current interest and applicability to research in child psychopathology are reviewed briefly. These include metaanalyses, structural equation modeling, and growth curve analysis. In the context of child psychopathology research, these approaches are particularly relevant because they offer the potential to: (a) integrate findings across diverse data sets and studies; (b) derive and test models that are sensitive to multiple determinants, direct and indirect effects, and alternative pathways of influence; and (c) conduct analyses that are especially sensitive to the parameters of developmental change.

Meta-analysis is a quantitative method for averaging and integrating the standardized results from a large number of independent studies. Using data from already published studies, metaanalysis provide for the statistical estimation of effect sizes (ES), most typically derived by subtracting the mean of the control group from the mean of the experimental or treatment group and dividing the difference by the standard deviation of the control group. The larger the ES, the greater the effect of the treatment condition. Once ESs from a large number of different studies are calculated, statistical analyses can then be used to answer different questions, for example, comparing different forms of therapy or different levels of therapist experience.

Meta-analyses have been used successfully to determine the efficacy along multiple parameters of psychotherapy with children (Weisz et al., 1987; Weisz & Weiss, 1993), to identify salient features of successful early intervention programs for young children with developmental disabilities (Shonkoff & Hauser-Cram, 1987) and to determine the relationship between marital discord and child behavior problems (Reid & Crisafulli, 1990). Meta-analysis has also found that adjustment to pediatric physical disorder leaves children vulnerable to both externalizing and internalizing problems (Lavigne & Faier-Routman, 1992).

Meta-analytic studies have been criticized with respect to the criteria used to generate a data base for statistical analysis, the inclusion and equal weighting of findings from studies of different quality, and the choice and nonindependence of dependent measures. Although these criticisms of meta-analysis are valid, it is also important to note that many of them are not inherent to meta-analysis per se, but rather, reflect inadequacies in the way in which meta-analyses have been conducted. Proponents of meta-analysis believe that integrative interpretations of data are fairer, more objective, and more comprehensive than qualitative literature reviews and that they optimize the possibility of cumulative scientific knowledge (Schmidt, 1992).

A second analysis strategy to enjoy recent popularity in research on child psychopathology is structural equation modeling (SEM). SEM is particularly useful for purposes of causal modeling and validation of measures. A valuable feature that distinguishes SEM (e.g., LISREL) from more traditional factor analyses is that it affords a way to test hypotheses about latent variables or structures. Latent (or unmeasured) constructs are inferred from measurable variables. General applications of SEM are described in Morris, Bergan, and Fulginiti (1991) and specific applications in the context of antisocial behavior are described in Patterson et al. (1992).

Finally, there have been recent advances in the methods used to analyze change. Many of these models and methods are presented by Collins and Horn (1991) and Newman and Howard (1991). Particularly well suited for measuring change, such as developmental changes in longitudinal studies, are growth curve analyses. As an example, Graham, Collins, Wugalter, Chung, and Hansen (1991) applied latent transition analysis procedures to test competing hypotheses about the steps in the development of substance use patterns in a large sample of adolescents. Through these procedures they were able to address the role of and identity of "gateway" drugs in the progression to more significant drug abuse in teen-agers.

ETHICAL AND PRAGMATIC ISSUES

Researchers have become increasingly sensitive to the possible ethical misuses of research procedures and correspondingly more aware of the need for principles and guidelines to regulate research practices in child psychopathology. Currently, ethical guidelines for research are provided through Institutional Review Boards, federal funding agencies, and professional organizations (e.g., Society for Research in Child Development, 1990). Ethical guidelines attempt to strike a balance between freedom of scientific inquiry and protecting the rights of privacy and the overall welfare of the research participants.

Informed Consent and Assent

The individual's fully informed consent to participate, obtained without coercion, serves as the single most protective regulation for research participants. Informed consent ensures that all participants be fully informed of the nature of the research and of the research procedures before they agree to participate. In the case of research with children, this is extended to obtaining the informed consent of the parents acting for the child, as well as the assent of the child. Guidelines for obtaining assent of the child include that assent is sought beginning when children enter school or when they are at the developmental level where they can recognize their printed name. Informed consent includes awareness of potential benefits as well as risks of the option to withdraw from the study at any time and of the fact that participation or nonparticipation in the research does not affect eligibility for other services.

In some instances, obtaining informed consent poses formidable challenges. For example, in research with uneducated individuals, special efforts must be taken to insure that they fully comprehend the research procedures. Research on child maltreatment often informs parents that the purpose of the study is to examine a range of caregiving practices. If parents were fully informed that the researchers were studying abuse, the research likely could not be conducted. In studying "street-kids," minors who are generally not legally emancipated but whose parents or guardian are unaware of their whereabouts, the possibility that efforts would be made to obtain informed consent from parents could lead to absolute refusal on the part of the adolescent to participate. Researchers must make every effort to consider the importance of the research goals in relation to the need to maintain the dignity of the participants and the need to minimize the likelihood of potential harm.

Voluntary Participation

Participation in research is to be voluntary; yet some individuals may be more susceptible to subtle pressure and coercion than others. The role of the researcher requires balancing successful recruiting and avoiding placing pressure on potential participants (Grisso et al., 1991). Protection for vulnerable populations, including children, has received considerable attention. Fisher (1991) identified families of high-risk infants and children as potentially more vulnerable, related in part to the families' distress over their child's high-risk status. Although instructed otherwise, parents recruited from social service agencies or medical settings may still feel that their treatment or quality of care will be threatened if they do not participate in the research. Maltreating parents may feel that their failure to participate in research could result in the loss of their child, jail sentence, or a failure to receive services.

Volunteerism is itself a biasing factor in research. Individuals agreeing to participate in research obviously differ from those who are approached but refuse, with the question remaining as to whether the volunteerism factor significantly biases findings on the variables of interest. To address this concern, some researchers have recommended the use of a semirandomized clinical trial design (Fisher, 1991). Potential participants who refuse to participate in the study because of the requirement that they be *randomly* assigned to a treatment or no-treatment condition are included in the study and are then provided treatment or no treatment as per their choice. Participants who agree to the random assignment procedures are similarly assigned to the treatment or no-treatment conditions, resulting in four groups. Although the design is no longer a true experimental design, the analyses do allow for estimating the effects of volunteerism.

Confidentiality and Anonymity

Information revealed by individuals through participation in research is to be safeguarded. Most institutions require that individuals be informed that any information that they disclose will be kept confidential and also if there are any exceptions to confidentiality. In research with children, one of the most frequently encountered challenges to confidentiality occurs when the child or parent reveals past abuse or information that would suggest the possibility of future abuse of the child. Procedures for handling this situation vary across studies and across states, depending on the circumstances of the disclosure (e.g., by an adult within the context of therapy) and the reporting requirements of the state. The quality of research data that is collected may vary with the degree to which the confidentiality of information is emphasized (Blanck, Bellack, Rosnow, Rotheram-Borus, & Schooler, 1992).

Information that is videotaped is regarded as particularly sensitive because it stores data that ordinarily would not be permanently recorded (Grisso et al., 1991) and because identities are difficult to mask. Most Institutional Review Boards have policies about the storing and eventual erasing of videotaped information. Particular sensitivity must be exercised in handling videotaped data and in sharing it with other researchers.

Nonharmful Procedures

No research operations should be used that may harm the child either physically or psychologically. Whenever possible, the researcher is also obligated to use procedures that are the least stressful to the child and family. In some instances, psychological harm may be difficult to define, but when in doubt, it is the researcher's responsibility to seek consultation from others. If harm seems inevitable, alternative methods must be found or the research must be abandoned. In cases where exposure of the child to stressful conditions may be necessary if therapeutic benefits associated with the research are to be realized, careful deliberation by an Institutional Review Board is needed.

Other Ethical Concerns

Sensitivity to ethical concerns is especially important when the research involves potentially invasive procedures, possible entrapment, deception, the use of punishment procedures, the use of subject payment or other incentives, or possible coercion. Investigators must be particularly sensitive, and especially so in longitudinal research, to the occurrence of unexpected crises, unforeseen consequences of research, and issues surounding the continuation of the research when findings suggest that some other course of action is required to ensure the child's well-being.

Some Pragmatic Issues

Many research problems that are typically addressed through standardized instructions and procedures and through a reliance on the prior experiences and expectations of the participants are compounded by children's generally limited experience and understanding of novel research tasks and by the particular characteristics of disturbed children and families. Hyperactive children, defiant children, or children with limited intellectual functioning, learning difficulties, or language and sensory impairments may present special research challenges associated with establishing rapport, motivating the children, keeping within time limitations, ensuring that instructions are well understood, maintaining attention, and coping with possible boredom, distraction, and fatigue. Similarly, the families of problem children often exhibit characteristics that may compromise their research participation and involvement. These include high levels of stress, marital discord, parental psychiatric disorders (e.g., anxiety and depression), substance abuse disorders, restricted resources and/or time for research, and limited verbal abilities.

SUMMARY

We have emphasized that research activities in child psychopathology are best conceptualized within a decision-making framework that is predicated on an understanding of the theoretical, methodological, and practical considerations that assist the researcher in making informed decisions about when certain research methods and strategies are appropriate, and when they are not. We have considered the kinds of questions that research in child psychopathology typically seeks to address, including those about the nature of childhood disorders, the determinants of childhood disorders, risk and protective factors, and treatment and prevention. Three fundamental issues in child psychopathology research are the relation between theory and research, the role of developmental factors, and the impact of the child's social context.

We have described research in child psychopathology as a process and have highlighted issues that are relevant at various stages of this process. These include general approaches to research, sampling considerations, types of research designs, methods of measurement, and approaches to data analysis. Finally, we have discussed some of the special ethical and pragmatic issues that may be encountered in conducting research with disturbed children and families. It is believed that our understanding of child psychopathology can best be advanced through the use of a variety of research methods and strategies.

ACKNOWLEDGMENTS

During the preparation of this chapter Eric Mash was supported by a Sabbatical Fellowship from the University of Calgary and by a grant from the Alberta Mental Health Research Fund. Gloria Krahn was supported by grant #HD23014 from NICHD. This support is gratefully acknowledged.

REFERENCES

Abidin, R. R., Jenkins, C. L., & McGaughey, M. C. (1992). The relationship of early family variables to children's subsequent behavioral adjustment. *Journal of Clinical Child Psychology, 21*, 60–69.

Achenbach, T. M. (1982). *Developmental psychopathology* (2nd ed.). New York: Wiley.

Achenbach, T. M. (1985). *Assessment and taxonomy of child and adolescent psychopathology*. Beverly Hills, CA: Sage.

Achenbach, T. M. (1990). Conceptualization of developmental psychopathology. In M. Lewis & S. M. Miller (Eds.), *Handbook of developmental psychopathology* (pp. 3–14). New York: Plenum.

Achenbach, T. M., & Edelbrock, C. (1981). Behavior problems and competencies reported by parents of normal and disturbed children aged four through sixteen. *Monographs for the Society of Research in Child Development, 46* (1, Serial No. 188).

Achenbach, T. M., Howell, C. T., Quay, H. C., & Conners, C. K. (1991). National survey of problems and competencies among four-to sixteen-year-olds: Parents' reports for normative and clinical samples. *Monographs of the Society for Research in Child Development, 56* (3, Serial No. 225).

Achenbach, T. M., McConaughy, S. H., & Howell, C. T. (1987). Child/adolescent behavioral and emotional problems: Implications of cross-informant correlations for situational specificity. *Psychological Bulletin, 101*, 213–232.

American Psychiatric Association. (1994). *Diagnostic and statistical manual of mental disorders* (4th ed.) Washington, DC: Author.

Appelbaum, M., & McCall, R. B. (1983). Design and analysis in developmental psychology. In W. Kessen (Ed.), *Handbook of child psychology (4th ed.): Vol 1. History, theory, and methods* (pp. 415–476). New York: Wiley.

Barkley, R. A. (1990). *Attention deficit hyperactivity disorder: A handbook for diagnosis and treatment*. New York: Guilford.

Barkley, R. A., Guevremont, D. C., Anastopoulos, A. D., & Fletcher, K. E. (1992). A comparison of three family therapy programs for treating family conflicts in adolescents with Attention-Deficit Hyperactivity Disorder. *Journal of Consulting and Clinical Psychology, 60*, 450–462.

Blanck, P. D., Bellack, A. S., Rosnow, R. L., Rotheram-Borus, M. J., & Schooler, N. R. (1992). Scientific rewards and conflicts of ethical choices in human subjects research. *American Psychologist, 47*, 959–965.

Blatt, S. J., Wein, S. J., Chevron, E. S., & Quinlan, D. M. (1979). Parental representation and depression in normal young adults. *Journal of Abnormal Psychology, 88*, 388–397.

Botvin, G. J. (1990). Preventing adolescent drug abuse through a multi-modal cognitive-behavioral approach: Results of a three year study. *Journal of Consulting and Clinical Psychology, 58*, 437–446.

Browne, A., & Finkelhor, D. (1986). Impact of child sexual abuse: Review of the literature. *Psychological Bulletin, 99*, 66–77.

Caron, C., & Rutter, M. (1991). Comorbidity in child psychopathology: Concepts, issues and research strategies. *Journal of Child Psychology and Psychiatry, 32*, 1063–1080.

Cicchetti, D., & Serafica, F. C. (1981). Interplay among behavioral systems: Illustrations from the study of attachment, affiliation, and wariness in young children with Down Syndrome. *Developmental Psychology, 17*, 36–49.

Cohen, J. (1988). *Statistical power analysis for the behavioral sciences* (2nd ed.). Hillsdale, NJ: Lawrence Erlbaum Associates.

Collins, L. M., & Horn, J. L. (1991). *Best methods for the analysis of change: Recent advances, unanswered questions, future directions.* Washington, DC: American Psychological Association.

Costello, E. J. (1989). Developments in child psychiatric epidemiology. *Journal of the American Academy of Child and Adolescent Psychiatry, 28*, 836–841.

Crockenberg, S., & Covey, S. L. (1991). Marital conflict and externalizing behavior in children. In D. Cicchetti & S. L. Toth (Eds.), *Rochester symposium on developmental psychopathology: Models and integrations* (Vol. 3, pp. 235–260). Rochester, NY: University of Rochester Press.

Danforth, J. S., Barkley, R. A., & Stokes, T. F. (1991). Observations of parent–child interactions with hyperactive children: Research and clinical implications. *Clinical Psychology Review, 11*, 703–727.

Egeland, B. (1991). A longitudinal study of high-risk families: Issues and findings. In R. H. Starr, Jr. & D. A. Wolfe (Eds.), *The effects of child abuse and neglect: Issues and research* (pp. 33–56). New York: Guilford.

Farrington, D. F. (1991). Longitudinal research strategies: Advantages, problems, and prospects. *Journal of the American Academy of Child and Adolescent Psychiatry, 30*, 369–374.

Fisher, C. B. (1991). Ethical considerations for research on psychosocial intervention for high-risk infants and children. *Register Reporter, 17*(2), 9–12.

Foster, S. L., & Cone, J. D. (1986). Design and use of direct observation procedures. In A. R. Ciminero, K. S. Calhoun, & H. E. Adams (Eds.), *Handbook of behavioral assessment* (2nd ed., pp. 253–324). New York: Wiley.

Frick, P. J., Lahey, B. B., Loeber, R., Stouthamer-Loeber, M., Christ, M. A., & Hanson, K. (1992). Familial risk factors to oppositional defiant disorder and conduct disorder: Parental psychopathology and maternal parenting. *Journal of Consulting and Clinical Psychology, 60*, 49–55.

Graham, J. W., Collins, L. M., Wugalter, S. E., Chung, N. K., & Hansen, W. B. (1991). Modeling transitions in latent stage-sequential processes: A substance use prevention example. *Journal of Consulting and Clinical Psychology, 59*, 48–57.

Greenberg, M. T., Speltz, M. L., Deklyen, M., & Endriga, M. C. (1991). Attachment security in preschoolers with and without externalizing behavior problems: A replication. *Development and Psychopathology, 3*, 413–430.

Greenspan, S. I., Harmon, R. J., Emde, R. N., Sameroff, A. J., & Wieder, S. (1991, December). *Emerging trends in the diagnosis of emotional problems in infants and toddlers.* Symposium conducted at the National Center for Clincal Infant Programs, Washington, DC.

Grisso, T., Baldwin, E., Blanck, P. D., Rotheram-Borus, M. J., Schooler, N. R., & Thompson, T. (1991). Standards in research: APA's mechanism for monitoring the challenges. *American Psychologist, 46*, 758–766.

Grossman, H. J. (Ed.). (1983). *Classification in mental retardation* (rev. ed.). Washington, DC: American Association on Mental Deficiency.

Humphries, T., Kinsbourne, M., & Swanson, J. (1978). Stimulant effects on cooperation and social interaction between hyperactive children and their mothers. *Journal of Child Psychology and Psychiatry, 19*, 12–22.

Jacob, T., Krahn, G. L., & Leonard, K. (1991). Parent–child interactions in families with alcoholic fathers. *Journal of Consulting and Clinical Psychology, 59*, 176–181.

Jacobson, N. S., & Truax, P. (1991). Clinical significance: A statistical approach to defining meaningful change in psychotherapy research. *Journal of Consulting and Clinical Psychology, 59*, 12–19.

Kazdin, A. E. (1988). *Child psychotherapy: Developing and identifying effective treatments.* New York: Pergamon.

Kazdin, A. E. (1989). Developmental psychopathology: Current research, issues, and directions. *American Psychologist, 44*, 180–187.

Kazdin, A. E., Bass, D., Ayers, W. A., & Rodgers, A. (1990). Empirical and clinical focus of child and adolescent psychotherapy research. *Journal of Consulting and Clinical Psychology, 58*, 729–740.

Kazdin, A. E., Siegel, T. C., & Bass, D. (1992). Cognitive problem-solving skills training and parent management training in the treatment of antisocial behavior in children. *Journal of Consulting and Clinical Psychology, 60*, 733–747.

Lavigne, J. V., & Faier-Routman, J. (1992). Psychological adjustment to pediatric physical disorders: A meta-analytic review. *Journal of Pediatric Psychology, 17*, 133–157.

Lochman, J. E. (1992). Cognitive-behavioral intervention with aggressive boys: Three-year follow-up and preventive effects. *Journal of Consulting and Clinical Psychology, 60*, 426–432.

Mash, E. J. (1991). Measurement of parent–child interaction in studies of child maltreatment. In R. Starr, Jr. & D. Wolfe (Eds.), *The effects of child abuse and neglect: Research issues* (pp. 203–256). New York: Guilford.

Mash, E. J., & Johnston, C. (1990). Determinants of parenting stress: Illustrations from families of hyperactive children and families of physically abused children. *Journal of Clinical Child Psychology, 19*, 313–328.

Mash, E. J., & Terdal, L. G. (1988). Behavioral assessment of child and family disturbance. In E. J. Mash & L. G. Terdal (Eds.), *Behavioral assessment of childhood disorders* (pp. 3–65). New York: Guilford.

Mash, E. J., & Wolfe, D. A. (1991). Methodological issues in research on physical child abuse. *Criminal Justice and Behavior, 18*, 8–29.

McCubbin, H. I., & Patterson, J. (1983). The family stress process: The double ABCX model of adjustment and adaptation. *Marriage and Family Review, 8*, 7–37.

Mendelson, M. J. (1992). Let's teach case methods to developmental students. *SRCD Newsletter*, Fall Issue, 9, 13.

Messick, S. (1983). Assessment of children. In W. Kessen (Ed.), *Handbook of child psychology (4th ed.): Vol 1. History, theory, and methods* (pp. 477–526). New York: Wiley.

Miles, M. B., & Huberman, A. M. (1984). *Qualitative data analysis: A sourcebook of new methods.* Beverly Hills: Sage.

Morris, R. J., Bergan, J. R., & Fulginiti, J. V. (1991). Structural equation modeling in clinical assessment research with children. *Journal of Consulting and Clinical Psychology, 59*, 371–379.

Murphy, L. B. (1992). Sympathetic behavior in very young children. *Zero to Three, 12*(4), 1–5.

Newman, F. L., & Howard, K. I. (1991). Introduction to the special section on seeking new clinical research methods. *Journal of Consulting and Clinical Psychology, 59*, 8–11.

Overton, W. F., & Horowitz, H. A. (1991). Developmental psychopathology: Integrations and differentiations. In D. Cicchetti & S. L. Toth (Eds.), *Models and integrations: Rochester symposium on developmental psychopathology* (Vol. 3, pp. 1–42). Rochester, NY: University of Rochester Press.

Patterson, G. R. (1982). *Coercive family process.* Eugene, OR: Castalia.

Patterson, G. R., Reid, J., & Dishion, T. (1992). *Antisocial boys.* Eugene, OR: Castalia.

Patton, M. Q. (1990). *Qualitative evaluation and research methods* (2nd ed.). Beverly Hills: Sage.

Pisterman, S. J., McGrath, P., Firestone, P., Goodman, J. T., Webster, L., & Mallory, R. (1989). Outcome of parent-mediated treatment of pre-schoolers with attention-deficit disorder. *Journal of Consulting and Clinical Psychology, 57*, 628–635.

Ramey, C. T., Bryant, D. M., Wasik, B. H., Sparling, J. J., Fendt, K. H., & La Vange, L. M. (1992). Infant Health and Development Program for low birth weight, premature infants: Program elements, family participation, and child intelligence. *Pediatrics, 89*, 454–465.

Rauh, V. A., Achenbach, T. M., Nurcombe, B., Howell, C. T., & Teti, D. M. (1988). Minimizing adverse effects of low birthweight: Four-year results of an early intervention program. *Child Development, 59*, 544–553.

Reid, W. J., & Crisafulli, A. (1990). Marital discord and child behavior problems: A meta-analysis. *Journal of Abnormal Child Psychology, 18*, 105–117.

Roosa, M., Gensheimer, L. K., Short, J. L., Ayers, T., & Shell, R. (1989). A preventative intervention for children in alcoholic families: Results of a pilot study. *Family Relations, 38*, 295–300.

Scarr, S., & Weinberg, R. A. (1983). The Minnesota Adoption Studies: Genetic differences and malleability. *Child Development, 54*, 260–267.

Schmidt, F. L. (1992). What do data really mean? Research findings, meta-analysis, and cumulative knowledge in psychology. *American Psychologist, 47*, 1173–1181.

Shonkoff, J., & Hauser-Cram, P. (1987). Early intervention for disabled infants and their families: A quantitative analysis. *Pediatrics, 80*, 650–658.

Society for Research in Child Development (1990, Winter). SRCD ethical standards for research with children. *SRCD Newsletter*, pp. 5–7.

Steinberg, L. (1988). Reciprocal relation between parent– child distance and pubertal maturation. *Developmental Psychology, 24*, 122–128.

Stevenson, J., Batten, N., & Cherner, M. (1992). Fears and fearfulness in children and adolescents: A genetic analysis of twin data. *Journal of Child Psychology and Psychiatry, 33*, 977–985.

Stoneman, Z. (1989). Comparison groups in research on families with mentally retarded members: A methodological and conceptual review. *American Journal on Mental Retardation, 94*, 195–215.

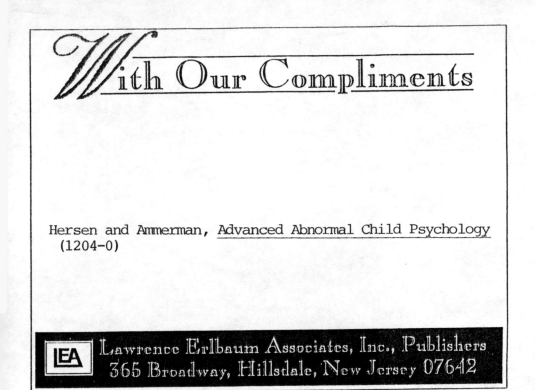

With Our Compliments

Hersen and Ammerman, <u>Advanced Abnormal Child Psychology</u>
(1204-0)

LEA Lawrence Erlbaum Associates, Inc., Publishers
365 Broadway, Hillsdale, New Jersey 07642

Verhulst, F. C., & Koot, H. M. (1991). Longitudinal research in child and adolescent psychiatry. *Journal of the American Academy of Child and Adolescent Psychiatry, 30*, 361–368.

Verhulst, F. C., & Van der Ende, J. (1992). Agreements between parents' reports and adolescents' self-reports of problem behavior. *Journal of Child Psychology and Psychiatry, 33*, 1011–1023.

Wasserman, G. A., Shilansky, M., & Hahn, H. (1986). A matter of degree: Maternal interaction with infants of varying levels of retardation. *Child Study Journal, 16*, 241–253.

Weissman, M. M., Wickramaratne, P., Warner, V., John, K., Prusoff, B. A., Merikangas, K. R., & Gammon, G. D. (1987). Assessing psychiatric disorders in children. *Archives of General Psychiatry, 44*, 747–753.

Weisz, J. R., & Weiss, B. (1993). *Effects of psychotherapy with children and adolescents.* Newbury Park, CA: Sage.

Weisz, J. R., Weiss, B., Alicke, M. D., & Klotz, M. L. (1987). Effectiveness of psychotherapy with children and adolescents: A meta-analysis for clinicians. *Journal of Consulting and Clinical Psychology, 55*, 542–549.

Wolfe, D. A., & Mosk, M. D. (1983). Behavioral comparisons of children from abusive and distressed families. *Journal of Consulting and Clinical Psychology, 51*, 702–708.

World Health Organization (1992). *International Classification of Diseases, Ninth Revision, Clinical Modification.* Geneva: Author.

Yoder, P. J., & Feagans, L. (1988). Mothers' attributions of communication to prelinguistic behavior of developmentally delayed and mentally retarded infants. *American Journal of Mental Deficiency, 93*, 36–43.

Part II

Assessment and Treatment

Assessment has always been the hallmark of clinical psychology. From its earliest days, measurement and testing provided the foundation for examining abnormal behavior, and have been the catalyst for the subsequent development of treatments. Assessment of intelligence, in particular, has been in the forefront of modern, empirically based approaches to measurement. More recently, as our definitions of what constitutes intelligence have broadened and our understanding of the antecedents of intelligence has deepened, measures of intellectual functioning have diversified to tap multiple cognitive domains and processes. Whereas the assessment of intelligence emanates from traditional psychometric approaches to test development, behavioral assessment focuses on measurement of overt, observable behaviors. Moreover, behavioral assessment is intricately linked with treatment in that the behaviors measured become the direct focus of intervention.

Research on the treatment of abnormal behavior in children has primarily involved behavioral interventions. Such approaches emphasize the assessment of target behaviors and the manipulation of environmental contingencies in an effort to increase or decrease the behavior(s). Behavioral interventions have become increasingly more sophisticated in the past decade, incorporating cognitive treatments and strategies that impact systems (e.g., family, classroom) where the child resides, plays, or works. As it has become increasingly evident that the etiologies of many child psychiatric disorders involve biological and environmental factors, pharmacological treatments have also emerged as impatient adjuncts to psychological interventions. Empirical research on the effectiveness of pharmacotherapy in children is in its early stages. Accordingly, firm recommendations for treatment are only now being developed. A third intervention approach that has gained considerable support in recent years is community prevention. In contrast to models of acute treatment, community prevention consists of identifying at-risk children and providing them with programs designed to forestall the future development of behavioral and emotional disorders. Such approaches are appealing given the ultimate savings in time and resources associated with successful early intervention.

The chapters in Part II cover assessment and treatment. In chapter 8, Lincoln, Kaufman, and Kaufman discuss intellectual and cognitive assessment. With a particular emphasis on traditional intelligence tests, the authors provide an in-depth coverage of test development, administration, and interpretation of results. In addition, the use of intelligence tests with specific clinical populations (e.g., conduct disorder, autism, learning disabilities) is addressed.

Beck (chapter 9) examines behavioral assessment. After contrasting the philosophical and procedural differences between behavioral and other forms of psychological assessment, Beck describes the specific methods used in behavioral assessment (e.g., naturalistic observation). Such strategies are considered within the context of advances in psychiatric diagnosis and developmental psychology.

In chapter 10, Graziano and Dorta cover behavioral treatment of childhood disorders. In addition to reviewing the most commonly used behavioral techniques, the authors point out that such interventions are always carried out within the systems in which the child lives and learns such as home and school. Multiple case examples are provided to illustrate how behavioral treatments are implemented.

Quintana and Birmaher review new developments in pharmacological treatment (chapter 11). Although the empirical data base in this area is small, the authors offer sound guidelines for when pharmacotherapy should be considered. Moreover, they examine specific psychiatric disorders in which pharmacotherapy shows promise, including conduct disorders, depression, and developmental disorders.

The final chapter in Part II, on community prevention (chapter 12), is written by Lorion, Brodsky, Flaherty, and Holland. The authors first examine theoretical formulations of prevention. They then review various types of preventive interventions, finishing up with an illustration of prevention principles involving conduct disorder and major depression.

Chapter 8

Intellectual and Cognitive Assessment

Alan J. Lincoln
Jennie Kaufman
California School of Professional Psychology, San Diego

Alan S. Kaufman
University of Alabama

Standardized tests of intelligence are now routinely employed as part of the clinical and psychoeducational assessment of children and adults. This routine and standard application of intelligence tests for both clinical and psychoeducational practice has largely developed because of the perceived usefulness of information derived from such tests. However, the types of information derived from intelligence tests are most useful when interpreted by a psychologist in the context of a broader battery of psychological tests, the individual's personal history, and direct behavioral observations. Therefore, when discussing the contribution of intelligence tests, one must consider their significance as a component of a much more comprehensive approach toward assessment and diagnosis.

Most measures of intelligence that psychologists utilize for clinical and psychoeducational assessment have been standardized on large groups of individuals. The better measures have well-documented reliability and validity. The reliability and validity of such measures are typically found through psychological, psychoeducational, or neuropsychological research studies examining diverse samples of individuals on dimensions of interest to the researcher.

However, in most instances of clinical and psychoeducational assessment, psychologists are not assessing large numbers of individuals. Rather, for the purpose of differential diagnosis, in either clinical or psychoeducational assessment, the psychologist is generally assessing a single person. The psychologist is therefore applying measures that have documented group reliability and validity to a single case. The potential problems associated with such an application of group data to a single case are, however, mitigated by utilizing a multimethod/multitrait approach for the clinical or psychoeducational assessment of the individual.

MULTIMETHOD/MULTITRAIT ASSESSMENT APPROACH

Multiple methods are applied by the psychologist in the assessment of the individual. These various methods can be conceptualized as individual data bases, separate but complementary toward one another. The individual being assessed is, after all, the common denominator. These methods or data bases include:

1. the presenting symptoms or problems;
2. the history of such symptoms;
3. the developmental, personal, and family history;
4. the school and work history;
5. the medical history;
6. a review of collateral information including aspects of history, previous test performance, medical history, and so forth;
7. direct observations of behavior during the interview;
8. performance on a range of specific psychological and/or neuropsychological measures;
9. feedback from additional evaluations (e.g., referral for hearing test, vision examination, neurologic examination); and
10. the literature known to be relevant to the ascertained history, test findings, and probable diagnosis.

Findings from an intelligence test are only one part of these more comprehensive methods for assessing and understanding the individual.

Why Intelligence Tests are Used for Clinical Assessment

There are five primary reasons for including a measure of intelligence as part of the clinical assessment. First, there are several specific diagnoses of children and adults that require a standardized measure of general ability or intelligence. These include the diagnoses of mental retardation, specific learning disabilities, and developmental language disorders (American Psychiatric Association, 1987, 1993).

Second, intelligence is perhaps the most predictive single measure of an individual's adaptive capabilities. This is why a measure of intelligence is employed to help ascertain the previous diagnoses and also employed to help evaluate individual potential (e.g., for determining giftedness). Intelligence may also either increase vulnerability or provide protection with respect to development of specific psychiatric disorders (e.g., schizophrenia; Aylward, Walker, & Bettes, 1984).

Third, intelligence as a construct is important to individual personality assessment. David Wechsler was one of the foremost psychologists instrumental in developing both an understanding of the nature of human intelligence and methods by which it could be operationally defined and measured. Wechsler (1958) operationally defined intelligence as:

> . . . the aggregate or global capacity of the individual to act purposefully, to think rationally and to deal effectively with his environment. It is aggregate or global because it is composed of elements or abilities which, though not entirely independent, are qualitatively differentiable. . . . But intelligence is not identical with the

mere sum of these abilities, however inclusive. There are three important reasons for this: 1) The ultimate products of intelligent behavior are a function not only of the number of abilities or their quality, but also the way in which they are combined. . . . 2) Factors other than intelligent ability, for example, drive and incentive, are involved in intellectual behavior. 3) Finally, . . . an excess of any given ability may add relatively little to the effectiveness of the behavior as a whole. (p. 7)

This operational definition of intelligence closely parallels the psychoanalytic, psychodynamic, and ego psychology attributes of functions of the ego. Wechsler (1958) believed that intelligence could no more be separated from "the total personality structure" (p. 5) than would the major theorists of the previous conceptual models separate the ego from the rest of human personality development.

The most widely used measures of intelligence in adults and children yield not only a single global IQ score, but more importantly, they yield standard scores across multiple intellectual ability domains (Kaufman, 1979, 1990; Sattler, 1992). These ability domains are organized and integrated differently from person to person even when such persons have identical global IQ scores. This multiscore aspect of the tests allows flexibility in assessing individual differences.

Fourth, the methods used to assess the specific intellectual abilities tend to be relatively clearly defined and well structured. This type of organization is in contrast to tests designed to maximize projection in order to assess personality functions and dynamic issues. Materials and questions used in intelligence tests tend to be fairly specific, easy to perceive, and call for certain correct responses. The format of the items and nature of the response process is also relatively familiar to the individual being tested. Less structured projective measures are designed to place a greater burden on the individual for both accurate perception and interpretation. With projective tests there are no right or wrong responses; there are, however, responses that tend to comform to both the salient characteristics of the projective test stimuli and the instructions given the individual. The clinician is interested in the stability of perceptual accuracy and the ability to evoke a well-integrated response across levels of tests ranging from those that are well-structured and clearly defined (e.g., intelligence tests, achievement tests, and tests of visual–motor integration) to those tests that are less structured and clearly defined (projective tests). For example, perceiving the image of a familiar object or person is more easily accomplished than the identification of an incomplete drawing, as in the Gestalt Closure subtest of the Kaufman Assessment Battery for Children (K–ABC; Kaufman & Kaufman, 1983). The identification of the incomplete drawing is in turn a more clearly defined perceptual task than the task of identifying a percept from a Rorschach inkblot. Even within the so-called more structured tests, there are frequently subtests that can evoke a wider range of response and thus have the capacity to be somewhat projective.

A fifth reason for the inclusion of an intelligence test in a psychological test battery is that it provides a sample of the individual's behavior in a fairly systematic manner. Individuals being tested are having their abilities sampled across a variety of domains, all of which contribute to their overall intellectual functioning. On the tests developed by Wechsler, such abilities include: verbal comprehension, attention, concentration, memory, abstract reasoning, knowledge of factual information, judgment, visual perception, visual–motor integration, planning, and cognitive flexibility. Each of these domains is not fully sampled by a single test; however, it is possible to acquire a great deal of information about an individual by what is sampled. Even a single response to a test item can provide significant information to the clinician. For example, an item from the Comprehension subtest from the Wechsler Intelligence Scale for Children: Third Edition (WISC–III; Wechsler, 1991) asks, "What should you do if you cut your finger?" A 9-year-old boy replies, "It bleeds, it is cut off. . . . I scream. . . . I'll bleed to death." In this single response, we learn that this child has difficulty thinking of the conventional response, "Wash it . . . put a band-aid on it," and instead becomes overly anxious and involved in the fantasy elicited by this test item. This child also personalizes the response in such a way that he seems to temporarily have difficulty differentiating a simple response to a test question from a real and threatening personal experience. In this example, the child does not receive credit for his response, and that has some effect on the score he achieves for the subtest. More importantly, however, this test item provided the clinician with a small sample of the child's behavior that when evaluated in the context of the boy's history and symptoms, may provide insight into vulnerabilities that he experiences.

INTERPRETING IQ TESTS

When psychologists look at a group of scores on an intelligence test such as the WISC–III, K–ABC, or the Stanford–Binet Intelligence Scale: Fourth Edition (S–B IV; Thorndike, Hagen, & Sattler, 1986), they generally follow a particular method to understand more adequately the individual's intellectual test profile. This systematic approach makes it possible to develop clear and descriptive hypotheses regarding the test taker's cognitive abilities. (The interpretation of the WISC–III is used in this chapter for the purpose of providing an example of how an IQ test can be interpreted. See Box 1 for a brief description of the WISC–III subtests).

The Three IQs

First, the global IQ score, or Full Scale IQ, is examined for a general placement of the person on the continuum of intellectual ability. IQ tests were first developed to help determine whether an individual was mentally retarded. Tests like the WISC–III allow the evaluator to determine whether the individual's intellectual functioning falls between the first and ninety-ninth percentile. The WISC–III is sensitive to measuring moderate mental retardation (IQ between 40 and 54) and very superior intellectual ability (IQ 130 or greater). However, this global score provides only a small piece of the puzzle that describes the individual's complex array of strengths and weaknesses.

The global, Full Scale IQ score on the WISC–III is derived from the sum of age-corrected scaled scores from two groups of subtests, the Verbal subtests and the Performance subtests. The Verbal subtests are generally more dependent on verbal comprehension and expression, whereas the Performance subtests are more dependent on visual analysis, visual–motor integration, and motor speed. The sum of the Verbal subtest age-corrected scaled scores is converted to a Verbal IQ score and the sum of the Performance subtest age-corrected scaled scores is converted into a Performance IQ Score.

Therefore, in order to evaluate how the Full Scale IQ score was derived, one must examine both the Verbal IQ score and the Performance IQ score. Some individuals score higher on the Verbal subtests, some score higher on the Performance subtests, and some score about evenly on both scales. It is possible to find evidence of uneven organization of intellectual abilities when there is a significant discrepancy between the Verbal and Performance subtests. For example, in both children and adults, it has been found that individuals with receptive developmental language disorder have significantly lower Verbal IQ scores compared to their Performance IQ scores (Lincoln, Courchesne, Harms, & Allen, 1993; Lincoln, Courchesne, Kilman, Elmasian, & Allen, 1988; Lincoln, Dickstein, Courchesne, Tallal, & Elmasian, 1992).

Factor Scores

However, even assessing the components of the global IQ (e.g., Verbal IQ versus Performance IQ in the case of Wechsler's child or adult intelligence tests; or the four domains that result in the composite intelligence score of the S-B IV; or the two domains, Sequential and Simultaneous processing that are converted to a global Mental Processing Composite standard score of the K-ABC) may not be the best way to assess an individual's intellectual strengths and weaknesses. This is because the factor analytic studies that attempt to validate such components of the more global IQ score sometimes yield factors or groupings of subtests that do not entirely overlap with the subtests that comprise the component IQ score. For example, the Verbal scale of the WISC-III has six subtests, five of which are used in the calculation of the Verbal IQ. However, factor analytic studies have repeatedly shown that only four of the Verbal subtests actually have significant factor loadings to a single factor.

The earlier version of the WISC-III was the Wechsler Intelligence Scale for Children-Revised (WISC-R; Wechsler, 1974) and its currently used adult counterpart, the Wechsler Adult Intelligence Scale-Revised (WAIS-R; Wechsler, 1981), were both explained best by a *three* factor solution, as opposed to the *two* factor (Verbal vs. Performance) solution as originally proposed by Wechsler (see Kaufman, 1990, pp. 234–262 for a review). The three factors (best three groupings of subtests) that emerge in factor analytic studies of the Wechsler scales are: *Factor I (Verbal Comprehension)* that includes the Information, Vocabulary, Comprehension, and Similarities subtests; *Factor II (Perceptual Organization)* that includes the Picture Completion, Picture Arrangement, Block Design, and Object Assembly subtests; and *Factor III (Freedom from Distractibility)* that includes the Arithmetic and Digit Span subtests for the WAIS-R and the Arithmetic, Digit Span, and Coding subtests for the WISC-R.

The factor structure of the WISC-III is a bit different. It is best explained by a four-factor solution. In order to evaluate a child's relative intellectual strengths and weaknesses on the WISC-III, the examiner must examine how the subtest scores are broken into the four factors: Verbal Comprehension (VC: comprised of Information, Vocabulary, Similarities, and Comprehension), Perceptual Organization (PO: comprised of Picture Completion, Picture Arrangement, Block Design, and Object Assembly), Freedom from Distractibility (FD: comprised of Digit Span and Arithmetic), and Processing Speed (PS: comprised of Coding and Symbol Search).

The VC factor primarily taps skills in verbal expression and reasoning. The PO factor is heavily influenced by an individual's visual analytic and visual–motor skills. The FD factor is sensitive to auditory attention, auditory short-term memory, sequential ability, concentration, and factors that might interfere in these abilities. Finally, the PS factor measures visual attention, visual encoding, and psychomotor processing speed (Wechsler, 1991). This factor structure helps to better understand the individual's abilities into known constructs so that they can be more fully explained. The PS factor is new with the revision from the WISC–R to the WISC–III, and so less is known about the construct that underlies processing speed (Sattler, 1992). The WISC–III manual provides tables for calculating standard scores and percentiles for each of the four factors. By comparing all pairwise combinations of the four factor standard scores (VC vs. PO vs. FD vs. PS), the examiner can evaluate relative intellectual strengths and weaknesses more accurately than by only evaluating the Full Scale IQ score, Verbal IQ score, or Performance IQ score.

Bannatyne's Approach

Another way of conceptualizing an individual's patterns of strengths and weaknesses is by applying another factor model, Bannatyne's regrouping of the WISC–III subtests. These factors are Spatial (comprised of Block Design, Object Assembly, and Picture Completion), Conceptualization (comprised of Vocabulary, Similarities, and Comprehension), Sequencing (comprised of Digit Span, Coding, and Arithmetic) and Acquired Knowledge (comprised of Information, Vocabulary, and Arithmetic). These categories are not as independent from one another as the four Wechsler factors, because Bannatyne's factors overlap slightly (Kamphaus, 1993). Kaufman (1979) pointed out that Bannatyne's first three factors are extremely similar to the first three Wechsler factors. However, it is sometimes more helpful to examine certain individuals' profiles using Bannatyne's factors. For example, if the person has a learning problem in school, the Acquired Knowledge factor is a valuable interpretive aid; also reading and learning disabled children usually perform poorly on the Sequential factor (Kaufman, 1979).

Intersubtest Scatter

After looking at the subtest scores through a factor structure approach, *intersubtest* scatter is examined, that is, shared strengths and weaknesses among subtests that do not fall into the neat factor structure are evaluated. First, two or more subtests that measure the same specific ability age grouped together if the person performed particularly well ("strength") or poorly ("weakness") on them. Finally, a single subtest that stands out as a strength or a weakness for the individual is examined if it is not feasible to group that subtest with one or more of the other subtests. A hypothesis or inference is more valid when it is derived from converging scores of multiple subtests, each having added shared variance from their common domain (Kamphaus, 1993). For example, one would have great convidence in the inference, "Billy has a relatively poor ability to evaluate verbal information," when that inference is supported by all of the subtests of the VC factor converging into a low VC factor score relative to significantly higher factor scores on PO, FD, and PS. In contrast, one would have less confidence in that inference if only the Vocabulary subtest score was low and not the other three subtests that also comprise the VC factor.

Intrasubtest Scatter

Finally, the *intrasubtest* scatter, or the pattern of right and wrong answers within the individual subtests, is examined to determine whether the ability or the skills tapped by the subtest are evenly applied. Most IQ tests have subtests that get progressively more difficult. Easier items come earlier and are followed by increasingly more difficult items. Early misses or patterns of misses in the context of more difficult items may suggest that the individual's knowledge has gaps (Kaufman, 1979) or that the individual has problems readily accessing information or organizing an appropriate response. By understanding a profile in this way, a clear picture of the client's abilities, strengths, and weaknesses is developed. The examiner can then form his or her hypotheses from the test data while considering the individual's presenting problem, his or her background history, and current behaviors. By combining these data sources, a more complete and clinically relevant formulation can be reached (Kamphaus, 1993).

SUBTEST PATTERNS IN SELECTED DIAGNOSTIC GROUPS

Although it is not appropriate to diagnose a client based on an intelligence test profile (Kamphaus, 1993), some research has been conducted on various diagnoses that have found certain test profiles or subtest fluctuations in certain categories of children's disorders.

Attention-Deficit Hyperactivity Disorder

Many researchers used the WISC–R to determine consistent subtest patterns for children who have Attention-Deficit Hyperactivity Disorder (ADHD), (see Appendix, "ADHD"). It is important to understand the cognitive functioning of children with ADHD because of the increased use of the diagnosis. Tests can be used along with behavioral observations to help identify these children (Sutter, Bishop, & Battin, 1987). These children frequently perform lower on the Freedom from Distractibility factor than other groups of children, including children with other diagnoses and those who are in the normal population. This factor, which was comprised of the Digit Span, Arithmetic, and Coding subtests on the WISC–R, has been suggested to measure not merely attention but the ability to store information while performing other mental operations simultaneously. For example, one study found that children with ADHD performed significantly lower than emotionally disturbed and normal control children on the Arithmetic and Coding subtests (Lufi, Cohen, & Parish-Plass, 1990). Sutter and his colleagues (1987) found that children with ADHD tend to have trouble understanding and remembering spoken words, numbers, and sentences, especially when they are distracted. They found auditory tasks to be the most discriminating, and the WISC–R's Arithmetic subtest best discriminated between ADHD children and other groups of children. Another study found that children with ADHD had a larger difference between the FD factor and the VC factor (VC > FD) than did children in special education or regular education (Zarski, Cook, West, & O'Keefe, 1987). The fact that children with ADHD tend to perform lower on this factor could mean that they have deficits in executive functioning and short-term memory (Wielkiewicz, 1990).

Recent research with the WISC–III supports the previous results of subtest patterns for ADHD children and adolescents. In one study, a sample of 65 individuals zages 7 to 16 years with the diagnosis of ADHD earned their lowest mean scores on Coding and Digit Span and had significantly depressed factor scores on both the FD and PS factors (Prifitera & Dersh, 1993). In a second investigation, 45 ADHD children (ages 8 to 11 years) earned their poorest subtest scores on Coding and Arithmetic and also scored significantly lower on the FD and PS factors than on the VC and PO factors (Schwean, Saklofske, Yackulic, & Quinn, 1993). With the WISC-R, deficits on the FD factor were consistently associated with ADHD; with the WISC-III, it appears that low PS score provides an additional diagnostic clue when assessing children or adolescents suspected of ADHD.

Conduct Disorder

Over the years, many researchers have studied the cognitive profiles of juvenile delinquents. Many of these delinquents could be diagnosed as having Conduct Disorder as described by the *DSM-III-R* and *DSM-IV*. Although Wechsler predicted that children with antisocial acting out patterns would have a Performance IQ (PIQ) greater than Verbal IQ (VIQ) profile, there has been conflicting evidence of this pattern in the literature for the past 45 years. Quay (1987) said that no unique subtest pattern has been found for delinquents, with the exception of the controversial PIQ > VIQ general pattern. He felt that the difference that has been observed is not a large difference and that this phenomenon is generally due to the lower performance of the delinquents on tasks that measure verbal skills such as word knowledge, verbally coded information, and verbal reasoning. Quay also reasoned that having lower intellect in the verbal sphere compared to children in the normal population may contribute to these children's ability to fit into a school environment, and it may interact with other variables like poor parenting in producing the behavioral acting out seen in juvenile delinquents.

Hogan and Quay (1984) suggested that the reason there may not be a clear intellectual pattern for delinquents is because they are such a heterogenous group that it is hard to find one pattern that fits all children in this category. By placing delinquents into subgroups, the chances of finding an intellectual pattern might increase. Some studies have found that IQ can be related to the severity of delinquent behaviors and, in some cases, early age of onset of delinquent behaviors.

A fairly recent study (Culbertson, Feral, & Gabby, 1989) divided delinquent boys into subgroups and found a pattern of high and low subtests for this population. Culbertson et al. (1989) found that 70% of delinquent boys had the PIQ > VIQ pattern. They examined the group as a whole, and separated out subgroups of boys who had a PIQ > VIQ of less than 13 points (Group 1), 13 points and higher (Group 2), and 15 points and higher (Group 3). They found that for the boys with the larger PIQ > VIQ split, as well as the group as a whole, the highest subtests were Object Assembly, Picture Completion, and Picture Arrangement. This is consistent with this populations strength in the visual–motor area. The lowest subtests for the whole group were Information, Vocabulary, and Coding. The lowest subtests for Groups 2 and 3 were Information, Vocabulary, and Comprehension. This triad of low scores for the subgroups would indicate that the more severe juvenile delinquents are lower on school-related skills, verbal expression, and concept formation, in addition to poor social judgment and reasoning.

Autism

In the past 16 years, there have been several studies which have evaluated the intellectual abilities of people with autism on the Wechsler scales. These studies demonstrate that many individuals with autism have a distinct pattern of intellectual ability (Bartak, Rutter, & Cox, 1975; Freeman, Lucas, Forness, & Ritvo, 1985; Lincoln et al., 1988; Lockyer & Rutter, 1970; Ohta, 1987; Rumsey & Hamburger, 1990). Most, but not all, studies report higher Performance IQ than Verbal IQ in samples of persons with autism (see Table 8.1).

Table 8.2 shows only those studies from Table 8.1 that reported scaled scores from the Wechsler subtests. The availability of scaled scores made it possible to calculate the mean scaled score for each of the three factors (e.g., Verbal Comprehension, Perceptual Organization, and Freedom from Distractibility). Results of the relative mean scaled scores across all of those studies clearly shows that the Verbal Comprehension factor is depressed relative to the Perceptual Organization factor. This finding is consistent with a verbal comprehension deficit in persons with autism compared to their more effective visual–motor and visual perception abilities.

Lincoln et al. (1988) reported how autistic individuals demonstrate even more profound differences among selected subtests derived from the Verbal Comprehension factor (Vocabulary and Comprehension) relative to selected subtests derived from the Perceptual Organization factor (Block Design and Object Assembly). Vocabulary and

TABLE 8.1
A Comparison of Verbal and Performance IQ Scores

Study	Sample	Test	VIQ	PIQ	PIQ-VIQ
Bartak et al. (1975)	Autism, mean age 7 years	WISC	66.6 $N = 9$	96.7 $N = 9$	30
Dawson (1983)	Autism, mean age 18 years	WAIS/WISC-R	64.1 $N = 10$	80.2 $N = 10$	16
Freeman et al. (1985)	Autism, mean age 8.8 years	WISC-R	90 $N = 21$	105 $N = 21$	15
Jacobson et al. (1988)	Autism, mean age 23 years	WAIS	83.0 $N = 9$	77.0 $N = 9$	− 6
Lincoln et al. (1988, Study 1)	Autism, mean age 17.6 years	WISC-R/WAIS-R	71.0 $N = 33$	83.3 $N = 33$	12
Lincoln et al. (1988, Study 2)	Autism, mean age 10 years	WISC-R	60.4 $N = 13$	84.1 $N = 13$	24
Lockyer & Rutter (1970)	Infantile psychosis, mean age 15 years	WAIS/WISC	73.5 $N = 21$	71.4 $N = 27$	− 2
Ohta (1987)	Autism, mean age 10 years	WISC	64.9 $N = 16$	85.3 $N = 16$	20
Rumsey (1985)	Autism, mean age 27 years	WAIS	103 $N = 9$	104 $N = 9$	1
Rumsey & Hamburger (1988)	Autism, mean age 26.4 years	WAIS	103.4 $N = 10*$	103.9 $N = 10*$	0
Schneider & Asarnow (1987)	Autism, mean age 10.7 years	WISC-R	80.1 $N = 15$	93.6 $N = 15$	13
Szatmari et al. (1990)	Autism, mean age 17 years	WISC-R/ WAIS-R	84 $N = 17$	81 $N = 17$	− 3

*Same subjects as Rumsey (1985).

TABLE 8.2
A Comparison of Mean Verbal Comprehension (VC), Perceptual Organization (PO), and Freedom from
Distractability (FD) Factors Obtained from Wechsler Subtest Scaled Scores

Study	Sample	Test	VC	PO	FD
Bartak et al. (1975)	Autism, mean age 7 years	WISC $N = 9$	3.6*	10.0	6.8
Dawson (1983)	Autism, mean age 18 years	WAIS/WISC-R $N = 10$	3.1*	9.8*	*
Freeman et al. (1985)	Autism, mean age 8.8 years	WISC-R $N = 21$	8.4	10.4	8.2
Lincoln et al. (1988, Study 1)	Autism, mean age 17.6 years	WISC-R/WAIS-R $N = 33$	4.6	8.2	6.1
Lincoln et al. (1988, Study 2)	Autism, mean age 10 years	WISC-R $N = 13$	2.8	8.0	4.8
Lockyer & Rutter (1970)	Infantile psychosis, mean age 15 years	WAIS/WISC $N = 21$	4.3	5.9	4.8
Ohta (1987)	Autism, mean age 10 years	WISC $N = 16$	4.7	7.7	5.7
Rumsey & Hamburger (1988)	Autism, mean age 26.4 years	WAIS $N = 10$	9.3	11.1	10.7
Szatmari et al. (1990)	Autism, mean age 17 years	WISC-R/ WAIS-R $N = 17$	7.2	7.8	7.4

*One or more subtests omitted.

Comprehension scaled scores were reported as being quite impaired compared to Block Design and Object Assembly scaled scores in almost all of the subjects with autism (see Fig. 8.1). Table 8.3 shows how these pairs of subtests compare across all of the studies shown in Table 8.2. It is clear from Table 8.3 that the more specific comparison of Vocabulary and Comprehension versus Block Design and Object Assembly more sensitively demonstrates the significant unevenness in these individuals' verbal and visual–motor cognitive abilities.

It is noteworthy that both Block Design and Object Assembly are generally considered good measures of fluid intellectual ability, whereas Vocabulary and Comprehension are good measures of crystallized ability (see Kaufman, 1990, for a review). Fluid intellectual ability is believed to relate closely to neurological development and is not a function of specific training or acculturation. Crystallized ability is influenced to a significant degree by environmental experience, learning, and culture. Furthermore, the ability to develop intellectual abilities based on environmental experience and learning is dependent on the efficacy of the fluid intellectual functions. Thus, early poor performance on measures sensitive to fluid ability may be more predictive of subsequent global intellectual deficits. The converse, however, may not be true. Adequate fluid ability may not necessarily facilitate crystallized intellectual functions.

Lincoln et al. (1988) described the characteristic pattern of scaled scores on the Wechsler scales (WAIS-R or WISC-R) obtained from one sample of 33 persons with autism (see Fig. 8.2), and another sample of 13 children with autism (see Fig. 8.3). The similarity of the scaled score profile was compared to subjects evaluated by Lockyer and Rutter (1970) and Bartak et al. (1975); see summary in Rutter, (1978).

As seen in Fig. 8.2, there is a consistent pattern across all of the studies reported in Table 8.3 in which verbal abilities and the evaluation of meaningful, nonverbal

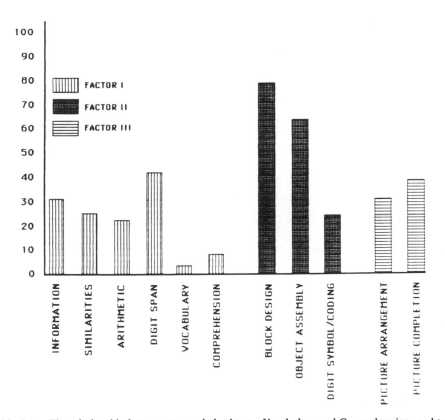

PERCENT OF SUBJECTS WITH WECHSLER SCALED
SCORES GREATER THAN 7

FIG. 8.1.   The relationship between two verbal subtests, Vocabulary and Comprehension, and two performance subtests, Block Design and Object Assembly, for 33 individuals with autism (adapted from Lincoln et al., 1988). Factor I shows the two verbal subtests, and Factor II shows the two performance subtests.

information are relatively depressed compared to the more intact visual–spatial and visual–motor integrative abilities. The latter set of abilities relates to the appraisal of less meaningful or context relevant information (Lincoln et al., 1988). The relatively lower scores consistently found on Digit Symbol/Coding are most likely related to its sensitivity for brain impairment in general (Reitan, 1985).

Figure 8.3 shows the specificity of the pattern of scaled scores derived from 13 autistic children reported by Lincoln et al. (1988) compared to three other groups of children. As seen in the figure, the children with autism from this study demonstrated severe verbal deficits relative to the other three groups. However, their performance on Block Design and Object Assembly was similar to that of the other children.

Learning Disabilities

A fundamental component of the evaluation of children, adolescents, or adults with learning disabilities requires the use of a measure of intelligence (*DSM-III-R* or

TABLE 8.3

A Comparison of the Mean Difference Between the Sum of Vocabulary and Comprehension to the Sum of Block Design and Object Assembly

Study	Sample	Test	$V+C$	$B+O$	$[(B+O) -$ $(V+C)]/2$
Bartak et al. (1975)	Autism, mean age 7 years	WISC $N = 9$	6.8	22.4	7.8
Dawson (1983)	Autism, mean age 18 years	WAIS/WISC-R $N = 10$	6.4	19.5	6.6
Freeman et al. (1985)	Autism, mean age 8.8 years	WISC-R $N = 21$	14.6	23.0	4.2
Lincoln et al. (1988, Study 1)	Autism, mean age 17.6 years	WISC-R/WAIS-R $N = 33$	7.4	19.1	5.9
Lincoln et al. (1988, Study 2)	Autism, mean age 10 years	WISC-R $N = 13$	3.3	19.6	8.2
Lockyer & Rutter (1970)	Infantile psychosis, mean age 15 years	WAIS/WISC $N = 21$	7.7	15.3	3.8
Ohta (1987)	Autism, mean age 10 years	WISC $N = 16$	9.5	21.1	5.8
Rumsey & Hamburger (1988)	Autism, mean age 26.4 years	WAIS $N = 10$	16.8	26.0	4.6
Szatmari et al. (1990)	Autism, mean age 17 years	WISC-R/WAIS-R $N = 17$	14.4	15.7	.65

DSM–IV; see Appendix, "Learning Disabilities"). In order to determine whether there is significant impairment of an academic skill, it is necessary to evaluate the level of that academic skill relative to the individual's general ability level. IQ tests are the best psychometric measures to evaluate an individual's general ability level. Thus, a learning disability diagnosis requires that the achievement measure should be significantly discrepant and below the measure of intelligence.

There are, however, not clearly agreed on criteria for how great that discrepancy should be nor how low the academic ability must be to make the diagnosis of a learning disability. Furthermore, there is no agreed on measure of academic achievement or intelligence on which such evaluations should be based. Such criteria and selection of tests are presently left to the discretion of clinicians, schools, researchers, or government agencies.

IQ tests may also prove useful in helping to evaluate characteristics of the learning disability (LD) in a particular child. Rose, Lincoln, and Allen (1992) identified a group of children who all had global problems in reading, spelling, and arithmetic. These children were compared to a group of children who all had a history of developmental receptive language disorder and also currently demonstrated equally impaired reading, spelling, and arithmetic skill. Thus, academically both groups of children showed similar impairment on standardized achievement tests. However, Rose et al. (1992) demonstrated that the children with developmental language disorder had significantly depressed Verbal IQ scores relative to their Performance IQ scores on the WISC–R, whereas the LD children without the history of language disorder demonstrated a more even relationship between Verbal and Performance IQ (see Fig. 8.4). Furthermore, typical subtest correlations among WISC–R Verbal subtests were not found for the group of children with developmental language problems but were maintained for the other group of LD children. Thus, it was possible to have the same

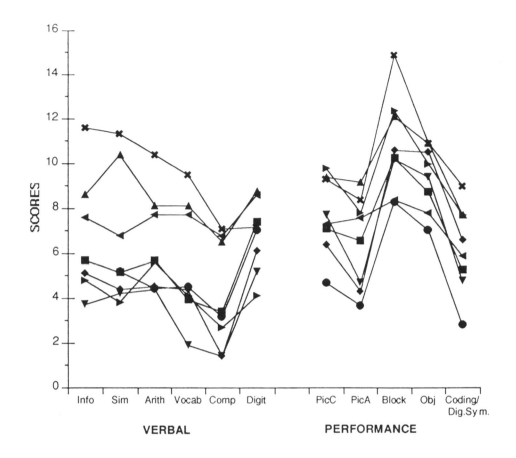

FIG. 8.2.   Wechsler mean scaled scores for individuals with autism taken from eight different studies.

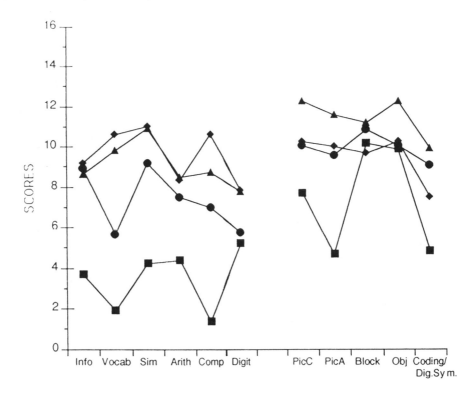

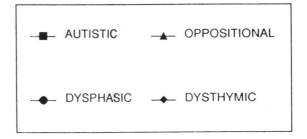

FIG. 8.3. WISC-R mean scaled scores for four groups of children with psychiatric disorders. Adapted from Lincoln et al. (1988).

magnitude of learning disability as measured by reading, spelling, and arithmetic achievement tests with very different language histories and current language abilities.

SUMMARY

The evaluation of intelligence has played an important role in the clinical and psychoeducational assessment of children and adolescents. As part of a comprehensive

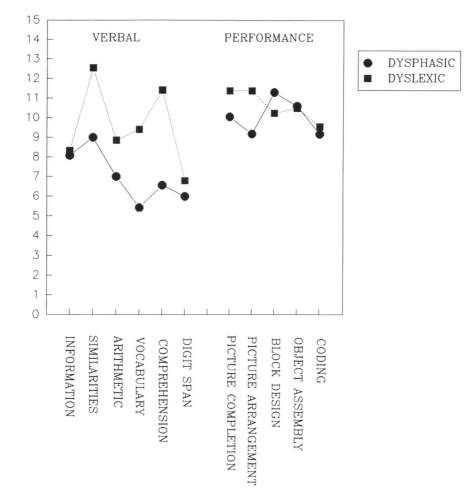

FIG. 8.4. Wechsler scaled scores for children with developmental language disorder (dysphasia) and developmental reading disorder (dyslexia). Adapted from Rose et al. (1992).

multimethod/multitrait evaluation process, the measurement of intelligence provides important quantitative and qualitative diagnostic information. For some specific diagnoses, a measure of intelligence provides an important reference on which other academic or adaptive deficits can be best understood. Intelligence is a good predictor variable of adaptive, learning, social, and language skill. Intelligence is an inherently complex psychological construct with a foundation of theory deeply rooted in essential and basic human abilities. Personality is integrated with intellectual ability and style. An individual's intelligence cannot be separated from the rest of his or her personality or character makeup.

The clinician can use intelligence tests to evaluate abilities in a context where the demands on the individual are clearly defined and the emergence of conflict-based associations or responses are minimized. In addition, intelligence tests allow the clinician in a relatively brief period of time to observe direct samples of behavior across a variety of intellectual domains.

Intelligence tests have been used in the evaluation of many types of psychological disorders. Such tests have helped improve our understanding of such disorders. Intelligence tests can provide important clinical and psychoeducational information about the organization of an individual's abilities and how such abilities might be affected in the context of a psychological disorder.

APPENDIX

WISC-III

Verbal Subtests

Influenced by High Verbal Ability

Information: Questions assess basic factual knowledge. Performance is influenced by cultural opportunities at home, outside reading, and school learning.

Similarities: Compare two objects/concepts and state how they are alike. Performance is influenced by reasoning ability, ability to distinguish essential from nonessential details, verbal expression, and abstract thinking.

Vocabulary: Define words. Performance is influenced by outside reading, school learning, verbal expression, and language development.

Comprehension: Assess social judgment by questions that tap development of moral sense, knowledge of practical information, and evaluation and use of past experiences.

Influenced by Attention and Concentration Abilities

Arithmetic: Mental arithmetic computation. Performance is influenced by attention span, anxiety, and concentration as well as sequencing ability, numerical facility, and school learning.

Digit Span: Repeat a sequence of numbers forward and backward. Influenced by attention span, anxiety, and distractibility. Taps short-term auditory memory.

Performance Subtests

Influenced by Visual–Spatial Abilities

Picture Completion: Pick out important missing element from incomplete picture. Influenced by visual perception of meaningful stimuli, distinguishing essential from nonessential detail, and long-term visual memory.

Picture Arrangement: Quickly place scrambled pictures into a sequence that makes sense. Influenced by creativity, anticipation of consequences, and sequencing ability.

Block Design: Quickly place blocks together to imitate a pictured pattern. Influenced by visual–spatial ability, analysis of whole into component parts, and nonverbal concept formation.

Object Assembly: Arrange puzzle pieces into complete object. Influenced by visual–motor coordination and ability to benefit from sensory–motor feedback, anticipation of relationship among parts, and flexibility.

Mazes: Influenced by planning ability, reasoning, and experience solving mazes.

Influenced by Rapid Processing Speed

Coding (A & B): Quickly write symbols in the appropriately coded boxes. Influenced by paper and pencil skill, working under time pressure, sequencing ability, anxiety, distractibility, and psychomotor speed.

Symbol Search: Scanning symbols. Influenced by anxiety, distractibility, visual processing speed, and working under time pressure.

Attention-Deficit Hyperactivity Disorder (ADHD)

As currently defined by the *Diagnostic and Statistical Manual of Mental Disorders*, Fourth Edition (*DSM-IV*), ADHD requires children to display either six of nine symptoms of inattention or four of six symptoms of hyperactivity/impulsivity. These children have the most difficulty in situations where they are required to sustain their attention, such as at school. However, to be diagnosed with ADHD they must manifest symptoms in at least two or more situations (e.g., school, home, sporting activities, etc.). Six to nine times more boys are diagnosed with the disorder than girls. Symptoms generally start to appear by age 4, but the disorder is frequently not diagnosed until the child begins school. Learning disabilities and conduct disorder frequently are also diagnosed in children who have ADHD. Treatments usually involve prescribing stimulant medications for the child, such as Ritalin. Drug therapies augmented with behavior modification and parent training are especially helpful.

Conduct Disorder

According to the *DSM-IV* (American Psychiatric Association, 1993), conduct disorder is a consistent way of behaving such that the basic rights of others as well as normal social rules are violated. Children with conduct disorder manifest behaviors such as stealing, lying, running away, truency from school, physical cruelty, and forcing someone into a sexual activity. Children are generally diagnosed with this disorder between prepuberty and age 17. Many juvenile delinquents are diagnosed with this disorder.

Autism

Autism is a pervasive developmental disorder that severely impacts social, language, and adaptive development. Individuals are generally diagnosed with autism prior to their fourth year of life. About four males to each female have the disorder and about three quarters of afflicted individuals also have mental retardation. Although early theories of autism suggested that it was etiologically due to severe psychological stress experienced in infancy, it is now believed to be due to abnormalities of the central nervous system.

Learning Disabilities

Learning disabilities are a heterogeneous group of neurologically based developmental disorders that result in impaired academic functioning. They are not due to specific sensory loss such as hearing impairment or visual impairment or due to general intellectual delay. Learning disabilities can involve single academic domains such as reading (dyslexia) or multiple academic domains such as reading, spelling, and arithmetic. Children, adolescents, and adults with learning disabilities most frequently require special academic assistance in order to develop their impaired academic ability.

REFERENCES

American Psychiatric Association. (1987). *Diagnostic and statistical manual of mental disorders* (3rd rev. ed.). Washington, DC: Author.

American Psychiatric Association. (1993). *DSM-IV:* Draft criteria. Washington, DC: Author.

Aylward, E., Walker, E., & Bettes, B. (1984). Intelligence in schizophrenia: Meta-analysis of the research. *Schizophrenia Bulletin, 10*, 430–459.

Bartak, L., Rutter, M., & Cox, A. (1975). A comparative study of infantile autism and specific developmental receptive language disorders. *British Journal of Psychiatry, 126*, 127–145.

Bartak, L., Rutter, M., & Cox, A. (1977). A comparative study of infantile autism and specific developmental receptive language disorders. III. Discriminant function analysis. *Journal of Autism and Childhood Schizophrenia, 7*(4), 383–396.

Culberton, F. M., Feral, C. H., & Gabby, S. (1989). Pattern analysis of Wechsler Intelligence Scale for Children—Revised profiles of delinquent boys. *Journal of Clinical Psychology, 45*(4), 651–660.

Dawson, G. (1983). Lateralized brain function in autism: Evidence from the Halstead-Reitan neuropsychological battery. *Journal of Autism and Developmental Disorders, 13*, 369–386.

Freeman, B. J., Lucas, J. C., Forness, S. R., & Ritvo, E. R. (1985). Cognitive processing of high functioning autistic children: Comparing the K-ABC and the WISC-R. *Journal of Psychoeducational Assessment, 4*, 357–362.

Hogan, A. E., & Quay, H. C. (1984). Cognition in child and adolescent behavior disorders. *Advances in Clinical Child Psychology, 7*, 1–34.

Jocobson, R., Le Couteur, A., & Rutter, M. (1988). Selective subcortical abnormalities in autism. *Psychological Medicine, 18*, 39–48.

Kamphaus, R. W. (1993). *Clinical assessment of children's intelligence.* Boston: Allyn & Bacon.

Kaufman, A. S. (1979). *Intelligent testing with the WISC-R.* New York: Wiley.

Kaufman, A. S. (1990). *Assessing adolescent and adult intelligence.* Boston: Allyn & Bacon.

Kaufman, A. S., & Kaufman, N. L. (1983). *Kaufman Assessment Battery for Children: Interpretive manual.* Circle Pines, MN: American Guidance Service.

Lincoln, A. J., Courchesne, E., Harms, L., & Allen, M. (1993). Contextual probability evaluation in autistic, receptive developmental language disorder, and control children: Event-related brain potential evidence. *Journal of Autism and Developmental Disorders, 23*(1), 37–58.

Lincoln, A. J., Courchesne, E., Kilman, B. A., Elmasian, R., & Allen, M. H. (1988). A study of intellectual abilities in people with autism. *Journal of Autism and Developmental Disorders, 18*(4), 505–524.

Lincoln, A. J., Dickstein, P., Courchesne, E., Tallal, P., & Elmasian, R. (1992). Auditory processing abilities in non-retarded adolescents and young adults with developmental language disorder and autism. *Brain and Language, 43*, 613–622.

Lockyer, L., & Rutter, M. (1970). A 5 to 15 year follow-up study of infantile psychosis: IV. Patterns of cognitive ability. *British Journal of Social and Clinical Psychology, 9*, 152–163.

Lufi, D., Cohen, A., & Parish-Plass, J. (1990). Identifying attention deficit hyperactive disorder with the WISC-R and the Stroop Color and Word Test. *Psychology in the Schools, 27*, 28–34.

Ohta, M. (1987) Cognitive disorders of infantile autism: A study employing the WISC, spatial relationship, conceptualization and gesture imitations. *Journal of Autism and Developmental Disorders, 17*(1), 45–62.

Prifitera, A., & Dersh, J. (1993). Base rates of WISC-III diagnostic subtest patterns among normal, learning-disabled, and ADHD samples. In B. A. Braken (Ed.), *Journal of Psychoeducational Assessment monograph series: Advances in psychoeducational assessment—Wechsler Intelligence Scale for Children: Third edition* (pp. 43-55). Germantown, TN: The Psychoeducational Corporation.

Quay, H. C. (1987). Intelligence. In H. C. Quay (Ed.), *Handbook of juvenile delinquency* (pp. 106-117). New York: Wiley.

Reitan, R. (1985). Relationships between measures of brain function and general intelligence. *Journal of Clinical Psychology, 41,* 245-253.

Rose, J., Lincoln, A. J., & Allen, M. (1992). Ability profiles in language impaired and reading disabled children: A comparative analysis. *Developmental Neuropsychology, 8*(4), 413-426.

Rumsey, J. (1985). Conceptual problem-solving in highly verbal, nonretarded autistic men. *Journal of Autism and Developmental Disorders, 15*(1), 23-36.

Rumsey, J., & Hamburger, S. (1990). Neuropsychological divergence in high-level autism and severe dyslexia. *Journal of Autism and Developmental Disorders, 20*(2), 155-168.

Rutter, M. (1978). Language disorder and infantile autism. In M. Rutter & E. Schopler (Eds.), *Autism: A reappraisal of concepts and treatment* (pp.247-264). New York: Plenum.

Sattler, J.M. (1992). *Assessment of children: WISC-III and WPPSI-R supplement.* San Diego: Sattler.

Schneider, S. G., & Asarnow, R. F. (1987). A comparison of cognitive/neuropsychological impairments of nonretarded autistic and schizophrenic children. *Journal of Abnormal Child Psychology, 15*(1), 29-45.

Schwean, V.L., Saklofske, D.H., Yackulic, R.A., & Quinn, D. (1993). WISC-III performance of ADHD children. In B.A. Braken (Ed.), *Journal of Psychoeducational Assessment monograph series: Advances in psychoeducational assessment—Wechsler Intelligence Scale for Children: Third edition* (pp. 56-70). Germantown, TN: The Psychoeducational Corporation.

Sutter, E., Bishop, P., & Battin, R.R. (1987). Psychometric screening for attention deficit disorder in a clinical setting. *Journal of Psychoeducational Assessment, 3,* 227-235.

Szatmari, P., Tuff, L., Finlayson, A., & Bartalucci, G. (1990). Asperger's syndrome and autism: Neurocognitive aspects. *Journal of the American Academy of Child and Adolescent Psychiatry, 29*(1), 130-136.

Thorndike, R.L., Hagen, E.P., & Sattler, J.M. (1986). *Stanford–Binet Intelligence Scale: Fourth edition.* Chicago: Riverside.

Wechsler, D. (1958). *The measurement and appraisal of adult intelligence.* Baltimore: Williams & Wikins.

Wechsler, D. (1974). *Wechsler Intelligence Scale for Children—Revised.* New York: The Psychological Corporation, Harcourth Brace Jovanovich.

Wechsler, D. (1981). *Wechsler Adult Intelligence Scale-Revised.* The Psychological Corporation, Harcourth Brace Jovanovich, Inc.: San Antonio, TX.

Wechsler, D. (1991). *Wechsler Intelligence Scale for Children: Third edition.* New York: The Psychological Corporation, Harcourth Brace Jovanovich.

Wielkiewicz, R.M. (1990). Interpreting low scores on the WISC-R third factor: It's more than distractibility. *Journal of Consulting and Clinical Psychology, 2*(1), 91-97.

Zarski, J.J., Cook, R., West, J., & O'Keefe, S. (1987). Attention deficit disorder: Identification and assessment issues. *American Mental Health Counselors Association Journal, 9*(1), 5-13.

Chapter 9

Behavioral Assessment

Steven J. Beck
The Ohio State University

Behavioral assessment of children's aberrant behavior is now a well-accepted approach in the armamentarium of identifying and treating children with behavior problems. The behavioral assessment approach was first introduced in the clinical literature in the 1960s, further discussed and delineated from more traditional assessment approaches in the 1970s, and more fully implemented and refined in the 1980s and 1990s. Much has been written about theoretical differences between traditional and behavioral assessment (e.g., Goldfried & Kent, 1972). However, during the last decade, while the original architects of the behavioral assessment approach have become less strident in emphasizing differences between traditional and behavioral approaches, behavioral assessment has become more accepted and mainstreamed into child clinical psychology. Nonetheless, an understanding of the principles of behavioral assessment is still best clarified against the backdrop of a more traditional, psychodynamic assessment approach.

The major differences between traditional and behavioral psychological assessment stem from theoretical conceptions of behavior. Traditional approaches to assessment are primarily concerned with identifying underlying personality constructs that are tied presumably to or the cause of behavior. Psychodynamic theories stress a basic "personality core" as important determinants of overt behavior. Traditional assessment approaches are typically based on indirect assessment strategies, such as projective instruments or sentence completion tests, where the ambiguous stimuli will discern or elicit signs of underlying behavior causes. The attempt to discern enduring internal traits or personality characteristics assumes that such characteristics remain relatively consistent or stable across situations and over time. For example, traditional assessment using projective techniques may determine, based on an 11-year-old boy's response to the shading of the inkblots or his comments on the white part of the cards, that the child displays "aggressive" tendencies or "oppositional" characteristics. Thus, the child's response is viewed as a "sign" or indirect manifestation of underlying personality traits.

Inasmuch as psychodynamic assessment views identifying core personality features as paramount, the classic behavioral position focuses on less inferential targets (e.g., observed behaviors) and emphasizes the situational and environmental determinants of behavior. Although the "trait-situation" explanation of behavior had provided heated discussion in personality theory and research for years, empirical evidence suggests that neither position is adequate as an explanatory model of behavior and that the determination of human behavior is more complex than implied by either trait theory or classic situationism (e.g., Endler & Magnussen, 1976).

Behavioral assessment has generally eschewed the more traditional notion of cross-situational and cross-consistency of behaviors. As Bem and Allen (1974) reported, we can only expect a modicum of behavioral consistency across diverse situations or over extended periods of time and only when there are similar environmental stimulus characteristics. Consequently, given that assessing individuals' responses to specific situations is viewed as too narrow, behavioral assessment has been expanded to include a broader range of methods. These methods include diverse procedures such as observational strategies, interviews, ratings by parents and teachers, and self-report measures in order to gather a composite picture of the target child.

The task then for a behaviorally oriented clinician is to derive information from multiple assessment methods and to develop functional analyses of the child's problematic behavior patterns. These analyses can attempt to discern similar stimulus characteristics across settings (e.g., discerning that a child appears to be noncompliant to her mother and teacher when similar requests made by these adults are difficult for the child to execute), environmental determinants (e.g., determining what elicits a child's aggressive behaviors on his school playground), and assess cognitive-mediated variables (e.g., such as a target child viewing a peer's ambiguous interaction with him as hostile). This analysis of behavior determines the selection and implementation of appropriate treatment procedures.

As Mischel (1968) noted, in behavioral analysis the task is to identify what a person *does* in specific situations rather than what attributes an individual *has* more globally. Thus, the difference between traditional and behavioral assessment lies not so much in its methods per se, but in the way in which data are derived from assessment methods and are integrated with regards to treatment formulations.

CONCEPTUAL FOUNDATIONS

Behavioral assessment is based on a set of underlying assumptions regarding behavior, its determinants, and focus of inquiry. These assumptions help organize and guide the child behavioral assessor's thinking and planning, the type of assessment methods used, and the search for causal explanations of target behaviors and possible intervention strategies. The purpose of this section is to examine four interrelated behavioral assessment assumptions as they relate to children: (a) a causal model emphasizing social–environmental determinants of behavior, (b) reciprocal determinism, (c) the importance of temporal contiguity of behavior, and (d) a reductionist view of childhood behavior problems. These conceptual underpinnings are not meant to be exhaustive of assumptions that guide behavior assessment, and the interested reader is referred to Haynes (1991).

A Social–Environmental Causal Model

A primary assumption that strongly influences and shapes the methods and focus of behavioral assessment is the view that determinants of behavior are mostly accounted for by social–environmental events. The determinants of behavior include response contingencies, situational contexts, antecedent cues, and associative learning experiences. A fundamental premise of behavioral assessment is that it is possible to account for a significant proportion of variance in the occurrence and maintenance of childhood behavior problems by assessing antecedent and consequent social–environmental events, particularly within learning paradigms. Within a broad social learning framework that takes into account cognitive mediated variables and modeling, behavioral clinicians can assess situational contexts and antecedental cues that are presumed to operate by classical conditioning or operant conditioning paradigms. As an example, behavioral assessors can explain why a young child who had previously been frightened in a thunderstorm (a conditioned stimulus) would become fearful and agitated (a conditioned response) when he sees a severe thunderstorm warning flashing on his TV screen. Similarly, an operant conditioning paradigm readily explains how a child is negatively reinforced for his whining when his mother gives him a command to put away his toys and the mother eventually withdraws the request because of her son's aversive response.

Reciprocal Determinism

Children are too often viewed as passive recipients of environmental stimuli. The premise of behavioral assessment is that children can be active arrangers and determiners of their environment. Children are viewed as both strongly influenced by the powerful shapers of their environment. This bidirectional child–environment interaction is exemplified by the New York Longitudinal Study (Thomas, Chess, & Birch, 1976). In this ongoing study, 136 children from middle- and upper middle-income families have been assessed since birth. The investigators report that a sample of children from their study have been identified as "difficult temperament" children. These children, who comprise approximately 10% of the sample, present with characteristics since birth as strong emotional reactivity, a general negative mood, and difficulty adjusting to new situations. Thomas et al. reported that by the age of 10, the majority of difficult temperament children appear to present with psychological adjustment problems. This study illustrates that largely regardless of family contextual factors and parenting styles, these children apparently interact with their environment in such a way as to impact negatively on themselves. Obviously, the mechanism through which person–environmental interaction operates are multiple and complex, yet the presumption of reciprocal determinism is that the manner in which a child interacts with his or her environment affects his or her environment, that in turn, affects how the child thinks, feels, and behaves.

Temporal Contiguity of Determinants

Behavioral assessment emphasizes the importance of determinants in close temporal proximity to the targeted behavior. There is an assumption that a greater proportion of variance in a child's behavior can be accounted for by reference to current rather than historical social–environmental influences. The de-emphasis on distal determinants in understanding childhood psychopathology should not be construed that behavioral assessors minimize earlier, historical determinants. It is hard to argue that longstanding aversive antecedental conditions that infringe on a child, such as marital distress, poverty, parental unemployment, or parental psychopathology, do not, in significant proportions, account for childhood adjustment problems. However, the child behavior treatment literature is replete with studies that have demonstrated clinically meaningful child behavior changes by focusing exclusively on current, contemporaneous interactional processes, for example, between parents and the target child. In fact, most naturalistic and analogue observations discussed in the next section are employed to detect ongoing, current determinants of proximal social–environmental events that occur with the target child towards his family, peers, and classmates.

A Reductionist View of Childhood Behavior Problems

Closely related to the concept of temporal contiguity is the position that behavior assessment attempts to take a reductionistic approach in the search for causal models of childhood behavior problems. This approach searches for increasingly smaller and narrower explanations of causal chains in the child's social–environmental interactions. A potential problem with the reductionist approach is the mistaken position that the most obvious, observable, least inferential cause of an event is the ultimate cause of a child's problematic behavior(s). In a car collision of automobiles, for example, one car causes damage to a second car immediately in front of it. It is obvious, however, that the movement of that car is caused by another behind it, and back to the car that began the collision. Even the car that began the chain collision cannot necessarily be thought of as the ultimate cause of the accident, because excess speed, faulty brakes, bad weather, or a combination of factors could account for the real source of the car collision.

As mentioned earlier, the behavioral assessor would not disagree with the premise that distal events may be important, powerful influences of childhood psychopathology. Parental psychopathology, such as longstanding maternal depression or paternal alcohol abuse, may be an impetus for the "chain car collision" in explaining a child's behavior problems, yet the child behavior assessor tends not to focus as much on the disorganizing or deleterious effects of such broad, negative effects (except perhaps to strongly encourage such parents to seek their own treatment). Instead, the behavioral clinician attempts to focus on "the car that causes damage to the last car in the collision chain" by attempting to search for more immediate, precise and observable behaviors (e.g., such as discrete parent–child interactions) that may be currently maintaining the child's behavior problems.

METHODS OF BEHAVIORAL ASSESSMENT

Although the boundaries of behavioral and traditional assessment methods are increasingly diffuse as psychologists become less rigid and more practical in the utilization of assessment methods, a useful distinction is found in understanding differences between indirect and direct assessment methods (Cone, 1978). Indirect assessment procedures collect information about relevant behaviors that are obtained at a time and place different than where the actual problematic behaviors occur. Clinical interviews, ratings, and checklists provide descriptions in which a significant person in the child's environment (parent or teacher) provides information about a child's behavior based on current or retrospective observations. Such assessment methods are considered indirect in that the relevant child behaviors are neither observed nor recorded by the assessor, and others provide information regarding the child's behaviors based on immediate past or even historical observations. Children's self-report instruments generally involve a child's retrospective rating of attitudes, feelings, and behaviors and as such, are also considered indirect methods of assessment.

Direct assessment procedures typically allows for the assessment of clinically relevant behaviors at the actual time and place of occurrence. These assessment methods are naturalistic observations, analogue observations, participant observations, and self-observations. A full discussion of the methodological issues surrounding these assessment methods are beyond the scope of this chapter. However, direct methods, although perhaps intuitively appearing more valid than indirect assessment methods, contain several sources of error, such as problems with observer bias, reactivity, and generalizability. Direct assessment procedures are oftentimes difficult to implement due to time, cost, and practical constraints. Consequently, each assessment method, direct or indirect, should be viewed as complementary to each other method with each providing slightly different and potentially valuable information.

DIRECT ASSESSMENT METHODS

Naturalistic Observations

The sine qua non of behavioral assessment is the direct observation of a child's behavior in his or her natural environment. Naturalistic observation is the systematic monitoring and recording of a representative sample of a child's behavior in the environment where the behaviors have been identified as being problematic. The development of naturalistic observation procedures represents a major contribution of the behavioral approach towards the assessment and treatment of children. Examples of common naturalistic observations are observing a child's "on task" behavior in a classroom or observing a child's interaction with peers on a playground. The frequent use of naturalistic observations, whereby target behaviors are operationally defined and are observed by trained, impartial observers who are not part of the child's natural environment, reflects the emphasis on minimizing the inferential nature of more indirect assessment methods. Furthermore, because deviant child behaviors rarely occur in an environmental vacuum, naturalistic observations typically allow for the observation and recording of possible antecedent and consequent factors that may be maintaining the problematic behaviors.

Naturalistic observations can provide information on behavior frequencies as well as length of duration. There are a variety of techniques for recording behaviors, but the most often used procedure appears to involve time sampling, in which observation periods are divided into circumscribed time frames (e.g., five 10-minute intervals in the morning and afternoon classroom to observe the frequency, duration, and antecedent conditions of a child's disruptive behavior in the classroom). Trained observers can then record the occurrence of preselected behaviors within each interval. Depending on the target behavior being recorded, target behaviors can be recorded in frequency tallies (e.g., the number of times the child interrupts the teacher or other children in the classroom), response chains (e.g., recording who the child is most often likely to interrupt and under which classroom conditions), or observer ratings (e.g., rating the child at the end of each timed interval on a 1 to 5 scale, with *1* representing no disruptive behaviors and a *5* denoting extreme disruptive behavior). Naturalistic observations have been used with a wide range of target behaviors, populations, and settings. Naturalistic observations have been instrumental in understanding such well-known clinical phenomena as the coercive process that occurs between conduct disordered children and their families (Patterson, 1982) by directly observing parent--child interactions in the home of conduct disordered children. Another example where naturalistic observations have made contributions to understanding childhood psychopathology is the systematic observation of the differing types of aggression displayed by rejected children towards their peers in the classroom and playground (e.g., Dodge, 1983).

Although naturalistic observations are the least inferential of all assessment methods, they should not necessarily be viewed as better than other methods of assessment. One potential problem with naturalistic observations is a phenomena called observer drift or observer bias. In this phenomenon, trained observers gradually "drift" from recording the preselected target behaviors, thereby threatening the validity of the observations. Although ongoing training sessions can minimize this potential source of error, recruiting, training, and then retraining observer-coders for naturalistic observations is expensive, often cumbersome, and thus not always practical in day-to-day child clinic settings.

Analogue Observations

Analogue observations involves the direct evaluation of children's behavior in settings that are structured to increase the occurrence of specific target behaviors. Typical analogue observations involve requesting a child to role-play a behavior (e.g., attempting to join a basketball game on the playground) or a parent–child interaction in a structured setting in which specific instructions are given (e.g., having a parent request the child to clean up the playroom). Analogue observations are particularly efficient and useful when the target behavior is of low frequency or the assessor wants to standardize or better control the situation to elicit relevant target behaviors relative to other children or families. Similar to naturalistic observations, the measurement method most often employed in analogue situations involves short time samples and the identification of specific, predetermined behaviors recorded within those intervals by trained observers or taped for later observation and recording.

Analogue observations have been instrumental in deriving clinically rich findings related to child behavior problems. For example, Dodge, McClaskey, and Feldman (1985) developed an empirically based taxonomy of social situations that has successfully differentiated children identified by teachers as socially competent from children identified as socially incompetent based on children's analogue performance on five social situations: entry into a peer group, responding to a peer provocation, responding to a school failure or school success, conforming to social expectations, and responding to teacher expectations. Similarly, based on analogue observations of child–mother semistructured interactions, Forehand and his colleagues identified parental behaviors that increase the probability of noncompliant child behaviors. Subsequently, Forehand and McMahon (1981) developed a parent training program that reduces child oppositionality and increases positive parent–child interactions as well as parent satisfaction of child rearing.

The two greatest threats to the validity of analogue observations are the reactive nature of the observational process and the issue of external validity. It is well known that the presence of an observer affects behavior and that several observational sessions may be required before reactive effects are reduced. In addition, child behavioral assessors assume that analogue situations closely mimic the relevant behaviors in the target child's more natural environment. Concurrent validity, or the degree of correlation between analogue observations and other assessment methods, such as parent or child self-report measures, can support the validity of analogue observation.

Participant Observations

An excellent alternative to when a target child may be reactive to external observers is participant observation. Participant observations involves an observer who is normally a part of the child's everyday environment, such as a parent, teacher, or even another child, such as a sibling, who monitors and records selected behaviors exhibited by the target child. Participant observation has certain advantages over naturalistic observations. It is an inexpensive method of collecting assessment data, particularly with the recording of low-rate behavior, such as stealing. Participant observation also has the obvious advantage over analogue observations of being recorded in the child's natural environment. Although this assessment method may appear to be promising, participant observation is subject to several sources of potential error that can limit its utility. Participant observations may be particularly susceptible to observer bias and observer inaccuracy. The presumed sensitivity of this assessment method accounts for the fact that participant observations have been used in research on children's behavior problems as a secondary rather than primary outcome measure.

Self-Observations

Self-observation is another direct method of assessment that requires a child to observe his or her own behaviors and then record its occurrence. Self-observation has the clear advantages of being cost efficient and portable (the child can record his or her behaviors anywhere). Thus, although this method has the unique advantage of having a child record his or her behavior without having to rely on observations of others, this fact also raises important validity issues. For example, in order for self-observation to be valid, the child must be aware of and discriminate between the presence of absence of specific target behaviors. Second, the occurrence of the response must be recorded systematically, which has been done with various types of recording devices such as record books, checklist forms, counters, and so forth. With children, successful self-monitoring is facilitated through the use of uncomplicated recording procedures for simple, well-defined behaviors (such as fighting with siblings, or using profanity). Reinforcement contingencies for accurate self-observation tend to increase the overall accuracy of the method.

Specific methods of self-observation reported in the literature have varied considerably, depending on the characteristics of the child, the types of target behavior recorded, and aspects of the setting in which the observation takes place. As an example, academic settings, and in particular classroom behavior and performance, have frequently used self-observation as an assessment method.

Self-observation is another hallmark of the behavioral assessment movement and as such, a significant amount of research has ben conducted with this assessment method (see Shapiro 1984, for a review. Studies generally suggest that children as young as 8 or 9 years of age can be reliable and accurate recorders of their own behavior, but that self-monitoring may result in behavior change due to the self-observation process itself and not necessarily to treatment interventions. In short, self-monitoring has been found to be useful, although basically as a secondary assessment method, for a wide range of child behavior problems.

In summary, even though problems related to their validity exist, behavioral observations are highly useful strategies and represent the hallmark of child behavioral assessment.

INDIRECT METHODS

Behavioral Assessment Interviews

The clinical interview is the most frequently used and the primary source of information about an identified child's problem, yet it is the least frequently researched assessment method. Haynes and Wilson (1979) defined the behavioral interview as a structured interaction between target subjects and the assessor with the following goals:

1. gather information about parental and the target child's concerns, expectations, and goals;
2. assess parental perceptions and feelings about the child's problems;
3. identify factors that may be maintaining or eliciting problem behaviors;
4. elicit historical information;
5. identify reinforcers for the target child;
6. assess cognitive/mediational potential;
7. educate the parents with respect to the nature of the childhood problems;
8. obtain informed consent; and
9. communicate clearly about the procedure and goals of the assessment and the ensuing treatment.

The behavioral interview compared to the more traditional assessment interview is more likely to focus on current behavior and its determinants and current child–environment interactions. Although the interview may often be supplemented by other assessment methods, it is generally considered the indispensable part of the assessment strategy.

The behavioral interview has several unique advantages over other assessment methods. The flexibility of the interview allows the psychologist to collect either broad based information (e.g., asking a couple how they believe their marital relationship affects their child's problematic behaviors) or very narrow, specific information (e.g., asking a mother how she "grounds" her adolescent when he or she comes home late from his or her curfew). The interpersonal, social interaction inherent in an interview process may make parents or the target child more likely to divulge relevant information. The flexibility inherent in the interview allows the clinician to build a relationship with the child and his or her family and to obtain information that otherwise might not be revealed. Finally, the interview allows the assessor an opportunity to directly observe a parent or child's social behavior, although such observations are more similar to analogue observations.

Like all assessment methods, behavioral interviews have sources of error. Major threats to the validity of information derived from an interview format include the veracity of the subjects retrospective information, the susceptibility to subject bias, and the demand by the interviewee to respond in a socially desirable (but erroneous) manner. One of the newest advances in behavioral assessment is the recent development and evaluation of structured interviews. For example, the Diagnostic Interview for Children and Adolescents-Revised (DICA–R) and similar structured interviews for children and their parents are now commonly used to more accurately diagnose and classify children. Structured interviews appear to reduce sources of error compared to more unstructured interviews.

Ratings and Checklists

Ratings and checklists are probably the second most frequently used behavioral assessment method for identifying children's behavior problems. These paper and pencil measures are usually completed by an adult, are easy to administer, and can encompass a wide range of items quickly. Paper and pencil measures are generally perceived as providing information that is more global than other assessment methods. Other assessment methods, such as interviews or naturalistic or analogue observations, allow for more flexibility and less subjective impressions compared to rating scales and checklists. Yet, ratings and checklists are ideal for identifying broad areas of child behavior problems and can ensure that significant areas not always covered in interview or observational methods are sampled. Another advantage of paper and pencil measures are that they often contain norms and traditionally have made attempts to emphasize psychometric properties, such as reliability and validity.

O'Leary and Johnson (1979) stated that four types of validity should be demonstrated in acceptable checklists and rating scales. First, an instrument should demonstrate predictive validity (sometimes referred to as criterion-related validity) that reflects the degree to which scores on an instrument accurately predict future performance on some relevant outcome or criterion measure. The second type of validity, concurrent validity, is the degree of relationship between scores on an instrument compared to similar paper or pencil or other assessment methods at approximately the same time. The third type of validity is content validity that measures how well items on the rating and checklists adequately represent what the investigator intends to measure. The fourth type of validity, and the most elusive, is construct validity that is the extent to which an instrument measures a theoretical construct or trait (e.g., anxiety). Construct validity is established by correlating test scores derived from a particular paper and pencil measure with similar and dissimilar ratings and checklists and other assessment methods.

Two well-known and frequently used rating scales and checklists for children are the Child Behavior Checklist (CBCL; Achenbach & Edlebrock, 1979) and the Conners Teacher Rating Scale (CTRS; Conners, 1969). The CBCL records in a standardized format the behavioral problems and competencies of children aged 4 to 16, as reported by a child's parent or teacher. The CBCL is unique because it reflects adaptive competencies, such as peer relationships and completing household chores, as well as behavior problems. The CBCL contains 118 behaviors and uses a weighted scoring system with a three-step response (e.g., *not true, somewhat or sometimes true*, and *very often true* for each item. The CBCL is preferred by many child clinicians because it has separate norms for boys and girls at three developmental stages, ages 4 to 5, 6 to 11, and 12 to 16.

The CTRS has been widely used for both research and clinical purposes in the child clinical literature. The CTRS is completed by the child's teacher and consists of 39 items or a shorter form consisting of 28 items. The CTRS also provides age and sex norms. The CTRS was specifically developed to aid in the identification of children with hyperactive characteristics and to specifically evaluate drug treatment interventions. However, the CTRS is now recognized as being able to identify social and behavior problems in the classroom setting.

Self-Report Instruments

Of the various behavioral assessment methods, children's self-report has received the least attention and empirical support. The primary reason for the underutilization of children's self-report measures is that children are not viewed as being capable of accurately reporting their psychological state. Self-report measures have often been eschewed because of the apparent lack of correspondence between self-report measures and observable behaviors. However, it is now recognized that a child's perception of his or her problem(s) can be valuable complement to other assessment methods. Furthermore, the lack of agreement between child self-report measures and other assessment methods does not necessarily suggest that one method is more accurate than the other, instead; it suggests that each method taps a different dimension of multifaceted problems.

Two popular child self-report measures are the Children's Depression Inventory (CDI; Kovacs, 1980–1981) and the Perceived Competence Scale (PCS; Harter, 1982). Within the last several years, no other area in child clinical psychology has received more attention than depression in children. The CDI is the standardized child self-report measure of dysphoria. The CDI is a 27-item severity measure of depression based on the well-known Beck Depression Inventory used with adults. Each of the 27 items consists of three sentences designed to range from mild to fairly severe and clinically significant depression. Kovacs reported that the instrument is suitable for children and adolescents from ages 8 to 17, but research has been done with the CDI with first and second grade children when items are read aloud. Overall, the CDI has been shown to be reliable, valid, and a clinically useful instrument for children and adolescents.

The PCS is a self-report measure that assesses children's perceived competence across cognitive, social, and physical domains. Unlike other self-esteem measures that just derive a global measure of self-worth, the PCS provides information on three skill subscales, as well as a fourth independent subscale, general self-worth. The PCS is a 28-question format presented in such a manner to offset the tendency of children to respond in socially desirable responses. The PCS can be used for children ages 8 to 14, although the measure typically needs to be read to 8- to 10-year-old children who are poor readers. The PCS also presents with acceptable psychometric properties, and although more frequently used for research purposes, this instrument can be valuable clinically because it assesses multifactorial dimensions of children's self-concept.

In summary, a variety of child self-report measures is available. Self-reports should be used with appropriate caution but can be used as an index of change following treatment.

SPECIAL CONSIDERATIONS OF BEHAVIOR ASSESSMENT OF CHILDREN

The most distinguishing characteristic of children is developmental change. With respect to generalizations about developmental change, the child clinicians' task is even more difficult because the most noteworthy characteristic of children's change is that it is often rapid and uneven (Mash & Terdal, 1988). Developmental change encompasses biological and physical growth as well as affective, behavioral, and cognitive fluctuations that characterize children at different age levels. Understanding children's developmental change has obvious implications for determining childhood deviancy and for ultimately assessing treatment effectiveness. As an example, childhood depression has only emerged in the last decade as a recognizable problem of childhood, because in part, symptoms of depression, such as crying, poor appetite, temper tantrums, and irritability, were considered normal childhood development phenomena. It was not until studies were able to show in large samples of children that approximately 5% of school age children present with extreme symptoms of dejection, loneliness, and inadequacy (e.g., Lefkowitz & Tesiny, 1980) that child psychologists and psychiatrists were willing to accept the diagnosis of childhood depression as distinct from normal, childhood developmental change.

Although child behavioral assessors need to take into consideration children's developmental levels during assessment, ways of integrating developmental concepts and principles are less clear. Edlebrock (1984) articulated three areas for synthesis of developmental and behavioral principles: (a) use of developmental fluctuations in behavior to develop normative baselines, (b) determination of age and gender differences in the expression and covariation of behavioral patterns, and (c) examination of stability and change in behavior over time as related to such variables as age of onset of behavior and diagnosis. Considerable work is still needed in understanding developmental change in the context of child behavior assessment.

Another important consideration when assessing children is the fact that children and usually adolescents are not self-referred; they are typically referred to child clinicians by parents, oftentimes based on recommendations made by teachers or physicians. As such, the child behavioral clinician may find it necessary to obtain descriptions from a variety of adults about the child's difficulties. Besides the parents being the primary informer, it is not uncommon for behavioral clinicians to collect information in interview format or to recruit as participant observers teachers, school principals, probation officers, pediatricians, and siblings. The inclusion of these additional sources is time consuming and complicates the assessment process but are indispensable parts of the child behavior assessment process.

FUTURE DIRECTIONS

The cornerstone of child behavior assessment is that the assessment methods described in this chapter are empirically validated. Child behavior assessment espouses a multimethod approach consisting of direct and indirect assessment methods, with the caveat that one method is not inherently better than another and that each method can provide a slightly different perspective of a child behavior problems. Yet, the development of empirically validated procedures still lags in child assessment. This problem is compounded by the fact that it may be difficult to apply conventional psychometric concepts such as reliability (i.e., that an assessment measure allows for a consistent or stable finding over time) and validity based on seemingly incompatible theoretical assumptions, such as situational specificity and developmental behavior changes. For example, how can an analogue observation of a child's social skills expect to possess concurrent validity when situational variability is the norm? However, as noted in the beginning of the chapter, some degree of consistency can be expected among procedures assessing similar behavior across similar situations. Therefore, psychometric properties, primarily different kinds of validity, are relevant and should be demonstrated in behavior assessment. Concurrent validity, that is, the extent to which information from one assessment method (e.g., direct observation of a child's classroom behavior) should be shown to correspond with information from another assessment method for the same behaviors (e.g., teacher ratings on the CTRS or teacher participant observations). Behavior assessment methods should also be expected to predict subsequent behavior with some degree of accuracy (predictive validity) and differentiate children referred for behavior problems (clinic-referred children) from children with similar demographics selected from the community (nonclinic-referred children) based on assessment procedures (discriminant validity).

Ollendick and Greene (1990) argued that the current goal of child behavior assessment is to demonstrate incremental validity when using different or additional assessment methods with children. One promising way incremental validity can be shown is the degree to which assessment strategies contribute to beneficial outcome findings by allowing for the selection of more relevant, critical target behaviors. It is worth noting that recent developments in the behavioral treatment literature allow for the assessment of treatment outcome evaluations not be limited to the effects of primary target behaviors but to include such dimensions as parent and child satisfaction and acceptance with treatment.

An increased attention to the assessment of cognitive factors in children that are developmentally sensitive is also needed. The child behavior treatment literature has begun to place an emphasis on such cognitive factors as imagery, expectations, and self-statements, particularly as they relate to childhood depression and anxiety disorders. There has been a corresponding increase of cognitive–behavioral interventions with children who are impulsive or who display dysphoric thoughts, low self-efficacy for particular tasks, and generalized concerns about perceived threats. Yet reliable and valid assessment of cognitive factors for such childhood problems are still in their infancy.

A final comment on the future direction of child behavior assessment is that more effort needs to be directed towards understanding gender differences between children. Numerous studies have shown that both the norms that are used in making judgments about children's behavior and reaction of parents and teachers vary as a function of whether the child is male or female. It is well known that gender differences exist for different childhood disorders (see Eme, 1979) and that some disorders, such as depression or attention-deficit hyperactivity disorder, may manifest itself in a different way, depending on the sex of the child. Yet, except for certain rating scales, such as the CBCL and the CTRS, gender differences are acknowledged by child clinicians but generally ignored when attempting to develop empirically sound assessment methods.

SUMMARY

Child behavioral assessment is based on assumptions regarding determinants of behavior. Behavioral assessment espouses that the majority of problem child behaviors occur and are maintained by antecedent and consequent social–environmental events and that children are not just influenced by but shape their environment. It is also assumed that behavior change is more likely to occur by focusing on current, specific, and observable behaviors, which is the primary focus of inquiry in behavioral assessment. Child behavioral assessment must also grapple with better understanding developmental change so as to better determine if change in child behavior is a normal developmental phenomenon or an indication of adjustment difficulties that warrants further examination. The scope of child behavioral assessment has also been broadened to further incorporate the impact of larger social systems, such as schools and other systems that affect children.

The comprehensive nature of a multimethod approach is perhaps the most salient characteristic of behavioral assessment. Behavioral assessment promotes using an array of assessment procedures, including more direct and less inferential strategies such as naturalistic, analogue, participant, and self-observations. The development of these observational methods has made a significant contribution to child clinical psychology. Behavioral assessment also includes information and data collected by clinical interviews, ratings and checklists, and child self-report measures. This multimethod approach, based on empirically validated instruments, allows for a composite picture of the child that is useful for identifying relevant target behaviors and assessing treatment intervention. However, the acceptability of the multiple assessment approach rests firmly on the availability of a range of psychometrically sound validity measures and the empirical demonstration of their incremental utility. The multimethod approach does not endorse a standard "test battery" mentality but a planned, step-by-step process of choosing complementary assessment methods that allows the behavioral clinician to obtain the best picture of a child.

REFERENCES

Achenbach, T. M., & Edlebrock, C. S. (1979). The Child Behavior Profile-II. Boys aged 12–16 and girls aged 6–11 and 12–16. *Journal of Consulting and Clinical Psychology*, *47*, 223–233.

Bem, D. J., & Allen, A. (1974). On predicting some of the people some of the time: The search for cross-situational consistencies in behavior. *Psychological Review*, *81*, 506–520.

Cone, J. D. (1978). The behavioral assessment grid (BAG): A conceptual framework and taxonomy. *Behavior Therapy*, *9*, 882–888.

Conners, C. K. (1969). A teachers rating for use in drug studies with children. *American Journal of Psychiatry*, *126*, 152–156.

Dodge, K. A. (1983). Behavioral antecedents of peer social status. *Child Development, 54,* 1386–1399.

Dodge, K. A., McClaskey, C. L., & Feldman, E. (1985). A situational approach to the assessment of social competence in children. *Journal of Consulting and Clinical Psychology, 53,* 344–353.

Edlebrock, C. S. (1984). Developmental considerations. In T. H. Ollendick & M. Hersen (Eds.), *Child behavioral assessment: Principles and procedures* (pp. 20–37). Elmsford, NY: Pergamon.

Eme, R. F. (1979). Sex differences in child psychopathology: A review. *Psychological Bulletin, 86,* 574–595.

Endler, N. S., & Magnusson, D. (1976). Toward an interactional psychology of personality. *Psychological Bulletin, 83,* 956–974.

Forehand, R., & McMahon, R. J. (1981). *Helping the noncompliant child: A clinician's guide to parent training.* New York: Guilford.

Goldfried, M. R., & Kent, R. N. (1972). Traditional versus behavioral assessment: A comparison of methodological and theoretical assumptions. *Psychological Bulletin, 77,* 409–420.

Harter, S. (1982). The perceived competence scale for children. *Child Development, 53,* 87–97.

Haynes, S. N. (1991). Behavioral assessment. In M. Hersen, A. E. Kazdin, & A. S. Bellack (Eds.), *The clinical psychology handbook* (2nd ed., pp. 430–464). Elmsford, NY: Pergamon.

Haynes, S. N., & Wilson, C. C. (1979). *Behavioral assessment.* San Francisco: Jossey-Bass.

Kovacs, M. (1980–1981). Rating scales to assess depression in school-aged children. *Paedopsychiatry, 46,* 305–315.

Lefkowitz, M. M., & Tesiny, E. P. (1980). Assessment of childhood depression. *Journal of Consulting and Clinical Psychology, 48,* 43–50.

Mash E. J., & Terdal L. G. (1988). Behavioral assessment of child and family disturbance. In E. J. Mash & L. G. Terdal (Eds.), *Behavioral assessment of childhood disorders* (2nd ed., pp. 3–65). New York: Guilford.

Mischel W. (1968). *Personality and assessment.* New York: Wiley.

O'Leary, K. D., & Johnson, S. B. (1979). Psychological assessment. In H. C. Quay & J. J. Werry (Eds.), *Psychopathological disorders of childhood* (pp. 210–246). New York: Wiley.

Ollendick, T. H., & Greene, R. (1990). Behavioral assessment of children. In G. Goldstein & M. Hersen (Eds.), *Handbook of psychological assessment* (2nd ed., pp. 403–422). Elmsford, NY: Pergamon.

Patterson, G. R. (1982). *Coercive family process.* Eugene, OR: Castalia.

Shapiro, E. S. (1984). Self-monitoring. In T. H. Ollendick & M. Hersen (Eds.), *Child behavior assessment principles and procedures* (pp. 148–165). Elmsford, NY: Pergamon.

Thomas, A., Chess, S., & Birch, H. G. (1976). *Temperament and behavior disorders in children.* New York: New York University Press.

Chapter 10

Behavioral Treatment

Anthony M. Graziano
Nelson J. Dorta
State University of New York at Buffalo

There are various ways of defining psychological treatment of children, most of which include the concept of child psychopathology (also referred to as Behavior Disorder). Children are referred for psychotherapy because they function in some psychologically maladaptive or abnormal manner that needs to be corrected so they can return to a more normal status. However, to know what is abnormal or maladaptive, one must first know a good deal about "normal" functioning; thus child psychotherapy is very much rooted in *knowledge of normal child development*.

Furthermore, children live within family contexts: the way a child develops, thinks, feels, and behaves is largely determined by the nature of his or her immediate family. Family influence is obviously greatest on infants (birth to 2 years old) and pre-schoolers (2–5 years old) who are completely dependent on their adult caretakers. The family continues to be a major factor in school-aged children (5–12 years old), although other social contexts that include children's friends and their friends' families also become important. Even for adolescents (13–18 years old), the family context continues to be important, although at times it is overshadowed by peers and the popular culture. As the child grows older the influence of family and his or her dependence on it gradually diminishes, but always remains a powerful factor.

The major points here are that the psychopathology of children and adolescents is best understood within the context of *normal child development*, and treatment is best carried out in the context of *family structure and interaction*. The successful child therapist knows this, has a good grounding in child development, and keeps a clear focus on the family when working with children.[1]

---

[1]In a longer work, these two important contexts would be discussed in far more detail. But the present brief chapter allows only the introductory comments noted above. The reader is referred to several good undergraduate textbooks on developmental psychopathology (Gelfand, Jensen, & Drew (1988); Kauffman, 1989; Wenar, 1990; Wicks-Nelson & Israel, 1991). A more advanced text is Lewis and Miller (1990).

MAJOR TYPES OF CHILDHOOD PROBLEMS THAT ARE TREATED

Children must develop a large array of skills and learn about themselves and the world. These are complex tasks, and all children run into problems involving personal upsets and conflicts with others. The toddler is stubborn, has temper tantrums, and sometimes resists toilet and other training; the preschooler argues, brags about imagined strengths and success, is often deliberately disobedient, and likes to show off; the young school-aged child develops new fears and anxieties, and may have academic problems; the pre-adolescent and the adolescent may become temporarily distanced from parents, may have emotional highs and lows, and may react to many normal social conflicts in adolescent life as if they are major catastrophes with no solutions. All children experience anxieties, disappointments, sadness, and uncertainties. It is all part of growing up, and most children—provided they have good parenting—will get through it all successfully.

But for many children, perhaps as high as 20%, normal development "goes awry" as Wenar (1990) noted, and those children have much greater personal, social, and academic difficulties. These are the children whose problems are beyond the normal level of difficulties—they have "clinical" problems, and they are the ones who come to the attention of counselors and therapists. Improving their functioning is the aim of child behavior therapy.

Clinical problems are clearly related to the normal tasks faced by children and the normal problems of growing up; the major difference is that the clinical problems are much more severe and exaggerated versions of the normal difficulties. For example, nearly all children go through a period of being stubborn, noncompliant, defiant, and even aggressive, but only a small proportion become severely defiant and aggressive so as to be considered "conduct disordered."

Children's clinical problems are typically grouped into several large categories.

Undercontrolled Disorders

These are disorders in which children have insufficient control over the ways in which they feel, think, and behave; they tend to act impulsively, without much thought about behavior or concern with consequences. This category includes:

Oppositional/Defiant Disorders. Some children seem to fight against adult authority far beyond the normal levels of noncompliance, making life difficult for parents.

Attention-Deficit Hyperactivity Disorder (ADHD). These children are also noncompliant, but in addition (a) they have difficulty sustaining attention, and (b) their general activity level is far beyond that of most children their age. Parents and teachers find them to be very difficult to be with.

Conduct Disorder. Like ADHD children, many of these children are hyperactive and have poor attention. But in addition, they seem to have a poorly developed moral sense. They lack a concern for others, will break any rules (e.g., steal, cheat), and often get into difficulties with parents, teachers and, later, other authorities, such as the police.

Aggressive Behavior, Delinquency, and Substance Abuse. Aggression is a very stable characteristic, and if it is high in 8–10-year-old children there is a high chance that they will be aggressive as adults. Similar to the Conduct Disordered children, these children have problems with authority but, in addition, they become actively delinquent as youths, often engaging in substance abuse, and may become adult criminals.

Overcontrolled Disorders

These are disorders in which children are "overly controlled," cautious, and tentative. When they feel anxious they try to "clamp down" to control the anxiety and this leads to sometimes bizarre, disorganized, or disruptive behavior. They experience high anxiety, and much of their problem behavior is in an attempt to avoid or escape upsetting (anxious) situations and feelings. Included are:

Anxiety Disorders. Some children are generally anxious and fearful. Their fears erupt in repeated attacks of panic. These children are nervous, restless, irritable, and they often also have somatic complaints like dizziness, nausea, sweating, and trembling.

Obsessive Compulsive Behavior. Repetitive ideas and ritualistic behaviors intrude on the child, who becomes very upset if the ritualistic behavior is interfered with, but understands that these behaviors are strange.

Post Traumatic Stress Disorder (PTSD). A severe trauma (such as a natural disaster, fire, or kidnapping) is re-experienced in various ways, causing more distress each time. These repeated reactions can be severe, frightening, and very debilitating. Most of the information about PTSD has been drawn from adults, such as Vietnam veterans but children have had similar experiences. Hyman (1990), for example, described cases of PTSD in children who have been physically beaten by teachers in school.

Fears and Phobias. Fear involves extreme anxiety that is associated with some object or idea (the fear stimulus). When that stimulus is present the child feels great anxiety, and tries to escape or avoid the stimulus. Feelings of dread and physical reactions such as nausea, stomach aches, sweating, and trembling may also occur. Phobias are severe and fears persistent. Fears and phobias are among the most common problems of childhood (Graziano, DeGiovanni, & Garcia, 1979).

Depression and Suicidal Behavior

This involves intense and prolonged feelings of sadness, guilt, and worthlessness, which can be associated with attempted and sometimes successful suicide. Suicide is a growing problem among adolescents (it is the third leading cause of death among adolescents).

Disorders of Physical Functions

These include disruptions of normal patterns in basic functions such as eating, sleeping, and bowel and bladder control. Eating disorders include, anorexia nervosa, in which an adolescent starves him- or herself in an effort to become and remain slim. Some actually die of starvation.

Pervasive Disorders

These disorders permeate all of the child's functioning. Although progress has been made in treatment, training, and education, they resist any complete "cure." They include:

Borderline Disorder. Children with this disorder are thought to stand somewhere between neuroses and the more severe psychoses. They are highly anxious and often become bizarre, with distorted thinking, and they lose contact with reality. Unlike psychotic children their adjustment fluctuates and at times they appear more normal. Borderline children seek reassurance in relationships with others, but they are socially unskilled and indiscriminate in their choices, thus repeatedly failing to find reassurance, and leaving themselves very vulnerable to other people's manipulations. They often cannot control their anger or inhibit their intrusive, frightening ideas.

Schizophrenia. This is a severe mental disorder that emerges after a period of apparently normal development. Schizophrenic functioning includes severe thought disorder, confusion, and delusions. The child can become severely withdrawn and separated from reality. Many experience auditory hallucinations.

Autism. Childhood autism is a severe developmental disability. It is diagnosed early in life, and these children, unlike schizophrenic children, are thought to have never developed normally. A high proportion of autistic children are also mentally retarded. They are characteristically aloof, have no language or, if they do, it is strange and distorted. They behave in rigidly repetitious patterns and become very upset if there is personal intrusion. Many autistic children can be taught (in school), but they tend to remain autistic all their lives.

Mental Retardation. This is another pervasive developmental disability in which children have significantly low intelligence and low social functioning. The retardation may be due to genetic factors or to traumas during pregnancy, birth, or childhood. Most (70%–75%) people labeled *retarded* are in the mildly retarded category, and most of them have no discernible physical or medical defect that might be causing the retardation. Persons with retardation can suffer most of the psychological disorders noted earlier, and need treatment as much as do any other psychologically disturbed children.

Sexual Disorders

The degree to which young children can be sexually motivated remains debatable, but children do engage in troubling behavior that has at least some sexual content. Intense, excessive, and inappropriate masturbation (e.g., in public), cross-sex dressing and other behavior, sexual promiscuity in young adolescents, homosexuality, and paraphelia (bizarre/perverted sexual behavior) are examples of sex-related child/youth problems treated in behavior therapy. Unlike most of the others listed, homosexuality in children is defined as a problem based largely on parents' personal values and whether the child or adolescent feels the homosexual urges are threatening.

Child Maltreatment

There are some two million suspected cases of child maltreatment annually in the United States (physical, sexual, and psychological abuse, and neglect). Psychological effects on children include low self-esteem, poor peer relations, heightened aggression, cognitive deficits, social deficiencies, and other problems, all of which may be lifelong. Nearly all of the treatment, however, is provided to the abusing parents and little is done to help the children directly (Graziano & Mills, 1992). A few studies are beginning to consider the direct psychological treatment of abused children.

Evaluation and Monitoring

In child behavior therapy careful evaluation of how the child functions is carried out at pre-treatment, during treatment, immediately at post-treatment, and at longer-term follow-ups. The first evaluation determines the type and direction of the treatment plan. Monitoring during treatment charts the progress of therapy, showing where goals have or have not been met and where changes need to be made. The posttreatment evaluations, including long-term follow-ups, provide the major assessments of the outcomes of therapy. It should be noted that long-term (more than one year) follow-up evaluations are critical in order to know if the treatment has had lasting effects.

Assumptions in Behavior Therapy with Children

There are many specific approaches used by therapists in behavioral treatment of children and their families. Despite some theoretical differences among them, there is general agreement on several basic ideas, as follows:

1. It is assumed that children's problem behaviors are largely learned according to systematic laws of learning in the course of the child's experiences within his or her environment; if the problem behaviors are learned, they can be unlearned or otherwise modified, according to the same laws of learning.

2. Maladaptive functioning is maintained largely by the reinforcing/punishing events in the environment (i.e., how the child is treated by parents and others) and by the ways in which the child thinks about, talks about, and evaluates him- or herself. Therefore detailed attention is paid to the nature of environmental events (stimuli) surrounding the child and the nature of the child's self-cognitions.

3. As discussed earlier, in order to help a child change maladaptive functioning the therapist must understand and work within the contexts of normal child development and the child's family structure and interactions.

4. Treatment involves the child and family actively. This includes direct practice of new behavior, home-based learning programs for child and parents, active programs of rewards for improvements, record keeping by the child and family, and so on. The therapist's roles include those of therapist, active teacher, and family consultant.

5. Behavioral and cognitive/behavioral therapy approaches are highly individualized for each specific child and family. This requires a *functional analysis*, which is a detailed analysis of how the child interacts with family members and friends, and thinks and responds particularly in problem situations (for example, when pressured in school or criticized by a parent).

6. The major focus is on observable *behavior* of the child and parents, and on the factors impinging on them which stimulate and maintain the behavior. Progress is measured in terms of observed behavioral improvements.

Thus as practiced, modern behavior therapy with children is based on concepts of learning principles, normal child development, and family interactions; it focuses on the client's overt, observable behavior as controlled by both external reinforcement and by internal cognitions; it is carried out with highly individualized treatment planning by an active therapist who promotes the active involvement of the clients.

THE MAJOR FORMS OF BEHAVIORAL AND COGNITIVE/ BEHAVIORAL TREATMENT

Behavioral treatment of childhood problems is based on several different theoretical models of how people learn. Modern behavior therapists apply a mix of those models, usually matching the models with the particular issues presented by the child. Although they are different from one another, the models also have considerable overlap, and the models we describe are not completely independent. For this chapter, we identify the major models as: contingency management; reciprocal inhibition; modeling; self-control training; and parent behavioral training (PBT). The latter, PBT, is not so much a different theoretical model of learning but, rather, combines all approaches in a parent-teaching focus.

Contingency Management Used in a Parent Behavioral Training Approach

Because much of the contingency management approaches are carried out through parent behavioral training (PBT), these two models are discussed together.

Contingency management includes a large array of approaches, and is used in one form or another in virtually all behavior therapy. The term refers to the careful arrangement and manipulation of reinforcements to increase or decrease the strength of targeted behaviors. In order to do this the behavior therapist must identify what behaviors are to be targeted, what the effective reinforcers are for that child and parents, and what the conditions are under which those targeted behaviors occur and can be modified. A careful *functional analysis* is carried out to make those determinations. This analysis can involve detailed interviews with the parents and/or the child, direct observations by the therapist in semi-structured situations (e.g., office) or in the home or at school, and through daily record-keeping by the parents, teachers, and/or the child.

Once the behaviors, reinforcers, and situations are identified, a treatment plan is made for applying those reinforcers (contingencies) in a systematic manner and monitoring the changes in the child's functioning. Often the program is carried out by teachers in school or parents at home, under the therapist's supervision. Progress records are kept by the teacher, parent, or child, and are reviewed by the therapist.

Among the many specific strategies used in such contingency management programs are time-out, token reinforcement systems, and contingency contracting. Two cases illustrate these three approaches.

Time-Out from reinforcement is a punishment procedure (i.e., it is designed to be contingent upon targeted undesirable behavior, and to have the effect of reducing the strength of that behavior). Typically, time-out involves removing the child from a setting in which he or she misbehaved, and putting him or her briefly in a presumably nonreinforcing setting.

The mother of a 3½-year-old boy, Roger, complained that he had become increasingly hyperactive, aggressive toward his younger sister, noncompliant and tantrumous, and frighteningly bizarre in his fantasies about chopping off heads and killing people.[2] A nursery school teacher was also concerned about his aggressive and bloody fantasies. Detailed functional analyses revealed that Roger was spanked harshly by his father frequently for misbehavior, and his mother was beginning to do the same. The physical punishment did not curb his behavior, but it seemed to increase and maintain his aggression toward his sister whom he repeatedly hit and pushed, making her cry. Neither parent spent much positive time with their son because he was so highly active and difficult to deal with. Instead, they focused their positive interactions on the 2-year-old sister. Roger's tantrums often occurred when he was ignored and his sister was being attended to, or when he was reprimanded or otherwise frustrated by his parents. The boy spent a great deal of time watching television, and often stayed up late at night watching television with his parents while his little sister slept. He enjoyed being with his parents. Unfortunately they observed a great deal of televised violence.

The parents agreed to try a home contingency management program, including weekly meetings with the therapist to evaluate progress and make needed adjustments to the program. The major goals were: (a) to help the parents end their use of physical punishment (spanking, slapping); (b) to reduce or eliminate the child's heavy diet of violent television (c) to increase the parents' positive interaction with the boy; (d) to decrease or eliminate the child's tantrums; (e) to eliminate his aggressive behavior toward his sister; (f) to increase their positive play together; and (g) to decrease his violent fantasy as expressed in his play and talking.

The parents were instructed how to play positively with Roger. His mother began having exclusive time with him to play games or read stories when his sister was napping. She was also to play with both children together at other times during each day. The mother agreed to at least three short, positive play sessions each day exclusively with Roger. His father agreed to do the same at least once each evening after work, and once each Saturday and Sunday. Taking short walks around the neighborhood became a favorite father–son interlude. Verbal praise and attention for "good" and cooperative behavior was to be given by the parents. All of this positive reinforcement (attention, praise, pleasant activity) was to be contingent upon his cooperative, appropriate behavior. That is, Roger would have several opportunities

---

[2]The cases used in this chapter have been chosen for their illustrative value and for their successes. However, as in all types of therapy, there are also problems and failures in child behavior therapy. For more discussion of these issues, see Graziano and Bythell (1983).

each day in which the parents would model appropriate play behavior, coach and direct him, and provide immediate contingent reinforcement.

At the same time the parents were to eliminate all spanking and substitute a time-out procedure contingent upon his tantrums and his aggressive behavior toward his sister. When he engaged in those negative behaviors, he was to be told "No! We don't do that!" (for tantrums) and "No! We don't hit!" (for aggression), and then immediately taken to a time-out chair in the corner where he had to remain until he quieted down, plus 2 minutes. It is obviously important that the parents refrain from spanking him once they began the "We don't hit" message.

His television viewing was to be sharply reduced and carefully monitored. All aggressive programs, such as cartoons, were not to be allowed. Nighttime viewing with his parents was to be limited to one half-hour of nonviolent programs. Some special children's program, such as those around holiday times (as long as they were suitably nonaggressive), were exceptions to the half-hour limit. In the evenings, instead of long television watching, the parents were to spend time with him in reading stories or in positive play.

Within 2 weeks his tantrums were significantly reduced and by 6 weeks they had virtually disappeared. Aggression toward his sister followed a similar decline. Both behaviors seem to have been controlled by the time-out procedure. Aggressive fantasies (as indicated in his play and talking) had not been targeted for time-out, but with his general improvement, they declined in another month.

Roger played more gently with his sister, as he was learning in the parent play-times. Mom's spankings stopped within the first 2 days; the father tapered off over a 3-week period.

Roger's demeanor at home and in school improved, and he enjoyed the new, increased, positive times with his parents, who reported greater ease and satisfaction with Roger.

After 3 months, all of the behavioral goals had been met and formal meetings with the therapist were reduced. They ended after 5 months. A 6-month and 1-year follow-up indicated continued good progress, and no recurrence of the high aggression, tantrums, or aggressive fantasies.

In this case, the contingency management program included time-out to reduce negative behaviors, and positive reinforcement plus modeling and direct teaching to increase positive behaviors. In the tradition of PBT, the parents were trained and monitored in carrying out the program at home.

With many children, a token reinforcement system is used in which specific behaviors are targeted for change, and clear, detailed rules are drawn up for how to reinforce those specified behaviors. With older children, especially adolescents, the decisions about what to reinforce and how to do it are made cooperatively with parents and child discussing and even bargaining over what is to take place. This is called "contingency contracting," and it provides an actual written contract of the agreement between the parents and child. It has been used with considerable success with adolescents who are beginning to show serious rebellion. Contingency contracting formalizes cooperative negotiations and agreements between parent and adolescent. The therapist becomes a negotiator, helping both to agree on how they are to behave toward each other.

In the following case of an 11-year-old girl, contingency contracting was attempted, but was soon dropped because the formalized negotiations were beyond the girl's ability. Instead, a contingency management program utilizing a token reinforcement system was drawn up by the therapist and the mother.

In the year since Mrs. M's divorce, life at home with 11-year-old Jan had become unbearable. The household was in constant turmoil, with Jan and her mother constantly at odds, screaming at each other, angry, and tearful much of the time. Jan, according to the mother, was completely oppositional, refusing to get up in the morning, eat breakfast, dress for school do the few chores requested by her mother, eat what her mother prepared for dinner, treat her 8-year-old sister nicely, and so on. Each day was a series of major battles over every simple request or expectation the mother had for Jan. It was, according to the mother, wearing her out. The sister was not a behavior problem—she just stayed timidly out of the way and said little to anyone.

The incident that precipitated their seeking help at our clinic occurred one rainy school-day morning when, after an hour of battles the mother found herself screaming, chasing Jan down the rain-filled street, both of them in pajamas and slippers. The child was too fast and she disappeared in the maze of neighbors' yards. The mother, sobbing, standing rain-soaked on the sidewalk with her wet pajamas clinging to her body, saw her neighbor, an elderly lady, peeking at her from behind a curtain, and suddenly realized how bizarre their lives had become.

Here was a case in which a family was in chaos; they lived a life of high stress and conflict and they were out of control—their emotions had taken over and none of them was able to exert any rational control over events.

The therapist believed that whatever the reasons for the child's severe negativistic behavior and the mother's total inability to control their emotional climate (all clearly related to the stresses and dislocations of the divorce), the most important immediate goal was to achieve some order and control in this otherwise chaotic situation. A token reinforcement system was to be the structure for that order and control.

When a contingency contracting approach was abandoned because Jan was not able even to discuss issues with her mother, it was decided that a token system would be designed by the therapist and the mother, and the child would simply have to live with it. This required several sessions with the mother reinforcing for her that, she was the responsible adult and had every right (and duty) to impose her order on the uncooperative child. Much of what we were to do was aimed at building up the mother's role as the family's responsible adult.

With the mother behind the plan and ready to assert her new role, it was then necessary to convince Jan to be at least minimally cooperative. She had attended all of the sessions, refusing to talk but listening to the discussions about parental responsibility and control.

Jan agreed that life was intolerable, that everyone in the family was unhappy, and that something had to be done to make it better. She refused to cooperate in any planning, said she did not care what we did or planned, but did agree to "try it out for 3 months" as requested by the therapist.

The token system was planned by the mother and therapist, with a silent Jan listening but not participating. She clearly did not like it when told "from now on" she would have to earn all of her privileges—television, movies, allowance, having friends visit or visiting them, favorite foods, after-school clubs, Saturdays with friends, new clothes, and so on. She was somewhat interested in learning that under the system, if she did well, she would actually have a good deal more freedom and privileges than she now had.

According to the plan, Jan would be immediately reinforced with tokens for specified behavior. The mother was to rely strictly on the system for rewards and punishments and was not to shout, hit, or otherwise punish the child anymore. They decided to focus first on the morning behavior and then, once that was improved, to extend the system gradually to the rest of the day.

In the morning, Jan was to be awakened by her mother and reminded about the system—if she got up without any complaint or obstructive behavior, she would receive two tokens (small paper "coupons" with Jan's name on them). Getting washed and dressed, eating breakfast, getting her coat on for school and being ready to be driven to school when mom was ready to leave, riding to school without complaint, and getting out of the car willingly and entering school, all with no problems from Jan, would each earn her another two tokens, for a total of 12 tokens possible each morning.

The tokens could be "cashed in" later in the day for her choice of back-up reinforcers such as television time, use of her telephone and record player, visiting friends, and so on. Each privilege cost a specified number of tokens and she could purchase only as much as she could "afford."

The system was, in essence, a highly detailed blueprint for daily living—it specified what she was supposed to do and what the rewards would be; it obviated the previous conflicts and punishments. In essence, it was a highly structured plan for bringing some degree of order into the family chaos.

Jan's room was emptied of all her "treasures"—telephone, posters, record player, records, and so on—to preclude her noncontingent access to them.

On the first day of the token system, Jan was awakened and reminded about the system. She refused to get up, to wash, dress, eat breakfast, or to get ready for school. Her mother told her she would have to remain in her near-empty room until she was ready to cooperate, and she had lost the opportunity to earn 12 tokens. After several failed attempts to turn on the television set in the living room, Jan remained in her room, with little to do. By 11 o'clock, a very bored Jan came out and asked her mother if she might have lunch and go to school that afternoon. That evening, because she had earned two tokens for going to school, she purchased a half-hour of television, but had to go to bed after that, while her sister stayed up. Because she had earned no additional tokens, she was not allowed access to other reinforcers, such as calling her friends.

The next morning Jan did manage to earn several tokens, and she cashed them in that evening for a half-hour's use of her telephone. From that point on her morning behavior improved, although still with some complaints and difficulties, but she sometimes even earned all 12 possible tokens. In the therapy sessions the therapist continued to coach the mother, to help correct and adjust the procedures where necessary. Most importantly, the therapist provided the mother with support and reinforcement for her good work, especially whenever the mother felt she was becoming overwhelmed and felt like giving up.

Within 2 weeks the morning situation had improved and the token system was extended gradually to the rest of the day (mealtimes, bedtime, chores, etc.). By the time the agreed-upon 3 months had elapsed, the family turmoil had disappeared. Jan and her mother still had conflicts and problems, but they were now talking with each other and to the therapist, instead of fighting. They were having increasing success in resolving their differences. A month later they terminated therapy, saying they had learned how to deal more effectively with the family issues and that the earlier chaos and conflict had ended. A 1-year follow-up showed continued improvement in the family system.

In this case the token economy had been used as a created—almost artificial— framework that imposed order in a chaotic situation. It served much as a training program in communication and other behaviors, with daily lessons and practice. The behavioral specificity made it clear to each of them what their appropriate, expected behavior was to be. It served to communicate clearly the relationships between one's behavior, one's rewards, and the behavior of other people. When they had learned their lessons well, mother and daughter no longer needed the token system, and they moved on to more "natural" interactions.

Reciprocal Inhibition

The concept of reciprocal inhibition holds that a response is weakened when it is in the presence of a stronger, incompatible response. For example, a person cannot be relaxed and anxious simultaneously. The two responses are incompatible, they cannot occur together, and one has to give way to the other. In a form of behavior therapy developed by Wolpe (1990), anxiety is assumed to be a set of conditioned responses. By pairing anxiety responses to specific anxiety-inducing stimuli with stronger relaxation responses to the same stimuli, the conditioned anxiety is de-conditioned (i.e., the conditioned bond is broken or inhibited). Wolpe's procedure of applying the reciprocal inhibition concept is called "systematic desensitization"

Barbara was a 16-year-old girl of low-normal intelligence. Her parents were successful business people and lived a comfortable suburban life with their three children.

Barbara attended a highly rated suburban public school. Despite her slight IQ disadvantage, she had always done well academically—earning "B" s and "C" s and receiving many commendations from teachers for her motivation and willingness to work hard. But at the end of her freshman year in high school she began to struggle academically. Her grades dropped and she had to attend summer school to make up two courses.

The difficulties continued in 10th grade, as Barbara failed nearly all of her examinations early in the year. She became generally upset, anxious, tearful, and mildly depressed. She was brought to the clinic on recommendation of her family doctor, who had examined her for recurrent headaches, stomach pains, and vomiting. No physical problems were found, and the physician concluded her problems were "emotional."

In several sessions with the parents and with Barbara individually, it was clear that her difficulties were school related. Barbara previously had a very healthy view of herself, recognizing her strengths and weaknesses. She knew that she was not as intellectually able as most of her friends and that she had to work hard just to pass with "B" and "C" grades, whereas many of her friends did little studying but often surpassed her on examinations. Her strength was in her sociability, her good skills in getting along well with people, her high motivation to succeed, and willingness to work harder than others had to. Basically she was psychologically stable and successful. Barbara's goals were clear: to graduate from high school with a respectable record, and then, when her friends went off to college, she would attend a local 1-year business school program. After that she would seek a job in a local business, perhaps in retail sales where her strengths could be used. Her parents had done a good job in raising Barbara.

A functional analysis revealed that Barbara had become test phobic—she had developed a strong fear of taking examinations. For some months she had feared that her abilities would someday fail her, and eventually she would not be able to pass examinations no matter how hard she studied for them. As her academic work became more demanding, her fear became so debilitating that it interfered with her concentration during examinations, and she began to fail them. Gradually her fear and anxiety generalized and she became unable to concentrate well enough to prepare for examinations. The more anxious she became the less she studied, and the more tests she failed. In time her whole adjustment was affected: Barbara became generally anxious, suffered stomach aches and sickness on school days, but not on weekends, lost touch with her friends, became tearful and moody at home, and began talking about quitting school because it had become too hard for her and she was developing a very low assessment of herself.

It was decided to focus first on the test anxiety, using Wolpe's systematic desensitization procedures. Barbara was taught how to relax deeply in therapy sessions and, when she had that under control, imaginal desensitization was introduced. This involved a series of imagined scenes having to do with examinations—imagining herself preparing for a test, reviewing a few days before, the night before, the morning of the test, and, finally, imagining sitting down to take the test itself. The scenes were arranged progressively, so she imagined coming closer and closer to the actual test. With each scene she felt anxiety, and was instructed to "turn on" her relaxation and to "keep it going" until she no longer felt anxious at that scene. She moved on progressively to each of the remaining scenes until she could imagine even the final one—taking the exam—without anxiety.

Over the next several weeks two more components of therapy were put into place: she began to practice relaxation and desensitization in vivo (in real life) at home each evening when she did homework, and she began developing more cognitive self-control skills, i.e., self-talk ("I can do this," "Relax and focus on this problem," etc.)

Soon she was able to do homework again, was performing better in classes, and was feeling more confident and more positive about herself. But midterm exams were coming up in a few weeks, and she still had the previous failed exams to contend with. At this point her teachers and guidance counselor, who had been consulted by the therapist at the start of treatment, were asked to help, and they agreed enthusiastically.

Each teacher agreed to provide Barbara with make-up study materials, and to go over the lessons with her each day after school. They also agreed to give her make-up tests, which she could take during school hours in the guidance counselor's office, with no time limits. Individual therapy sessions continued and she discussed her progress and carried out numerous behavioral and cognitive rehearsals with the therapist.

It was not an easy year, but Barbara worked hard in therapy and in school. By the end of the year, she had successfully made up enough of the previous work and did well enough on the examination to pass all of her courses—although some were very minimally passing. She had overcome her test anxiety and was able again to study effectively. Her general mood improved, she maintained passing grades over her junior and senior years, and successfully graduated from high school with a few "D" s and "B"s, but mostly "C" grades. A follow-up 2 years after high school showed she had completed the 1-year business course, and was successfully working in the office of a local department store.

Modeling

Modeling procedures have been used in behavior therapy since the late 1950s and comprise a range of techniques that share certain critical aspects. Modeling involves procedures in which the child is exposed to a person (model) who performs behaviors that he or she has difficulty performing (are not in the child's behavioral repertoire). The model can present the new behaviors to the child in the session (in vivo), filmed/video, or by having the child imagine him-or herself performing the actions (symbolic/covert). The person who models provides the child with a learning experience to acquire new behaviors, and an opportunity to learn and to practice those behaviors in an appropriate context.

The model provides the child with the opportunity to learn specific behaviors that he or she may lack (how to ask another child appropriately if he or she wants to play). This aspect of modeling is referred to as the *acquisition or behavior attainment function*. Models also help the child discriminate when these new behaviors should be implemented. In the previous example, it would be inappropriate for the child to ask his or her peer to play catch during a reading lesson in school. Modeling helps children to recognize when these new learned behaviors should be tried and with whom they should be tried. This aspect of modeling is called the *facilitation and discrimination function*. Another beneficial aspect of modeling for some children is its ability to decrease their anxiety, fear, and/or hesitancy in performing these newly learned behaviors. For example, anxious children are overconcerned about their ability to carry out certain behaviors. Modeling provides them with the opportunity to observe and practice these behaviors in a supportive and less stressful environment. This effect of modeling to diminish a child's fear or anxiety about performing certain behaviors is its *disinhibition function*. Modeling may also serve to eliminate the fear or anxiety the child has about performing certain behaviors, this is the *extinction function* (Masters, Burish, Hollon, & Rimm, 1987).

Bandura (1977) outlined four central processes in modeling. The first step in effectively teaching new behavior through modeling is to gain and hold the attention of the child. Second, models need to help the child retain and store what has been learned. Several techniques that help with retention are: (a) rehearsal (motoric, symbolic, and cognitive), (b) providing a specific and detailed organization for the new behavior, and (c) having different people in different settings of the child's environment ask for the child's recall of the newly learned behavior. Third, the model must help the child reproduce the behavior. In our previous example, this entails not only having the child ask another child to play catch, but also to develop appropriate accompanying nonverbal behavior. This is critical for children because many are unable to reproduce behavior without the model's guidance. Last, for the model to be an effective "teacher" he or she must motivate the child to attend, learn, and try the behavior. Some techniques that increase motivation in children are: providing rewards for performing the modeled behavior or developing a system where the child gives him-or herself reinforcement for trying the new behavior (self-reinforcement).

Modeling techniques have been used for a variety of behavioral and emotional problems in children. Modeling is routinely used to teach social skills to children who are extremely shy/withdrawn and are thereby socially isolated. Modeling has also been used to teach social skills to children who are aggressive and lack appropriate interaction skills. Thus, an aggressive child may be taught nonaggressive alternative behavior by being shown (modeled) appropriate behavior, given the opportunity and support to practice it, and rewarded (reinforced) for the new, nonaggressive behavior. Many aggressive children have never been taught such nonaggressive alternatives.

Modeling has also been used to help children with high anxiety or fear. For example, modeling techniques are routinely used with children who are school phobic (i.e., they are extremely fearful of going to school and leaving their caretakers). These children tend to protest vehemently, act aggressively, and/or cry for long periods of time under demands to go to school. A therapist can model for the child some of the demands likely to be made by the school situation, such as how to say "goodbye" to parents for the day, how to greet the teacher and friends, and so on. With the therapist's help, the child can also imagine having fun in school, enjoying activities, stories, and so on with classmates. Such modeling can help the child learn new behaviors appropriate for school, as well as decrease the anxiety and fear about going to school (the facilitation and disinhibition-extinction functions of modeling).

Modeling has also been applied to autistic children. Lovaas, Berberich, Perloff, and Schaeffer (1966) used guided, reinforced rehearsal to train one mute, autistic child to use some language. They began by modeling to the child very simple sounds as "b" and "a." Every time the child made utterances similar to those sounds he was reinforced (in this case given an M&Mcondy). The child's attempts to imitate the sound were reinforced and, with practice, the imitation improved until it was close to the modeled vocal sound. This systematic, step-by-step process of moving progressively closer to the goal behavior is termed *successive approximation* of the goal or target behavior. After repetitions of this procedure the therapist began combining sounds (chaining) to form words-*baby* for example. Each correct repetition of the word was again reinforced. The therapists then proceeded to reinforce the child for accurate use of the words, in this case when the child said *baby* to an actual infant or doll. In this procedure (discriminating training) the child is taught to make the correct sound when the appropriate stimulus is presented, and not when inappropriate stimuli are presented.

Graziano (1974) described an entire social learning program for groups of autistic children in which modeling and imitation procedures were central. The children progressed from simple social interactions, through more complex behavior such as cooperative, sharing behavior at brief snack times, to longer mealtimes, to appropriate school behavior and, eventually, to academic achievement. Modeling, imitation, rehearsal, and reinforcement, all arranged along sequences of successive approximations to defined goals, were consistently used.

Self-Control Training

Self-control training is largely based on the work of B.F. Skinner in the 1950s. It continued to develop through the 1970s and 1980s to comprise a host of techniques with a common rational. Basically, self-control training is an extension of operant contingency management, with the addition of some cognitive behavior modification techniques. In essence it holds that if a psychologist can bring about significant changes in another person through the systematic application of learning principles such as contingency management, then any person should be able to learn to use these principles of learning to plan and bring about their own behavior changes. Thus, self-control training is largely cognitive-behavior modification that is planned and carried out by a person (with the therapist's guidance) whose goal it is to change his or her own functioning. The person is an active, decisive participant in the therapy process when self-control training is used. A central idea is that the changes a child can make in therapy will endure if he or she is an active participant in the change process. Therapists are advised to help their clients be responsible for change.

With children it is assumed that the improvements brought about through self-control training will be stable and generalizable, because the procedure relies on the child developing his or her own new, useful coping strategies and problem-solving techniques. Self-control training has been used to teach children to reduce fears and anxieties, to control aggressive behavior, to improve studying and practicing, and even to become more assertive when appropriate. Self-control training programs include self monitoring, self-evaluation, and self-reinforcement.

Self-Monitoring.   The child is first trained in self-monitoring; that is, how to recognize and to keep track of his or her thoughts (cognitions), feelings (emotions), and actions (behavior) in problem situations. For example, a boy who frequently starts fights can be trained to think about what kinds of things make him angry, how he feels in those situations, and how he typically acts when angry.

Self-Evaluation.   The second characteristic of a self-control program is to teach the child self-evaluative skills. The self-evaluative aspect of the training teaches the child to understand his or her behavior and provides opportunities for perspective taking, problem solving, and goal setting. For example, with the child who gets into fights, the therapist would teach the child to see how others feel when he or she gets angry and hits (perspective taking), develop strategies to avoid getting so angry or, when angry, to act assertively, but nonaggressively (problem solving), and to develop a plan on how to know that goals to avoid fighting are being accomplished (goal setting).

Self-Reinforcement.   The final aspect of self-control training is to help the child establish a system of self-reinforcement. The self-reinforcement training has the child reward him or herself every time he or she accurately self-monitors, takes the perspective of others, problem solves and/or accomplishes a goal in his or her plan.

The self-monitoring phase is very important, because it enables the therapist to assess the problem behavior's baseline. The child is instructed to write down what was happening prior to the occurrence of the problem behavior (e.g., child fighting). This record enables the therapist to assess what stimuli occasion the problem behavior. It has been found that self-monitoring in itself tends to decrease the frequency of problem behavior because the child becomes more aware of that behavior.

Self-control training must also provide the child with a set of new skills and behaviors to carry out in those problem situations. It is not enough for children to be told how not to get into fights, the child must be taught these skills directly. The therapist does this by discussing with the child specific things to do in the problem situation and by giving him or her opportunities to practice these new skills. For example, with our aggressive child the therapist would discuss situations that cause anger and find what alternate behaviors he can perform instead of hitting. The first part of the self-control program might have him or her yell at the other child instead of hitting. Later, when the child is able to inhibit hitting behavior successfully, the therapist can work on having him walk away from the situations that cause anger, to talk more calmly with the other children, and to seek solutions other than aggression.

That is, effective alternative behaviors are taught. Throughout such training the child is also trained in self-reinforcement for success.

Self-control training programs have been developed for children who are aggressive, depressed, and/or anxious. Recently self-control programs have also been developed for children with ADHD (e.g., Hinshaw Erhardt, 1991). They maintained that the first part of self-control training with these children is to have them develop more internalized speech (self-talk). Everyone with self-control ability talks to him or herself, giving self-instructions, guidance, and reviewing information one might need in any particular situation. The ADHD children, however, are deficient in such self-talk. In Hinshaw and Erhardt's program, these children were instructed to monitor self-talk (i.e., at what times during the day they talked to themselves, and what they talked about). Once a baseline was established, the children were taught to evaluate the effectiveness of their self-talk and to develop new verbal strategies for problem situations. The therapists then taught the children to self-reinforce, using a token system, for effective self-talk.

Think of a 10-year-old boy who has problems paying attention to his teacher and staying seated in class. In a self-control approach this child would first monitor how many times and under what conditions he gets out of his chair during the day and when it is hard for him to pay attention. The boy would also be asked to write down what he says to himself in those situations. With this information, the therapist would discuss with the child the effective things he is saying to himself that help him pay attention. The child would then be shown how to reinforce himself with tokens when he uses this self-talk. The therapist would also develop other self-statements the child can use. For example, with this boy who cannot stay seated, the therapist might have him say, "I know I am fidgety because my legs are moving and I did not hear what the teacher just said. I can stay in my seat by crossing my legs and looking at my teacher's funny glasses." The child practices these self-statements in the therapy session and is encouraged to use them in school. He is also given a chart to record each time he uses the self-statement and stays in his seat. Each mark counts for a token that can be turned in for a prize.

SUMMARY

Behavior therapy with children encompasses a number of approaches based on cognitive and behavioral learning theory concepts, and these have been applied to virtually every type of child behavior problem. Each case includes careful functional analysis, a treatment plan, systematic application of methods aimed at specified goals, continuous monitoring, and follow-up evaluations. In any one case a number of different procedures can be used as therapy progesses.

REFERENCES

Bandura, A. (1977). *Social learning theory*. Englewood Cliffs, NJ: Prentice-Hall.

Gelfand, D. M., Jensen, W. R., & Drew, C. J. (1988). *Understanding child behavior disorders* (2nd. ed.). New York: Holt, Rinehart & Winston.

Graziano, A. M. (1974). *Child without tomorrow*. New York: Pergamon Press.

Graziano, A. M., & Bythell, D. L. (1983). Failures in child behavior therapy. In E. B. Foa & P. M. G. Emmelkamp (Eds.). *Failures in behavior therapy* (pp. 406–424). New York: Wiley.

Graziano, A. M., DeGiovanni, I. S., & Garcia, K. A. (1979). Behavioral treatment of children's fears: A review. *Psychological Bulletin, 86*, 804–830.

Graziano, A. M., & Mills, J. R. (1992). Treatment for abused children: When is a partial solution acceptable? *Child Abuse & Neglect, 16*, 217–228.

Hinshaw, S., & Erhardt, D. (1991). Attention Deficit Hyperactivity Disorder. In P. Kendall (Ed.), *Child and adolescent therapy: Cognitive behavioral techniques.* (pp. 98–130). New York: Guilford Press.

Hyman, I. (1990). Reading, writing, and the hickory stick. Lexington, MA: D. C Heath

Kaufmann, J. M. (1989). *Characteristics of behavior disorders of children and youth.* (4th ed.). Columbus, OH: Merrill.

Lewis, M., & Miller, S. M. (Eds.). (1990). *Handbook of developmental psychopathology.* New York: Plenum Press.

Lovaas, O., Berberich, J. P., Perloff, B. F., & Schaeffer, B. (1966). Acquisition of imitative speech by schizophrenic children. *Science, 151*, 705–707.

Masters, J., Burish, T., Hollon, S., & Rimm, D. (1987). *Behavior therapy: techniques and empirical findings* (3rd ed.). New York: Harcourt Brace Jovanovich.

Wenar, C. (1990). *Developmental psychopathology from infancy through adolescence.* New York: McGraw-Hill.

Wicks-Nelson, R., & Israel, A. C. (1991). *Behavior disorders of childhood* (2nd ed.). Englewood Cliffs, NJ: Prentice-Hall.

Wolpe, J. (1990). *The practice of behavior therapy* (4th ed.). New York: Pergamon Press.

Chapter 11

Pharmacological Treatment

Humberto Quintana
University of Pittsburgh Medical Center

Boris Birmaher
University of Pittsburgh Medical Center

A psychopharmacology for childhood and adolescent disorders did not exist before the 1930s. During the 1930s and 1940s, the emphasis was on the use of benzedrine sulfate and dilantin sodium with hyperactivity (Bender & Cottington, 1942), brain-damaged, and behavior-disordered children. With the introduction of the "tranquilizers" in the 1950s, there grew an increase in the number of studies on the use of drugs for childhood and adolescent disorders.

By contrast to the earlier decades, the decade of the 1960s was a period of great advances in childhood psychopharmacology. This period saw the use of antidepressant drugs, specifically the tricyclic compounds and the monamine oxidase (MAO) inhibitors, in depressive and disruptive disorders in childhood and adolescence. During this period, the major tranquilizers—thioxanthenes, butyrophenones, piperazines, and piperidine compound-thioridazine (Mellaril)—were used for the first time in children. Also, during this period, there were many studies on stimulant effects in children with hyperactivity and, beginning in 1965, reports on the use of antidepressants for the treatment of hyperactivity and depression in children (Lucas, Lockett, & Grimm, 1965).

Research in the 1970s was dominated by studies on the diagnosis and treatment of depression in childhood and on the indications for antidepressants, as well as the efficacy of tricyclic antidepressants (TCAs) in separation anxiety, affective disorders, anorexia nervosa, hyperactivity, and enuresis.

In the mid 1970s and during the 1980s, more sophisticated studies on the psychostimulants, methylphenidate (MPH) and dextro-amphetamine, were completed (Barkley, 1977; Connors & Werry, 1979; Gittleman-Klein, Klein, Katz, & Pollack,

1976). For example, Barkley's (1977) review of over 110 studies demonstrated an approximate 75% improvement rate when children with Attention-Deficit Hyperactivity Disorder are treated with MPH. It was research during this period that gave credence to the formulation, which is the current opinion, that psychostimulants only treat the attention span—behavioral impulsivity symptoms of this disorder and not the often found concurrent learning disability.

In the last decade, the side effects of the stimulants have been closely examined and, as a result, some of the contra-indications for the use of psychostimulants have been more clearly identified. Studies looking into height inhibition did not substantiate the early claims made in the 1970s. In fact, Mattes and Gittleman (1983) found that MPH dosage accounted for a very small effect in variance in final height. However, several studies have brought to our attention a correlation between stimulant medication and motor tics. Shapiro and Shapiro (1981) and Lowe, Cohen, Detlor, Kremenitzer, and Shaywitz (1982) presented evidence that stimulant medication may precipitate tics. Therefore, the presence of Tourette's Disorder or motor tics requires a reconsideration as to whether psychostimulants should be used or discontinued and a generally more cautious approach to psychopharmacological treatment with psychostimulants in general.

Significant contributions to the treatment of infantile autism with haloperidol (Haldol) were made by Campbell et al. (1982). Essentially, results indicate that haloperidol is superior to placebo in decreasing withdrawal and stereotypic movements in autistic children, and also, they reported that haloperidol and behavior therapy are more effective than either treatment alone. Another major use for haloperidol has been in Tourette's Syndrome (Seignot, 1961). Later, Shapiro and Shapiro (1981) reported that haloperidol decreased tic symptoms in upwards to 80% of Tourette's patients followed for 8 years.

During the 1980s, studies on the use of lithium and the anticonvulsant medications in childhood and adolescence were numerous. There was a special interest in looking at the use of these medications in affective disorders and aggressive disorders in childhood and adolescence.

In summary, in the 1970s and 1980s, there were a number of very significant developments that affected childhood and adolescent psychopharmacology: the establishment of more precise diagnostic criteria, such as *Diagnostic and Statistical Manual DSM–III–R*; (American Psychiatric Association, 1987) and Research Diagnostic Criteria (RDC; Spitzer, Endicott, & Robins, 1978); the development of a number of reliable assessment instruments; increased knowledge about pharmacokinetics; growing attention and concern about long-and short-term adverse medication effects; and an increase in the number of researchers in child and adolescent psychiatry (Wiener & Jaffe, 1985). Now in the 1990s, studies are underway looking at treatment outcome, exploring the use of different medications on established disorders, delineating genetic contributions to childhood and adolescent disorders, evaluating the comparative efficacy of various treatment approaches, and the use of new classes of medications (such as serotonin uptake inhibitors) for depression and disruptive behavior disorders. In addition, we are now seeing and will continue to see in the future an ever increasing integration of our knowledge in the neurosciences (neuroanatomy, neurobiology, neuro-imaging and neurotransmitter theories) with our future pharmacological approaches and interventions.

NEUROTRANSMITTERS IN PSYCHOPHARMACOLOGY

In order to understand and treat psychiatric disorders, it is becoming increasingly important to consider neurochemistry and pharmacology. For example, communication between neurons takes place by the release of specialized chemical substances called neurotransmitters. There is a large number of neurotransmitters that act on specialized sites of action, the receptor sites. The neurotransmitters regulate information handling, memory, mood, and behavior. It appears that functional and structural areas of the brain appear to be at least partially differentiated by their relative concentrations of neurotransmitters that are chemically distinct. Once the neurotransmitter has completed its function, it must be removed to stop its continued action. A failure to terminate the action of a neurotransmitter results in a prolongation, inhibition, or exaggeration of its action. Similarly, the release of an excessive amount of neurotransmitter or an excessive sensitivity to the neurotransmitter produces an excessive effect at the level of the cell. Either of these consequences may produce functional or clinical abnormalities. Similarly, deficiencies in production and release of neurotransmitters or a decrease in receptor sensitivity may likewise cause functional or clinical abnormalities. The clinical abnormalities may manifest themselves as disturbances in cognitive or thought processes, disturbances of mood, and disturbances of behavior. The following is a review of the commonly identified neurotransmitters (Coyle, 1987; Wiener & Jaffe, 1985):

Neurotransmitters

1. Gamma-aminobutyric acid (GABA): accounts for 25% to 40% of brain synapses. GABA inhibits the firing of some neurons and seems to act as the major inhibitory neurotransmitter.
2. Glycine, an amino acid, seems to function as an inhibitory transmitter in a number of spinal cord/brain stem synapses.
3. Glutamic Acid and Aspartic Acid, also amino acids, seem to function as excitatory neurotransmitters.
4. Opiate-like peptides, called enkephalins, bind to sites in the central nervous system and mediate pain perception.
5. Substance P, another polypeptide, seems to have a role as a transmitter mediating pain sensation.
6. Norepinephrine appears to have a role in affective behaviors, including euphoria/depression. Norepinephrine pathways to the cerebral cortex may be linked with the control of alertness.
7A. Dopamine/dopaminergic neurotransmitters: Dopamine is believed to have an influence on a number of areas. The deterioration of cell bodies in the substantia nigra and the axons that terminate in the caudate nucleus and putamen is well recognized as giving rise to the motor disorders and tremors seen in Parkinson's disease. The administration of a dopamine precursor, levodopa, helps restore the neurotransmitter depletion and bring some alleviation of symptoms.
7B. Dopamine also seems to have a role with emotional behavior, essentially, the antipsychotics function by directly blocking the dopamine receptors.

7C. Current studies indicate that there may be three or more species of dopamine-sensitive receptors. The DA-2 receptors may be most important in the action of neuroleptic drugs.

8A. Serotonergic neurotransmitters: Cell bodies of the serotonin containing neurons are localized in nuclei in the lower midbrain and upper pons (raphe nuclei). Destruction in animals of the raphe nuclei produces insomnia and agitation.

8B. Serotonin and norepinephrine have both been implicated in the etiology of affective disorders.

8C. Current studies are linking serotonin neurotransmitters with aggression and certain externalizing disorders (Coyle, 1987; Weiner, 1980).

Peptide Neurotransmitters in the Brain

Dysfunction of endogenous opiate peptides systems has been hypothesized in a number of psychiatric disorders, including affective illness, anxiety disorders, and anorexia. Given the lengthy list of other neuropeptides that are thought to serve as neurotransmitters, it may be anticipated that future research will uncover a considerable array of neuropsychiatric disorders associated with chemical pathology of the peptide neurotransmitter systems in the brain (Coyle, 1987).

ATTENTION-DEFICIT HYPERACTIVITY DISORDER

The psychostimulants are the major agents used in the psychopharmacological treatment of Attention-Deficit Hyperactivity Disorder (ADHD) as described in *DSM–III–R* and Attention-Deficit Hyperactivity Disorder as described in *DSM–IV*. This condition is characterized by inattentiveness, distractibility, hyperactivity, and intrusiveness or destructiveness due to impulsivity. In *DSM–IV*, it is characterized by at least six out of nine symptoms of inattention or by at least 4 out of 6 symptoms of Hyperactivity-Impulsivity. In addition, these symptoms must have their onset no later than 7 years of age and have persisted for at least 6 months in two or more situations (e.g., at school, home, and/or work). Children with this disorder often suffer from academic difficulties and underachievement and varying degrees of impairment in social learning and peer interactions. Therefore, this disorder causes clinically significant distress or impairment in social, academic, or occupational functioning.

Stimulants have been used for over 50 years, and they have been established to improve motor behavior, attention, distractibility, impulsiveness, and short-term memory in about 75% of affected children (Dulcan, 1990). Stimulant treatment of adults with ADHD has also shown similar improvements (Jacobvitz, 1990). Whereas there are many short-term controlled studies on the pharmacological treatment of ADHD with stimulants, there are no controlled studies of the long-term effects of stimulant treatments of ADHD on achievement, social relationships, and interpersonal relationships (Franz, 1980; Silvester, 1993).

Although the stimulants have been proven to be effective for ADHD, it is important to note before discussing this topic further that not all children may need to take medications. A careful psychiatric evaluation is done and the decision to use medication is dependent on the severity of symptoms, degree of disturbance in overall functioning—including academic and home functioning; the ability of the child, parents, and school to deal with problem behaviors; and last, the history of previous interventions or treatments. Most common contraindications to the use of the psychostimulants are the presence of a thought disorder or overt psychosis. The presence of tics, severe anxiety, or medical conditions—such as cardiovascular or compromised respiratory states—are considered to be relative contra-indications.

Methylphenidate (MPH; Ritalin) and dextroamphetamine (DAM; Dexedrine) are the most commonly used stimulants, followed by pemoline. It has been our clinical experience that a child may not respond to one but yet will respond to one of the other drugs. The use of two psychostimulants concurrently is not indicated and the use of a stimulant and another psychotropic is infrequent (Silvester, 1993).

The starting dose for MPH is 5 mg b.i.d., for Dexedrine 2.5 mg q.d. or b.i.d. (for under 6), and Dexedrine 5 mg q.d. or b.i.d. (for ages 6 and older). The maximum recommended dose of MPH is 60 mg and the maximum dose for Dexedrine is 30 mg. Many clinicians use MPH in the range of .3 mg/kg to .6 mg/kg. Routinely advancing MPH beyond .6 mg/kg/dose in the interest of further improving behavioral control may cause a decrease in cognitive performance (Jacobvitz, 1990). The other stimulant used but with less frequency is magnesium pemoline (Cylert). This longer acting stimulant, magnesium pemoline, is recommended for use at a dose of 18.75 mg or 37.5 mg and the maximum recommended dose is 112.5 mg/day. Most often the medication is increased slowly over 3 to 7 days (but only 1x/wk for pemoline) until a clinical therapeutic effect or adverse effect occurs. The dosage needs to be reevaluated as the child grows and matures (Gittleman-Klein & Mannuzza, 1988).

Methylphenidate is one of the psychostimulants that has a sustained release form. However, recent pharmacokinetics and clinical evidence suggest that the slow release form gives comparable results to the standard regimen (Birmaher, Greenhill, Cooper, Frieo, & Maminski, 1989; Fitzpatrick, Klorman, Brumaghim, & Borgstedt, 1992). Therefore, the timing of the dose has to do with the duration of action of the individual psychostimulant used and may routinely require two to three doses during the day.

Both methylphenidate and dextroamphetamine are absorbed easily when given orally, readily crosses the blood brain barrier, and reaches peak plasma levels in 1 to 2 hours. They have a half-life of 2 to 3 hours, and their overall duration of action is reported to be up to 6 hours (Wiener & Jaffe, 1985). Once again, like amphetamines, these compounds show large individual fluctuations in clearance (Green, 1992). MPH is metabolized in the liver where 80% of the dose is mainly de-esterified to ritalinic acid (Franz, 1980).

Magnesium pemoline (Cylert) functions in a manner similar to amphetamines and MPH, but it has a different structure and its sympathomimetic effects are minimal (Connors & Taylor, 1980). Pemoline attains its peak serum levels in children within 2 to 4 hours and its half-life is 12 hours. Thus, its half-life is longer than the amphetamines and MPH. Also, whereas clinical improvement with the amphetamines and MPH may be seen within 1 to 2 hours, in magnesium pemoline the clinical improvement may not be seen until 3 to 4 weeks (Friedman et al., 1981; Wiener & Jaffe, 1985).

Parents are often concerned about addiction or abuse of the stimulants. However, this is usually nonexistent. Despite the need sometimes for children to be on a stimulant for several years, the development of tolerance in children to stimulants is extremely rare. However, as mentioned before increase in growth may require dose readjustment (Gittleman-Klein, Abikoff, Mattes, & Klein, 1983; Roche, Lipman, Overall, & Hung, 1979).

One of the biggest problems encountered when treating children or adolescents with psychostimulants has to do with the decision of when to discontinue the medication. Generally, a failure of a child to respond to a psychostimulant after 2 weeks at the maximum dose of MPH or dextroamphetamine or after 5 weeks of treatment with pemoline is an indication to stop the medications. At this point, an antidepressant (desipramine, imipramine), clonidine, or in some cases for short periods a neuroleptic may be considered as an alternative treatment (Gittleman-Klein et al., 1976; Hunt, Capper, & O'Connell, 1990; Klein, 1991; Whitaker & Rao, 1992). Treatment with stimulants should include "drug holidays," during which the clinician reassesses the need for the medications and evaluates potential adverse effects. Because the long-term benefits derived from the use of these drugs has not been clearly demonstrated, a periodic reassessment with drug holidays on weekends, during holidays, and during the summer seems worthwhile.

The most frequently seen adverse effects of stimulants are anorexia and insomnia. Generally, modification of dosage administration to after meals diminishes the severity of the decreased appetite and usually giving the last dosage of the day before 5 p.m. eliminates the insomnia problem (Chan et al., 1983). However, sometimes these problems persist and result in the discontinuation of the particular psychostimulant. Other less often seen side effects are headaches, weight loss, and abdominal discomfort (Grob & Coyle, 1986). Usually these effects are transient, and with dose adjustment and taking of medications with meals, they are eliminated. Other reported but rare adverse effects are mood changes, dizziness, and toxic psychosis (Gualtieri, Quade, Hicks, Mayo, & Schroeder, 1984). Adverse effects are minimized when dosages are kept below the range of .5 mg/kg of dextroamphetamine or .6 mg/kg of MPH. The risk for psychostimulants lowering the seizure threshold has not been substantiated (Dulcan, 1990). Psychotic symptoms may be a side effect or a toxic effect. Methylphenidate may reduce the white blood cell count and magnesium pemoline may cause elevation in liver enzymes so the cellular blood count (CBC) and liver function test (LFT) should be monitored at least every 8 months (Green, 1992).

In terms of cognitive effects, it appears that high stimulant dosages may help with behavioral control. However, Sprague and Sleator (1977) reported that there is an optimal dose that produces the least attentional errors and higher doses interfere with cognitive function. Pelham and Sams (1992) believed that optimal dosing of an individual child with ADHD must be done carefully on an empirical basis, adjusting the dose level to correct for the child's most serious area of difficulty (see also Conners, Rothchild, Eisenberg, Schwartz, & Robinson, 1969). One of the greatest concerns regarding the use of the psychostimulants has been concerns regarding their suppression of height and weight. Recent research indicates that the effect of MPH dosage accounts for a very small variance in final height (Gittleman-Klein, Landa, Mattes, & Klein, 1988; Gittleman-Klein & Mannuzza, 1988; Roche et al., 1979). Nevertheless, despite this finding, we regularly take weight and height measurements and recommend that this should be performed as part of a standard medication follow-up visit.

Other Medications Used in ADHD

When there are contra-indications against the use of the stimulants, such as the presence of tics or reported unresponsiveness to the stimulants, the most commonly used second line agents are the antidepressants. The most carefully studied antidepressant for ADHD is desipramine. This medication has not been associated with delays in height, unlike the stimulants. The recommended dosage is above 3.5 mg/kg/day and the dosage needs to be monitored with periodic blood levels and ECGs (Biederman et al., 1989). Wilens and Biederman (1982) suggested that nortriptyline may be an effective alternative to desipramine in ADHD. Also, it has been recently reported that in patients with ADHD and a comorbid tic disorder, both nortriptyline and desipramine may improve both conditions (Spencer, Biederman, Kerman, Steingard, & Wilens, 1992).

The concurrent use of a psychostimulant and an antidepressant is not recommended or indicated because it may cause affective lability, aggression, and agitation. This iatrogenically induced condition may make it difficult to differentiate these states from the development or acute onset of other psychiatric disorders such as bipolar disorder, conduct disorder, or anxiety disorders. Also, the addition of a psychostimulant may raise the therapeutic level of an antidepressant and result in an antidepressant toxicity (Grob & Coyle, 1986).

Clonidine (Catapres) has been used in cases of hyperactivity when a stimulant is contraindicated or cannot be used. It is also used in children with tics, oppositional disorders, or when there is a hyperarousal as is seen in Post-traumatic Stress Disorder (Hunt et al., 1990). Clonidine does not act on the same site as the stimulants and is usually not as effective in improving inattention or managing distractibility. Nevertheless, it may yield general or global improvement especially in children with comorbid ADHD and tics (Bruun, 1988; Gadow, Nolan, & Sverd, 1992), whereas in children with ADHD alone it does not seem to be as effective. Clonidine is given in two to three doses during the day in the range .15 to 3 mg/day. This medication is usually started at bedtime and increased gradually every 3 days by .5 mg/kg doses. Although mild hypotension, orthostatic hypotension, and lowered pulse have been reported, they are usually not clinically significant when the patients are monitored closely and regularly. When stopping the medicine, a gradual slow decrease is required, and rapid cessation is not recommended. This is mostly because serious rebound hypertension has been reported upon abruptly discontinuing the medication (Hunt et al., 1990). In children, this appears to be less common.

Biological Basis of ADHD—Stimulants and Dopamine

In terms of their central action, stimulants excite the respiratory center in the medulla but do not affect respiratory rate. They generally stimulate the reticular activating system (RAS), thereby enhancing attention and task performance (Barkley, 1977; Wiener & Jaffe, 1985). The psychostimulants have some peripheral effects that include mild elevations in blood pressure and heart rate, but generally these effects are either not clinically significant or their clinical significance is not clear (Green, 1992).

The pharmacological properties of the stimulants relate to their central as well as to their peripheral action. In general, these drugs can alter biogenic amine metabolism and influence the release, uptake, and turnover of dopamine, norepinephrine, and serotonin in the central nervous system. Therefore, a prevailing mechanism of psychostimulants is the inhibition of the presynaptic uptake of dopamine. Behavioral stimulants also strongly promote the synaptic release of dopamine. Amphetamine psychostimulants are potent releasers of dopamine from the reserpine-insensitive cytoplasmic pool of dopamine that is dependent upon replenishment by newly formed amine. In contrast, the nonamphetamine class of stimulants, such as methylphenidate, cocaine, and nomifensine, can be distinguished from amphetamine in that these latter stimulants promote release of dopamine from the granular storage pool of vesicular dopamine that is reserpine-sensitive. Therefore, stimulants that enhance central dopaminergic neurotransmission, such as d-amphetamine and methylphenidate, reduce motor activity and increase attention span in these children (Hauger, Angel, Janowsky, Berger, & Hulihan-Giblin, 1990).

Biological Basis of ADHD — Neuroleptics and Dopamine

Neuroleptics that block dopamine receptors can also reduce hyperactivity, although their effects on cognitive functions may be less salutary (Werry & Aman, 1975). Shaywitz, Klopper, Yager, and Garden (1976) demonstrated that neonatal destruction of the dopaminergic neurons results in a marked enhancement of the normally increased motor activity of prepubescent rat pups and that this hyperactivity can be reduced by administration stimulants.

CONDUCT DISORDERS

According to *DSM–IV* criteria, Conduct Disorder is a repetitive and persistent pattern of behavior in which either the basic rights of others or major age-appropriate societal norms or rules are violated, lasting at least 6 months, during which at least 3 of an enumerated 15 behaviors are present. *DSM–IV* replaces the previous designations of solitary aggressive and group types with specific types based on the age of onset: childhood onset type (onset of at least one conduct problem prior to age 10) and adolescent onset type (no conduct problems prior to age 10). Specific descriptors of severity ranging from mild to moderate are also included.

The literature on the pharmacotherapy Conduct Disorders has to be considered with because aggressive and nonaggressive conduct disorders appear in children and adolescents who suffer from different psychiatric and neurological disorders. Aggressive behavior can be associated with depressive disorders, Attention Deficit Hyperactivity Disorder, mental retardation, or with nonspecific organic brain dysfunction. Therefore, Conduct Disorders, which are often the most common childhood psychiatric presentation to mental health centers and outpatient psychiatry, are frequently comorbid with other disorders, especially with ADHD and learning or developmental disorders. For example, in a report by Puig-Antich (1982), 16 children diagnosed as having both Major Depression and Conduct Disorder were treated with imipramine. In the 13 cases that had a full response to imipramine, Conduct Disorder disappeared in 11 after the antidepressant treatment.

Although Conduct Disorder and ADHD alone are more common in males than in females, generally females have a greater risk (40:1) for comorbid Conduct Disorder (Szatmari, Boyle, & Offord, 1989). The prognosis is poor for children with conduct disorders, with later diagnosis manifesting as psychosis, substance abuse disorders, depression, sucidality with and without depression, and sociopathy (Offord et al., 1992; Robins, 1966). Therefore, in providing an appropriate treatment for Conduct Disorder, a comprehensive psychiatric evaluation that recognizes comorbid conditions, such as ADHD, depressive disorders, and developmental disorders that may aggravate aggressive behavior, is often necessary.

The medications most often used in the pharmacological treatment of childhood aggression include the neuroleptics (which have fallen out of favor in recent years), lithium, carbamazepine (Tegretol), propranolol (Inderal), and trazadone (Desyrel) (Campbell, Cohen, & Small, 1982; Kuperman & Stewart, 1987; Popper, 1987; Trimble, 1990; Whitaker & Rao, 1992).

Whereas the neuroleptics, most commonly chlorpromazine and haloperidol, have been approved and used for nonspecific behavioral control in children and adolescents (Whitaker & Rao, 1992), our current knowledge regarding their multiple adverse effects and long-term potential dangerousness currently limits their use in childhood and adolescence (Gualtieri et al., 1984). An additional problem with the neuroleptics is their interference with cognitive functioning in children (Campbell, 1985; Campbell et al., 1982).

Lithium has been used in childhood aggressive disorders and has been shown to interfere less with learning than the nonsedating high potency neuroleptics — such as haloperidol (Haldol) (Campbell & Deutsch, 1985; Campbell, Perry, & Green, 1984; Campbell, Schulman, & Rapoport, 1978). Lithium treatment is started in children at 150 mg p.o. twice a day and in older children at 300 mg twice a day. This dose is gradually titrated upward with careful monitoring of lithium levels. The blood lithium level is kept in the range of .6 to 1.2 and regular follow-up involves examining for signs of toxicity such as dizziness, stomachaches, diarrhea, nausea or vomiting, increased tremors, and ataxia (Arana & Hyman, 1991; Weller, & Fristad, 1986).

An anticonvulsant, carbamazepine, has also been used in the management of aggression and of behavioral dyscontrol. Carbamazepine (Tegretol) has gained an increase in use because it has no risk for tardive dyskinesia, and the risk for development of blood dyscrasias is now considered to be less than the risk of developing tardive dyskinesia with the neuroleptics. Carbamazepine dose ranges may vary in order to maintain blood levels in the range of 8 to 12 ug/ml.

Propranolol (Inderal), a beta blocker, has been found to be helpful in aggressive children with or without mental retardation (Kuperman & Stewart, 1987; Williams, Mehl, Yudofsky, Adams, & Roseman, 1982). Also, the beta blockers have been used in the treatment of rage attacks in children with brain damage (Arnold & Aman, 1991).

Recent attention is turning to agents that act on the serotonergic system. New agents, recently approved by the Federal Drug Administration (FDA), which are serotonin uptake inhibitors such as fluoxetine and sertraline, will be studied in children and adolescents in the near future. Trazadone has been studied in 22 prepubertal children with indications that it may be potentially useful in disruptive disorders (Zubieta & Alessi, 1992). The development of priapism in adult males is a significant adverse effect that may limit this agent's usefulness (Sher, Krieger, & Juergens, 1983).

MOOD DISORDERS

Major Depression and Dysthymia

Children with Major Depression and Dysthymic Disorder may not be brought to treatment until they are seriously impaired. Often in children and adolescents the affective disorders may present as academic problems, disruptive behaviors, or sleep or appetite disturbances (Silvester, 1993).

In *DSM-IV*, the Mood Disorder section has undergone some changes, however, the diagnostic criteria remain applicable to adults and to children/adolescents. *DSM-IV* requires that a major depressive episode have at least one of these symptoms — depressed mood or loss of interest or pleasure. In addition, 5 of 9 symptoms ennumerated under category A need to be present during the same 2-week period, and their occurrence must represent a change from previous functioning. As in *DSM-III-R*, in *DSM-IV* the symptoms for the diagnosis of a mood disorder must cause clinically significant distress or impairment in social, occupational, or other important areas of functioning. New inclusions in *DSM-IV* are the category of Mood Disorder Due to a General Medical Condition and Substance-Induced Mood Disorder. Another addition in *DSM-IV* is the inclusion of a section on cross-sectional symptom features, course specifiers, and longitudinal course specifiers for Major Depressive and Bipolar I Disorders.

The lack of good psychopharmacological studies does not allow yet for definite claims that tricyclic medication is clinically effective in child and adolescent depression (Bernstein, 1984). In other words, the antidepressant treatment of major depression in children has not been supported by double-blind placebo controlled studies (Ambrosini, Bianche, Rabinovich, & Elia, 1993). Also, at this time, in neither open-label or randomized controlled clinical trials is there any compelling evidence of the efficacy of antidepressant drugs in the treatment of major depression in adolescents (Ryan, 1990). However, the main question that remains unanswered is the long-term stability of antidepressant response to placebo. Therefore, in future studies the question of differential patterns and types of drug–placebo response in depressed youngsters needs to be addressed (Wiener & Jaffe, 1985). For example, one suggestion is that the monitoring of plasma levels and the dexamethasone suppression test be used in children in order to provide a better definition and determination of the depressed children who may respond to antidepressants (Ryan, 1990).

The recommended tricyclic antidepressants TCA; (imipramine, desipramine, and amitriptyline) have a starting dose of 1.5 mg/kg/day with increases of 1 to 1.5 mg/kg/day every 3 days (Weller & Weller, 1990). Increasing the amount of antidepressant by 25 mg/day is usually a satisfactory way of maximizing the patient's comfort, reducing the toxicity, and increasing compliance (Bartels, Varley, Mitchell, & Stamm, 1991; Wiener & Jaffe, 1985). Commonly, two to three divided doses are recommended because of the tendency for children to metabolize these agents rapidly. There is a need to monitor blood levels regularly, and for imipramine and amitriptyline, these therapeutic levels are above 150 mg/ml (Ryan, 1990).

Antidepressants have been used in a number of conditions other than depression, including hyperactivity, school phobia, enuresis, Conduct Disorder with Depression, anorexia and bulimia, panic disorder, and obsessive compulsive disorder (Carlson, 1984; Carlson & Cantwell, 1979).

Most commonly, imipramine (Tofranil) has been used to treat enuresis effectively (Bindelglass, Dec, & Enos, 1968; Shaffer, 1984). Generally a lower dose is necessary than the dose required in the treatment of depressive disorders; specifically, 25 mg to 50 mg at bedtime is usually sufficient. However, the results are palliative because the problem returns when treatment is stopped.

The association between anorexia nervosa and bulimia with affective disorder has prompted several studies that have attempted to treat these disorders with antidepressant medication. Although there were some initial expectations and suggestions that the antidepressants might be beneficial, other studies do not demonstrate appreciable benefits from antidepressants treatment of anorexia nervosa (Biederman et al., 1982; Lacey & Crisp, 1980).

There are several antidepressants in addition to imipramine in current usage. These include nortriptyline (Pamelor), amitriptyline (Elavil, Endep), desipramine (Norpramine), clomipramine (Anafranil), and fluoxetine (Prozac), which is chemically unrelated to the tricyclics, being a tetracyclic serotonin uptake inhibitor. In addition, another two newly released serotonin uptake inhibitors used as antidepressants but not approved for use with children are Zoloft and Paxil.

Because the tricyclic, imipramine, has been the most widely used clinically in children and adolescents, it serves as the prototype for our discussion on the effects of withdrawal of tricyclic medications, tricyclic interactions with other drugs, and for our discussion of the adverse effects of tricyclics.

When withdrawn from a tricyclic, some children may experience a flu-like withdrawal syndrome, with gastrointestinal symptoms including nausea, abdominal discomfort, pain, vomiting, headache, and fatigue. These symptoms usually result from cholinergic rebound and may be considered a cholinergic overdrive phenomenon. Ryan (1990) reported that because of their rapid metabolism of the tricyclics, some prepubertal children and younger adolescents may experience daily withdrawal effects if the receive their entire daily tricyclic medication in one dose. Therefore, for this reason, it may be necessary to divide the medication into two or three doses. Generally, when maintenance medication is discontinued, tapering the medication down over 10 days to 2 weeks rather than abruptly withdrawing the medication will avoid the development of a clinically significant withdrawal syndrome. In some patients with poor compliance, the resulting withdrawal symptoms may be confused with adverse effects of medication, inadequate treatment, or worsening of the underlying condition.

The most common contra-indications for the tricyclic antidepressants include known hypersensitivity to tricyclic antidepressants (which is an absolute contra-indication), cardiac abnormalities, lowering of seizure threshold (which means they must be used cautiously in individuals with seizure disorders), potential exacerbation of psychotic symptoms in schizophrenic patients, and the recommended contra-indication of using tricyclics concomitantly with a monamine oxidase inhibitor (MAOI). With respect to this last contra-indication, it is recommended that at least a 14-day period elapse after discontinuing a MAOI before a tricyclic antidepressant is started (Silvester, 1993; Wiener & Jaffe, 1985).

In addition to the interaction of tricyclic antidepressants with the monamine oxidase inhibitors (MAOIs), which can produce a hyperpyretic crisis or severe convulsive seizures, other interactions may also occur. For example, anticholinergic effects of the tricyclic antidepressants may be additive with those of the antipsychotic (neuroleptic) medications resulting in central nervous system anticholinergic crisis. Also, the central nervous system (CNS) depressive effects of tricyclic antidepressants may be additive with those of alcohol, benzodiazepines, barbiturates, and antipsychotics. In addition to their effects on diminishing or decreasing the efficacy of antihypertensive agents, many other interactions with various drugs have also been reported (Green, 1992).

Adverse Effects of Tricyclic Antidepressants

The cardiovascular side effects that are caused by the tricyclic antidepressants are of concern to all age groups, but they are especially relevant in children and younger adolescents. This is because children may be particularly vulnerable due to the relative efficiency with which they convert tricyclic antidepressants to potentially cardiotoxic 2-OH metabolites and especially because children are more sensitive to cardiotoxic effects than are adolescents or adults (Biederman et al., 1989). In terms of cardiac effects the greatest concern comes from the TCA's effects on cardiac conduction as seen on the ECG by increases in P–R and Q–R intervals, cardiac arrhythmias, tachycardia, and heart block (Bartels et al., 1991).

The tricyclic antidepressants may also cause some additional untoward effects that can include central nervous system effects such as drowsiness, incoordination, seizures, EEG changes, anxiety, insomnia and nightmares, and anticholinergic effects such as dry mouth, blurred vision, constipation, and blood dyscrasias (Green, 1992).

Monamine Oxidase Inhibitors

Monamine oxidase inhibitors (MAOIs) are primarily used in treating adults with depressive disorder that have usually not been responsive to other classes of antide-pressants. MAOIs that have been used in children include clorgyline (a selective monamine oxidase-A [MAO-A] inhibitor), tranylcypromine sulfate (Parnate, a mixed MAO-A and MAO-B inhibitor), and phenelzine sulfate (Nardil, a selective central MAO-B inhibitor). The various dietary restrictions, potentially very serious drug interactions, and untoward effects of the MAOIs, limit their use in children and adolescents. Also, only a few research reports are available for this age group using these agents. Ryan et al., (1988) concluded that the MAOIs (tranylcypromine and phenelzine) appeared useful in treating some adolescents with major depression that had not responded to tricyclic antidepressants. However, the authors concluded that only very reliable adolescents are suitable for treatment with MAOIs.

MAOIs may cause adverse effects including orthostatic hypotension, dizziness, headache, sleep disturbances, sedation, fatigue, hyperreflexia, and gastrointestinal disturbance. Interactions with tyramine and concomitant use of a tricyclic antidepres-sant can cause a hypertensive crisis or severe seizures (Arana & Hyman, 1991; Green, 1992).

In cases of childhood depression that are resistant to tricyclic treatment, lithium has been added with the result that it has augmented the antidepressant response (Ryan, Meyer, Dachille, Mazzi, & Puig-Antich, 1988).

The recently FDA approved agents, fluoxetine and sertraline, which are serotonin uptake inhibitors, show promise but have not yet been adequately studied in children. There are indications that these agents have fewer anticholinergic or cardiotoxic effects (Riddle et al., 1991). Associated side effects seen with these agents include gastroin-testinal upset and hypomanic symptoms including irritability, increased psychomotor activity, silliness, and insomnia. Despite their potential, their use in children awaits additional information from adult treatments and controlled studies.

Biological Basis of Affective Disorders — Norepinephrine and Serotonin

The noradrenergic neuronal system appears to mediate arousal and anxiety, two primitive defenses needed for survival. The noradrenergic system has also been implicated in the pathophysiology of mood disorders and the action of antidepressant drugs. As discussed in this chapter, the last decade has witnessed mounting evidence of the occurrence of major depressive disorders in adolescents and in prepubertal children (Kovacs et al., 1984). Although not yet fully confirmed, it is believed that these mood disorders may respond to antidepressant treatment in a manner similar to that in adults. The vulnerability to severe mood disorders in infancy and early childhood may be related to the early development of the noradrenergic system.

The serotonergic system has been implicated as having a potential role in mood disorder. The mechanism of action of the new serotonin uptake inhibitors, Prozac, Zoloft and Paxil, is based on the ability of these agents to increase serotonin level in specific areas of the brain.

Bipolar Disorder

Bipolar Disorder in prepubertal children is rare. The more common presentation is of a prepubertal onset of a major depression that in early adolescence, presents as a manic episode (Carlson, 1984). Occasionally, treatment with stimulants or antidepressants exacerbates or uncovers the underlying condition, and the result is a classical manic episode (Silvester, Burke, McCauley, & Clark, 1984).

A change seen in *DSM-IV* is that Bipolar Disorder now appear as a separate category in the Mood Disorder section. Included in this Bipolar Disorder category are manic episode, hypomanic episode, Bipolar I Disorder (Single manic episode or most recent episode hypomanic, or manic), Bipolar I Disorder (mixed type), Bipolar II Disorder (recurrent major depressive episodes with hypomania), Bipolar Disorder not otherwise specified, and cyclothymic disorder.

The psychopharmacological treatment for children with Bipolar Disorder is lithium. The recommended dosages for children under 6 years of age is 300 to 600 mg/day and in 6 to 12 year olds, 30 mg/kg/day in two to four divided doses. The therapeutic lithium level range is .6 to 1.2 Meq/L (Silvester, 1993; Weller, Weller, & Fristad, 1986). It is extremely important to closely monitor lithium levels at the initiation of treatment and throughout the course of treatment. It has been reported that children clear lithium rapidly and that they may sometimes require higher doses than adults. Nevertheless, caution must be taken when lithium treatment is implemented. Lithium side effects include sedation, tremors, polydypsia, and polyuria (Campbell et al., 1984). In addition, in young pubertal children, there may be a worsening of acne that is extremely discomforting to the patient and creates problems with compliance. Generally a referral to a dermatologist and reassurance by the clinician is effective in dealing with this often disturbing problem. Although lithium may induce hypothyroidism, a review of the studies of children treated with lithium over a 10-year period indicates that it seems better to provide thyroid replacement rather than to stop lithium treatment (Strober, Morrell, Lampert, & Burroughs, 1990).

In cases of childhood mania, a neuroleptic may be useful in the management of the acute agitation. Of course, in these cases all the necessary precautions and monitoring is necessary.

Another agent, carbamazepine (Tegretol), which has been used in seizure disorders, is now used in the treatment of childhood Bipolar Disorder. The use of carbamazepine has increased in children because the incidence of blood dyscrasias (which it can cause) has been reported to be less than neuroleptic-induced effects (e.g., tardive dyskinesia, Aman, 1987; Arana & Hyman, 1991). It must be used cautiously, however, because it has been reported to cause agitation and manic symptoms (Pleak,

Birmaher, Gavrilescu, Abichandani, & Williams, 1988). The range of therapeutic blood level is 4 to 12 ug/ml, and this usually requires 400 to 800 mg/day. It is recommended that an amount of 1 g/day not be exceeded. Usually, the normal range is 10 to 50 mg/kg/day (Trimble, 1990).

Contraindications for carbamazepine include hypersensitivity to tricyclic antidepressants, ingestion of MAOIs within 14 days, and previous history of bone marrow suppression (Green, 1992). Because carbamazepine can cause aplastic anemia, monitoring of CBC, including platelet count and baseline LFT, weekly for a month and then monthly for 4 months, then every 3 months is recommended. Observations for signs of viral syndrome during the course of this treatment is important because aplastic anemia symptoms may mimic this type of condition (Silvester, 1993; Trimble, 1990).

ANXIETY DISORDERS

Anxiety ranges from a mild emotional response of everyday life, to moderately intense states that may be associated with normal developmental stages, to prominent and severe symptoms of psychiatric disorders (Adams, 1979; Coffey, 1990). Unfortunately, there are a few methodologically sound studies in childhood and adolescence that provide significant information on pharmacological treatments for anxiety disorder in childhood. For example, there are no controlled studies of the medication treatments of children with the diagnosis of avoidant or overanxious disorders. Only separation anxiety disorder (a variation of school phobia) has been studied and has provided an effective pharmacological treatment.

In the new *DSM-IV*, only separation anxiety remains grouped in the section on disorders of infancy, childhood, and adolescence. Overanxious disorder of childhood is now included under generalized anxiety disorder. Also included in the anxiety disorder section are specific phobias (social phobia, obsessive compulsive disorder, and Post Traumatic Stress Disorder) thereby indicating that other than time of onset there is no difference in the childhood and adult forms of these disorders.

The pharmacological treatment of anxiety disorders in childhood and adolescence has consisted of tricyclic antidepressants (especially imipramine), benzodiazepines, antihistamines, beta-adrenergic blockers, or clonidine (Bernstein, 1984; Bernstein, Garfinkel, & Borchart, 1991; Coffey, 1990). However, as mentioned previously, there are no double-blind studies of the treatment of childhood anxiety disorders that use medication alone (Klein & Last, 1989).

Gittleman-Klein and Klein (1971) replicated the efficacy of imipramine hydrochloride (Tofranil) at doses of 100–200 mg/day in the treatment of school phobia in children. In their study, children who were unresponsive to initial attempts to return to school were put into a study (double-blind placebo control) that combined drug and placebo with family and individual psychotherapy treatment approaches. Their results showed that the active drug group (imipramine) returned to school significantly sooner than the placebo group. It is important to clarify that not all cases of school phobia have separation anxiety, and similarly not all cases of separation anxiety have school phobia. In some cases, school phobia is considered as an expression of the most severe form of separation anxiety (Bernstein et al., 1991). A recent study that attempted to replicate the use of imipramine in separation anxiety failed; subjects in this group were hypothesized to be less impaired with less school refusal than in the original classic report (Klein, Koplewicz, & Kanner, 1992). Nevertheless, a cognitive–behavioral approach combined with imipramine (or other tricyclic antidepressant) may be useful in moderately severe separation anxiety disorder when school refusal is present (Silvester, 1993).

Alprazolam (Xanax) has been reported as helpful in treating anticipatory and acute anxiety in some children whose separation anxiety does not respond to therapy (Klein & Last, 1989; Pfefferbaum et al., 1987). Alprazolam has been found to be safe in children at a dose.25 to 2 mg/day; usually the dosage is gradually increased every 3 to 4 days by.25 to a maximum of 4 mg/day that is given in two to three divided doses (Bernstein, 1984; Silvester, 1993). Therefore, the benzodiazepines are the second group of drugs used to treat anxiety in children and adolescents (Coffey, 1990). Members of this group are diazepam (Valium), chlordiazepoxide (Librium), oxazepam (Serax), and more recent compounds such as lorazepam (Ativan), clorazepate (Tranxene), and alprazolam (Xanax). The benzodiazepines are rapidly dispersed to brain tissue because they are bound highly to plasma proteins and highly lipid-soluble (Coffey, 1990, Klein & Last, 1989).

Diazepam (Valium) is often used in pediatrics, especially because it is metabolized rapidly in children (Riddle et al., 1991). The pediatric dose is usually 1 to 10 mg/day in divided doses, two to four per day (Coffey, 1990), and in prepubertal children the recommended maximum is 15 mg/day (Silvester, 1993). Alprazolam, another benzo-diazepine that is long acting has been used in panic attacks in children in doses.5 to 3 mg/day in divided doses. However, panic attacks in children are uncommon. Side effects of the benzodiazepines include drowsiness, dizziness, disinhibition, incoordi-nation, and varying degrees of sedation. Also, psychological and physical dependence may develop, and seizures have been reported upon abrupt withdrawal. More rare side effects are ataxia, constipation, and syncopy (Coffey, 1990; Green, 1992). Therefore, when planning treatment with these agents, the potential side effects and the benefits versus risk involved need to be carefully considered.

The antihistamines are used based on anecdotal reports for episodes of mild anxiety. The reports available on their use in childhood and adolescence are generally inconclusive. The benzodiazepines are likewise not well studied, and their established uses in children and adolescents need to be more intensely investigated. However, because recent evidence makes the use of neuroleptics increasingly more potentially detrimental, the use of more benign alternatives seems to be imperative (Whitaker & Rao, 1992; Wiener & Jaffe, 1985).

Obsessive-compulsive disorder (OCD) has been identified in children as young as age 3. It is reported that the onset is between 7 and 9 years of age. Clomipramine hydrochloride (Anafranil) is a tricyclic antidepressant that has shown significant improvement to resolution of the symptoms of obsessive-compulsive disorder and is now considered an established treatment for this disorder (DeVeaugh-Giess et al., 1992; Leonard et al., 1989). Rapoport, Elkins, and Mikkelsen (1980) reported that clomipramine is more effective than placebo in treating obsessive-compulsive disorder in children. It was found that, as for adults, 50% of drug-treated children improve. The maximum daily dosage as reported in the multicenter study of 31 children over 10 years old was 200 mg or 3 mg/kg, whichever amount is less (DeVeaugh-Giess et al., 1992). Side effects such as palpitations and hepatic enzyme elevation may cause the withdrawal of this medication. The recommended precautions that include a physical examination, baseline red and white blood count, liver function tests (LFT), and electrocardiogram (EKG) as well as periodic clomipramine blood levels is indicated.

Although the antianxiety agents have been and can be used to treat the anxiety associated with obsessive-compulsive disorder, there is no empirical evidence that these agents relieve the symptoms of obsessive-compulsive disorder.

Fluoxetine (Prozac), a serotonin uptake inhibitor, may soon become an alternative treatment for OCD in children, however, more studies are needed to determine the safety and efficacy of this agent (Riddle et al., 1991).

Biological Basis of Anxiety Disorders — Antianxiety Agents and GABA

The central nervous system effects of the benzodiazepines are sedation and disinhibition, slowing of psychomotor function, and muscle relaxation occurring largely on a central basis. Tyrer (1982) emphasized the selective antianxiety effects in the limbic system. Benzodiazepine receptors were discovered in the central nervous system in 1976, and benzodiazepine specifically binds to a special recognition site on the Gabaminergic (GABA) receptor that itself is functionally linked to the benzodiazepine receptor (Wiener & Jaffe, 1985). In addition, there are data showing that the benzodiazepine receptor is involved in the mediation and modulation of aggressive behavior (Hauger et al., 1990). In essence, the major pharmacological actions of the benzodiazepines agonists, inverse agonists, and antagonist can be explained by their ability to modulate GABA-mediated chloride ion flux within the central nervous system (CNS, Hauger et al., 1990).

CHILDHOOD SCHIZOPHRENIA

Schizophrenia is a very rare condition in children and usually does not manifest before age 8 (McClellan & Werry, 1992; McClellan, Werry & Ham, 1992). The diagnostic evaluation and treatment of such children should follow the same principles as those of adult schizophrenia. In fact, according to *DSM-III-R*, in order for children to be diagnosed with this condition, they must meet the criteria for this condition that is the same for children as for adults (American Psychiatric Association, 1987). *DSM-IV* continues to use the term Schizophrenia to describe the occurrence of this disorder in adults and/or children, however it now further identifies the disorders by the ages of onset as follows: very early onset schizophrenia (VEOS) and early onset schizophrenia (EOS). The diagnosis still requires the presence of two of five criteria including delusions, hallucinations, disorganized speech (e.g., frequent derailment or incoherences), grossly disorganized or catatonic behavior, or negative symptoms (e.g., affective flattening; American Psychiatric Association, 1993). It is extremely important to understand that we now know that hallucinations may occur in a number of nonpsychotic conditions in children (Teicher & Glod, 1990). Therefore, an extensive evaluation is essential whenever one is assessing early onset psychosis (McClellan et al., 1992).

Despite the fact that there are no double-blind controlled studies of any pharmacological treatment for childhood schizophrenia, the neuroleptics have had extensive use in child psychiatry. The most commonly used neuroleptics have been chlorpromazine (Thorazine) and thioridazine (Mellaril). Although in children the development of dystonic reactions is less, they usually experience more of the sedation, that is an anticholinergic side effect. One of the major concerns that has been raised with respect to the use of neuroleptics in children is the potential for these agents to interfere with cognitive processes and academic functioning (Klein, 1991). With regard to this interference of neuroleptics with learning, it has been reported that haloperidol (Haldol) and thiothixene (Navane), which are high potency neuroleptics, interfere less with learning (Campbell, 1985, Campbell et al., 1982). These two neuroleptics also have less anticholinergic activity, and it has been reported that thiothixene may cause less akathisia than haloperidol (Teicher & Glod, 1990). The increased knowledge and awareness regarding the incidence and prevalence of withdrawal dyskinesia and tardive dyskinesia in children and adolescents treated with neuroleptics has made clinicians increasingly cautious and vigilant when they use these medications (Whitaker & Rao, 1992).

Haloperidol is used at a dose range of .01 to .05 mg/kg/day in two divided doses; it can be increased gradually every 3 to 4 days by .25 to .5 mg (Campbell, 1985; Silvester, 1993). Generally, the dose can be maintained at low levels because children are usually more sensitive to neuroleptic effects. The standard practices of obtaining a red and white blood cell count, liver functions, and an electrocardiogram are also recommended prior to starting this medication. For schizophrenia, the particular neuroleptic should be used for approximately 4 weeks to adequately assess effectiveness. Generally the use of a single neuroleptic has been preferred, especially because no additive or synergistic effects have been reported when two neuroleptics are used. In the treatment of disorders in children and especially when treating a psychotic disorder, an adequate treatment period should take place before proceeding to increasing the dosage or using a combination of medications. The long-term use of neuroleptics is not recommended, and, in fact, after 6 months in most cases, the medication can be discontinued and the need for further medication reassessed (Campbell, 1985; Campbell, Adams, Perry, Spencer, & Overall, 1988).

Therefore, in summary, the current psychopharmacological practice is to minimize the use of neuroleptics, to minimize the period of time during which they are used when indicated, and also to seriously consider using alternative medications whenever possible. These guidelines are aimed at avoiding the multiple risks and dangers associated with adverse effects such as tardive dyskinesia and neuroleptic malignant syndrome (Addonizio, 1991).

Biological Clues to the Nature of Psychosis (Schizophrenia, Tourette's Disorder) — Neuroleptics and Dopamine

The gradual development of striatal-limbic dopaminergic pathways may account for the age-related emergence of symptoms of Tourette's disorder and schizophrenia. Tourette's disorder symptoms include hyperactivity, motor tics, and vocal tics, and it typically emerges between ages 5 and 12. The symptoms of the disorder are exacerbated by stimulants that enhance dopaminergic neurotransmission and are attenuated by neuroleptics that block dopamine receptors; therefore, the emergence of symptoms may result from the altered development of dopaminergic neurotransmission. In light of the evidence of decreased levels of the dopamine metabolite homovanillic acid in the cerebrospinal fluid of Tourette's patients, there is reason to believe that the syndrome involves an increased postsynaptic response to dopamine, possibly due to a supersensitivity of the dopamine receptors (Singer, Butler, Tune, Siefert, & Coyle, 1982).

Schizophrenia with onset in childhood represents merely an earlier appearance of the disorder, which typically has its onset in mid to late adolescence. The criteria for schizophrenia include "positive" symptoms, such as hallucinations, delusions, and thought disorder that are most responsive to antidopaminergic neuroleptic medications (Crow, 1980). Antipsychotic potencies of neuroleptic agents are correlated with their in vitro blockade of D2 dopamine receptors (Creese, Burt, & Snyder, 1976). Positron emission tomography (PET) reveals elevated D2 dopamine receptor density in the caudate nuclei of nonmedicated schizophrenics in vivo.

DEVELOPMENTAL DISORDERS

DSM-IV Pervasive Developmental Disorders (PDD) section retains the three major descriptive categories of Infantile Autism — qualitative impairment in social interaction, qualitative impairments in communication, and restricted repetitive and stereotypic patterns of behavior, interest, and activities — but slightly modifies and generalizes the item descriptions for each. However, now included under the Pervasive Developmental Disorders is Rett's Disorder, which is described as having the following characteristics: (a) a deceleration of head growth, (b) loss of previously acquired purposeful hand movements with the development of stereotyped hand movements, (c) loss of social engagement early in course, (d) appearance of poorly coordinated gait or trunk movements, and (e) marked delay and impairment of expressive and receptive language with severe psychomotor retardation. Also included in the PDD section is the diagnosis of Childhood Disintegrative Disorder and Asperger's Disorder. Childhood Disintegrative Disorder is characterized by apparently normal development for the first 2 years of life as manifested by the presence of age-appropriate verbal and nonverbal communication, social relationships, play, and adaptive behavior. However, there is a clinically significant loss of previously acquired skill in at least two of the following areas: expressive or receptive language, social skills or adaptive behavior, bowel or bladder control, play, and motor skills. These deficits must also be associated with at least two qualitative impairments in social interactions and at least one qualitative impairment in communication. Asperger's Disorder is a disorder in which patients lack any clinically significant general delays in language or cognitive developments. However, they demonstrate restricted, repetitive, and stereotyped patterns of behavior, interest, and activities and qualitative impairments in social interactions, as manifested by two of the following criteria: (a) impairments in the use of multiple nonverbal behaviors, (b) failure to develop peer relationships, (c) impaired expression of pleasure in other people's happiness, and (d) lack of social or emotional reciprocity (American Psychiatric Association, 1993).

Pervasive Developmental Disorder differs from infantile autism in that its onset occurs after 30 months of age, and from childhood schizophrenia by the absence of delusions, hallucinations, and a formal thought disorder.

There exist no established pharmacological treatments for Rett's, Childhood Disintegrative, or Asperger's Disorder. The pharmacological treatment of Infantile Autism and other Pervasive Developmental Disorders consists of the use of medications, usually neuroleptics, that attempt to control the marked agitation, hyperactivity, and destructive behavior of the child. Successful pharmacotherapy can prevent hospitalization by making the child more manageable so he or she can stay at home (Aman & Singh, 1986).

Campbell et al. (1982) and Campbell and Deutsch (1985) reported that haloperidol combined with behavior therapy was more effective than placebo in decreasing stereotypy and withdrawal in autistic children aged 4 years or older. Haloperidol did not affect other behaviors such as angry affect and abnormal object relations. In treating autistic disorder, haloperidol, in doses ranging from .5 to 4 mg/day, can reduce irritability, uncooperativeness behavior, and labile affect. Unfortunately, dose decrease or discontinuation results in a rapid return of symptoms (Perry et al., 1989).

Other medications may be used in the developmental disorders to decrease specific target symptoms. For example, propranolol may reduce rage outburst and aggression in these disorders (Arnold & Aman, 1991; Williams et al., 1982). Buspirone (Buspar), an anxiolytic agent, has been used for the management of agitation and aggression in autistic children and mentally retarded adults. Although it is potentially beneficial, caution must be used because of its sedation effects that may be subtle at first and then gradually increasing because it takes 2 to 3 weeks for buspirone's full effect to develop (Coffey, 1990; Klein & Last, 1989). Buspirone may also precipitate mania or psychotic deterioration of children at risk (Soni & Weintraub, 1992). Therefore, doses are started low and slowly increased.

Naltrexone (Trexan), a narcotic antagonist, may be useful in managing those patients with developmental disorder who have self-injurious behavior. A potential problem that may limit its use is the hepatotoxicity it may cause in immature individuals (Campbell et al., 1988). The recommended dosage ranges from 50 mg two times a day to 50 mg three times a day (Arana & Hyman, 1991).

Biological Basis of Developmental Disorders (Infantile Autism) and Serotonin

The serotonergic system has also been implicated in the pathophysiology of infantile autism. Todd and Ciaranello (1985) demonstrated the presence of auto-antibodies both in serum and in the cerebrospinal fluid against one subtype of brain serotonin receptor. Approximately 40% of the autistic individuals tested exhibited this receptor antibody, whereas the incidence is quite low in controls. Thus, infantile autism, a complex disorder or group of disorders, may be the developmental consequence of early serotonergic dysfunction because it appears within the first 18 months of life (Coyle, 1987).

SUMMARY

Progress has definitely been made since the 1950s in the relatively young field of child and adolescent pharmacological treatments. However, the 1990s seem to promise greater advances in psychopharmacology with many studies already underway looking at treatment outcome, exploring the use of different medications on childhood and adolescent disorders, delineating genetic contributions to childhood disorders, evaluating the comparative efficacy of various treatment approaches, and examining the use of new classes of medications for depression and disruptive behavior disorders in childhood and adolescence. In addition, our increasing knowledge about the basic neurotransmitters in psychopharmacology and the discovery of new neurotransmitters is essential to future pharmacological interventions. The current understanding regarding the mechanism of action that was included at the end of most of the sections will receive confirmation and validation or will be disproven in the near future.

In this chapter, we reviewed several *DSM–III–R* and *DSM–IV* diagnostic categories (Attention-Deficit Hyperactivity Disorder, Conduct Disorder, depression, anxiety disorders, psychosis, and pervasive developmental disorders) and the medications used for these disorders. Treatment indications and uses, dosages, and associated side effects were also discussed. We stressed how the therapist must be knowledgeable as to the potential side effects of medications so that they may be better able to separate these effects from other psychological factors.

In our discussion, we also stressed that in children and adolescent pharmacological treatments the dosage levels are variable and not always reliable and that there are few guidelines such as age, weight, or body surface to indicate dosage range. Therefore, this means that pharmacological treatment in children and adolescents requires some flexibility and that readjustments in medication dosage may be necessary to maintain effects. Also, it may be necessary to sometimes use more than one medication to decrease multiple symptoms. Whenever possible, the lowest dose should be used in order to minimize side effects and increase the overall compliance. Drug holidays are now the rule rather than the exception. These periods are used to reassess the need for medications and to minimize the potential adverse effects associated with the use of the medications (Bernstein, 1984).

In conclusion, medications are rarely the only treatment used, but when a pharmacological treatment is implemented in children and adolescents, this entails a collaboration between the therapist, child psychiatrist, the patient or client, and the family. Often the advantages of a medication must be weighted against the disadvantages. Therefore, good psychopharmacology is based on an understanding of the physiological and neurological underpinning of a given disorder rather than a random selection of medication that may have been found to work for unknown reasons.

REFERENCES

Adams, P. (1979). Psychoneurosis. In J. Noshpitz (Ed.), *Basic handbook of child psychiatry* (Vol. 2, pp. 231–252). New York: Basic Books.

Addonizio, G. (1991). The pharmacologic basis of neuroleptic malignant syndrome. *Psychiatric Annals, 21,* 152–156.

Aman, M. G. (1987). Overview of pharmacotherapy: Current status and future directions. *Journal of Mental Deficiency Research, 31,* 121–130.

Aman M. G., & Singh N. N. (1986). A critical appraisal of recent drug research in mental retardation: The cold water studies. *Journal of Mental Deficiency Research, 30,* 203–216.

Ambrosini, P. J., Bianche, M. D., Rabinovich, H., & Elia, J. (1993). Anti-depressant treatments in children and adolescents: I. Affective disorders. *Journal of the American Academy of Child and Adolescent Psychiatry, 32,* 1–6.

American Psychiatric Association. (1987). *Diagnostic and statistical manual of mental disorders* (3rd rev. ed.). Washington, DC: Author.

American Psychiatric Association, Task Force on DSM-IV. (1993). *DSM-IV draft criteria.* Washington, DC: Author.

Arana, G. W., & Hyman, S. E. (1991). *Handbook of psychiatric drug therapy* (2nd Ed., pp. 38–107). Boston: Little, Brown.

Arnold, L. E., & Aman, M. G. (1991). Beta blockers in mental retardation and development. *Journal of Child and Adolescent Psychopharmacology, 1*, 361–373.

Barkley, R. (1977). A review of stimulant drug research with hyperactive children. *Journal of Child Psychology and Psychiatry, 18*, 137–165.

Bartels M. G., Varley C. K., Mitchell J. C., & Stamm, S. J. (1991). Pediatric cardiovascular effects of imipramine and desipramine. *Journal of the American Academy of Child and Adolescent Psychiatry, 30*, 100–103.

Bender, L., & Cottington, F. (1942). The use of amphetamine sulfate (benzedrine) in child psychiatry. *American Journal of Psychiatry, 99*, 116–121.

Bernstein, G. A., Garfinkel, B. D., & Borchart, C. M. (1991). Comparative studies of pharmacotherapy for school refusal. *Journal of the American Academy of Child and Adolescent Psychiatry, 30*, 100–103.

Bernstein, J. G. (1984). Neurotransmitters and receptors in pharmacopsychiatry. In J. G. Bernstein (Ed.), *Clinical Psychopharmacology* (2nd Ed. (pp. 59–74). Littleton, MA: John Wright, PSG Inc.

Biederman, J., Baldessarini, R. J., Wright, V., Knee, D., Harmatz, J. S., & Goldblatt, A. (1989). A doubleblind controlled study of desipramine in the treatment of ADD: II. Serum drug levels and cardiovascular findings. *Journal of the American Academy of Child and Adolescent Psychiatry, 28*, 903–911.

Biederman, J., Herzog, D. B., Rivinus, T., Haber, G., Feber, R., Rosenbaum, J., Harmatz, J. S., Tandorf, R., Orsulak, P., & Schildkraut, J. (1982, October). *Amitriptyline in the treatment of anorexia nervosa: A double blind placebo controlled study.* Paper presented at the annual meeting of the American Academy of Child and Adolescent Psychiatry, Washington, DC.

Bindelglass, P. M., Dec, G. H., & Enos, F. A. (1968). Medical and psychosocial factors in enuretic children treated with imipramine hydrochloride. *American Journal of Psychiatry, 124*(4), 1107–1112.

Birmaher, B., Greenhill, L. L., Cooper, T. B., Frieo, J., & Maminski, B. (1989). Sustained release methylphenidate: Pharmacokinetic studies in ADHD males. *Journal of the American Academy of Child and Adolescent Psychiatry, 28*, 768–772.

Bruun, R. D. (1988). Subtle and underrecognized side effects of neuroleptic treatment in children with Tourette's Disorder. *American Journal of Psychiatry, 145*, 621–624.

Campbell, M. (1985). On the use of neuroleptics in children and adolescents. *Psychiatric Annals, 15*, 104–107.

Campbell, M., Adams P., Perry, R., Spencer, E., & Overall, J. E. (1988). Tardive and withdrawal dyskinesia in autistic children: A prospective study. *Psychopharmacology Bulletin, 24*, 251–255.

Campbell, M., Anderson, L. T., Small, A. M., Perry, R., Green, W. H., & Caplan, R. (1982). The effects of haloperidol on learning and behavior in autistic children. *Journal of Autism and Developmental Disorder, 12*, 167–174.

Campbell, M., Cohen, I. L., & Small, A. M. (1982). Drugs in aggressive behavior. *Journal of the American Academy of Child Psychiatry, 21*, 107–117.

Campbell, M., & Deutsch, S. I. (1985). Neuroleptics in children. In T. R. Norman & B. Davis (Eds.), *Antipsychotics* (pp. 213–238). New York: Elvseveir.

Campbell, M., Perry, R., & Green, W. H. (1984). Use of lithium in children and adolescents. *Psychosomatics, 25*, 95–106.

Campbell, M., Schulman, D., & Rapoport, J. L. (1978). The current status of lithium therapy in child/adolescent psychiatry. *Journal of the American Academy of Child Psychiatry, 17*, 717–720.

Carlson, G. A. (1984). Classification issues in bipolar disorders in childhood. *Psychological Development, 2*, 273–285.

Carlson, G. A., & Cantwell, D. P. (1979). A survey of depressive symptoms in a child and adolescent psychiatric population. *American Journal of Psychiatry, 137*, 445–449.

Chan, Y. P., Swanson, J. M., Soldin, S. S., Thiessen, J. J., Macleod, S. M., & Logan, W. (1983). Methylphenidate hydrochloride given with or before breakfast: II. Effects on plasma concentration of methylphenidate and ritalinic acid. *Pediatrics, 72*, 56–59.

Coffey, B. J. (1990). Anxiolytics for children and adolescents: Traditional and new drugs. *Journal of Child and Adolescent Psychopharmacology, 1*, 57–83.

Conners, C. K., Rothchild, G., Eisenberg, L., Schwartz, L. S., & Robinson, E. (1969). Dextroamphetamine sulfate in children with learning disorders. *Archives of General Psychiatry, 21*, 182–190.

Conners, C. K., & Taylor, E. (1980). Pemoline, methylphenidate, and placebo in children with minimal brain dysfunction. *Archives of General Psychiatry, 37*, 922–930.

Conners, C. K., & Werry, J. S. (1979). Pharmacotherapy. In H. C. Quay & J. S. Werry (Eds.), *Psychopathological disorders of childhood* (2nd Ed., pp. 336–386). New York: Wiley.

Coyle, J. T., (1987). Biochemical development of the brain: Neurotransmitters in child psychiatry. In C. Popper (Ed.), *Psychiatric pharmacosciences of children and adolescents* (pp. 3–26). Washington, DC: American Psychiatric Press.

Creese, I., Burt, D. R., & Snyder, D. H. (1976). Dopamine receptor binding predicts clinical and pharmacological potencies of antischizophrenic drugs. *Science, 192*, 481–483.

Crow, T. J. (1980). Positive and negative schizophrenia symptoms and the role of dopamine. *British Journal of Psychiatry, 137*, 383–386.

DeVeaugh-Giess, J., Moroz, G., Biederman, J., Cantwell, D., Fontaine, R., Griest, J. H., Reichler, R., Katz, R., & Landau, P. (1992). Clomipramine hydrochloride in childhood and adolescent obsessive-compulsive disorder — a multi-center trial. *Journal of the American Academy of Child and Adolescent Psychiatry, 31*, 45–49.

Dulcan, M. K. (1990). Using psychostimulants to treat behavior disorders of children and adolescents. *Journal of Child and Adolescent Psychopharmacology, 1*, 7–20.

Fitzpatrick, P. A., Klorman, R., Brumaghim, J. T., & Borgstedt, A. D. (1992). Effects of sustained-release and standard preparations of methylphenidate on attention deficit disorder. *Journal of the American Academy of Child and Adolescent Psychiatry, 31*, 226–234.

Franz, D. (1980). Central nervous system stimulants. In L. Goodman & A. Gilman (Eds.), *The pharmacological basis of therapeutics* (6th Ed., pp. 585–591). New York: Macmillan.

Friedmann, N., Thomas, J., Carr, R., Elders, J., Ringdahl, I., & Roche, A. (1981). Effects on growth on pemoline-treated children with attention deficit disorder. *American Journal of Diseases of Children, 135*, 329–332.

Gadow, K. D., Nolan, E. E., & Sverd, J. (1992). Methylphenidate in hyperactive boys with comorbid tic disorder: II. Short-term behavioral effects in school settings. *Journal of the American Academy of Child and Adolescent Psychiatry, 31*, 462–471.

Gittleman-Klein, R., Abikoff, H., Mattes, J., & Klein, D. (1983). A controlled trial of behavior modification and methylphenidate in hyperactive children. In C. Whalen & B. Henker (Eds.), *Hyperactive children: The social ecology of identification and treatment*. New York: Academic Press.

Gittleman-Klein, R., & Klein, D. F. (1971). Controlled imipramine treatment of school phobia. *Archives of General Psychiatry, 25*, 204–207.

Gittleman-Klein, R., Klein, D. F., Katz, S., & Pollack, E. (1976). Comparative effects of methylphenidate and thioridazine in hyperkinetic children. *Archives of General Psychiatry, 33*, 1217–1231.

Gittleman-Klein, R., Landa, B., Mattes, J. A., & Klein, D. F. (1988). Methylphenidate and growth in hyperactive children: A controlled withdrawal study. *Archives of General Psychiatry, 45*, 1127–1130.

Gittleman-Klein, R., & Mannuzza, S. (1988). Hyperactive boys almost grown up: III. Methylphenidate effects on ultimate height. *Archives of General Psychiatry, 45*, 1131–1134.

Green, W. H. (1992). *Child and adolescent clinical psychopharmacology*. Baltimore: Williams and Wilkens.

Grob, C. S., & Coyle, J. T. (1986). Suspected adverse methylphenidate-imipramine interactions in children. *Developmental Behavioral Pediatrics, 7*, 265–267.

Gualtieri, C. T., Quade, D., Hicks, R., Mayo, J., & Schroeder, S. (1984). Tardive dyskinesia and other clinical consequences of neuroleptic treatment in childhood and adolescence. *American Journal of Psychiatry, 141*, 20–23.

Hauger, R. L., Angel, I., Janowsky, A., Berger, P., & Hulihan-Giblin, B. (1990). Brain recognition sites for methylphenidate and the amphetamines. In S. I. Deutsch, A. Weizman, & R. Weizman (Eds.), *Application of basic neuroscience to child psychiatry* (pp. 77–100). New York: Plenum.

Hunt, R. D., Capper, L., & O'Connell, P. (1990). Clonidine in child and adolescent psychiatry. *Journal of Child and Adolescent Psychopharmacology, 1*, 87–102.

Jacobvitz, D. (1990). Treatment of attentional and hyperactivity problems in children with sympathomimetic drugs: A comprehensive review. *Journal of the American Academy of Child and Adolescent Psychiatry, 29*, 677–688.

Klein, R. G. (1991). Thioridazine effects on the cognitive permanence of children with attention-deficit hyperactivity disorder. *Journal of Child and Adolescent Psychopharmacology, 1*, 263–270.

Klein, R. G., Koplewicz, H. S., & Kanner, A. (1992). Imipramine treatment of children with separation anxiety disorder. *Journal of the American Academy of Child and Adolescent Psychiatry, 31*, 21–28.

Klein, R. G., & Last, C. G. (1989). *Anxiety disorders in children*. Newbury Park, CA: Sage.

Kovacs, M., Feinberg, T. L., Crouse, M. A., Paulauskas, S. L., Pollock, M., & Finkelstien, R. (1984). Depressive disorders in childhood: A longitudinal study of the risk for a subsequent major depression. *Archives of General Psychiatry, 41*, 643–649.

Kuperman, S., & Stewart, M. A. (1987). Use of propranolol to decrease aggressive outbursts in younger patients. *Psychosomatics, 28*, 315–319.

Lacey, J. H., & Crisp, A. H. (1980). Hunger, food intake, and weight: The impact of clomipramine on a refeeding anorexia nervosa population. *Postgraduate Medical Journal, 56* (Suppl. 1), 79–85.

Leonard, H. L., Swedo, S. E., Rapoport, J. L., Koby, E. V., Lenane, M. C., Chesion, D. L., & Hamburger, S. D. (1989). Treatment of obsessive-compulsive disorder with clomipramine and desipramine in children and adolescent: A double-blind crossover comparison. *Archives of General Psychiatry, 46,* 1088–1092.

Lowe, T. L., Cohen, D. J., Detlor, J., Kremenitzer, M. W., & Shaywitz, B. A. (1982). Stimulant medications precipitate Tourette's Disorder. *Journal of the American Medical Association, 247,* 1729–1731.

Lucas, A. P., Lockett, H. J., & Grimm, F. (1965). Amitriptyline in childhood depression. *Diseases of the Nervous System, 28,* 105–113.

Mattes, J., & Gittleman, K. (1983). Growth of hyperactive children on a maintenance regimen of methylphenidate. *Archives of General Psychiatry, 40,* 317–321.

McClellan, J. M., & Werry, J. S. (1992). Schizophrenia. *Psychiatric Clinics of North America, 15,* 131–148.

McClellan, J. M., Werry, J. S., & Ham, M. (1992). Diagnostic outcome in early onset psychotic disorders. In J. H. Newcorn (Ed.), *Scientific proceedings* (p. 64). Washington, DC: American Academy of Child and Adolescent Psychiatry.

Offord, D. R., Boyle, M. H., Racine, Y. A., Fleming, J. E., Ladman, D. T., Blum, K. M., Byrne, C., Links, P. S., Lipman, E. L., MacMillan, H. L., Grant, N. I., Sanford, M. N., Szatmari, P., Thomas, H., & Woodward, C. A. (1992). Outcome, prognosis, and risk in a longitudinal follow-up study. *Journal of the American Academy of Child and Adolescent Psychiatry, 31,* 916–923.

Pelham, W. E., & Sams, S. E. (1992). Behavior modification. In G. Weiss (Ed.), *Child and adolescent psychiatric clinics of North America - Attention-deficit hyperactivity disorder* (pp. 505–518). Philadelphia: Saunders.

Perry, R., Campbell, M., Adams, P., Lynch, N., Spencer, E. K., Curren, E. L., & Overall, J. E. (1989). Long-term efficacy of haloperidol in autistic children: Continuous versus discontinuous drug administration. *Journal of the American Academy of Child and Adolescent Psychiatry, 28,* 87–92.

Pfefferbaum, B., Overall, J. E., Boren, H. A., Frankel, L. S., Sullivan, M. P., & Johnson, K. (1987). Alprazolam in the treatment of anticipatory and acute situational anxiety in children with cancer. *Journal of the American Academy of Child and Adolescent Psychiatry, 26,* 532–535.

Pleak, R. R., Birmaher, B., Gavrilescu, A., Abichandani, C., & Williams, D. T. (1988). Mania and neuropsychiatric excitation following carbamazepine. *Journal of the American Academy of Child and Adolescent Psychiatry, 27,* 500–503.

Popper, C. (1987). Medical unknowns and ethical consent: Prescribing psychotropic medications for children in the face of uncertainty. In C. Popper (Ed.), *Psychiatric pharmacosciences of children and adolescents* (pp. 125–161). Washington, DC: American Psychiatric Press.

Puig-Antich, J. (1982). Major depression and conduct disorders in prepuberty. *Journal of the American Academy of Child and Adolescent Psychiatry, 21,* 118–128.

Rapoport, J. L., Elkins, R., & Mikkelsen, E. (1980). Clinical controlled trial of clomipramine in adolescents with obsessive compulsive disorder. *Psychopharmacology Bulletin, 16,* 61–63.

Riddle, M., King, R. A., Hardin, M. T., Scahill, L., Ort, S. I., Chappell, P., Rasmusson, A., & Leckman, J. F. (1991). Behavior side effects of fluoxetine in children and adolescents. *Journal of Child and Adolescent Psychopharmacology, 1,* 193–198.

Robins, L. N. (1966). *Deviant children grown up.* Baltimore: Williams and Wilkens.

Roche, A. F., Lipman, R. S., Overall, J. E., & Hung, W. (1979). The effect of stimulant medication on the growth of hyperkinetic children. *Pediatrics, 63,* 847–850.

Ryan, N. D. (1990). Heterocyclic antidepressants in children and adolescents. *Journal of Child and Adolescent Psychopharmacology, 1,* 21–31.

Ryan, N. D., Meyer, V., Dachille, S., Mazzi, D., & Puig-Antich, J. (1988). Lithium antidepressant augmentation in TCA-refractory depression in adolescents. *Journal of the American Academy of Child and Adolescent Psychiatry, 27,* 371–376.

Ryan, N. D., Puig-Antich, J., Rabinovich, H., Frieo, J., Ambrosini, P., Meyer, V., Torres, D., Dachille, S., & Mazzie, D. (1988). MAOIs in adolescent major depression unresponsive to tricyclic antidepressants. *Journal of the American Academy of Child and Adolescent Psychiatry, 27,* 755–758.

Seignot, J. J. N. (1961). A case of the syndrome of tics of Gilles de la Tourette controlled by R1625. *Annals Medico-Psychologiques, 119,* 578–579.

Shaffer, D. (1984). Enuresis. In M. Rutter & L. Hersov (Eds.), *Child and adolescent psychiatry: Modern approaches* (2nd Ed., pp. 129–137). Oxford: Blackwell Scientific.

Shapiro, A., & Shapiro, E. (1981). Do stimulants provoke, cause or exacerbate tics or Tourette's Syndrome? *Comprehensive Psychiatry, 22,* 265–273.

Shaywitz. B. A., Klopper, J. H., Yager, R. D., & Gorden, J. W. (1976). Paradoxical response to amphetamine in developing rats treated with 6-hydroxydopamine. *Nature, 261,* 153–155.

Sher, M., Krieger, J. N., & Juergens, S. (1983). Trazadone and priapism. *American Journal of Psychiatry, 140,* 1362–1363.

Silvester, C. E. (1993). Psychopharmacology of disorders in children. *Psychiatric clinics of North America.* 16(4), 779–791.

Silvester, C. E., Burke, P. M., McCauley, E. A., & Clark, C. J. (1984). Acute mania psychosis in childhood: Report of two cases. *Journal of Nervous and Mental Diseases, 172,* 12–15.

Singer, H., Butler, I. J., Tune, L. E., Siefert, W. E., & Coyle, J. T. (1982). Dopamine dysfunction in Tourette syndrome. *Annals of Neurology, 12,* 361–366.

Soni, P., & Weintraub, A. L. (1992). Buspirone-associated mental status changes. *Journal of the American Academy of Child and Adolescent Psychiatry, 31,* 1098–1099.

Spencer, T., Biederman, J., Kerman, K., Steingard, R., & Wilens, T. (1992). Desipramine treatment of children with attention deficit hyperactivity disorder and tic disorder. In J. H. Newcorn (Ed.), *Scientific proceedings* (p. 75). Washington, DC: American Academy of Child and Adolescent Psychiatry.

Spitzer, R., Endicott, J., & Robins, E. (1978). *Research Diagnostic Criteria (RDC) for a selected group of functional disorders.* New York: Biometrics Research.

Sprague, R. L., & Sleator, E. K. (1977). Methylphenidate in hyperkinetic children: Differences in dose effects on learning and social behavior. *Science, 198,* 1274–1276.

Strober, M., Morrell, W., Lampert, C., & Burroughs, J. (1990). Relapse following discontinuation of lithium maintenance therapy in adolescents with bipolar I illness: A naturalistic study. *American Journal of Psychiatry, 147,* 457–461.

Szatmari, P., Boyle, M., & Offord, D. (1989). ADDH and conduct disorder: Degree of diagnostic overlap and differences among correlates. *Journal of the American Academy of Child and Adolescent Psychiatry, 28,* 865–872.

Teicher, M. H., & Glod, C. A. (1990). Neuroleptic drugs: Indications and rational use in children and adolescents. *Journal of Child and Adolescent Psychopharmacology, 1,* 33–56.

Todd, R. D., & Ciaranello, R. D. (1985). Demonstration of inter- and intraspecies differences in serotonin binding sites by antibodies from an autistic child. *Proceedings of the National Academy of Science USA, 82,* 612–616.

Trimble, M. R. (1990). Anticonvulsants in children and adolescents. *Journal of Child and Adolescent Psychopharmacology, 1,* 107–124.

Tyrer, P. J. (Ed.). (1982). *Drugs in psychiatric practice.* Cambridge: Butterworth.

Weiner, N. (1980). Norepinephrine, epinephrine, and the sympathomimetic amines. In A. G. Gilman, L. S. Goodman, & A. Gilman (Eds.), *Goodman and Gilman's the pharmacological basis of therapeutics* (6th Ed.), pp. 138–175). New York: Macmillan.

Weller, E. B., & Weller, R. A. (1990). Depressive disorders in children and adolescents. In B. D. Garfinkel, G. A. Carlson, & E. B. Weller (Eds.), *Psychiatric disorders in children and adolescents* (pp. 3–36). Philadelphia: Saunders.

Weller, E. B., Weller, R. A., & Fristad, M. A. (1986). Lithium dosage guide for prepubertal children: A preliminary report. *Journal of the American Academy of Child and Adolescent Psychiatry, 25,* 92–95.

Werry, J. S., & Aman, M. G. (1975). Methylphenidate and haloperidol in children: Effects on attention, memory, and activity. *Archives of General Psychiatry, 32,* 790–96.

Whitaker, A., & Rao, U. (1992). Neuroleptics in pediatric psychiatry. *Psychiatric Clinics of North America, 15,* 243–276.

Wiener, J. M., & Jaffe, S. L. (1985). Historical overview of childhood and adolescent psychopharmacology. In J. M. Wiener (Ed.), *Diagnosis and psychopharmacology of childhood and adolescent disorders* (pp. 3–50). New York: Wiley.

Wilens, T. E., & Biederman, J. (1982). The stimulants. *Psychiatric Clinics of North America, 15,* 191–222.

Williams, D. T., Mehl, K., Yudofsky, S., Adams, D., & Roseman, B. (1982). The effects of propranolol on uncontrolled rage outbursts in children and adolescents with organic dysfunction. *Journal of the American Academy of Child and Adolescent Psychiatry, 21,* 129–135.

Zubieta, J. K., & Alessi, N. E. (1992). Acute and chronic administration of trazodone in the treatment of disruptive behavior disorders in children. *Journal of Clinical Psychopharamacology, 12,* 346-351.

Chapter 12

Community
and Prevention

Raymond P. Lorion
Anne Brodsky
Mary Jo Flaherty
Cheryl Cole Holland
University of Maryland at College Park

Effective preventive interventions offer society strategies for correcting past mistakes, righting existing wrongs, and, most importantly, proactively shaping the future of its citizens. Preventive interventions targeted early in life may, by definition, have the greatest capacity for long-term impact on the welfare of individuals and society (Cowen, 1986; National Mental Health Association, 1986). Such preventive interventions can at best preclude or at least reduce the proportion of life characterized by disorder, emotional distress, and impaired development. Unencumbered by disorder and dysfunction, youth can encounter and master significant stages of cognitive, emotional, interpersonal, and behavioral development. The foundation for future growth is thereby built on health and adaptation rather than pathology and struggle. In combination, these effects optimize the possibility of achieving one's individual potential (Lorion, Price, & Eaton, 1989).

To be involved in the design and implementation of preventive interventions targeting youth one must be optimistic about the behavioral and developmental sciences' capacity to influence the future. One must assume that links among genetic, familial, and environmental circumstance as well as impaired development and problematic lives can be modified. The designers of preventive interventions replace the determinism of dynamic theories of development (e.g., Freud, 1964) with the flexibility of continuously transactional perspectives (e.g., Hobbs, 1982; Sameroff & Chandler, 1975; Sameroff & Fiese, 1989). Prevention advocates assume that proactive interventions can influence present experience in ways that increase the likelihood of health and reduce that of pathology (Albee, 1982; Cowen, 1986, 1991).

Beyond their effects on individuals and families, effective preventive interventions have the capacity to redress imbalances between pathogenic and health promotive processes inherent in high-risk settings (Lorion, 1985, 1991a). The overarching message of this chapter is that, if carefully designed, implemented, evaluated, and disseminated, such interventions can both increase the resistance of children and adolescents to the psychologically toxic elements in their environments and decrease that very toxicity as well (Wandersman & Hess, 1985).

Ideally, changes in the environment will have positive short-and long-term consequences. In the short term, preventive interventions will frequently reduce pathogenic qualities of children's experiences in their families, their classrooms, and their neighborhoods. Freed from what otherwise would have been development marked by psychological impairment, emotional and behavioral conflicts, and maladaptive coping, the recipients of preventive interventions may instead successfully resolve expected developmental challenges (Erikson, 1963). In doing so, they may also accumulate the psychological resources needed to cope with the unexpected, critical life events that so threaten children's futures (Bloom, 1984; Sandler, Wolchik, Braver, & Braver, 1991).

Long-term benefits may be seen as the initiation of a sustainable environmental press toward optimal human development. Reasonably, just as pathogens appear to have a self-perpetuating quality (Sameroff & Fiese, 1989; Sroufe & Rutter, 1984), so too may the development and application of adaptive skills combined with a lessening of environmental stressors be self-sustaining. In other words, if preventive interventions change the interactional, childrearing, and educational experiences of one generation, those experiences will themselves define the expected ways of interacting with children and youth of the next generation (Garmezy, 1971; Sarason, 1972).

If, as argued, this effect is sustainable, responding proactively and effectively to the needs of youth currently at-risk for emotional, cognitive, and behavioral disorders increases the human resource pool from which subsequent generations of adjusted and adaptive adults will emerge. Thus, in their adult years, as parents, teachers, and workers, these youth will sustain and expand the further promotion of subsequent generations. Through such an intergenerational sequence, high-risk settings and populations can be mitigated and even made health promotive. In summary, the psychosocial environments of high-risk settings will change to reflect the changing lives and resources of their inhabitants.

Evidence supporting the mental health disciplines' potential for promoting health and preventing disorder in children and adolescents via community-based prevention is available in recent compendia of promising interventions (Dryfoos, 1990; Koretz, 1991; Lorion, 1990a; Lorion & Ross, 1992; National Mental Health Association, 1986; Price, Cowen, Lorion, & Ramos-McKay, 1988). Interested readers are referred to these sources for descriptions of currently available strategies. It is hoped that the information provided in this chapter will encourage readers to design preventive interventions informed by considerations of the salience of the child's environment to pathogenic and health processes.

LINKING PREVENTION AND ABNORMAL CHILD PSYCHOLOGY

The design and implementation of preventive interventions are relevant to abnormal child psychology in multiple ways. By definition, effective preventive interventions protect children and adolescents from the direct and indirect effects of emotional and behavioral disorders. As these interventions are identified and disseminated, the disruptive impact of targeted disorders on the normal developmental processes of youth and on members of their families is lessened.

Second, preventive interventions represent a valuable methodological strategy for identifying and confirming etiological pathways (Lorion, 1990b, 1991b). Such interventions represent unique windows of opportunity for the examination of causal links among developmental mechanisms, risk and protective factors, and normative and pathological outcomes. Even ineffective preventive interventions, carefully applied and researched, can contribute to the understanding of disorder and dysfunction and the design of strategies for their treatment (Kellam et al., 1991).

Moreover, the inclusion of preventive interventions in the mental health caregivers' service repertoire can have far-reaching implications for professional roles and definitions (Price, 1983). The emergence of preventive interventions has and will continue to redefine the emphases and activities of the child care, mental health, and human development professions. Gradually, caregivers and researchers will shift their emphases from repair, treatment, and rehabilitation to the design and implementation of strategies to prevent pathology, optimize development, and promote growth.

Inevitably, their activities will involve both person-oriented and system-oriented initiatives (Cowen, 1991). Over time, a portion of their efforts may increasingly be focused on the creation of risk-reducing and health promoting environments (Sarason, 1971, 1972). Thus, gradually, the human development disciplines will apply their skills and knowledge less frequently in professional settings and designated child care facilities and more frequently in homes, schools, playgrounds and other sites where daily life occurs.

With that change, these same disciplines may even begin to approach the redefinition of their priorities and procedures sought after by critics such as Sarason (1981, 1983). For more than a decade, Sarason focused attention on how solving human problems is really limited by the longstanding mental health emphasis on individuals rather than systems and settings. He noted that solutions derived in this traditional fashion tend to be limited in their scope, frequently temporary in their impact, and rarely ripple throughout affected communities. Sarason (1988) argued that this approach is fostered by bifurcations of educational theory and practice and of the mental health sciences and professions. In his view, these divisions were the inevitable consequences of attempts to understand and treat cognitive, emotional, and behavioral problems apart from their social and community contexts. By contrast, preventive interventions require nurturance of the complementary relationships between science and services and maximization of the fit between programs and the settings in which they are delivered.

The locus of preventive interventions within community settings is an important component of their potential for long-term impact. In many cases, these interventions are designed to enable their recipients to sense and respond appropriately to the demands of the settings in which they live. In effect, problems are confronted and resolved or avoided entirely under the conditions in which they normally arise. Consequently, what would have been a problematic encounter is experienced in an adaptive and health-promotive manner. Thus, one of the chapter's emphases is on the salience of community settings as the "where" of effective preventive interventions.

It must also be noted that, in some cases, the settings themselves (e.g., a child's home, school, or neighborhood) may be pathogenic, presenting unresolvable or unavoidable risks for their residents. To be effective, in this case, an intervention must not only be located within the community, it must also modify relevant environmental characteristics. In effect, an intervention may require the transformation of the setting's pathogenic characteristics by: (a) weakening or reducing their level to fit within the residents' coping capacities, (b) neutralizing those characteristics so they no longer impact on the residents, or (c) modifying them such that their encounter actually represents a health-promotive interaction for the residents.

Thus, an additional emphasis of this chapter is on the salience of community settings and characteristics of natural environments as one of the "hows" of effective preventive interventions. In this sense, aspects of the community become the focus as well as the locus of the preventive processes. Childhood pathology becomes not only an individual but also a social and community phenomenon. Interventions, therefore, may target the individual child, the family, the neighborhood, or even the systems (e.g., the schools or the recreational programs) that impact on youth.

This chapter examines the salience of community factors to the design and implementation of effective preventive interventions for disorders of childhood and adolescence. First, however, a brief review of the epidemiological bases of preventive interventions and alternatives for their categorization is presented to provide a common perspective and language. To this epidemiological base is added an overview of defining concepts of an ecological or interactive individual–environmental orientation. Together, the merger of these perspectives (i.e., prevention and ecology) provides the foundation for community-based prevention. This integration offers a promising route to the design of effective and sustainable interventions.

CONCEPTS OF PREVENTION

Space does not allow for a comprehensive review of the history of preventive interventions in the mental health disciplines. Interested readers are referred to Kessler and Goldston (1986), Kazdin (1993), and Lorion, Myers, Bartels, and Dennis (in press) for perspectives on that history. All agree that Caplan's (1964) *The Principles of Preventive Psychiatry* was an early, seminal catalyst for the emergence of prevention in the mental health sciences. Caplan argued that the basic principles of the nation's public health efforts could be applied to emotional and behavioral disorders. His rationale reflected the public health truism that no major disease had ever been controlled by its treatment but only by its prevention. Caplan's work nurtured efforts to adapt public health principles to mental health disorders.

Those principles included recognition of the triad of elements relevant to public health practitioners' understanding of the occurrence and spread of disease. Components of that triad include the "host," the "agent," and the "environment." The elements of this triad were originally applied to describe the etiology of physical disorders involving an identifiable cause (i.e., the agent) that affects an individual (i.e., the host) under a specific set of circumstances (i.e., the environment). Interventions may target one or more of these elements in the service or reducing prevalence. With relative success, this triad has been applied wholesale as a model for public health interventions to respond to and prevent diverse physical disorders (Lilienfeld & Lilienfeld, 1980). The elegance of the model lies in the simplicity with which etiological processes can be reduced to the invasion of the host by the agent under identifiable circumstances/environments.

Within this model lies the assumption that public health interventions can be introduced at any point during the developmental timeline of the disorder. Simply stated, one's efforts could be focused prior to the invasion, at or soon after the time of the invasion, or even after the invasion. Interventions targeted prior to symptomatic expression, for example, define the category of "primary prevention." Interventions within this category are designed to interrupt the pathogenic process early enough to avoid the disorder entirely. Epidemiologically, the success of such interventions is reflected in reductions in the incidence (i.e., the rate at which new cases appeared in a population) of the targeted disorder.

Alternatively, interventions may be targeted to initial subclinical or clinical symptomatic expression. Labeled *secondary prevention*, such efforts require psychometrically sound screening procedures capable of accurately detecting effected individuals. Early case-finding is an essential component of secondary efforts. Once identified, cases are referred to treatments designed to interrupt the ongoing pathogenic process and thereby avoid further symptomatic expression. Because the duration of symptomatic expression is thereby limited, secondary efforts are reflected epidemiologically in reductions in the prevalence (i.e., total number of cases in a population) of the targeted disorder.

Finally, the traditional public health conception of preventive interventions includes strategies designed to minimize the secondary consequences and sequelae of an established disorder. Labeled *tertiary prevention*, such strategies involve the application of effective treatment and rehabilitation strategies. If effective, tertiary efforts limit or preclude the long-term disabilities that can accompany serious emotional disorder. Such efforts can also reduce the recurrence of disorder.

The classic model's triad has served public health efforts for infectious diseases quite well. Applied to such childhood disorders as polio, measles, smallpox, and PKU, interventions based on the concepts of host, agent, and environment have been mounted with remarkable success in reducing the incidence and prevalence of these threats to well-being and life. The model and the intervention categories (i.e., primary, secondary, and tertiary) associated with it however, apply less well to emotional and behavioral disorders. In these instances, identifying the agent and the environment has been considerably more difficult. An important aspect of this difficulty is the apparent overlap of the concepts of agent (i.e., cause) and environment (i.e., conditions that bring the cause and the host together).

Agent and environmental factors tend to be interactive, even transactional, and thus their distinct relevance to etiology uncertain. Moreover, unlike many physical disorders, emotional and behavioral disorders rarely have an identifiable onset and continuity in their progression. For those reasons, interventions to prevent emotional and behavioral disorders cannot accurately be categorized in terms of the chronology of disorder. Appreciating the etiological complexity of behavioral disorders, Gordon (1983) offered an alternative approach to conceptualizing and categorizing preventive interventions. He proposed that such interventions be considered in terms of the degree of risk assumed for their recipients.

Universal interventions, for example, are targeted broadly to the population. Efforts such as public service announcements, national campaigns (e.g., "Just Say No!"), and educational curricula exemplify such approaches. Typically, they can be delivered at relatively little cost per individual and are designed so that their effects, at worse, are neutral. Given their wholesale delivery with little possibility of influencing who receives how much of the intervention, assessment of their impact on the prevalence of targeted disorders is very difficult. By contrast, *selective interventions* are targeted to specific segments of the population whose heightened risk for disorder has been epidemiologically confirmed. These interventions tend to be more specifically targeted both to their recipients and the disorder of concern. Consequently, the potential for iatrogenic effects (i.e., unanticipated negative side effects) is heightened albeit justified by the increased risk of those targeted. Evaluations of selective interventions tend to be methodologically easier than their universal counterparts.

Finally, Gordon described *indicated interventions* as strategies targeted to individuals demonstrating early signs of disorder. The intensity of such interventions is typically greater than that of either universal or selective, again balancing the relative risk of disorder faced by the recipients. Understandably, that increased intensity includes an increased potential for iatrogenic consequences. For that reason, the screening and problem assessment procedures used to select individuals for participation must be carefully designed, psychometrically sound, and systematically applied. If these conditions are met, however, indicated interventions frequently represent an efficient approach to reducing the prevalence of mental health disorders (Gordon, 1987; Lorion et al. 1989).

There is a growing realization that specific emotional or behavioral outcomes (e.g., conduct problems) can result from diverse sets of antecedents and, conversely, that specific risk factors (e.g., ranging from parental divorce to early childhood abuse) that reflect different interactions between host and environment are linked to a variety of dysfunctional outcomes (Lorion et al., 1989 Sroufe & Rutter, 1984). To that complexity must be added Bell's (1986) description of the developmental nature of risk. In his work, Bell argued that presumed risks (e.g., parental conflict) vary in their pathogenic quality across time and situations. As the parental discord waxes and wanes, for example, or other influences come and go in a child's life (e.g., a supportive grandparent or teacher), the potency of familial tension varies (e.g., Sandler et al., 1991). Thus, the riskiness of individual (host) or agent/environment characteristics rises and falls over time and across circumstances (Bell, 1986).

This discontinuous, "multiple-paths–multiple outcomes" quality of emotional disorders underlines the importance of examining environmental factors for etiological processes. This importance is reflected in developmental models such as that offered by Sameroff and colleagues (Sameroff & Chandler, 1975; Sameroff & Fiese, 1989). Within such models, the unique contributions of individual and environmental factors to developmental outcomes are considered relative to their synergistic influences on each other. In effect, development of normal or pathological conditions becomes understandable as an ongoing sequence of *transactions* between individual and environmental states, each of which influences subsequent states of the other.

The value of such a model to the design and evaluation of preventive interventions targeting children's mental health has received increasing attention (e.g., Felner, Farber, & Primavera, 1983; Lorion, 1990b; Lorion et al., 1989). Although complicating the identification of etiological factors, the model clarifies opportunities and processes relevant to influencing developmental outcomes. Interventions, for example, can be introduced into developmental pathways that alter individual or environmental factors or their transactional sequences. In this way, outcomes in adolescence resulting from preschool interventions, for example, can be monitored over time (Lorion et al., 1989; West, Sandler, Pillow, Baca, & Gersten, 1991).

BASIC ISSUES IN ECOLOGICAL SCIENCE

Application of transactional developmental models such as Sameroff's requires a basic grasp of the nature of the "environment." This shift in perspective challenges those steeped in individually oriented perspectives. It also confronts one with the need to fill an important gap in psychology and the other mental health sciences, that is, the absence of a "branch devoted to the observation of phenomena in their natural states" (Levine & Perkins, 1987, p. 87). This gap has contributed to the mental health discipline's tradition of studying, diagnosing, and even intervening in behavior without considering or involving the settings, circumstances, and conditions under which the disorders develop, intensify, and dissipate (Barker, 1968).

Kelly's (1966) ecological principles provide a valuable foundation for conceptualizing the dynamic environment referenced in models such as Sameroff's. As such, these principles may greatly contribute to the design of effective preventive interventions for youth whether the salient environment is the family, school, neighborhood, or larger community (Trickett, Birman, & Watts, in press).

The first of Kelly's principles, *interdependence*, refers to the mutual influence among components or systems within the environment. A change in one component inevitably ripples through other elements of the environment. Understanding the interdependence among the components of a community, for example, alerts one to the potential both to impact that setting and to have that impact obstructed by countervailing forces. Interdependence argues for rooting the intervention deeply within the salient system and involving many environmental components. Doing so should both accelerate the rate of change and insulate the intended impact from other influences.

The second ecological principle identified by Kelly (1966) focuses on the *cycling of resources*. Given the interdependence of elements within a family, school, or neighborhood, it is reasonable to assume that any intervention alters existing resource exchanges within a system. The resource may be access to prenatal health care, parent counseling, social support, academic tutoring, peer relationship skills, and so forth. Whatever the case, that alteration can have both immediate and subsequent effects resource availability, utilization, and demand.

This principle also leads one to appreciate that the likely success of an intervention depends, in part, on knowledge of the ways in which the community distributes and uses its resources, adds to its available pool of resources, and responds to shortages of resources. Because the intervention will influence each of these aspects, it reminds one that one should know a system and its tributaries before attempting to use, change, or replace that system. Such knowledge can clarify the relevance of the behaviors that one wishes to modify to the contexts in which it appears. In this way, one comes to understand the ecological fit of the "adaptive behaviors" with which one wishes to replace the "pathology."

The third ecological principle is *adaptation*. As change occurs within a community, resources increase or decrease, behavioral expectations and options vary, and individuals respond accordingly. Effective preventive interventions targeted to preschoolers, for example, will create impetus for changes in primary grade curricula. Altering the parent–teacher relationship will increase the expectations on each for further communication, involvement, etc. Facilitating mothers' access to day care may result in increased pursuit of vocational training, postsecondary education, and employment. Whatever the change, those effected will adapt their behavior accordingly. As they do so, those with whom they relate will also adapt to their modification.

The final principle involves the concept of *succession*. As Levine and Perkins (1987) noted, environments are not static entities. Change initiates subsequent changes. This principle highlights the temporal nature of community interventions. Like the ripples in a pond or the dominoes in a series, the impacts of interventions move from their immediate point of contact to other components of the environment. The rate at which the sequence proceeds depends on the intensity and, we believe, diversity (i.e., across multiple contextual elements) of the intervention.

It must also be noted that not all of the ripples will be in the intended direction. In many instances, some forces within the community will respond counter to the intervention. Rather than facilitate the possibility of change, elements in the system will react to maintain the status quo. This interplay between forces of change and forces of continuity exemplifies the dynamism integral to the transactional-development approach to the prevention of children's emotional disorders.

Bronfenbrenner (1977) modeled the environment within which these principles occur as a system of concentric environmental components. Development represents the reciprocal interactions (transactions in Sameroff's terms) between the child and this multilayered environment. Most immediate is the *microsystem* that includes the immediate interpersonal interactions, roles, activities, and settings in which the developing person operates. The *mesosystem* comprises interrelationships among two or more microsystems (e.g., the home and school, the church and local recreational facilities). These systems, in turn, operate within the *exosystem* that encompasses community systems (e.g., the School Board or Health Department) perhaps not directly involved with a particular child but affecting him or her nevertheless. Finally, the *macrosystem* refers to the subculture or culture, including belief systems and values that impact all other levels.

Jasnoski's (1984) ecosystemic view of human development offers a similar multilayered model. In this case, the individual is central within an ecosystem of concentric influences expanding from the interpersonal, to the family, to the peer group or friendship network, to the community, and even to the culture. Consistent with Sameroff's model, the reciprocal interactions within and across levels must be considered temporally to understand the process of development across the life span.

Incorporation of the ecological perspective within the design of preventive interventions directed to children addresses several important concerns. Key among these is the recognition that successfully disseminated and adopted preventive interventions must fit the settings in which they are to be delivered (Lorion & Lounsbury, 1982; Munoz, Snowden, & Kelly, 1979; Price & Lorion, 1989). The importance of such a fit is reflected in use of *ecological validity* as a critical yardstick for examining the viability of an intervention (Bronfenbrenner, 1977). The concept of ecological validity emerged from Bronfenbrenner's (1977) appreciation of the methodological significance of naturalistic, descriptive research to understanding how developmental processes actually evolve. Simply matching in the laboratory the objective characteristics of the presumably salient setting seemed inadequate. Bronfenbrenner also stressed that the environment as perceived and experienced by targeted individuals must also be considered.

From this assumption arose Bronfenbrenner's proposal that research designs and experimental interventions be evaluated in terms of their ecological validity. To meet this recommendation, research and intervention designs must incorporate questions, constructs, and measures that are relevant and meaningful to the life experience of research and program participants. Ignorance of the match between the real life and the proposed designs is, in Bronfenbrenner's view, unlikely to produce findings or procedures generalizable and acceptable to real people. When applied to policy decisions, the consequences can be especially unfortunate given the frustration likely to arise when help is offered in forms that are unacceptable or counterproductive (Lorion, 1991b).

The ecological principles models and the concept of ecological validity direct the prevention researcher to new target populations and strategies for intervention. The focus extends beyond children to those people and settings who participate in the developmental processes of concern for emotional and behavioral health.

In our view, the works of Sameroff, Bronfenbrenner, Jasnoski, and Kelly provide a solid theoretical foundation on which to establish preventive interventions to avoid or to minimize emotional and behavioral disorders in youth. From that foundation, should arise interventions that are multilayered, contextually sensitive, and informed by an understanding of relevant pathogenic and health-promotive processes as they occur naturally. Ecologically valid interventions would incorporate information from youth, families, schools, neighborhoods, and segments of the larger communities in the design, implementation, and evaluation of intervention processes.

Bronfenbrenner (1977) appreciated the unique challenges of research in which those studied are involved in the discovery of their "real" experience. Would not such participation alter the very "real life" circumstances under study? Analogous to the Heisenberg principle in physics, the reactive impact on natural processes of their study must be examined. Yet, procedures for minimizing such reactivity and criteria for assessing its level remain elusive (Reppucci, 1990). Thoughtful calls for increasing collaboration between researchers and participants (Kelly, 1986; Trickett et al., in press) provide clues for how to proceed. As yet, however, the differential level of reactivity associated with alternative approaches is unknown. Presumably, the systematic application and evaluation of such approaches will provide successively closer approximations to accurate models of the processes relevant to health and pathology in youth (Lorion & Lounsbury, 1982).

Numerous methodologies for conducting interactive research have been proposed. Among these is the practice of grounded theorizing. Within this methodology, theory follows rather than precedes the acquisition of information by a participant-observer in the natural setting (e.g., Glazer & Strauss, 1967). Other qualitative approaches include ethnographic (Agar, 1980), key informant (Warren & Warren, 1977), and resource collaborator methods (Tyler, Pargament, & Gatz, 1983). Each of these strategies rely on the input and integral participation of setting participants at all stages of information gathering. The results of such efforts inform the development of interventions consistent with the actual experiences of participants and are therefore, presumably, ecologically valid.

Beyond increasing the match between interventions and the individuals and settings to which they are applied, participatory information gathering strategies may contribute to the achievement of intended effects. Acquisition of information can be an intervention as people and systems become more self-reflective and involved in shaping their future direction (Bronfenbrenner, 1977). Settings in which, through participatory decision making, people are empowered to increase responsiveness to their needs are expected to support optimal development. Such empowerment includes an appreciation of those characteristics of a setting relevant to acceptance of the "pathology" to be avoided or reduced and the "health" to be promoted (Hiltonsmith & Keller, 1983 Jasnoski, 1984; Kelly, 1968).

In the following sections of this chapter, we apply this contextual perspective to conduct disorder in girls and affective disorder in boys. Given limited attention in the literature, these nonintuitive conditions may serve as helpful vehicles for highlighting the relevance of contextual factors to the onset, evolution, maintenance, and alteration of pathological processes. As such, these examples may stimulate innovation in the design of interventions to prevent disorder and promote health in youth.

CONDUCT DISORDER

According to the DSM-III-R (American Psychiatric Association, 1987) diagnostic criteria, a conduct disorder is present based on "a persistent pattern of conduct in which the basic rights of others and major age-appropriate societal norms or rules are violated" (p. 53). Diagnosable behaviors include chronic lying, stealing, deliberate property damage, physical aggression, truancy, and running away from home. Although each of these behaviors has interpersonal aspects, the various ecosystems within which such interactions occur have received little attention. Rather, diagnostic criteria consider extraindividual effects only as "associated" (rather than possibly integral) symptomatic features and predisposing factors. The research literature on conduct disorder is similarly noninteractionist. In general, identification of factors differentiating conduct disordered and nonconduct disordered individuals has been emphasized. The results of such research is intended to inform individual treatment. Admittedly, studies of the relevance to conduct disorder of factors such as sociodemographic characteristics (Offord, Alder, & Boyle, 1986), family history (Lewis & Bucholz, 1991), quality of relationships (Fujita, Miura, & Hosomizu, 1985; Moos & Fuhr, 1982), and environmental structure (Baron, 1987) have been reported. Yet, in each of these instances, findings have been considered primarily relative to individual diagnosis and intervention.

Missing from this work has been consideration of the intervention options that might emerge were figure and ground reversed and focus shifted from the individual to such associated features. Sipila (1985), for example, in his community-based work, identified three community characteristics that might impact on the formation of "deviance." Poor living conditions, lack of opportunity, and voluntary or involuntary social segregation were each studied. In attempting to separate the differential contributions of individual and setting, Sipila was unable to identify unambiguously "good" communities whose structure could be duplicated in communities that were overall "poor" at protecting its youth from deviant behavior. Ecological principles, however, would argue against Sipila's separation of setting and individual. Each influences the other and defines, in part, which behaviors can and will be expressed. From that perspective, the intervention must somehow reflect that setting and individual are one.

Consider the ecological parameters of girls diagnosed with conduct disorder. Approximately 9% of males and 2% of females under 18 are diagnosed with conduct disorder (American Psychiatric Association, 1987). Sipila (1985) attributed this and other apparent gender-related differences (e.g., the differential prevalence of depression in females and males) to the observation that females tend toward internalizing or passive behaviors and males toward externalizing or active behaviors. Given both its low prevalence and noninternalizing quality, the tendency to focus at an individual level on females with conduct disorder is as understandable as its limitations are obvious.

Can one understand what makes the conduct disordered girl different from 98% of her counterparts without understanding the settings within which her behaviors evolved? If, as generally assumed, emotional conflicts were to have been expressed through passive, internalizing symptoms, which setting and socialization factors obstructed that path and opened a less normative expression? Answers to such questions seem quite relevant to selecting interventions that fit the etiological ecology of female conduct disorder. Setting is certainly relevant given that rehabilitative interventions for conduct disordered youth typically remove them from their homes and communities.

Significantly missing from these modal treatment decisions is an explicit analysis of their match with the problem behavior's ecological bases. That lack may explain the limited generalization of treatment effects. Changes observed in the treatment environment are rarely sustained in the youth's natural community. Ecologically, one could conclude that the intervention was inconsistent with ecological parameters of the ecosystem within which the conduct problem arose.

Predictably, attempting to change the individual without addressing the interdependence of her behavior to interpersonal and systemic qualities of her environment has little chance of being sustained over time. Given the array of factors that may contribute to the initiation and maintenance of her aggressive response patterns, preventing its establishment through early detection and intervention may represent the most likely avenue of success. To reach that goal, however, requires considerably more information about the setting characteristics associated with development of so atypical a pattern of situational adaptation by a female youth.

Consider the following case example. "April" is an 8-year-old African-American girl assigned to a residential treatment center for foster care children. Her placement removed her from an alcoholic, unemployed mother. April had spent her first 6 years living with her mother, three younger siblings, and her mother's physically abusive boyfriend. Prior to her placement, April was described by her teachers as a gifted student. The girl's behavior at school provided no easy clues to her physical abuse or to her traumatic reactions to witnessing her mother's abuse.

Treatment for April was also to be "protective," that is, removal and separation from home, mother, and siblings. Prior to residential care, April had been removed from four foster homes. Each time, she had repeatedly initiated physical confrontations with foster parents and foster siblings. Reportedly, April stole food and money from her foster parents. Repeatedly, she ran away to find her mother or obtain housing from her grandmother. April's earlier academic success ended when she was moved from her neighborhood school. Suddenly she became truant and in serious academic difficulty. Residential treatment included behavior modification and individual therapy.

Understanding the etiology of April's conduct disorder has traditionally involved recreating the basis for her behavior. Perhaps some consideration would even be given to examining why she responds in this way to her environment. By contrast, an interactionist approach requires far more information. For example, is her behavior in some measure due to the setting conditions? Does her gender influence which behaviors are considered problematic? Under the same circumstances, would a boy be so labeled? Does there exist a safe setting in the community for mothers and children? How and why would one condition a child not to fight when her acting-out may have protected her, helped her mother, and would remain necessary when she returns to that setting, if the environment remains unchanged?

An alternative would be to understand the conditions leading to April's conduct and determine the feasibility of altering those conditions. Clearly, continuation of her aggression in spite of significant positive changes in her *natural* environment would be diagnostically significant. Ecologically, an appropriate intervention would involve family, school, and community. Rather than focus solely on her behavior, an early intervention might have trained teachers to identify subtle signs of an increasingly stressful and abusive homelife. Building on April's positive experiences at school, an intervention might have offered resources to the family and support to April. Important for her would have been acquiring alternatives to aggression and acting-out as responses to experienced stress and fear.

Ideally, the resulting preventive intervention would be designed so that both individual *and* setting become less pathogenic and more health promotive. Aspects of the environment and of those who live within it would be modified to enhance the congruence between individual and setting. In April's case, early detection and a multilayered contextual approach may have allowed her to avoid what is likely to become a long-term sequence of problematic encounters with others.

CHILDHOOD DEPRESSION

Throughout this chapter, we have emphasized that conceptions of childhood psychopathology and its etiology, treatment, and prevention are seriously limited when relevant phenomena are examined only at the individual level. Many contemporary models of psychopathology reflect awareness of diathesis-stress concepts (Cicchetti 1984; Sameroff & Fiese, 1989). Yet, typically, their focus on individual symptoms emphasizes the "diathesis." Little attention, however, is given to either the external sources of "stress" or the dynamic interaction between diathesis and stress.

Consideration of extraindividual levels of analysis along a developmental timeline offers, we believe, radically different conceptions of the etiology of childhood depression and of its prevention and treatment. Cicchetti and Schneider-Rosen (1984), Quay, Routh, and Shapiro (1987) and Kazdin (1990, 1993) also argued convincingly for adopting a developmental perspective toward the etiological study of psychopathology. Research on the developmental psychopathology of childhood depression has raised significant findings that correct the past assumption that this condition parallels the etiology, symptoms, and treatment of adult depression. Jorm (1987) reviewed data from 36 studies to compare the prevalence of depression in male and female youth. The assumption that more girls than boys were affected was found to be age related. Overall, little difference between the genders was found in childhood depression prevalence rates. Based on his analyses, Jorm concluded that the disorder was significantly more common among females only during midlife.

Other investigators have examined this question of differences from the adult condition using cross-sectional or longitudinal research. They have focused on identifying the condition's developmental sequence. Relative to the gender distribution of childhood depression, the findings have been enlightening. Huntley, Phelps, and Rehm (1986), for example, found that the 6-and 10-year-old boys in their study reported significantly *greater* depressive symptomatology than did girls of those ages. Similarly, Nolen-Hoeksema, Girus, and Seligman (1991) found consistently higher reporting of depressive symptoms among elementary school boys than girls. These patterns confirmed the observations of McGee and Williams (1988) in their 4-year longitudinal study of 9-year-olds. At the conclusion of the study, depression was more prevalent and persistent among boys, who also displayed considerably more "antisocial" behavior than girls.

Craighead (1991) proposed that childhood depression, particularly in adolescent males, represents both a continuous personality construct and a diagnosed conduct disorder. He concurred with McKnew, Cytryn, and Yahraes (1983) that estimates of the prevalence of childhood depression among males are frequently lowered in the presence of expected comorbid or co-occurring externalizing behaviors such as aggressively acting-out. Generally, these and related findings offer insights into the interactions of gender across the developmental trajectory of childhood depression.

Efforts have been made to model the multilevel impact of individual–environmental transactions of this disorder, albeit at the loss of the developmental focus. Teichman's (1989) model of childhood depression, for example, is consistent with contextual perspectives including Bronfenbrenner's (1977) emphasis on interactive systems and Sameroff and Fiese's (1989) focus on transactional relationships between individual and environmental factors. Teichman's model highlights reciprocal patterns between parent and child that contribute to the development and maintenance of depression. Teichman explained that this phenomenon occurs within the family system that is, in turn, nested within sociocultural systems and subsystems. Each of these systems are assumed to be mutually interactive. Consequently, according to Teichman, reciprocities external to the family can also produce and reinforce depression. If so, preventive interventions must identify and understand the mechanisms of such reciprocities. Information must be obtained about which specific reciprocities engender and maintain the evolution of depressive symptoms and also which are accessible to intervention. To do so, the application of the aforementioned collaborative, observational, and qualitative methods seems essential.

Cicchetti and Schneider-Rosen's (1984) model of childhood depression incorporates both the transactional system features apparent in Teichman's model and the developmental approach stressed by Bronfenbrenner (1977), Sameroff (Sameroff & Chandler, 1975; Sameroff & Fiese, 1989), and others. Cicchetti incorporated consideration of "potentiating" factors that increase the risk of a depressive episode and "compensatory" factors that increase the avoidance of a depressive episode. These factors must be determined at the individual, familial, social, and broader environmental levels. This approach acknowledges the aforementioned alternate pathways characteristic of childhood disorder.

Comprehensive application of this model remains rare. Efforts in that direction beyond that of Cicchetti and Schneider-Rosen (1984) include work by Friedrich, Reams, and Jacobs (1988). These investigators report that depression in early adolescent boys correlates with life stress, low family cohesion, limited family expressiveness, and academic difficulty. For girls of the same age, depression correlates with different factors including low family cohesion, high family control, patterns of social support, and academic difficulty. Feldman, Rubenstein, and Rubin (1988) found family cohesion and friendship support to be key, independent factors in depression of both early adolescent boys and girls. Low measures of each constituted potentiating factors, whereas strong measures of each were seen as potent compensatory factors. In both cases, a summative effect of both sets of factors was observed.

In their longitudinal study of youth ages 7 to 17, Myers et al. (1991) linked suicidality with depressive thinking and conduct problems. They speculated that the link with conduct problems may reflect that the suicidal youth came from apparently chaotic homes. Asarnow and Carlson (1988) expanded their inquiry into the etiology of child suicide to include consideration of the affective nature of the child's immediate environment. Interestingly, suicide attempters in their 8- to 13-year-old inpatient sample differed from nonattempters (regardless of gender) in terms of perceived family support as measured by Moos Family Environment Scale. This measure correctly discriminated 88% of attempters and nonattempters. The addition of individually oriented measures of hopelessness and depression did not increase the accuracy of this distinction.

Generally, therefore, low family support appears to be a risk factor for a number of negative mental health outcomes, including childhood depression and suicidality. From a preventive perspective, an intervention that increases family support, especially in high-risk families, may simultaneously reduce an exogenous risk factor and increase externally based protective factors. Understanding the developmental impact of transactional factors between individual and environmental characteristics informs the designers of interventions about the timing and form of maximally acceptable strategies (Lorion et al., in press, Lorion et al., 1989).

If, for example, a community's cultural codes provide limited emotional or practical support for high family cohesion, low family support may be endemic throughout its households. So informed, a collaborative team could then design and introduce an intervention at the community or macrosystem level as an initial step. From this programmatic foundation would emerge further preventive efforts focused at the family or mesosystem level. Teichman (1989) stressed the need for programs that have identified and incorporated accessible key reciprocities between a child and the context.

In this hypothetical program, the collaborative team may determine that peer support, as a protective factor, is more readily accessible via community centers or neighborhoods than in the schools or families. The extrafamilial intervention components will build on that strength. A school-based primary prevention program, for example, aimed at improving children's ability to cope with poor peer support could result in fundamental changes in the school's structure and processes and thereby in the child's attitudes toward school and its academic demands. Family-based components, in turn, may build a child's increased sense of academic mastery and peer competence and use them as resources enhancing the child's contribution to a redefinition of familial roles and procedures. These same resources may also protect the child in the event that family changes are minimal. In combination, perhaps with a school-based support program to enhance children's adaptive skills, these multilevel interventions are likely to have sustainable effects.

SUMMARY

In its various forms, community prevention may be offered as the ultimate "right stuff" of mental health intervention. Unquestionably, we are interested in the continuing acceptance and refinement of this thorough approach to understanding and responding to the needs of children and adolescents. We firmly believe that interventions that prevent disorder and promote health are important tools for the mental health professions to acquire and apply. We do not, however, wish to imply either that they are the only tools or that their implementation is without risks. As we and others have noted (Levin & Trickett, 1990; Lorion, 1987; Weithorn, 1987), preventive interventions are as vulnerable to iatrogenic consequences as other forms of human service. Stating this fact should add caution to, but not reduce, continuing enthusiasm for the development of this most challenging scientific and professional focus.

Included within that caution should be an appreciation of the unique complications associated with community level interventions. For example, in the community and school-based intervention described earlier, who should provide informed consent? Should it be the school administration, the parents, the school children, or community residents? How can confidentiality be maintained? In this complicated milieu, how can we adequately assess the risks of planned interventions so that individuals at each of the impacted levels can be monitored and, if necessary, alerted? In fact, who exactly is the client or subject?

The proposed conceptualization of preventive interventions as contextually based strategies that impact across the multiple levels of influence on child and adolescent development is admittedly challenging. Problem analysis and intervention development must be carried out with populations of concern ranging from a single individual to the children, families, and residents of entire communities. Obviously, the fundamental theory and techniques of community-based prevention require the collaboration of developmental scientists, child clinicians, educators, urban planners, systems planners, but especially of the families, adults, and children living within those communities. A complex and challenging field such as community prevention cannot hope to achieve its potential unless it reflects the very contextual, multilevel quality of the phenomena on which it focuses.

REFERENCES

Agar, M. (1980). *The professional stranger: An informal introduction to ethnography.* New York: Academic Press.

Albee, G. W. (1982). Preventing psychopathology and promoting human potential. *American Psychologist, 37,* 1043–1050.

American Psychiatric Association. (1987). *The diagnostic and statistical manual of mental disorders* (3rd rev. ed.). Washington, DC: Author.

Asarnow, J. R., & Carlson, G. (1988). Suicide attempts in preadolescent child psychiatry inpatients. *Suicide and Life-Threatening Behavior, 18*(2), 129–136.

Barker, R. G. (1968). *Ecological psychology: Concepts and methods for studying the environment.* Stanford, CA: Stanford University Press.

Baron, K. (1987). The model of human occupation: A newspaper treatment group for adolescents with conduct disorder: Evaluation and treatment of adolescents and children (Special issue). *Occupational Therapy in Mental Health, 7*(2), 89–104.

Bell, R. Q. (1986). Age specific manifestations in changing psychosocial risk. In D. C. Farran & J. D. McKinney (Eds.), *The concept of risk in intellectual and psychosocial development* (pp. 169–185). New York: Academic Press.

Bloom, B. (1984). *Community mental health: A general introduction* (2nd ed.). Monterey: Brooks-Cole.

Bronfenbrenner, U. (1977). Toward an experimental ecology of human development. *American Psychologist, 32,* 513–531.

Caplan, G. (1964) *The principles of preventive psychiatry.* New York: Basic Books.

Cicchetti, D. (1984). The emergence of developmental psychopathology. *Child Development, 55,* 1–7.

Cicchetti, D., & Schneider-Rosen, K. (1984). Toward a transactional model of childhood depression. In D. Cicchetti & K. Schneider-Rosen (Eds.), *Childhood depression* (pp. 1–28). Washington, DC: Jossey-Bass.

Cowen, E. L. (1986). Primary prevention in mental health: Ten years of retrospect and ten years of prospect. In M. Kessler & S. E. Goldston (Eds.), *A decade of progress in primary prevention* (pp. 3–46). Hanover, NH: University Press of New England.

Cowen, E. L. (1991). In pursuit of wellness. *American Psychologist, 46,* 404–408.

Craighead, W. E. (1991). Cognitive factors and classification issues in adolescent depression. *Journal of Youth and Adolescence, 20*(2), 311–326.

Dryfoos, J. G. (1990). *Adolescents at risk: Prevalence and prevention.* New York: Oxford University Press.

Erikson, E. (1963). *Childhood and society.* New York: Norton.

Feldman, S. S., Rubenstein, J. L., & Rubin, C. (1988). Depressive affect and restraint in early adolescents: Relationships with family structure, family processes, and friendship support. *Journal of Early Adolescence, 8*(3), 279–296.

Felner, R. D., Farber, S. S., & Primavera, J. (1983). Transitions and stressful life events: A model for primary prevention. In R. D. Felner, L. A. Jason, J. N. Moritsugu, & S. S. Farber (Eds.), *Preventive psychology: Theory, research, and practice* (pp. 199–215). New York: Pergamon.

Freud, S. (1964) *A general introduction to psychoanalysis.* New York: Washington Square.

Friedrich, W. N., Reams, R., & Jacobs, J. H. (1988). Sex differences in depression in early adolescents. *Psychological Reports, 62,* 475–481.

Fujita, H., Miura, M., & Hosomizu, R. (1985), Delinquent girls and their families: With special reference to mother – daughter relationships. *Japanese Journal of Criminal Psychology, 123* (1), 49–58.

Garmezy, N. (1971). Vulnerability research and the issue of primary prevention. *American Journal of Orthopsychiatry, 41,* 101–116.

Glazer, B., & Strauss, A. (1967). *The discovery of grounded theory.* Chicago: Aldine.

Gordon, R. S. (1983). An operational classification of disease prevention. *Public Health Reports, 98,* 107–109.

Gordon, R. S. (1987). An operational classification of disease prevention. In J. A. Steinberg & M. M. Silverman (Eds.), *Preventing mental disorders: A research perspective* (DHHS Publication No. ADM 87–1492, pp. 20–26). Washington, DC: U.S. Government Printing Office.

Hiltonsmith, R., & Keller, H. (1983). What happened to the setting in person-setting assessment. *Professional Psychology: Research and Practice, 14,* 419–434.

Hobbs, N. (1982). *The troubled and troubling child: Reeducation in mental health, education and human services programs for children and youth.* San Francisco: Jossey-Bass.

Huntley, D. K., Phelps, R. E., & Rehm, L. P. (1986). Depression in children from single-parent families. *Journal of Divorce, 10* (1–2), 153–161.

Jasnoski, M. (1984). The ecosystemic perspective in clinical assessment and intervention. In W. O'Connor and B. Lubin (Eds.), *Ecological approaches to clinical and community psychology (pp. 41–56).* New York: Wiley.

Jorm, A. F. (1987). Sex and age differences in depression: A quantitative synthesis of published research. *Australian and New Zealand Journal of Psychiatry, 21,* 46–53.

Kazdin, A. E. (1990). Childhood depression. *Journal of Child Psychology and Psychiatry, 31,* 121–160.

Kazdin, A. E. (1993). Adolescent mental health: Prevention and treatment. *American Psychologist, 48,* 127–142.

Kellam, S. G., Werthamer-Larsson, L., Dolan, L. J., Brown, C. H., Mayer, L. S., Rebok, G. W., Anthony, J. C., Laudoff, J., Edelsohn, G., & Wheeler, L. (1991). Developmental epidemiologically based preventive trials: Baseline modeling of early target behaviors and depressive symptoms. *American Journal of Community Psychology, 19,* 563–584.

Kelly, J. G. (1966). Ecological constraints on mental health services. *American Psychologist, 21,* 535–539.

Kelly, J. G. (1968). Towards an ecological conception of preventive interventions. In J. W. Carter, Jr. (Ed.), *Research contributions from psychology to community mental health. (pp. 75–97)* New York: Behavioral Publications.

Kelly, J. G. (1986). Content and process: An ecological view of the interdependence of practice and research. *American Journal of Community Psychology, 14*, 581–589.

Kessler, M., & Goldston, S. E. (Eds.). (1986). *A decade of progress in primary prevention.* Hanover, NH: University Press of New England.

Koretz, D. S. (1991). Prevention-centered science in mental health. *American Journal of Community Psychology, 19*, 453–458.

Levin, G. B., & Trickett, E. J., & Hess, R. E. (Eds.). (1990). *Ethical implications of primary prevention.* New York: Haworth.

Levine, M., & Perkins, D. V. (1987). *Principles of community psychology: Perspectives and applications.* New York: Oxford University Press.

Lewis, C. E., & Bucholz, K. K. (1991). Alcoholism, antisocial behavior and family history. *British Journal of Addiction, 86*(2), 177–194.

Lilienfeld, A. M., & Lilienfeld, D. E. (1980). *Foundations of epidemiology* (2nd ed.). New York: Oxford University Press.

Lorion, R. P. (1985). Environmental approaches and prevention: The dangers of imprecision. In A. Wandersman & R. Hess (Eds.), *Beyond the individual: Environmental approaches and prevention* (pp. 193–205). New York: Haworth.

Lorion, R. P. (1987). The other side of the coin: The potential for negative consequences of prevention interventions. In J. A. Steinberg & M. M. Silverman (Eds.), *Preventing mental disorders: A research perspective* (DHHS Publication No. ADM 87-1492, pp. 243–250). Washington, DC: U.S. Government Printing Office.

Lorion, R. P. (Ed.). (1990a). *Protecting the children: Strategies for optimizing emotional and behavioral development.* New York: Haworth.

Lorion, R. P. (1990b). Basing preventive interventions on theory: Stimulating a field's momentum. In R. P. Lorion (Ed.), *Protecting the children: Strategies for optimizing emotional and behavioral development* (pp. 7–32). New York: Haworth Press.

Lorion, R. P. (1991a). Prevention and public health: Psychology's response to the nation's health care crisis. *American Psychologist, 46*, 516–519.

Lorion, R. P. (1991b). Targeting preventive interventions: Enhancing risk estimates through theory. *American Journal of Community Psychology, 19*, 859–866.

Lorion, R. P., & Lounsbury, J. W. (1982). Conceptual and methodological considerations in evaluating preventive interventions. In W. R. Tash & G. Stahler (Eds.), *Innovative approaches to mental health evaluation* (pp. 23–59). New York: Academic Press.

Lorion, R. P., Myers, T. G., Bartels, C., & Dennis, A. (in press). Preventive intervention research: Pathways for extending knowledge of child/adolescent health and pathology. In T. Ollendick & R. Prinz (Eds.), *Advances in clinical child psychology.* New York: Plenum.

Lorion, R. P., Price, R. H., & Eaton, W. W. (1989). The prevention of child and adolescent disorders: From theory to research. In D. Shaffer, I. Philips, & N. B. Enzer (Eds.), *Prevention of mental disorders, alcohol and other drug use in children and adolescents.* OSAP Prevention Monograph-2 (DHHS Publication No. ADM 89-1646, pp. 55–96). Washington, DC: U.S. Government Printing Office.

Lorion, R. P., & Ross J. G. (Eds.). (1992). Programs for change: Office for Substance Abuse Prevention demonstration models [Special issue]. *Journal of Community Psychology.*

McGee, R., & Williams, S. (1988). A longitudinal study of depression in nine-year-old children. *Journal of the American Academy of Child and Adolescent Psychiatry, 27*(3), 342–348.

McKnew, D. H., Cytryn, L., Yahraes, H. (1983). *Why isn't Johnny crying? Coping with depression in children.* New York: Norton.

Moos, R., & Fuhr, R. (1982). The clinical use of social–ecological concepts: The case of an adolescent girl. *American Journal of Orthopsychiatry, 52*, 111–121.

Munoz, R. F., Snowden, L. R., & Kelly, J. G. (Eds.). (1979). *Social and psychological research in community settings: Designing and conducting programs for social and personal well-being.* San Francisco: Jossey Bass.

Myers, K., McCauley, E., Calderon, R., Mitchell, J., Burke, P., & Schloredt, K. (1991). Risks for suicidality in major depressive disorder. *Journal of the American Academy of Child and Adolescent Psychiatry, 30*(1), 86–94.

National Mental Health Association. (1986). *The prevention of mental-emotional disabilities: Report of the National Mental Health Association Commission on the Prevention of Mental-Emotional Disabilities* (Vols. 1–2). Washington, DC: Author.

Nolen-Hoeksema, S., Girus, J. S., & Seligman, M. E. P. (1991). Sex differences in depression and explanatory style in children. *Journal of Youth and Adolescence*, 20(2), 233–245.

Offord, D. R., Alder, R. J., & Boyle, M. H. (1986). Prevalence and sociodemographic correlates of conduct disorder [Special Issue: Psychiatric Epidemiology]. *American Journal of Social Psychology*, 6(4), 272–278.

Price, R. H. (1983). The education of a prevention psychologist. In R. D. Felner, L. A. Jason, J. N. Moritsugu, & S. S. Farber (Eds.), *Preventive psychology: Theory, research, and practice* (pp. 290–296). New York: Pergamon.

Price, R. H., Cowen, E. L., Lorion, R. P., & Ramos-McKay, J. (Eds.). (1988). *14 ounces of prevention: A casebook for practitioners*. Washington, DC: American Psychological Association.

Price, R. H., & Lorion, R. P. (1989). Prevention programming as organizational reinvention: From research to implementation. In D. Shaffer, I. Philips, & N. B. Enzer (Eds.), *Prevention of mental disorders, alcohol and other drug use in children and adolescents*. OSAP Prevention Monograph-2 (DHHS Publication No. ADM 89-1646, pp.97–123). Washington, DC: U.S. Government Printing Office.

Quay, H. C., Routh, D. K., & Shapiro, S. K. (1987). Psychopathology of childhood: From description to validation. *Annual Review of Psychology*, 38, 491–532.

Reppucci, N. D. (1990). Ecological validity and deritualization of process. In P. Tolan, C. Keys, F. Chertok, & L. Jason (Eds.), *Research community psychology issues of theory and method* (pp. 160–163). Washington DC: American Psychological Association.

Sameroff, A. J., & Chandler, M. J. (1975). Reproductive risk and the continuum of caretaking casualty. In F. D. Horowitz, M. Hetherington, S. Scarr-Salapatek, & G. Siegel (Eds.), *Review of child development research* (Vol. 4, pp. 187–244). Chicago: University of Chicago Press.

Sameroff, A. J., & Fiese, B. H. (1989). Conceptual issues in prevention. In D. Shaffer, I. Philips, & N. B. Enzer (Eds.), *Prevention of mental disorders, alcohol and other drug use in children and adolescents*. OSAP Prevention Monograph-2 (DHHS Publication No. ADM 89-1646, pp.23–53). Washington, DC: U.S. Government Printing Office.

Sandler, I., Wolchik, S., Braver, S., & Braver, B. (1991). Stability and quality of life events and psychological symptomatology in children of divorce. *American Journal of Community Psychology*, 19, 501–520.

Sarason, S. B. (1971). *The culture of schools and the problem of change*. Boston: Allyn & Bacon.

Sarason, S. B. (1972). *The creation of settings and the future societies*. San Francisco: Jossey-Bass.

Sarason, S. B. (1981). *Psychology misdirected*. New York: The Free Press.

Sarason, S. B. (1983). *Schooling in America: Scapegoat and salvation*. New York: The Free Press.

Sarason, S. B. (1988). *The making of an American psychologist: An autobiography*. San Francisco: Jossey-Bass.

Sipila, J. (1985). Community structure and deviant behavior among adolescents. *Youth and Society* 16(4), 471–497.

Sroufe, L. A., & Rutter, M. (1984). The domain of developmental psychopathology. *Child Development*, 55, 17–29.

Teichman, Y. (1989). Childhood depression: A family perspective. *Israel Journal of Psychiatry and Related Sciences*, 26(1–2), 45–57.

Trickett, E. J., Birman, D., & Watts, R. (in press). Human diversity and community psychology: Still hazy after all these years. *Journal of Community Psychology*.

Tyler, F. B., Pargament, K. I., & Gatz, M. (1983). The resource collaborator role. *American Psychologist*, 38, 488–398.

Wandersman, A., & Hess, R. (1985). *Beyond the individual: Environmental approaches and prevention*. New York: Haworth.

Warren, R. I., & Warren, D. K. (1977). *The neighborhood organizer's handbook*. South Bend, IN: University of Notre Dame Press.

Weithorn, L. A. (1987). Informed consent for prevention research involving children: Legal and ethical issues. In J. A. Steinberg & M. M. Silverman (Eds.), *Preventing mental disorders: A research perspective* (DHHS Publication No. ADM 87-1492, pp. 226–242). Washington, DC: U.S. Government Printing Office.

West, S. G., Sandler, I., Pillow, D. R., Baca, L., & Gersten, J. C. (1991). The use of structural equation modeling in generative research: Toward the design of a preventive intervention for bereaved children. *American Journal of Community Psychology*, 19, 459–480.

Part III

Description
of the Disorders

Until relatively recently, it would have been impossible to organize a textbook of abnormal behavior in children based on specific disorders. Prior to *DSM-III* and *DSM-III-R,* the diversity of children's behavioral and emotional disorders was not so clearly delineated. As indicated in chapter 2, the rich literature in behavioral classification had long distinguished between externalizing and internalizing behavior problems. In the past 20 years, however, a considerable body of research has enhanced our understanding of previously neglected conditions, such as anxiety disorders, affective disorders, and eating disorders. Moreover, new and distinct areas have emerged, including pediatric psychology and substance use and abuse in children and adolescents.

As an increasingly sophisticated body of well-controlled research has been amassed, several general observations can be made regarding the etiology, assessment, and treatment of child and adolescent psychopathology. First, disorders must be understood within the context of the child's family and social environment. Factors such as a dysfunctional family system, poverty, and neighborhood violence, to name but a few, can contribute to the etiology and/or maintenance of the disorder and may impede treatment. Second, most disorders occur as a function of the interaction between biological and environmental risk factors. Treatment, therefore, must derive from an assessment of psychological, environmental, and psychophysiological systems. Third, in order to maximize successful outcome, treatment should target the multiple settings (e.g., family, school) that ultimately impact the child's behavior. And fourth, the chronic course of several disorders (e.g., mental retardation, autism) necessitates long-term treatment and frequent follow-ups.

The 10 chapters in this section examine specific disorders of childhood and adolescence. Included is a chapter on the assessment of and intervention with pediatric illness that is often accompanied by behavioral and emotional distress.

In chapter 13, Rabian and Silverman examine anxiety disorders. Subsumed under this rubric are disorders unique to childhood (e.g., overanxious disorder, separation anxiety disorder) and disorders exhibited by both children and adults (e.g., phobia, obsessive-compulsive disorder, post-traumatic stress disorder). The etiology of anxiety disorders in children is not well understood, although evidence points toward the role of learning in the development of at least some types of anxiety disorders. Several therapies have been developed for the anxiety disorders, all of which ultimately require that the child be exposed to the feared stimulus to ensure recovery.

Stark, Ostrander, Kurowski, Swearer, and Bowen cover affective and mood disorders in chapter 14. The authors point out that it has only been recently that depression has been recognized as a distinct disorder in children and adolescents. Etiologic formulations, on the whole, mirror those developed for adults, and emphasize vulnerabilities in cognitive, physiological, and social domains. Given the often chronic course of depression, early intervention is critical. The authors describe several models of treatment, the most promising of which incorporates cognitive therapy and social skills training.

Mental retardation is reviewed by Baumeister and Baumeister in chapter 15. By definition, mental retardation emerges in childhood and is characterized by low IQ and deficits in functional ability. Although there are a number of possible causes of mental retardation, broad distinctions are typically made between cultural-familial retardation, characterized by mild impairment in response to environmental deprivation, and organic retardation, involving more severe impairment and emanating from organic pathology or genetic factors. Mental retardation is chronic, and early intervention is needed to maximize developmental and cognitive potential. For severe behavior problems, both behavior therapy and pharmacotherapy have been used, although the authors caution against the abuse of these procedures.

In chapter 16, Harris examines autism. Although relatively rare, this disorder is chronic in its course and has profound implications for social, emotional, and cognitive functioning. The precise etiology of autism has eluded researchers, although most evidence points toward a biological basis. Behavior therapy is the treatment of choice for autism, with particular emphasis on enhancing social skills in these children.

Specific developmental disorders are covered by Johnson in chapter 17. These disorders involve children who exhibit deficits in academic, language, and motor domains. Although there are multiple causative factors implicated in specific developmental disorders, it is generally accepted that an underlying cerebral dysfunction plays an important role. Intensive educational interventions are used in an effort to reverse what can be a long lasting condition.

In chapter 18, Webster-Stratton and Dahl examine conduct disorder. Children with this diagnosis are heterogeneous in their presentation, exhibiting various degrees of noncompliance, oppositionality, lying, stealing, and antisocial behavior. Numerous factors are associated with the onset of conduct disorder, including difficult temperament, poor academic performance, and parents' psychopathology. Treatment has primarily focused on skills training that can be implemented at the individual, family, and community levels.

Attention-Deficit Hyperactivity Disorder (ADHD) is reviewed by Rapport in chapter 19. Unlike several other child and adolescent disorders, ADHD is comparatively well-researched. The etiology of ADHD is complex. Recent research has implicated dysfunction of the regulation process in the brain as a potentially important contributer. ADHD is typically long term in its course. Optimal treatment involves the concurrent use of psychostimulants to enhance attention and behavior therapy to increase on-task behavior and decrease disruptive behavior.

Eating disorders are examined by Mizes in chapter 20. Included here are anorexia nervosa, characterized by severe weight loss and distortion in body image, and bulimia nervosa, consisting of alternating binge eating and purging behavior. Cultural pressures promoting thinness as an ideal, negative attitudes about one's body, and genetics have all been implicated in the etiology of eating disorders. Cognitive–behavior therapy and antidepressant medications appear to be the treatments of choice at this point in time.

In chapter 21, Tarnowski and Brown examine psychological aspects of pediatric disorders. The authors address the psychological consequences of pediatric illness and injury, as well as psychological and behavioral contributions to illness. They then review the literature for two types of pediatric disorders: burn injuries and sickle cell disease. In pediatric psychology, assessment is comprehensive, involving both children and their families. Interventions must be tailored to the needs of the child and family to maximize adaptation and recovery.

Finally, in chapter 22, Newcomb and Richardson discuss substance use disorders. Risk factors for use and abuse are many and varied, ranging from models emphasizing social influences (e.g., peer pressure) to those focusing on biological vulnerabilities. The authors distinguish between experimentation, which is relatively widespread, and substance dependence and abuse, which is less common but has profound negative implications for psychosocial functioning. Intervention programs for adolescents engaged in substance abuse are only now being subjected to empirical scrutiny. It is evident, however, that active participation in treatment by adolescents and their families is important for eventual rehabilitation.

Chapter 13

Anxiety Disorders

Brian Rabian
University of Southern Mississippi

Wendy K. Silverman
Florida International University

CLINICAL DESCRIPTION

In recent years, a great deal of research attention has been directed to the anxiety disorders of childhood. This surge in attention is due, in part, to the increased coverage allotted to the anxiety disorders in the third edition of the *Diagnostic and Statistical Manual of Mental Disorders* (*DSM-III*; American Psychiatric Association, 1980), as well as its revision, *DSM-III-R* (American Psychiatric Association, 1987). Unlike its predecessor, *DSM-II*, that contained only one childhood anxiety diagnostic category called Overanxious Reaction, *DSM-III* added two more childhood anxiety categories. These were: Separation Anxiety Disorder and Avoidant Disorder. Overanxious reaction was retained in *DSM-III* and *DSM-III-R* as a third category, though its name was changed to Overanxious Disorder. Also new to *DSM-III*, and retained in *DSM-III-R*, was the creation of the major and broader heading, "Anxiety Disorders of Childhood and Adolescence," under which these three childhood anxiety categories (Separation Anxiety Disorder, Avoidant Disorder, and Overanxious Disorder) were now subsumed.

In addition to the Anxiety Disorders of Childhood and Adolescence, *DSM-III* and *DSM-III-R* contained several other categories of anxiety disorders, not specific to youth (i.e., disorders that children may present with, but so too may adults). These additional anxiety disorder categories included: Generalized Anxiety Disorder, Panic Disorder, Obsessive-Compulsive Disorder, Posttraumatic Stress Disorder, and Phobic Disorder (consisting of simple phobia, social phobia, and agoraphobia).

At the time of the writing of this chapter, *DSM-III-R* was still the classification scheme being used. However, there are several major changes in the revision of DSM, namely, *DSM-IV* (American Psychiatric Association, 1993). Specifically, the broad category Anxiety Disorders of Childhood and Adolescence is no longer retained, and the diagnosis separation anxiety disorder is now be subsumed under the category "Other Disorders of Childhood and Adolescence" (American Psychiatric Association,

1993). Because of problems with the overanxious disorder category (outlined later in this chapter), this disorder is now be subsumed under the adult category of generalized Anxiety Disorder. In addition, avoidant disorder is eliminated altogether from *DSM–IV*. Thus, this disorder is rarely discussed from hereon. Other changes, although specific to the adult anxiety diagnostic categories, also affect the use of these diagnoses with children. Specifically, simple phobia is now referred to as specific phobia, and social phobia is also referred to as social anxiety, that is, social phobia (Social Anxiety Disorder).

In this chapter, the terminology that is used is largely that of *DSM–III–R*, but, whenever possible, our eyes are cast toward *DSM–IV*. In addition, because of the developmental specificity of Separation Anxiety Disorder and Overanxious Disorder, these disorders are the focus here. Also considered in this chapter are childhood simple and social phobia. Because the other anxiety disorders (e.g., panic disorder and agoraphobia) have relatively lower prevalence rates in children, they are not included in the discussion to follow.

Before turning to a description of the clinical features of phobic and anxiety disorders in children, it is important to mention some of the broader issues relating to classification of these disorders, as codified in the *DSM*. In general, many questions remain about the reliability and validity of the *DSM* childhood diagnostic categories, in general, and the anxiety categories, in particular (see Silverman, 1992, 1993). When it comes to reliability, questions remain about the extent to which clinicians are able to independently agree in their diagnoses. When it comes to validity, questions remain about the extent to which anxiety disorders in children are clearly distinct disorders. For example, although significant differences have been found among Anxiety Disorder diagnoses in children along such as factors as age at time of referral, gender, and socioeconomic status, thereby lending support to distinctiveness (e.g., Last, Strauss, & Francis, 1987), absence of differences among the subcategories in terms of family history, scores on questionnaire measures, and course weakens support of distinctiveness (e.g., Cantwell & Baker, 1989; Last, Hersen, Kazdin, Orvaschel, & Perrin, 1991; Rabian, Peterson, Richters, & Jensen, 1993). This has led several investigators to question the subtyping of anxiety disorders in children; perhaps it would be wiser to have just one amalgamate category (e.g., Cantwell & Baker, 1989; Werry, Reeves, & Elkind, 1987), similar to what had existed with *DSM–II*. On the other hand, this approach was also viewed as problematic, leading to the changes that appeared in *DSM–III*.

There also is the problem of comorbidity: that is, the common finding that children frequently display multiple problems and thus, receive multiple diagnoses. With respect to anxiety disorders in children, depression has frequently been found to be a concurrent diagnosis (see Brady & Kendall, 1992). Externalizing behavior problems, such as Attention-Deficit Hyperactivity Disorder and conduct disorder, have also been found to frequently co-occur with anxiety disorders in children (e.g., Walker et al., 1991; Woolston et al., 1989). In general, it is important to keep in mind that comorbidity is the rule—not the exception in abnormal child psychology. However, the implications of comorbidity are not yet well understood, especially when it come to treatment planning, although attempts to delineate possible treatment strategies for work with anxious/depressed youth have recently been undertaken (Kendall, Kortlander, Chansky, & Brady, 1992). Clearly, this is an avenue of research that is wide open and deserving of attention.

Separation Anxiety Disorder

Separation Anxiety Disorder is characterized by excessive anxiety or distress upon separation or upon threat of separation from a major attachment figure (usually the parent) or from home. According to *DSM-IV*, the child must meet three of nine criteria to receive this diagnosis. These criteria are presented in Table 13.1.

Although *DSM-IV* specifies that the individual must be "younger than 18-yearsold" to be diagnosed with separation anxiety disorder, the precise age range is not indicated. Specification of age would seem important, however, given that anxiety about separation is a common developmental occurrence in all young children. For instance, for an 18-month-old child who is displaying "normal" distress upon separation from his or her caretaker, it would be inappropriate to view him or her as suffering from separation anxiety disorder. It would be appropriate, however, if the child were 12 years of age. Thus, diagnosis of Separation Anxiety Disorder is appropriate only to those cases where observed distress surrounding separation is extremely severe and is beyond what one would expect, given the particular developmental level of that child.

In a mental health setting, separation anxiety is a problem that can be readily ascertained in a child—at times, even immediately upon his or her presentation. The child with Separation Anxiety Disorder is one who is clinging to his or her parent or who refuses to meet with the clinician, unless the parent can also be present. The child may also cry or beg the parent not to leave him or her when the parent is asked to meet with the clinician alone.

Outside the clinic setting, the child's separation difficulties may be observed in a variety of other circumstances that require separation from loved ones or anticipation of separation. These include having to go to school, having to be left with a babysitter,

TABLE 13.1
Criteria for DSM-IV Diagnosis of Separation Anxiety Disorder

A. Developmentally inappropriate and excessive anxiety concerning separation from home or from those to whom the child is attached, as evidenced by at least three of the following:
  1. Persistent and excessive worry about losing, or possible harm befalling, major attachment figure
  2. Persistent and excessive worry that an untoward event will lead to separation from a major attachment figure (e.g., getting lost or being kidnapped)
  3. Persistent reluctance or refusal to go to school or elsewhere because of fear of separation
  4. Persistently and excessively scared or reluctant to be alone or without major attachment figures at home or without significant adults in other settings
  5. Persistent reluctance or refusal to go to sleep without being near a major attachment figure or to sleep away from home
  6. Repeated nightmares involving the theme of separation
  7. Repeated complaints of physical symptoms, e.g., headaches, stomachaches, nausea, or vomiting, when separation from major attachment figures is anticipated or involved
  8. Recurrent excessive distress when separation from home or major attachment figures is anticipated or involved
B. Duration of disturbance of at least four weeks
C. Onset before the age of 18
D. The disturbance causes clinically significant distress or impairment in social, academic (occupational), or other important areas of functioning
E. Occurrence not exclusively during the course of a Pervasive Developmental Disorder, Schizophrenia, or any other psychotic disorder

Note. Reprinted with permission from *DSM-IV Draft Criteria* (1993). Copyright 1993 American Psychiatric Association.

or having to go to sleep at night by oneself. Somatic complaints (e.g., stomachaches, headaches) also are common among these children.

Although Separation Anxiety Disorder is present in both children and adolescents, the disorder is more common among preadolescent children, and in general, younger and older children appear to differ in the symptoms that are most frequently reported (Francis, Last, & Strauss, 1987). In older children (ages 12 to 16) with separation anxiety disorder, the presenting problem is often that they cannot sleep away from home overnight, for example, at a friend's house or at a camp-out. Another problem may be that they are reluctant to go to school on most days. In younger children (ages 5 to 11), the presenting problem is often excessive worry about harm befalling parents upon separation and reported nightmares with separation themes.

Overanxious Disorder/Generalized Anxiety Disorder

In *DSM–III–R*, Overanxious Disorder (OAD) was characterized by excessive worry and fearful behavior not focused on a specific object or situation and not due to a recent stressor. According to *DSM–III–R*, a child had to meet 4 of 8 criteria to receive the diagnosis. These criteria included symptoms such as "excessive or unrealistic worry about future events," "excessive or unrealistic concern about competence in one or more areas (e.g., athletic, academic)," "somatic complaints, such as headaches or stomachaches, for which no physical basis can be established," and "marked feelings of tension or inability to relax." In *DSM–IV*, to receive a diagnosis of generalized anxiety disorder, a child must experience excessive anxiety and worry about a number of events (such as school), where the worry is associated with at least 3 of 6 symptoms. A full listing of the criteria for Generalized Anxiety Disorder (GAD) is contained in Table 13.2.

Although developmental differences in the expression of the *DSM–IV* category of GAD has not yet been examined, developmental differences in the manifestation of the *DSM–III–R* sub category of OAD has been noted. Specifically, an examination of such differences in youth was reported by Strauss, Lease, Last, and Francis (1988), who

TABLE 13.2
Criteria for DSM-IV Diagnosis of Generalized Anxiety Disorder

A. Excessive anxiety and worry (apprehensive expectation), occurring more days than not for at least six months, about a number of events or activities (such as work or school performance)
B. The person finds it difficult to control the worry
C. The anxiety and worry are associated with at least three of the following six symptoms:
   1. Restlessness or feeling keyed up or on edge
   2. Being easily fatigued
   3. Difficulty concentrating or mind going blank
   4. Irritability
   5. Muscle tension
   6. Sleep disturbance (difficulty falling or staying asleep, or restless unsatisfying sleep)
D. The focus of anxiety and worry is not confined to features of an Axis I disorder
E. The anxiety, worry, or physical symptoms cause clinically significant distress or impairment in social, occupational, or other important areas of functioning.
F. Not due to the direct effects of a substance or a general medical condition

Note. Reprinted with permission from *DSM-IV Draft Criteria* (1993). Copyright 1993 American Psychiatric Association.

divided a sample of 55 children and adolescents with Overanxious Disorder into two age groups: those younger than 12 years of age and those 12 years of age and older. A greater number of the youth in this sample fell within the older age group ($n = 32$) than the younger age group ($n = 23$). Compared to the younger children, the older children endorsed a greater number of symptoms, with "worry about future events" endorsed as the most common symptom.

As noted earlier, a number of problems contributed to the decision to subsume OAD under GAD in *DSM–IV* (Silverman, 1992; Werry, 1991). First, research found the reliability of OAD to vary considerably across studies. Second, high prevalence of OAD in epidemiological studies suggested that the threshold (i.e., the number of symptoms required to be present to receive the diagnosis) was too low. Third, probably because of the nonspecific nature of its symptoms, OAD was found to be highly comorbid with other disorders, most notably social phobia. For the previous reasons and also because OAD already shared a number of features with GAD, the decision was made to eliminate the subcategory of OAD in *DSM–IV* and to subsume it under the previous adult category of GAD (American Psychiatric Association, 1993).

Simple/Specific Phobia and Social Phobia/(Social Anxiety Disorder)

A specific phobia is a "marked and persistent fear that is excessive or unreasonable, cued by the presence or anticipation of a specific object or situation," such that the stimulus is avoided whenever possible or is endured only with intense anxiety (American Psychiatric Association, 1993). Typically, the intensity of the fear is severe enough to lead to interference in the child's functioning in school, home, or social relations.

To properly differentiate specific phobia from other anxiety disorders, it is important to ensure that the child's fear is not related to other fears such as separation (as in separation anxiety), panic attacks (as in panic disorder), or social humiliation or embarrassment (as in social phobia/social anxiety; see later discussion). Common specific phobias observed in children include small animals such as dogs, darkness, thunder/lightning, and doctors/dentists.

Social phobia (Social Anxiety Disorder) is a persistent fear of situations in which the individual is exposed to possible scrutiny by others and fears that he or she may act in a way that will be humiliating or embarrassing. This problem may be manifested in the school setting, where the child may avoid activities such as giving a speech in class or asking a question in class. Outside the school setting, a child with social phobia may avoid attending social gatherings such as birthday parties, boyscout or girlscout meetings, and so on.

CAUSES OF THE DISORDERS

At the present time, causes of anxiety and phobias in children are still not well understood, but they appear to be multifaceted. The most theorizing about cause has centered on separation anxiety disorder and simple phobia.

In terms of Separation Anxiety Disorder, psychodynamic formulations emphasize the hostile wishes of the child toward the attachment figure, usually the mother. Fearing the possible fulfillment of these hostile wishes, the child avoids separation from mother as a way to suppress such thoughts and to help ensure her safety. According to the psychodynamic formulation, the child's insistence to be with mother serves to satisfy the dependency needs and internal conflicts of both the child and the mother. Unfortunately, little is said about the father's role in this process (Wicks-Nelson & Israel, 1991).

Evidence for the psychodynamic formulation of separation anxiety is based primarily on clinical case studies. Although the clinical case study can richly describe phenomena, the reliability and validity of such descriptions are weak. In terms of reliability, because the descriptions in a case study are based on the reporting of past events, accuracy and completeness of such retrospective data are often suspect. In terms of validity, when case studies go beyond descriptions to interpretations, there are few guidelines to judge their veracity (Wicks-Nelson & Israel, 1991).

A behavioral formulation of separation anxiety disorder points to a combination of both classical and operant learning factors. For example, a behavioral explanation of school avoidance as a symptom of separation anxiety presumes that the child has learned to stay away from school because of some association of the school with an intense fear of losing the mother or other attachment figure. Once avoidance behavior has occurred, it may be reinforced by attention and other rewards (e.g., watching television when at home) received by the child (Wicks-Nelson & Israel, 1991).

With respect to simple phobia of childhood, Freud's case of "Little Hans" has come to serve as the prototype in psychodynamic theory (Freud, 1953). According to Freud's formulation, the experience or threat of helplessness (from physical or psychic danger) is key. For example, in the case of Little Hans, his phobia of horses was viewed as arising from desire for his mother and desire to do away with his father: the competitor. However, for Hans to act on such instinctual wishes would put him in conflict with his father. His father would then want to be rid of or harm him, and Hans would then be in a position of helplessness. According to Freud, flight or repression (from internal or instinctual danger) was the response to this threat of helplessness. Because Hans' repression was incomplete, unconscious anxiety was displaced onto some external object that in some way was related to or symbolic of the unconscious wish. For Hans, the horse was related to such things as playing "horsie" with his father, his father's appearance (the horse's muzzle symbolized his father's mustache), and castration (symbolized by the horse's biting). Displacement allowed Hans to avoid the phobic object — the horse — whereas he could not avoid his father (Silverman & Rabian, in press).

As was true for the psychodynamic formulation of separation anxiety, the psychodynamic formulation of specific phobias is based primarily on clinical case studies. And thus, the reliability and validity of such descriptions may be questioned on scientific grounds.

Several behavioral theories, derived from principles of learning, have been proposed to explain the causes of phobias in children. According to Rachman (1977), simple phobias may develop either through direct acquisition (e.g., conditioning) or through indirect acquisition (e.g., vicarious exposure and/or the transmission of information or instruction). Support for these pathways in the development of childhood phobia has recently been provided by Ollendick and colleagues (Ollendick, King, & Hamilton, 1991). Specifically, Ollendick et al. (1991) administered a questionnaire, designed to assess the pathways for 10 highly prevalent fears (e.g., nuclear war, fire — getting burned, etc.), to 1,092 Australian and American children (ages 9 to 14 years). Results indicated that vicarious and instructional factors were most influential (56% and 89%, respectively). However, these factors were frequently combined with direct conditioning experiences as well.

Although results of Ollendick et al. (1991) are based exclusively on retrospective reports of a nonclinical sample of children, the findings are consistent with what is frequently heard from clinical samples of phobic children and their parents. It is not unusual for many parents of children with phobias to indicate that they too share the same fear as their child. Moreover, the child is aware of or has observed parental fear behavior. Similarly, it is not unusual for parents of phobic children to report that they have told their child "to be careful" of certain aspects of a particular object or event. Thus, the influence of parental modeling, or what Rachman (1977) referred to as "vicarious exposure," as well as "transmission of information and instruction," is apparent in the etiology of childhood phobia, based on the anecdotal reports of clinical samples (Silverman & Rabian, in press).

In addition to the pathways proposed by Rachman (1977), phobias may be acquired through operant conditioning. Specifically, the positive consequences that follow a fearful response (e.g., avoidance) may initiate and maintain that fearful response. For example, a youngster who exhibits avoidance behavior upon encountering a certain object or event, such as swimming in a pool or lake, and whose parents attend to this avoidance behavior may be positively reinforcing that behavior.

The notion that phobias are acquired via classical conditioning (the pairing of a neutral stimulus with an aversive unconditioned stimulus produces the initial fear or anxiety) but are maintained via operant conditioning (the reduction of visceral arousal via avoidance) is the basic premise of the two-factor model (Mowrer, 1939). Because questions have been raised about the relationship between avoidance to fear reduction, a revision of the two-factor model has been proposed (Delprato & McGlynn, 1984). Briefly, the revision emphasizes positive reinforcement that results from the relaxation and relief experienced following avoidance, rather than negative reinforcement (due to fear avoidance).

In addition to psychodynamic and learning theory, cognitive theories of etiology have also been proposed (e.g., Beck & Emery, 1985). Cognitive models are generally based on the assumption that emotional and behavioral problems, including anxieties and phobias, are due to maladaptive thinking. For example, unlike their nonphobic counterparts, phobic children are viewed as being more likely to hold faulty cognitions about a specific stimulus (e.g., I'll get hit by lightning) and have difficulty in controlling these cognitions.

Finally, some attention has been paid to identifying risk factors that might predispose individuals' development of phobic and anxiety disorders. One such set of risk factors is that of stressful life events. In this connection, investigators have found that stressful life events are associated with the manifestation of anxious symptomatology (Kashani & Orvaschel, 1990). Costello (1989) found an association between parental stress and OAD, although McGee et al. (1990) found that stressful life events were no more characteristic of OAD than any other disorder. Certainly, the influence of stressful life events and other risk factors, such as low socioeconomic status, poor social support, and so on, in the development of anxiety and phobic disorders in children requires further study (Velez, Johnson, & Cohen, 1989).

COURSE OF THE DISORDERS

There are few data on the course of anxiety disorders in children. As a result, findings from available studies do not allow for a definitive conclusion as to whether the course of these disorders is chronic or transient over time. In one of the few longitudinal studies, Cantwell and Baker (1989) followed 151 children and adolescents over a 5-year period after an initial outpatient evaluation. At the time of the initial evaluation, 14 children were identified with a *DSM-III-R* diagnosis of avoidant disorder, 9 children with separation anxiety, and 8 children with overanxious disorder. At the 5-year follow-up, the majority of the children who initially presented with an anxiety disorder either showed spontaneous remission or now met criteria for a different disorder—usually another anxiety disorder. Of the anxiety disorders, avoidant disorder was the most stable at follow-up, with 29% of the children still meeting criteria for that disorder. This contrasts with separation anxiety disorder, where only 1 child still met criteria for this disorder 5 years later, and overanxious disorder, where only 2 children continued to meet criteria. Cantwell and Baker (1989) also reported that at the 5-year follow-up, 44% of children with the original diagnosis of separation anxiety were completely recovered. This compares to 36% for children with the diagnosis of overanxious disorder and 25% for children with the diagnosis of avoidant disorder.

Several investigators have hypothesized that children with separation anxiety disorder grow up to be adults with agoraphobia or panic disorder (e.g., Gittelman & Klein, 1984; Zitrin & Ross, 1988). This view was espoused in *DSM-III-R*'s description of panic disorder that stated that "separation anxiety disorder in childhood and sudden loss of social supports or disruption of important interpersonal relationships apparently predisposes to the development of" panic disorder (American Psychiatric Association, 1987, p. 237). Research support for continuity between childhood separation anxiety disorder and adult agoraphobia or panic disorder is mixed, however. For example, although several studies, based on the retrospective reports of patients with agoraphobia, found that many patients (approximately 20% to 35%) experienced separation anxiety disorder as children (e.g., Gittelman & Klein, 1985; Klein, Zitrin, Woerner, & Ross, 1983; Zitrin, Klein, Woerner, & Ross, 1983), just as many studies failed to find such a relationship (e.g., Breier, Charney, & Heninger, 1986; Mendel & Klein, 1969; Thyer, Himle, & Fischer, 1988). To date, therefore, it is difficult to draw any conclusions about the nature of the relationship, if any, between separation anxiety disorder in childhood and agoraphobia in adulthood. Moreover, due to limitations of patients' retrospective reports (e.g., memory loss, distortion, bias)—which has been the primary method used in this research—it is necessary for future research to employ prospective, longitudinal designs.

Similarly, to date, there is little evidence that there is continuity between chronic worrying in childhood (or what was referred to as OAD in *DSM-III-R*) and chronic worrying in adulthood (or GAD), Werry, 1991). As Werry (1991) pointed out, children of parents with GAD do not appear to display an increased rate themselves for this disorder (or *DSM-III-R*, OAD). In addition, there is evidence that the symptoms of OAD in children tend to disappear or abate significantly in the majority of cases after only a few years.

With respect to phobic disorders in children, although evidence suggests that milder fears and phobias are relatively transient, some types of simple phobias appear to persist into adulthood, if untreated (Silverman & Rabian, in press). In one of the few longitudinal studies on the natural history of phobia, Agras, Chapin, and Oliveau (1972) followed 30 phobic individuals (10 of whom were children) who reported a variety of fears over a 5- year period. During this time, none received treatment. All of the children were viewed as "improved" after 5 years, compared to 43% of the adults. However, most of the children still exhibited symptomatology at follow-up.

Although these results appear encouraging, especially for children with phobias, Ollendick (1979) pointed out that "improved" children in the Agras et al. study were not completely free from symptoms. In fact, the majority of children assessed at follow-up continued to exhibit symptoms of sufficient intensity to be rated between "no disability" and "maximum disability." Thus, Ollendick's reinterpretation of the Agras et al. (1972) data suggests that phobias, or at least some of the symptoms of phobias, persist over time for some children.

Studies that examine age of onset of phobias are yet another means by which their course may be evaluated (e.g., Ost, 1987; Sheehan, Sheehan, & Minichiello, 1981; Thyer Nesse, Cameron, & Curtis, 1985). Although these studies are limited as they are based on subjects' retrospective reports, some interesting trends can be gleaned from this work, nevertheless. For example, Ost (1987) reported that among a sample of adults with agoraphobia, social phobia, and simple phobia (mean age = 34-years-old), their phobia problems developed, on average, between the ages of 7 and 28 years, with the simple phobias having the earliest age of onset. Thus, consistent with Ollendick's (1979) reinterpretation of the longitudinal study of Agras et al. (1972), these data suggest that simple phobias tend to persist into adulthood for some proportion of children.

FAMILIAL CONTRIBUTIONS

There is a growing literature on the familial contributions to the anxiety disorders in children. Two types of studies in this area have been most common: those examining the offspring of adults with anxiety disorders ("top-down") and those examining the first-degree relatives of children with anxiety disorders ("bottom-up", Last, 1993).

In general, studies on adults diagnosed with anxiety disorders demonstrate an increased likelihood of anxiety disorders among their children (Silverman, Cerny, Nelles, & Burke, 1988). For example, Turner, Beidel, and Costello (1987), in a top-down study on the offspring of mothers with anxiety disorders (obsessive-compulsive disorder or agoraphobia), found that these children were seven times more likely to be diagnosed with an anxiety disorder as children of "normal" parents. Also, they were twice as likely to have an anxiety disorder as compared to children of depressed mothers (although the latter was not a significant difference).

Although findings such as these are tantalizing, what is not clear from such top-down studies is whether the increased risk observed among offspring is for a specific disorder or for psychopathology in general. Nor is it clear why some offspring whose parents suffer from severe anxiety symptoms appear to be unaffected by their parents' pathology. The mechanisms used by youngsters to help cope with parental problem.behaviors are also not clear. Overall, the issue of resilience and coping among the offspring of parents with anxiety disorders is a critical area requiring future research attention.

In addition to top-down studies, several bottom-up studies have evaluated the first-degree relatives of children with anxiety disorders. Last, Phillips, and Statfeld (1987) examined prevalence of separation anxiety and OAD in the histories of mothers whose children had these disorders and in mothers whose children had a nonanxiety psychiatric disorder. Overall, results indicated that the rate of OAD was significantly higher in mothers of overanxious children than in mothers of children with separation anxiety or a nonanxiety disorder.

In another study, Last, Hersen, Kazdin, Francis, and Grubb (1987) evaluated rates of both past and current psychiatric disorders among mothers of children with an anxiety disorder (separation anxiety and OAD; $N = 58$) versus mothers of children with a nonanxiety disorder (e.g., conduct disorder or attention deficit disorder). Overall, mothers of children with anxiety disorders were significantly more likely to report a past history of some anxiety disorder, or to currently meet criteria for an anxiety disorder, relative to mothers of children in the comparison group. Specifically, more than 80% of the mothers of children with anxiety disorders reported a past history of anxiety disorder, and more than 50% were currently symptomatic.

In a more recent effort, Last and colleagues (1991) compared first- and second-degree relatives of children with anxiety disorders ($N = 94$) with relatives of children with Attention-Deficit Hyperactivity Disorder ($N = 58$) and children with no history of psychopathology ($N = 87$). The findings of this study showed higher rates of anxiety disorders in the relatives of children with anxiety disorders compared to the relatives of either children with Attention-Deficit Hyperactivity Disorder or children with no disorder.

All together, as was the case with top-down studies, evidence from bottom-up studies suggests that there is a familial contribution to the development of anxiety disorders in children. The evidence is mixed, however, as to whether this familial contribution is specific to anxiety disorders or to psychopathology in general. Thus, additional work is necessary to clarify this issue.

With respect to familial contributions to the development of phobias in children, to date, only a small number of studies have been conducted. For example, interviewing the first-degree relatives of adults with simple phobia and those of "normal" adults, Fyer et al. (1990) found that the relatives of simple phobia were more likely to exhibit simple phobia themselves (31%) compared to the relatives of the "normal" group (11%). Moreover, the relatives of the adults with simple phobia were more likely to display simple phobia specifically, rather than any other anxiety or phobic disorder. Similarly, other investigators have found the first-degree relatives of adults with social phobia to be more at risk for social phobia than for another anxiety disorder (e.g., Reich & Yates, 1988).

In summary, results from top-down and bottom-up studies have yielded valuable information pertaining to the familial contribution to phobic and anxiety disorders in children. However, such studies do not allow for the disentanglement of the relative contributions of genetic and environmental factors. Rather, what family studies can provide is "negative proof." That is, "If a higher frequency of a disorder is not observed among biological relatives, then genetic factors cannot be involved" (Last, 1993, p. 109). To specifically answer questions about the genetic influences in anxiety disorders, it is necessary to examine evidence from twin and adoptive studies; such work is summarized in the next section.

GENETIC INFLUENCES

There are a number of methods to examine genetic influences on the development of anxiety in children. These include: twin studies, adoptive studies, and the recently developed "genetic linkage" studies. An excellent summary of each of these methods is provided by Torgersen (1993). Briefly, twin studies examine concordance rates between monozygotic twins (MZ), who share identical genes, and dizygotic twins (DZ), who are no more similar genetically than nontwin siblings. Evidence showing higher concordance rates for a disorder between MZ twins than between DZ twins would indicate the influence of genetics on the appearance of the disorder. Adoptive studies examine twins reared in separate homes, thereby eliminating the possibility that high concordance rates for a disorder between twins simply reflect the fact that they were raised in the same environment. Genetic linkage studies attempt to use genetic markers to pinpoint the chromosomal location of a gene that may carry a particular disorder.

To date, few studies using the previous methods have been conducted in the area of childhood anxiety and phobia. Those studies that have been conducted have largely focused on temperamental variables such as withdrawal or on now outdated diagnostic labels such as anxiety neurosis (Torgersen, 1985). Twin studies, using adult subjects, have focused on more diffuse concepts, such as neuroticism (Eysenck, 1959) or on fears and phobias.

Given the paucity of research, what conclusions can be drawn regarding genetic influences on the development of anxiety and phobias in children? Overall, research findings suggest that anxious or fearful characteristics, in general, may be at least partly influenced by genetic features, although there is little evidence that genetic transmission takes place for a specific disorder. That is, it appears that offspring of adults with anxiety or phobic disorders may inherit a tendency to anxiousness or fearfulness that may manifest itself in a number of ways but not necessarily in the same specific way as that observed in the parent (Torgersen, 1993). This general conclusion holds true for most of the anxiety and phobic disorders; however, there is growing evidence that panic disorder is caused by dominant genetic factors (Torgersen, 1993).

CURRENT TREATMENTS

Currently, the research literature focusing specifically on the treatment of anxiety disorders in children is meager. Although there is a more extensive literature on the treatment of phobias in children, most of this literature consists of case studies. Well-controlled studies using experimental designs are lacking.

The most widely used treatment approaches for childhood phobic and anxiety disorders are the behavioral, psychodynamic, and pharmacological. Each of these is briefly described.

Behavior Therapy

Behavioral strategies used to treat childhood anxiety and phobia include the following:

1. contingency management, in which external agents (parents, therapists) rearrange the environment to ensure that positive consequences follow exposure tasks;

2. systematic desensitization, which involves gradually exposing the child to the fear-evoking situation while he or she engages in an activity incompatible with fear, usually some form of relaxation;
3. implosion and flooding, which involve prolonged exposure;
4. modeling, which involves observing a model—either live or symbolic—confront the feared stimulus; and
5. self-control, which involves teaching the child cognitive strategies that are to be applied when he or she experiences feelings of fear or anxiety or is in a situation that elicits fear or anxiety.

At present, the data are not yet available as to which is the "best" behavioral strategy to use. However, there is one conclusion that can be stated rather confidently: Exposure to the fearful or anxiety-provoking object or situation is essential for a successful fear or anxiety reduction program (Marks, 1975). With the exception of implosion and flooding procedures, when exposure has been used, it has been carried out in a gradual fashion. That is, the child is usually asked to conduct exposure exercises along the "steps of a fear hierarchy." Use of the hierarchy provides an opportunity for the child to gradually gain confidence (and reduce fear or anxiety) when in the presence of the phobic or anxious stimulus, as he or she successful completes each "step" of the hierarchy.

An example of a fear hierarchy for a child with a phobia of dogs might be: (a) seeing pictures of dogs in magazines, (b) going to a pet shop and looking at a dog through the window, (c) going to a pet shop and petting a small puppy that is being held by somebody, (d) petting a larger size dog that is on a leash, and (e) petting yet a larger dog that is running around (Silverman & Eisen, 1993).

Similarly, Eisen and Silverman (in press) described hierarchies that were devised for four children with OAD. For each child, each step of the hierarchy consisted of the situations or events that he or she predominantly thought or worried about (from lowest to highest). These children were taught how to control worrisome thoughts through use of cognitive coping strategies (i.e., self-control training). Then, the child practiced using these strategies each week while confronting—either in imagination or in vivo—each situation or event on the hierarchy. Overall, treatment was found to be effective in reducing overanxious symptoms in these youngsters. In summary, further research is needed to clearly demonstrate the efficacy of behavioral approaches in reducing phobic and anxiety disorders in children. Also important is to examine how variables such as the child's developmental level, comorbidity and familial factors (e.g., parental psychopathology, marital discord, etc.) influence treatment effectiveness.

Psychodynamic Therapy

Even more than the behavioral therapies, evidence for efficacy of the psychodynamic approach in the treatment of childhood phobia and anxiety is based almost exclusively on reports from case studies. In general, psychodynamic therapies are based on the notion that the focus of the child's anxiety or fear is a symbolic manifestation of some underlying intrapsychic conflict. Psychodynamic therapy, therefore, addresses the child's emotional conflict. To pursue this aim, play therapy is frequently employed, where the therapist uses the content and process of the child's play activities to provide interpretations about the perceived source of the conflict. In older children, psychodynamic therapy might also involve interpretations about the child's attitudes and behaviors toward the therapist. Lack of empirical study of psychodynamic therapy in the treatment of anxiety and phobic disorders in children renders it difficult to recommend its routine application.

Pharmacological Therapy

As with psychodynamic approaches, the literature on pharmacotherapy with anxious children consists largely of clinical reports, many with methodological limitations. As a result, it is difficult to draw conclusions from this work (Gittelman & Koplewicz, 1986). Antidepressants, such as imipramine and clomipramine, are the most frequently administered class of drugs. These medications have been tested in double-blind, placebo-controlled studies, examining their use for school refusal and associated symptoms of anxiety and depression (Bernstein & Borchardt, 1991). However, the findings have been mixed. Although antidepressants appear to be effective in helping separation anxious children return to school, some evidence suggests that they may be no more effective than placebos. Certainly, more work in this area is warranted before such agents with potential side effects are widely used with youngsters.

Case Study

Jerry is a 9-year-old boy who was referred to a childhood anxiety program by the school psychologist because of repeated absences from school. Jerry's parents reported that he is very fearful of school and cries almost every morning when preparing for that setting. In particular, Jerry, an only child, complains to his parents about how uncomfortable he feels around the other children. Both in and out of school, Jerry has few friends and avoids participation in group activities whenever he can. In addition, Jerry's parents indicated that he is a "worry wart," who is almost constantly seeking reassurance from others about his abilities and performance. Although Jerry had experienced these problems for some time, they became problematic (repeated absences from school) only recently.

Jerry and his parents were individually administered a structured interview. Results of the structured interviews indicated that Jerry met criteria for overanxious disorder and for social phobia. Although Jerry and his parents also reported some depressive symptomology, he did not meet sufficient criteria to warrant a diagnosis of affective disorder. Depression was seen as secondary to Jerry's difficulties in establishing social contacts with peers.

Jerry's mother indicated that she had experienced similar problems herself when in school, although she does not currently experience significant anxiety in social settings. Nevertheless, Jerry's parents considered themselves "homebodies" and reported that they did not engage in social activities outside of the home very often. Similarly, they had never encouraged Jerry to become involved in extracurricular activities. Apart from anxiety experienced by Jerry's mother during childhood, no other family history of anxiety was reported, although Jerry's parents were uncertain of the histories of many extended relatives.

Because of Jerry's excessive worrying and need for reassurance, it appeared important to provide him with skills that would help him manage his feelings of anxiety on his own. Thus, self-control training was initiated. The focus of this training was on teaching Jerry specific thinking styles and on how to apply these styles when experiencing feelings of anxiety, fear, or worry.

In addition to self-control training, graduated in vivo exposure (where Jerry was required to confront his fear of interacting with other children at school) was conducted. Contingency contracting procedures were instituted to help him carry out these exposure tasks each week. Specifically, Jerry's parents were taught how to rearrange the environment to ensure that positive consequences followed each exposure task. To ensure that positive consequences followed each exposure, Jerry and his parents signed a written contract each week that stated that "if Jerry does (a specified exposure task) then (a specified reward) is provided by the parents." To assist Jerry in dealing with the social exposure tasks, he received coaching in social skills, such as making conversation, asking questions, and maintaining eye contact.

After approximately seven sessions of treatment, Jerry reported that he felt less anxious about attending school and better able to control his anxiety during most interactions with peers at school. By the tenth (and last) session, Jerry had accepted an invitation to a classmate's birthday party, and he expressed interest in joining a soccer team with a new friend from school. Most importantly, Jerry had not missed a day of school in the past 5 weeks.

Following treatment, Jerry and his parents continued to work on their own in devising exposure exercises, so that he could continue to practice his newly acquired self-control skills. Follow-up visits, conducted at intervals of 3 months, 6 months, and 12 months, revealed that treatment gains had been maintained. Jerry was attending school regularly, was involved in extracurricular activities both in and out of school, and reported feeling more comfortable interacting with peers. He now worried less than before initiation of treatment. Furthermore, he was no longer seeking constant reassurance from his parents. Overall, both Jerry and his parents indicated that much progress had occurred.

SUMMARY

Whereas *DSM-III-R* contained three disorders under the broad heading of Anxiety Disorders of Childhood and Adolescence (i.e., separation anxiety disorder, avoidant disorder, and overanxious disorder), *DSM-IV* maintains only separation anxiety, now under the category Other Disorders of Infancy, Childhood, or Adolescence. *DSM-III-R's* diagnosis of overanxious disorder has been subsumed under generalized anxiety disorder in *DSM-IV*, and avoidant disorder has been eliminated altogether. As in *DSM-III-R*, *DSM-IV* allows for additional adult anxiety diagnoses to be used with children. Of these, specific phobia (previously simple phobia) and social phobia/ (social anxiety disorder, previously just social phobia) are the most common in youth.

Questions remain about the reliability and validity of the *DSM* anxiety categories. In terms of reliability, questions remain about the extent to which clinicians are able to agree in their diagnoses. In terms of validity, questions remain about the extent to which the disorders listed are distinct. There also is the problem of comorbidity, that is, the common finding that children with anxiety disorders tend to receive multiple diagnoses.

Separation anxiety disorder is characterized by excessive anxiety or distress upon separation or upon threat of separation from major attachment figures, such as parents. Because anxiety about separation is a common developmental occurrence in the young child, the diagnosis of separation anxiety is appropriate only to those cases where the child's distress is severe and is not typical of the current developmental level. The symptoms of this disorder, which are more common among preadolescent children, may be readily observed in a variety of settings, such as having to go to school, having to be left with a babysitter, and so on.

Generalized anxiety disorder (or overanxious disorder in *DSM–III–R*) is characterized by excessive worry and fearful behavior not focused on a specific object or situation and not due to a recent stressor. Like separation anxiety disorder, there appear to be developmental differences in the manifestation of this disorder.

Specific phobia refers to a persistent fear of a circumscribed stimulus, usually leading to avoidance. Common phobias in children include small animals, darkness, thunder/lightning, and the dentist. Social phobia (anxiety) refers to a persistent fear of situations in which the person is exposed to possible scrutiny by others and fears that he or she may act in a way that will be humiliating or embarrassing.

At the present time, causes of anxiety and phobic disorders in childhood are not well understood and appear to be multifaceted. Although several models have been proposed to explain onset of these disorders, behavioral and cognitive–behavioral theories have gained the most attention and support in the research literature.

Few conclusions, if any, can be drawn about the course of anxiety disorders in children. At the present time, evidence is mixed as to whether children with separation anxiety disorder grow up to become adults with agoraphobia. Also mixed is the evidence as to whether children with generalized excessive worry (or with what was referred to as overanxious disorder) grow up to become adults with generalized anxiety disorder. With regard to phobic disorders, evidence suggests that milder fears and phobias tend to be transient, whereas more severe fears and phobias persist into adulthood for some proportion of children.

Overall, findings from top-down and bottom-up studies indicate that there is a trend for anxiety and phobic disorders to aggregate in families. However, with the exception of the phobias, the findings suggest that what may be transmitted within families is a risk for developing some anxiety disorder, in general, rather than a specific anxiety disorder. Some studies suggest that genetics may play a part in this transmission. No definitive conclusions can be made, however, about the influence of genetics versus the environment until further work is conducted.

The most widely used treatment approaches for childhood phobic and anxiety disorders are behavioral, psychodynamic, and pharmacological. Currently, most of the treatment literature consists of case reports. Controlled experimental studies are lacking. Despite the paucity of research in this area, evidence is strong that an effective fear and anxiety reduction program should include exposure to the fear or anxiety-provoking stimulus.

The writing of this chapter was supported in part by NIMH grants #44781 and #49680.

REFERENCES

Agras, W. S., Chapin, H. N., & Oliveau, D. C. (1972). The natural history of phobia. *Archives of General Psychiatry, 26*, 315–317.

American Psychiatric Association. (1980). *Diagnostic and statistical manual of mental disorders*. (3rd ed.). Washington, DC: Author.

American Psychiatric Association. (1987). *Diagnostic and statistical manual of mental disorders*. (3rd rev. ed.). Washington, DC: Author.

American Psychiatric Association. (1993). *DSM-IV draft criteria*. Washington, DC: Author.

Beck, A. T., & Emery, G. (1985). *Anxiety and phobias: A cognitive perspective*. New York: Basic Books.

Bernstein, G. A., & Borchardt, C. M. (1991). Anxiety disorders of childhood and adolescence: A critical review. *Journal of the American Academy of Child and Adolescent Psychiatry, 30*, 519–532.

Brady, U., & Kendall, P. C. (1992). Comorbidity of anxiety and depression in children and adolescents. *Psychological Bulletin, 111*, 244–255.

Breier, A., Charney, D. S., & Heninger, G. R. (1986). Agoraphobia with panic attacks: Developmental, diagnostic stability and course of illness. *Archives of General Psychiatry, 43*, 1029–1031.

Cantwell, D. P., & Baker, L., (1989). Stability and natural history of DSM-III childhood diagnoses. *Journal of the American Academy of Child and Adolescent Psychiatry, 29*, 691–700.

Costello, E. J. (1989). Developments in child psychiatric epidemiology. *Journal of the American Academy of Child and Adolescent Psychiatry, 28*, 836–841.

Delprato, D. J., & McGlynn, F. D. (1984). Behavioral theories of anxiety disorders. In S. M. Turner (Ed.), *Behavioral treatment of anxiety disorders*. New York: Plenum.

Eisen, A. R., & Silverman, W. K. (in press). Should I relax or change my thoughts? A preliminary study of the treatment of overanxious disorder in children. *Cognitive Psychotherapy Research: An International Quarterly*.

Eysenck, H. J. (1959). *Maudsley personality inventory*. London: University of London.

Francis, G., Last, C. G., & Strauss, C. C. (1987). Expression of separation anxiety disorder: The roles of age and gender. *Child Psychiatry and Human Development, 18*, 82–89.

Freud, S. (1953). Analysis of a phobia in a five-year-old boy. In J. Strachey (Ed. and Trans.), *Standard edition*, of the complete psychological works of Sigmund Freud (Vol. 10). London: Hogarth. (Original work published 1909)

Fyer, A. J., Mannuzza, S., Gallops, M. S., Martin, L. Y., Aaronson, C., Gorman, M., Liebowitz, M. R., & Klein, D. F. (1990). Familial transmission of simple phobias and fears: A preliminary report. *Archives of General Psychiatry, 47*, 252–256.

Gittelman, R., & Klein, D. F. (1984). Relationship between separation anxiety and panic and agoraphobic disorders. *Psychopathology, 17*, 56–65.

Gittelman, R., & Klein, D. F. (1985). Childhood separation anxiety and adult agoraphobia. In A. H. Tuman & J. Maser (Eds.), *Anxiety and the anxiety disorders* (pp. 389–402). Hillsdale, NJ: Lawrence Erlbaum Associates.

Gittelman, R., & Koplewicz, H. S. (1986). Pharmacotherapy of childhood anxiety disorders. In R. Gittelman (Ed.), *Anxiety disorders of childhood*, (pp. 188–201). New York: Guilford.

Kashani, J. H., & Orvaschel, H. (1990). A community study of anxiety in children and adolescents. *American Journal of Psychiatry, 147*, 313–318.

Kendall, P. C., Kortlander, E., Chansky, T. E., & Brady, E. U. (1992). Comorbidity of anxiety and depression in youth: Treatment implications. *Journal of Consulting and Clinical Psychology, 60*, 869–880.

Klein, D. F., Zitrin, C. M., Woerner, M. G., & Ross, D. C. (1983). Treatment of phobias: 2. Behavior therapy and supportive psychotherapy: Are there any specific ingredients? *Archives of General Psychiatry, 40*, 139–145.

Last, C. G. (1993). Relationship between familial and childhood anxiety disorder. In C. G. Last (Ed.), *Anxiety across the lifespan: A developmental perspective* (pp. 94–112). New York: Springer.

Last, C. G., Hersen, M., Kazdin, A. E., Francis, G., & Grubb, H. J. (1987). Psychiatric illness in the mothers of anxious children. *American Journal of Psychiatry, 144*, 653–657.

Last, C. G., Hersen, M., Kazdin, A. E., Orvaschel, H., & Perrin, S. (1991). Anxiety disorders in children and their families. *Archives of General Psychiatry, 48*, 928–934.

Last, C. G., Phillips, J. E., & Statfeld, A. (1987). Childhood anxiety disorders in mothers and their children. *Child Psychiatry and Human Development, 18*, 103–112.

Last, C. G., Strauss, C. C., & Francis, G. (1987). Comorbidity among childhood anxiety disorders. *Journal of Nervous and Mental Disease, 175*, 726–730.

Marks, I. M. (1975). Behavioral treatment of phobic and obsessive-compulsive disorders: A critical appraisal. In M. Hersen, R. M. Eisler, & P. M. Miller (Eds.), *Progress in behavior modification* (Vol. 1). New York: Academic Press.

McGee, R., Feehan, M., Williams, S., Partridge, F., Silva, P. A., & Kelly, J. (1990). DSM-III disorders in a large sample of adolescents. *Journal of the American Academy of Child and Adolescent Psychiatry*, *29*, 611–619.

Mendel., J., & Klein, D. F. (1969). Anxiety attacks and subsequent agoraphobia. *Comprehensive Psychiatry*, *10*, 476–478.

Mowrer, O. H. (1939). A stimulus-response analysis of anxiety and its role as a reinforcing agent. *Psychological Review*, *46*, 553–565.

Ollendick, T. H. (1979). Fear reduction techniques with children. In M. Hersen, R. M. Eisler, & P. M. Miller (Eds.), *Progress in behavior modification* (Vol. 8, pp. 127–168). New York: Academic Press.

Ollendick, T. H., King, N. J., Hamilton, D. I. (1991). Origins of childhood fears: An evaluation of Rachman's theory of fear acquisition. *Behaviour Research and Therapy*, *29*, 117–123.

Ost, L. (1987). Age of onset in different phobias. *Journal of Abnormal Psychology*, *96*, 123–145.

Rabian, B., Peterson, R., Richters, J., & Jensen, P. R. (1993). Anxiety sensitivity among anxious children. *Journal of Child Clinical Psychology*, *22*, 441–446.

Rachman, S. (1977). The conditioning theory of fear acquisition: A critical examination. *Behaviour Research and Therapy*, *15*, 375–387.

Reich, J., & Yates, W. (1988). Family history of psychiatric disorders in social phobia. *Comprehensive Psychiatry*, *29*, 72–75.

Sheehan, D. V., Sheehan, K. E., & Minichiello, W. E. (1981). Age of onset of phobic disorders: A reevaluation. *Comprehensive Psychiatry*, *22*, 544–553.

Silverman, W. K. (1992). Taxonomy of anxiety disorders in children. In G. D. Burrows, M. Roth, & R. Noyes, Jr. (Eds.), *Handbook of anxiety (Vol. 5): Contemporary issues and prospects for research in anxiety disorders*. Amsterdam: Elsevier.

Silverman, W. K. (1993). DSM and classification of anxiety disorders in children and adults. In C. G. Last (Ed.), *Anxiety across the lifespan: A developmental perspective* (pp. 7–36). New York: Springer.

Silverman, W. K., Cerny, J. A., Nelles, W. B., & Burke, A. (1988). Behavior problems in children of parents with anxiety disorders. *Journal of the American Academy of Child and Adolescent Psychiatry*, *27*, 779–784.

Silverman, W. K., & Eisen, A. E. (1993). Phobic disorders. In R. T. Ammerman, C. G. Last, & M. Hersen (Eds.), *Handbook of prescriptive treatments for children and adolescents*. Boston: Allyn & Bacon.

Silverman, W. K., & Rabian, B. (in press). Simple phobias. In T. H. Ollendick, N. J. King, & W. Yule (Eds.), *Handbook of phobic and anxiety disorders of children*.

Strauss, C. C., Lease, C. A., Last, C. G., & Francis, G. (1988). Overanxious disorder: An examination of developmental differences. *Journal of Abnormal Child Psychology*, *16*, 433–443.

Thyer, B. A., Himle, J., & Fischer, D. (1988). Is parental death a selective precursor to either panic disorder or agoraphobia? A test of the separation anxiety hypothesis. *Journal of Anxiety Disorders*, *2*, 333–338.

Thyer, B. A., Nesse, R. M., Cameron, O. G., & Curtis, G. C. (1985). Agoraphobia: A test of the separation anxiety hypothesis. *Behaviour Research and Therapy*, *24*, 209–211.

Torgersen, S. (1985). Hereditary differentiation of anxiety and affective neuroses. *British Journal of Psychiatry*, *146*, 530–534.

Torgersen, S. (1993). Relationship between adult and childhood anxiety disorders: Genetic hypothesis. In C. G. Last (Ed.), *Anxiety across the lifespan: A developmental perspective* (pp. 113–127). New York: Springer.

Turner, S. M., Beidel, D. C., & Costello, A. (1987). Psychopathology in the offspring of anxiety disorders patients. *Journal of Consulting and Clinical Psychology*, *55*, 229–235.

Velez, C. N., Johnson, J., & Cohen, P. (1989). A longitudinal analysis of selected risk factors for childhood psychopathology. *Journal of the American Academy of Child and Adolescent Psychiatry*, *28*, 861–864.

Walker, J. L., Lahey, B. B., Russo, M. F., Frick, P. J., Christ, M., McBurnett, K., Loeber, R., Stouthaser-Lober, M., & Green, S. B. (1991). Anxiety inhibition and conduct disorder in children: I. Relations to social impairment. *Journal of the American Academy of Child and Adolescent Psychiatry*, *30*, 187–191.

Werry, J. S. (1991). Overanxious disorder: A review of taxonomic properties. *Journal of the American Academy of Child and Adolescent Psychiatry*, *30*, 533–544.

Werry, J. S., Reeves, J. C., & Elkind, G. S. (1987). Attention deficit, conduct, oppositional, and anxiety disorders in children: I. A review of research on differentiating characteristics. *Journal of the American Academy of Child and Adolescent Psychiatry*, *26*, 133–143.

Wicks-Nelson, R., & Israel, A. (1991). *Behavior disorders of childhood* (2nd ed.). Englewood Cliffs: Prentice-Hall.

Woolston, J. L., Rosenthal, S. L., Riddle, M. A., Sparrow, S. S., Cicchetti, D., Zimmerman, L. D. (1989). Childhood comorbidity of anxiety/affective disorders and behavior disorders. *Journal of the American Academy of Child and Adolescent Psychiatry*, *28*, 707–713.

Zitrin, C. M., Klein, D. F., Woerner, M. G., & Ross, D. C. (1983). Treatment of phobias: 1. Comparison of imipramine hydrochloride and placebo. *Archives of General Psychiatry*, *40*, 125–138.

Zitrin, C. M., & Ross, D. C. (1988). Early separation anxiety and adult agoraphobia. *Journal of Nervous and Mental Disease*, *176*, 621–625.

Chapter 14

Affective and Mood Disorders

Kevin D. Stark
University of Texas

Rick Ostrander
Georgetown University

Cynthia A. Kurowski
Susan Swearer
Blair Bowen
University of Texas

Although depressive disorders may be the most widely studied and best understood psychological disorders among adults, our empirical knowledge of depressive disorders in children just began to emerge in the 1980s. This rather recent emergence stems in part from the many debates surrounding the existence and nature of depressive disorders during childhood. Initially, the debate centered on the possibility that a child could experience a depressive disorder. Psychodynamic theorists believed that depression was a superego phenomenon and because children do not have a well-developed superego, theoretically speaking, they could not be depressed. Subsequently, the debate progressed to recognizing that children could experience a depressive disorder as an underlying pathological phenomenon that caused a variety of overtly expressed disturbances including virtually all psychological disorders of childhood. Thus, if a child had an attention-deficit disorder for example, it was assumed that it was the result of an underlying depressive disorder. This phenomenon was referred to as *masked depression* because another disorder is presumed to mask the underlying depressive disorder. The shortcomings of this position were soon recognized (e.g., when was a childhood disorder a disorder other than depression?), and this position was abandoned. Next it was argued that depressive disorders during childhood and adolescence are a normal developmental phenomenon that did not warrant clinical attention. In other words, they are a normal part of growing up and they naturally go away, so why bother to deal with them. Clearly this is not the case. They are not the norm and, although they are episodic, they tend to be of long duration and to recur within a few years. During the 1980s, the *Diagnostic and Statistical Manual of Mental Disorders (DSM–III)* formally recognized the existence of depressive disorders during childhood, and the debate moved to the failure of *DSM–III* and its revision to recognize the developmental expression of depressive symptoms. In the *DSM–III* and *DSM–III–R*, adult criteria are used to diagnose depressive disorders in children. Currently, the debate appears to have returned to some of the earlier controversies. Are depressive disorders unique, or are they part of a broader disturbance referred to as negative affectivity (which is discussed later)? Are depressive and anxiety disorders part of the same disturbance that is expressed differently over the course of time? Are depressive disorders a secondary reaction to the existence of another primary debilitating disorder? These questions remain to be answered through future research. However, they exemplify the continued controversy surrounding depressive disorders during childhood.

As we learn more about depressive disorders during childhood, it is becoming increasingly clear that most children who are depressed are also experiencing another psychological disorder. This phenomenon is referred to as comorbidity. In fact, it appears as though less than one third of children who are diagnosed as depressed are experiencing a pure depressive disorder. This phenomenon of comorbidity creates some difficulties for the practitioner when trying to assess, diagnose, and treat a youngster with a depressive disorder. The phenomenon of comorbidity is referred to throughout the chapter.

To date a paucity of research into the treatment of depressive disorders during childhood has been completed. Based on our own research and clinical experience, it is evident that a multimodal approach to intervention that includes psychosocial as well as pharmacological interventions is most effective. Not only should the child receive individual treatment, but the youngster's parents should be involved in treatment in a variety of capacities ranging from serving as a cognitive–behavioral coach for the child to involvement in their own personal therapy as it relates to the child's problems and/or through involvement in family therapy.

In this chapter, the reader is introduced to the clinical picture of depressive disorders and the diagnostic categories used to capture and communicate the child's symptom picture. We have chosen to emphasize unipolar depressive disorders because they are more widely researched and more common among children. Thus, after describing the two major types of mood disorders (unipolar and bipolar), we no longer discuss the bipolar disorders (episode of mania and depression). The interested reader is referred to Fristad, Weller, and Weller (1992) for a discussion of bipolar disorders among children.

In addition to describing the clinical picture and course of depressive disorders during childhood, the major psychological and physiological models of depression are briefly described. Research related to the potential influence of family variables, both psychosocial and genetic, on the development of depressive disorders during childhood is discussed. Finally, the various treatment models that have been applied to depressed youths are described.

CLINICAL DESCRIPTION

When deciding whether a child is experiencing a mood disorder, it is important to consider the combination of symptoms that he or she is experiencing because dysphoric mood, and many of the other symptoms associated with mood disorders, are commonly experienced by children without any diagnosis as well as those with other psychological disturbances. A mood disorder can best be conceptualized as a syndrome in which a group of symptoms reliably co-occur (Carlson & Cantwell, 1980). It has been argued that the essential symptoms of mood disorders, especially unipolar depressive disorders, are identical between youths and adults (e.g. Cantwell, 1983; Kaslow & Rehm, 1983), this is the current position of the Third Edition of the *Diagnostic and Statistical Manual-Revised (DSM–III–R*; American Psychiatric Association, 1987). It appears as though the essential diagnostic criteria are the same across ages, but there are some additional symptoms that are unique to the individual's age and developmental stage (e.g., running away from home). These latter symptoms are referred to as age-specific associated features.

The principle feature of mood disorders is a disturbance in mood either excessively elevated (mania), dysphoric, irritable, or anhedonic (loss of interest or pleasure in most previously enjoyed activities) that occurs to a significant degree for a specified duration of time. A child with a mood disorder experiences a number of additional affective, cognitive, motivational, or physical disturbances (Kovacs & Beck, 1977). Dependent on the specific symptoms the child experiences, the youngster receives a diagnosis of a unipolar depressive disorder (the youngster is experiencing a depressive episode and has no history of a manic episode) or a bipolar disorder (a disorder in which at least a manic episode has occurred).

In addition to dysphoric mood, children who are experiencing a unipolar depressive episode may experience additional affective symptoms including anhedonia, irritability, excessive weepiness, feeling unloved, a sense of worthlessness, self-pity, and self-deprecation. Included among the possible cognitive symptoms are negative self-evaluations, excessive guilt, hopelessness, difficulty concentrating, and indecisiveness. Possible motivational symptoms include suicidal ideation and behavior, social withdrawal, and impaired academic functioning. A depressed child may experience any of the following physical symptoms: fatigue, sleep disturbance, change in appetite or weight, psychomotor agitation and retardation, and/or somatic complaints.

Children who are experiencing a manic episode have a feeling of extreme elation. They also may experience a number of cognitive symptoms including flight of ideas, racing thoughts, elevated self-esteem that may reach the point of grandiosity, distractibility, over-optimism, and especially creative or sharpened thinking. Motivational disturbances might include increased productivity, excessive involvement in activities with the potential for producing painful consequences, increased energy, and uninhibited people seeking. Among the possible physical symptoms are restlessness, talkativeness, and a decreased need for sleep.

Dependent on which of the symptoms are present, for how long, and to what level of severity, the youngster may receive a diagnosis of a mood disorder. A child who is experiencing a mood disorder may experience as few as three of the previously noted symptoms or most of them. The typical child who is experiencing an episode of unipolar depression reports experiencing at least eight symptoms that negatively impact the youngster's emotional, cognitive, physiological, and interpersonal functioning. An episode of depression tends to be time limited and to recur again later in the child's life. Research indicates that the episodes typically last for between 1 to 3 years, although a portion of the youngsters experience chronic difficulties.

Prevalence rates for unipolar depressive disorders in the general population of children range from 2% to 5%. Much higher rates are reported for children from psychiatric populations, children of depressed parents, medically ill youth, and children with educational and learning problems. Prior to adolescence, an equal proportion of girls and boys are depressed. Following puberty, more girls than boys are depressed and this disproportion eventually grows to the 2 to 1 ratio found among adults. Although there is very little research on the effects of other demographic variables, it appears as though more children from lower income families and families that have experienced divorce are depressed.

Diagnostic Categories

The *DSM–III–R* (American Psychiatric Association, 1987) is the most widely utilized diagnostic system for classifying mood disorders (Stark, Dempsey, & Christopher, 1993). Within the *DSM–III–R,* mood disorders are grouped into two basic categories: bipolar and unipolar depressive disorders. Both types of disorders are characterized by depressive episodes. However, bipolar disorders include an episode of mania. The manic episode can occur in isolation or in a temporal sequence with a depressive episode. Each of the two categories of mood disorders is further divided into major syndromes that are characterized by a full-blown disorder, minor syndromes that are less severe disorders of long duration (at least 1 year), and disorders not otherwise specified that have a disturbance in mood as their central characteristic but cannot be classified into one of the major or minor syndromes. The unipolar depressive disorders are divided into three diagnostic categories based on symptom expression, severity, and duration: major depression, dysthymic disorder, and depressive disorder not otherwise specified. Bipolar disorders are divided into three diagnostic categories including bipolar disorder, cyclothymia, and bipolar disorder not otherwise specified. For a list of the specific symptoms required for each of the previously mentioned diagnoses, see the *DSM–III–R* or the *DSM–IV.* However, we would like to note a few of the differences between the diagnostic criteria in *DSM–III–R* and *DSM–IV.* Although the changes are not dramatic, they appear to better represent the nature of depressive disorders in youths and the clinical realities of diagnosing these youngsters. The two major diagnostic categories of unipolar depressive disorders, major depression and dysthymic disorder, continue to be used and the diagnostic criteria for each disorder have changed only slightly. The primary change in the diagnostic criteria for major depression is the addition of rule-out criteria for medical conditions that present as depressive disorders such as withdrawal from substance abuse and hyperthyroidism. Another change is the delineation of a time frame for differentiating between a depressive disorder and the natural grieving that follows the loss of a loved one. The depressive symptoms are not considered to be a reflection of a depressive disorder if they occur within 2 months of the loss of a loved one. In this case, they would be a reflection of the normal grieving process.

Some significant changes are evident in the diagnostic criteria for dysthymic disorder. In *DSM–III–R,* the youngster had to demonstrate a mood disturbance plus two of six possible additional symptoms. In the fourth edition, in addition to the mood disturbance, the individual has to experience three of nine possible symptoms. The pool of additional symptoms has been both changed and expanded. The physical or vegetative symptoms of a disturbance in eating and sleeping have been dropped. The new symptoms include social withdrawal, anhedonia, excessive guilt, irritability or anger, and decreased activity, effectiveness, or productivity. The latter symptom would be especially evident in a youngster's behavior in school. In general, the changes are consistent with our research on the nature of depressive disorders among youths and assist in the often difficult process of differentially diagnosing youngsters with possible depressive disorders. Now that the diagnostic distinction between unipolar depressive disorders and bipolar disorder has been made, the remainder of this chapter emphasizes unipolar depressive disorders.

Issues in Differential Diagnosis

One of the first diagnostic questions that needs to be asked when a child is exhibiting symptoms of a depressive disorder is whether this is a depressive disorder or the normal grieving process that is a result of a significant loss, such as the death of a loved one. The *DSM-III-R* (American Psychiatric Association, 1987) refers to this experience as uncomplicated bereavement, and the person is not given a diagnosis unless suicidal ideation, marked functional impairment, or prolonged duration suggests that bereavement is complicated by a major depressive episode. If a depressive disorder is present, then it is important to look for symptoms that would suggest the presence or history of an episode of mania.

Although it would seem as though it would be very easy to determine whether a youngster is experiencing a unipolar depressive disorder or a bipolar disorder, it is not as straightforward as it seems. The distinction is clouded by the fact that the hypomanic periods between depressive episodes among bipolar disordered children may appear to the children or their parents to be periods in which the children are symptom-free. This stems from the fact that the child appears to be doing so much better that no one thinks that the child could be experiencing another disorder. It appears to be a return to normality. Another factor that can create some diagnostic confusion is the fact that a relatively large proportion of children who are experiencing a depressive disorder are also experiencing an Attention-Deficit Hyperactivity Disorder (ADHD). In some of these cases, it is difficult to distinguish this combination of disorders from cyclothymic disorder. It is important to note that a diagnosis of a bipolar disorder precludes a diagnosis of ADHD.

When a bipolar disorder is ruled out by the fact that an episode of mania is not and has not been present and a depressive episode clearly is present, it is possible to fail to recognize that the youngster may be experiencing a case of double depression. In such cases, an episode of major depression is superimposed on a pre-existing dysthymic disorder. This misdiagnosis may be due to overlooking the dysthymic disorder because of the more dramatic presentation of major depression. Recognition of the double depression diagnosis is important because this disorder has a different course than either disorder alone, and it is more detrimental.

One of the more common differential diagnoses the clinician faces is between a depressive disorder and an adjustment disorder that includes a mood disturbance, such as adjustment disorder with depressed mood and adjustment disorder with mixed emotional features. Children with either a mood disorder or an adjustment disorder may report the same symptoms. However, the definitive characteristic is the presence of a psychosocial stressor (e.g., parents get a divorce) that has occurred in the past 3 months and seems to have triggered the depressive symptoms. If a stressor is identified and could have accounted for the disturbance, then an adjustment disorder diagnosis would be most appropriate. However, if a stressor has been identified, but the depressive symptoms remain for more than 6 months and are sufficiently severe, the diagnosis would be major depression.

Given that the predominant mood in children and adolescents with a depressive disorder can be irritability that may be expressed through angry acting-out, there may be some confusion as to whether a child is actually depressed, experiencing a disruptive behavior disorder (e.g., conduct disorder or oppositional defiant disorder), or both. Further clouding this picture is the fact that many depressed children have a comorbid conduct disorder. Puig-Antich (1982) found that one third of a sample of preadolescent boys with a diagnosis of a depressive disorder also met criteria for conduct disorder. It is necessary, therefore, to consider the constellation of symptoms before making the decision about which of these disorders the child is experiencing.

From the previous discussion, it is apparent that most depressed youths are experiencing a comorbid disorder. In fact, research indicates that a "pure" depressive disorder is relatively uncommon. This phenomenon of comorbid disorders creates a more complex clinical picture to assess and diagnose. Other common comorbid disorders are eating disorders and substance abuse disorders, although a dual diagnosis of a depressive disorder and a substance abuse disorder is more common among adolescents than children (Gotlib & Hammen, 1992). Probably the most common disorders that are comorbid with depression among children are anxiety disorders (Brady & Kendall, 1992).

Because depression and anxiety co-occur so frequently together and share many of the same symptoms, some investigators believe that they are the same disorder expressed differently over the evolution of the disturbance, with anxiety disorders predating the depressive disorder (Kendall & Ingram, 1987; Kovacs, Gatsonis, Paulaskas, & Richards, 1989). They share a number of symptoms such as somatic complaints, crying, feelings of tension, social withdrawal, and sleep problems. Watson and Clark (1984) suggested that anxiety and depression are part of the same mood-based construct that they referred to as *negative affectivity*. However, Kendall and Watson (1989) suggested that positive affect is useful in distinguishing between the two disorders. Whereas both anxiety and depressive disorders involve high negative affect, low positive affect appears to be more characteristic of depressive disorders.

CAUSES OF THE DISORDERS

A number of models of depression have emerged to the fore of theory, research, and clinical practice. These models are briefly described in this section. The models that were chosen for inclusion have generated the most research with depressed adults and children, and each has spawned its own approach to therapy. All of these models were developed with depressed adults as the focus. Given the many similarities between depressive disorders in adults and children, it has been common practice to apply these adult models to children (c.f. Kaslow & Rehm, 1983). However, as it becomes apparent later, we believe that there are many critical developmental differences that need to be encompassed within a model of depressive disorders during childhood (Stark, Rouse, & Livingston, 1991). Furthermore, it would appear as though depression is the final common pathway for a variety of disturbances that are not captured by any single existing model of depression.

Psychological Models of Depression

Lewinsohn's Behavioral Model.   Lewinsohn (1974) proposed a behavioral model of depression that states that part of the depressive syndrome is caused by a prolonged lack of contingency between the emission of adaptive behavior and subsequent reinforcement. This places the individual's adaptive behavior on an extinction schedule. In addition, the individual is reinforced for not emitting adaptive behavior. The low rate of response-contingent positive reinforcement leads to the central depressive symptom, dysphoric mood. In addition, it directly leads to fatigue and other somatic complaints. A number of secondary cognitive complaints including decreased self-esteem, pessimism, and guilt stem from the difficulty associated with labeling the feeling of dysphoria. The label the individual attaches to the feeling determines the nature of the symptom. For example, if the individual perceives the dysphoria as a sign of illness, this leads to somatic symptoms, whereas labeling the sensation as "I am weak/inadequate" leads to decreased self-esteem.

Lewinsohn (1974) stated that the amount of positive reinforcement a person receives is a function of three variables. One of them is assumed to be subject to individual differences that may be biologically or experientially determined. The person who is prone to depression is assumed to have a restricted range of potentially reinforcing events. Another is the availability of positive reinforcement in the environment. The depressed person either has few potential reinforcements in his or her environment or is experiencing a sudden reduction in the amount of reinforcement available in the environment due to the loss of a loved one, a financial crisis, or social isolation.

The third and most important variable according to Lewinsohn (1974) is the amount of social skill the individual has to elicit positive reinforcement from the environment. In addition to possessing these skills, the person must also emit the socially skilled behaviors that elicit positive reinforcement. Thus, a depressed individual may not receive response-contingent positive reinforcement either because he or she does not have the skill to elicit the reinforcement or because they have the skill in their repertoire but fail to perform the behavior for some reason. Consequently, he or she is unable to elicit positive reinforcement even when it is potentially available.

Once the individual begins to exhibit depressive symptomatology, significant others in the social milieu inadvertently reinforce the depressive behavior by showing increased interest, concern, or sympathy for the person. However, even this positive reinforcement is short lived because interactions with depressed people are aversive. Eventually, the significant others withdraw from the person, resulting in a further reduction in the amount of reinforcement available to him or her.

Rehm's Self-Control Model.   Rehm (1977) extended Kanfer's three stage (self-monitoring, self-evaluation, self-consequation) model of self-control (Kanfer, 1970) by adding an attributional dimension and applied it as a heuristic model for studying the symptoms, etiology, and treatment of depression. Within Rehm's self-control framework, depression is conceptualized as a failure to adjust to, or cope with, change or an undesirable outcome. Depressed individuals either disengage from the self-regulatory process early in the chain, or they may suffer from a deficit in a self-regulatory skill.

Rehm identified two maladaptive means of self-monitoring in depressed individuals. These individuals demonstrate a proclivity for attending to negative events to the exclusion of positive events, and they tend to selectively attend to immediate rather than the delayed outcomes of their behavior.

Depression may result from either of two forms of maladaptive self-evaluation including setting excessively stringent criteria for positive self-evaluation or failure to make accurate internal attributions for causality. Self-evaluative standards may be stringent due to a high threshold requiring great quantitative or qualitative excellence for self-approval, low thresholds for negative self-evaluation (a minimal deficiency is considered to be a total failure), and a sense of excessive breadth (failure in one instance is taken as a failure in an entire class of behaviors).

The final disturbance in self-regulation is in the area of self-consequation. Depressed individuals self-administer relatively low rates of reinforcement and high rates of self-punishment. The self-punishment also produces an internal dialogue that is dominated by negative self-statements.

The Reformulated Theory of Learned Helplessness.   The basic premise of Seligman's (1975) original learned helplessness model of depression was learning that outcomes are uncontrollable results in the motivational, cognitive, and emotional symptoms of depression. Due to the identification of basic shortcomings in the original model, Abramson, Seligman, and Teasdale (1978) reformulated the model within an attributional framework. The reformulated theory, like the original theory, holds the expectation of response-outcome independence to be the crucial determinant of learned helplessness. However, Abramson et al. hypothesized that mere exposure to noncontingency is not enough to produce helplessness. Rather, the individual must first perceive the noncontingency, and then the causal attribution he or she makes for this lack of contingency determines the expectations the individual holds for the future. These expectations in turn "determine the generality, chronicity, and type of his helplessness symptoms" (Abramson et al., 1978, p. 52).

In order to construct a comprehensive model, Abramson et al. (1978) refined attribution theory by hypothesizing the existence of three attributional dimensions: specificity (global–specific), stability (stable–unstable), and internality (internal–external). The first two dimensions predict when and where the expectations of helplessness occur. An attribution to specific factors predicts that the expectation of helplessness only occurs in situations that are very similar to the original situation. An attribution to global factors predicts that the expectation of helplessness recurs across many situations. An attribution to stable factors predicts that the expectations of helplessness will become chronic. An attribution to unstable factors predicts that the expectation need not recur after a time lapse. The internality dimension determines whether the helplessness is experienced as personal or universal. Individuals who make external attributions for failure are universally helpless, whereas those who make internal attributions for failure are personally helpless. Individuals who make internal attributions for failure experience lower self-esteem.

Abramson et al. (1978) postulated that depressed individuals make internal, global, and stable attributions for failure. Thus, they attribute the cause of their failure to themselves across many situations and over an extended period of time. In addition, when a depressed individual experiences success, it is attributed to external sources, to the specific situation, and is not necessarily be expected to occur in the future.

Beck's Cognitive Model.   Beck (1967) proposed a cognitive model of depression that has at its core the premise that depression stems from negatively distorted information processing. Central to Beck's theory is the cognitive construct of schemata. A schema is hypothesized to have both a structural and functional component. Structurally, a schema is an organized cluster of knowledge about aspects of the domain of interest that has been derived from lifetime experiences. Functionally, a schema is believed to act as a filter through which incoming stimuli are interpreted. When individuals encounter a situation, their conceptualization and evaluation of it is dependent on which of a vast array of stimuli are attended to. Schemata serve as filters and determine which stimuli are attended to and help the individual derive meaning from the situation. The interpretation of a situation is dependent on which schemata are activated and the appropriateness of these schemata. In the healthy individual, a schema that is relevant to the situation and enables accurate and adaptive information processing would be activated. Beck (1967) believes that depressed individuals' conceptualizations and evaluations of situations are distorted to "fit" prepotent dysfunctional schemata. This distortion is evident in, and supported by, errors in information processing such as selective abstraction and overgeneralization (Beck, Rush, Shaw, & Emery, 1979). These negative schemata give rise to negative automatic thoughts. Of particular relevance to depressive disorders is a constellation of depressive thoughts about the self, the world, and the future that Beck referred to as the depressive cognitive triad. The negative thoughts are assumed to underlie and support the depressive symptoms.

COURSE OF THE DISORDERS

Although relatively few longitudinal studies have been conducted with depressed children, the available research indicates that many children and adolescents experience persistent and recurrent episodes of depressive disorders. Kovacs et al. (1984) found that the mean length of an episode of major depression is 32 weeks and that 41% of children were still depressed after 1 year. The average length of an episode of dysthymic disorder was in excess of 3 years. In addition, they reported that children were at-risk for experiencing another episode of depression within 5 years. The best predictor of a future episode of depression appears to be a past episode of depression (Gotlib & Hammen, 1992). An earlier age of onset of a depressive disorder predicts a more negative and protracted course (Bland, Newman, & Orn, 1986). In addition, Gotlib and Hammen (1992) suggested that the presence of comorbid disorders appears to worsen the course of a depressive disorder in terms of poorer functioning and lower recovery rates. However, several investigators have found that a depressive disorder followed rather than preceded the onset of another disorder (Brady & Kendall, 1992; Rohde, Lewinsohn, & Seeley, 1991). It is common for some depressive symptoms to remain in between episodes and evidence suggests that the longer a person is generally symptom-free, the less likely he or she is to relapse (Keller, 1988). Although a paucity of longitudinal research has been conducted with depressed children, it would appear as though the course of the disorder is both protracted and that the youngsters are at a very high risk for experiencing future episodes of depression.

FAMILIAL CONTRIBUTIONS

The contribution of the family to the development and maintenance of depressive disorders during childhood remains an area in need of further empirical exploration. Overall, as will become apparent to the reader, current research suggests that disturbances in family functioning may contribute to the development and mainte-nance of unipolar depressive disorders during childhood. However, it is too simplistic to assume that a disturbance in family functioning is always found among depressed youths. Furthermore, when a disturbance in family functioning is found, it is a mistake to assume that the dysfunction led to the development of the depressive disorder. It also is possible that the expression of the youngster's depressive symptoms may lead to the disturbance in family functioning, a point that is discussed in more detail below.

The nature of the disturbance in family functioning, when it exists, is not well-defined nor empirically established. However, the consistencies that have emerged from the literature are highlighted. It appears as though family variables may have both a direct and indirect effect on the youngster's development of a depressive disorder. An example of a direct effect would be passing along a genetic predisposition toward depressive disorders. An example of a direct psychosocial effect would be a family in which a parent is allowed to chronically abuse or neglect a child. An indirect path would stem from a family environment that fails to teach a child the necessary coping skills to deal with stress. Consequently, when an external stressor is present in the child's life, the youngster becomes overwhelmed and eventually depressed. Of critical importance in the study of child psychopathology is research that helps us understand the mechanism through which disturbances in family functioning might contribute to the youngster's depressive disorder. Some of our hypotheses about this very important question is noted in a later section of this chapter. However, we first review the relevant research.

Parenting Style

Based on observations during our clinical work, we have begun studying the parenting styles in families with a depressed child. An emerging pattern is that the parents' method of managing their children's behavior is dominated by punitive and restrictive techniques that are enacted in a way that belittles or demeans the youngster and cuts the child off from external social, emotional, material, or activity rewards. In other instances, accompanying the aforementioned punishment is an angry attacking out-burst in which the angry affect appears to dramatically magnify the negative impact on the child's sense of self-worth, which subsequently plummets. This atmosphere of heightened emotionality appears to leave a more lasting and damaging imprint. Other investigators have reported similar observations.

Arieti and Bemporad (1980) described a destructive parenting style in which one dominant and highly critical parent uses punitive and psychologically damaging methods such as guilt, shame, and threats of abandonment to enforce rules and coerce compliance. Affection is expressed by these parents contingent on compliance with parental expectations. Poznanski and Zrull (1970) culled the hospital case notes of 14 children between the ages of 3 and 12 who were depressed. They reported a pattern in which the parents had frequent temper outbursts and employed severe, punitive disciplinary techniques. The children were rejected when they misbehaved or experi-enced difficulty mastering a situation. Similarly, in another study of the interactions of depressed children and their parents, Kashani, Venzke and Millar (1981) reported that the parents were excessively critical of their children and teased them in a mean-spirited fashion.

In addition to the body of clinical reports of disturbances in parenting style, there are a handful of empirical reports that also suggest that disturbances in parenting style are associated with depression during childhood. Amanat and Butler (1984) reported that parents of depressed children exerted nearly total control over the decision making of their children and that their primary tool for exerting this control was oppression. Cole and Rehm (1986) found that parents, and mothers in particular, of depressed children set high standards for their children and only express affection contingent on achievement of these high standards. However, the authors noted that this constriction in the expression of affection may have been a product of the mothers' own depression. In one of our own investigations, Stark, Humphrey, Crook, and Lewis (1990) found that parenting style in families with a depressed child was characterized by less democracy as the children had minimal say in decisions that were being made within the family. This took place within a more hostile and conflictual family environment. Puig-Antich et al. (1985a) reported that the relationship between mothers and their depressed children was characterized as cold, hostile, and sometimes rejecting. Parents of depressed children reported using more severe forms of punishment. In a follow-up study, Puig-Antich et al. (1985b) evaluated the same psychosocial variables 4 months after the youngster's depressive episode had remitted, and results indicated that the disturbance in child–parent interactions had lessened. They concluded that the disturbances in parent–child interactions were a result of the youngster's depressive symptoms rather than vice versa.

Activity Level

Our clinical experience working with families of depressed children indicates that they engage in fewer pleasant activities than families with nondisturbed children. This seems to stem from both a failure of the family to engage in pleasant activities and from the parents restricting their children from engaging in pleasant activities. Research indicates that the families of depressed children engage in fewer recreational (Puig-Antich et al., 1985a; Stark et al., 1990), social, intellectual or cultural, and religious activities than families of nondisturbed children (Stark et al., 1990). The reasons for this failure to engage in pleasant activities is not clear. In some cases, it appears as though this is due to the parents' belief that recreational activities are of no value or a waste of time. In other families, it seems to stem from the fact that the parents' work schedule prevents them from engaging in such activities, or the parents believe that they can't afford to engage in pleasant activities. However, as Stark, Raffaele, and Reysa (in press) noted, there are numerous no-cost or low-cost activities that families of all incomes can do and children enjoy. Furthermore, because many parents have to work into the evening and on weekends, the children are restricted from going out of the house due to fears for the children's safety. In many of these families, the oldest child is responsible for babysitting the younger children while the parents are at work, and this child cannot spend time socializing or engaging in other age-appropriate activities.

Family Milieu

The family milieu of depressed youths has been examined in a few studies. Our own research (Stark et al., 1990) indicates that families with a depressed child are described by the children, and to a lesser degree by their mothers, as being more conflictual and hostile. Conflict within the family has been reported by a number of investigators (Forehand, McCombe, Long, Brody, & Fauber, 1988; Puig-Antich et al., 1985a) using a variety of methodologies, suggesting that this could be a significant contributor to the development of depressive disorders in children. The mechanism through which this leads to depressive symptoms is unclear. However, based on an information processing perspective, it is possible that this conflict sends the child the message that he or she is not worthwhile, lovable, or acceptable. This, in turn, is internalized and structuralized into a negative self-schema. The child may develop a sense of hopelessness as he or she begins to believe that any action leads to conflict or punishment; so why bother to try? The affect within the home is angry and unpleasant; this combines with the youngster's negative cognitions that arise from the negative self-schema to produce a mood disturbance. The impact of this conflict and hostility is heightened by the fact that the families seem to be insulated from the outside world by not engaging in an adequate number of activities (social, recreational, cultural, or religious) outside of the home that could provide family members with some respite from the hostility. In addition, the failure to engage in enjoyable activities reduces the family's opportunities to spend pleasurable time together. This impedes their opportunity to develop positive relationships that are built on good feelings. This failure to engage in enjoyable activities stifles the building of appropriate positive relationships between family members and may lead the children to learn an aversive and hostile style of interacting. Furthermore, this pattern would be reciprocated by similarly hostile interactions and rejection, thereby confirming the child's sense of worthlessness and the belief that he or she is unlikable. In fact, our own research (Stark, Linn, & Mc Guire, 1993) indicates that depressed youths behave in a more hostile and irritable fashion with peers. Depressed youths also rate their families as less supportive, which could stem from the conflict, and they perceive their families to be less desirable than their peer's families.

Abuse and Neglect

Results of a pair of case studies completed by Kashani and colleagues (Kashani & Carlson, 1987; Kashani, Ray, & Carlson, 1984) on depressed preschoolers clearly implicated extreme family chaos, parental psychopathology, abuse, neglect, and substance abuse in their families. Poznanski and Zrull (1970), in their retrospective study of hospital case files, also reported a high rate of abuse among depressed youths. More recent research indicates that there is a relationship between abuse and elevated levels of depressive symptoms (Toth, Manly, & Cicchetti, 1992). When abuse is combined with parental psychopathology, the children are at especially high risk for developing depressive symptoms. Although this more recent research implies a relationship between child maltreatment and depressive disorders, it does not firmly implicate maltreatment as a cause. However, additional support for the destructive nature of child abuse and its potential involvement in depressive disorders is emerging from current research that is being conducted in a residential treatment center, in which we are finding a very high rate of concordance between depressive disorders and child maltreatment. However, it is important to note that there is a very high rate of abuse in the history of the children in this facility regardless of their diagnosis. Thus, child maltreatment may contribute to the development of psychological disorders in general and may be part of a constellation of variables that contributes to the development of depressive disorders in particular. Once again, the implications of maltreatment for an information processing model are staggering. The abuse and the surrounding patho-logical behavior could lead to the development of a variety of maladaptive schemata and patterns of behavior.

Marital Discord

At the core of some family systems theories of childhood psychopathology is the tenet that the child's disorder stems from a disturbance in the parents' marital relationship (Fine & Carlson, 1992). The marital relationship of parents with a depressed child has been examined in several studies. Overall, results are mixed and inconclusive. In one study (Kashani et al., 1981), marital discord was found to be "intense" in families with a depressed child. In another study (Grossman, Poznanski, & Banegas, 1983), marital distress was expressed openly in front of the depressed youngster who appeared to be trying to create a wedge between the parents. The source and character of the marital discord is not clear. One possible source of the distress is evident in a study conducted by Forehand and colleagues (Forehand et al., 1988) who reported that the parents of depressed youths experienced conflict over childrearing practices. However, disagree-ment over childrearing is a common source of friction between parents and this is an even greater problem among families with a child who has special needs. In contrast to the previous findings reported in nonempirically based case studies, Puig-Antich et al. (1985a) did not find marital discord to be a significant factor in families with a depressed child. The investigators did not find any evidence of elevations in irritability, hostility, complaining, or quarrels, nor did they find that the marital dyads engaged in fewer activities together, nor was there less affection, satisfaction, warmth, problem solving, or sharing of housework.

Based on our clinical observations, it seems as though marital discord can lead to the development and maintenance of a depressive disorder through a number of different avenues. However, it would appear to depend on the way the discord is expressed and the duration of time that the child is exposed to it. In addition, the parent's reaction to the discord and the eventual outcome for the family all enter into the formula. Marital discord could lead to bitterness between the parents that may be expressed through an angry, conflictual, negatively charged family environment in which a parent or both parents displace their anger for their spouse onto their children. This anger may be expressed through excessively punitive behavior (Arieti & Bempo-rad, 1980; Poznanski & Zrull, 1970) and rejection (Puig-Antich et al., 1985a), or personalized criticism (Kashani et al., 1981). Because the parents do not enjoy each other's company, the family may engage in fewer enjoyable and social activities together (Stark et al., 1990), and the parents may drift apart physically as well as emotionally, which may leave a child with a sense of loss. The emotional loss also may be real as parents become withdrawn and incapable of providing their children with adequate nurturance and support.

Parental Psychopathology

Based on the belief that there is a strong genetic basis to depressive disorders, investigators began studying the prevalence of depressive disorders in the offspring of depressed parents. Results of this research and research on the prevalence of depressive disorders among offspring of parents with other psychological disorders indicates that children of parents with psychological disorders, and depressive disorders in particular, are at-risk for developing a depressive disorder. A very large literature exists in this area, and a complete discussion is beyond the scope of this chapter. Therefore, the primary conclusions that can be drawn from this research are discussed. For more detailed reviews see Beardslee, Bemporad, Keller, and Klerman (1983), Hammen (1991), and Orvaschel, Weissman, and Kidd, (1980).

Results of early studies, which were limited by a number of methodological shortcomings (see Hammen, 1991), indicate that children of unipolar depressed parents are at risk for disturbances in functioning including depressive symptoms (Orvaschel et al., 1980), depressive disorders, anxiety disorders, impulsivity, and attention deficit disorders (Beardslee et al., 1983). A number of well-designed studies indicate that children of depressed parents, relative to normal controls, were three times more likely to have a diagnosable disorder, with depressive disorders being the most common (Weissman et al., 1984). Klein and colleagues (Klein, Clark, Dansky, & Margolis, 1988) reported that one in six children of a unipolar depressed adult suffered from a low-grade chronic depressive disorder. They also are more likely to have a lifetime diagnosis of major depression, substance abuse disorder, multiple comorbid disorders, and to be hospitalized for a psychological disturbance. Furthermore, the age of onset of a depressive disorder was much earlier for the offspring of depressed parents (Weissman et al., 1987).

The degree to which the youngster is at-risk of developing a depressive disorder appears to be related to a number of parental variables. The offspring are at greater risk if the parent's depressive disorder had an early onset, has been recurrent (Orvaschel, Walsh-Allis, & Ye, 1988), and if the parent had been hospitalized a number of times (Hammen, 1991). In addition, as the number of relatives with an affective disorder increases, so does the risk for the offspring. Hammen (1991) also noted that the severity of the offspring's depressive disorder is related to their mothers experiencing more episodes of depression and that the chronicity of the child's disorder is related to the number of relatives who have depressive disorders. Another variable that portends an unfavorable outcome is the loss of the child's father.

Children of parents who are experiencing a number of other disorders are at-risk for developing a depressive disorder. Children of alcoholics are most likely to develop an externalizing disorder, but they also are at-risk for developing a depressive disorder (West & Prinz, 1987). Bipolar disorder is another risk factor (Weintraub, 1987), especially if the mother is experiencing a bipolar disorder (Klein, Depue, & Slater, 1985). Children of parents with a personality disorder, especially if there is hostility in the home, are at-risk for developing a depressive disorder (Rutter & Quinton, 1984). We believe that this is an area in need of much more research as there appears to be a disproportionately large number of youngsters with depressive disorders who have parents with a personality disorder.

Although the research is consistent in demonstrating that offspring of depressed parents are at-risk for developing depressive disorders, the mechanism underlying this is unclear. It appears as though the negative outcome may be due to a number of psychosocial risk factors in addition to the parent's depressive disorder. Additional risk factors include assortative mating (the tendency of depressed individuals to marry a person with a psychological disorder), marital conflict, and parent–child conflict (Gotlib & Hammen, 1992). Furthermore, as Hammen's research indicates, there is an interaction between the mother's impaired parenting behavior and stressful events within the child's life. When the mother is experiencing a depressive disorder, she is unavailable to support her children and bolster their coping behaviors in the face of adversity.

Conclusions

From the previously cited research it appears as though family variables play an important role in the etiology of depressive disorders in many children. The emerging picture of the family of a depressed youth is one in which the child is given a genetic predisposition (see the next section of this chapter) for a depressive disorder from a parent who has a psychological disturbance, most commonly a depressive disorder. The parent's own disturbance has a negative impact on the family and prevents the child from receiving support when help is needed to cope with a stressor. The family environment is one that is quite dysfunctional, and in the case of the depressed preschool aged child, it is likely to include substance abuse as well as child maltreatment. The family milieu of depressed school-aged children is characterized by conflict and hostility that is exacerbated by the fact that family members are entrapped within this environment by a failure to engage in pleasant activities outside of the home. The parents are controlling and make the decisions that affect the children with a minimum of input. They rely on punitive, critical, and psychologically damaging means of coercing the youngsters into behaving the way that they want. Affection is not expressed in a consistent and supportive fashion. Rather, it is expressed contingently on compliance with parental expectations. Research on the health of the marital relationship is equivocal with some studies reporting marital discord whereas other more well-controlled studies fail to report any disturbance. There also is some evidence that the disturbance in family functioning may stem from the expression of the youngster's depressive symptoms as the disturbance in the depressed child–mother relationship improves after the youngster's depressive episode subsides (Puig-Antich et al., 1985b).

In one of our most recent investigations (Stark, Schmidt, & Joiner, 1993), we hypothesized that the severity of children's depressive symptoms would be related to their cognitive triad and that their thoughts about the self, world, and future would be related to the messages they receive from their mothers and fathers about the self, world, and future. Furthermore, we evaluated the relationship between the parents' cognitive triad and the children's perceptions of their family environment on their own sense of self, world, and future. Using a path analysis, we found that the children's perceptions of the messages they received from their mothers and fathers predicted their cognitive triad ratings, which in turn predicted the severity of depressive symptoms. This suggests that a possible mechanism for the development of children's depressive thinking is the messages that they receives about the self, world, and future within the family. These messages are communicated directly through verbalizations such as "You are useless!" and "This sure is a crazy world you are growing up in, and it just seems to be getting worse!" and indirectly through actions such as excessive punishment and abusive behaviors. As the children repeatedly experiences these messages, they become structuralized as schemata and begin to drive the children's information processing. Once structuralized, due to the confirmatory bias (Turk & Salovey, 1985), the youngsters seek information that confirms their schemata thus perpetuating a maladaptive pattern. This model is discussed in greater detail in Stark et al. (1991).

PSYCHOPHYSIOLOGICAL AND GENETIC INFLUENCES

Psychophysiology and Depression

In the past decade, depression has been viewed by researchers as a combination of psychological stress and biological vulnerability that impact the individual. Psychophysiological variables have been widely researched in depressed adults and are now being explored in depressed children (e.g., Burke & Puig-Antich, 1990). Researchers have delineated several psychophysiological variables that may be implicated in childhood depressive disorders (Burke & Puig-Antich, 1990; Kalat, 1992; Shelton, Hollon, Purdon, & Loosed, 1991) including neurotransmitter systems, neuroendocrine dysfunction, and biological rhythms. These variables are thought to underlie the expression of depressive symptomatology.

The monoamine neurotransmitter system model of depression implicates the central nervous system monoamine neurotransmitters (norepinephrine, serotonin, and dopamine) in the expression of depressive symptoms. This model is based on the fact that certain drugs that decrease norepinephrine and serotonin produce depression, and drugs that increase these neurotransmitters alleviate depressive symptoms.

When drugs that increase monoamines in the depressed individual are administered, a time delay of 2 to 3 weeks occurs before the individual experiences a relief from depressive symptoms. However, the biochemical effects of the drugs take only 2 to 3 hours. This temporal dilemma led researchers to realize that depression was affected by not only a deficit in neurotransmitters but also a deficit in the number of binding sites for the neurotransmitters. A synapse, the space between neurons, responds to a neurotransmitter deficit by increasing the number of receptor sites on the postsynaptic neuron. The depressed individual may not only be suffering from a deficit in neurotransmitters but also from an abnormally high number of binding sites that have formed in response to the neurotransmitter deficit. This indicates that depression is more than a deficit (or excess) in neurotransmitters and that depression is a combination of irregularities in the neuroendocrine system and normal biological rhythms. Monoaminergic mechanisms play a critical role in the nervous system and affect sleep, arousal, and response to incoming stimuli. Thus, disruptions in this system seem to explain the symptomatic expression of depression (Shelton et al. 1991).

Norepinephrine and serotonin are directly linked to the functioning of the limbic system. The limbic system, consisting of the amygdala, hippocampus, and hypothalamus, regulates the individual's drives, instincts, and emotions. The hypothalamus exerts control over the endocrine and autonomic nervous systems that coordinate physiological and behavioral responses to stimuli. The noradrenergic neurotransmitter system illuminates the link between monoamines and the expression of depression. Carstens and colleagues (Carstens, Engelbrecht, Russell, van Zyl, & Talijaard, 1987) found that elevated a2-adrenoceptor and imipramine Kd values were found in children with major depressive disorder and a suicide attempt. The authors proposed that these elevated values may be biological markers for suicide attempts in children with major depressive disorder. This finding supports the presence of noradrenergic abnormality in depression that also involves the neuroendocrine system (Siver & Davis, 1985).

The monoamine neurotransmitters and neuroendocrine systems are closely linked. Serotonin and norepinephrine are found in the limbic system that elucidates the connection between behaviors controlled by the limbic system such as eating, sleeping, and emotion and depression. Two endocrine systems, the hypothalamic-pituitary-thyroid (HPT) axis and the hypothalamic-pituitary-adrenal (HPA) axis are closely linked to depression. The dexamethasone suppression test (DST) has been used to assess dysregulation in the HPA axis. As a biological marker of depression, the DST has been used in adult studies of depression with mixed results. The DST is sensitive to the failure of dexamethasone to inhibit cortisol secretion after giving the individual the drug, dexamethasone. This reaction assesses dysregulations in the HPA axis that modulates the individual's response to stress (Shelton et al., 1991). In children and adolescents, DST results are contradictory (Fristad, Weller, Weller, Teare, & Preskorn, 1988; Puig-Antich, 1986), and age is hypothesized to have an interactive effect with depression (Burke & Puig-Antich, 1990). Stress triggers the increase in levels of cortisol, a stress hormone, that has been linked to depressive disorders. Stress may account for differences in cortisol secretion studies among children and adolescents (Burke & Puig-Antich, 1990) and further research in this area is needed.

Neuroendocrine dysfunction and the role of both the HPA axis and the HPT axis in depressives have been examined in adults and children (Shelton et al., 1991). Mild hypothyroidism is seen in patients with clinical depression and thyroid hormone replacement decreases depressive symptoms. This suggests that the HPT axis is implicated in depression. However, these responses to thyroid hormone replacement have not been found in prepubertal depressed children (Burke & Puig-Antich, 1990). Further research is needed in this area, as this response may be mediated by age.

Hormonal changes, particularly the presence of estrogen in girls, have also been linked to depressive disorders. Estrogen accounts for some individual differences between boys and girls in growth hormone (GH) secretion, with girls secreting significantly more GH than boys (Burke & Puig-Antich, 1990). GH release during sleep in depressed prepubertal children was found to be significantly greater than in controls, however, this finding was not found in depressed adolescents (Burke & Puig-Antich, 1990). These authors hypothesize that age and puberty may interact in the control of GH release. The complex relationship between hormones and the HPA and HPT axes that are mutually regulated with the monoamine neurotransmitters contribute to the complexity of biological explanations for depression.

Biological rhythms determine human functioning and involve natural circadian and ultradian rhythms. These physical processes provide another competing explanation for the biological basis of depression and focus on the mutual influences of the sleep–wake cycle, neuroendocrine activity, and body temperature that follow the daily light–dark cycle. Disruptions in these processes are potential links to the expression of depressive symptoms. One of the most important rhythmic patterns in the body is sleep, and the association between sleep and depression has been widely studied. Sleep disturbances are implicated via electroencephalographic (EEG) studies in depressed patients. A shortened latency to the onset of rapid eye movement (REM) sleep has been found in depressed adults and adolescents (Cowen & Wood, 1991; Shelton et al., 1991). However, before puberty there are no changes in EEG sleep among depressed children (Burke & Puig-Antich, 1990). Both an underlying depressive trait or a past episode of depression have been hypothesized to be determined by a shortened first REM latency period. This effect seems to only implicate the individual after puberty. Therefore, EEG studies lead us to view depression as possibly having distinct stages at different points in life. It also points to the value of an integrated developmental model of depression across the life span that includes biological and psychological variables.

These biological models provide explanations for some depressive symptoms. However, they do not suffice as an all-inclusive explanation for depression in children and adolescents. There is a need to integrate biological and psychological phenomena in order to elucidate the depth and breadth of clinical manifestations of depression (Shelton et al., 1991), and it is likely that multiple biological and psychological precursors influence depression.

Age and puberty appear to affect most psychobiological markers of depressive disorders in children and adolescents (Burke & Puig-Antich, 1990; Puig-Antich, 1986). To date, there is no identified biological marker of depression that reliably separates depressed individuals from healthy or psychiatric controls (Cowen & Wood, 1991). Future research will continue to examine possible biological markers that are triggered via environmental stresses that influence the expression and progression of child and adolescent depression.

Genetic Influences

Several investigations have been conducted to determine whether there is a genetic basis to depressive disorders during childhood. Overall, the evidence supporting such a link is compelling (Clarkin, Haas, & Glick, 1988). The data gathered in support of the genetic factor in depressive disorders are based on studies of twins, families, and adopted children.

Twin studies compare the concordance rates between monozygotic (MZ) and dizygotic (DZ) twins. Although results vary according to the research methodology employed in a particular study, these investigations find substantially higher concordance rates for depressive disorders among MZ twins relative to DZ twins (Tsuang & Farone, 1990). In fact, MZ twins are approximately three times more likely to develop a depressive disorder than DZ twins (Clarkin et al., 1988). Because twins not only share the same genes but also the same psychosocial environment, studies of twins who grew up together versus those who grew up in separate environments are important. Investigators have compared the concordance rates of MZ twins who were reared apart and found a concordance rate of (67%) for the development of depressive disorders (Coppen & Walk, 1968). Results of these studies suggest that genetics play a significant role in who is at-risk for development of a depressive disorder during childhood.

Family research also gives credence to the genetic link in depressive disorders. Family studies usually compare the rates of a disorder in first-degree relatives, consisting of parents, children, and siblings of subjects sharing 50% of their genes, to second-degree relatives, consisting of grandparents, aunts, uncles, nieces, and nephews who have 25% of their genes in common. Family studies of depressive disorders have found a considerably higher rate of depressive disorders in first-degree relatives of depressed probands than in the general population (Gershon et al., 1982). In fact, children with a depressed parent have a 15% risk of developing a depressive disorder, which is six times greater than for children with nondepressed parents (Downey & Coyne, 1990). Furthermore, if both parents have a depressive disorder, the child's chances increase to 40% (Goodwin, 1982). Interestingly, children who have second-degree relatives with a depressive disorder are not at any greater risk for developing a depressive disorder than anyone else in the general population (Tsuang & Farone, 1990). Although the results of these studies provide support for the genetic link to depressive disorders in children, it is important to note that these studies are confounded by the sharing of a common family environment in the studies of first-degree relatives. Once again, adoption studies can help us understand the contribution of genetic and environmental factors.

From a methodological standpoint, adoption studies suffer from fewer confounding variables when children are adopted at birth rather than later in life, because the children have the genes of their biological parents but live in an environment that is different from that of their biological parents. Mendlewicz and Rainer (1977) conducted a study using individuals who were adopted as infants and developed a depressive disorder. A depressive disorder was found in 31% of the subject's biological parents versus 12% in adoptive parents. Because the concordance rate is higher among biological as compared to adoptive parents, the results once again suggest that there is a genetic link to depression. Although adoption studies have not led to unequivocal proof, these results do strengthen the case for the involvement of genetic factors in the development of depressive disorders in children.

CURRENT TREATMENTS

The psychosocial approaches for treating depressed children vary considerably, although, they tend to be associated with a few approaches to therapy including psychodynamic, cognitive–behavioral, and family systems interventions. Unfortunately, research concerning the relative efficacy of these approaches with depressed children is limited. Prior to briefly describing each of these approaches to treating depressed youths, we highlight a few issues that complicate the treatment picture.

When discussing the treatment of depressed youths, one needs to consider comorbidity, developmental, and environmental issues. Although some depressed children may be viewed as exhibiting a "pure" or uncomplicated depressive disorder, this is more likely the exception rather than the rule. It would appear that less than one third of all children diagnosed as depressed have no additional diagnoses (Anderson, Williams, McGee, & Silva, 1987; Bird et al., 1988). Certainly, a co-existing anxiety or conduct disorder can complicate treatment (see Stark et al., 1993).

Variations in the child's level of development are reflected by variations in the clinical presentation of depressive symptoms. For instance, adolescents present with more lethal suicide attempts and more anhedonia when compared to prepubertal children (Ryan et al., 1987). Similarly, developmental considerations may also influence treatment considerations. Some researchers would contend that the immature cognitive development of the prepubescent child limits treatment options; consequently, therapeutic approaches that attempt to change cognitive structures may be less effective for younger children (e.g., McCracken & Cantwell, 1992).

Most of the approaches to treatment recognize that childhood depression evolves within an environmental context. As a result, it is often crucial to recognize the most salient environmental factors that can influence the etiology and maintenance of mood disorders in young people. This should include not only the family but also encompass other environmental factors, such as peer interactions (Barrera & Garrison-Jones, 1992).

Psychodynamic Approaches to Therapy

The goal of treatment through psychodynamic approaches involves core changes in the way the personality is organized. This process requires a reduction in the use of maladaptive defense mechanisms. The goal is to replace maladaptive defense mechanisms with a more realistic sense of self. This in turn allows for normal psychosocial development. Although most adolescents are typically able to respond to more conventional face-to-face discussions, the principal form of therapeutic communication with children involves the use of play. Through play, the therapist gains an understanding of the child's wishes, fantasies, and coping strategies. The therapist then uses play as a metaphor for unresolved issues that may contribute to feelings of guilt or abandonment. With play as the main therapeutic vehicle, the therapist relates past experiences to current feelings. Eventually, the child acquires a greater awareness of the factors that contribute to feelings of sadness. In the process, the child acquires greater freedom to make more adaptive responses to life challenges (McCracken & Cantwell, 1992).

One of the major criticisms of this approach involves the over reliance on the therapist–child relationship and the de-emphasis of working with parents and significant others. However, recent psychodynamic treatments recognize the link between depression and interpersonal relationships or social considerations. Within the context of treating depressed youths, "interpersonal psychotherapy" attempts to effectively intervene with the parents and additional significant others in order to facilitate a child's psychosocial development (Moreau, Mufson, Weissman, & Klerman, 1991). Throughout the assessment and treatment process, the involvement of significant others is encouraged through techniques such as parent education, co-joint sessions, and role playing.

Research efforts are represented by several individual case studies. Although these studies provide some assistance in understanding the essential nature of treatment, they provide only support concerning the relative efficacy of this specific approach to treatment.

Cognitive–Behavioral Approaches

Rational Emotive Therapy.   Cognitive approaches for treating depressive disorders in children are predicted on the contention that maladaptive patterns of thinking lead to depression. The early work of Albert Ellis in the 1950's led to treatment through Rational–Emotive Therapy (RET; Ellis & Bernard, 1983). Many of Ellis's techniques have served as the foundation for subsequent cognitive–behavioral interventions. All such interventions share Ellis's premise that by changing cognitions one can effectively treat depression.

The central goal of RET is to first have the child or adolescent understand the relationship between the ABCs–DE of emotional disturbance. That is, the individual is taught how the emotional consequence (C) such as sadness is a direct result of irrational beliefs (B) concerning a particular activating event (A). Treatment requires the therapist to actively assist the client to dispute (D) these beliefs and to replace irrational beliefs with more adaptable alternatives, so that the net effect (E) of therapy is maximized (Ellis & Bernard, 1983).

The next stage of therapy builds upon this understanding by applying RET to the child's own circumstances. Rational alternatives are examined as a replacement for the child's or adolescent's irrational assumptions. Prescriptions or homework assignments are given for activities that help the child or adolescent practice ways of generalizing the lessons learned during the discussions and role playing offered during the actual therapy session. Some authors suggested that the process can be enhanced by having the parent included during each part of therapy and to serve as therapists at home (e.g., Carey, 1993). Although the principles offered by RET have been well accepted, only a few case studies have offered empirical support for RET's effectiveness.

Cognitive Therapy. Aaron Beck's cognitive therapy is perhaps the most widely cited cognitive–behavioral treatment for depression (Beck et al., 1979). The goals of therapy evolve directly from Beck's cognitive model of depression noted earlier in the chapter. The goals of therapy are to modify negative views about one's self, the world, and the future as well as systematic errors in information processing including selective abstraction, over-generalization, personalization, and dichotomous thinking.

Stark (1990) adapted Beck's approaches for children. In order to allow young people to better recognize and label a broad range of emotions, "affective education" provides the foundation for cognitive restructuring procedures that are used later in treatment. Affective education also serves as the initial means of linking thoughts with feelings and behaviors. Concepts are introduced through the use of cartoons and role playing. Techniques for children and adolescents also include a process whereby daily events, affects, and reactions are logged for later review (Stark, 1990). Over time, maladaptive cognitions are identified, and the linkages between distorted assumptions and depression are examined by both the therapist and the child. As this process evolves, the child and therapist begin to systemically question the validity of these assumptions, and more adaptive alternatives are proposed. Homework assignments also make the process of cognitive restructuring more personally relevant. Through repeated applications of logical analysis and cognitive restructuring, the child or adolescent becomes accustomed to rational evaluation and modification of his or her beliefs.

Several studies have incorporated aspects of Beck's therapy in treating depressed children and adolescents. However, there has been only one research effort that specifically examined the relative efficacy of cognitive restructuring. Butler and associates (Butler, Miezitis, Friedman, & Cole, 1980) found cognitive restructuring to be superior to waiting list and attention only controls. However, it proved no more effective than another active treatment (e.g., social problems solving). Subsequent studies (Kahn, Kehle, Jensen, & Clark 1990; Lewinsohn, Clark, Hops, & Andrews, 1990; Reynolds & Coates, 1986; Stark, 1990; Stark, Reynolds, & Kaslow, 1987) have included cognitive restructuring as one component of their treatment program. In general, interventions that have included cognitive restructuring have been superior to nonspecific treatments, attention only conditions, or waiting list controls. However, most studies failed to demonstrate much difference in the relative efficacy of approaches that include cognitive restructuring to other active treatments, such as relaxation training.

Rehm's Model of Treatment. The primary focus of Rehm's self-control treatment is on changing the deficits in self-regulation associated with depression. These deficits include disturbances in self-monitoring, negative self-evaluations, inadequate rates of reinforcement, and high rates of self-punishment (Kaslow & Rehm, 1983). Self-control therapy is a didactic treatment that is often conducted in a group setting. Intervention techniques stress the importance of homework assignments between therapy sessions.

The initial treatment is concerned with teaching the child or adolescent how depressed individuals tend to selectively ignore positive experiences while they focus unduly on negative experiences. Early homework assignments require the child to monitor pleasant events and daily mood. The child subsequently learns about the relationship between mood and pleasant activities. This offers the child a concrete illustration of how high rates of pleasant events and elevated mood are related. The goal of therapy is then to increase the rate of pleasant events, while continuing to monitor daily mood (Stark, 1990). The child or adolescent can also be encouraged to differentiate immediate versus long-term consequences of behavior. As such, the child is taught how positive consequences may not result immediately from their behavior, but other consequences may be delayed and evolve over a longer period of time. As the child continues to monitor behavior and mood, he or she may be instructed to identify a delayed effect of behavior on a regular basis (Carey, 1993).

The tendency of depressed individuals to set unrealistic goals, and to also define success in absolute terms, is another target of the therapy (Stark, 1990). First, the client is taught to identify realistic goals. Once realistic goals are set, the client is taught to task analyze the primary goal into subgoals; self-reinforcement is provided for obtainment of these subgoals. Teaching the principles of covert and overt self-praise and reinforcement is an important aspect of therapy. In order to increase the rate of self-reinforcement, it is incorporated into other components of therapy. For example, the individual is taught how to self-reward after completing homework assignments. Increasing the rate of self-reinforcement serves two functions. First, self-reinforcement may lead to an elevation in mood. Second, as the rate of self-reinforcement increases, the child has less opportunity to self-punish.

In two separate studies, Stark and colleagues (Stark, 1990; Stark et al., 1987) evaluated the efficacy of self-control techniques for the treatment of depressed children. Reynolds and Coates (1986) also used similar techniques for treating depressed adolescents. These studies provide general support for the efficacy of self-control techniques as one component of treatment of depressed youngsters. The results of these studies indicate that treatment involving self-control techniques provide significant improvement in depressive symptoms relative to waiting-list controls. However, self-control approaches appear to be no more effective than other active treatments, such as relaxation training or behavior therapy. It is also noteworthy that no study has examined the efficacy of self-control techniques with clinic-referred populations. To date, self-control approaches have been evaluated using nonreferred, school-based populations. As a result, further studies are needed to evaluate the efficacy of self-control techniques with clinic-referred populations.

Lewinsohn's Model of Treatment.   Lewinsohn and associates (Clarke, Lewinsohn, & Hops, 1990) designed treatment approaches that focus on the relationship between reinforcement and punishment rates, that are proposed to be the primary factors that contribute to depression (Lewinsohn, Hoberman, Teri, & Hautzinger 1985). This treatment approach is designed for both adolescents and their parents. Treatment is in the form of a formal class, one attended by the adolescent and another class provided for the parent. The curriculum for these sessions involves the introduction of a particular skill during the course of several sessions. Skill review and practice is individualized through the use of homework assignments. Specific skills include ways to control irrational maladaptive thoughts, strategies for increasing pleasant events, and social skills training, in conjunction with communication and conflict resolution between parent and child (Lewinsohn, Clarke, Hops, Andrews, & Williams, 1990).

In the only large scale treatment study of cognitive–behavioral methods as applied to clinic populations, the Lewinsohn approach to treatment has resulted in both immediate and long-term improvement in the severity of depressive symptoms. Moreover, parent involvement appeared to heighten treatment effectiveness. It is noteworthy, however, that adolescents with a comorbid diagnosis were excluded from the study and that the study only included middle to late adolescents. Adolescents were also excluded from the study if they did not possess a seventh-grade reading level (Lewinsohn et al., 1990). These limitations make generalizations to clinically complicated, lower-functioning, or younger populations tentative.

Conclusions.   The various models of cognitive-behavior therapy have common characteristics. For example, each model emphasizes the need to introduce specific skills during therapy and the need to apply those skills outside of the therapy session through the use of homework assignments. For the most part, the various approaches incorporate traditional behavioral approaches with cognitive procedures. Differences typically arise in the emphasis placed on one technique over another. For example, the approaches based on Beck and Ellis target the cognitions that foster depression, whereas approaches developed by Rehm tend to focus on behavioral considerations. Intervention studies generally support the efficacy of cognitive–behavioral treatments; however, it is unclear which techniques, or set of techniques, represent the most parsimonious treatment approach. Most of the various studies have been confined to nonreferred samples of depressed children and/or adolescents. However, the findings of Lewinsohn and colleagues suggest that CBT can be an effective treatment approach for clinically depressed adolescents as well. Moreover, this study also provides qualified support for a strong family component to treatment.

Family Therapy

Despite the research that links parental psychopathology and other family considerations with childhood depression, there is little research that includes family-based interventions as a major component of treatment. The families of depressed children tend to be oppressive, conflictual, controlling, and less supportive than families of nondepressed young people. Moreover, parents of depressed children are often psychiatrically involved themselves. Parental psychopathology can in turn lead to parent–child interactions that are maladaptive.

Despite the absence of empirical efforts that have addressed the efficacy of treating depressed children through family-based interventions, several authors have indicated that the family should play an essential role in the treatment of the depressed child or adolescent (Lewinsohn, Hoberman, & Clarke, 1989; McCracken & Cantwell, 1992; Stark et al., 1991). Parental psychopathology often needs to be treated apart from the child focused therapy. In many families, the goals of therapy can be to lower family conflict through behavior-management or problem-solving techniques. However, even in relatively healthy families, parental involvement is often essential to insure homework assignments are completed and to help generalize skills beyond the confines of therapy.

One group study has included a significant family component in treatment

(Lewinsohn et al., 1989). These researchers incorporated parent training as an adjunct component to individual treatment of adolescents with depression. Parent training provided an overview of the skills presented to the adolescent in addition to specific instruction concerning conflict resolution for managing parent–child difficulties. By including a significant parental component to treatment, the adolescent appeared to demonstrate a more pervasive and long lasting improvement in their depressive symptoms (Lewinsohn et al., 1989). In our most recent set of treatment materials (Stark et al., in press), we have outlined a 10-session family therapy component to treatment that accompanies and parallels the child component. We believe that both family therapy and parent training are necessary for the successful treatment of depressed youths.

Psychopharmacological Treatments

For adult depression, the primary psychopharmacological treatments involve tricylic medications. The most common tricyclic medications are nortriptyline, imipramine, and amitriptyline. Over 200 studies have demonstrated the efficacy of antidepressant medication with adults. In particular, imipramine has resulted in good to marked improvement in the majority of depressed adults. Yet, there have been few well-designed studies that have examined the benefits of tricyclic medications with children and adolescents. Open experimental trials initially yielded very promising data concerning use with young people. However, more rigorous, double-blind placebo studies have failed to confirm the overall efficacy of antidepressants with depressed youths.

In the only double-blind placebo study to date, Puig-Antich and colleagues studied the therapeutic effects of imipramine with prepubertal children (Puig-Antich et al., 1987). In this study, 56% of depressed children who received antidepressant medication had a positive response to treatment. In contrast, 68% of subjects who received a placebo had a positive response. It is noteworthy that treatment response tended to be significantly related to plasma levels of imipramine. In fact, 85% of depressed subjects with high plasma levels (over 150mg/ml) had a positive response to imipramine, whereas only 30% of subjects with lower plasma levels responded favorably. Unfortunately, the authors were unable to identify any factor that predicted plasma levels, including dosage. In addition to plasma levels, the researchers demonstrated other factors associated with a differential response to imipramine. Specifically, more severely depressed subjects, and subjects who exhibit psychotic features, tended to demonstrate a particularly poor response to the medication.

Double-blind placebo studies with adolescents have also failed to demonstrate empirical support for the efficacy of antidepressant medications over placebo (Kramer & Feiguine, 1983; Ryan et al., 1986). Unlike depressed adults, treatment response for adolescents was unrelated to plasma levels. The authors suggest that the higher levels of sex hormones in adolescents may interfere with the antidepressive effects of imipramine (Ryan et al., 1986).

There is some support for the use of monoamine-oxidase inhibitors (MAOIs) in adolescents who have responded inadequately to trials of a tricyclic antidepressant (Ryan et al., 1988). However, this research has involved open trials and further study is clearly needed in order to determine if these results can be replicated with more rigorous double-blind placebo studies.

Recently available antidepressants (i.e., fluoxetine, buproprion, clomipramine) have demonstrated promise with adults and typically have fewer side effects than other tricyclics. However, little is known about their relative effects on children or adolescents.

In short, compared with the psychopharmacological literature with depressed adults, research with children has been very limited. Clearly, the encouraging effects of standard psychopharmacological treatment with adults have not been replicated with children or adolescents. Additional studies are needed in order to clarify whether alternative psychopharmacological treatments might have a positive effect on children and adolescents. There have been a number of plausible explanations for the age-related differences in response to tricyclic medications. For example, children and adolescents may differ from adults in the pathophysiol`gcal causes of depression, comorbid symptoms may limit positive outcomes, children may be particularly responsive to the therapeutic climate engendered by taking a placebo, and/or environmental influences may override the effects of medication (McCracken & Cantwell, 1992).

Case Study

Bryan is a 10-year-old boy who manifests many of the signs of childhood depression. He expresses sadness, social withdrawal, disinterest in sports, and increasing complaints of stomach aches. Over the past 10 weeks, Bryan has become increasingly disinterested in his studies. Although he continues to display excellent scores on standardized achievement tests, he has been receiving failing grades in many subject areas. His grades began deteriorating immediately after his father and mother separated. The separation resulted after a protracted period of conflict between his parents that ultimately included both verbal and physical aggression. During the interval that immediately preceded the separation, the parents admit to being preoccupied and had little inclination to interact with Bryan. Both parents have experienced depression in the past, and Bryan's mother is currently involved in therapy and receiving antidepressants. Bryan believes that he is at fault for his parents' separation and that there is little hope for a reconciliation between his parents. Although his father visits him on a weekly basis, Bryan is afraid that each visit is the last and that he will never see his father again.

Bryan's treatment included several cognitive–behavioral and family components. First, further investigation indicated that his mother was experiencing signs of depression. Consequently, she was encouraged to seek treatment. In addition to supportive psychotherapy, she was prescribed imipramine. Although his father refused to play an active role, Bryan's mother agreed to participate in Bryan's treatment. Within the context of cognitive–behavior therapy, Bryan and his mother were taught how to enhance mood by increasing the rate of pleasant events. They were also instructed how maladaptive cognitions can effect mood and how to evaluate cognitions more realistically. In order to insure these skills were practiced at home, his mother acted as co-therapist. Bryan's mother was encouraged to model more adaptive cognitions herself and to reinforce Bryan for completing homework assignments. Over the course of therapy, Bryan and his mother became quite adept at supporting each other for viewing the world more realistically. Bryan increasingly engaged in pleasant activities, both with his mother and independently. Over a 3-month period, Bryan's and his mother's depression gradually lifted. These positive results were maintained at a 1-year follow-up visit.

SUMMARY

The study of depressive disorders during childhood is at an early stage in which many new questions about the disorder are arising. It is apparent that depressive disorders negatively impact a child's emotional, cognitive, motivational, and physical functioning. The diagnostic criteria for depressive disorders for children are similar to those for adults. Between 2% to 5% of children from the general population are experiencing either major depression or dysthymic disorder. Although depressive disorders are episodic, the episodes tend to be long lasting and to recur. In most cases, the depressive disorder is accompanied by another psychological disorder. A number of models of depressive disorders have been proposed. Currently it would appear as though none of these models adequately explains the etiology of depressive disorders during childhood, nor do they adequately take into account the developmental nature of childhood depressive disorders. It behooves theoreticians to consider the reciprocal interplay of cognitive, affective, physiological, and environmental variables in the construction of models that explain the development and maintenance of unipolar depressive disorders. It is apparent that each of these systems along with stress plays a crucial role in depressive disorders.

The family plays an important role in the development, maintenance, and prevention of depressive disorders during childhood. A pattern of family dysfunction appears to be emerging from the literature in which the families are characterized by elevated levels of conflict, a less democratic style of management, and the use of coercive and psychologically destructive punitive techniques. These families are insulated from external sources of pleasure due to the fact that they engage in fewer pleasant activities of a social, recreational, or religious nature. There is also strong evidence for a genetic basis to depressive disorders. It is highly likely that this genetic predisposition is activated in families that are characterized by the aforementioned family environment and parenting style.

A variety of adult treatment models have been used as models for the development of intervention programs for depressed youths. To date, the bulk of the evidence that supports their utility is based on nonclinic populations from school settings. In general, results suggest that a multicomponent and multimodal intervention that combines psychosocial, both individual and family intervention, along with pharmacological intervention, is most likely to be effective.

REFERENCES

Abramson, L. Y., Seligman, M. E. P., & Teasdale, J. D. (1978). Learned helplessness in humans: Critique and reformulation. *Journal of Abnormal Psychology*, *87*, 49–74.

Amanat, E., & Butler, C. (1984). Oppressive behaviors in the families of depressed children. *Family Therapy*, *11*, 65–77.

American Psychiatric Association. (1987). *Diagnostic and statistical manual of mental disorders* (3rd rev. ed.). Washington, DC: Author.

Anderson, J. C., Williams, S., McGee, R., & Silva, P. A. (1987). DSM III disorders in pre-adolescent children. *Archives of General Psychiatry*, *44*, 69–76.

Arieti, S., & Bemporad, J. R. (1980). The psychological organization of depression. *American Journal of Psychiatry, 137*, 1360–1365.

Barrera, M., & Garrison-Jones, C. (1992). Family and peer support as specific correlates of adolescent depressive symptoms. *Journal of Abnormal Child Psychology, 20*, 1–16.

Beardslee, W. R., Bemporad, J., Keller, M. B., & Klerman, G. L. (1983) Children with parents with major affective disorder: A review. *American Journal of Psychiatry, 140*, 825–832.

Beck, A. T. (1967). *Depression: Clinical experimental, and theoretical aspects.* New York: Harper & Row.

Beck, A. T., Rush, A. J., Shaw, B. F., & Emery, G. (1979). *Cognitive therapy of depression.* New York: Guilford.`

Bird, H. R., Canino, G., Rubio-Stripes, M., Gould, M. S., Ribera, J., Sesman, M., Woodbury, M., Huertas-Goldman, S., Pagan, A., Sanchez-Lecay, A., & Moscaso, M. A. (1988). Estimates of prevalence of childhood maladjustment in a community survey in Puerto Rico. *Archives of General Psychiatry, 45*, 1120–1126.

Bland, R. C., Newman, S. C., & Orn, H. (1986). Recurrent and nonrecurrent depression: A family study. *Archives of General Psychiatry, 43*, 1085–1089.

Brady, E. U., & Kendall, P. C. (1992). Comorbidity of anxiety and depression in children and adolescents. *Psychological Bulletin, 111*, 244–255.

Burke, P., & Puig-Antich, J. (1990). Psychobiology of childhood depression. In M. Lewis & S. M., Miller (Eds.), *Handbook of developmental psychopathology* (pp. 327–339). New York: Plenum.

Butler, L., Miezitis, S., Friedman, R., & Cole, E. (1980). The effects of two school-based intervention programs on depressed symptoms in preadolescents. *American Educational Research Journal, 17*, 111–119.

Cantwell, D. P. (1983). Childhood depression: A review of current research. In B. B. Lahey & A. E. Kazdin (Eds.), *Advances in clinical child psychology* (Vol. 5, pp. 39–93). New York: Plenum.

Carey, M. P. (1993). Child and adolescent depression: Cognitive–behavioral strategies and interventions. In A. J. Finch, W. M. Nelson, & E. S. Ott (Eds.), *Cognitive–behavioral procedures with children and adolescents* (pp. 289–314). Needham Heights, MA: Allyn & Bacon.

Carlson, G. A., & Cantwell, D. P. (1980). Unmasking masked depression in children and adolescents. *American Journal of Psychiatry, 137*, 445–449.

Carstens, M. E., Engelbrecht, A. H., Russell, V. A., van Zyl, A. M., & Talijaard, J. F. (1987). Biological markers in juvenile depression. *Psychiatry Research, 23*, 77–88.

Clarke, G., Lewinsohn, P. M., & Hops, H. (1990). *Leader's manual for adolescent groups: Adolescent coping with depression course.* Eugene, OR: Castalia.

Clarkin, J. F., Haas, G. L., & Glick, I. D. (Eds). (1988). *Affective disorders and the family: Assessment and treatment.* New York: Guilford.

Cole, D. A., & Rehm, L. P. (1986). Family interaction patterns and childhood depression. *Journal of Abnormal Child Psychology, 14*, 297–314.

Coppen, A., & Walk, A. (Eds.), (1968). The genetics of depressive behavior [Special issue #2]. *British Journal of Psychiatry.*

Cowen, P. J., & Wood, A. J. (1991). Biological markers of depression. *Psychological Medicine, 21*, 831–836.

Downey, G., & Coyne, J. C. (1990). Children of depression parents: An integrative review. *Psychological Bulletin, 108*, 50–76.

Ellis, A., & Bernard M. (1983). *Rational-emotive approaches to the problems of children.* New York: Plenum.

Fine, M. J., & Carlson, C. (1992). *The handbook of family-school intervention: A systems perspective.* New York: Allyn & Bacon.

Forehand, R., McCombe, A., Long, N., Brody, G., & Fauber, R. (1988). Early adolescent adjustment to recent parental divorce: The role of interparental conflict and adolescent sex as mediating variables. *Journal of Consulting and Clinical Psychology, 56*, 624–627.

Fristad, M. A., Weller, E. B., Weller, R. A., Teare, M., & Preskorn, S. H. (1988). Self-report vs. biological markers in assessment of childhood depression. *Journal of Affective Disorders, 15*, 339–345.

Fristad, M. A., Weller, E. B., & Weller, R. A. (1992). Bipolar disorder in children and adolescents. *Children and Adolescent Psychiatric Clinics of North America, 1*, 13–29.

Gershon, E. S., Hamovit, J., Guroff, J. J., Dibble, E., Leckman, J. F., Sceery, W., Targum, S. D., Nurnberger, J. I., Goldin, L. R., & Bunney, W. E. (1982). A family study of schizoaffective, bipolar I, bipolar II, unipolar, and normal control probands. *Archives of General Psychiatry, 39*, 1157–1167.

Goodwin, F. (1982). *Depression and manic-depressive illness.* Bethesda, MD: National Institutes of Health.

Gotlib, I. H., & Hammen, C. L. (1992). *Psychological aspects of depression: Toward a cognitive-interpersonal integration.* New York: Wiley.

Grossman, J. A., Poznanski, E. O., & Banegas, M. E. (1983). Lunch: Time to study family interactions. *Journal of Psychosocial Nursing and Mental Health Services, 21,* 10–22.

Hammen, C. (1991). *Depression runs in families.* New York: Springer Verlag.

Kahn, J. S., Kehle, T. J., Jensen, W. R., & Clark, E. (1990). Comparison of cognitive–behavioral, relaxation, and self-modeling interventions for depression among middle-school students. *School Psychology Review, 19,* 196–.

Kalat, J. W. (1992). *Biological Psychology.* Belmont, CA: Wadsworth.

Kanfer, F. H. (1970). Self-regulation: Research, issues and speculations. In C. Neuringer & J. L. Michael (Eds.), *Behavioral modification in clinical psychology* (pp. 178–220). New York: Appleton-Century-Crofts.

Kashani, J. H., & Carlson, G. A. (1987). Seriously depressed preschoolers. *American Journal of Psychiatry, 144,* 348–350.

Kashani, J. H., Ray, J. S., & Carlson, G. A. (1984). Depression and depressive-like states in pre-school-age children in a child development unit. *American Journal of Psychiatry, 141,* 1397–1402.

Kashani, J. H., Venzke, R., & Millar, E. A. (1981). Depression in children admitted to hospital for orthopaedic procedures. *British Journal of Psychiatry, 138,* 21–25.

Kaslow, N. J., & Rehm, L. P. (1983). Childhood depression. In R. J. Morris & T. R. Kratochwill (Eds.), *The practice of child therapy* (pp. 27–51). New York: Pergamon.

Keller, M. B. (1988). Diagnostic issues and clinical course of unipolar illness. In A. J. Frances & R. E. Hales (Eds.), *Review of psychiatry* (pp. 188–212). Washington, DC: American Psychiatric Press.

Kendall, P. C., & Ingram, R. E. (1987). The future of the cognitive assessment of anxiety: Let's get specific. In L. Michelson & M. Ascher (Eds.), *Anxiety and stress disorders: Cognitive–behavioral assessment and treatment* (pp. 89–104). New York: Guilford.

Kendall, P. C., & Watson, D. (1989). *Anxiety and depression: Distinctive and overlapping features.* New York: Academic Press.

Klein, D. N., Clark, D. C., Dansky, L., & Margolis, E. T. (1988). Dysthymia in offspring of parents with primary unipolar affective disorder *Journal of Abnormal Psychology, 97,* 265–274.

Klein, D. N., Depue, R. A., & Slater, J. F. (1985). Cyclothymia in the adolescent offspring of parents with bipolar affective disorder *Journal of Abnormal Psychology, 94,* 115–127.

Kovacs, M., & Beck, A. T. (1977). An empirical clinical approach towards a definition of childhood depression. In J. G. Schulterbrandt & A. Raskin (Eds.), *Depression in childhood: Diagnosis, treatment, and conceptual models* (pp. 1–25). New York: Raven.

Kovacs, M., Feinberg, T. L., Crouse-Novak, M., Paulauskas, S. L., Pollack, M., & Finkelstein, R. (1984). Depressive disorders in childhood: I. A longitudinal prospective study of characteristics and recovery. *Archives of General Psychiatry, 41,* 643–649.

Kovacs, M., Gatsonis, C., Paulauskas, S. L., & Richards, C. (1989). Depressive disorders in childhood: IV. A longitudinal study of comorbidity with and risk for anxiety disorders. *Archives of General Psychiatry, 46,* 776–782.

Kramer, E., & Feiguine, R. (1983). Clinical effects of amitriptyline in adolescent depression. *Journal of the American Academy of Child Psychiatry, 20,* 636–644.

Lewinsohn, P. M. (1974). A behavioral approach to depression. In R. J. Friedman & M. M. Katz (Eds.), *The psychology of depression: Contemporary theory and research* (pp. 157–184). New York: Wiley.

Lewinsohn, P. M., Clarke, G., Hops, H., & Andrews, J. (1990). Cognitive–behavioral treatment for depressed adolescents. *Behavior Therapy, 21,* 385–401.

Lewinsohn, P. M., Hoberman, H. M., & Clarke, G. N. (1989). The Coping with Depression Course: Review and future directions. *Canadian Journal of Behavioral Science, 21,* 470–493.

McCracken, J. T., & Cantwell, D. P. (1992). Management of child and adolescent mood disorders. *Child and Adolescent Psychiatric Clinics of North America, 1,* 229–255.

Mendlewicz, J., & Rainer, J. D. (1977). Adoption study supporting genetic transmission in manic-depressive illness. *Nature, 268,* 327–329.

Moreau, D., Mufson, L., Weissman, M. M., & Klerman, G. L. (1991). Interpersonal psychotherapy for adolescent depression: Description of modification and preliminary application. *Journal of the American Academy of Child and Adolescent Psychiatry, 30,* 642–651.

Orvaschel, H., Walsh-Allis, G., & Ye, W. (1988). Psychopathology in children of parents with recurrent depression. *Journal of Abnormal Child Psychology, 16,* 17–28.

Orvaschel, H., Weissman, M. M., & Kidd, K. K. (1980). Children and depression. *Journal of Affective Disorders, 2,* 1–16.

Poznanski, E. O., & Zrull, J. P. (1970). Childhood depression: Clinical characteristics of overtly depressed children. *Archives of General Psychiatry, 23,* 8–15.

Puig-Antich, J. (1982). Major depression and conduct disorder in prepuberty. *Journal of the American Academy of Child Psychiatry, 21,* 118–128.

Puig-Antich, J. (1986) Psychobiological markers: Effects of age and puberty. In M. Rutter, C. Izard, & P. B. Read (Eds.), *Depression in young people* (pp. 341–381). New York: Guilford.

Puig-Antich, J., Lukens, E., Davies, M., Goetz, D., Brennan-Quattrock, J., & Todak, G. (1985a). Psychosocial functioning in prepubertal major depressive disorders: I. Interpersonal relationships during the depressive episode. *Archives of General Psychiatry, 42,* 500–507.

Puig-Antich, J., Lukens, E., Davies, M., Goetz, D., Brennan-Quattrock, J., & Todak, G. (1985b). Psychosocial functioning in prepubertal major depressive disorders: II. Interpersonal relationships after sustained recovery from affective episode. *Archives of General Psychiatry, 42,* 511–517.

Puig-Antich, J., Perel, J. M., Lupatkin, W., Chambers, W. J., Tabrizi, M. A., King, J., Goetz, T., Davies, M., & Stiller, R. L. (1987). Imipramine in prepubertal major depression disorders. *Archives of General Psychiatry, 44,* 81–89.

Rehm, L. P. (1977). A self-control model of depression. *Behavior Therapy, 8,* 787–804.

Reynolds, W. M., & Coates, K. I. (1986). A comparison of cognitive-behavioral therapy and relaxation training for the treatment of depression. *Journal of Consulting and Clinical Psychology, 54,* 654–660.

Rohde, P., Lewinsohn, P., & Seeley, J. (1991). Comorbidity of unipolar depression: II. Comorbidity with other mental disorders in adolescents and adults. *Journal of Abnormal Psychology, 100,* 214–222.

Rutter, M., & Quinton, P. (1984). Parental psychiatric disorder: Effects on children. *Psychological Medicine, 14,* 853–880.

Ryan, N. D., Puig-Antich, J., Ambronisi, R., Rabinovich, H., Tobinson, D., Nelson, B., Iyengar, S., & Twomey, J. (1987). The clinical picture of major depression in children and adolescents. *Archives of General Psychiatry, 44,* 854–861.

Ryan, N. D., Puig-Antich, J., Cooper, T. B., Rabinovich, H., Ambrosini, P., Davis, M., King, J., Torres, D., & Fried, J. (1986). Imiprimaine in adolescent major depression: Plasma level and clinical response. *Acta Psychiatrica Scandinavia, 73,* 275–288.

Ryan, N. D., Puig-Antich, J., Rabinovich, H., Fried, J., Ambrosini, P., & Myer, V. (1988). MAOIs in adolescent major depression unresponsive to tricyclic antidepressants. *Journal of the American Academy of Child and Adolescent Psychiatry, 27,* 755–758.

Seiver, L. J., & Davis, K. L. (1985). Overview: Toward a dysregulation hypothesis of depression. *American Journal of Psychiatry, 142,* 1017–1031.

Seligman, M. E. P. (1975). *Helplessness.* San Francisco: Freeman.

Shelton, R. C., Hollon, S. D., Purdon, S. E., & Loosen, P. T. (1991). Biological and psychological aspects of depression. *Behavior Therapy, 22,* 201–228.

Stark, K. D. (1990). *Childhood depression: School-based intervention.* New York: Guilford.

Stark, K. D., Dempsey, M., & Christopher, J. (1993). Depressive disorders. In R. T. Ammerman, C. Last, & M. Hersen (Eds.), *Handbook of prescriptive treatment for children and adolescents.* (pp. 115–143) Boston: Allyn & Boston.

Stark, K. D., Humphrey, L. L., Crook, K., & Lewis, K. (1990). Perceived family environments of depressed and anxious children. *Journal of Abnormal Child Psychology, 18,* 527–547.

Stark, K. D., Linn, J., & McGuire, M. (1993). *The interpersonal functioning of depressed and anxious children: Social skills, social knowledge, automatic thoughts, and physical arousal.* Manuscript submitted for publication.

Stark, K. D., Raffaele, L., & Reysa, A. (in press). The treatment of depressed children: A skills training approach to working with children and families. In C. W. LeCroy (Ed.), *Handbook of child and adolescent treatment manuals.* New York: Wiley.

Stark, K. D., Reynolds, W. M., & Kaslow, N. (1987). A comparison of the relative efficacy of self-control therapy and a behavioral problem solving therapy for depression in children. *Journal of Abnormal Child Psychology, 15,* 91–113.

Stark, K. D., Rouse, L. W., & Livingston, R. (1991). Treatment of depression during childhood and adolescence: Cognitive and behavioral procedures for the individual and family. In P. C. Kendall (Ed.), *Child and adolescent therapy: Cognitive-behavioral procedures* (pp. 165–206). New York: Guilford.

Stark, K. D., Schmidt K., & Joiner, T. E. (1993). *Depressive cognitive triad: Relationship to severity of depressive symptoms in children, parents' cognitive triad, and perceived parental messages about the child, him or herself, the world, and the future.* Manuscript submitted for publication.

Toth, S., Manly, J. T., & Cicchetti, D. (1992). Child maltreatment and vulnerability to depression. *Development and Psychopathology, 4,* 97–112.

Tsuang, M. T., & Farone, S. V. (1990). *The genetics of mood disorders,* Baltimore: The Johns Hopkins University Press.

Turk, D., & Salovey, P. (1985). Cognitive structures, cognitive processes, and Cognitive–Behavior Modification: I. Client issues. *Cognitive Therapy and Research, 9,* 1–19.

Watson, D., & Clark, L. A. (1984). Negative affectivity: The disposition to experience aversive emotional states. *Psychological Bulletin, 96,* 455–490.

Weintraub, S. (1987). Risk factors in schizophrenia: The Stony Brook high-risk project. *Schizophrenia Bulletin, 13*(3), 439–450.

Weissman, M. M., Gammon, G. D., John, K., Merkangas, K. R., Warren, U., Prusoff, B. A., & Sholomkas, D. (1987). Children of depressed parents: Increased psychopathology and early onset of major depression. *Archives of General Psychiatry, 44,* 847–853.

Weissman, M. M., Prusoff, B. A., Gammon, G. D., Merkangas, K. R., Leckman, J. F., & Kidd, K. K. (1984). Psychopathology in children (6–10) of depressed and normal parents. *Journal of the American Academy of Child Psychiatry, 23,* 78–84.

West, M. O., & Prinz, R. J. (1987). Parental alcoholism and childhood psychopathology. *Psychological Bulletin, 102,* 204–218.

Chapter 15

Mental Retardation

Alan A. Baumeister
Louisiana State University

Alfred A. Baumeister
Vanderbilt University

The most general description of mental retardation is typically presented in terms of an individual's failure to demonstrate skills that are age appropriate. Mental retardation is a problem of human development, an expression of behavioral differences among people as reflected in quality of adaptation and adjustment to changing demands of our environments. Behavioral accommodations are judged according to appropriateness for different age and cultural groups. Although adaptation can take many forms in different situations, the essence of this fundamental "quality" or attribute, for layman and professional alike, is inherent in the term commonly known as *intelligence*.

Despite obvious individual differences in many characteristics among people with mental retardation, they do, both by our intuition and by formal definition, share one common characteristic: diminished intelligence. The concepts of mental retardation and intelligence by tradition and practice are inextricably interwoven. An understanding of the former demands a consideration of the latter, not withstanding the ageless and acrimonious debate as to the essential nature or meaning of intelligence. For this and other reasons, mental retardation is as much a part of our sociology as it is our biology because although we sometimes may be able to identify specific causes of intellectual delay, the interpretation of the significance of that delay often lies in the expression societal values.

Because of the linkage of mental retardation to the construct of intelligence, along with a myriad of other social implications concerning causes and consequences, as a human condition mental retardation has been buffeted about in divisive and often contradictory ways by changing values and attitudes. The practical effects of such value judgments are enormous because they determine who is included and who is excluded from health and education services and even which services are to be available. In fact, the concept of mental retardation is so heavily laden with sociopolitical ramifications that scientific and professional distinctions frequently become obscured or compromised with respect to such basic issues as definition, etiology, clinical description, epidemiology, treatment, and prognosis. For the individual who is affected, these are not trivial considerations because of the direct influence on the service system.

In point of fact, the constellation of etiologies, symptoms, impairments, and outcomes that encompass mental retardation is enormous. Although in some instances a particular biological cause may be observed or inferred, in most instances factors that control an individual's fate are complex and culturally determined. Of course, there are those cases where the impairments are so profound that an individual would be handicapped in practically every setting, and there is little doubt about diagnosis. This extreme degree of intellectual deviation could be therefore considered *absolute*. More common, however, are those instances in which impairments are particularly significant in one context but not another. This would be considered a *relative* form of retardation, in which an understanding of cultural norms and expectations is as relevant to diagnosis and classification as scientific or clinical information.

Basic and applied scientific considerations are, or course, important to understanding mental retardation. Indeed, the only linear and predictable features of the knowledge base are to be found in research domains. But where treatment, broadly construed, is concerned the history of the field has been characterized by an erratic course.

CLINICAL DESCRIPTION

Definition of Mental Retardation

Numerous systems of classification and terminology are currently used in the United States, although the differences among them tend to be variations of degree rather than of kind. The most widely employed definition, classification, and terminology system is that advanced by the American Association on Mental Retardation (AAMR). The first AAMR manual on terminology was published in 1921. Up-dated and expanded editions have appeared in 1959, 1961, 1973, 1977, 1983, and 1992. In some respects, the most recent version represents the greatest departure from previous conceptions of mental retardation, particularly with respect to the issue of classification. The most notable change is that traditional classification according to IQ-defined levels of mental retardation have been abandoned in favor of classification based on the specific needs of the individual. Nevertheless, the three basic operational characteristics remain: (a) subaverage intellectual functioning—an IQ of between 70 to 75 or less, (b) concurrent limitations in adaptive behavior or functioning, and (c) existing before age 18.

Intelligence as the Primary Feature.   Subaverage intellectual functioning refers to an IQ that is two standard deviations or more below the mean as determined from a standardized general intelligence instrument, typically the Stanford–Binet or one of the Wechsler Scales. The most recent definition of mental retardation advocated by the AAMR in 1992 (Luckasson et al., 1992) eschews reference to measurement of IQ expressed in terms of standard deviations—a curious departure from informed professional practice and conventional psychometric principles because standardized tests do vary according to precision of measurement and variability in scores as expressed by the standard deviation. The practical effect of this change is to diagnose mental retardation by a low IQ score (70 to 75 or less), irrespective of the psychometric properties of the instrument.

The term intelligence—a relatively recent addition to psychological terminology (Tuddenham, 1962)—has been and continues to be a rich source of controversy. Few other human characteristics have been the subject of more speculation, interest, and polemics. Nevertheless, a century of debate and research have failed to elucidate the essential meaning of intelligence, and there probably exists today a wider array of views and theories than ever before.

In a pragmatic sense, we are dependent on a "stipulative nominal" definition of intelligence and, therefore, of mental retardation. A stipulative nominal definition refers to how a word is used as specified by the user, not unlike Humpty Dumpty who observed, "When I use a word, it means just what I choose it to mean—neither more nor less." Similarly, the eminent historian of psychology, Edwin Boring, perhaps out of exasperation, concluded that "intelligence is what intelligence tests measure" (Boring, 1923). Nevertheless, the IQ is almost always the principal defining feature of mental retardation.

Reliance on the IQ, however, conceals enormous heterogeneity with respect to etiology, symptomatology, and outcome. Although intelligence tests often serve administrative needs well, they are of limited professional and scientific value. Results of intelligence testing yield little information pertaining to the myriad causes and consequences of mental retardation. Indeed, there is often greater intra- and interperson variability within groups of people designated as mentally retarded than among people considered to be within the normal range of ability. For example, when two individuals have IQs of 50, both may be diagnosed as mentally retarded—but very little else can be said about their comparability. The diagnosis for one may be Down Syndrome; for the other, fetal alcohol syndrome. The only shared aspect, and not a very programmatically useful one at that, is moderate or serious retardation. Measured intelligence tells us nothing about how these deviations in development occur, whether they are endogenous or exogenous, whether they present differing medical complications, whether the basic underlying condition is alterable, how individual growth and adaptation are likely to proceed, how generalized the disabilities are, or how to evaluate prognosis. Moreover, the focus of the IQ is more on what the child might be able to do in an abstract or idealized environment rather than on what he or she typically does.

Adaptive Behavior.   Functional limitations include deficits in adaptive skill areas such as communication, self-care, home living, social skills, community use, self-direction, health and safety, functional academics, leisure, and work. The most recent AAMR definition requires demonstrable limitations in two or more of these domains. Furthermore, impairments should be construed and evaluated in terms of what is typical for the individual's age group and cultural milieu. The relatively high prevalence of mental retardation during the school years is undoubtedly due to the fact that academic skills, which can be readily and reliably measured, are salient indicators of adaptation. This is a circumstance that has led to the identification of the so-called "six-hour retarded child"—that is, the child who displays relatively poor academic performance but whose behavior outside of school is not noticeably deficient.

Measurement of adaptive skills in areas other than academic, however, is not so clear cut nor is the failure to meet the standard of adequacy so clearly apparent. In fact, reliable clinical evaluation of functional deficits has proven to be an elusive goal. It is in this aspect of ascertainment where clinical judgment, often notoriously unreliable, greatly influences the diagnostic process and, not incidentally, accounts for the greatest amount of disagreement among clinicians. Primarily for these reasons, along with other theoretical considerations, some have argued that the IQ should be the *only* formal basis for identification of mental retardation (e.g., Zigler, Balla, & Hodapp, 1984). They contend that objective measures of adaptive behavior may provide useful adjunctive information for diagnostic refinement, treatment, and education. But such indices are not as central to definition and classification as is the intelligence quotient.

The AAMR Adaptive Behavior Scale (Nihira, Foster, Shellaas, & Leland, 1974) and the Vineland Social Maturity Scale (Sparrow, Balla, & Cichetti, 1984) are both widely applied behavior assessment instruments. Measurements are typically obtained through interviews with informants, such as parents and teachers, who are presumed to be very familiar with the client. However, there are significant shortcomings. For example, standardized scales pay relatively little formal attention to the constraints and demands of the environment, in turn, leading to a person-oriented defect model of mental retardation. The quandary facing educators and clinicians is generally one of what particular individuals can do in the environment in which they must function — not of what they could do if environmental circumstances were ideal. Despite limitations in such interview-based adaptive behavior scales, psychologists, in all likelihood, will continue to use them, for they do provide some information about specific behavioral deficits that may be useful in program development.

Systems of Classification

A number of different classification systems have been proposed. Medical taxonomy is important from the point of view of treatment and prognosis. The World Health Organization International Classification of Diseases (ICD–9; 1978) is the most widely used because it is a comprehensive system for classifying medical conditions. In 1985, the Health Care Finance Administration issued a regulation that requires use of ICD codes for Medicaid reimbursement. Given that huge sums of money are involved, it is not surprising that this ruling has had a significant influence on medical classification systems employed at the state level.

Recently the AAMR has proposed a coding system for purposes of classification based on etiologic considerations (Luckasson et al., 1992). Most of these are biomedical etiologies, but the system does include mental retardation resulting from psychosocial factors. The system moves from a broad category, reflecting timing of occurrence, to increasingly specific conditions. The major categories are are presented in Table 15.1.

Within this etiologic classification system literally hundreds of distinct conditions can be enumerated. Of course, not all inevitably result in mental retardation for every afflicted individual and, furthermore, there is considerable variability of phenotypic expression. But, nevertheless, the risk for mental retardation is significantly elevated when a child presents with one or more of these diagnoses. This is a system of classification that is constantly changing because of rapid growth of medical knowledge and burgeoning technology. Consider, for instance, that we are now capable of identifying over 5,000 genetic diseases, with many more to come. One obvious con-

TABLE 15.1
Disorders Resulting in Mental Retardation

1. Prenatal Causes
   A. Chromosome disorders (e.g., Down Syndrome)
   B. Syndrome disorders (e.g., Tuberous sclerosis)
   C. Inborn error of metabolism e.g., Phenylketonuria)
   D. Developmental disorders (e.g., Spina bifida)
   E. Intrauterine malnutrition (e.g., Fetal alcohol syndrome and other prenatal toxicants)
   F. Unknown
2. Perinatal Causes
   A. Intrauterine disorders (e.g., Prematurity)
   B. Neonatal disorders (e.g., Intra-cranial hemorrhage)
3. Postnatal Causes
   A. Head injuries (e.g., Cerebral concussion)
   B. Infections e.g., (Pediatric HIV)
   C. Demyelinating disorders (e.g., Schilder disease)
   D. Degenerative disorders (e.g., Rett syndrome)
   E. Seizure disorders (e.g., Myoclonic epilepsy)
   F. Toxic metabolic disorders (e.g., lead exposure)
   G. Malnutrition e.g., (Protein-caloric deficiency)
   H. Environmental deprivations (e.g., Psychosocial disadvantage)

Note. This is an abbreviated adaption of the classification system progosed by Luckasson et al. (1992).

sideration, having both theoretical and immediate practical implications, involves the problem of relying on "mental retardation" as a unitary and inclusive diagnostic entity, even for administrative purposes. The causes, needs, outcomes, and strategies for intervention and prevention are so diverse that serious questions must be raised as to whether such a heterogeneous array of biological and behavioral manifestations can be meaningfully embraced under a common rubric. From a etiologic point of view, it appears that the general concept of mental retardation is no longer a particularly useful designation, expect as a starting point for much more refined analysis.

Another major classification system for mental retardation has evolved within educational settings in order to devise teaching methods and content according to ability to learn. Basically three categories have been commonly used, roughly corresponding to different IQ ranges as follows: educable (50 to 75), trainable (25 to 55) and severe (< 25). Lately, this system seems to be yielding to a more individualized education plan. As educational technology becomes more refined and knowledge within the domain of cognitive science, including neuroscience, expands and is applied more universally, other more useful systems will be described for educational purposes.

Classification is a necessary process for purposes of resource allocation, program development, prevention and treatment, and research. Clearly, different systems are appropriate depending on the purpose. The problem, of course, with any system that purports to cluster people according to fairly broad characteristics is that relevant information is sacrificed. The challenge is to devise taxonomies that are compatible and that when used in tandem provide a comprehensive and useful model for managing the problem of mental retardation.

Incidence and Prevalence

There is great variability in the empirical and statistical estimates of the number of persons with mental retardation in the United States. This uncertainty stems from definitional inconsistencies, poor ascertainment, regional and time differences in diagnostic procedures, situational determinants, and even confusion over the terms, incidence, and prevalence. Incidence is essentially a longitudinal measure that yields the number of new cases appearing relative to the population during a certain time frame. Prevalence is assessed by determining a ratio of the number of people who express the disorder at a specified or designated time point relative to the population.

Estimates of rates of mild mental retardation range from 1% to 3% of the total population. When these estimates are translated into numbers of people affected, the discrepancy has enormous professional and policy implications because service systems cannot effectively and flexibly provide for thousands of people whose eligibility is questionable. In the United States, where prevalence is typically estimated through statistical rather than empirical epidemiological methods, between 6,000,000 and 7,000,000 people are assumed to be mildly mentally retarded.

Recently, the Department of Health and Human Services has placed the number of serious instances of mental retardation, including moderate, profound, and severe cases, at 2.7 per 1,000 (Department of Health and Human Services, 1990). Other researchers have reported figures that range from 3 to 4 per 1,000. Because of methodological weaknesses in many of these epidemiologic studies, there are some who claim that even these are underestimates of the true prevalence of serious mental retardation (McLaren & Bryson, 1987).

The National Health Interview Survey, despite some limitations, is one of the continuing barometers of the health profile of our citizens. Data obtained from this survey indicated that in 1988 there were approximately 2,000,000 people identified with mental retardation or other developmental disabilities (LaPlante, 1989). Clearly, this figure is significantly below other estimates of prevalence whether obtained from statistical models or extrapolated from samples with known characteristics. Because of the indirect methods of ascertainment employed in the National Health Interview Survey, these data are likely to produce an underestimate of the true prevalence of mental retardation, especially the mild cases.

In any case, the most common of the developmental disabilities is mental retardation, accounting for about 18% of the chronic activity limitations for children under 18. The economic costs associated with developmental disabilities are stunning. For instance, data from the National Medical Care Utilization and Expenditure Survey revealed that in 1988, children with chronic disabilities accounted for $4.4 billion health care expenditures. This does not take into account costs for special education, social services, residential treatment, and lost productivity.

Associated Disorders

Many people diagnosed as mentally retarded present with other serious disabilities, a problem that has enormous service implications. The more severe the mental retardation, as measured by IQ, the greater the variety of associated disabilities, both in number and severity. Cerebral palsy, epilepsy, behavior disturbances, sensory disorders, and other health problems are common and affect developmental course. Fortunately, some of these accompanying problems can be treated or alleviated.

For some specific etiologies, associated disabilities are particularly frequent and of such serious nature as to command attention prior to dealing with the mental retardation per se. For instance, heart defects are a common, and sometimes life-threatening, consideration in children with Down Syndrome. Children with a genetic disorder known as galactosemia are at risk for cataracts, whereas children born with Lesch-Nyhan syndrome, another inborn error of metabolism, experience extremely severe self-injurious behavior.

A long-standing concern in the field has been the connection between mental retardation and psychopathology. Depending on how one defines affective disorder, persons with mental retardation are 3 to 10 times more likely to have a serious emotional disturbance than are nonretarded children. Various studies have shown that persons with mental retardation frequently experience disorders such as stereotyped movements, hyperactivity, destructive behavior, pica, aggression, and extreme noncompliance. Intensity and frequency of these problems increases as IQ decreases, implicating pervasive or focal central nervous system damage. There are a considerable number of genetic and other biological risk factors for mental retardation that are also associated with behavior disturbances, including childhood psychoses, attention deficits, conduct disorders, and neurosis.

CAUSES OF THE DISORDERS

Historically, diagnostic and intervention strategies have been and, generally still are, couched within a dichotomous view of primary causes of mental retardation: for example, organic versus psychosocial, exogenous versus endogenous, cultural versus biological. This is a distinction borne of clinical experience that repeatedly has shown that those individuals with very low IQs (below 50) are much more likely to present some type of clear physical abnormality. In fact, actual frequency distributions of intelligence test scores are known to be bimodal in that there is a substantial number of individuals concentrated at the lower end of the range, far greater than would be statistically predicted from the commonly accepted normal symmetrical distribution of scores. Dingman and Tarjan (1960) gathered IQ data from numerous sources and found that there is considerable excess of cases in the range from 0 to 50, forming its own distribution with an average IQ of 32 and a standard deviation of 16. This departure from the normal distribution has come to be known as the "bump of pathology."

Cultural–Familial Mental Retardation.   A long-standing and widely accepted discrimination has been made between those cases of mental retardation resulting from biologic perturbations (e.g., Down Syndrome) and those due to cultural–familial factors. Persons in the latter category, which includes most cases of mild mental retardation, tend to show few gross physical stigmata, come from the lower socioeconomic strata, and have close relatives who score in the subaverage intelligence range.

In practice, the distinction between biologic and cultural–familial mental retardation is really one of exclusion; that is, the diagnosis of cultural–familial retardation is most often made merely because no *known* biologic causative agent is apparent. Two other criteria that are commonly used for diagnosing cultural–familial retardation include mild mental retardation and evidence of subnormal intelligence in at least one sibling and/or a parent.

It is widely believed that cultural–familial mental retardation is an expression of both polygenically inherited low intelligence that is within the normal range of human variability and environmental circumstances that are not conducive to optimal cognitive development. This view of cultural–familial mental retardation has been supported by its strong association with poverty, data from family studies, and by analyses of performance on cognitive tasks showing that for most children with retardation, the difference is one of degree, not of kind. With regard to family studies, heritability for IQ (i.e., variance in IQ explained by genetic variance) is much higher among those with mild mental retardation than among the more serious forms where there is much greater likelihood that a specific biological perturbation is implicated. Notwithstanding family studies, however, the term cultural–familial retardation is currently in disfavor in some quarters due to its ethnic and racial genetic implications. Consequently, other terms have been used to describe this group such as "psychosocial disadvantage." By whatever term one wishes to apply, the numbers of people subsumed under this category is substantial, accounting for perhaps a many as half of the population with mental retardation.

Given that cultural–familial mental retardation results from complex biologic and environmental processes that act in concert to condition the individual outcome in a synergistic manner, a multiple-risk approach is appropriate to gauge and measure predisposition for signs and symptoms. Baumeister, Kupstas, and Klindworth (1992) described an elaborate model, termed the *New Morbidity* in which five classes of variables (predisposing, catalytic, resource, proximal, and outcome) interact to produce the general outcome of mental retardation and accompanying features. The generalizer model is presented in Fig. 15.1. A brief account of these variables follows:

1. *Predisposing variables* include demographic factors such as race, parental education, and socioeconomic status; behavioral influences such as personal habits; and genetic/biologic factors.
2. *Catalytic variables* involve acute and chronic poverty or other political, economic, and social conditions that act as catalysts to initiate or limit the operation of other factors, such as resources, that affect the outcome.
3. *Resource variables* refer to the array of health, education, social support systems, programs, and services that are not universally or equitably available to all people.
4. *Proximal variables* include those events and circumstances, greatly influenced by the preceding variables, that are the most immediately relevant to the outcomes or symptomatology (e.g., medical complications in the pre- or perinatal period).
5. *Outcome variables* are the product of various combinations and interactions among the other classes of variables.

This model is not only designed to serve as a comprehensive clinical descriptive system for delivery of services but also to provide a unified basis for truly effective prevention of mental retardation and other health problems of children. The dichotomous view of mental retardation is a gross and harmful oversimplification. Only when we identify the complex multivariate causes of psychosocial mental retardation, can we begin systematically to intervene and to employ preventive methods on a wide-scale basis.

Mental Retardation Due to Organic Pathology.   Abnormalities is the nervous (structural or chemical) system account for at least 25% of all cases of mental

Proximal Variables

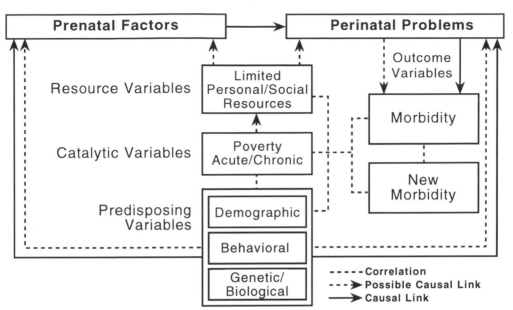

FIG. 15.1.   Schematic representation of the New Morbidity model of mental retardation.

retardation. Mental retardation due to organic pathology is more evenly distributed across social class than cultural–familial mental retardation, accounting for the vast majority of persons functioning in the severe and profound ranges. Organic mental retardation can have either genetic or environmental causes.

Genetic disorders associated with mental retardation can be caused by inheritance of defective genes or by chromosome abnormalities. Disorders attributable to inheritance of defective genes can be classified according to whether the defective genes are dominant or recessive and whether they are located on the autosomes or the X sex chromosome. Genetic problems due to inheritance of dominant genes are relatively rare and are characterized by incomplete penetrance (the gene is not expressed in some individuals) and variable expression (the severity and nature of the disorder varies). The variable nature of such disorders is explained by the fact that genetic transmission of a dominant gene that consistently produced conditions that reduced reproductive fitness (e.g., mental retardation) would be diminished or precluded. If, on the other hand, some individuals who carry a defective dominant gene are only mildly affected, they can reproduce and transmit the gene to their offspring. A group of diseases involving the skin and nervous system have a dominant autosomal mode of inheritance. Representative examples include neurofibromatosis, tuberous sclerosis, and Sturge–Weber syndrome. Mental retardation may occur in each of these diseases.

Autosomal disorders caused by the inheritance of two recessive genes are more common and less variable in expression than are dominant gene disorders. Included in this category are the inborn errors of metabolism. This is a large group of disorders in which inherited enzyme defects block biosynthesis in particular metabolic pathways. Representative diseases that are associated with mental retardation include phenylke-tonuria, galactosemia, and Tay-Sachs disease. The biochemical consequences of a metabolic block are an accumulation of the enzyme substrate and its metabolites and a deficiency of the enzyme products. Mental retardation is often associated with the former consequence and may, therefore, be prevented by reducing enzyme substrate in the body through dietary restrictions or other means. A classic example is phenyl-ketonuria (PKU), which is caused by an inherited deficiency of phenylalanine hydroxylase, the enzyme that catalyzes the conversion of phenylalanine to tyrosine. If untreated, PKU results in severe mental retardation. However, when phenylalanine in the diet is restricted beginning shortly after birth, mental retardation can be prevented. It was once thought that the low phenylalanine diet could in some cases be discontinued without harmful consequence when the child reached school age. However, mainte-nance of the dietary restriction throughout life is now thought to be the better practice. It is particularly important that women with PKU be placed on low phenylalanine diets prior to and during pregnancy. Due to the teratogenic effect of phenylalanine, there is an extremely high probability of mental retardation in offspring who are not homozygous for PKU but who are born to mothers with elevated phenylalanine.

Mental retardation can also be caused by inheritance of defective genes on the X sex chromosome. It has long been known that the population of persons with mental retardation has a preponderance of males. This sex difference is attributable in large part to disorders that are caused by X-linked genes. An example of such a disorder is the Lesch-Nyhan syndrome, a metabolic disease that is caused by an inherited deficiency of a particular enzyme. An especially interesting aspect of this syndrome is the nearly invariable occurrence of severe self-injurious behavior.

The other major category of genetic disorders associated with mental retardation are those caused by abnormalities in the number (aneuploidy) or structure of chromosomes. The most common form of aneuploidy associated with mental retar-dation is Down syndrome. Several distinct chromosomal abnormalities are recognized in Down syndrome, the most common being the presence of an extra chromosome number 21. This condition, called trisomy 21, results from nondysjunction of the chromosome during a stage of cell division called meiosis. Other chromosome abnormalities that result in Down syndrome are translocation, in which extra material from chromosome 21 is attached to another chromosome and mosaicism, in which both trisomic 21 and normal cell lines exist.

Down syndrome has a distinctive phenotype. Classic physical features include a flat round face, upward slanting palperable fissures, epicanthal folds, flat nasal bridge, thick protruding tongue, short broad neck, short stature, and short stubby extremities. Mental retardation, usually severe to moderate, is a consistent feature of Down syndrome. Gross neuropathological findings include reduced brain size and simplifi-cation of the convolutional pattern of the cortex. In addition, persons with Down syndrome who live beyond 30 or 40 years invariably develop dementia and the neuropathological changes characteristic of Alzheimer's disease.

Prevalence of Down syndrome in the general population is just under 1 in 1,000 live births. The principal risk factor for Down syndrome is maternal age. Risk increases dramatically as maternal age increases. In women under 30 years of age, the rate is 1 in 1,500; the rate rises to 1 in 40 when maternal age exceeds 45 years. But lest there be confusion about the effects of maternal age on incidence, it should always be kept in mind that most children with Down syndrome are born to mothers under 40 due to the greater fecundity of this group. Down syndrome also appears to be related to paternal age.

Mental retardation can also be linked to abnormalities in the structure of chromosomes. The most common such disorder is the fragile X syndrome that is associated with a gap or break near the distal end of the long arm of the X chromosome. The prevalence of fragile X syndrome has been estimated to be approximately 1 in 1,000. However, because of under-ascertainment, this figure appears to be too low (Baumeister, Kupstas, & Zanthos, 1993). In fact, fragile X syndrome probably accounts for more cases of mental retardation than any other single genetic cause, including Down syndrome. Compared to other X-linked disorders, fragile X syndrome is unusual in that the frequency of nonpenetrant males and the percentage of heterozygous females with phenotypic manifestations (approximately 30%) are relatively high. The physical phenotype in the male is variable, but typical findings include elongated face, enlarged ears, mandibles, and testes and hyperextensible joints. Recently a neuropsychiatric phenotype has been defined consisting of mental retardation (usually moderate to mild), social impairment, attentional deficits, stereotyped behavior, and a variety of cognitive deficits. The syndrome in females is less severe but qualitatively similar to the male syndrome.

Organic mental retardation can also be caused by environmental insults. Included in this category are infectious diseases, toxicant exposure, and trauma. These etiologic factors may be further categorized according to whether they occur prenatally or postnatally. The severity and nature of the abnormalities caused by environmental insults depends greatly on the developmental timing of the insult. Risks for significant neurological sequelae are often greatest during prenatal development due to a variety of factors such as heightened susceptibility of the nervous system and immaturity of protective systems such as the blood brain barrier and immunological responses. Among the prenatal insults that have been associated with mental retardation are maternal malnutrition, anoxia, radiation, physical injury, intrauterine infections, mother–infant blood incompatibilities, and maternal exposure to toxicants.

A variety of infectious diseases, including cytomegalovirus, HIV/AIDS, rubella, toxoplasmosis, and syphilis can be transmitted from the mother to the fetus and cause congenital mental retardation. The most common infectious agent transmitted in utero is cytomegalovirus (CMV), a member of the herpesvirus group. Between 1% and 2% of infants are infected with CMV at birth. The majority of these infants (85% to 90%) are asymptomatic at birth. Among those who are symptomatic at birth, approximately 25% have nervous system involvement, and the vast majority of these children (approximately 90%) have mental retardation.

One of the most serious and long-range threats to our children's health is the pandemic of symptomatic pediatric HIV. Virtually all infected children (almost always by transmission from mother to child in utero) demonstrate prominent central nervous system damage. An examination of epidemiologic data and disease transmission patterns confirms the alarming fact that HIV infection promises to become the primary infectious cause of developmental disabilities and neurologic impairment in children. AIDS in the 1-to 4-year age group is now the ninth leading cause of pediatric death in the United States and projections for the 1990s indicate that AIDS will soon become the fifth leading cause of suffering, disability, and death among children.

Congenital rubella (German measles) was once a significant cause of birth defects in the United States. Among the sequelae of congenital rubella are heart defects, visual and auditory impairment, microcephaly, and mental retardation. The nature and severity of the defects produced by congenital rubella depend on the gestational timing of the disease. Exposure during the first trimester is especially critical. The development of effective vaccines for rubella, combined with compulsory vaccination in school-aged children, nearly eradicated congenital rubella in the United States by the 1980s. However, in recent years, there has been an alarming trend toward increasing prevalence of rubella and congenital rubella infections in this country (Baumeister et al., in press).

Toxoplasmosis is caused by a protozoan parasite that may be acquired by exposure to cat feces or ingestion of raw meat. Approximately 40% of offspring of infected mothers have the infection at birth, though most are asymptomatic at this time. Among those who are infected, 10% to 15% develop severe symptoms, usually months or years after birth, which include growth retardation, seizures, microcephaly, hydrocephaly, and mental retardation.

Although historically, congenital syphilis has been a common cause of mental retardation, with the advent of premarital and prenatal screening along with antibiotic treatment, this disease has been greatly reduced. However, a resurgence of primary and congenital syphilis in the United States since 1985 has raised new concerns about this disease (Baumeister et al., 1993).

Another significant cause of mental retardation is prenatal exposure to toxic agents. The most significant of these agents is alcohol. Alcohol is a small water soluble molecule that is readily distributed to the fetus. If consumed in sufficient quantities during pregnancy, alcohol is associated with a variety of abnormalities in the offspring referred to as fetal alcohol syndrome (FAS). Characteristics of FAS include growth retardation, facial abnormalities, microcephaly, motor dysfunction, and mental retardation. Estimates of the prevalence of FAS vary from 1 in 750 to 1 in 2,000 live births. Among children of alcoholic mothers, the prevalence may be as high as 1 in 3. The dose of alcohol required to produce deleterious effects is the subject of considerable debate. It is generally accepted that consumption of between 2 to 3 ounces of alcohol per day during pregnancy produces FAS. However, some authorities believe that alcohol consumption in much lower doses may produce subtle behavioral and cognitive abnormalities in the absence of any clear physical teratogenic effect. Thus, there may be no level of alcohol exposure during pregnancy that is entirely safe. Alcohol also enters breast milk, which can be a source of intoxication in newborns. Other teratogenic agents that have been associated with mental retardation include lead, maternal smoking, and maternal drug use.

A variety of other biological disorders resulting from unknown prenatal influences are also associated with mental retardation. Included in this group of disorders are primary microcephaly, craniostenosis, hydrocephaly, and anencephaly.

Most cases of mental retardation due to events occurring postnatally are associated with encephalitis (inflammation of the brain tissue) or meningitis (inflammation of the meninges). Encephalitis and meningitis are most often caused by viral and bacterial infections, respectively. The most important infectious agent that causes mental retardation is the bacterium Haemophilus influenza type b (Hib). Infections with Hib are most likely to occur between 4 months and 4 years of age. Hib is responsible for approximately 80% of cases of childhood meningitis after the neonatal period. Vaccines that are effective against Hib have been recently developed.

Mental retardation can also be a sequela of postnatal encephalopathies, such as that produced by lead. Lead from flaking paint, gasoline emissions, leaded and lead-soldered pipes, pottery, industrial sources, and so forth is ubiquitous in the environment. Children, who have a propensity for putting inedible substances in their mouths, often get lead poisoning from ingesting paint chips, dust, or dirt contaminated with lead. Exposure to high levels of lead produces widespread cerebral damage and neurologic signs such as ataxia, convulsions, and coma. The CNS damage is irreversible, and children who survive frank lead encephalopathy often have mental retardation. Exposure to subclinical levels of lead may produce subtle behavioral and cognitive deficits.

COURSE OF THE DISORDERS

As previously mentioned, there are literally hundreds of known causes of mental retardation, ranging from specific genetic defects, through a veritable myriad of acquired diseases and exogenous hazards, to complex psychosocial factors. Even within one specific disorder, say neurofibromatosis, differences in symptomatology and ultimate outcome can be enormous. Taken across conditions, it is very difficult to offer anything other than general statements concerning the course of the disorder of mental retardation. Some conditions always lead to early death, such as Tay-Sachs disease or Pediatric AIDS, whereas others are severely debilitating and life is so compromised that the affected child is said to exist in a "vegetative state," such as in the case of severe hydrocephaly. Yet, many conditions produce much more subtle signs detected, for instance, only when the child does poorly in school, such as in the case of low level of lead exposure. Given that fewer than 50% of diagnosed cases of mental retardation can be traced to identifiable causes in which some sort of prognostic statement is possible, our ability to make definitive statements about the course of the mental retardation disorder is seriously compromised.

Another factor to be considered has to do with treatment and intervention. Mental retardation is not always the hopeless condition that popular (and often professional) attitudes convey. There are, in fact, effective treatments for some disorders that if left unattended would produce severe and profound mental retardation. Probably the best known of these is the previously mentioned phenylketonuria (PKU), an inborn failure to metabolize phenylalanine, an essential amino acid. An inexpensive blood test of the newborn infant enables the physician to determine whether the child has the disease. If so, a dietary treatment is usually initiated with the result that the child develops normally. Without dietary prophylaxis, the prognosis is very grim.

There are a number of other conditions that yield to medical, dietary, or behavioral intervention, significantly influencing the course of development. On the other hand, the generalization can be made that mental retardation associated with organic brain disease, with exceptions as noted, presents relatively poor prognosis compared with mental retardation stemming from psychosocial factors. When there is explicit brain damage, serious intellectual deficits are seen early, are more severe, not as amenable to education interventions, and are much more likely to be chronic and progressive.

Secondary problems, such as heart defects, cerebral palsy, epilepsy, blood disorders, skeletal contractions, speech defects, behavior disturbances, social acceptability, and the like obviously must be considered in an evaluation of the course of development of children with mental retardation. The problems may be life threatening. Certainly, many related health and behavior problems complicate primary treatment of mental retardation. Children with mental retardation are at relatively high risk for multiple handicapping conditions. As unfair as it may seem, adversity begets adversity.

FAMILIAL CONTRIBUTIONS

As we have previously noted, mental retardation, both with respect to cause and course, is best regarded within a multivariate framework, along continua that include vulnerability, expression of symptomatology, and causality. There is no doubt that familial factors weigh heavily in all these respects. In evaluating the impact of familial contributions, a number of general considerations must be taken into account. The first is that there are known to be many specific single gene effects, both dominant and recessive, that produce conditions that are linked to mental retardation. In some of these instances, almost all affected individuals are phenotypically mentally impaired. However, there is also usually variability in the degree of handicap. This may be due to operation of other genetic and/or environmental influences. In certain cases, nevertheless, single gene effects are very profound and universal, such as in untreated phenylketonuria.

Perhaps in half the cases of mental retardation, a specific cause can be identified. Even this estimate is misleading, however, because frequently medical diagnosis, although having the appearance of precision, is apt to fall within a poorly defined and general category such as "of prenatal origin, cause unknown." As previously noted, in those instances of mild mental retardation where the cognitive disability cannot be attributed to a specific etiology or circumstance, the prevailing theory is that the observed IQ deficit is an expression of normal human variability, mediated by polygenic factors in combination with environmental factors.

No other field of inquiry can match that of intelligence theory for acrimonious confrontation when it comes to a consideration of the relative influence of nature versus nurture. Although the basic arguments have persisted from the writings of the ancient Greeks to the present, the relative contributions of genome and environment to intelligence remain unresolved.

Much of the debate has evolved from the problem of mental retardation and societal responsibility to deal with that problem. Early in this century, many of our social ills were attributed to the prolific breeding of people who were themselves from "weak and poor stock." Thus, the eugenics movement gained prominence because it promised to cast out the weak, infirm, and "depraved." Immigration laws were enacted to control entry of people into the United States who, in reproducing, might mix bad seed into good. Many states passed sterilization laws to control the fecundity of the "mental deficient." In 1924, the Supreme Court upheld the sterilization law of Maryland in the case of Carrie Buck who had been diagnosed as "feebleminded" as had been her mother and her illegitimate child. The mood of much of the country was reflected in the opinion handed down by Justice Oliver Wendell Holmes who said:

> It is better for all the world, if instead of waiting to execute degenerate offspring for crime, or to let them starve for their imbecility, society can prevent those who are manifestly unfit from continuing their kind. The principle that sustains compulsory vaccination is broad enough to cover the cutting of fallopian tubes. Three

generations of imbeciles are enough. (American Association for the Study of the Feebleminded, 1930, p. 54)

Holmes was speaking of that group of persons with mental retardation who have variously been described as *imbecile, moron, feebleminded, educable mentally retarded, mildly mentally retarded, psychosocially mentally retarded,* and *cultural-familial mentally retarded* (although the terms do not always overlap precisely). And this, the largest subgroup in the population of people with mental retardation, is the group whose etiology is least understood.

During the height of the "eugenics alarm," researchers such as Ivan Pavlov and Vladimir Bechterev in Russia and John B. Watson in the United States were refining a school of thought that came to be known as behaviorism—a conceptual model concerned with behavior and its relationship to environmental stimulation. Only two years after Holmes delivered the Supreme Court ruling in the case of Carrie Buck, Watson said, in what has become one of the most famous statements in the history of psychology:

> Give me a dozen healthy infants, well-formed, and my own specified world to bring them up in and I'll guarantee to take any one at random and train him to become any type of specialist I might select—a doctor, lawyer, artist, merchant-chief and, yes, even into beggarman and thief, regardless of his talents, penchants, tendencies, abilities, vocations and race of his ancestors. (Watson, 1926, p. 10)

And the fight was on.

The fact is that there is evidence to partially support both sides, and, ironically, it is sometimes the same evidence. For example, Higgins, Reed, and Reed (1962) reported the results of a study that indicated that children born to two normal parents have an average IQ of 107, children born to one retarded and one normal parent have an average IQ of 90, and children born to two retarded parents have an average IQ of 74. But, whereas the nature proponents point to the study as strong evidence in support of the heritability notion, the nurture faction interprets the findings as important environmental evidence, assuming that retarded parents provide an impoverished intellectual environment for their children. An elementary point, too often lost in the debate, is that heritability refers to and only to differences between people within a specified population. In other words, one may infer that a great deal of the variation in IQs, say 60%, is attributable to genetic differences within a well-defined population. But it is not appropriate to say that 60% of an individual's IQ is due to genetic influences.

In any discussion of the nature versus nurture controversy, it is important to distinguish between the phenotype and the genotype. The former is what we see, what we are, what we might well be. That is, the phenotype is the combination of our experience and our DNA. The genotype is our genetic composition and, until recently, has had to be inferred from classical family studies. Ethical considerations preclude randomized, controlled studies that might separate the respective influences of environment and heredity on the development of intelligence. (Consider the implications of placing large numbers of children born to two parents of known high IQ into the homes of impoverished, retarded adults for research purposes.) However, current developments in cytogenetics are enabling a more direct look at the genetic makeup of the individual. For the first time since the writings of the ancient Greeks, a resolution to the heredity versus environment question may be on the horizon.

PSYCHOPHYSIOLOGICAL AND GENETIC INFLUENCES

Psychophysiological and genetic influences in mental retardation are discussed in detail in other sections. As we have previously emphasized, diagnosis, treatment, and prognosis of mental retardation involves an almost bewildering constellation of psychological, social, and biological influences. These are often interactive and synergistic in conditioning individual outcomes, both immediate and long term. Uncertainties about etiology, symptomatology, and intervention are not likely to be resolved by unidimensional explanatory models because specific causative factors rarely act in isolation. Understanding, prevention, and treatment of mental retardation must be approached from a multiple risk perspective.

CURRENT TREATMENTS

As we have repeatedly observed, mental retardation is a very general and inclusive categorical term that conceals all manner of variability with respect to causation, behavioral, and medical sequelae, course of development, and amenability to treatment. In addition, mental retardation has been the object of vigorous political and legal advocacy, especially in the last two decades. As an example, the principle of "normalization" has been widely adopted as integral to treatment goals and methods. Taken together, all these considerations have a profound effect on treatment strategies, whether medical, behavioral, educational, or sociological. In addition, the advocacy movement has raised serious questions about whether certain procedures (e.g., contingent electric shock to suppress self-injurious responding) should ever be applied, regardless of efficacy. The basic argument is rooted in an appeal to ethical dogma stating that people with mental retardation, because of their limited ability to participate in their own treatment, should not be subjected to atypical, aversive, or dehumanizing procedures. Of course, just about everyone agrees with this general premise, but there is considerable controversy as to what the term "normalized" means especially in regard to people who are behaving in decidedly abnormal or destructive ways and who do not respond to less intrusive interventions.

The concept of treatment with respect to mental retardation covers a wide range of activities, some of which are circumscribed and fairly well-defined and others that involve consideration of the entire milieu.

The most clinically and educationally salient feature of the mental retardation picture is diminished capacity to learn and retain information. Children with mental retardation have relatively great difficulty in acquiring language and academic skills. Problems with higher level functioning, such as maintenance, transfer and generalization, and concept formation have long been an educational challenge with respect to persons with mental retardation.

In fact, the first formal intelligence tests, developed by Binet and his collaborator Simon in the early part of this century, were constructed on the premise that cognitive processes could be modified and the intellect could be trained. The tests were intended to identify children in the public schools who would profit from special training toward this end. Although the trend recently has been again to equate intellectual deficiency with higher level cognitive impairment, the notion of educability of higher order functions has not always been the predominant assumption, and dispute continues today over the viability of the concept.

At the heart of the debate is the question of whether "control processes" (i.e., essentially modifiable characteristics) or "structural features" (i.e., fixed limitations) are the essence of retarded behavior. Baumeister (1984) proposed a "reaction range" concept in which intrinsic biological factors, or structural fractures, establish a limit beyond which control processes, particularly educational interventions, exert little influence on adaptive behavior. Rather heated arguments have been aroused by the distinction between the roles played by control processes and structural features because of exceedingly significant theoretical, practical, and even legal implications.

Another aspect of mental retardation that is often the focus of treatment is aberrant behavior. Aggression, self-injury, and stereotyped behavior (repetitious movements such as body rocking), for example, are common problems among mentally retarded persons, especially those with severe functional and intellectual impairments. Such behaviors are often given high priority in habilitation plans because they may be physically harmful or they may interfere with socialization and efforts to develop cognitive skills and adaptive behavior. The two most widely used approaches to dealing with problem behaviors are behavior modification and psychopharmacology.

Behavior modification refers to a technology for behavior change that is based on the principles of instrumental conditioning. This technology is widely applied in efforts to educate and habilitate persons with mental retardation. The emphasis in behavior modification programs with mentally retarded persons is to shape and strengthen desirable behavior through the contingent application of appetitive stimuli (e.g., positive reinforcement). Appetitive procedures are often employed in efforts to reduce problem behavior. For example, behavior may be reduced by reinforcing low rates of the behavior or by reinforcing competing responses — techniques respectively referred to as differential reinforcement of low rates (DRL) and differential reinforcement of other behavior (DRO). Undesirable behavior may also be reduced by contingent withdrawal of appetitive stimuli (e.g., response cost) or contingent application of aversive stimuli (e.g., punishment). The latter technique is only used for severe problem behavior (e.g., self-injurious behavior) and then only after nonaversive techniques have been tried without success. However, as previously mentioned, there are some who believe that no circumstance justifies the use of aversive techniques. In any event, recent meta-analyses of published research reports indicate that some excessive claims may have been made in support of behavior analytical interventions, especially in regard to difficult behavior problems. For example, despite widely held assumptions to the contrary, in approximately 40% to 50% of published studies on this topic, the interventions have been ineffective or have had questionable effectiveness (Scotti, Evans, Meyer, & Walker, 1991).

Psychotropic medications are widely used to control aberrant behavior in persons with mental retardation. Approximately 55% of mentally persons who reside in institutions and 40% of those residing in community settings receive such medications. Antipsychotics (e.g., chlorpromazine, thioridazine, and haloperidol) and anticonvulsants (e.g., carbamazipine) are the medications that are most frequently prescribed. To a degree the high use of anticonvulsants represents the high frequency of seizure disorders in this population. However, these medications are also widely used to control behavior, though the rationale for this use is not well-developed. The extent and manner in which antipsychotic medications are used in this population borders on abuse. Approximately 1 in 3 residents of state institutions receives such medication. In the vast majority of these cases, the drug is administered to control aberrant behavior, not to treat psychotic disorders. Although antipsychotic drugs appear to be somewhat effective in controlling aberrant behavior, they have a number of serious side effects. For example, these drugs tend to suppress behavior generally and may therefore interfere with adaptive behavior. In addition, chronic treatment with antipsychotics (with the possible exception of clozapine) produces a potentially irreversible movement disorder called tardive dyskinesia. Other drugs with more selective actions and fewer side effects are also used. For example, naltrexone, an opioid antagonist, may be effective in reducing self-injurious behavior in some cases. Methylphenidate seems to be very effective in treating Attention-Deficit Hyperactivity Disorder, especially among mildly mentally retarded persons.

Perhaps the most widely employed general treatment or prevention strategy is early intervention. The literature on the effects of early intervention on children who are developmentally disabled or at-risk is enormous, diverse, and continues to grow. The best known of these programs, of course, is Head Start. But there are many others focusing on children with Down Syndrome, low-birthweight babies, children with sensory disorders, and many others. The effectiveness of early intervention is often characterized by excessive claims on both sides of the issue.

The long-term gains resulting from early intervention programs are not yet clearly understood. Nevertheless, comprehensive early childhood educational interventions are often reported to produce a number of direct and indirect positive effects for children and their families. Among these are: facilitating intellectual gains, enhancing interactions between children and their families, instructing parents to become effective teachers, enhancing socialization, improving motivation, and increasing family awareness of other social programs. It should be emphasized that early intervention efforts must be grounded in and address the child's broader life contexts, not just IQs. Although early interventions typically yield short-term intellectual gains, "one-shot" interventions are not generally inoculations that provide enduring effects.

Case Illustration

Emma dropped out of school when she became pregnant in the tenth grade. There was no discussion of marriage between Emma and the father of the child, nor was adoption or abortion considered as an option. Emma neither sought nor received prenatal care until early in the third trimester of the pregnancy when she experienced abdominal cramping and a small amount of vaginal bleeding. Two weeks after she began experiencing these symptoms and 1 week after her first prenatal visit, Emma's grandmother took her to the emergency room of a local public hospital where Emma gave birth to a son whom she named Derek. At his birth, Derek weighed slightly under 1400 g (or about 3 lbs.). He was sent to the hospital's Neonatal Intensive Care Unit (NICU) where his progress was monitored, and he was treated for a number of problems common to low-birthweight infants.

After 6 weeks, Derek was discharged to his mother who had agreed to participate in a long-term study of low-birthweight children. When Derek was tested at 1 year, his developmental score fell within the normal range. At 2 years, however, developmental tests indicated that Derek's progress had failed to keep pace with that of the comparison group, a decline that was even more pronounced at the 4-year testing. Midway through Derek's first year in school, his teacher recommended that he be tested by a school psychometrist to determine if he was eligible for special educational placement. On the WISC–R, Derek scored 73 on the performance section of the test and 61 on the verbal section, yielding a full-scale IQ of 68. Derek was labeled Educable Mentally Retarded (EMR) by the school system and placed in a special class for those so labeled. Derek, now in the sixth grade, has remained in special education classes. He reads on the first grade level and has mastered some addition, subtraction, and multiplication facts. His favorite subjects are art, physical education, and lunch.

In his neighborhood, Derek enjoys riding his bicycle and playing "pick-up" basketball with his friends. He loves MTV, drawing, skateboarding, the Chicago Bulls, and pepperoni pizza.

The results of the study in which Derek was a participant indicate that Derek's low birthweight, by itself, probably had little influence on his later academic performance. Low-birthweight children whose mothers had some college education, were married, and were from a higher income group than Derek's mother performed no different academically from normal-birthweight children of similar circumstances.

Is Derek mentally retarded? Derek's case is representative of millions of school-aged children in the United States whose "borderline" status makes it difficult for epidemiologists to agree on the prevalence of persons with mental retardation in this country.

What "caused" Derek's low IQ and learning difficulties? Sociodemographic factors, especially race, income level, and maternal level of education along with followed by mother's marital status and age at the child's time of birth are the most potent predictors of outcomes such as that of Derek. By no means, however, do these factors provide a clear-cut answer to the roles played by biologic and environmental factors in mild mental retardation.

SUMMARY

Mental retardation is defined primarily by two criteria: (a) subaverage intellectual development and (b) deficiencies in adaptive behavior. The former refers to intelligence test scores below the range of 70 to 75 and the latter to a number of domains of adjustment to norms of behavior that are age and culturally appropriate. Mental retardation is also a developmental concept in that, by most definitions, the onset must be during childhood and diagnosis is made in terms of age-graded standards. Despite the heavy reliance on IQs for diagnostic purposes, heterogeneity is a hallmark of mental retardation in that there are many causes and many effects, encompassing an enormous diversity of disabilities that require different approaches to intervention with varying degrees of success.

There are many known causes of mental retardation, numbering in the hundreds. The largest category, sometimes referred to as cultural–familial or psychosocial mental retardation, is comprised mostly of individuals with mild impairments, who lack obvious signs of nervous system pathology and who fall in low socioeconomic strata. This type of mental retardation is thought to be caused by a complex interaction between inherited low "normal" intelligence and environmental deprivation that precludes optimal intellectual development. In other cases, mental retardation is clearly the result of organic pathology caused by genetic factors (e.g., inheritance of defective genes or chromosome abnormalities) or environmental insults (e.g., congenital syphilis or prenatal toxicant exposure). Mental retardation associated with clear signs of organicity tends to be more severe, more evenly distributed across social class, and far less common than cultural–familial mental retardation. In most cases, however, the precise etiology of mental retardation is unknown.

Incidence and prevalence estimates are not very precise. But, in the United States, there are several million cases of mental retardation. Most of these are in the mild category, although there are a great many individuals whose disabilities are so severe that they are in constant need of care. Costs for health care, social services, special education, and other needs run into the billions of dollars. For some individuals with mental retardation there are effective treatments and preventions. Yet, for the vast majority treatment consists of providing supportive environments during the entire life span.

ACKNOWLEDGMENT

The authors are indebted to Dr. Pamela Zanthos for her significant contributions to the preparation of this chapter. Work on this manuscript was supported, in part, by PHS Grant HD15051 and HD27336.

REFERENCES

American Association for the Study of the Feebleminded. (1930, May). Proceedings, 1930 Annual Meeting. *Journal of Psycho-Asthenics, 35,* 54.

Baumeister, A. A. (1984). Some conceptual and methodological issues in the study of cognitive processes. In P. Brooks, R. Sperber, & C. McCauley (Eds.), *Learning and cognition in the mentally retarded* (pp. 1–38). Hillsdale, NJ: Lawrence Erlbaum Associates.

Baumeister, A. A., Kupstas, F., & Klindworth, L. M. (1992). The New Morbidity: A national plan of action. In T. Thompson & S. Hupp (Eds.), *Saving children at risk* (pp. 143–177). San Francisco: Sage.

Baumeister, A. A., Kupstas, F. D., & Zanthos, P. W. (1993). *Guide to state planning for the prevention of mental retardation and related disabilities associated with socioeconomic conditions.* Washington, DC: President's Committee on Mental Retardation.

Boring, E. G. (1923). Intelligence as the tests test it. *New Republic, 35,* 35–37.

Department of Health and Human Services. (1990). *Healthy people 2000: National health promotion and disease prevention objectives.* Washington, DC: Author.

Dingman, H. F., & Tarjan, G. (1960). Mental retardation and the normal distribution curve. *American Journal of Mental Deficiency, 64,* 991–994.

Higgins, J. V., Reed, E. W., & Reed, G. C. (1962). Intelligence and family size: A paradox resolved. *Eugenics Quarterly, 9,* 84–90.

LaPlante, M. P. (1989). Disability in basic life activities across the life span. In *Disability Statistics Report I.* San Francisco: University of California, Institute for Health and Aging.

Luckasson, R. R., Coulter, D. L., Polloway, E. A., Reiss, S., Schalock, R. L., Snell, M. E., Spitalnik, D. M., & Stark, J. A. (1992). *Mental retardation: Definition, classification, and systems of supports.* Washington, DC: American Association on Mental Retardation.

McLaren, J., & Bryson, S. E. (1987). Review of recent epidemiological studies of mental retardation: Prevalence, associated disorders, and etiology. *American Journal of Mental Retardation, 92,* 243–254.

Nihira, K., Foster, R., Shellhaas, M., & Leland, H. (1974). *Adaptive behavior scales.* Washington, DC: American Association on Mental Deficiency.

Scotti, J. R., Evans, I. M., Meyer, L. H., & Walker, P. (1991). A meta-analysis of intervention research with problem behavior: Treatment validity and standards of practice. *American Journal on Mental Retardation, 96*, 233–256.

Sparrow, S. S., Balla, D. A., & Cicchetti, D. V. (1984). *Vineland Adaptive Behavior Scales*. Circle Pines, MN: American Guidance Service.

Tuddenham, R. D. (1962). The nature and measurement of intelligence. In L. J. Postman (Ed.), *Psychology in the making* (pp. 469–525). New York: Knopf.

Watson, J. B. (1926). What the nursery has to say about instincts. In C. Murchison (Ed.), *Psychologies of 1925*. Worchester, MA: Clark University Press.

World Health Organization. (1978). International classification of diseases (9th ed.). Geneva: Author.

Zigler, E., Balla, D., & Hodapp, R. (1984). On the definition and classification of mental retardation. *American Journal of Mental Deficiency, 89*, 215–230.

Chapter 16

Autism

Sandra L. Harris
Rutgers, The State University of New Jersey

CLINICAL DESCRIPTION

It is impossible to ignore the child with autism. The profound aloneness, bizarre rituals, and lack of language make this a striking and perplexing disorder that has commanded the attention of several generations of scientists, educators, and clinicians.

Although first identified by Leo Kanner in the early 1940s (Kanner, 1943), autism did not become an official part of psychiatric nomenclature for 40 years, upon the publication of the third *Diagnostic and Statistical Manual of Mental Disorders* (*DSM-III*; American Psychiatric Association, 1980). The definition was further refined in the the revised edition of that manual (*DSM-III-R*; American Psychiatric Association, 1987) and most recently in *DSM-IV* (American Psychiatric Association, 1994). Although the subtle details of the diagnosis continue to be debated, the basic symptoms of autism remain consistent. These symptoms fall under three broad headings: social, communication, and behavior.

This relatively rare disorder occurs in 4 or 5 out of every 10,000 children, effects more boys than girls, begins in infancy or early childhood, and has been identified in children around the world. Autism is often accompanied by mental retardation, but some children may have average or even above average intelligence while still suffering from autism.

The specific symptoms of autism vary with the mental age of the person who is affected and also with chronological age. People with autism typically show a decrease in the intensity of many symptoms as they grow older, and their skills for dealing with the environment increase, although a significant subgroup may show a decline in behavior when they enter adolescence. It is therefore important to take into account the developmental age as well as the calendar age of the person with autism.

Impaired Social Behavior

Persons with autism exhibit major deficits in their ability to relate to others. Children with autism often appears content to dwell in a separate world, showing little interest in parents or siblings. Unlike normally developing babies, children with autism may not raise their arms to be picked up or may stiffen in protest when cuddled by his parent. Their lack of social interest may make some of these babies seem like "easy babies" because they may not seek parental attention, appearing content to remain in their cribs, watching a mobile or staring at their hands. As they get older, this lack of demandingness is soon recognized for the indifference it actually reflects.

Children with autism may not seek others for comfort when they are hurt or upset, finding little consolation in gentle words and hugs. Not only do the children not ask for comfort, they are typically quite indifferent to the distress of other people as well. A sibling's tears or a parent being upset may elicit no response from children with autism.

Children with autism show little interest in the domestic imitation that is part of most children's play. For example, unlike normally developing children, children with autism usually do not want to use their miniature snow shovel to shovel snow just like daddy or use a screwdriver to repair a toy when mommy is doing the same. This lack of interest in imitation interferes with one of the primary channels for learning by young children, their ability to model adult behaviors and master them though role play.

Social play is one of the primary activities of childhood. A few simple toys can create the backdrop for long hours of companionship. Children with autism do not know how to enter into this kind of play, sometimes completely ignoring other children, or perhaps standing on the sidelines, not comprehending how to become part of the group. Not surprisingly, given the range of social deficits they exhibit, children with autism are very impaired in their ability to make childhood friends.

The nature and intensity of the social deficits in autism may be altered as the person with autism grows older. Many parents report that their child begins to show a differential attachment to them and to develop at least a rudimentary awareness of other people's needs, as the child grows up. However, these changes are of a relative nature, and when compared with their normally developing peers, the young person with autism is sadly deficient in the ability to form intimate relationships.

Impaired Communication

Children with autism are impaired in verbal and nonverbal communication. For very young children, this may mean a lack of communicative babbling and substantial delays in the onset of rudimentary speech. Early nonverbal communication may be similarly delayed with a failure to use eye to face gaze for communication and a lack of facial expression.

For those children who do develop speech, there typically are abnormalities in production including problems with volume, rate, and intonation. Some children with autism are said to sound like "robots" because they do not appear to be aware of the importance of variations in inflection and pace as part of the process of communication.

Children with autism also demonstrate abnormalities in the content of the speech itself, for example, rotely repeating back what others have said, a behavior called *echolalia*. Echolalia can occur in immediate response to a question or at a later time. An example of immediate echolalia would be the child who, being asked "Who did you see at school today?" responds, "see at school today." In the case of delayed echolalia, the child might repeat something heard days or even years before. It is not uncommon for children with autism to recite entire pieces of dialogue from a television show or videotape. Another abnormality of speech exhibited by some children with autism is called *pronominal reversal*. This refers to a tendency to reverse pronouns, often confusing *I* and *you*. For example, when asked, "Do you want juice?" the child might answer, "Yes, you want juice."

Older, higher functioning persons with autism may have complex speech but be unable to sustain a conversation because they are insensitive to the reactions of their audience. For example, one young man can identify all of the trains that pass through his local railroad station but fails to comprehend that other people have little interest in a repeated description of the train numbers, time of arrival, and ultimate destination.

Abnormalities of Routine and Behavior

Children with autism often show repetitive stereotyped body movements such as rocking, hand waving, or head banging. They may become quite absorbed in these movements, often to the exclusion of an awareness of other events around them. For example, a boy with autism may hold his hand up the light and wave his fingers back and forth staring at the pattern created as his fingers weave before his eyes. Under these conditions, he may not hear his mother calling him to come to dinner or notice that his younger sister has come into the room and turned on the television.

Seemingly trivial changes in their environment may trigger intense emotional responses in some children with autism who insist that things remain in the same pattern. For example, a child with autism may spend long periods of time lining up tiny doll figures in a row, with each having the same precise relationship to the other, day after day, and then tantrumming if one of the dolls is moved out of line.

Changes in routine may also be upsetting to the child with autism. For example, if the parents of a child with autism always turn left out of the driveway to visit grandmother, and one day the car turns right because they are going to pick up Aunt Sally before they go to grandmother's, the child may scream in protest until they return to the driveway and turn left. At the more advanced level of development this ritualistic behavior may manifest itself in a narrow interest in a specific topic such as train schedules or air conditioners.

Although none of these symptoms is unique to autism and may be seen in some form in normally developing children as well as children with other disorders such as mental retardation, it is the grouping of the constellation of symptoms that distinguishes autism from other related disorders.

CAUSES OF THE DISORDER

Until the mid-1960s, most people believed that autism was the result of poor parenting. The best known advocate of this view, Bruno Bettelheim (1967), argued that these children recognized the incapacity of their parents to be loving and withdrew from that harsh reality. Scientific research failed to provide support for this point of view, and in the past 15 years, there has been accumulating evidence to support the notion that autism is a biologically based disorder.

It may be more accurate to speak of autism*s* in the plural rather than autism as a single disorder. We are gradually uncovering a variety of different biologically based disorders that are known to be linked to autistic behavior. For example, one of the first known infectious diseases associated with autism was identified when it was noted that a disproportionate number of babies whose mothers had german measles during pregnancy, demonstrated autistic behaviors (Chess, 1977).

Symptoms of autism have been been traced to some chromosomal defects. One of the most common of these is called Fragile-X syndrome. This disorder was long known to be a cause of mental retardation but has now been found to be related to autism as well (Coleman, 1987). Autism has similarly been found to be linked to seizure disorders, Tay-Sachs disease, and phenylketonuria (PKU; Batshaw & Perret, 1981).

Continuing research will doubtless gradually disentangled the many separate disorders that have been lumped under the single heading of autism and enable the prevention or treatment of some of these disorders. Later in the chapter, some of the current research on the biological bases of autism is discussed in greater depth.

COURSE OF THE DISORDER

For most children, autism lasts a life time. Although early intervention for some children with autism has produced major developmental changes, the technology has not yet reached the point where most children show dramatic changes. As a result, most children with autism become adults with autism. It is therefore important to understand how the symptoms of autism manifest themselves across the lifespan.

The symptoms of autism typically increase gradually through the child's second year, reach a peak between the ages of 2 and 4 years, and then show some improvement. Young children with greater cognitive ability who receive early intensive treatment may show dramatic improvement at this age, whereas those who are more impaired show more modest changes.

In general, the troubling behaviors of children with autism tend to improve as the children grow older (Mesibov, 1983). Activity level declines, ritualistic and compulsive behaviors improve, and self-care improves. A similar pattern is observed for social and interpersonal behaviors that tend in general to improve in adolescence and adulthood. Similarly, speech and language skills get better as children with autism mature.

The outcome for cognitive skills is generally positive as persons with autism grow up. However, there is a group of youngsters with autism who show a decline in this area at puberty. Mesibov (1983) noted that many children with autism first develop seizure disorders in adolescence or early adulthood, a factor that may contribute to the cognitive decline seen in some young people with autism. The course of change for self-injurious and aggressive behavior is not yet clearly defined. It is however clear that aggression or self-injury in an adolescent or adult is far more serious than the same behavior in a small child, and therefore these behaviors are a source of serious clinical concern if they persist beyond the early years.

FAMILIAL CONTRIBUTIONS

Although it was once believed that poor parenting was the cause of autism, research over the years has revealed few if any differences between parents of children with autism and other parents. Today, there is a general understanding that parents of children with autism are "ordinary people" to whom an extraordinary thing has happened. Although there is a greater than chance probability that a family with one child with autism will have a second child with the disorder, these family patterns seem more closely linked to genetic factors than to environmental variables.

Understanding the etiology of autism will improve as we begin to separate out the several disorders that fall under that broad heading. The criteria for Pervasive Developmental Disorders in *DSM–IV* (American Psychiatric Association, 1994) make potentially useful discriminations among a group of disorders along the continuum of autistic behavior. This includes Autistic Disorder, with diagnostic criteria closely resembling those in *DSM–III–R* (American Psychiatric Association, 1987). In addition, the new system includes Rhett's Disorder, a neurological condition in which apparently normal development in early infancy is followed by a decline in motor function, language, and social behavior. These children, although suffering from a degenerative neurological disorder show behavioral similarity to children with autistic disorder, especially in the early stages of Rhett's Disorder (Tsai, 1992).

Another category in *DSM–IV* is Childhood Disintegrative Disorder, which is characterized by apparently normal development for at least the first 24 months followed by a loss of function in areas such as language, social skills, and play. Unlike children with Rhett's Disorder, these children do not show a continuing loss of function. Asperger's Disorder is also included *DSM–IV*. Although children with Asperger's Disorder show the impairment in social relatedness that accompanies Autistic Disorder, they are not delayed in general language or cognitive development.

PSYCHOPHYSIOLOGICAL AND GENETIC INFLUENCES

We do not yet know what causes autism. However, considerable research in the past decade has suggested that there are significant genetic patterns for some persons with autism and that genetic, neurological, neurochemical, and biochemical factors will ultimately be found to underlie autism. It is probably important not to look for a single etiology but to recognize that multiple causes may eventually be identified. In this sense, autism is similar to mental retardation, where we know that different conditions such as microcephaly and Down Syndrome have different causes, although they share the common symptom of cognitive deficits.

Genetic Factors

There appears to be a genetic contribution to at least some kinds of autism. For example, Fragile-X syndrome is a chromosomal disorder long known to be related to mental retardation, and more recently shown to be linked to autism. This disorder gets its name from a narrowing near the end of the long arm of the X chromosome that sometimes makes the tip fragile. Fragile-X syndrome shows an X-linked (sex gene linked) recessive pattern of inheritance. As a result, this disorder is typically transmitted to boys by their mothers. Fragile-X syndrome accounts for a small but significant number of boys diagnosed as autistic (Coleman, 1987). Similarly, tuberous sclerosis and PKU are heredity disorders usually accompanied by mental retardation, which have been identified in some people with autism (Folstein & Rutter, 1987).

If one identical twin has autism, the odds are very great that the second does as well. Ritvo, Freeman, Mason-Brothers, Mo, and Ritvo (1985) found a 95.7% concordance rate for autism in identical twins, and only 23.5% in fraternal twins. The familial factor in autism may also be seen in the siblings of these youngsters, who exhibit a greater than chance frequency of problems with general intelligence, reading, and language (Folstein & Rutter, 1987). For example, August, Stewart, and Tsai (1981) found that 15% of the siblings of children with autism had cognitive abnormalities such as mental retardation, whereas only 3% of the siblings of children with Down Syndrome exhibited similar problems.

Physiological Factors

General support for the notion that the symptoms of autism reflect underlying physiological dysfunction comes from research showing that autism occurs more often than would be predicted by chance among children whose mothers had german measles during pregnancy (Chess, 1977), that these children experience a higher than expected rate of problems during pregnancy and/or birth (Schreibman, 1988), and that they are at greater risk for seizures than are other children (DeLong & Bauman, 1987). Findings such as these raise important questions about where in the brain abnormalities may occur and how these neurochemical, biochemical, or neurological factors may be specifically linked to the development of the language, social, affective, and behavioral symptoms that characterize autism.

The neurological approach to autism searches for those portions of the brain that are specifically involved. Much of this research is based on comparing what we know about the behaviors observed in people with autism with the behaviors of persons who are known to have suffered damage in specific areas of the brain (Reichler & Lee, 1987). Although a few of these studies have been done on postmortem examination of people with autism who died from other causes (e.g., Ritvo et al., 1986), the development of noninvasive methods for studying brain structure in living persons is enabling us to look more closely at the brains of people with autism than was possible in the past.

Two of the most commonly used methods of studying brain structure are computerized tomographic scans (CT scans) and magnetic resonance imaging (MRI). CT scans involve passing multiple x-ray beams through the brain in a step wise or circular pattern and measuring the intensity of these beams as they exit the head. These measurements are analyzed by computer and displayed as a picture of the brain on a cathode ray tube (Brahme, 1982). Brain lesions show a different density on the CT scan than does healthy tissue, thus making it possible to see abnormalities of brain structure. The MRI procedure takes technology one step further than the CT scan because it does not use x-rays beams and thereby further reduces any risk to the patient. Rather than x-rays, the MRI measures the magnetic properties of hydrogen and phosphorus in the brain and with the use of a computer, converts these into pictures of the living brain, a measure that is often more detailed than the CT scan (Elliott & Ciaranello, 1987).

DeLong and Bauman (1987) in a review of research on brain structure in autism concluded that a high proportion of these children have a recognizable neurological disorder. Nonetheless, the specific locations of these lesions is quite variable, and we have not yet identified the relationships between these observed brain abnormalities and specific behaviors of autism.

In addition to CT scans and MRIs to inspect brain structure, another noninvasive way of studying brain functioning is to measure the electrical activity of the brain. This is done by placing electrodes on the surface of the scalp that record the minute electrical impulses constantly emitted by the living brain. We know, for example, that epilepsy is characterized by specific abnormalities of brain electrical activity as measured by an electroencephalogram (EEG). Similar abnormalities may occur with autism. Courchesne (1987) measured highly localized brain responses called event-related potentials (ERPs) in people with autism by placing electrodes on the scalp and then presenting a specific stimulus event. This measurement differs from an EEG in that the ERP allows for a direct link between a specific response and a specific stimulus. The results of his work are consistent with the notion that there is abnormal brain processing in the person with autism that interferes with attending and awareness. He speculates that these abnormalities of brain function are analogous to, although perhaps different from, epilepsy.

In addition to looking for specific lesions or areas of anatomical abnormality in the brains of persons with autism, it is also possible to examine the neurotransmitters in the brain to determine whether there are abnormalities in brain chemistry. Neurotransmitters are the chemicals that enable information to be transferred from one neuron to another. Because these chemicals control sleep, arousal, affect, motor coordination, and so forth, they are major targets of investigation for the etiology of any psychiatric disorder (Yuwiler & Freedman, 1987). For example, one neurotransmitter called dopamine has been linked to the development of movement disorders in Parkinsonism and to schizophrenia. Similarly, norepinephrine has been implicated in bipolar affective disorder.

The neurotransmitter serotonin has thus far been the brain chemical most closely examined as a possible cause of autism. Serotonin is found in the blood as well as the brain, and research typically has focused on this indirect measure of the chemical's presence. Elevated blood levels of serotonin, which occur in about 30% of children with autism, led to considerable interest in this neurotransmitter as a possible cause of autism (Yuwiler & Freedman, 1987) and a potential basis for treatment. However, we have not yet identified any consistent relationships between specific autistic behaviors and blood serotonin levels, nor can we be confident of the relationship between blood and brain levels of serotonin. Furthermore, elevated serotonin levels are common in a number of disorders including bipolar affective disorder and chronic schizophrenia, thus raising questions about how specific these findings may be to autism (Yuwiler & Freedman, 1987).

In general, the research on the role of brain anatomy, biochemistry, and neurotransmitters in autism has not yet provided sufficient information to allow us to draw any definitive conclusions about the role of these factors in autism. Inconsistency of diagnosis from one study to another, the use of small samples, variability in diagnosis, and the technological limits of the tools available to study brain function have all impeded progress. However, the research is growing in technical sophistication, and as we gain a greater data base it becomes possible to ask increasingly precise questions that doubtlessly will ultimately yield important answers about the specific biological etiologies of autistic behavior.

CURRENT TREATMENTS

The most common approach to the treatment of people with autism is behavior therapy. Since the mid-1960s, when Ivar Lovass and his colleagues (Lovaas, Berberich, Perloff, & Schaeffer, 1966) first demonstrated that children with autism could respond to carefully planned operant conditioning techniques, there has been extensive research on the use of these methods to treat autism. More than two decades of research have contributed to the development of a substantial array of specific behavioral treatment techniques and of documentation to support the efficacy of these methods in treating the symptoms of autism. This research has also demonstrated the essential role that parents can play in the treatment of their children by providing a consistency of intervention between home and school (Handleman & Harris, 1986)

Traditionally operant conditioning procedures have relied on a technique called the *discrete trial format* to convey small units of information to the child with autism. In this format the teacher first gains the child's attention, gives a brief command (e.g., "show me the dog"), waits for the child's response, and reinforces a correct response with praise and perhaps with a small treat. The teacher then records whether the child's response was correct and goes on to the next trial. In the event that the child fails to respond or makes an error, a correct response would be prompted. Hundreds of discrete trials might be necessary to teach a child a skill such as putting on his or her socks or discriminating red from blue. This discrete trial format remains an important tool for teaching children with autism, but in recent years there has also been a heavy emphasis on teaching in a more naturalistic context that resembles the setting in which the child will actually be living. For example, if one were teaching a child to discriminate colors, it might be done during the course of picking crayons to color a picture or selecting a ball to play catch.

When they first enter treatment, children with autism may have little if any motivation to do the kinds of things their teachers and parents wish they would do. Paying attention to an adult's instructions, speaking, eating with a fork, and using the toilet have little if any interest for many children with autism, and as a result, it is sometimes necessary to offer them artificial reinforcers at the early stages of treatment. For example, the child who sits quietly for a few moments may be praised and given a small taste of ice cream. Gradually these artificial rewards are replaced by the more natural reinforcements that occur in interactions between children and adults.

Social Skills

Children with autism often have to be taught in considerable detail all of the complexities of social interactions such as how to play a game with another child, how to express affection, to wait one's turn, to console another child who is crying, or to initiate a play interaction. Normally developing peers can be useful in this training by providing age-appropriate models of behavior and by learning to be responsive to the first, tentative social efforts of the child with autism (Odom & Strain, 1986). Twenty years of research have documented the feasibility of teaching these many discrete skills to the child with autism, although mastery of all of these individual behaviors does not necessarily result in the child's being able to hold his or her own in the spontaneous, rough and tumble of daily childhood living.

My colleagues and I taught young adolescents at our center how to offer assistance to other people who were having difficulty with a task (Harris, Handleman, & Alessandri, 1990). For example, for 14-year-old Rick, we first conducted a baseline observation period during which we noted that he essentially ignored other people who were struggling to do such tasks as putting a key in a lock, tearing off a piece of tape, or buttoning a button. Then we taught Rick to say, "Can I help you?" when another person was having trouble with a task. When Rick made the offer of assistance, the second person would reply, "Thanks a lot. Could you please button my jacket?" Rick was then praised for his helpful behavior. Under these conditions, his offers of assistance increased to an average of 88%, and he began to offer assistance at home as well as in school.

Treatment for the child with autism can be helpful to the rest of the family as well. David Celiberti and I (1992) taught siblings of children with autism how to play with their brother or sister. In one family, Jack, a 4-year-old boy with autism, was a source of distress to Alice, his 8-year-old sister. Alice would have liked nothing better than to play with her little brother, but her efforts were ignored or actively rebuffed by his tantrums. This was vividly clear during a baseline assessment where Jack ignored his sister's efforts to get him to play, and she in turn was quickly discouraged and withdrew from her brother. During the training program, Alice was taught the behavioral skills necessary to get her brother's attention and invite him to play with interesting toys, how to prompt him to play appropriately, and to reinforce his play behaviors. By following these steps, she transformed their playtime into experiences enjoyable to both children, and their parents were delighted to see the youngsters share fun time together.

Speech and Language

Although there were a number of early demonstrations that children with autism could acquire simple speech through operant conditioning techniques, there were also serious limitations to these methods because the children tended to become relatively dependent on the specific cues of the instructional context and therefore to have difficulty transferring their language to other settings. As a result, recent research has focused on techniques for enhancing spontaneity and generality of communication by children with autism. This has been addressed in part by creating a more richly varied instructional setting, by encouraging the child to take the lead in initiating communication, and by trying to ensure that language use is met by rich and varied natural reinforcers (Harris, in press). An example of such work by Koegel, O'Dell, and Koegel (1987) documents the value of learning speech as an integral aspect of the natural interactions that occur between an adult and a child.

Disruptive Behaviors

One of the areas in which major advances have been made in the treatment of persons with autism is in the management of disruptive or dangerous behaviors such as self-injury, stereotyped behavior, and aggression. We have learned that there is often a link between environmental events and disruptive behaviors. Much of this research on what is called *functional analysis* has focused on behaviors that have an escape function or that are attention seeking in nature (e.g., Carr & Durand, 1985). If the function of the behavior can be determined, then it is often possible to teach a substitute behavior that will create the desired outcome without being disruptive. For example, the child who tantrums to avoid work can be taught to ask from a break from work. Similarly, the youngster who throws toys to seek adult attention can be taught to raise his or her hand and ask the teacher to look at his or her work.

Determining which variables are functional for a client may require highly sophisticated behavioral assessment including detailed recording of such data as the nature of the disruptive response, the day, time, physical location, persons present, specific antecedent, and consequent events, and so forth. Careful inspection of these data often reveals patterns of responding that can then be verified through the use of analog assessments in which variables of interest such as attention or escape factors are deliberately manipulated to assess their impact on behavior.

Although substituting a new, adaptive response for an old, disruptive behaviors is often effective is reducing unwanted behaviors, sometimes it may be necessary to suppress the disruptive behavior directly as well. The use of physical exercise, brief restraint, or time-out from a reinforcing situation are among the range of mildly aversive techniques that are available to help persons with autism learn to control their disruptive behaviors (Harris, in press). Sometimes, when less aversive alternatives fail and the behavior is of a life threatening nature such as severe self-injury, it may be necessary to use a more potent aversive technique including very brief, but not physically dangerous electrical shock. Such methods are only used as a last resort and must be done by persons well-trained in their application in order to avoid the risk of abuse (Harris & Handleman, 1990). Many facilities have special student rights advocates who would review these methods to ensure they are necessary; parental consent would also be required.

Most often, disruptive behaviors can be treated without resorting to powerfully aversive procedures. For example, my colleagues and I used physical exercise to help Mark, 7-year boy with autism, learn to control his disruptive, out-of-seat behavior (Gordon, Handleman, & Harris, 1986). During a 5-day baseline before treatment, we determined that Mark was jumping out of his seat an average of 77 times during the school day. We then introduced a treatment procedure that required him to go jogging with his teacher each time he got out of chair without permission. Using this procedure the frequency of his out-of-seat behavior quickly declined to an average of four times a day.

Medication

Drugs may be useful adjunct treatment for some children with autism. Medication is most likely to be considered for students who are aggressive or self-injurious and do not respond to behavioral techniques. Among the most commonly used drugs are haloperidol, naloxone, and naltrexone (Spencer & Campbell, 1990). Because of the wide range of individual responses to medication, these and other drugs must be closely monitored for side effects, with careful behavioral measures to demonstrate efficacy.

Early Intervention — A Case Illustration

Pauline M. was admitted to the Douglass Developmental Disabilities Center at the age of 4 years, 2 months. The intake report notes that she was a cute little girl with a lovely smile, who left her parents to go with the examiner without a backward glance. She had little interpersonal eye contact, was aloof, noncompliant, and several times pinched the examiner. She exhibited a number of behaviors consistent with a diagnosis of autism including smelling objects, putting her hands over her ears, lining up crayons in a precise row, and making a variety of odd noises. She also engaged in immediate and delayed echolalia.

According to Mrs. M, the pregnancy was full term and uneventful. Pauline's motor milestones such as sitting up, standing, and walking were all on time. However, her language development was very slow, with a few words emerging around her first birthday and very little speech after that time. At the age of 4, Pauline had a number of single words and a few two-word combinations.

At home, Pauline engaged in a great deal of stereotyped behavior including rocking, spinning in circles, and posturing her fingers. She tantrummed when someone disrupted the pattern of objects she had arranged or when she was otherwise frustrated. She also liked to lick and sniff objects. She was an emotionally removed child who often seemed to be in her "own world."

Pauline's behavior fit the criteria for a diagnosis of Autistic Disorder. Because of her limited speech and her tantrums, we admitted her to the Center's specialized class for children who need one-to-one instruction.

Within the framework of intensive, behavioral intervention, Pauline made impressive progress during her first year at the center. Her tested IQ on the the Stanford–Binet IV went from 37 at the time of admission to 63, a very impressive 26 point gain at the end of the school year. On the Preschool Language Scale her language quotient showed a similarly substantial gain, from 55 at the time of admission to 83 at the end of the year.

Pauline's progress on these objective tests was paralleled by her gains in instructional programming. At the end of the first quarter, her progress report showed that she had mastered 41% of her instructional goals for that period. In the second period, this rose to 56%; in the third period, 63%, and in the final period of the year, she had mastered 73% of an ever growing pool of programs. Her progress was evident in every domain including behavior management, speech and language, cognitive skills, fine and gross motor, and self-help activities. Her most impressive progress was in the area of cognitive skills where she mastered 33 out of 35 programs by the end of the year. This included such activities as naming colors, counting objects, naming shapes, matching numerals, and telling time by the hour. She had also stopped tantrumming and learned to ask for what she wanted when frustrated. Socially, she showed an increasing awareness of the presence of other people and an interest in being with them.

Pauline's developmental progress at school was paralleled at home where her parents instituted a number of behavior management, self-help, speech, and socialization programs to ensure the transfer of school based activities to the home.

SUMMARY

Autistic disorder is a relatively rare, but very serious disorder that begins in infancy or early childhood and requires early, intensive intervention for maximum treatment benefits. The symptoms of autism include pervasive problems of social behavior and emotional expression, communication deficits, and disruptive behavior including stereotyped behavior, self-injury, and resistance to change.

Although once believed to be the result of poor parenting, autism is now known to be related to a variety of biologically based disorders. There appear to be genetic patterns for some cases of autism, and other neurological and neurochemical bases are being explored for this disorder.

Behavior therapy is the most common treatment for autism, and there exists an extensive data base to document the benefits of behavioral procedures for treating the social, communication, and behavior problems exhibited by the child with autism.

REFERENCES

American Psychiatric Association (1980). *Diagnostic and statistical manual of mental disorders* (3rd ed.). Washington DC: Author.

American Psychiatric Association (1987). *Diagnostic and statistical manual of mental disorders* (3rd rev. ed.). Washington DC: Author.

American Psychiatric Association (1994). *Diagnostic and statistical manual of mental disorder (4th ed)*. Washington DC: Author.

August, G. J., Stewart, M. A., & Tsai, L. (1981). The incidence of cognitive disabilities in the siblings of autistic children. *British Journal of Psychiatry, 138*, 416–422.

Batshaw, M. L., & Perret, Y. M. (1981). *Children with handicaps: A medical primer*. Baltimore MD: Brooks.

Bettelheim, B. (1967). *The empty fortress*. New York: The Free Press.

Brahme, F. J. (1982). Neuroradiology. In W. C. Wiederholt (Ed.), *Neurology for non-neurologists* (pp. 107–142). New York: Academic Press.

Carr, E. G., & Durand, V. M. (1985). Reducing behavior problems through functional communication training. *Journal of Applied Behavior Analysis, 18*, 111–126.

Celiberti, D. A., & Harris, S. L. (1992). *The effects of a skills based intervention on the play behavior of children with autism and their normally developing siblings*. Manuscript submitted for publication.

Chess, S. (1977). Follow-up report on autism in congenital rubella. *Journal of Autism and Childhood Schizophrenia, 7*, 69–81.

Coleman, M. (1987). The search for neurological subgroups in autism. In E. Schopler & G. B. Mesibov (Eds.), *Neurobiological issues in autism* (pp. 163–178). New York: Plenum.

Courchesne, E. (1987). A neurophysiological view of autism. In E. Schopler & G. B. Mesibov (Eds.), *Neurobiological issues in autism* (pp. 285–324). New York: Plenum.

DeLong, G. R., & Bauman, M. L. (1987). Brain lesions in autism. In E. Schopler & G. B. Mesibov (Eds.), *Neurobiological issues in autism* (pp. 229–242). New York: Plenum.

Elliott, G. R., & Ciaranello, R. D. (1987). Neurochemical hypotheses of childhood psychoses. In E. Schopler & G. B. Mesibov (Eds.), *Neurobiological issues in autism* (pp. 245–261). New York: Plenum.

Folstein, S. E., & Rutter, M. L. (1987). Autism. Familial aggregation and genetic implications. In E. Schopler & G. B. Mesibov (Eds.), *Neurobiological issues in autism* (pp. 83–105). New York: Plenum.

Gordon, R., Handleman, J. S., & Harris, S. L. (1986). The effects of contingent versus non-contingent running on the out-of-seat behavior of an autistic boy. *Child and Family Behavior Therapy, 8*, 337–344.

Handleman, J. S., & Harris, S. L. (1986). *Educating the developmentally disabled. Meeting the needs of children and families*. San Diego CA: College-Hill Press.

Harris, S. L. (in press). Educational strategies in autism. In E. Schopler & G. B. Mesibov (Eds.), *Learning and cognition in autism*. New York: Plenum.

Harris, S. L., & Handleman, J. S. (Eds). (1990). *Aversive and nonaversive interventions: Controlling life-threatening behavior by the developmentally disabled*. New York: Springer.

Harris, S. L., Handleman, J. S., & Alessandri, M. (1990). Teaching youths with autism to offer assistance. *Journal of Applied Behavior Analysis, 23*, 297–305.

Kanner, L. (1943). Autistic disturbances of affective contact. *Nervous Child*, *2*, 217–240.

Koegel, R. L., O'Dell, M. C., & Koegel, L. K. (1987). A natural language teaching paradigm for nonverbal autistic children. *Journal of Autism and Developmental Disorders*, *17*, 187–200.

Lovaas, O. I., Berberich, J. P., Perloff, B. F., & Schaeffer, B. (1966). Acquisition of imitative speech by schizophrenic children. *Science*, *151*, 705–707.

Mesibov, G. B. (1983). Current perspectives and issues in autism and adolescence. In E. Schopler & G. B. Mesibov (Eds.), *Autism in adolescents and adults* (pp. 37–53). New York: Plenum.

Odom, S. L., & Strain, P. S. (1986). A comparison of peer-initiation and teacher-antecedent interventions for promoting reciprocal interactions of autistic preschoolers. *Journal of Applied Behavior Analysis*, *19*, 59–71.

Reichler, R. J., & Lee, E. M. C. (1987). Overview of biomedical issues in autism. In E. Schopler & G. B. Mesibov (Eds.), *Neurobiological issues in autism* (pp. 13–41). New York: Plenum.

Ritvo, E. R., Freeman, B. J., Mason-Brothers, A., Mo, A., & Ritvo, A. M. (1985). Concordance for the syndrome of autism in 40 pairs of afflicted twins. *American Journal of Psychiatry*, *142*, 74–77.

Ritvo, E. R., Freeman, B. J., Sheibel, A. B., Duong, T., Robinson, R., Guthrie, D., & Ritvo, A. M. (1986). Lower Purkinje cell counts in the cerebella of four autistic subjects: Initial findings of the UCLA-NSAC autopsy research report. *American Journal of Psychiatry*, *143*, 862–866.

Schreibman, L. (1988). *Autism*. Newbury Park, CA: Sage.

Spencer, E. K., & Campbell, M. (1990). Aggressiveness directed against self and others: Psychopharmacological intervention. In S. L. Harris & J. S. Handleman (Eds.), *Aversive and nonaversive interventions: Controlling life-threatening behavior by the developmentally disabled* (pp. 163–181). New York: Springer.

Tsai, L. Y. (1992). Is Rhett syndrome a subtype of pervasive developmental disorders? *Journal of Autism and Developmental Disorders*, *22*, 5, 651–561.

Yuwiler, A., & Freedman, D. X. (1987). Neurotransmitter research in autism. In E. Schopler & G. B. Mesibov (Eds.), *Neurobiological issues in autism* (pp. 263–284). New York: Plenum.

Chapter 17

Specific Developmental Disorders

Cynthia R. Johnson
Western Psychiatric Institute and Clinic

Specific Developmental Disorders refer to a group of disorders characterized by severe deficiencies in the development of skills in the academic, language, and motor domains. These disorders are included under Axis II in the *Diagnostic and Statistical Manual of Mental Disorders-III-Revised* (American Psychiatric Association, 1987) classification system. The Academic Skills Disorders are further divided into Developmental Reading Disorder, Developmental Expressive Writing Disorder, and Developmental Arithmetic Disorder. Included in the language and speech disorders are Developmental Articulation Disorder, Developmental Expressive Language Disorder, and Developmental Receptive Language Disorder. Lastly, under Motor Skills Disorder is Developmental Coordination Disorder.

In the *DSM-IV Draft Criteria* (American Psychiatric Association, 1993), the Specific Developmental Disorders are reclassified under the diagnoses of Learning Disorders, Motor Skills Disorder, and Communication Disorders. The subtypes of these diagnostic labels closely parallel *DSM-III-R* nomenclature. Learning disorders are divided into Reading disorder, Mathematics Disorder, Disorder of Written Expression, and Learning disorder Not Otherwise Specified (NOS). The Motor Skills disorder will remain the same with Developmental Coordination Disorder as the sole subtype. Under Communication Disorders, the subtypes include Expressive Language Disorder, Mixed Receptive/Expressive Language Disorder, Phonological Disorder, delete a new separate diagnosis of Stuttering, and Communication Disorder NOS, are included.

Although these are the psychiatric diagnostic labels, Specific Developmental Disorders (*DSM-III-R*), or Learning Disorders and Communication Disorders (*DSM-IV*) are subsumed under various labels by other classification systems to include learning disability, learning disorder, specific learning disability, language impairment, and communication disorder. Historically, many terms have also been used to describe Specific Developmental Disorders. Earlier labels commonly applied included minimal brain dysfunction, congenital word blindness, dyslexia, developmental aphasia, and congenital aphasia (Baker & Cantwell, 1989; Silver & Hagin, 1990). According to Silver (1991), children with significant learning difficulties were considered mentally retarded before the 1940s. Since this time, the possibility of other influences has been considered.

Within the educational system, Specific Developmental Disorders are encompassed under the terms learning disability and speech and language impairment. According to the Public Law 94-142, Education for Handicapped Children, learning disability is defined as follows:

> A disorder in one or more of the more basic psychological processes involved in understanding or in using language, spoken or written, which may manifest itself in an imperfect ability to listen think, speak, read, write, spell, or to do mathematical calculations. The term includes such conditions as perceptual handicaps, brain injury, minimal brain dysfunction, dyslexia, and developmental aphasia. The term does not include children who have learning problems primarily the result of visual, hearing, or motor handicaps or mental retardation, or emotional disturbance, or of environmental, cultural, or economic disadvantage. (Federal Register, 1976, p. 46977)

The separate educational category of speech and language impairment is more narrowly defined as impairments in language, voice, fluency, or articulation that are not as a result of sensory impairment or developmental delay. It should be underscored here that the definitions of Specific Developmental Disorders in *DSM-III-R* and learning disability and speech and language disorders in the education system are problematic in that the degree of deficits in skill development is not specified or standardized. This lack of precision in definitions has led to differing criteria applied to diagnosing Specific Developmental Disorders, thus resulting in a heterogenous group. This is further complicated by the accepted view that learning disabilities present on a continuum from mild to severe impairment in skill development.

Critical features for each of the Specific Developmental Disorders included in *DSM-III-R* are described, the course of the disorder, an account of factors influencing these disorders, and intervention strategies commonly employed are reviewed in this chapter. The terms learning disability and speech and language impairment are used interchangeably with the Specific Developmental Disorders.

CLINICAL DESCRIPTION

Academic Skill Disorders

Central to the diagnosis of the disorders falling under this domain is impairment in skill development than would expected based on intellectual ability. In the educational system, the three disorders here are subsumed under the learning disabilities classification. The learning disability classification is the most prevalent of the educational handicapping conditions identified. Although the prevalence of learning disabilities is unclear, it is estimated that 3% to 15% of school-age children have some learning disability (Heaton, 1988).

Developmental Arithmetic Disorder.   According to *DSM–III–R*, the primary characteristic for Developmental Arithmetic Disorder is marked impairment in arithmetic skills that is not attributable to mental retardation, school issues, or sensory impairment such as blindness or deafness. The level of significance must be such that impairment hinders achievement or living skills requiring arithmetic skills. A diagnosis is typically made when a severe discrepancy between overall cognitive ability and arithmetic achievement level is determined from the administration of standardized measures. These measures may be administered after the child has experienced difficulty in the school setting. Specific areas of impairment may include deficits in understanding math terminology, concepts, and operations, problems with the recognition of symbols; attention difficulties; and math problems requiring multiple skills. According to *DSM–III–R*, the prevalence of Developmental Arithmetic Disorder is not known but is thought to be less common than Developmental Reading Disorder.

Developmental Reading Disorder.   The critical feature of this Specific Developmental Disorder is significant impairment in skill development related to reading such as word recognition, decoding skills, and comprehension. Again, the diagnosis is made when a discrepancy exists between intellectual ability and reading achievement levels and when mental retardation, sensory impairment, and environmental factors have been excluded as causes. The prevalence of developmental reading disorder has been estimated to be 3% to 10% of school-age children (American Psychiatric Association, 1987). It is common that children who meet the diagnostic criteria for a reading disorder also have deficits in other academic and language areas, possibly warranting other specific developmental disorder diagnoses. There has been much recent speculation that children with Developmental Reading Disorder may in fact have a primary Developmental Language Disorder that has caused or at least strongly influenced the reading difficulty (Mann & Brady, 1988).

Developmental Expressive Writing Disorder.   The main facet of this disorder is severe impairment in the development of expressive writing abilities. These include spelling, grammatical and punctuation skills, and poor paragraph organization. The presence of this disorder may become evident in the first couple of years of school if severe. The disorder, however, may not become evident until later elementary levels if there is only mild impairment. Developmental Reading Disorder is very often associated with this diagnosis. As with the other academic skill disorders, a diagnosis is made with the help of standardized masures of ability and writing achievement.

Language Disorders

Developmental Articulation Disorder.   Consistent with the label, the essential clinical manifestation of this disorder is failure to develop correct articulation at appropriate ages. Omissions and substitutions for speech sounds are also likely. Often considered the most common developmental disorder, a prevalence rate of 5% to 10% of young children has been reported (Arnold, 1990). Other Specific Developmental Disorders are often present in the same individual with an articulation disorder.

Developmental Expressive Language Disorder.   This diagnostic label implies significant deficiencies in the development of expressive language that may not be explained by other causes. From 3% to 10% of children are reported to be affected with this language disorder (Arnold, 1990). Areas of difficulty may include a limited (small) vocabulary, limited sentence structure, omissions in spoken sentences, delayed speech development, and idiosyncratic word ordering. Other language disorders may coexist in an individual, particularly developmental articulation disorder. A diagnosis usually depends on the demonstration of an expressive language score on a standardized test that is well below assessed intellectual ability and interferes with daily or academic functioning.

Developmental Receptive Language Disorder.   The hallmark characteristic for this diagnostic label is inadequacy in the development of the ability to comprehend language that significantly hinders academic progress or daily living activities. The prevalence of this disorder is thought to be similar to that of Developmental Expressive Language Disorder. As with the other developmental disorders, there is a continuum from mild to severe impairment in the capability in understanding words. Impairment is usually noticed in the toddler or preschool years depending on the severity level. A standardized language measure of receptive skills in comparison to assessed intellectual functioning is used to make a diagnosis.

Motor Skills Disorders

Developmental Coordination Disorder.   This diagnostic category is reserved for significantly impaired coordination given chronological age and intellectual ability. The motor coordination must interfere with achievement or daily living activities including physical activities typical for age. An estimated 6% of young children are suspected to meet criteria for this diagnosis (Arnold, 1990). However, very little is reported about this category in comparison to the attention the other specific developmental disorder diagnoses have received.

Other Developmental Disorders

Specific Developmental Disorder Not Otherwise Specified.   This category is included in *DSM-III-R* for disorders in the academic, language, or motor domains that do not meet the criteria for one of the earlier discussed disorders. An example that is provided in *DSM-III-R* is Landau-Kleffner Syndrome that refers to acquired aphasia associated with abnormal EEG findings.

CAUSES OF THE DISORDERS

It is generally accepted that the causes of Specific Developmental Disorders are multiple. A general underlying assumption regarding the etiology is the presence of cerebral dysfunction that may be of unknown origin (Obrzut & Boliek, 1991). Although in many cases the particular reasons of a child's learning or language difficulty may be unclear, commonly cited etiological factors associated with Specific Developmental Disorders include perinatal and neonatal insult. There is a correlation between Specific Developmental Disorders and factors such as low birth weight, maternal smoking and alcohol consumption during pregnancy, and exposure to other toxins (Silver, 1991). Fifty percent of children with elevated lead levels have a reading disorder (Needleman, Schell, Bellinger, Leviton, & Allred, 1990). Additionally, specific infections such as a particular type of meningitis (Silver & Hagin, 1990) have also been related to later developmental disorders.

Although research findings have been equivocal, recurrent otitis media has been implicated in at least placing a child at-risk for a specific language disorder (Bishop & Edmundson, 1986). This is suggested as particularly the case when other perinatal risks are also present. Other causative or at least contributing risk factors involve early deprivation and malnutrition (Arnold, 1990). These is also speculation that a relationship between learning and language disorders and seizure disorders exists (Klein, 1991; Silver & Hagin, 1990).

The mechanisms by which these etiologic factors lead to the emergence of specific developmental disorders is far from clear. Alternations in the development of the central nervous system have been suggested to include specific anomalies in the cerebral cortex (Galaburda, Sherman, Rosen, Aboitiz, & Geschwind (1985). Cerebral asymmetry and aberrant neuronal migration have also been offered as the consequence of early insults correlated with the development of the Specific Developmental Disorders (Galaburda et al., 1985)

COURSE OF THE DISORDERS

Academic Skills Disorders

The three disorders in this category, Specific Arithmetic Disorder, Specific Reading Disorder, and Specific Expressive Writing Disorder, progress in similar courses across time. These three disorders are most commonly identified during the early elementary school years, although the types of academic difficulty depends on the grade level such tasks required. Depending on the degree of impairment, improvement in the development of skills may be realized over time or conversely, the impairment may interfere more as the child moves through school and academic tasks become increasingly challenging. Recent investigations of adults with learning disabilities add further support for this mixed prognosis. Although some young adults with learning disabilities experience minimal difficulty in securing and maintaining satisfying employment, other persons with learning disabilities may have difficulty finding employment and may be quite dissatisfied with their attainments (Spreen, 1988). Variables likely influencing the prognosis include the level of impairment, early educational experiences, vocational track demands, and the coexistence of any other disabilities or illness.

There has been much speculation about the psychosocial adjustment of children with learning disabilities. More recently, findings have refuted that *all* children with learning disabilities are social–emotional disturbed (Rourke, 1989), although it is generally held that among the learning disorder group is a disproportionate number who also experience psychosocial problems. Of particular interest is recent work suggesting that one proposed subtype of learning disability (i.e., better arithmetic skills than reading skills) places children more at-risk for social–emotional and psychiatric problems (Rourke & Fuerst, 1991). Students labelled as learning disabled have been found to have lower status among their peers and are thought to be deficient in social skills or social competency (Bryan & Lee, 1990). There is a significant overlap of children with both an Academic Skills Disorder and Attention-Deficit Hyperactivity Disorder (ADHD). However, it is important to note that many children with learning disabilities experience no psychosocial difficulties (Pearl, 1992).

Language and Speech Disorders

Among the language and speech disorders, Developmental Articulation Disorder is the most likely to be resolved. Because this disorder is typically identified during the preschool years, early detection and intervention lead to a positive treatment outcome. However, children with severe articulation problems may need continued intensive treatment throughout childhood. In contrast, the prognosis of both Developmental Expressive and Receptive Language Disorders is more variable and depends on the severity of the impairment, but difficulty is more likely to be experienced through childhood and adulthood. Not surprisingly, the course of language disorders is closely tied to the demands placed on the individual. A person with a language disorder who remains in a line of employment where language skills are not critical may be very minimally affected by a language disorder. Conversely, the young adult who enters a vocational area where language skills are in demand is more likely to continue to be hindered by a language disorder.

Children with language and speech disorders are at increased risk for behavior and other psychiatric problems (Beitchman, Nair, Clegg, Ferguson, & Patel, 1986). In a recent extensive study conducted by Cantwell and Baker (1991), children with language and speech disorders had increased rates of psychiatric disorders when compared with the general population. As with the Academic Skills Disorder group, there is significant overlap between language disorder and Attention-Deficit Hyperactivity Disorder.

Motor Coordination Disorder

As mentioned earlier, Developmental Coordination Disorder has received little investigative attention. It is thought that the course of this disorder is variable with lack of coordination continuing through adulthood (American Psychiatric Association, 1987). The impact of the disorder has not been clearly elucidated.

In summary, there is significant overlap or comorbidity of learning or Academic Skill Disorders, language disorders, and other psychiatric disorders. From a theoretical standpoint, it is logical to assume that children who experience difficulty in comprehending, mastering academic demands, and encounter failure repeatedly are more likely to develop behavioral or emotional problems. In this case, psychiatric and behavior problems are secondary to the learning or language disorder. It has been suggested as well that the underlying mechanisms for the different disorders are similar. Thus, if one disorder emerges, there is an increased likelihood that another will. For example, the cerebral dysfunction assumed to be present in learning disorders may also be present in other disorders.

FAMILIAL CONTRIBUTIONS

As with most childhood disorders, socioeconomic and familial variables play a significant role in the development and the prognosis of the disorder. The putative effects of neglect and abuse, for example, on the development of children in general has been clearly documented (Garbarino, 1982). Ironically this contributing cause of delay also places the child more at-risk for future neglect and abuse. Although little has been noted particularly about Specific Developmental Disorders, the presence of developmental and physical disabilities has been demonstrated to put children at increased risk for abuse (see Ammerman, Van Hasselt, & Hersen, 1988).

Not surprisingly, functioning of the family impacts the prognosis of the child with a Specific Developmental Disorder. Ziegler and Holden (1988) described different family characteristics that may influence the outcome and intervention needs of a child with a learning disability. Although a "healthy" family may adequately cope with parenting a child with learning disorders, families described as "disorganized" and "blaming" have more difficulty responding to the child's needs and providing appropriate support and intervention (Ziegler & Holden, 1988).

PSYCHOPHYSIOLOGICAL AND GENETIC INFLUENCES

Electrophysiologic Studies

Electroencephalographic (EEG) investigations of children with learning and language disorders have attempted to uncover a specific abnormality in brain functions. Although no conclusive evidence has been obtained, there has been some noted differences in EEG findings in children with and without a reading disorder (Willis, Hooper, & Stone, 1992). However, no common EEG pattern typical of learning and language problems has been determined. Another electrophysiological indicator is event-related potentials (ERPs) that are averaged electrical response to a stimulus that purportedly requires cognitive processing. Differences in waveforms have been shown on this measure between reading disordered subjects and a control group (Willis et al., 1992).

Other physiological measures that have revealed dissimilarities in learning disordered individuals and comparison groups are computed topography (CT scan), positron emission tomography (PET scan), and regional cerebral blood flow. Although no conclusive results can be made at this point, it is clear that there are differences among those individuals with learning and language disorders. A full understanding of these differences on these measures will require much more investigative efforts.

Neuropsychological Assessment

Neuropsychological assessment serves as an adjunct to traditional psychoeducational testing and is used to evaluate specific information processing strengths and weaknesses of an individual and make inferences regarding areas of possible brain insult or dysfunction. Within this framework, specific deficits in brain structure or regions of dysfunction are inferred from performance on a battery of neuropsychological instruments. Though neuropsychological assessments have been shown to accurately identify areas of learning difficulties and predict academic problems (Taylor, 1988), further research is necessary before any conclusive statements may be made about specific patterns on neuropsychology testing in children with specific developmental disorders.

Genetic Contributions

There is mounting evidence that at least some of the disorders falling under the rubric of Specific Developmental Disorders are significantly influenced by genetics. Reading and language disorders have received the most attention with respect to genetic contributions. Support of the heritability of Specific Learning Disorders is provided by findings that there is a higher rate of these disorders in biological relatives than what would be expected in general (American Psychiatric Association, 1987; Arnold, 1990; Pennington & Smith, 1983). Twin studies have provided further evidence of a genetic predisposition for certain Specific Developmental Disorders with monozygotic (identical) twins showing higher concordance of reading disorders than dizygotic (fraternal) twins. Studies of chromosomal abnormalities suggest that some sex chromosome anomalies are correlated with learning disorders. For example, boys with 47 XXY have been shown to have poor reading skills (Bender, Puck, Salenblatt, & Robinson, 1986) and both 47 XXX and 47 XXY karotypes are correlated with language and motor skill delay (Bender et al., 1983). Much recent attention has been devoted to the relationship of Fragile X syndrome, an abnormality of the X chromosome, and Developmental Language Disorders (Hagerman & Sobesky, 1989). Learning and language disorders have also been associated with low-incidence, known genetically transmitted syndromes. The disorder may be a primary or secondary feature of the syndrome. Examples include syndromes resulting in cleft palate, some lysosomal storage diseases, and some craniofacial syndromes (Shprintzen & Goldberg, 1986).

Overall, evidence from genetic research and investigations indicate that the genetic transmission of learning and language disorders is likely to be heterogeneous with multiple paths of transmission (Pennington & Smith, 1983). There are likely many genetic mechanisms that produce the same phenotype. Furthermore, the expression of this genetic transmission is likely to be highly variable and at this point not fully understood.

CURRENT TREATMENTS

Educational Placement and Services Models

Within the education system where children with learning and language disorders are served, several service options are typically considered. Service delivery options have most typically included regular classroom placement with and without consultation services, itinerant services, resource room services, self-contained classrooms, and separate special schools. An estimated 16% of children labeled as learning disabled are served in regular classrooms (Silver & Hagin, 1990). An advantage of educating the child classified as learning disabled in the regular classroom is the hope of removing the stigma of a special placement. However the disadvantage is that the child with special learning needs may be in a large classroom with a regular education teacher who is not equipped to instruct such a student. Consultation services may be provided to the classroom teacher with special methods of instruction and curricula. Typical itinerant models involve a special education teacher with training in instructional methods for children with learning and language disorders to provide services to a child within the regular classroom setting. A majority of children classified as learning disabled are served in a resource room where educational intervention efforts are undertaken in the particular area of weaknesses while the child spends the remaining part of the day in a regular classroom. An estimated 21% of children classified as learning disabled are enrolled in self-contained classrooms (Silver & Hagin, 1990) where they spend all or most of the day for academic instruction. Lastly, a small percentage of children with learning disabilities attend a special school. In keeping with the "least restrictive environment" mandate of Public Law 94–142, children classified as learning disabled or speech or language impaired are to be placed in the educational service that is least restrictive within this continuum of service options. Thus, this latter option is rarely used.

Specific modes of intervention that might be applied within any of these educational settings are described later. Intervention strategies taken for specific developmental disorders rest in the assumptions made about the etiology of the disorder and the deficits targeted for treatment.

Behavioral Interventions

Behavioral theory and principles have been implemented extensively in educational settings with a significant influence on instructional strategies for both Academic Skills Disorders and language and speech disorders. Within the framework of behavior management, the probability that a behavior will occur is a function of environmental antecedents and consequences of that particular behavior. The focus is on observable behavior and not on underlying inferred processes.

Specific behavioral procedures may be divided into consequence strategies or stimulus control strategies. Consequence strategies refer to the presentation of a reinforcer or punisher contingent on an observer behavior. Examples include the implementation of token or tangible reinforcement contingent on the performance of a prespecified target behavior. Error correction methods as a consequence such as feedback, feedback with rehearsal, and positive practice have also been demonstrated to promote academic progress (Singh, Deitz, & Singh, 1992). Stimulus control strategies include modeling, stimulus fading, prompting, and delayed prompting. With modeling procedures, the correct response may be first modeled for the students by the teacher. This is often used in teaching sight words (Singh et al., 1992). Stimulus fading refers to a technique by which difficult discriminations are taught by slowly moving from an easy discrimination to the more difficult target discrimination skill needed. For example, to teach a discrimination between the letters *N* and *M*, the first letter might be presented initially as much larger than the second. As the student consistently identifies the letters appropriately, the size of the letters are systematically changed until the child is able to discriminate the letters when presented in equal sizes. Prompting refers to the presentation of an addition cue or discriminative stimulus to elicit a particular response in a particular manner. For example, showing a picture of a ball when presenting the word *ball*. Delayed prompting refers to simply delaying the presentation of the cue or prompt with the goal of systematically fading out the need to have the prompt presented. Although presented separately here, it is often the case that a combination of behavioral approaches are implemented to ameliorate academic deficits. Some published educational curricula incorporate these behavioral techniques in their programs. One example is the Corrective Reading Program (Engelmann 1978) that incorporates modeling, behavioral rehearsal, immediate corrective feedback, and frequent delivery of reinforcement from the teacher.

Case Illustration 1: Developmental Reading Disorder

Bobby, an 11-year-old boy, was the product of a breech delivery with Erb's palsy noted in the right arm immediately after birth, but he recovered soon afterwards. Major developmental milestones were achieved at appropriate ages. On the Stanford–Binet Intelligence Scale: Fourth Edition, a total composite score of 104 was obtained, placing him in the average range of global cognitive functioning. Scores on the subscale areas of this scale were as follows: Verbal Reasoning - 107, Abstract/Visual, Reasoning - 115, Quantitative Reasoning - 102, and Short-term Memory - 98. Extensive academic testing indicated that Bobby was approximately 3 years below his sixth grade level in reading with a grade equivalent score of 3.2 on the Metropolitan Achievement Test. Bobby was having no difficulty in math and was approximately a year below grade level in language skills. Specific reading skill deficits involved decoding skills and comprehension of passages.

Based on these findings and specific skill deficits, Bobby was placed in a resource room where he participated in the Corrective Reading Program. This highly structured program (which facilitates increased student attention by incorporating modeling, behavioral rehearsal, immediate corrective feedback, and high levels of reinforcement) involves decoding and comprehension lessons. Additionally, a home-school token program for students in this reading program was implemented. Students could earn a token in the form of play money every 10 minutes for correct responding and participation. The money earned was used to purchase special privileges at home at the end of the school week such as a later bedtime, renting a video, and choosing the menu for a meal. This reinforcement system was viewed as an important intervention component given Bobby's lack of motivation and cooperation around reading activities because of his earlier experiences of failure in mastering reading skills. After 1 year in this specialized instructional program, Bobby was tested to be on grade level in reading. Although he no longer needed the intensive remedial services in the resource room, during the subsequent school year, the resource room teacher provided consultation to the regular classroom teacher to facilitate ongoing academic adjustment.

Cognitive–Behavioral Interventions

A primary assumption made with cognitive–behavioral interventions is that thoughts and cognitions as well as environmental consequences influence overt behavior. This model further posits a reciprocal interaction between overt behavior and cognitions or feelings. Children with specific learning disorders are said to be deficient in their ability to regulate, organize, and execute cognitive functions in an efficient manner. Furthermore, some children may then lack effective verbal mediation skills (Meichenbaum & Genst, 1980). Based on these premises, goals of cognitive–behavioral interventions are to teach self-control and self-regulation. Commonly employed techniques include self-assessment, self-monitoring, self-recording, and self-reinforcement. Likewise, application of problem-solving or self-instructional strategies are often chosen for treatment. In the educational arena, these strategies are often collectively referred to as learning strategies. Instruction in specific learning strategies involves teaching and providing practice in using the strategy tied to the academic material.

Psychoeducational, Neuropsychological, and Information Processing Interventions

The psychoeducational model postulates that academic problems result from the inability to accurately perceive and integrate information received. The goal within this framework is to assess strengths and weaknesses and then teach according to these assessed abilities. This is often referred to as "teaching to the modality" of strength or preference. The efficacy of this approach has yet to be proven; to date little academic gains have been noted implementing this approach (Lyon & Moats, 1988).

The psychoeducational approach shares similarities with the information processing and neuropsychological approaches. Akin to the psychoeducational model is the assumption that the underpinning of learning disorders are deficits in how information is processed (see Lyon & Moats, 1988; Solman & Stanovich, 1992). The neuropsychological model posits that these processing deficits are manifestations of dysfunction in specific brain regions. The processes are inferred from observed behaviors and are the target of remediation or compensation, not specific academic skills as with behavioral and cognitive–behavioral interventions.

Pharmacological Interventions

Although the use of pharmacological interventions for Specific Developmental Disorders remains controversial, children with diagnosed learning disorders often receive medication. One estimate has been that 10% to 20% of children enrolled in special education services for learning disabilities are prescribed psychoactive medication (Gadow, 1991). The primary class of medications used are psychostimulants (Aman & Rojahn, 1992). This group includes methylphenidate (Ritalin), dextroamphetamine (Dexedrine), and pemoline (Cylert). The efficacy of these medications in the management of children with Attention-Deficit Hyperactivity Disorder has been well established. Given the significant overlap between ADHD and specific developmental disorders, it is not surprising that this class of medication has been thought to be indicated. In a recent review of numerous studies investigating the effects of stimulants on Specific Developmental Disorders, improvement on perceptual–cognitive tasks and academic tasks were realized in approximately 30% to 40% of the measures with medication having a larger impact on the perceptual–cognitive tasks (Aman & Rojahn, 1992). Furthermore, the effects of stimulant therapy has been suggested to be more short term in nature (Aman & Rojahn, 1992). Gadow (1991) concluded that although immediate academic productivity and efficacy increases, long-term gains on academic tests have not been demonstrated.

Other medications that have received some attention with regard to their effects on learning problems include antianxiety agents, antidepressants, and neuroleptics or major tranquilizers. Although the number of studies evaluating the effects of these classes of medication on learning performance have been minimal, it is generally thought that unless the medication is indicated for other behavioral or psychiatric reasons, it is not indicated as treatment of Specific Developmental Disorders. The use of vitamin therapy for treatment of these disorders has similarly met with the same conclusion. Though the use of megavitamins, mineral supplements, and specific dietary regimens quickly gained popularity, findings have been equivocal and inconclusive with regard to learning and behavior improvements. Hence, currently there is only minimal support for pharmacological intervention for Specific Developmental Disorders. Medication is most likely to be indicated and effective if comorbid disorders are present that respond to a particular medication. Moreover, Aman and Rojahn (1992) warned that in fact, adverse effects on learning may result from medication and should be kept in consideration in prescribing psychoactive medications.

Case Illustration 2: Developmental Reading Disorder, Developmental Math Disorder, Developmental Expressive Language Disorder, Developmental Receptive Language Disorder, and Attention-Deficit Hyperactivity Disorder (ADHD)

Danny was an 8-year-old boy with a history of recurrent otitis media. In school he was described as a cooperative student who tried very hard to please others. Academically Danny had made no progress in the past year. He was also observed to be frequently off task and was distracted easily when doing independent seat work. On the recent administration of the Woodcock–Johnson Test of Achievement: Revised, Danny was assessed to have academic skills at the kindergarten level. The lack of academic gains were alarming in view of his average intellectual potential with a recent score of 98 on the Stanford–Binet Intelligence Scale: Fourth Edition achieved.

According to guidelines, Danny qualified for services for students labeled learning disabled. This was based on the significant discrepancy between his ability level and current academic functioning. Danny was placed in a self-contained classroom for students with learning disabilities. In this classroom, the curriculum employed was the Direct Instructional System for Teaching Arithmetic and Reading (DISTAR; Englemann & Bruner, 1974) and the DISTAR Language Program (Englemann & Osborn, 1976). As with the Corrective Reading Program for older students, the DISTAR curriculum is highly structured and incorporates modeling, behavioral rehearsal at a fast pace, prompting and delayed prompting, corrective feedback, and immediate reinforcement. Additionally, Danny's attentional difficulty and distractibility were treated with pharmacological therapy and cognitive–behavioral intervention. Ritalin, a stimulant, was prescribed for Danny. In combination, Danny was taught to self-monitor and self-record his on-task behavior. At the signal of a random bell, Danny was instructed to record whether he was paying attention or not and record this with a plus or minus sign on an index card taped to his desk. Initially, Danny was rewarded for all self-monitoring efforts but was later rewarded only when he was in agreement with the teacher's recording of his on-task behavior. This type of intervention promoted self-control and would thus be more likely to generalize to other academic settings. The combination of medication and self-monitoring increased Danny's attention in the classroom. Steady academic gains in math and reading were made because enrollment in the specialized curriculum through ongoing intervention is warranted to continue remediating areas of deficits.

SUMMARY

Specific Developmental Disorders comprise a group of disorders characterized by significant deficiencies in the development of skills related to academic, language, and motor abilities. Similarly, for all the Specific Developmental Disorders, the delay in development must seriously interfere with the individual's function for a diagnosis to be made. A discrepancy between expected level of development based on current development in the specific domain is a necessary criterion for a Specific Developmental Disorder diagnosis. This discrepancy is typically determined by the administration of standardized tests of cognitive or intellectual potential and achievement in academic, language, or motor skills. It is likely that the causes of Specific Developmental Disorders are multiple. Currently, some associations between various environmental factors and genetic predispositions have been determined, but much more must be learned about the etiology of these disorders. Treatment approaches that are commonly utilized include behavioral interventions, cognitive–behavioral treatments, information-processing and psychoeducational interventions, and pharmacologic therapy. Educational services for children classified as learning disabled range in levels of restrictiveness from services in the regular classroom to special school placements. Although current treatment approaches have met with some degree of success, it is hoped that a more complete understanding of these developmental disorders will lead to more specific, effective therapy.

REFERENCES

Aman, M. G., & Rojahn, J. (1992). Pharmacological intervention. In N. N. Singh & I. L. Beale (Eds.), *Current perspectives in learning disabilities: Nature, theory, and treatment* (pp. 478–525). New York: Springer-Verlag.

American Psychiatric Association. (1987). *The diagnostic and statistical manual of mental disorders* (3rd rev. ed.). Washington, DC: Author.

American Psychiatric Association. (1993). *DSM-IV draft criteria*. Washington, DC: Author.

Ammerman, R. T., Van Hasselt, V. B., & Hersen, M. (1988). Maltreatment of handicapped children: A critical review. *Journal of Family Violence, 3*, 53–72.

Arnold, L. E. (1990). Learning disorders. In B. D. Garfinkel, G. A. Carlson, & E. B. Weller (Eds.), *Psychiatric disorders in children and adolescents* (pp. 237–256). Philadelphia: Saunders.

Baker, L., & Cantwell, D. P. (1989). Specific language and learning disorders. In T. H. Ollendick & M. Hersen (Eds.), *Handbook of child psychopathology* (2nd ed., pp. 93–104). New York: Plenum.

Beitchman, J. H., Nair, R., Clegg, M. A., Ferguson, B., & Patel, P. G. (1986). Prevalence of psychiatric disorders in children with speech and language disorders. *Journal of the American Academy of Child Psychiatry, 25*, 528–535.

Bender, B., Fry, E., Pennington, B., Puck, M., Salenblatt, J., & Robinson, A. (1983). Speech and language development in 41 children with sex chromosome anomalies. *Pediatrics, 71*, 262–267.

Bender, B., Puck, M., Salenblatt, J., & Robinson, A. (1986). Cognitive development of children with sex chromosome abnormalities. In S. D. Smith (Ed.), *Genetics and learning disabilities* (pp. 175–201). San Diego, CA: College-Hill.

Bishop, D. V. M., & Edmundson, A. (1986). Is otitis media a major cause of specific language disorders? *British Journal of Disorders of Communication, 21*, 321–338.

Bryan, T., & Lee, J. (1990). Social skills training with learning disabled children and adolescents: The state of the art. In T. E. Scruggs & B. Y. L. Wong (Eds.), *Intervention research in learning disabilities* (pp. 263–278). New York: Springer-Verlag.

Cantwell, D. P., & Baker, L. (1991). *Psychiatric and developmental disorders in children with communication disorder*. Washington, DC: American Psychiatric Press.

Engelmann, S., & Bruner, E. (1974). *DISTAR: An instructional system*. Chicago: Science Research Associates.

Engelmann, S., Johnson, G., Hanner, S., Carnine, L., Meyers, L., Osborn, S., Haddox, P., Becker, W., Osborn, W., & Becker, J. (1978). *Corrective reading program*. Chicago: Science Research Associates.

Engelmann, S., & Osborn, J. (1976). *DISTAR: An instructional approach*. Chicago: Science Research Associates.

Federal Register. (1976). *Education of handicapped children and incentive grants program* (vol. 41, No. 46977). U.S. Department of Health, Education, and Welfare.

Gadow, K. (1991). Psychopharmacological assessment and intervention. In H.L. Swanson (Ed.), *Handbook on the assessment of learning disabilities* (pp. 351–372). Austin, TX: Pro-ed.

Galaburda, A. M., Sherman, G. F., Rosen, G. D., Aboitiz, F., & Geschwind, N. (1985). Developmental dyslexia: Four consecutive patients with cortical anomalies. *Annuals of Neurology, 18,* 222–223.

Garbarino, J. (1982). *Children and families in the social environment.* Chicago: Aldine.

Hagerman, R. J., & Sobesky, W. E. (1989). Psychopathology in fragile X syndrome. *American Journal of Orthopsychiatry, 59,* 142–152.

Heaton, R. K. (1988). Introduction to the special series. *Journal of Consulting and Clinical Psychology, 56,* 787–788.

Klein, S. K., (1991). Cognitive factors and learning disabilities in children with epilepsy. In O. Devinsky & W. H. Theodore (Eds.), *Epilepsy and behavior* (pp. 171–179). New York: Wiley-Liss.

Lyon, G. R., & Moats, L. C. (1988). Critical issues in the instruction of the learning disabled. *Journal of Consulting and Clinical Psychology, 56,* 830–835.

Mann, V. A., & Brady, S. (1988). Reading disability: The role of language deficiencies. *Journal of Consulting and Clinical Psychology, 56,* 811-816.

Meichenbaum, D., & Genest, M. (1980). Cognitive behavior modification: An integration of cognitive and behavioral methods. In F. H. Kanfer & A. P. Goldstein (Eds.), *Helping people change* (2nd ed., pp. 390–422). Elmsford, NY: Plenum.

Needleman, H. L., Schell, A., Bellinger, D., Leviton, A., & Allred, E. (1990). The long-term effects of exposure to low doses of lead in childhood. *New England Journal of Medicine, 322,* 83–88.

Obrzut, J. E., & Boliek, C. A. (1991). Neuropsychological assessment of childhood learning disorders. In H. L. Swanson (Ed.), *Handbook on the assessment of learning disabilities* (pp. 121–145). Austin, TX: Pro-ed.

Pearl, R. (1992). Psychosocial characteristics of learning disabled students. In N. N. Singh & I. E. Beale (Eds.), *Current perspectives in learning disabilities: Nature, theory, and treatment* (pp. 96–125). New York: Springer-Verlag.

Pennington, B., & Smith, S. D. (1983). Genetic influences on learning disabilities and speech and language disorders. *Child Development, 54,* 369–387.

Rourke, B. P. (1989). *Nonverbal learning disabilities: The syndrome and the model.* New York: Guilford.

Rourke, B. P., & Fuerst, D. R. (1991). *Learning disabilities and psychosocial functioning.* New York: Guilford.

Silver, L. B. (1991). Developmental learning disorders. In M. Lewis (Ed.), *Child and adolescent psychiatry: A comprehensive textbook* (pp. 522–528). Baltimore: William & Wilkins.

Silver, L. B., & Hagin, R. A. (1990). *Disorders of learning in childhood.* New York: Wiley.

Shprintzen, R. J., & Goldberg, R. B. (1986). Multiple anomaly syndromes and learning disabilities. In S. D. Smith (Ed.), *Genetics and learning disabilities* (pp. 153–174). San Diego, CA: College-Hill.

Singh, N. N., Deitz, D. E., & Singh, J. (1992). Behavioral approaches. In N. N. Singh & I. E. Beale (Eds.), *Current perspectives in learning disabilities: Nature, theory, and treatment* (pp. 375–414). New York: Springer-Verlag.

Solman, R. T., & Stanovich, K. E. (1992). Information processing models. In N. N. Singh & I. E. Beale (Eds.), *Current perspectives in learning disabilities: Nature, theory, and treatment* (pp. 352-371). New York: Springer-Verlag.

Spreen, O. (1988). Prognosis of learning disability. *Journal of Consulting and Clinical Psychology, 56,* 836–842.

Taylor, H. G. (1988). Neuropsychological testing: Relevance for assessing children's learning disabilities. *Journal of Consulting and Clinical Psychology, 56,* 795–800.

Willis, W. G., Hooper, S. R., & Stone, B. H. (1992). Neuropsychological theories of learning disabilities. In N. N. Signh & I. E. Beale (Eds.), *Current perspectives in learning disabilities: Nature, theory, and treatment* (pp. 201–245). New York: Springer-Verlag.

Ziegler, P., & Holden, L. (1988). Family therapy for learning disabled and attention-deficit disordered children. *American Journal of Orthopsychiatry, 58,* 196–210.

Chapter 18

Conduct Disorder

Carolyn Webster-Stratton
Rebecca W. Dahl
University of Washington

Clinicians working with families typically encounter children who exhibit persistent patterns of antisocial behavior—where there is significant impairment in everyday functioning at home or school, or when the child's conduct is considered unmanageable by parents or teachers. The term *externalizing* has generally been used to summarize a set of negativistic behaviors that commonly co-occur during childhood. These include noncompliance, aggression, tantrums, and oppositional-defiant behaviors in the preschool years; classroom and authority violations such as lying and cheating in school years; and violations of community such as shoplifting in adolescence. The referral of children to clinicians for treatment of these externalizing and aggressive behaviors comprises one third to one half of all child and adolescent clinic referrals. These children and their families utilize multiple social and educational services provided to manage such children on a daily basis. Moreover, the prevalence of these behavioral disorders is increasing, creating a need for service that far exceeds available resources and personnel. Recent projections suggest that fewer than 10% of children who need mental health services actually receive them (Hobbs, 1982).

Although most parents at one time or another have problems with children lying, cheating, stealing, hitting, and noncompliance to parental requests, it is the degree of destruction and disturbance, the occurrence of the behaviors in more than one setting (e.g., at home and at school), and the persistence of these behaviors over time beginning at an early age that causes concern for families and clinicians alike.

This chapter deals with features that characterize young children to whom the label of oppositional defiant disorder and/or conduct disorder is frequently applied. These children typically exhibit a "complex" or pattern of behaviors (e.g., lying, cheating, stealing, hitting, and noncompliance to parental requests) and to a lesser extent, display violations of social rules.

The following case description illustrates the type and severity of problems represented by the conduct problem child. Eric is an 8-year-old boy living at home with his father, mother, younger brother, and an infant sister. He was referred to the clinic because of excessive aggressive behavior. Eric made a recent attempt to stab his younger brother, and makes frequent threats of violence towards both younger siblings. Eric's history reveals an escalation in aggressive activity including the initiation of physical fights with his peers, destruction of household property, and refusal to do what his parents request. Eric's parents express exasperation and exhaustion in dealing with Eric and talk about placing him in a boarding school. They have experienced difficulties managing his behavior since he was a toddler, and although initially they were told by professionals he would "outgrow" these problems, they found he became increasingly aggressive and defiant. He was kicked out of four preschools before he started grade school. The parents reported that they had tried every discipline strategy they could think of, such as time-out, yelling, hitting and spanking, taking away privileges, and grounding him. They felt none of these approaches worked with him. The parents reported feeling isolated and stigmatized by other parents with more "normal" children and felt teachers blamed them for his misbehaviors.

An evaluation of his behavior in Grade 3 reveals inattentiveness and distractibility in the classroom, aggression towards his peers—particularly during recess and frequent reports of teacher calls to his mother to take him home from school because of misbehavior. His intellectual performance is within the normal range (WISC-R full scale IQ = 105) and his academic performance is barely passing. His school absences and physical fights have constituted frequent contact with his parents and threats of expulsion.

Eric's home life includes the following characteristics: a mother with moderate depression and a father who drinks heavily. The father becomes abusive when he drinks, and often the children as well as the mother are targets of the abuse. Less than a year ago, the mother had another child, that has increased the stress in the family in that the mother is unable to take responsibility for the care and supervision of the older children.

CLINICAL DESCRIPTION

DSM-IV Draft Criteria

According to the *DSM-IV*, (American Psychiatric Association, 1994), externalizing behavior problems are referred to collectively as "Disruptive Behavior Disorders and Attention Deficit Disorders." There are three subgroups related to this larger category: Oppositional Defiant Disorder (ODD), Attention-Deficit Hyperactivity Disorder (ADHD), and Conduct Disorder (CD). As Conduct Disorder is rarely diagnosed before age 6, most young children with externalizing symptoms fit the criteria for ODD, ADHD, or a combination of the two disorders. The primary features of conduct disorder are are conduct disturbance lasting at least 6 months, the number of conduct problems, and violation of the rights of others. A diagnosis of conduct disorder requires a disturbance lasting for at least 6 months during which three of the following symptoms are present: often bullies, threatens, or intimidates others; often initiates physical fights; has used a weapon that can cause serious physical harm; has stolen with confrontation with a victim; has been physically cruel to people; has been physically cruel to animals; has forced someone into sexual activity; often lies or breaks promises; often stays out at night despite parental prohibitions, beginning before age 13; has stolen items of nontrivial value; has deliberately engaged in fire setting; has deliberately destroyed another's property; has run away from home overnight at least twice while living in parental home; often truant from school beginning before age 13; has broken into someone else's house, building, or car (APA, 1993).

The *DSM-IV* (American Psychiatric Association, 1994) mentions three subtypes of Conduct Disorder. The childhood onset type that consists of at least one conduct problem occurring before age 10 and the adolescent onset type where there are no conduct problems prior to age 10. Also severity is rated from mild to moderate to severe.

The diagnosis of ODD requires a pattern of negativistic, hostile, and defiant behavior lasting 6 months during which four of the following are present: often loses temper; often argues with adults; often actively defies or refuses to comply with adults' rules; often deliberately does things that annoy other people; often blames others for his or her mistakes; is often touchy or easily annoyed; is often angry and resentful and is often vindictive.

Other Classifications

Another method for classifying conduct disorder is through empirically derived syndromes. Two distinct syndromes that consistently emerge from the literature are undersocialized aggressive and socialized aggressive (Quay, 1986). The undersocialized-aggressive syndrome includes such behaviors as fighting, disobedience, temper tantrums, destructiveness, uncooperative, and impertinence. The socialized-aggressive syndrome includes truancy from school, absence from the home, stealing with peers, loyalty to delinquent friends, and gang involvement (Quay, 1986). It is important to remember that conduct disorder, although relatively stable, is manifested by different patters of behavior in different age/gender children.

Another method of categorization is known as the salient symptom approach. This method suggests subcategorizing conduct disorder based on the specific behaviors displayed by the child. The dimensions of the subcategorization are the overt dimension (e.g., physical aggression, disobedient, destruction of property) and the covert dimension (e.g., lying, stealing, truancy). The overt–covert dimensions are supported by evidence that certain behaviors tend to cluster together and that the two dimensions differ in their response to treatment (Wicks-Nelson & Israel, 1991).

Comorbidity

There seems to be considerable diagnostic ambiguity between CD, ODD, and ADHD in the young preschool age group as well as true comorbidity (i.e., hyperactive, impulsive, inattentive children have externalizing problems). Current reports suggest that as many as 75% of children who are identified as a attention deficit disorder with hyperactivity (ADHD) can also be identified as conduct disordered (Safer & Allen, 1976). It has been proposed that hyperactivity may influence the emergence of conduct disorder. Loeber (1985) suggested that hyperactivity is inherent in conduct disordered children. However, careful assessment of the child may reveal that the child actually meets the criteria for one and not the other. The criteria for ADHD and conduct disorder, although similar, are not identical, and it is important that ODD and ADHD be differentiated for both clinical and empirical reasons. Furthermore, those children who display concurrent ODD and ADHD appear to be at heightened risk for development of severe antisocial behavior than children with either single-disorder category.

Developmental Progression from ODD to CD

A number of theorists have shown high continuity between disruptive and externalizing problems in the preschool years and externalizing problems in adolescents (Loeber, 1990; Rutter, 1985). Recently developmental theorists have suggested that there may be two developmental pathways related to conduct disorders: the "early starter" versus "late starter" model (Patterson, DeBaryshe, & Ramsey, 1989). The hypothesized early onset pathway begins formally with the emergence of oppositional disorders (ODD) in early preschool years and progresses to aggressive and nonaggressive symptoms of conduct disorders in middle childhood and then to the most serious symptoms by adolescence (Lahey, Loeber, Quay, Frick, & Grimm, 1992). For the adolescents who develop conduct disorders later in their adolescent years, the prognosis seems more favorable than for the adolescents who have a chronic history of conduct disorders stemming from their preschool years. Adolescents who are most likely to be chronically antisocial are those who first evidenced symptoms of ODD in the preschool years. Thus, the primary developmental pathway for serious conduct disorders in adolescence and adulthood appears to be set in the preschool period. ODD is a sensitive predictor of subsequent CD, in that nearly all CD youths have shown previous ODD.

CAUSES OF THE DISORDER

It is widely accepted that multiple influences and factors contribute to the development and maintenance of child conduct disorder. It is important to briefly review the major categories influencing the establishment of conduct disorder. These include child, parent, and school-related factors.

Child Biological Factors

The "child deficit" hypothesis argues that some abnormal aspect of the child's internal organization at the physiological, neurological, and neuropsychological level — which may be genetically transmitted — is at least partially responsible for the development of externalizing behavior problems.

Temperament has perhaps been researched the most in regard to conduct problems. Temperament refers to aspects of the personality that show consistency over time and across situations, and are identified as constitutional in nature. These personality characteristics include activity of the child, emotional responsiveness, quality of mood, and social adaptability (Thomas & Chess, 1977). It appears that there is support for the mother's objective rating of child temperament and independent observations of the child and that these objective components are not overwhelmed by subjective components. Research has indicated that there are links between specific temperament scales and specific behavior problem scales. For example, there is a strong correlation between unadaptability and later aggressive problems. Frequent and intensive negative child affect also consistently predicts behavior problems. In one longitudinal study mother reports of infant difficultness (at 6 months) and infant resistance to control (at 1 year) showed significant predictions to maternal report of externalizing problems at ages 6 and 8 years (Bates, Bayles, Bennett, Ridge, & Brown, 1991).

Although studies have shown that early assessments of temperament predict later behavior problems, the amount of variance accounted for in the outcome is relatively small. Factors such as family conflict or support and quality of parent management strategies appear to interact with temperament to influence outcome. Several recent studies have shown that extreme (difficult) infant temperament in the context of favorable family conditions is not likely to increase the risk of disruptive behavior disorder at age 4 (Maziade, Cote, Bernier, Boutin, & Thivierge, 1989). In general the findings on temperament clearly support the notion of Thomas and Chess (1977) that "no temperamental pattern confers an immunity to behavior disorder, nor is it fated to create psychopathology" (p. 4).

In addition to temperament, other organic factors related to cognition have been implicated. It is suggested that conduct disordered children distort social cues during peer interactions (Milich & Dodge, 1984). This distortion includes attributions of hostile intent during neutral situations. Aggressive children also search for fewer cues or facts when determining another's intentions (Dodge & Newman, 1981) and focus more on aggressive cues. The child's perception of hostile intentions from others may subsequently encourage aggressive behavior. There are also data that indicate that deficits in social problem-solving skills contribute to poor peer interactions. These children may generate fewer alternative solutions to social problems, seek less information, define problems in hostile ways, and anticipate fewer consequences for aggression (Slaby & Guerra, 1988).

The findings bearing on the relationship between empathy and aggression also merit some attention. An inverse relationship exists between aggressive children and empathy across a wide age range, although the converse of aggression–prosocial behavior does not reflect as stable a relationship (Feshbach, 1989).

School-Related Factors

Academic performance has been implicated in child conduct disorder. Low academic achievement and low intellectual functioning often manifest themselves in conduct disordered children early on during the elementary grades and continue through high school (Kazdin, 1987). Reading disabilities, in particular, are associated with conduct disorder (Sturge, 1982). One study especially indicated that conduct disordered children exhibited reading deficits defined as a 28-month lag in reading ability, compared with the reading ability of normal children (Rutter, Tizard, Yule, Graham, & Whitmore, 1976). The relationship between academic performance and conduct disorder is not merely unidirectional but is considered a bidirectional relationship. It is unclear whether disruptive behavior problems precede or follow low intelligence, language delay, or neuropsychological deficits. However, there is some evidence that cognitive and linguistic problems may precede disruptive behavior problems (Schonfeld, Shaffer, O'Connor, & Portnoy, 1988).

The school setting has been studied as a risk factor contributing to conduct disorders. Rutter and his colleagues (1976) found that characteristics such as emphases on academic work, teacher time on lessons, teacher use of praise, emphasis on individual responsibility, teacher availability, school working conditions (e.g., physical condition, size), and teacher–student ratio were related to delinquency rates and academic performance.

Parent Psychological Factors

Parent psychopathology places the child at considerable risk for conduct disorder. Specifically, depression in the mother, alcoholism in the father, and antisocial behavior in either parent have been implicated in increasing the child's risk for conduct disorder. Maternal depression is associated with misperception of a child's behavior. For example, mothers who are depressed perceive their child's behavior as maladjusted or inappropriate. Depression also influences the parenting behavior directed toward a child's misbehavior. For example, depressed mothers often increase the number of commands and criticisms they give to their children. The child, in response to the increase in parent commands, displays an increase in noncompliance of deviant child behavior (Webster-Stratton & Hammond, 1988). Therefore, it is hypothesized that maternal depression and irritability indirectly lead to behavior problems as a result of negative attention reinforcing inappropriate child behaviors, inconsistent limit setting, and emotional unavailability. In a recent community study, maternal depression, when the child was 5, was related to parent and teacher reports of behavior problems at age 7 (Williams, Anderson, McGee, & Silva, 1990).

As might be expected, presence of antisocial behavior in either parent places the child at greater risk for conduct disorders. In particular, criminal behavior and alcoholism in the father are consistently demonstrated as parental factors increasing the child's risk. Grandparents of conduct disordered children are also more likely to show antisocial behavior compared to grandparents of children who are not antisocial.

COURSE OF THE DISORDER

Research has indicated that a high rate of childhood aggression, even in children as young as age 3, is fairly stable over time. Richman, Stevenson, and Graham (1982) found that 67% of children with externalizing problems at age 3 continued to be aggressive at age 8. Other studies have have reported stability correlations between between.5 and.7 for externalizing scores. Loeber (1991) contended that these estimates of stability may actually be higher because manifestations of the problems are episodic, situational, and change in nature (e.g., from tantrums to stealing). Early onset of ODD appears to be related to later aggressive and antisocial behavior and the development of severe problems later in life (e.g., school drop out, alcoholism, drug abuse, juvenile delinquency, adult crime, marital disruption, interpersonal problems, and poor physical health, Kazdin, 1987). However, not all conduct disordered children incur a poor prognosis as adults. Data suggest that less than 50% of the most severe conduct disordered children become antisocial as adults. The fact that less than one half of conduct disordered children continue into adulthood with significant problems represents an usually high percentage; one that cannot be ignored.

Although not all ODD children become CD and not all conduct disordered children become antisocial adults, certain risk factors contribute to the continuation of the disorder: (a) early age of onset (preschool years), (b) breadth of deviance (across multiple settings such as home and school), (c) frequency and intensity of antisocial behavior, (d) diversity of antisocial behavior (several versus few) and covert behaviors at early ages (stealing, lying, firesetting), and (e) family and parent characteristics (Kazdin, 1987). However, a delineation of contributing risk factors does not convey a complete understanding of the complex nature of variables involved and the relationship of the variables with one another.

FAMILIAL CONTRIBUTIONS

Divorce, Marital Distress, and Violence

Specific family characteristics have been found that contribute to the development and maintenance of child conduct disorder. Interparental conflict leading to and surrounding divorce are associated with, but are not strong predictors of, child conduct disorder (Kazdin, 1987). In particular, boys appear to be more apt to show significant increases in antisocial behaviors following divorce. However, some single parents and their children appear to do relatively well over time postseparation, whereas others are chronically depressed and report increased stress levels. One explanation might be that for some single parents the stress of divorce sets in motion a series of stages of increased depression and increased irritability; such increased irritability leads to a loss of friendships and social support, placing the mothers at increased risk for more irritable behaviors, ineffective discipline, and poor problem-solving outcomes; the poor problem solving of these parents in turn results in increased depression and stress levels, completing the spiraling negative cycle. Irritability simultaneously sets in motion a process whereby the child also becomes increasingly antisocial (Forgatch, 1989).

Once researchers began to differentiate between parental divorce, separation, and discord, they began to understand that it was not the divorce per se that was the critical factor in the child's behavior but rather the amount and intensity of parental conflict and violence (O'Leary & Emery, 1982). For example, children whose parents divorced but whose homes were conflict-free were less likely to have problems than children whose parents stayed together but experienced a great deal of conflict; children whose parents divorce and continue to have conflict have more conduct problems than children whose parents experience conflict-free divorce. In our own studies with conduct problem children, half of the married couples reported experiences with spouse abuse and violence. Taken together, these findings highlight the importance of parents' marital conflict and violence (not family structure per se) as a key factor influencing children's externalizing problems.

Marital conflict is associated with more negative perceptions of the child's adjustment, inconsistent parenting, use of increased punitiveness and decreased reasoning, and fewer rewards with children. Conflictual, unhappy marriages that display aggressive behavior are more likely to incite the formation of conduct disorder. It is consistently demonstrated that if aggressive behavior is present in the marital relationship, the likelihood of conduct disorder is greater than if conflict is present alone (Jouriles, Murphy, & O'Leary, 1989). The explanation here is that the aggressive parent may serve as a model to the child.

Frick, Lahey, Hartdagen, and Hynd (1989) proposed two models to account for the correlation between marital distress and child conduct disorders. One model proposes a direct and an indirect path from marital satisfaction to child conduct disorders, whereas the other model predicts that the significant correlations between marital satisfaction and child conduct problems are more an artifact of the common effects of maternal antisocial personality and social class. They found the relationship between marital satisfaction and child conduct problems was based primarily on the common association with maternal antisocial personality but that social class did not play an important role as a third variable. These findings seem to argue the importance of the parents' psychological adjustment as a primary determinant of the effects of stress on parent–child interactions.

Family Adversity

Research suggests that life stressors such as poverty, unemployment, crowded living conditions, and illness have deleterious effects on parenting and are related to a variety of forms of child psychopathology including conduct disorders (Rutter & Giller, 1983). Families with conduct disordered children report the incidence of major stressors two to four times greater than for nonclinic families (Webster-Stratton, 1990a). Parents of conduct disordered children indicate that they experience more day-to-day hassles as well as major crises than nonclinic families. An accumulation of minor day-to-day chronic life hassles is related to more aversive maternal interactions, for example, higher rates of coercive behavior and irritability in the mothers' interactions with their children. Recent reports have also shown maternal stress to be associated with inept discipline practices, such as explosive discipline and "nattering" with children (Forgatch, Patterson, & Skinner, 1988; Webster-Stratton, 1990a).

The link between social class and child conduct disorder probably does not exist. Often social class includes multiple confounding variables such as overcrowding, poor supervision, and other potential risk factors (Kazdin, 1987). When control is obtained for these risk factors, social status shows little relation to conduct disorder. Social class as a summary label that includes multiple risk factors can influence child conduct disorder (Kazdin, 1987).

Family Insularity

Maternal insularity is another parental factor implicated in child conduct disorder. Insularity is defined as "a specific pattern of social contacts within the community that are characterized by a high level of negatively perceived social interchanges with relatives and/or helping agency representatives and by a low level of positively perceived supported interchanges with friends" (Wahler & Dumas, 1984, p. 387). This definition is important because it appears that rather than the number of social contacts, it is the individual's perception of whether the social contact is supportive or helpful that makes the social contact advantageous. Mothers characterized as insular are more aversive and use more aversive consequences with their children than noninsular mothers. Insularity and lack of support have also been reported to be significant predictors of a family's relapse or failure to maintain treatment effects (Webster-Stratton, 1985).

Parent–Child Interactions

Parenting interactions are clearly the most well-researched and most important proximal cause of conduct problems. Research has indicated that parents of conduct disordered children lack certain fundamental parenting skills. For example, parents of such children have been reported to exhibit fewer positive behaviors; to be more violent and critical in their use of discipline; to be more permissive, erratic, and inconsistent, to be more likely to fail to monitor their children's behaviors; and to be more likely to reinforce inappropriate behaviors and to ignore or punish prosocial behaviors (Patterson & Stouthamer-Loeber, 1984; Webster-Stratton, 1985; 1991; Webster-Stratton & Spitzer, 1991). Patterson and his colleagues called this the *coercive process* (Patterson, 1982), a process whereby children learn to escape or avoid parental criticism by escalating their negative behaviors, that in turn leads to increasingly aversive parent interactions. These negative responses, in turn, directly reinforce the child's deviant behaviors. In addition, it is important to note the affective nature of the parent–child relationship. There is considerable evidence that a warm, positive bond between parent and child leads to a more socially competent child.

Conduct disordered children engage in higher rates of deviant behaviors and noncompliance with parental commands than nonconduct disordered children. Children interacting with their mothers exhibit fewer positive verbal and nonverbal behaviors (smiles, laughs, enthusiasm, praise) than nonconduct disordered children. In addition, conduct disordered children exhibit more negative nonverbal gestures, expressions, and tones of voice in interactions with both mothers and fathers. These children have less positive affect, seem depressed, and are less reinforcing to their parents, thus setting in motion the cycle of aversive interactions for mothers as well as fathers.

Other Family Characteristics

Other family characteristics contributing to the formation of conduct disorder include birth order (delinquency and antisocial behaviors are found more often in middle children); Wadsworth, 1979), and family size (increased family size is associated with higher rates of delinquency but only when there is a greater number of male children, Offord, 1982).

PSYCHOPHYSIOLOGICAL AND GENETIC INFLUENCES

Earlier we noted the cognitive difficulties in relation to CD children's attributions and problem solving as well as their academic and language difficulties. Neurological abnormalities are inconsistently correlated with conduct disorder. An association exists more generally with childhood dysfunction than with conduct disorder in particular (Kazdin, 1987). There is some evidence and much speculation that deficits in verbal functioning, language comprehension, impulsivity, and emotional regulation may be related to the left frontal lobe and its relation to the limbic system in aggressive children (Gorensten & Newman, 1980). However, it is important also to note that conduct disordered children have an increased likelihood of abuse and subsequent head and facial injuries resulting in neurological abnormalities (e.g., soft signs, EEG aberrations, seizure disorders).

Other psychophysiological variables have been implicated in child conduct disorder. Low resting heart rate (lower vagal tone) among antisocial youth has received some support (Raine & Venables, 1984). Skin conductance responses have been found to differentiate between conduct disordered youth and nonconduct disordered controls in both adolescents and younger children (Schmidt, Solanto & Bridger, 1985).

Longitudinal studies suggest that conduct disorder is stable across generations. However, this does not implicate genetic influences as the cause of conduct disorder. There is little direct evidence as to genetic contributions to child conduct disorder. However, twin studies have shown greater concordance of antisocial behavior among monozygotic rather than dizygotic twins (Kazdin, 1987). Adoption studies, where the child is separated from the biological parent, indicate that offspring show a greater increase in antisocial behavior (Kazdin, 1987). The increased risk due to antisocial behavior in the biological parent establishes some credence for the inclusion of genetics in accounting for a portion of the variance in conduct disorder. Yet, it has also been established that genetic factors alone do not account for the emergence of the disorder. Rather, these studies affirm the effect of genetic influences in conjunction with environmental factors such as adverse conditions in the home (e.g., marital discord, psychiatric dysfunction) and ineffective family problem-solving and coping techniques.

CURRENT TREATMENTS

A variety of interventions have been proposed to decrease the prevalence (i.e., the number of existing cases at a given point in time) and incidence (i.e., the number of new cases) of oppositional-defiant and conduct disorders. The former are directed towards treatment efforts and the latter toward prevention efforts. Treatment and prevention are not separate entitles; prevention represents the onset when the child has not yet manifested the disorder, and treatment consists of reducing or eliminating the severity, duration, and manifestation of the disorder. The initial question to ask when considering prevention treatment is whether identified risk factors contributing to conduct disorder can contribute to the development of intervention programs designed to eliminate or curtail the disorder.

Child Training

Several prominent strategies are emphasized as a means of preventing child conduct problems. One view that has received particular attention is the development of child competence. Competence refers to "the ability of the child to negotiate the course of development including effective interactions with others, successful (adaptive) completion of developmental tasks and contacts with the environment (e.g., school performance), and use of approaches that increase adaptive functioning (e.g., problem solving)" (Kazdin, 1990). However, development of competence in children has not been specifically applied to conduct disordered children. Rather, it has been found to be useful in protecting the child against risk factors that can lead to maladjustment and psychopathology (Kazdin, 1990).

Treatment interventions have been aimed toward altering the child's cognitive processes (e.g., problem-solving skills, self-control, and self-statements) and developing prosocial rather than antisocial behaviors (e.g., play skills, friendship and conversational skills). The first type of intervention is based on a hypothesized skills relationship. Such programs coach children in positive social skills such as greeting, joining, inviting, asking, sharing, cooperating, praising, and apologizing. The second type of intervention relies on verbal instructions and discussions, opportunities to practice the skill with peers, role playing, games, stories, and therapist feedback and reinforcement. Most of these programs have not specifically focused on children with conduct disorders. Those that do specify this population tend to intervene with older school-age children and adolescents (rather than preschool and early school-age children).

Parent/Family Intervention

In many parent/family interventions, the purpose has been to reduce or eliminate the severity, duration, and manifestation of conduct problems. The modification of problematic parenting skills can serve as the primary mechanism for change in child conduct disorder. The rationale for this approach is supplied by research indicating that parents of conduct disordered children have an underlying deficit in certain fundamental parenting skills.

The most highly influential parent training program was developed by Patterson, Reid, and their colleagues at the Oregon Social Learning Center (Patterson, 1982). The parent training program was originally developed for children ages 3 to 12 years, who are engaged in overt conduct disorders. Program content has also been modified for use with adolescents. Parents begin by reading a programmed text, *Living with Children* (Patterson, 1976). They then participate in learning five family management practices that include pinpointing and tacking problem behaviors, social tangible reinforcement techniques, discipline procedures, monitoring or supervision of the children, and problem-solving and negotiation strategies.

A second important parent training program was designed to treat noncompliance in young children, ages 3 to 8 years. Originally developed by Hanf (Hanf & Kling, 1973), the program was later modified and evaluated extensively by McMahon and Forehand (1984). Phase one of the program teaches parents how to play with their children in a nondirective way and how to identify and reward children's prosocial behaviors through praise and attention. Phase two of the program includes teaching parents ways to give direct, concise and effective commands and how to use 3- minute time-outs for noncompliance.

A third example of a comprehensive and extensively evaluated parent training program for young conduct disordered children was a videotape training program developed by Webster-Stratton (1984). The content of the BASIC program, a series of 10 videotapes (250 vignettes) designed for parents with children ages 3–8 years, includes components of Hanf and Kling (1973) as well as the strategic use of differential-attention and effective use of commands. The content incorporates Patterson's (1982) discipline components concerning time-out, logical and natural consequences, and monitoring. Finally, the content includes teaching parents problem solving and communication strategies with their children.

A fourth family-based intervention called *Functional Family Therapy* (FFT); (Alexander & Parsons, 1982) was developed for delinquent adolescents. This approach integrates family systems and behavioral and cognitive perspectives. The program consists of several components. The first component is concerned with identifying and modifying family members' blaming attributions and inappropriate expectations through relabeling. The next component involves teaching behavioral management strategies such as communication skills, behavioral contracting, and contingency management. During the final component the therapist helps parents generalize and maintain their new skills.

Reviews of these parent training programs are highly promising. The short-term treatment outcome success has been quantified by significant changes in parents' and children's behavior and in parental perceptions of child adjustment. Home observations have indicated that parents are successful in reducing children's levels of aggression by 20%–60%. Generalization of behavior improvements from the clinic setting to the home over reasonable follow-up periods (1 to 4 years) and to untreated child behaviors has also been demonstrated (e.g., McMahon & Forehand, 1984; Patterson, Chamberlain, & Reid, 1982; Webster-Stratton, 1984; Webster-Stratton, Kolpacoff, & Hollinsworth, 1988). Nonetheless, for about one third of the families, these parent management strategies are not enough. Parent and family characteristics, such as marital distress, spouse abuse, lack of a supportive partner, maternal depression, poor problem-solving skills, and high life stress, are associated with fewer treatment gains (Forehand, Furey, & McMahon, 1984; Forgatch, 1989; Webster-Stratton, 1985; 1989; 1990a).

A more comprehensive approach that encompasses parents' cognitive, psychological, marital and/or social adjustment would seem to be more appropriate given the number of issues faced by these families. Several programs have instituted expansions to their standard parent training treatment. Dadds, Schwartz, and Sanders (1987) incorporated Partner Support Training (PST) to their Child Management Training (CMT) program. A parent enhancement therapy designed by Griest, Forehand, Wells, and McMahon (1980) augments general family functioning, marital adjustment, parent personal adjustment, and the parents' extrafamilial relationship. Recently an advanced videotape program (ADVANCE) has been developed by Webster-Stratton and her colleagues to focus on personal parent issues other than parent skills and cognitive perspectives such as anger management, how to cope with depression, effective communication skills, problem solving and conflict resolution skills, ways to give and get support, how to teach children to problem solve and manage their anger, and finally how to support children's education (Webster-Stratton, 1994).

School and Community Interventions.

Several preventive interventions relevant to conduct disorder have focused on the school and the community. The High/Scope Perry Preschool Program was designed to aid children who are considered at-risk for school failure. The parents of these children were low income, living in stressful environments, and had low levels of education. The children began the program at age 3 and participated for a 2-year period (Schweinhart & Weikart, 1988). The program addressed intellectual, social, and physical needs necessary for the development of decision-making and cognitive processes.

Another strategy aimed at preventing conduct disorder emphasizes the development of conventional values and behaviors as a way of protecting the child against deviance. Social bonding refers to the integration of commitment, attachment, and adherence to the values of the family, school, and peers (Hawkins & Lam, 1987). The intervention included several components. The classroom component addresses issues of deportment, interactive teaching, and cooperative (peer involved) learning techniques. The family component consists of parent management training and assists family members in conflict resolution. Peer social-skills training and community-focused career education and counseling are also included. The multiple contexts of family, school, and peers may increase the bonding necessary to reduce the onset of antisocial behavior (Kazdin, 1990).

The School Transitional Environmental Program (STEP; Felner, & Adan, 1988) was developed to help children through the normal process of entering a new school (e.g., middle to high school). Transitions are associated with decreased academic performance and psychological problems including antisocial behavior. The STEP attempts to reduce the effect of school transitions and increase the child's coping responses.

In addition to prevention programs, efforts have also focused on populations where conduct disorder is evident. One school-based program was designed to prevent further adjustment problems among children who evinced signs of low academic motivation, family problems, and a record of disciplinary referrals (Bry & George, 1980). The program included meetings with students where rewards were given for appropriate classroom behavior, punctuality, and a reduction in the amount of disciplinary action. Meetings were also scheduled with teachers and parents to focus on specific problems with individual children.

Another school-based approach targeted anger control in an Anger Coping Program (Lochman, Lampron, Gemmer, & Harris, 1987). The content includes teaching interpersonal problem-solving skills, strategies for increasing physiological awareness, and learning to use self-talk and self-control during problem situations. Another example for older school-age children with conduct disorders is the Problem-Solving Skills Training (PSST) program (Kazdin, Esveldt-Dawson, French, & Unis, 1987), which was based on the programs developed by Kendall and Braswell (1985) and focuses on the child's cognitive processes (perceptions, self-statements, attributions, expectations, and problem-solving skills) that presumably underlie maladaptive behavior. The primary focus of treatment is on the thought processes rather than on the behavioral acts that result and teaches children a step-by-step approach to solving problems. Shure and Spivak (1982) also developed an interpersonal problem-solving training program that has been used with a variety of populations to train children to be socially competent. Finally, Webster-Stratton (1991) developed a videotape-based curriculum for young children ages 3–8 years that focuses on understanding feelings, problem solving, anger management, how to be friendly, how to talk to friends, and how to succeed in school. This program uses life-size puppets, real (nonacted) videotape examples of children at home and in school situations, cartoons, and homework assignments to parents and teachers.

Community-based interventions address prevention (for those youth at-risk for antisocial behavior) and treatment (those youth identified with signs of antisocial behavior). One extensive program targeted a housing project with over 400 children from poverty stricken families (ages 5 to 15) considered to be at risk for antisocial behavior (Offord & Jones, 1983). Youths were involved in activity programs and trained specific skill areas (e.g., swimming, hockey, dancing, and musical instruments). Children were evaluated on their progress in the programs and rewards were provided for attendance and participation.

Another program was designed for youth who were identified as delinquent. The intervention assigns the youth to a college student volunteer who works with the youth 6 to 8 hours per week in the community (Davidson & Basta, 1988). Weekly supervision for the volunteers was provided by a juvenile court staff member, and supervision took place in the court worker's office.

Community-based interventions have also addressed both prevention and treatment. One program utilized existing community facilities in order to intervene with delinquent youth and youth who had no history of prior arrests (O'Donnell, Lygate, & Fo, 1979). Adults were recruited from the community and trained to conduct behavior modification programs with the youth. They also involved the youth in various activities (e.g., arts and crafts, fishing, and camping). Individualized reward programs focused on such behaviors as home activity, fishing, and truancy (Kazdin, 1990).

The programs reviewed have provided some evidence to indicate that early preventive interventions can reduce risk factors that place children at-risk for conduct disorders (e.g., abusive child rearing practices) and can reduce the onset of a variety of antisocial behaviors.

Case Illustration

Mr. and Mrs. W. came into the Parenting Clinic with their 7-year-old son Doug. Mrs. W. describes Doug's behavior as unmanageable at home. Her concerns include: (a) hitting and other aggressive behaviors, especially when Doug does not get what he wants, (b) noncompliance with his mother's requests, and (c) intense negative exchanges between Doug and herself.

When the parents were asked how they usually discipline Doug, they reported that they put him in "time-out for a couple of minutes" or take away a privilege. They also yell a great deal, use threats, and administer spankings. Mrs. W., however, expressed concern that none of the discipline techniques have really achieved any success, and she reported feelings of helplessness and discouragement. Mr. W. quickly established himself as a management expert and claimed that it is his wife who lacks the ability to deal with Doug. He felt that she was not a "tough enough" disciplinarian.

Mr. and Mrs. W. stated that Doug's problems hitting other children began in the preschool and that he always has had difficulties in making transitions from one activity to the next. Doug's previous teacher reported frequent conflicts between Doug and his peers. Both parents talked about long months during which they waited for Doug to get older, in the expectation that things would get easier for them. However, they agreed that things had not changed with time and instead their child had become increasingly defiant and noncompliant.

Mrs. W. was working full time and was pregnant with her second child. Mrs. W. stated that she had not had any recent psychological treatment but said she had dealt with depressions several times and had taken antidepressants on one occasion. However, she was not taking medication at the time and stated that she was not depressed. Mrs. W. also admitted that she received very little support from friends with similar aged children and feared rejection from other parents if they "knew what my child really was like."

Mrs. W. also had no support from her own family. She stated that her mother was an alcoholic and was verbally abusive toward her. Also, several years ago Mrs. W. and her mother had a major break in communication, although currently she continued to make contact with her mother once or twice a week. According to Mrs. W., her father was a very capable and responsible man.

Mr. W.'s mother was recently hospitalized and was quite ill. Mr. W.'s father was an alcoholic and continued to drink moderately. Mr. W. described his mother as caring and very giving. He stated that his father "didn't have much in the way of parenting skills" and punished excessively. Mr. W. was completing a graduate degree and was in the process of interviewing for a job that would lead to a family move in the near future.

The stressors that have occurred in this family involved attending graduate school, potential move to a new residence, and responsibility for one difficult child with a second pregnancy. Positive indicators included a supportive marriage, no alcohol or drug use, and no indication of child or spousal abuse.

Assessment of both the parents and child indicated that parent training would be appropriate for this family and plans are made for Mr. and Mrs. W. to attend the 12-week group training sessions. As they participated in the videotape training program, the attitude of Mr. and Mrs. W. at first oscillated between despair and guilt concerning their previous parenting approaches to Doug's problems and the irrational hope that they would have a "quick fix" to his problems, before the new baby arrived.

As Mr. and Mrs. W. participated in the parent training program and learned new parenting strategies such as play skills, effective reinforcement, and nonviolent discipline approaches, they came to realize that different children required different degrees of parental supervision and different parenting skills in order to be successfully socialized. They began to blame themselves less and focused more constructively on which parenting techniques would work to bring out Doug's prosocial behaviors and personality strengths as well as decrease his noncompliance and aggression. Initially they experienced some immediate success with Doug using the play and praise strategies.

As the program progressed, Mrs. W. noticed that Mr. W. appeared to become increasingly critical of the program. Mr. W. believed strongly that spanking was the optimal discipline strategy for Doug and that it worked to manage his behaviors. He had difficulty with the use of strategies such as sticker charts, ignore, logical consequences, and problem solving. This resistance to the program and conflict with his wife's viewpoint resulted in marital stress. Also, Doug's behavior began to regress in spite of the parents' initial hard work. Mrs. W.'s reaction was depression and anger as she experienced setbacks and stated that she was having difficulty motivating herself to complete program assignments. Both parents experienced feelings of resignation as the therapist collaborated with them and helped them realize the chronic nature of Doug's problems requiring them to agree on strategies that would be used consistently by both of them over the "long haul." Mr. W. was helped to understand that many of his attitudes towards discipline came from his father's approach that he readily admitted were an approach that lead to alienation and resentment in their relationship. Working towards the long-term benefits of nonviolent discipline rather than the short-term benefits of spanking became an objective they both agreed on.

In learning to cope more effectively with Doug's problems, the therapist collaborated with Mr. and Mrs. W. to tailor the concepts shown in the standardized videotape examples to their own family situation and parenting style. Mrs. W. acknowledge difficulty generalizing certain parenting techniques to various problem behaviors. However, the parent group sharing and problem solving provided a variety of different examples for Mrs. W. and helped her understand how to generalize the skills she had learned to new situations and problems.

During the final weeks of treatment, Mr. and Mrs. W. were supportive of each others' efforts and began to discover they could cope successfully with the daily hassles of having a conduct disordered child. They gained confidence in themselves and their ability to cope with future problems. Both parents indicated that they had also gained an acceptance and understanding of Doug's temperament and needs and were better able to emphasize with his feelings and perspectives. Mrs. W. was particularly encouraged because the parent group provided support and a safe place where she could be honest and vulnerable about her feelings and difficulties with Doug. She felt that the parent group provided a tremendous sense of connection with other parents who had experienced similar problems and thereby reduced her feelings of isolation and loneliness.

SUMMARY

Conduct disorder is highly prevalent in our society and has an impact on the school, community, family and peer relationships. Conduct disordered children are character-ized by a "complex" pattern of behaviors including lying, cheating, stealing, hitting, and noncompliance to parental requests.

Multiple influences, including child, parent, and school-related factors, con-tribute to the development and maintenance of child conduct disorder. The association between conduct disorder and psychophysiological or genetic influence is inconsistent. Rather, studies affirm that genetics in conjunction with environmental factors are influential in the development and maintenance of the disorder.

The course of the disorder indicates that early oppositional and conduct problems often persist into adulthood and appear to be related to aggressive and antisocial behavior later in life. The primary factors contributing to the continuation of conduct disorder include age of onset, deviant behavior across multiple settings, several versus few behaviors, and parent and family characteristics.

Current treatments have been proposed to decrease the prevalence and incidence of conduct disorder; the former directed toward prevention efforts. Intervention measures have been proposed on various levels (community, school, family, peer, and child) and have achieved varying success. The importance of developing prevention and treatment programs designed to arrest or curtail child conduct disorder cannot be over emphasized. An integrated approach treating both the child and the family, in the home and in the broader social context—particularly in schools—will produce better results than if multiple factors are not included. Program design must also consider that conduct disorder is often a chronic problem transmitted across generations. Therefore, successful intervention necessitates periodic training and support offered at critical stages throughout the child's and family's development and within a variety of contexts.

REFERENCES

Alexander, J., & Parsons, B. (1982). *Functional family therapy*: *Principles and procedures*. Carmel, CA: Brooks/Cole.

American Psyciatric Association (1994). *Diagnostic and statistical manual of mental disorders* (4th ed.). Washington, DC: American Psyciatric Association.

Bates, J. E., Bayles, K., Bennett, D. S., Ridge, B., & Brown, M. M. (1991). Origins of externalyzing behavior problems at eight years of age. In D. J. Pepler & K. H. Rubin (Eds.), *The development and treatment of childhood aggression* (pp. 93–120). Hillsdale, NJ: Lawrence Erlbaum Associates.

Bry, B., & George, F. (1980). The preventive effects of early intervention on the attendance and grades of urban adolescents. *Professional Psychology, 11*, 252–260.

Dadds, M., Schwartz, S., & Sanders, M. (1987). Marital discord and treatment outcome in behavioral treatment of child conduct disorders. *Journal of Consulting and Clinical Psychology, 55*, 396–403.

Davidson, W., & Basta, J. (1988). Diversion from the juvenile justice system: Research evidence and a discussion of issues. In B. B. Lahey & A. E. Kazdin (Eds.), *Advances in clinical child psychology vol. 12*. New York: Plenum.

Dodge, K. A., & Newman, J. P. (1981) Biased decision-making processes in aggressive boys. *Journal of Abnormal Psychology, 90*, 375–379.

D'Zurilla, T., & Nezu, A. (1982). Social problem-solving in adults. In P. C. Kendall (Ed.), *Advances in cognitive behavioral research and therapy 1 (Vol. 1)*. New York: Academic Press.

Felner, R., & Adan, A. (1988). The school transitional environmental project: An ecological intervention and evaluation. In R. H. Price, E. L. Cowen, R. P. Lorion, & J. Ramos-McKay (Eds.), *14 ounces of prevention*: *A casebook for practitioners* (pp. 111–122). Washington, DC: American Psychological Association.

Feshbach, N. (1989). The construct of empathy and the phenomenon of physical maltreatment of children. In D. Cicchetti & V. Carlson (Eds.), *Child maltreatment*: *Theory and research on the causes and consequences of child abuse and neglect* (pp. 349–373). Cambridge, MA: Cambridge University Press.

Fo, W., & O'Donnell, C. (1975). The buddy system: Effect of community intervention on delinquent offenses. *Behavior Therapy, 6*, 522–524.

Forehand, R. L., Furey, W. M., & McMahon, R. J. (1984). The role of maternal distress in a parent training program to modify child noncompliance. *Behavioral Psychotherapy, 12*, 93–108.

Forehand, R. L., & McMahon, R. (1981). *Helping the noncompliant child*: *A clinicians' guide to parent training*. New York: Guilford.

Forgatch, M. (1989). Patterns and outcome in family problem-solving: The disrupting effect of negative emotions. *Journal of Marriage and the Family, 51*, 115–124.

Forgatch, M., Patterson, G., & Skinner, M. (1988). A mediational model for the effect of divorce in antisocial behavior in boys. In E. M. Hetherington & J. D. Arasteh (Eds.), *Impact of divorce, single parenting, and step-parenting on children* (pp. 135–154). Hillsdale, NJ: Lawrence Erlbaum Associates.

Frick, P., Lahey, B., Hartdagen S., & Hynd, G. (1989). Conduct problem in boys: Relations to maternal personality, marital satisfaction, and socioeconomic status. *Journal of Clinical Child Psychology, 18*, 114–120.

Gorensten, E. E., & Newman, J. P. (1980). Disinhibitory psychopathology: A new perspective and model for research. *Psychological Review, 87*, 301 315.

Goutz, K. (1981). Children's initial aggression level and the effectiveness of intervention strategies in moderating television effects on aggression.

Griest, D., Forehand, R., Wells, K., & McMahon, R. (1980). An examination of differences between nonclinic and behavior-problem clinic-referred children and their mothers. *Journal of Abnormal Psychology, 89*, 497–500.

Hanf, E., & Kling, J. (1973). *Facilitating parent–child interactions*: *A two-stage training model*. Unpublished manuscript, University of Oregon Medical School.

Hawkins, J., & Lam, T. (1987). Teacher practices, social development and delinquency. In J. D. Burchard & S. N. Burchard (Eds.), *Prevention of delinquency behavior* (pp. 241–274). Newbury Park, CA: Sage.

Hawkins, J., & Weis, J. (1985). The social development model: An integrated approach to delinquency prevention. *Journal of Primary Prevention, 6*, 73–97.

Hobbs, N. (1982). *The troubled and the troubling child*. San Francisco: Jossey-Bass.

Jouriles, E., Murphy, C., & O'Leary, K. (1989). Interspousal aggression, marital discord, and child problems. *Journal of Consulting and Clinical Psychology, 57*, 453–455.

Kazdin, A. (1986). *Treatment of antisocial behavior in children and adolescents*. Homewood, IL: Dorsey.

Kazdin, A. (1987). Treatment of antisocial behavior in children: Current status and future directions. *Psychological Bulletin, 102*, 187–203.

Kazdin, A. (1990, June). *Prevention of conduct disorder*. Paper presented at the National Conference on Prevention Research, NIMH, Bethesda, MD.

Kazdin, A., Esveldt-Dawson, K., French, N., & Unis, A. (1987). Effects of parent management training and problem-solving skills training combined in the treatment of antisocial child behavior. *Journal of the American Academy of Child and Adolescent Psychiatry, 25*, 416–424.

Kendall, P., & Braswell, L. (1985). *Cognitive-behavioral therapy for impulsive children*. New York: Guilford.

LaGreca, A., & Santogrossi, D. (1980). Social skills training with elementary school students: A behavioral group approach. *Journal of Consulting and Clinical Psychology, 48*, 220–227.

Lahey, B. B., Loeber, R., Quay, H. C., Frick, P. J., & Grimm, J. (1992). Oppositional defiant and conduct disorders: Issues to be resolved for DSM-IV. *Journal of Academy of Child Psychiatry, 31*(3), 539–546.

Lochman, J., Lampron, L., Gemmer, T., & Harris, S. (1987). Anger coping intervention with aggressive children: A guide to implementation in school settings. In P. A. Keller & S. R. Heyman, (Eds.), *Innovations in clinical practice: A source book* (Vol. 6, pp. 339–356). Sarasota, FL: Professional Resource Exchange.

Loeber, R. (1985). Patterns and development of antisocial and delinquent child behavior: A review. *Child Development, 53*, 1431–1446.

Loeber, R. (1990). Development and risk factors of juvenile antisocial behavior and delinquency. *Clinical Psychology Review, 10*, 1–41.

Loeber, R. (1991). Antisocial behavior: More enduring than changeable? *Journal of the American Academy of Child and Adolescent Psychiatry, 30*, 393–397.

Maziade, M., Cote, R., Bernier, H., Boutin, P., & Thivierge, J. (1989). Significance of extreme temperament in infancy for clinical status in pre-school years I. *British Journal of Psychiatry, 14*, 535–543.

McMahon, R., & Forehand, R. (1984). Parent training for the noncompliant child: Treatment outcome, generalization, and adjunctive therapy procedures. In R. F. Dangel & R. A. Polster (Eds.), *Parent training: Foundations of research and practice* (pp. 298–328). New York: Guilford.

McMahon, R., & Forehand, R. (1988). Conduct disorders. In E. J. Mash & L. G. Terdal (Eds.)., *Behavioral assessment of childhood disorders*. New York: Guilford Press.

Milich, R., & Dodge, K. (1984). Social information processing in child psychiatric populations. *Journal of Abnormal Child Psychology, 9*, 127–140.

O'Donnell, C., Lygate, T., & Fo, W. (1979). The buddy system: Review and follow-up. *Child Behavior Therapy, 1*, 161–169.

Offord, D. (1982). Family backgrounds of male and female delinquents. In J. Gunn & D. P. Farrington (Eds.), *Abnormal offenders: Delinquency and the criminal justice system*. Chichester: Wiley.

Offord, D., & Jones, M. (1983). Skill development: A community intervention program for the prevention of antisocial behavior. In S. B. Guze, F. J. Earls, & J. E. Barrett (Eds.), *Childhood psychopathology and development* (pp. 165–188). New York: Raven.

O'Leary, K. D., & Emery, R. E. (1982). Marital discord and child behavior problems. In M. D. Levine & P. Satz (Eds.), *Middle childhood: Developmental variation and dysfunction* (pp. 345–364). New York: Academic Press.

Patterson, G. (1975). *Families: Applications of social learning to family life*. Champaign, IL: Research Press.

Patterson, G. (1976). *Living with children: New methods for parents and teachers*. Champaign, IL: Research Press.

Patterson, G. R. (1982). *Coercive family precess*. Eugene, OR: Castalia.

Paterson, G. R., Chamberlain, P., & Reid, J. B. (1982). A comparative evaluation of a parent training program. *Behavior Therapy, 13*, 638–650.

Patterson, G. R., DeBaryshe, B. D., & Ramsey, E. (1989). A developmental perspective on antisocial behavior. *American Psychologist, 44,* 329–335.

Patterson, G. R., & Stouthamer-Loeber, M. (1984). The correlation of family management practices and delinquency. *Child Development, 55,* 129–307.

Quay, H. (1986). Classification. In H. C. Quay & J. S. Werry (Eds.), *Psychopathological disorders of childhood* (3rd ed.). New York: Wiley.

Raine, A., & Venables, P. (1984). Tonic heart rate level, social class and antisocial class and antisocial behavior in adolescents. *Biological Psychology, 18,* 123–132.

Richard, B. A., & Dodge, K. A. (1982). Social maladjustment and problem solving in school-aged children. *Journal of Consulting and Clinical Psychology, 50,* 226–233.

Richman, N., Stevenson, L., & Graham, P. J. (1982). *Pre-school to school: A behavioural study.* London: Academic Press.

Robins, L. (1981). Epidemiological approaches to natural history research: Antisocial disorders in children. *Journal of Consulting and Clinical Psychology, 50,* 226–233.

Rose, S. L., Rose, S. A., & Feldman, J. (1989). Stability of behavior problems in very young children. *Development and Psychopathology, 1,* 5–20.

Rutter, M. (1985). Resilience in the face of adversity: Protective factors and resistance to psychiatric disorder. *British Journal of Psychiatry, 147,* 598–611.

Rutter, M., & Giller, H. (1983). *Juvenile delinquency: Trends and perspectives.* Harmondsworth, Middlesex: Penguin.

Rutter, M., Tizard, J., Yule, W., Graham, P., & Whitmore, K. (1976). Research report: Isle of Wight studies. *Psychological Medicine, 6,* 313–332.

Safer, D., & Allen R., (1976). *Hyperactive children: Diagnosis and management.* Baltimore, MD: University Park Press.

Schmidt, K., Solanto, M., & Bridger, W. (1985). Electrodermal activity of undersocialized aggressive children: A pilot study. *Journal of Child Psychology and Psychiatry, 26,* 653–660.

Schonfeld, I. S., Shaffer, D., O'Connor, P., & Portnoy, S. (1988). Conduct disorder and cognitive functioning: Testing three causal hypotheses. *Child Development, 59,* 993–1007.

Schweinhart, L., & Weikart, D. (1988). The high/scope perry preschool program. In R. H. Price, E. L. Cowen, R. P. Lorion, & J. Ramos-McKay (Eds.), *14 ounces of prevention: A casebook for practitioners* (pp. 53–66). Washington, DC: American Psychological Association.

Slaby, R., & Guerra, N. (1988). Cognitive mediators of aggression in adolescent offenders: vol. 1. Assessment. *Development Psychology, 24,* 580–588.

Spivak, G., Platt, J., & Shure, M. (1976). *The problem-solving approach to adjustment.* San Francisco, CA: Jossey-Bass.

Stonemen, Z., Brody, G., & Burke, M. (1988). Marital quality, depression, and inconsistent parenting: Relationship with observed mother–child conflict. *American Journal of Orthopsychiatry, 59,* 105–117.

Sturge, C. (1982). Reading retardation and antisocial behavior. *Journal of Child Psychology and Psychiatry, 23,* 21–31.

Thomas, A., & Chess, S. (1977). *Temperament and development.* New York: Brunner/Mazel.

Wadsworth, M. (1979). Roots of delinquency: Infancy adolescence and crime. New York: Barnes & Noble.

Wahler, R., & Dumas, J. (1984). Changing the observational coding styles of insular and noninsular mothers: A step toward maintenance of parent training effects. In R. F. Dangel & R. A. Polster (Eds.), *Parent training: Foundations of research and practice* (pp. 379–416).

Wahler, R., & Dumas, J. (1985). Maintenance factors in coercive mother–child interactions: The compliance and predictability hypothesis. *Journal of Applied Behavioral Analyses, 19*(1), 13–22.

Walker, J. L., Lahey, B. B., Hynd, G. W., & Frame, C. L. (1988). Comparison of specific patterns of antisocial behavior in children with conduct disorder with or without hyperactivity. *Journal of Consulting and Clinical Psychology, 55,* 910–913.

Webster-Stratton, C. (1981a). Modification of mothers' behaviors and attitudes through a videotape modeling group discussion program. *Behavior Therapy, 12,* 634–642.

Webster-Stratton, C. (1981b). Videotape modeling: A method of parent education. *Journal of Clinical Psychology, 10*(2), 93–98.

Webster-Stratton, C. (1982a). The long term effects of a videotape modeling parent training program: Comparison of immediate and 1-year followup results. *Behavior Therapy, 13,* 702–714.

Webster-Stratton, C. (1982b). Teaching mothers through videotape modeling to change their children's behaviors. *Journal of Pediatric Psychology, 7*(3), 279–294.

Webster-Stratton, C. (1984). Randomized trial of two parent-training programs for families with conduct disordered children. *Journal of Consulting and Clinical Psychology, 52*(4), 666–678.

Webster-Stratton, C. (1985). Comparisons of behavior transactions between conduct disordered children and their mothers in the clinic and at home. *Journal of Abnormal Child Psychology, 13* (2), 169–184.

Webster-Stratton, C. (1990a). Stress: A potential disrupter of parent perceptions and family interactions. *Journal of Clinical Psychology, 19*(4), 302–312.

Webster-Stratton, C. (1990b). Predictors of treatment outcome in parent training for families with conduct problem children. *Behavior Therapy, 21,* 319–337.

Webster-Stratton, C. (1989). *The advanced videotape parent training programs.* Seth Enterprises, 1411 8th Avenue West, Seattle, WA 98119.

Webster-Stratton, C. (1991) *The dinosaur videotape social skills and problem-solving curriculum for young children.* Seth Enterprises, 1411 8th Avenue West, Seattle, WA 98119.

Webster-Stratton, C., & Hammond, M. (1988). Maternal depression and its relationship to life stress, perceptions of child behavior problems, parenting behaviors, and child conduct problems. *Journal of Abnormal Child Psychology, 16*(3), 299–315.

Webster-Stratton, C., & Hammond, M. (1990). Predictors of treatment outcome in parent training for families with conduct problem children. *Behavior Therapy, 21,* 319–337.

Webster-Stratton, C., Kolpacoff, M., & Hollinsworth, T. (1989). The long-term effectiveness and clinical significance of three cost-effective training programs for families with conduct problem children. *Journal of Consulting and Clinical Psychology, 57,* 550–553.

Webster-Stratton, C., & Spitzer, A. (1991). Reliability and validity of a parent daily discipline inventory (DDI). *Behavioral Assessment, 13,* 221–239.

Webster-Stratton, (1994). Advancing videotape parent training: A comparism study. *Journal of Consulting and Clinical Psychology, 62,* 538–594.

White, J., Moffit, T., Earls, F., & Robins, L. (1990). Preschool predictors of persistent conduct disorder and delinquency. *Criminology, 28,* 443–454.

Wicks-Nelson, & Israel, (1991). *Behavior disorders of childhood.* Englewook Cliffs, NJ: Prentice Hall.

Williams, S., Anderson, J., McGee, R., & Silva, P. A. (1990). Risk factors for behavioral and emotional disorder in preadolescent children. *Journal of the American Academy of Child and Adolescent Psychiatry, 29,* 413–419.

Chapter 19

Attention-Deficit Hyperactivity Disorder

Mark D. Rapport
University of Hawaii

CLINICAL DESCRIPTION

Chapter Overview

In the initial section of this chapter, introductory comments concerning children with Attention-Deficit Hyperactivity Disorder (ADHD) are offered, followed by a historical overview and detailed clinical description of the disorder. The second section discusses current thinking and recent empirical findings concerning both unlikely and probable causes of the disorder. It will become apparent that researchers have been unable to satisfactorily unravel the mystery to date, but evidence is mounting to suggest that ADHD is a complex and chronic disorder of brain, behavior, and development whose behavioral and cognitive consequences affect multiple areas of functioning. In the third section of the chapter, information is presented concerning the developmental course of the disorder, beginning with early childhood and continuing through adolescence to adulthood. The ensuing two chapter sections discuss whether ADHD is inherited or more common in certain families (familial contributions) and the role brain-based and genetic mechanisms play in affecting how children with ADHD think and act (psychophysiological and genetic influences). The remainder of the chapter focuses on current treatments for children with ADHD, ranging from pharmacological (medication) to highly specialized behavioral interventions.

Introduction

This chapter is about children with Attention-Deficit Hyperactivity Disorder. ADHD is estimated to affect literally millions of children throughout the world (i.e., between 3% and 5% of the childhood population or approximately one child in every classroom). It accounts for an estimated 30% to 60% of clinical case loads in child psychiatry and mental health outpatient clinics in the United States. And, there is presently no known cure. As a result, ADHD is considered to be one of the most serious and perplexing clinical disorders of childhood.

Historical Overview

While reading through the clinical description section of this chapter, the reader will discover that he or she probably knew several classmates affected by ADHD—only the name of the disorder was different. Historically, children with ADHD were referred to as having "Minimal Brain Damage" (1947 to early 1950s). The association between brain damage and behavioral deviance was a logical one and introduced following the 1918 encephalitis epidemics. Many of the postencephalitic children were observed to be motorically overactive, inattentive, and aggressive, in addition to displaying a wide variety of emotional and learning difficulties. Subsequent attempts to validate the concept of minimal brain damage, however, were unsuccessful. Neither "soft neurological signs"—that is, objective physical evidence that is perceptible to the examining physician as opposed to the subjective sensations or symptoms of the patient—nor a positive history of brain damage or birth difficulties were evidenced in a majority of children with a history of behavioral problems.

The concept of a clinical disorder resulting from brain damage was gradually discarded and replaced with the more subtle but nebulous concept, "Minimal Brain Dysfunction," or MBD (late 1950s to mid 1960s). The distinction between brain damage and and brain dysfunction was an important one. It implied an *hypothesis* of brain dysfunction resulting from manifestations of central nervous system dysfunction, as opposed to brain damage as an assumed *fact* in affected children. It also suggested that a wide range of learning and behavioral disabilities could accompany the hypothesized deviations of the central nervous system. These symptoms could be inferred from various combinations of impairment in attention, impulse control, gross motor activity, perception, language, and memory, among others.

The concept of minimal brain dysfunction was eventually replaced with the moniker, "Hyperkinetic Reaction of Childhood," in the American Psychiatric Association's second edition of its *Diagnostic and Statistical Manual* (American Psychiatric Association, 1968). The change in diagnostic labels reflected a general dissatisfaction with the untestable notion of brain dysfunction and concomitantly suggested that an excessive degree of and difficulties in regulating gross motor activity best represented the core symptoms of the disorder.

The concept of an independent syndrome of *hyperactivity* prevailed between 1968 and 1979, during which time considerable effort was spent trying to validate the notion of a hyperactive child syndrome. An upsurge in child psychopathology research directly affected the evolution of thinking over this time period and resulted in a focus on *attentional difficulties* or deficits as the core disturbance of the disorder. Excessive gross motor activity was subsequently relegated to an associative feature role in defining the disorder, which in turn, was considered to be neither sufficient nor necessary to establish a formal diagnosis. This rather dramatic shift in diagnostic emphasis was reflected in the third edition of the *Diagnostic and Statistical Manual* (American Psychiatric Association, 1980), wherein the disorder was renamed "Attention Deficit Disorder" (ADD) and could occur with hyperactivity (ADDH) or without hyperactivity (ADD).

A second important change in the *DSM-III* nomenclature involved the conceptualization of the disorder itself. Earlier diagnostic conceptualizations of the disorder required, among other clinical criteria, that a child meet a specified number of symptoms from a prepared list to qualify for a diagnosis (e.g., *any* eight criteria on the list). This type of diagnostic conceptualization, in which no single behavioral characteristic is essential or sufficient for group membership and members having a number of shared characteristics or clinical features are grouped together, is referred to as a *polythetic* schema. The *DSM-III* nomenclature, however, incorporated a *monothetic* schema for the first time, wherein an individual was now required to present with a specified number of symptoms from *each* of three assumably independent behavioral categories for a diagnosis to be established: inattention, impulsivity, and overactivity. The difference may appear subtle, but it has important implications for diagnostic categorization and defining what constitutes a particular clinical disorder. In the case of ADDH, for example, it would be much more difficult to meet multiple criteria in three distinct behavioral domains (versus from a single list of symptoms), which in turn, would have the effect of refining the disorder to a more homogeneous (similar) grouping of children.

As a consequence of this conceptual shift, researchers began focusing their efforts on establishing whether or not inattention, impulsivity, and hyperactivity were in fact independent behavioral domains — primarily by conducting factor analytic studies on child behavior rating scale data obtained from classroom teachers. In factor analytic studies, researchers use statistical techniques to discern whether certain rating scale items or descriptions of specific types of behavior co-vary or "go together" to form one or more independent domains of behavior. If all items correlate highly with one another (i.e., they are significantly related to one another), then a single factor such as "inattention" is thought to account for the different rating scale items. A two-factor solution suggests that some items or behavioral descriptions of behavior co-vary with one another but not with the remaining behavioral descriptions entered into the equation. These remaining items might subsequently be found to co-vary or go together in a statistical sense to form a second behavioral domain such as "impulsivity."

What emerged from factor analytic studies was a mixed and often confusing picture. Most studies failed to find evidence of independent factors or behavioral domains to support the three dimensions associated with ADDH. Several of the studies found evidence for a separate "attentional disturbance" domain, whereas impulsivity and hyperactivity appeared to load together on a second factor. That is, items making up these latter two domains were frequently inseparable from one another, suggesting that impulsivity and hyperactivity were probably different but related behaviors of a single dimension of behavior.

The evolution from the *DSM-III* to the revised *DSM-III-R* edition (American Psychiatric Association, 1987) was much quicker than had been the case with earlier evolutions. In fact, many researchers were displeased with the rapidity of the change. Information was still being collected and analyzed concerning critical questions having a direct bearing on the independence of factors or behavioral dimensions assumed to be integral components of ADDH. And insufficient evidence was available concerning whether ADD represented a special subtype of the disorder that could occur without the hyperactivity component.

Nevertheless, the disorder was renamed in the *DSM-III* revised edition, with hyperactivity re-emerging as a central feature of the disorder. Several other important changes were adopted in the revised 1987 nomenclature. The modified monothetic classification schema that required the presence of behavior problems in three different dimensions (inattention, impulsivity and hyperactivity) was discarded. And the new classification schema reverted back to a polythetic dimensional approach—that is, a diagnosis now required that 8 out of 14 behaviors from a single list be present in a child for a minimum of 6 months duration, with onset of difficulties occurring prior to age 7. ADD without hyperactivity was abandoned as a distinct subtype of the disorder, and a secondary category termed "undifferentiated attention deficit disorder" was added to subsume those children with attentional problems occurring without hyperactivity. Finally, the "residual ADDH" category, which was used in the earlier edition to describe older individuals (usually adolescents) who no longer presented with the full complement of ADHD symptoms, was discarded.

Readers may wish to note, however, that the new *DSM-IV* edition reflects additional changes both in the formal name of the disorder and the specific criteria used in arriving at a formal diagnosis. The *DSM-IV* contains three subtypes under the "attention-deficit and disruptive behavior disorders" of childhood. These include (a) Attention-Deficit Hyperactivity Disorder, predominantly inattentive type; (b) Attention-Deficit Hyperactivity Disorder, predominantly hyperactive-impulsive type; and (c) Attention-Deficit Hyperactivity Disorder, combined type (inattentive and hyperactive-impulsive). The first category is used to describe those children who were previously diagnosed as ADD without hyperactivity in the earlier *DSM-III-R* (APA, 1980) nomenclature. It requires children to exhibit at least six (from a list of nine) inattentive behaviors for a minimal duration of at least 6 months and to a degree that is considered developmentally inappropriate for their age. Moreover, the "inattentive" subtype children must not exhibit more than five behaviors from a second list of hyperactivity-impulsivity items listed under the symptom checklist for "ADHD, predominantly hyperactive-impulsive subtype". To meet diagnostic criteria for the second subtype, children must exhibit a minimum of six developmentally inappropriate behaviors from the hyperactivity-impulsivity symptom checklist but less than six from the inattention list for a minimum duration of 6 months. For the combined subtype, children must meet criteria for both "inattention" and "hyperactivity." Additional changes reflected in the *DSM-IV* (APA, 1994) include requiring that symptoms (or problem behaviors) be exhibited pervasively (as opposed to situationally) across settings (e.g., in two or more settings such as at school and at home) and that the disturbance cause clinically significant impairment in social, academic, or occupational functioning. Finally, ADHD cannot occur exclusively during the course of a pervasive developmental disorder, schizophrenia, or other psychotic disorder and cannot be better accounted for by another mental disorder such as mood disorder, anxiety disorder, or personality disorder.

Description and Distinguishing Features

The first distinction that should be noted in understanding children with ADHD is that it is not the type or kind of behavior they exhibit that is particularly deviant but the quantity or degree and intensity of their behavior. That is, they tend to exhibit higher rates of behavior and frequently with greater intensity in situations that demand lower rates or more subtle kinds of behavior (e.g., becoming disruptive and behaving inappropriately in school or while interacting with others) and at other times, lower rates of behavior when higher rates are demanded (e.g., not paying attention and completing academic assignments in the classroom). Overall, they appear to be out of sync with environmental demands and expectations, especially in situations that require careful sustained attention and protracted effort at tasks that are not particularly interesting or stimulating to the child.

Children's behavior must also be viewed in an appropriate developmental context. For example, younger children typically are more active, cannot pay attention to a particular task for as long a time interval, and tend to spend less time in making decisions or analyzing problems compared to older children. Other factors, such as gender and cultural differences, may also play a defining role in determining what constitutes normality, and it is only when a child's behavior consistently and significantly exceeds these expectations that it is considered deviant.

In ADHD, the developmental behavioral pattern typically observed is associated with an early onset, a gradual worsening of symptoms over time, and an unrelenting clinical course until late adolescence when the child is no longer in school. Most children with ADHD continue to exhibit symptoms of the disorder as adults, the severity of which depends upon a number of factors. As we see later in the chapter, many believe that the disorder is inherited and thus present from birth.

A third feature characteristic of children with ADHD is that their behavioral difficulties tend to be pervasive across situations and settings. Most people have been "hyper" at one time or another, have experienced difficulty concentrating, and have acted impulsively in particular situations. These occurrences tend to be isolated events, and one can usually point to particular environmental circumstances, situations, or contingencies as responsible for or contributing factors associated with the behavior (e.g., feeling ill or having to study for a particularly uninteresting class). The child with ADHD, on the other hand, exhibits this pattern of behavior in most situations and settings, day after day, year after year. A gradual worsening of behavioral and academic difficulties is usually observed as the child grows older. This is because the environment demands that one be able to pay attention, sit still, and control one's impulses for longer periods of time with increasing age. Difficulties are especially conspicuous upon entry into the fourth and seventh grades, when classroom demands and academic assignments become increasingly more complex, take longer to complete, and rely heavily on one's ability to work independently.

Children with ADHD are also known for their "consistently inconsistent" behavior. That is, they tend to behave rather erratically both within and across days even when their home and school environments are relatively stable. Teachers frequently report, for example, that the child appears relatively settled and able to pay attention and complete academic assignments on some days, although most days are characterized by disruptiveness, inattention, and low work completion rates. Parents report a similar phenomena at home, even among those who are highly skilled in managing their child's behavior. The reasons for the ADHD child's inconsistent pattern of behavior are varied, and as is discussed, may be related to a complex interaction between brain regulation mechanisms and prevailing environmental stimulation and contingencies.

Primary Symptoms and Diagnostic Criteria

The primary symptoms or clinical features of ADHD are developmentally inappropriate degrees of inattention, impulsivity, and gross motor overactivity. The current
DSM-IV (APA, 1994) diagnostic criteria for ADHD are presented in Table 19.1 and
require a child to exhibit a minimum of six symptoms (or problem behaviors) listed
under the A(1) criteria (Attention-Deficit Hyperactivity Disorder, predominantly
inattentive type) but less than six symptoms from the "hyperactivity-impulsivity" list;
a minimum of six symptoms listed under the A(2) criteria (Attention-Deficit Hyperactivity Disorder, predominantly hyperactive-impulsive type) but less than six symptoms from the "inattentive" list; or a minimum of six symptoms from both lists
(Attention-Deficit Hyperactivity Disorder, combined type).

Individuals with the disorder generally display some disturbance in each of these
areas and in most settings, but to varying degrees. Conversely, signs of the disorder
may be minimal or even absent in novel settings (e.g., being examined in a doctor's
office or clinical setting), when receiving individualized attention, or under conditions
in which stimulation or interest level is relatively high.

At home, inattention is commonly displayed by frequent shifts from one
uncompleted activity to another and a failure to follow through and/or comply with
instructions. The impulsivity component is often expressed by acting without considering either the immediate or delayed consequences of one's actions (e.g., running into
the street, accident proneness), interrupting the conversation of other household
members, and grabbing objects (not with malevolent intent) in the store while on
shopping trips. Problems with overactivity are often expressed by difficulty remaining
seated during meals, while completing homework or riding in the car, and excessive
movement during sleep.

At school, inattention is usually evidenced by difficulty deploying and maintaining adequate attention (i.e., staying on-task), a failure to complete academic
assignments, and deficient organizational and informational processing skills. Impulsivity is expressed in a variety of ways, such as interrupting others, beginning
assignments before receiving (or understanding) complete instructions, making careless
mistakes while completing assignments, blurting out answers in class, and having
difficulty waiting one's turn in both small group and organized sport activities.
Hyperactivity is frequently manifested by fidgetiness, twisting, and wiggling in one's
seat or changing seat positions, dropping objects on the floor, and emitting noises or
playing with objects during quiet assignment periods. One should be careful to note,
however, that all of these behaviors may be diminished or exacerbated by subtle
changes in the environment. Teachers frequently comment, for example, that an
identified child with ADHD who is absorbed in a particular activity of high interest
value or who is working in a one-on-one situation with an adult can attend for normal
time expectations and not move a muscle while doing so. Parents also report that their
children with ADHD can sit perfectly still while engaged in high stimulation activities
such as watching movies (e.g., "Star Wars") and while playing interactive computer or
video games. This may have a direct bearing on the extant nature of the disorder.

Secondary Symptoms or Associated Features of ADHD

Secondary features are those behaviors and difficulties that occur at a greater than
chance frequency in children with a particular disorder but are not necessary or

TABLE 19.1
DSM–IV Diagnostic Criteria for Attention-Deficit Hyperactivity Disorder

A. Either (1) or (2):
  (1) Six (or more) of the following symptoms of *inattention* have persisted for at least 6 months to a degree that is maladaptive and inconsistent with developmental level:
  Inattention
   (a) often fails to give close attention to details or makes careless mistakes in schoolwork, work, or other activities
   (b) often has difficulty sustaining attention in tasks or play activities
   (c) often does not seem to listen when spoken to directly
   (d) often does not follow through on instructions and fails to finish schoolwork, chores, or duties in the workplace (not due to oppositional behavior or failure to understand instructions)
   (e) often has difficulty organizing tasks and activities
   (f) often avoids, dislikes, or is reluctant to engage in tasks that require sustained mental effort (such as schoolwork or homework)
   (g) often loses things necessary for tasks or activities (e.g., toys, school assignments, pencils, books, or tools)
   (h) is often easily distracted by extraneous stimuli
   (i) is often forgetful in daily activities
  (2) Six (or more) of the following symptoms of *hyperactivity-impulsivity* have persisted for at least 6 months to a degree that is maladaptive and inconsistent with developmental level:
  Hyperactivity
   (a) often fidgets with hands or feet or squirms in seat
   (b) often leaves seat in classroom or in other situations in which remaining seated is expected
   (c) often runs about or climbs excessively in situations in which it is inappropriate (in adolescents or adults, may be limited to subjective feelings of restlessness)
   (d) often has difficulty playing or engaging in leisure activities quietly
   (e) is often "on the go" or often acts as if "driven by a motor"
   (f) often talks excessively
  Impulsivity
   (g) often blurts out answers before questions have been completed
   (h) often has difficulty awaiting turn
   (i) often interrupts or intrudes on others (e.g., butts into conversations or games)
B. Some hyperactive-impulsive or inattentive symptoms that caused impairment were present before age 7 years.
C. Some impairment from the symptoms is present in two or more settings (e.g., at school [or work] and at home).
D. There must be clear evidence of clinically significant impairment in social, academic, or occupational functioning.
E. The symptoms do not occur exclusively during the course of a Pervasive Developmental Disorder, Schizophrenia, or other Psychotic Disorder and are not better accounted for by another mental disorder (e.g., Mood Disorder, Anxiety Disorder, Dissociative Disorder, or a Personality Disorder).

Code based on type:
314.01 *Attention-Deficit/Hyperactivity Disorder, Combined Type*: if both Criteria A1 and A2 are met for the past 6 months
314.00*Attention-Deficit/Hyperactivity Disorder, Predominantly Inattentive Type*: if Criterion A1 is met but Criterion A2 is not met for the past 6 months
314.01 *Attention-Deficit/Hyperactivity Disorder, Predominantly Hyperactive-Impulsive Type*: if Criterion A2 is met but Criterion A1 is not met for the past 6 months

Coding note: For individuals (especially adolescents and adults) who currently have symptoms that no longer meet full criteria, "In Partial Remission" should be specified.

Note. From APA (1994). Adapted by permission.

sufficient to serve as formal diagnostic criteria. Many of these symptoms or behaviors are reported early in the developmental course of the disorder and may thus, represent less prominent features of the disorder. These include lability of mood, temper tantrums, low frustration tolerance, social disinhibition, cognitive impairment with associated learning disability, and perceptual motor difficulties (Barkley, 1990). Other aspects of disturbance or behavioral difficulties may be secondary to or direct and indirect consequences of the disorder. For example, disturbed peer and interpersonal relationships, academic underachievement, school failure, decreased self-esteem, depressed mood, and conduct problems are characteristic of many children with ADHD. The presence or absence of attendant aggressive or conduct features is especially important and may be of both diagnostic and prognostic value.

CAUSES OF THE DISORDER

Speculations concerning the cause or causes of ADHD have proliferated in recent years, ranging from brain-based mechanisms to environmental toxins. Although definitive answers remain elusive, recent discoveries suggest several possible factors that may be related to the etiology of ADHD.

Environmental Toxins

A variety of environmental toxins and factors has been suggested as causal or contributing agents to the development of ADHD. The most popular of these include elevated blood lead levels, food additives (particularly salicylates, food dyes, and preservatives), sugar, cigarette smoking or alcohol consumption during pregnancy, exposure to cool-white fluorescent lighting, and radioactive rays emitted from televisions. Although comprehensive coverage of these topics is beyond the scope of this chapter, it is worthwhile to point out that none of the environmental agents has received empirical support as important contributing factors to the developmental of ADHD in a majority of children.

Neurological and Neurophysiological Factors

Results of routine neurological examinations are usually found to be normal in children with ADHD. Research investigating the presence of neuromaturational signs (i.e., signs that a person's brain represents a more immature form of development) has been equivocal but generally suggests either nonspecific or no increased frequency of soft signs in this population. Also, as noted previously, the overwhelming majority of children with ADHD does not have a history of brain injury or damage. More recent studies using advanced brain scanning techniques, such as computed tomography (CT) scan analysis, have also failed to reveal differences in brain structure, although preliminary findings using the higher-resolution magnetic resonance imaging (MRI) have been conflicting.

Neurochemical abnormalities, particularly those involving the monoamines, comprising the catecholamines (dopamine and norepinephrine) and an indoleamine (serotonin) have been implicated as potential contributing factors in the pathophysiology of ADHD. The evidence to date remains speculative but suggests a possible selective deficiency in the availability of dopamine and/or norepinephrine.

More promising results have emerged in three recent studies. Using single photon emission computed tomography (SPECT) to measure cerebral blood flow in the brain, Lou (1990) reported hypoperfusion (reduced) and low neural activity in the striatal and orbital prefrontal regions of children with ADHD compared with controls, whereas the primary sensory and sensorimotor regions were hyperperfused (overly active). Ongoing studies by Satterfield (1990), using EEG brain electrical activity mapping (BEAM) techniques, have been relatively consistent with Lou's findings in showing abnormality in information processing in the frontal lobes of children with ADHD. Finally, Zametkin et al. (1990), in studying adults who had been hyperactive since childhood, reported reduced glucose metabolism in various areas of the brain, particularly the premotor and superior prefrontal regions—areas known to be associated with the regulation of attention, motor activity, and information processing.

Collectively, these findings implicate a central nervous system mechanism in the development of ADHD, most likely involving connections between the prefrontal areas and the limbic system of the brain. The findings are also consistent with speculations concerning a possible selective deficiency in the availability of two of the brain's neurotransmitter systems: dopamine and norepinephrine. Prefrontal–limbic connections are known to contain relatively high amounts of these neurotransmitters, psychostimulants (the primary pharmacological treatment for children with ADHD) are known agonists (they increase neurotransmitter function) of these systems, and the brain areas implicated are thought to underlie several aspects of inattention, behavioral inhibition (impulsivity, executive planning abilities), emotion, and learning. Overall, the findings move one closer to understanding both the pathogenesis of and treatment response observed in children with ADHD.

Comment

Although the cause(s) of ADHD remains unknown, current thinking suggests that a primary component of the disorder involves the regulatory processes of the brain—that is, the brain's ability to regulate itself appropriately (which include both the initiation and inhibition of behavior and activity) on a ongoing basis and under a range of normally occurring circumstances and conditions. These differences in regulatory processes appear to be governed by at least two of the best studied neurotransmitters: dopamine and norepinephrine.

Several scientists have speculated that dopamine may be more directly related to regulating the reward centers of the human brain and attentional processes, whereas the noradrenergic system plays a more important role in regulating behavioral inhibition and higher-order learning processes. The implications of these theories on a behavioral level are that both systems are probably affected to some degree in all children with ADHD and that differences in symptomatology may reflect the degree to which one or both systems are affected. For example, a child who experiences greater deficits in attention and learning from positive reinforcement may have especially lower or more poorly regulated levels of the neurotransmitter dopamine. Similarly, children who are highly impulsive (fail to inhibit themselves under appropriate circumstances) and fail to learn from aversive environmental events may be found to have lower or more poorly regulated levels of the brain neurotransmitter norepinephrine. Following this general theoretical model, the worse case scenario would be those children who evidence significant disturbance in both neurotransmitter systems. These individuals would likely exhibit poorly regulated attention, a high degree of impulsivity, and a panoply of serious behavioral and learning problems.

Before leaving this section, one may wish to ask oneself what role a child's gross motor activity level may play in the theoretical reasoning expressed in the preceding paragraphs. Researchers have learned, for example, that brain-behavior relationships are not unidirectional—That is, ongoing activity within the human brain clearly affects how one behaves—but one's behavior and the environment also affect how one's brain functions. One example of this phenomenon is the well-documented finding that increased activity level can increase the level or availability of dopamine in the human brain. Following this logic, one might speculate that the higher than average gross motor activity observed in children with ADHD while they attempt to concentrate on school work or learning tasks represents the body's attempt to "self-medicate" itself. It could theoretically do so by increasing the availability of dopamine to areas of the brain concerned with executive functions, such as the prefrontal and frontal areas. The next decade of research is likely to shed light on these and other hypotheses concerning the causes of ADHD.

COURSE OF THE DISORDER

Early Childhood

Several well-controlled studies indicate that difficulties with attention and overactivity are relatively common among preschoolers. Only a small subset of these children continues to manifest symptoms characteristic of ADHD by the time they are 4 to 5 years of age. These symptoms are strongly predictive of continued difficulties and a probable clinical diagnosis by ages 6 and 9 (Campbell, 1990). Thus, the necessity of considering both the degree *and* duration of behavioral disturbance cannot be overemphasized, especially in very young children.

Parents describe children in this age group—who continue to exhibit a durable pattern of ADHD symptoms—as always on the go, fearless, restless, continually getting into things, not obeying parental commands, oppositional, highly curious about their environment, and requiring high levels of adult supervision. Other problems, such as perceptual motor difficulties, sleep and eating difficulties, accident proneness, speech and language difficulties, and toilet training difficulties are reported in a subset of these children. Those with advanced intellectual and cognitive skills and who tend not to be aggressive are generally easier to manage both at home and in preschool settings. Needless to say, the parents (and especially mothers) of these children are under enormous daily stress in their parental roles, the reciprocal interaction of which frequently results in psychiatric disability, marital problems, alcoholism, and increased risk for child abuse.

Middle Childhood

Between the ages of 6 and 12 years, children with ADHD continue to demonstrate difficulties with attention, impulsivity, overactivity, and compliance with adult requests. These difficulties are exacerbated after such children enter elementary school, with a subsequent rise in outpatient referral rates owing to two primary factors: the increased familiarity of classroom teachers with age-appropriate norms for behavior; and the increased demands to sit still, pay attention, and engage in increasingly more difficult academic tasks and organized activities for longer periods of time. In some cases, however, the child is excused as "immature" by well-meaning school personnel and forced to repeat the grade or passed marginally with the expectation that the child will magically "mature" over the summer months.

Increasing social and academic demands impact on their already handicapping condition to an even greater extent during these primary school years and cause the greatest level of stress to already overburdened parents and teachers. Homework assignments add an additional source of conflict to the familial environment, and 25% or more of the children experience significant difficulties with reading and/or develop other academic skill disorders. Their inattention, impulsivity, and higher than normal activity level predestines them to develop poor peer and interpersonal relationships, with a resulting pattern of social isolation and eventual low self-esteem in later years.

Adolescence

One of the prevailing myths about children with ADHD is that they "outgrow" the disorder when they reach adolescence. Follow-up and long-term outcome studies, however, reveal that approximately 80% of children diagnosed as having ADHD in childhood continue to display symptoms of and meet diagnostic criteria for ADHD as adolescents. Primary difficulties with attention/concentration, impulsively, and difficulty following directions remain, whereas the overactivity component of the disorder diminishes somewhat and transforms into fidgeting and restlessness with increasing age.

Perhaps more unsettling are the findings that between 40% and 60% of adolescents with ADHD also meet diagnostic criteria for Conduct Disorder (CD) — a disorder characterized by serious and pervasive antisocial behavior. These comorbid adolescents, in turn, are also more likely to engage in substance use (e.g., cigarette smoking) and abuse (e.g., alcohol and marijuana).

One of the strongest predictors during early childhood for becoming a well-functioning, stable, successful adult is academic achievement. Follow-up studies of children with ADHD during their adolescent years, particularly those comorbid for CD, have been alarmingly negative with regard to academic outcome. They are significantly more likely to have been suspended or expelled from school, three times more likely to have failed at least one grade, and their standardized achievement test scores are below normal in math, reading, and spelling. Of even greater concern is that an estimated 10% to 30% of them quit school and do not graduate with even a high school diploma. Overall, adolescents with ADHD, and especially those carrying a dual diagnosis of CD, represent a population at high risk for a variety of negative outcomes associated with psychiatric disability, social, and adult occupational functioning.

Adult Outcome and Long-Term Prognosis

At least three different clinical models have been postulated concerning the long-term outcome of children with ADHD: developmental delay, developmental decay, and continuous display. The first model presumes that ADHD is primarily a neuromaturational problem and that associated difficulties eventually diminish with age. The second model holds that the primary symptom picture worsens with increasing age and that specific clinical features are manifested somewhat differently in older children. The third model postulates that the primary symptom picture continues to be manifested with increasing age to a more or less similar degree of severity but, similar to the decay model, that the topography of clinical features (e.g., inattention, impulsivity) changes to reflect difficulties related to adolescence and adulthood.

Each of the three outcome models presented previously is supported in part by the existing, albeit scant, literature concerning adults diagnosed during childhood as having ADHD. Between 50% and 65% of diagnosed children continue to experience difficulties with core clinical symptoms and related behavioral problems as adults; and only 11% are estimated to be free of any psychiatric diagnosis and to be well-functioning adults. These rather bleak estimates are tempered somewhat, when one considers that only about a third of the "normal" population of children is free of psychiatric disability as adults.

Other areas of adult functioning are equally impaired. Relatively few adults with a childhood diagnosis of ADHD go on to complete a university degree program (approximately 5% vs. 41% of control children). A significant minority of them (20% to 25%) continue to display a persistent pattern of antisocial behavior. Poor work records, lower job status, difficulties getting along with supervisors, and overall lower socioeconomic status attainment are common. And greater difficulties with social skills, unstable marriages, and lower self-esteem prevail. Conversely, other adults with ADHD appear to function normally and even exceptionally well as adults. The limited evidence available indicates that a supportive, stable family environment, milder ADHD symptoms, higher intelligence, greater emotional stability, and no concomitant conduct disorder and especially aggression during childhood are the best predictors of positive adult outcome.

FAMILIAL CONTRIBUTIONS

Studies examining the families of children with ADHD represent an important avenue of inquiry concerning the inheritability of the disorder. Although one cannot completely separate the role of genetics from that of deviant child rearing practices, family-genetic studies can nevertheless improve one's understanding of the psychobiology of ADHD and specifically address whether it tends to run in families (i.e., by establishing familial risk).

In the most comprehensive and methodologically eloquent study conducted to date, Biederman, Faraone, Keenan, Knee, and Tsuang (1990) evaluated family-genetic and psychosocial risk factors for ADHD among 457 first-degree relatives of clinically referred children and adolescents with ADHD compared with psychiatric and normal controls. Age-corrected rates of illness, termed *morbidity risks*, were used to adjust upwards the degree to which an individual was counted as "healthy" as a function of increasing age. Use of this technique has been woefully absent in a majority of family-genetic studies but is necessary because many psychiatric disorders have a variable age of onset (e.g., major depression). Consequently, the fact that one may not have lived through the "risk period" must be taken into account and corrected for statistically.

Several important findings emerged from the Biederman et al. study. The first of these was that parents of children with ADHD were significantly more likely to be separated or divorced relative to the psychiatric and normal comparison groups. This finding must be interpreted cautiously, however, as it could indicate a greater degree of psychopathology among the parents or alternatively, reflect the strain placed on a marriage in raising a child with ADHD. A second major finding of the study was that the probability or risk of having ADHD among relatives of ADHD children were 7.6 and 4.6 times the odds for having ADHD among the relatives of normal or psychiatric control groups, respectively. In examining these odds ratios, it was found that nearly 65% of the children with ADHD had at least one relative with ADHD compared with 24% and 15% of the psychiatric and normal control groups, respectively. Relatives of ADHD children were also at higher risk for both antisocial disorder and mood disorders—that is, these disorders were significantly more prevalent in the families of children with ADHD. Finally, both parents as well as brothers of children with ADHD had a significantly higher risk for ADHD compared to relatives of control groups: 44% of the fathers, 19% of the mothers, and 39% of the brothers of ADHD children also had ADHD. Finally, all of the aforementioned findings remained significant even after controlling for social class and intactness of families among the different groups.

The conclusion that can be drawn from this and other studies is that ADHD is a highly familial disorder that places affected individuals at significant risk for adult psychopathology and dysfunctional marriages.

PSYCHOPHYSIOLOGICAL AND GENETIC INFLUENCES

Psychophysiological Influences

Psychophysiological functions in children with ADHD have been investigated in numerous studies over the past 20 years. Investigations in this field have generally sought to examine topics related to general autonomic arousal of the nervous system and cortical electrical activity of the brain, using measures such as galvanic skin response and electroencephalogram (EEG), respectively. Although popular several years ago, theories purporting that children with ADHD experience a general pattern of nervous system underarousal have not been supported by recent, better controlled studies.

More recent work in the field has essentially abandoned the notion of a simple difference model of brain activity and has sought instead to investigate brain activity while children are actively engaged in cognitive tasks known to differentiate them from normals. This line of inquiry may prove more informative, as it recognizes the accepted fact that the difficulties experienced by children with ADHD are not static, but dynamic, and depend on a panoply of prevailing environmental conditions. Related advances in the field were described previously under the chapter section entitled, "Neurological and Neurophysiological Factors."

Genetic Factors

The role of hereditary transmission of ADHD has been investigated in several studies over the past 30 years. Unfortunately, the bulk of this research is uninterpretable because of numerous methodological problems and poorly defined diagnostic groups of children. More recent twin studies, however, indicate a significantly greater concordance (agreement) for hyperactive symptoms between identical than between fraternal twins, with heritability of ADHD estimated to be 30% to 50%. Thus, genetic factors are likely to play an important role in the development of ADHD but must be accounted for by something other than a direct genetic model of transmission.

Comment

In summary, ADHD is most likely an inheritable condition, the symptomatology of which may be diminished or exacerbated by prevailing environmental conditions. There is also some evidence to indicate that different etiological factors involving pregnancy, birth complications, exposure to lead or drugs, and a variety of central nervous system insults may be the primary culprit in a small subset of these children. The majority, however, probably inherits the disorder through some yet unknown mechanism, with resulting underactivity of the prefrontal–striatal–limbic regions of the brain. A different and admittedly speculative view of the disorder is that the brains of children with ADHD are not abnormal per se but simply operate differently under certain environmental conditions—primarily conditions that involve sustained concentration for routine and nonstimulating tasks as is the case with the majority of classroom learning and homework assignments. From an evolutionary perspective, it could be argued that many of the behavioral characteristics that typify children with ADHD may have had high survival value in earlier societies and cultures that relied on acting and shifting attention quickly without undue reflection.

CURRENT TREATMENTS

Introduction

Current treatments for children with ADHD fall within two broad categories: behavioral and pharmacological. In a majority of cases, variants of these two treatments must be combined to obtain optimal results, especially in those children with more severe ADHD symptoms.

Behavioral Treatment

A wide variety of behavioral interventions has been used in an attempt to treat children with ADHD. Most have focused on improving classroom functioning and school-based behavior, whereas more recent interventions have emphasized enhancing peer relationships and social skills. The discussion that follow focuses exclusively on classroom interventions.

Historical Overview of Behavioral Interventions for Children with ADHD

Early behavioral interventions tended to focus on decreasing disruptive behavior in children with ADHD but were eventually abandoned when it was discovered that reduced disruptiveness did not necessarily translate into improved academic performance. This was an important finding, because academic achievement is one of the best indicators of a good prognosis and favorable long-term outcome in children. It was also found that many of the behavioral interventions that required teachers to deliver positive feedback (using verbal praise or by administering points, stars, or checks on a sheet containing descriptions of desirable behavior) involved several drawbacks. One was that the systems required a disproportionate amount of teacher time and were thus not considered "cost effective." A second criticism was that many children with ADHD tended to be drawn off-task by the delivery of positive feedback and experienced difficulty getting back on-task — an effect opposite of that intended by the intervention.

Empirical studies examining the relative efficacy of behavioral interventions beginning in the early 1970s and continuing through the 1980s revealed a rather interesting finding. If the behavioral intervention directly targeted improved academic performance as its main goal (e.g., by making consequences specific for completing academic work successfully), disruptive behavior nearly always showed a concomitant decline in frequency. The "incompatible response approach" was subsequently coined to refer to these procedures. It implied that increased academic performance was incompatible with disruptive conduct in the classroom and should be the primary target of intervention efforts.

During the 1980s and continuing to present, the most successful classroom interventions followed this general principle and focused on developing incentive and/or feedback systems that directed the child's attention to the completion of his or her school work. It was also established that a combination of positive and mild aversive corrective feedback worked better than either one alone. This type of intervention relies upon a behavioral principle termed *response cost*, wherein a child earns or is awarded points that reflect some value (e.g., earned minutes of structured free-time or specific classroom activities) on an ongoing basis but also loses (or is "costed") points for not attending to his or her academic assignments.

Newly Developed Behavioral Interventions

A prototypical example of the response cost procedure for classroom use is the recently developed Attentional Training System (ATS). A small electronic device is placed on the child's desk during periods of in-seat academic work (see Fig. 19.1). The child receives basic instructions concerning how the system works and what he or she needs to do to earn points during the ensuing academic period. Then the device is switched on, whereafter points (one per minute) are accumulated on the display counter while the child is attending to his or her academic assignments. The classroom teacher has in his or her possession a handheld remote control device (see Fig. 19.1) that can be used anywhere within the classroom to control as many as four different student units. This allows the teacher to work with other students throughout the academic period, either in small groups or individually, while still being able to monitor the ADHD child's behavior. The teacher simply glances periodically at the ADHD child to determine whether he or she is on-task. If the student is attending to his or her classroom assignment, the teacher does nothing, as the student's desk module awards points on a cumulative basis throughout the academic assignment period for appropriate behavior. If the student is not paying attention to his or her assignment, the teacher activates his or her handheld device that in turn, illuminates the red dome on the student's desk module for 15 seconds (signaling the student that he or she is off-task) and

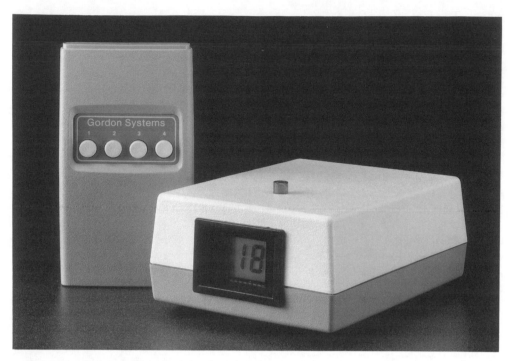

FIG. 19.1.   The Attentional Training System (ATS). Developed by M. D. Rapport (see Rapport, Murphy, & Bailey, 1982) for treating children with ADHD. Manufactured and distributed for commercial use by Gordon Systems, DeWitt, NY.

simultaneously deducts one point from the student's accumulated point total. The teacher immediately returns to whatever he or she was doing and reviews the student's progress again in a minute or 2. At the end of the academic period, the accumulated point total is transferred to a recording sheet, and the student is allowed to engage in a variety of structured learning activities that he or she enjoys (e.g., listening to tapes, art projects, using the computer). The student engages in these activities for either an equivalent or ratio (e.g., 1 minute for every two points earned) amount of time earned during the academic period. The desk module is subsequently set aside until the next scheduled academic period. An empirical demonstration and a case example using the ATS are provided later under the pharmacological treatment section.

Pharmacological Treatment

Pharmacological treatment of children with ADHD usually involves the use of psychostimulants and less frequently, one of the tricyclic antidepressants. In this section, the focus is exclusively on discussing one of the psychostimulants, methylphenidate (Ritalin). As it is used in approximately 90% of the cases, it represents the "first line defense" in treating children with ADHD and is by far the most well-studied of the medications.

Overview and Rationale

Most students studying psychopathology, and particularly, children with ADHD, raise serious questions concerning the use of medications with children. The topic is often "moralized" and children are viewed as "being medicated or drugged" unnecessarily, with blame placed on the adults (parents and teachers) who cannot cope with their behavior or academic difficulties. A useful analogy, however, might be to contrast the use of medication with that of using eyeglasses for reading. Eye glasses or contact lenses, like medication, represent an "unnatural" intervention and clearly do not *cure* visual problems. They do, however, allow one who is experiencing visual problems to read or view the environment more normally. When they are removed, the original vision problems are as they were before. Similar to the child with ADHD, individuals with vision problems (e.g., far sightedness) could in fact alter their environment so that they did not require glasses, for example, by having all written material they come in contact with printed in very large letters. This would require a great deal of cooperation and effort by those in the individual's environment, and similar to the child with ADHD, is not considered a cost-effective alternative, it is much easier and just as effective to simply wear one's glasses.

For the child with ADHD, his or her brain simply does not work optimally in a variety of situations, especially those requiring sustained concentration and the ability to reflectively approach and complete difficult tasks that characterize much of school work. Thus, there are two alternatives. One can dramatically alter the child's academic environment by asking teachers to provide feedback, create a different curriculum, and supply unnatural incentives for the child throughout the day. Or, the child can ingest a small tablet once or twice a day and achieve the same effect.

Titrating and Assessing Psychostimulant Response in Children with ADHD

Using methylphenidate (MPH) as an ongoing (i.e., maintenance) treatment intervention for children with ADHD requires careful attention by a knowledgeable professional. First, it must be established that the child is a "positive responder" to the medication, which holds true in approximately 80% of the cases. This is relatively easy to accomplish, because MPH is not what is referred to as a steady-state medication. That is, it does not require a buildup in the bloodstream for several days or weeks. Rather, it affects behavior as well as cognitive performance within 30 to 45 minutes following ingestion, and the effects of a single tablet last approximately 4 hours. Thus, positive treatment effects are easily recognized on the first day of treatment, and the degree of change may be easily quantified using a variety of behavioral, medication-sensitive rating scales completed by the child's classroom teacher or by means of direct observation.

The second step is more difficult and somewhat controversial. It involves establishing the appropriate dosage for a particular child. The primary difficulty is that, unlike other medications, a child's gross body weight is not a useful determinant of how much MPH to administer — in fact, body weight has been found to be unrelated to behavioral response (Rapport, DuPaul, & Kelly, 1989). The task is further complicated by the fact that children with ADHD cannot be relied on to provide useful information concerning medication response. Positive and even dramatic changes in their behavior and cognitive performance that are glaringly obvious to others are usually unrecognized by the ADHD child. As a result, two alternatives remain. One can request parents and teachers to complete standardized rating scales on a weekly basis as a means to adjust dosage, or one can attempt to establish optimal dosage in the clinic by observing the child under a range of dosages while he or she completes a battery of neurocognitive instruments that attempt to mirror the cognitive demands associated with successful school performance and learning.

Teacher rating scales are by far the more cost-effective and traditional method for establishing dosage. Their primary drawback, with the lone exception being the recently developed Academic Performance Rating Scale (APRS; DuPaul, Rapport, & Perriello, 1991), is that the scales target changes in children's *behavior* and fail to consider changes in *academic performance* or *learning*. This has become a highly controversial issue over the years, as some have demonstrated that behavior and cognitive performance (or learning) may be optimized at different dosages (Sprague & Sleator, 1977). More recent investigations, however, have failed to confirm these findings (see Rapport & Kelly, 1991, for a comprehensive review). Nevertheless, it would be prudent to obtain some measure of a child's academic and/or learning performance when establishing optimal dosage.

Use of a dose-sensitive neurocognitive battery that mimics a child's school performance would also be tremendously valuable. Various computer-administered instruments have been developed to assist with clinical titration in recent years but await standardization and empirical validation before they can be recommended for clinical titration purposes.

Case Illustration

Mitch was an 8-year-old boy with a chronic history of multiple behavioral and academic problems. He was brought to an outpatient mental health facility for evaluation by his mother, following a school conference in which issues were raised concerning his ability to perform on grade level and generally "immature" behavior.

Assessment. A semistructured clinical interview was conducted with Mitch's mother, in which her son's developmental, medical, educational, and mental health history were reviewed. Age, onset, course, and duration of the symptoms or behaviors related to each of the clinical disorders described in the *Diagnostic and Statistical Manual of Mental Disorders* (*DSM*) were also reviewed for diagnostic formulation purposes. Following the clinical interview a battery of standardized, age-appropriate teacher and parent rating scales was administered and scored to help quantify the degree and pervasiveness of difficulties experienced by Mitch. Finally, a standardized battery of intelligence and academic achievement tests was administered to assess Mitch's abilities and current level of functioning (see Rapport, 1993, for a review of appropriate instruments). Results were compared directly to both his recent and past academic records obtained from the school.

Diagnosis. The results obtained from the assessment work-up indicated that Mitch met diagnostic criteria for pervasive Attention-Deficit Hyperactivity Disorder as well as for a Developmental Arithmetic Disorder (considered a "learning disability" in his state). Problems were also noted with peer relationships, compliance with adults, following oral and written directions, short-term memory, and self-esteem.

Treatment. A meeting was scheduled with Mitch's parents and treatment recommendations were offered that specifically targeted their son's behavior and academic performance in school. It was felt that Mitch's academic problems, low self-esteem, and at least some interpersonal problems were directly related to his difficulties paying attention and completing academic assignments correctly in school on a consistent basis. The parents agreed to an alternating trial of MPH and a behavioral intervention, consisting of attentional training (response cost), to determine the relative benefits of each. As with most parents, they were very skeptical about using medication with their son.

Pharmacological treatment consisted of a closely monitored trial of MPH (Ritalin) at each of four doses: 5-mg (.23 mg/kg), 10-mg (.46 mg/kg), 15-mg (.64 mg/kg) and 20-mg (.92 mg/kg) following baseline (no medication) assessment. Each dose was tried for a minimum of 2 weeks before titrating (adjusting) dosage upward to a higher dose. The behavioral intervention (attentional training using response cost technology) was used during two of Mitch's most difficult morning academic periods (phonicn and math) and was instituted for a 3-week period initially, then a 4-week period during the last experimental condition (See Figures 19.2 and Fig. 19.3). Teacher ratings were obtained weekly with the teacher blind to medication conditions.

Results of Treatment. An ABACBC (reversal) within-subject design was used to compare the effects of MPH at different doses with no-medication conditions (baseline) and then to contrast the most effective MPH dose with the behavioral intervention (response cost). Direct observations of Mitch's attention (see on-task in

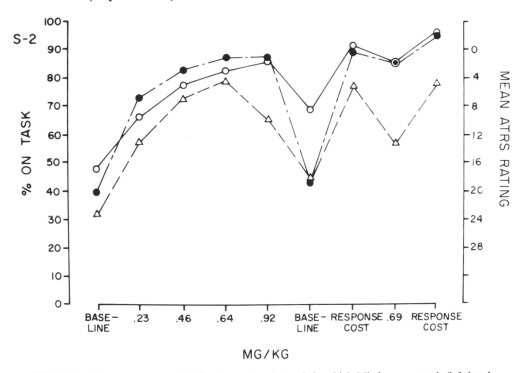

FIG. 19.2.   Mean percentage of daily observation intervals in which Mitch was on-task (left-hand ordinate) during the two morning academic assignment periods (math = closed circles; phonics = open circles) during no-treatment (baseline), methylphenidate treatment (.23 mg/kg through .92 mg/kg doses), and behavioral treatment (response cost) conditions. Weekly teacher ratings (ATRS) are shown as open triangles and interpreted using the right-hand ordinate. Improvement on all measures is indicated by upward movement on the vertical axis.

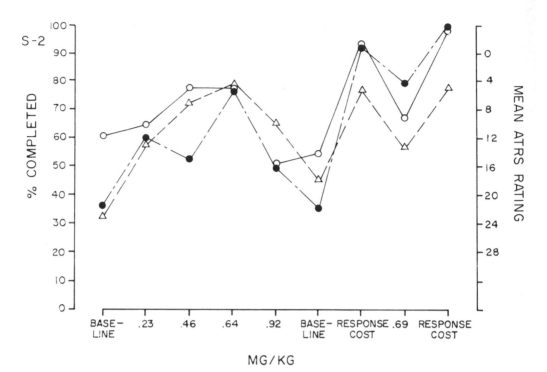

FIG. 19.3.   Mean percentage of academic assignments completed daily (left-hand ordinate) during the two morning assignment periods (math = closed circles; phonics = open circles) during no-treatment (baseline), methylphenidate treatment (.23 mg/kg through.92 mg/kg doses), and behavioral treatment (response cost) conditions. Weekly teacher ratings (ATRS) are shown as open triangles and interpreted using the right-hand ordinate. Improvement on all measures is indicated by upward movement on the vertical axis.

Fig. 19.2) and completion of academic assignments (see percentage completed and percentage correct in Fig. 19.3) were conducted daily and at the same time each morning—approximately 45 minutes after ingestion of the morning medication and at the same time on no-medication days.

Prior to any intervention (see first baseline condition in Fig. 19.2), Mitch experienced serious difficulty paying attention, as evidenced by his 40% to 48% on-task rate during the two morning academic assignment periods. Consistent with this low rate of attention, he completed between 35% and 60% of his academic assignments on a daily basis during the initial 3-week baseline (no intervention) period. A clear and somewhat dramatic increase in attention was observed under each of the medication conditions, with a concomitant increase in the percentage of academic assignments completed (see.23 through.92 mg/kg MPH dose conditions in Fig. 19.2 and Fig. 19.3). Academic assignment accuracy remained relatively high and stable throughout the course of both interventions, which was a very positive finding given his increase in academic productivity. Teacher ratings using the Abbreviated Conners Teacher Rating Scale (ATRS) generally paralleled changes observed in attention and academic performance (see open triangles and corresponding right-hand ordinate of Fig. 19.2 and Fig. 19.3).

A return to baseline (no intervention) conditions was initiated following the medication trial to help insure that changes were due to active drug as opposed to some other phenomena (e.g., developmental maturity in which improvement might be observed with the passage of time regardless of intervention). Clearly this was not the case. Mitch's attention and academic productivity returned to near pretreatment levels (see second baseline in Fig. 19.2 and Fig. 19.3).

The second stage of the evaluation was established such that the MPH dose deemed most therapeutic during the initial titration trials could be directly compared with the attentional training program (response cost). The 15-mg (.69 mg/kg) dose was selected instead of the 20-mg dose because Mitch's academic performance showed a decline under the higher dose condition, despite slightly higher levels of attention (see "% on-task" compared with "% completed" under the.92 mg/kg dose condition in Fig. 19.2 and Fig. 19.3, respectively).

Introduction of attentional training (for details, see previous section, "Newly Developed Behavioral Interventions" resulted in clear and sustained increases in Mitch's attention and academic performance, as well as improved teacher ratings during the ensuing 3-week period. These effects, when contrasted with the 15-mg (.69 mg/kg) MPH condition, indicate that both interventions affected Mitch's attention to a similar degree, with somewhat higher rates of academic performance associated with attentional training. Discontinuation of MPH and a return to the Attentional Training intervention for the final 4-weeks of observation essentially replicated the effects observed previously.

The results were shared with both Mitch's parents and his classroom teacher. It was agreed that he would continue with the Attentional Training intervention for the remainder of the school year. The training apparatus itself (see Fig. 19.1) was removed approximately 4 weeks later according to suggestions provided in the training manual, and a free-time product completion contingency was instituted in which Mitch completed all of his academic work with an established degree of accuracy in exchange for a fixed amount of in-class structured free time (approximately 10 minutes following each academic period).

Follow-up at the end of the school year indicated that Mitch maintained the therapeutic gains made during the formal assessment period of the evaluation and was promoted to the third grade. His third grade teacher, however, was not interested in establishing an ongoing behavioral management system in the classroom. He was subsequently prescribed a 15-mg b.i.d. (twice a day) regimen of MPH by his pediatrician that proved to be relatively successful throughout the course of the school year.

Comments.   Several points are worth noting. First, a combined behavioral and medication intervention is nearly always required for more severe cases of ADHD. Second, just as medication must be carefully titrated to achieve optimal results, behavioral interventions must be created using great care and attention to detail, and nearly always require periodic adjustment to maintain their effectiveness. Finally, a host of parameters must be considered when creating a behavioral program. Questions concerning what will serve as an effective incentive for the child, how well the teacher will cooperate given the existing classroom demands, and how to intervene at other times during the day when the program is not operative, must be addressed.

SUMMARY

In this chapter, it was suggested that ADHD may best be viewed as a complex and chronic disorder of brain, behavior, and development whose behavioral and cognitive consequences affect multiple areas of functioning. Mounting evidence also suggests that the disorder is significantly more common in certain families. Differences in the neurophysiological functioning of the brain, particularly executive and regulatory functioning, may help explain why these children experience such profound difficulties in maintaining attention, regulating their arousal, inhibiting themselves in accordance with environmental demands, and getting along with others—yet only at specific times and under certain conditions. Behavioral and pharmacological interventions, both alone and in combination, represent the most efficacious treatments currently available for children with ADHD. They must be viewed as "maintenance" therapies, however, as neither *cures* the disorder. Indeed, both must be maintained on an ongoing, long-term basis. Alternative therapies, computerized assessment instruments, and dramatic changes in classroom instructional design are evolving and represent only a smattering of the exciting developments expected during the next decade.

REFERENCES

American Psychiatric Association. (1968). *Diagnostic and statistical manual of mental disorders* (2nd ed.). Washington, DC: Author.

American Psychiatric Association. (1980). *Diagnostic and statistical manual of mental disorders* (3rd ed.). Washington, DC: Author.

American Psychiatric Association. (1987). *Diagnostic and statistical manual of mental disorders* (3rd rev. ed.). Washington, DC: Author.

American Psychiatric Association. (1994). *Diagnostic and statistical manual of mental disorders* (4th ed). Washington, DC: Author.

Barkley, R. A. (1990). *Attention deficit hyperactivity disorder: A handbook for diagnosis and treatment.* New York: Guilford.

Biederman, J., Faraone, S. V., Keenan, K., Knee, D., & Tsuang, M. T. (1990). Family-genetic and psychosocial risk factors in DSM-III attention deficit disorder. *Journal of the American Academy of Child and Adolescent Psychiatry, 29*, 526–533.

Campbell, S. B. (1990). *Behavior problems in preschoolers: Clinical and developmental issues.* New York: Guilford.

DuPaul, G. J., Rapport, M. D., & Perriello, L. M. (1991). Teacher ratings of academic skills: The development of the Academic Performance Rating Scale. *School Psychology Review, 20*, 284–300.

Lou, H. C. (1990). Methylphenidate reversible hypoperfusion of striatal regions in ADHD. In K. Conners & M. Kinsbourne (Eds.), *Attention deficit hyperactivity disorder: ADHD; clinical, experimental and demographic issues* (pp. 137–148). Munich, Germany: MMV Medizin Verlag.

Rapport, M. D. (1993). Attention deficit hyperactivity disorder. In T. H. Ollendick & M. Hersen (Eds.), *Handbook of child and adolescent assessment* (pp. 269–291). Boston: Allyn & Bacon.

Rapport, M. D., DuPaul, G. J., & Kelly, K. L., (1989). Attention-deficit hyperactivity disorder and methylphenidate: The relationship between gross body weight and drug response in children. *Psychopharmacology Bulletin, 25*(2), 285–290.

Rapport, M. D., & Kelly, K. L. (1991). Psychostimulant effects on learning and cognitive function: Findings and implications for children with attention deficit hyperactivity disorder. *Clinical Psychology Review, 11*, 61–92.

Rapport, M. D., Murphy, H. A., & Bailey, J. S. (1982). Ritalin vs response cost in the control of hyperactive children: A within-subject comparison. *Journal of Applied Behavior Analysis, 15*, 205–216.

Satterfield, J.H. (1990). BEAM studies in ADD boys. In C.K. Conners & M. Kinsbourne (Eds.), *Attention deficit hyperactivity disorder* (pp. 127–136) Munich, Germany: Medizin Verlag.

Sprague, R. L., & Sleator, E. K. (1977). Methylphenidate in hyperkinetic children: Differences in dose effects on learning and social behavior. *Science, 198*, 1274–1276.

Zametkin, A. J., Nordahl, T.E., Gross, M., King, A. C., Semple, W. E., Rumsey, J., Hamburger, S., & Cohen, R. M. (1990). Cerebral glucose metabolism in adults with hyperactivity of childhood onset. *The New England Journal of Medicine, 323*, 1361–1366.

Chapter 20

Eating Disorders

J. Scott Mizes
Case Western Reserve University

CLINICAL DESCRIPTION

"Starving for Beauty" was the headline for the February 17, 1992, issue of *People* magazine. The lead story and accompanying cover photo chronicled the ravages of anorexia nervosa on Tracey Gold, an actress in the popular television situation comedy *Growing Pains* (Sporkin, Wagner, & Tomashoff, 1992). The 5′3″ Tracey, having wasted away to a mere 90 pounds, had been forced to leave the television show and enter inpatient treatment. The article described how she was first diagnosed with anorexia nervosa at the age of 12, but recovered from the initial bout after 4 months of psychotherapy. At the age of 19, she started to relapse, beginning as a compulsive dieter. Her dieting was a reaction in part to becoming 133 pounds and being teased about her weight by a casting agent. By the time of the *People* article, at age 22, she was locked into the mental tyranny of full-blown anorexia nervosa. Reflecting on her desperation and lack of control, Tracey related, "I feel like the anorexia is trying to drown me. . . . There are all these hands reaching out to me, and my hand is reaching above the water. Everything inside me is fighting to pull up above the surface" (p. 93). The story also highlighted her parents' horror, with her mother describing how she went to her daughter's room every night while she was sleeping to check her pulse and breathing to make sure Tracey was still alive.

Sadly, this was not the only *People* magazine article on a star who had succumbed to anorexia nervosa. In 1983, the periodical published a story on the death of the popular singer Karen Carpenter due to anorexia nervosa. As revealed in the 1992 *People* article, the list of stars suffering from or previously afflicted with anorexia nervosa, or its diagnostic sister, bulimia nervosa, is extensive. Janine Turner of the television show *Northern Exposure* suffered with anorexia nervosa, and several actresses have struggled with the binging and purging of bulimia nervosa. These include Gilda Radner of *Saturday Night Live* fame and movie actresses Sally Field and Ally

Sheedy. Of particular note is the 20-year struggle of Jane Fonda with binging and purging. After a successful movie career, ironically she has now made her mark as the queen of exercise workout video tapes. Competitive female athletes have also struggled with eating disorders. The United States Olympic gymnast Cathy Rigby has described her 12 years of battling bulimia nervosa in the video *Faces of Recovery*. The salience of stories like Ms. Rigby's was strengthened by the bright light of the 1992 Summer Olympics. Watching the young female gymnasts compete, one could not help but notice their ribs protruding under their skin tight leotards. Equally as noticeable was the fact that, among sports that did not have competitive weight classes, only the female gymnasts routinely had their height and weight highlighted by the television commentators. One can only shudder while speculating about the pressures these young girls must feel.

The high profile of these women's struggles has turned dramatic attention to what are surely serious and, sadly, common disorders. Among women, it is estimated that 4% will develop bulimia nervosa at some time in their life, with another 4% developing near bulimia symptoms (Kendler et al., 1991). Although the incidence per year of anorexia nervosa is only estimated at as many as 1.6 cases per 100,000 people, it is estimated that as many a 5% of young adolescent women may have some form of subclinical anorexia nervosa (Szmukler, 1985). Though the stories of these famous women may have drawn much needed attention to these serious disorders, they may have also contributed to the assumption that eating disorders afflict mainly high achieving, high socioeconomic status females. Although early research studies lent some support to this belief, more recent well-executed research has found no relationship between prevalence and educational level, income, or occupation, at least for bulimia nervosa (Kendler et al., 1991).

The human significance of various forms of eating pathology is only partly conveyed by the prevalence of clinically severe anorexia and bulimia nervosa. Many people, particularly women, are unhappy with what they perceive to be a fat body, preoccupied with food and weight, and are caught in a seemingly endless struggle to eat less and exercise more. For many, the psychological result is self-criticism, lower self-esteem, a sense of failure, and feelings of depression. Sadly, the varying levels of subclinical eating pathology are the rule and not the exception. For example, Klesges, Mizes, and Klesges (1987) reported that in a sample of university students, 89% of the women and 54% of the men had engaged in some form of dieting in the previous 6 months. This was despite the fact that only 20% were overweight according to medical criteria. In this same group, 80% of the females and 46% of the males had been involved in some form of physical activity to lose weight.

Weight and eating concerns appear to start as early as elementary school age. Thelen, Lawrence, and Powell (1992) noted that studies suggest that older elementary school girls (Grades 3 to 6) are concerned about becoming overweight and are dissatisfied with their bodies, with over half wanting to be thinner. In addition, as many as 40% have attempted to lose weight. Subclinical eating pathology is sufficiently pervasive that there is discussion of the "normative discontent" that females experience regarding their bodies (Rodin, Silberstein, & Striegel-Moore, 1984). Others have called for the treatment of "normal eating" because what is "normal" reflects pathological eating attitudes and behaviors (Polivy & Herman, 1987).

This chapter discusses the eating disorders from among those disorders that usually begin in infancy, childhood, or adolescence. For completeness, the reader should note that the classification "eating disorders" in the *Diagnostic and Statistical Manual of Mental Disorders III–Revised* (*DSM–III–R*; American Psychiatric Association, 1987) includes not only anorexia and bulimia nervosa, but pica and rumination disorder of childhood as well. Briefly, pica is a disorder where children repeatedly eat nonnutritive substances, such as paint, plaster, animal droppings, or small rocks. In rumination disorder, the infant regurgitates partially digested food. The food may then be spit out, or chewed, and reswallowed. Severe malnutrition can result, and in some cases the disorder can be fatal. Though pica and rumination disorder are important clinical problems, they are not nearly as prevalent as anorexia and bulimia nervosa, nor do pica and rumination have an extensive prevalence of associated subclinical pathology as is reflected in anorexia and bulimia. Thus, this chapter focuses exclusively on anorexia and bulimia nervosa. Those readers interested in pica or rumination disorder are referred to recent reviews (Bell & Stein, 1992; Whitehead & Schuster, 1985).

The most prominent features of bulimia nervosa are frequent binge eating and purging behavior or other severe weight regulation measures such as fasting or extensive exercise primarily for weight control (American Psychiatric Association, 1987). Although persons not suffering with bulimia nervosa may at times binge, the frequency and size of the binges of a bulimic woman can be quite dramatic. Among persons seeking treatment, 10 to 12 binge episodes per week is common; however, there is great variability. Some patients binge only 2 to 3 times per week, others as often as 30 to 40 times. Although the size of the binge is quite variable, consumption of as much as 1300 calories is common, often consisting of cereals, grains, snack foods, and desserts. The high risk times for binges tend to be in the late afternoon or early evening, often after coming home from work or school or in association with the evening meal.

After binging, the bulimic woman engages in a "corrective" behavior, most often purging by self-inducing vomiting. Though occurring less frequently, purging by abusing laxatives is common, and occasionally the women use diuretics (i.e., water pills) in order to lose weight. Other frequently used forms of corrective behavior include skipping meals or fasting for a day in order to compensate for the binge or vigorously exercising in an attempt to "work off" the calories consumed in the binge (for a summary, see Mizes, 1985). Binge purge episodes are also characterized by intense emotions (Mizes & Arbitell, 1991). Feeling anxious or depressed before a binge is common, although many binges are preceded by a perceived violation of one's diet. After binging, strong anxiety and/or guilt is present, feelings that are substantially reduced by purging or engaging in other corrective behaviors. Bulimics also experience a marked overconcern with body weight or shape. This can be expressed in many ways. For example, whereas normal women wish to weigh on average about 11 pounds less than a statistically average weight for their age and height, bulimic women want to weigh nearly 18 pounds less (Mizes, 1992a).

Weight loss of 15% or more of expected weight is the most prominent feature of anorexia nervosa (American Psychiatric Association, 1987). Additionally, for women, three conaacutive menstrual periods should have been missed in order to meet the diagnostic criteria. Cessation of periods is due to loss of the amount of body fat necessary to maintain menstrual functioning. Anorectics express a pervasive fear of gaining weight and becoming fat and artfully dodge the attempts of others to encourage or coerce weight gain. Many anorectics fear that even a few pounds of weight gain, despite their emaciated condition, will lead to uncontrolled weight gain that will eventually result in massive obesity. Body image distortion is also present, reflecting negative attitudes about the body as well as misperceptions of the degree of "fatness." Anorectics often wish to weigh 30 pounds less than an expected average weight and become markedly fearful and self-critical if their weight rises even a pound or two above this unrealistic self standard (Mizes, 1992a). Although some anorectics acknowledge their thin, gaunt appearance, eating "forbidden" foods or slight increases in weight activate intense feelings that certain body parts, if not their whole body, is fat.

Although the *DSM-III-R* diagnostic criteria specify anorexia and bulimia as two separate entities, there is much overlap between the two disorders. Two subtypes of anorexia have long been described in the literature, though this had not been explicitly delineated in the *DSM-III-R* diagnostic criteria. One subtype is the *restricting anorectic*, who met the *DSM-III-R* diagnostic criteria for anorexia. The term comes from the marked restriction in eating behavior, often less than 500 calories per day. Such restriction of eating may be supplemented with purging or other corrective behavior including intense exercise. The bulimic subtype of anorexia combines the features of bulimia and anorexia nervosa, and under the older *DSM-II* diagnostic scheme, received both diagnoses. Thus, in addition to low weight, absent periods, and low food intake (separate from binges), the person experiences the marked binging and purging behavior characteristic of bulimia nervosa. The blurring of the two disorders is also evident in the fact that the same person may go through phases where she alternatively is anorectic, bulimic, or both (Yager, Landsverk, & Edelstein, 1987).

The third major eating category in *DSM-III-R* (American Psychiatric Association, 1987) is that of Eating Disorder Not Otherwise Specified (NOS). This is largely a "catch all" category for individuals with significant eating pathology who nonetheless do not meet all the criteria for either anorexia or bulimia. Research on a series of patients seeking treatment suggested that the persons diagnosed as NOS clustered in two groups (Mitchell, Pyle, Hatsukami, & Eckert, 1986). One group of "near bulimics" met all the criteria for bulimia nervosa, except that, rather than binging, they ate only small amounts of "forbidden" foods prior to purging. The second group of "near anorectics" either continued to have their periods and/or did not quite meet the weight loss criterion.

In *DSM-III-R*, the NOS category was also often used for a group clinically referred to as compulsive binge eaters (Mizes, 1993). Usually these patients were substantially overweight and binge ate frequently, however they did not engage in purging or other extreme corrective behaviors. In the process of revising the *Diagnostic and Statistical Manual*, the *DSM-IV* Work Group on Eating Disorders proposed a new diagnostic category labeled Binge Eating Disorder (BED; Soltzer et al., 1992). BED has been listed as a provisional diagnosis requiring further study in *DSM-IV* (American Psychiatric Association, 1994). Due to its provisional status, BED will continue to be listed as a specific example of Eating Disorder NOS. BED is defined by the presence of binge eating, specified to be the consumption of a larger than normal amount of food in a specific time period, as well as the person's subjective sense of loss of control of eating. The eating behavior also needs to reflect some behavioral indices of loss of control, such as eating rapidly or eating until uncomfortably full. Binges have to occur minimally twice weekly for 6 months, and the person has to experience distress about the eating binges.

In terms of other changes in the diagnostic scheme for eating disorders, new subclassifications for anorexia and bulimia have been adopted in *DSM–IV* (American Psychiatric Association, 1994). The suggestion that the criteria for anorexia include an anorexia nervosa-restrictor type and an anorexia nervosa-bulimic type (DaCosta & Halmi, 1992) has been adopted. This replaces the former practice, described previously, of diagnosing bulimic anorectics with both anorexia nervosa and bulimic nervosa. There has been dissenting opinion regarding the possible utility of subtypes of bulimia nervosa (Mitchell, 1992). Nonetheless, the *DSM–IV* classification for bulimia nervosa includes two subtypes: the purging subtype for those who vomit or use laxatives or diuretics; the nonpurging subtype for those who use "compensatory behaviors" including fostery, excessive exercise, or diet pills.

In addition to the specific diagnostic features of anorexia and bulimia, both disorders are associated with patterns of general psychological characteristics, as well as often co-occur with other specific psychological disorders such as depression (Mizes, 1994). Bulimics tend to be concerned about receiving approval from others, have high personal expectations for achievement or performance, tend to be concerned about approval, and have perfectionistic self-expectations. However, anorectics tend to be socially and emotionally withdrawn, and they tend to deny the presence of a problem and often resist or refuse treatment. Initial research suggests that bulimics often have other specific disorders, such as depressive disorders, anxiety disorders, and personality disorders. Though much less research is available, anorectics seem to frequently suffer from these same problems. However, it is possible that anorectics and bulimics tend to experience different anxiety and personality disorders, though it is too early to make firm conclusions.

CAUSES OF THE DISORDERS

Although research into the causes of eating disorders is in its infancy, sociocultural, psychological, and biological variables appear to contribute to the etiology of anorexia and bulimia nervosa. This section addresses societal factors relating to cultural expectations for thinness, psychological variables including the onset of dieting, body dissatisfaction, and psychological distress, and the biologic variable of weight gain. The contribution of family functioning, genetics, and biologic risk factors are discussed in later sections.

There is extensive evidence that Western culture strongly values physical attractiveness and defines this in terms of thinness. Furthermore, there is a corresponding denigration of obesity (Striegel-Moore, Silberstein, & Rodin, 1986). These attitudes start as early as elementary school and continue well into the adult years. The pressures for attractiveness via thinness are strongest for females. Consistent with these pressures, women rate it as much more important to maintain or achieve their self-stated ideal weight than do men (Klesges et al., 1987). It is difficult to link specific societal factors as directly causing eating disorders. However, there has been speculation about the increasingly extreme thinness standard and the presumed increased prevalence of eating disorders. In one of the most frequently cited studies (Garner, Garfinkel, Schwartz, & Thompson, 1980), the more stringent thinness standard is shown in the increasingly thinner female ideal as reflected in the stature of Playboy centerfolds and Miss America Pageant contestants over the 20 years spanning the 1960s and 1970s. Correspondingly, there has been an increased frequency of dieting articles in women's magazines during the same period.

The differences in cultural approaches to body weight are illustrated by a few personal experiences. A few months after my marriage, I ran into a Jamaican colleague. She noted that marriage must be agreeing with me, as I was looking good, had on a new suit, and had gained weight! After noting in jest that her comment about my weight balanced out her compliment about my suit, she exclaimed, "You Americans are all alike, you all worry about your weight." She went on to explain that in her culture, where poverty is common, gaining weight was a sign that you were prospering and doing well, rather than having barely enough food to get by. Thus, weight gain for a newlywed was a sign that the marriage was prospering. Similarly, in another experience, a visiting Greek professor described his culture as also viewing weight as a sign of prosperity. He relayed that Greek parents often lie about the birth weight of their children, stating that they were heavier than the actually were.

Sociocultural influences have also been examined in segments of Western culture that place an even more extreme emphasis on thinness. For example, in a series of studies on ballet dancers by Brooks-Gunn and colleagues (cf. Attie & Brooks-Gunn, 1992), they have found clinically severe eating disorders in about one third of ballerinas. Increased eating pathology in women athletes has been shown in sports that emphasize thinness. In a study of competitive adolescent female figure skaters, swimmers, ballet dancers, and nonathletes, it was found that skaters and dancers weighed less than swimmers and nonathletes, and they also had more pathological eating attitudes. This is consistent with the greater thinness pressures for dancers and skaters.

Only since the late 1980s have there been any longitudinal studies of factors potentially associated with the development of subclinical eating disturbances or eating disorders. Patton (1988) assessed a large group of London school girls twice over the course of a year. Patton found that most of the adolescent girls who dieted did not later develop clinical eating disorders. However, those girls who did develop eating disorders had previously engaged in otherwise normal dieting. Weight gain was the strongest predictor of level of eating pathology at the end of the study. Another study assessed adolescent girls over a 4-month period (Rosen, Tacy, & Howell, 1990). It was found that weight reducing behavior predicted development of psychological stress. However, psychological stress and symptoms did not predict eventual onset of weight reducing behavior. Thus, dieting appears to have a key causal role rather than being one type of eating pathology resulting from psychological distress or symptoms. A study of college freshman at the beginning and end of the academic year examined variables associated with worsening of eating symptoms (Striegel-Moore, Silberstein, Frensch, & Rodin, 1989). Several weight-related variables were quite predictive, especially negative feelings about one's body. Other weight related variables that were predictive were feeling less attractive, increased body weight, and increased body dissatisfaction. Additional variables included feeling stressed and ineffective. In a 2-year study of young adolescent girls (Attie & Brooks-Gunn, 1989), only body image predicted changes in level of eating pathology over the course of the study.

These studies suggest that changes in weight, negative attitudes about the body, and dieting could potentially put someone at-risk to progress along a path that could result in an eating disorder. It is not clear what variables determine how far one proceeds down this path. Regarding weight change and relative weight, it has been noted that females are confronted with unique challenges (Striegel-Moore et al., 1986). The normal course of physical maturation for girls is to gain weight, primarily in fat, during puberty. This occurs at a time when girls are showing an increased interest in dating, which is crucial to the young girl due to the relative importance that females place on interpersonal relationships as a component of self-esteem. After puberty, the normal circumstance is for women to have a substantially higher percentage of body fat than do men. They also have lower metabolic rates than do men and thus need to consume fewer calories to maintain their weight. All of these factors pit women's biology against a thinness standard that is usually below statistically average weights.

COURSE OF THE DISORDERS

Bulimia nervosa barely qualifies as a disorder that usually begins in adolescence, as the average age of onset is about age 21 (Kendler et al., 1991). However, approximately 68% of cases of bulimia nervosa start between age 15 and 27. Thus, a substantial number do begin in adolescence. Though research is sparse, it appears that bulimia tends to alternatively worsen and abate over several years if left untreated (Drewnowski & Garn, 1987). However, this chronic course may be representative of those persons with severe enough symptoms to have sought treatment. Little is known about those who do not seek treatment. However, there is some anecdotal evidence that at least some people have brief, time-limited bulimia of moderate levels.

A recent study of the course of bulimia following treatment illustrates the waxing and waning course (Drewnowski & Garn, 1987). Over the course of 3 to 4 years, about 70% had at least one period of recovery, with most of those occurring in the first year after treatment. However, relapse after recovery was frequent, with 60% relapsing within a year. Even during periods of improvement, one third of bulimic patients showed subclinical eating disturbance, such as chronic dieting or compulsive exercise.

Because bulimia nervosa was formally identified as a diagnostic entity only in 1980 (American Psychiatric Association, 1980), little is known about the course over the span of decades nor about factors that predict the severity of the course. Factors suggested to be associated with poor treatment outcome include chemical abuse, borderline personality disorder, and severe body image disturbance (Mizes, in press-b). Depression is inconsistently related to treatment outcome, and there is no information on the effect of anxiety disorders on treatment outcome. In general, duration of the bulimia, frequency of binging and purging, and history of anorexia have not been associated with response to treatment. However, factors that affect response to treatment can only suggest factors that lead to a more chronic and severe course in the absence of treatment.

Anorexia nervosa is more clearly a disorder that begins in adolescence. The average age of first onset is about 17, with 68% of the cases beginning between ages 14 and 20 (Willi, Giacometti, & Limacher, 1990). However, anorexia can begin in adulthood, well into the twenties and thirties. Theander (1985) presented observations of the course of anorexia nervosa, spanning a period of 30 years on average. Anorexia appears be a chronic and refractory disorder, though there is a trend toward gradual improvement over several years. After 24 years, Theander found that three quarters of the anorectics had improved, with most of the recoveries occurring in the first 12 years. However, those who had improved were far from "cured," as most continued to have a pronounced preoccupation with weight and dieting. Unfortunately, 6% of the patients continued to have severe symptoms even after 30 years. Unlike bulimia, anorexia nervosa frequently results in death. In Theander's study, 8% of the anorectics had died in the first 5 years. After 30 years had passed, Theander found that 18% of the anorectics had died, two thirds from anorexia and the remainder from suicide. Patients who die of anorexia tend to die of complications such as heart failure rather than starvation per se. Heart failure can occur due to loss of heart muscle tissue because of starvation, via ingesting ipecac syrup to induce vomiting or due to electrolyte imbalances caused by vomiting or abuse of laxatives or diuretics. Recent improvements in hospital treatment to increase body weight appears to have resulted in lower initial death rates in the last several years.

FAMILIAL CONTRIBUTIONS

Early accounts of the clinical presentation of anorexia nervosa vividly described pathological patterns in these patients' families. Additionally, these early writings attempted to relate the observed family pathology to the etiology of anorexia nervosa. Influential writings by psychodymanic and family systems theorists emphasized difficulties the anorectic adolescents had in the developmental task of separating from the family and becoming autonomous (Strober & Humphrey, 1987). Consistent with this, families of anorectics were described as enmeshed. That is, mothers in particular were considered to be intrusively overinvolved in their daughters' lives, with inadequate boundaries between mother and daughter and a lack of opportunities for the development of the daughters' autonomy. Family therapy perspectives in particular highlighted the proposed role of the anorectic's symptoms in maintaining a pathological family structure by diverting family attention toward her problems and away from parental conflicts. Compared to anorexia, relatively little has been done to offer theoretical accounts of the family pathology and potential etiologic influences in bulimia nervosa, though a few writings have appeared in the past few years (Wonderlich, 1992).

In general, the modest number of research studies has suggested that families of eating disordered patients do tend to have more family distress than normal families. However, this research has not clearly supported the specific hypotheses regarding family pathology offered by psychodynamic and family theorists. For example, in a study assessing predictions from family systems theory (Kog, Vandereycken, & Vertommen, 1985), only the behavior pattern of enmeshment was found to be common in the families studied. In general, families of anorectics and bulimics tend to have more hostility and difficulty resolving conflict, less support and nurturance, more enmeshment, and more of a sense of isolation and noncohesiveness within the family (Strober & Humphrey, 1987; Wonderlich, 1992).

In viewing these general descriptors of the families of eating disordered persons, it is important to note that there is much variation in the pattern of pathology in individual families, if it indeed exists. Many families are normal in their level of functioning. For example, a recent study of nondepressed bulimic patients found that they did not perceive their families as more distressed than did a nonpsychiatric comparison group (Blouin, Zuro, & Blouin, 1990). Among those families suffering with dysfunctional patterns, some may have had pathology that predated the development of the daughter's eating disorder. In others, the pathology may be, in part, a response to it. For example, many parents, particularly those of anorectics, are frightened by the potentially dire consequences of their daughter's disorder. Not knowing what to do, they resort to ineffective and often hostile and coercive strategies to try to get their daughter to eat.

In contrast to psychodynamic and family systems perspectives that hypothesize a strong etiologic role of family pathology in eating disorders, recent research suggests a diminished causal role for family pathology. Crowther and Mizes (1992) discussed a heuristic that suggests examination of variables related to the development of core eating disorder symptoms and inspection of different variables casually related to associated psychopathology and comorbid conditions. Several recent studies have compared the families of eating disordered patients with a specific comorbid disorder to those without the comorbid condition. In general, the patients with a comorbid disorder have more family pathology, whereas those without the comorbid disorder have family functioning that is very similar to normal families. This has been found for eating disordered patients with and without borderline personality disorder (Johnson, Tobin, & Enright, 1989; Wonderlich, & Swift, 1990) and depression (Blouin et al. 1990). Importantly, the level of eating disorder symptoms has been the same in the patients with and without the comorbid disorder. Other studies have shown that the level of family disturbance is related to level of personality disturbance in eating disordered patients but is unrelated to level of eating pathology (Head & Williamson, 1990; Steiger, Liquornik, Chapman, & Hussain, 1991). Thus, family pathology may be more casually related to the presence of associated psychopathology or comorbid conditions rather than to the core eating disorder symptoms per se. It is important to keep in mind that this maybe true for the broad family variables (e.g., conflictual, enmeshed, etc.) that have been examined to date. It is possible that other family variables, such as specific attitudes and behaviors regarding food and weight, are directly related to the development of eating disorder symptoms. However, such possibilities have not yet received research attention.

PSYCHOPHYSIOLOGICAL AND GENETIC INFLUENCES

Both anorexia and bulimia result in medical complications, although physical problems are more prominent in anorexia. Bulimics can potentially suffer from a number of physical complaints (see Mitchell, Specker, & de Zwaan, 1991; Mizes, 1993). However, most of these are not life threatening and most bulimics suffer from only a few of these difficulties. General problems include fatigue, lethargy, weakness, bloating while eating, dizziness, faintness, and puffy cheeks. Vomiting may lead to sore throats, dental cavities, or wearing away of tooth enamel. Use of laxatives may result in chronic constipation. Purging behavior, including vomiting, laxatives, and diuretics, can result in potassium loss. This condition, called hypokalemia, can be serious. At mild levels, it results in fatigue and lethargy. However, at more severe levels, irregular heart beats and heart failure can occur. Purging can also lead to dehydration, and marked dehydration can be medically serious. Irregular periods may occur, which is likely due to low body fat or wide fluctuations in food intake.

Anorectics who binge and purge can develop the symptoms listed previously. However, anorectics also suffer from a variety of medical symptoms due to the effects of starvation (for a summary, see Kaplan & Woodside, 1987). Their skin is often dry and cracked, there may be a blue cast to their hands and feet due to inadequate blood flow to the extremities, and a fine, downy hair (lanugo hair) may develop. Heart rate is often slowed, and blood pressure may be low. Orthostatic hypotension, a drop in blood pressure upon standing, may occur. Delayed emptying of ingested food from the stomach after eating may occur, as well as constipation. Periods stop due to the loss of the necessary body fat needed for menstruation. Ammenorhea is associated with marked changes in the hormones that control menstruation and ovulation, with the anorectic's hormone functioning reverting to that seen in prepubertal or pubertal girls. Body temperature may be reduced, and coldness may be experienced in the hands and feet in particular. Due to the loss of muscle tissue, muscle weakness is often present. Osteoporosis and bone fractures can occur, and onset of anorexia before reaching physical maturity can cause stunted growth. Starvation can lead to distinct psychological changes including preoccupation with food, irritability, fluctuating emotions, and decreased concentration and alertness. These factors may make it difficult if not impossible for the person to benefit from psychotherapy until refeeding and substantial restoration of weight has occurred.

Anorectics show a variety of abnormalities in neuroendocrine functioning. Rather than being causes of anorexia, they appear to be due to the effects of starvation because these changes return to normal once weight is gained (Yates, 1989). There has been recent research suggesting biologic abnormalities that may be risk factors for bulimia. These abnormalities are in systems involved in the regulation of appetite and feeding (Kaye & Weltzin, 1991). Bulimics have shown excesses of peptide YY, that stimulates eating behavior. They have also shown decreased cholecystokinin, a peptide that reduces or stops eating. Research has suggested that bulimics have altered neurotransmitter function, specifically in serotonin (which inhibits eating) and in norepinephrine (which initiates eating). Though these biologic abnormalities have been suggested as contributing to the development of bulimia, it is possible that they are the result of chronic binging and vomiting or other eating irregularities.

Recent research reviews (Drewnowski & Garn, 1987; Strober, 1991) show that eating disorders tend to run in families, suggesting a genetic influence in etiology. A higher than expected rate of eating and weight difficulties has been reported in the parents of anorectics. In one study, a broad range of related difficulties (low adolescent weight, weight phobias, and anorexia nervosa) was found in 27% of the mothers and 16% of the fathers (Kalucy, Crisp, & Harding, 1977). More specific near-anorexia difficulties were found in 16% of the mothers and 11% of the fathers. Other research shows that female siblings of anorectics are more likely to develop anorexia; this occurs approximately 3% to 10% of the time. There appears to be a shared risk for transmission of anorexia and bulimia. Relatives of anorectics have shown an increased risk for both anorexia and bulimia. Approximately 2% to 4% of first degree relatives of anorectics have suffered from anorexia, and a similar number have had bulimia nervosa. Similarly, first degree relatives of bulimics have shown a substantial increased risk of bulimia and anorexia, with 9.6% having had bulimia and 2.2% having had anorexia (Kassett, Gershon, & Maxwell, 1989).

Twin studies have strongly suggested a genetic component to eating disorders. Among female identical twins, the sister of the anoretic also has the disorder 44% to 50% of the time. Anorexia nervosa occurs in both of nonidentical fraternal twins about 7% of the time, which is about the same rate as for nontwin sisters. Kendler et al.

(1991) reported one of the best studies of twins in eating disorders, notable because of the large sample (2000 plus female twins). For identical twins, both had bulimia nervosa 29% of the time, whereas for fraternal twins both had the disorder only 9% of the time. These authors estimated that 55% of the risk for bulimia came from genetic rather than sociocultural or psychological factors.

Though the studies are few, a genetic risk for the development of eating disorders appears to be present. However, there are no data on which inherited vulnerability confers this risk. Strober (1991) suggested that, at least for anorexia, the vulnerability is due to the heritability of dispositional traits. He suggested that these dispositions include cognitive rigidity, vigilance toward harm avoidance, and a tendency toward anxious and depressed worry. The accuracy of this speculation awaits verification.

CURRENT TREATMENTS

Studies on the treatment of bulimia nervosa have been primarily on young adult women. Thus, the description of treatments of bulimia assumes that these interventions can be applied to adolescents. The vast majority of studies have been of cognitive–behavioral treatments, which have been shown to be effective with little relapse after improvement (Garner, Fairburn, & Davis, 1987; Hartmann, Herzog, & Drinkman, 1992: Agras, 1991). In general, patients reduce their frequency of binging and purging by 75% to 80%, with about 30% to 40% stopping binging and purging altogether. Unfortunately, 25% to 30% of patients drop out of treatment.

Treatments have included individual and group therapy formats. Generally, the situations that are associated with binge purge episodes are examined (such as time of day, upsetting emotions, interpersonal stressors). The examination occurs via self-monitoring of food intake and sets the stage for developing alternative coping strategies. A specific emphasis is placed on making concrete changes in eating behaviors, with the goal of reducing restrictive dieting and restoring nutritional balance. Patients are also helped to reduce a variety of rigid food rules, correct inaccurate beliefs about food and body weight, decrease their extreme emphasis on body weight and shape as a basis of self-esteem and approval from others, and decrease their belief that their self-control of food and weight increases their self-worth. Modification of these beliefs is thought to be necessary because of evidence showing their prominence in the thought processes of bulimics and anorectics (Garner & Bemis, 1982; Mizes, 1988, 1992b).

Exposure and response prevention (ERP) has been successfully used for bulimia (Rosen & Leitenberg, 1985) and is drawn from the cognitive behavioral treatment of anxiety disorders. Its use is based on a view that emphasizes the fear-of-weight-gain aspect of bulimia nervosa. The basic idea in ERP is to repeatedly expose the persons to the situation they fear, prevent their avoidance response, and gradually allow their fear to diminish. ERP applied to bulimia involves having the patients eat "forbidden foods" while refraining from purging. With repeated exposures, the patients find that their anxiety after eating is diminished or eliminated, thus there is no need to purge. Though effective, a notable minority of patients refuse ERP, and it is unclear if it is a necessary addition to the cognitive–behavioral approaches described previously (Agras, 1991).

Various antidepressant medications are about equally as effective in reducing binging and purging in bulimia as is psychotherapy (Walsh, 1991). However, relapse after stopping the medication is a problem, and some patients cannot or will not take the antidepressants because of side effects (Mizes, 1993). Combining psychotherapy and antidepressant medications does not seem to result in greater reductions in binging and purging but may lead to greater improvement in food preoccupation and depression (Agras, 1991; Agras et al., 1992).

The case of Erica illustrates the use of cognitive–behavior therapy in treating bulimia nervosa. Erica (age 27) began binge eating at age 15 and vomiting at 16. She averaged 4 binge episodes per week, and she vomited 2 times per month, representing a case of moderate severity. Though previously overweight, she was presently of normal weight. However, she wanted to weigh 14 pounds less than her medically acceptable average weight. In the previous year, she had been treated for moderate depression via psychotherapy and antidepressant medication. At least part of her depression was related to her low self-esteem due to self-criticism for being "fat," and loneliness due to her withdrawal from others because of her embarrassment about her weight.

In treatment, Erica kept self-monitoring records of her eating behavior. They showed that she was more likely to binge, and sometimes purge, when she violated one of her rigid food rules (such as having a candy bar at work). She would criticize herself for being "weak and a failure" and would come home and binge. Binging often occurred on nights that her husband was working, and she would reduce her eating during the day in anticipation of this. The main changes in her eating behavior were to stop reducing food intake prior to an anticipated binge, to regularly eat previously forbidden foods, and to practice eating larger meals to increase her tolerance for feeling full. She was also instructed to resist the urge to vomit, so that she could observe that the urge to vomit would pass. Several strategies were utilized to change her eating disordered attitudes. She was given correct nutritional information, such as the importance of genetics in determining one's body weight. She was also helped to value herself more for her desirable personal characteristics rather than for weight and appearance. Toward the end of treatment, she began to think that her current weight was acceptable. Her binges and purges dropped to zero, an improvement that was maintained at a 2-month follow-up visit. Her depression also improved, mainly due to her significantly decreased self-criticism.

As compared to bulimia nervosa, much less is known from the research literature about the treatment of anorexia nervosa. More is know about techniques for achieving short-term weight restoration, whereas little is known about effective psychotherapy approaches. A major hurdle for any treatment approach is to overcome the marked resistance to treatment that anorectics often exhibit. The cooperation of the anorectic is made more likely by not challenging her desire for extreme thinness and her self-perception of fatness directly, as this can quickly become confrontational. Rather, the focus should be on her distress about the effects of her disorder, such as depression, physical problems, the burden of extreme food and weight preoccupation and associated rituals, and the effects on family members (Hsu, 1986).

In general, techniques for restoration of weight in an inpatient hospital setting are successful with about 80% of patients over the short term (Hsu, 1986). However, little is known about long-term effectiveness, though relapse occurs in about 50% of patients. Also, although weight may have improved, many significant aspects of the disorder are often continue to persist. A typical treatment program includes a behavior modification component where weekly weight gain of 2 to 3 pounds per week is needed to earn various privileges on the ward (Yates, 1990), such as visiting privileges, access to social activities, or access to moderate physical activities. Occasionally, contingent bed rest for not gaining weight is used (Hsu, 1986). Patients are usually weighed a few times to once a week, before breakfast and in a hospital gown, in order to minimize the patients' attempts to manipulate their weight. The nutritional plan (Yates, 1990) has the patient initially eating 1200 to 1500 calories per day, with a gradual increase in the calories per day in 500 to 750 calorie increments. Often, patients need to eat 3500 to 5000 calories per day in order to show steady weight gain. Typically, a discharge weight is set, often between 80% to 95% of the patient's expected average weight. Recently there has been an increased trend toward conducting these programs on an outpatient rather than inpatient basis when possible (Bemis, 1987).

Most writers feel that psychotherapy is also important in the treatment of anorexia (Hsu, 1986). However, due to the cognitive effects of starvation, psychotherapy is usually difficult at best until some normalization of eating and weight gain has occurred. Psychodynamic theorists usually recommend that treatment focus on the anorectic's pervasive perfectionism, extreme self-criticism and doubt, and her belief that her worth depends on others' approval (Hsu, 1986). Garner and Bemis (1982) outlined a cognitive–behavioral approach to treatment that emphasizes changing basic maladaptive attitudes, including beliefs about excessively rigid regulation of food and weight, the extreme importance of weight and shape to determining self-worth, and the need for exaggerated self-control or "will power" over eating and weight. One preliminary study of a limited number of patients suggests that cognitive–behavioral techniques may be helpful with at least some anorectic patients (Cooper & Fairburn, 1984).

The case of Becky, a severe anorectic, illustrates some of the difficulties in treating these patients. Becky (age 16) had suffered from anorexia nervosa for 3 years. She was 5'3" tall, and weighed 75 pounds, as compared to an expected average weight of 115 pounds. Her eating was limited to a small breakfast, an apple for lunch, and a piece of bread and some vegetables for dinner. She had seen several previous therapists and had been hospitalized twice without benefit for weight restoration. Previous outpatient therapy had not been helpful. In fact, the patient had refused to talk to the last therapist she saw, and she had found something wrong with all of her previous therapists causing her to prematurely terminate therapy. Becky was a straight "A" student and had previously been a competitive gymnast. Her parents were concerned that she pushed herself very hard in school, despite their requests that she relax and accept a few "Bs" and enjoy more social activities. Interviews with the parents, as well as psychological testing, revealed that the parents currently suffered from no notable psychological problems. However, one parent previously suffered from major depression. Interestingly, the patient's older sister, who was "driven" scholastically, also had previously suffered a brief period of near-anorexia nervosa.

Despite their initial resistance, the parents reluctantly agreed to an outpatient behavior modification contract for their daughter to achieve weight gain. Despite attempts, the patient refused to participate in the development of the contract. The contract specified 2 pounds a week as the weight gain goal, with a goal weight of 92 pounds. The contract was presented to the patient and family as a trial to see if outpatient treatment could be effective, in lieu of more intensive inpatient treatment. Thus, the contract specified that not reaching the weekly weight goal would indicate that outpatient treatment was not working and that hospitalization was needed. The patient did not respond to attempts to incorporate positive rewards into the contract. Her initial suggested daily calorie level was 1500 calories, which the patient and her parents gradually increased to about 3000 calories. During twice a week psychotherapy, her extreme self-criticism and sense of worthlessness were explored. However, she remained extremely resistant to any weight gain. Her parents were seen once weekly for adjunct treatment. The patient's weight increased from 78 to 90 pounds. However, she did not meet the final weight goal in the last week of the contract. In part, this was because her parents wavered in their commitment to hospitalize her, and they refused to write a new outpatient contract to continue her weight gain. As had happened with previous therapists, the patient convinced her parents that she could not work with the current psychologist, and they switched to yet another therapist.

SUMMARY

Anorexia and bulimia nervosa are fascinating disorders, and they have received much media attention. Several well-known public personalities have suffered with one or both disorders. It is likely that many public personalities have also suffered from other psychological disorders that are prevalent in the general population. However, they do not appear to draw the same media attention. Perhaps this heightened media focus is a reflection of our own fears about weight and insecurities in self-esteem. This allows us to identify more deeply with the struggles of the anorectic or bulimic, than say with a schizophrenic whose experiences are foreign to our own.

Both anorexia and bulimia appear to be chronic disorders among the population that seeks treatment. There appears to be a gradual improvement over several years, though this improvement does not usually result in remission. A substantial minority have very chronic symptoms with little improvement, and for anorectics, the outcome can be death. Eating disorders are most assuredly multidetermined, with societal, psychological, and biological risk factors. Though much attention has been given to societal factors, such as the cultural thinness preoccupation, recent research suggests a much stronger role for a genetic predisposition to eating disorders than previously thought. Work on physiologic abnormalities in eating disorders may clarify the nature of the genetic predisposition. In particular, research on abnormalities in the neurochemisty of bulimics' feeding systems may hold promise. Psychological risk factors have only barely been examined. Exploration of psychological risk factors may be assisted by distinguishing between variables associated with development of the core psychopathology of eating disorders versus those associated with emergence of secondary psychopathology or cooccurring conditions.

On a note of optimism and hope, psychotherapy and medication treatments have been developed that result in substantial improvements in two thirds to three fourths of bulimics, with one third becoming binge and purge free. There is still substantial room, however, for treatments to improve. On the other hand, treatment of anorexia nervosa is discouraging. Though short-term weight gain can often be achieved via hospitalization, relapse is common. There is little scientific evidence regarding effective psychotherapy approaches for anorexia nervosa.

REFERENCES

Agras, W. S. (1991). Nonpharmacological treatments of bulimia nervosa. *Journal of Clinical Psychiatry, 52,* 29–33.

Agras, W. S., Rossiter, E. M., Arnow, B., Schneider, J. A., Telch, C. F., Raeburn, S. D., Bruce, B., Perl, M., & Koran, L. M. (1992). Pharmacologic and cognitive–behavioral treatment for bulimia nervosa: A controlled comparison. *American Journal of Psychiatry, 149,* 82–87.

American Psychiatry Association. (1980). *Diagnostic and statistical manual of mental disorders* (3rd ed.). Washington, DC: Author.

American Psychiatric Association. (1987). *Diagnostic and statistical manual of mental disorders–Revised* (3rd rev. ed.). Washington, DC: Author.

American Psychiatric Association. (1994). *Diagnostic and statistical manual of mental disorder* (4th ed.). Washington, DC: Author.

Attie, I., & Brooks-Gunn, J. (1989). The development of eating problems in adolescent girls: A longitudinal study. *Developmental Psychology, 25,* 70–79.

Attie, I., & Brooks-Gunn, J. (1992). Developmental issues in the study of eating problems and eating disorders. In J. H. Crowther, D. L. Tennenbaum, S. E. Hobfoll, & M. A. P. Stephens (Eds.), *The etiology of bulimia nervosa: The individual and familial context* (pp. 35–58). Washington, DC: Hemisphere.

Bell, K. E., & Stein, D. M. (1992). Behavioral treatments for Pica: A review of empirical studies. *International Journal of Eating Disorders, 11,* 377–390.

Bemis, K. M. (1987). The present status of operant conditioning for the treatment of anorexia nervosa. *Behavior Modification, 11,* 432–463.

Blouin, A. G., Zuro, C., & Blouin, J. H. (1990). Family environment in bulimia nervosa: The role of depression. *International Journal of Eating Disorders, 9,* 649–658.

Cooper, P. J., & Fairburn, C. G. (1984). Cognitive behavior therapy for anorexia nervosa: Some preliminary findings. *Journal of Psychosomatic Research, 28,* 493–499.

Crowther, J. H., & Mizes, J. S. (1992). Etiology of bulimia nervosa: Conceptual, research, and measurement issues. In J. H. Crowther, D. L. Tennebaum, S. E. Hobfoll, & M. A. P. Stephens (Eds.). *The etiology of bulimia nervosa: The individual and familial context* (pp. 225–244). Washington, DC: Hemisphere.

DaCosta, M., & Halmi, K. A. (1992). Classification of anorexia nervosa: Question of subtypes. *International Journal of Eating Disorders, 11,* 305–314.

Drewnowski, A., & Garn, S. M. (1987). Concerning the use of weight tables to categorize patients with eating disorders. *International Journal of Eating Disorders, 6,* 639–646.

Garner, D. M., & Bemis, K. M. (1982). A cognitive–behavioral approach to anorexia nervosa. *Cognitive Therapy and Research, 6,* 123–150.

Garner, D. M., Fairburn, C. G., & Davis, R. (1987). Cognitive–behavioral treatment of bulimia nervosa: A critical appraisal. *Behavior Modification, 11,* 398–431.

Garner, D. M., Garfinkel, P. E., Schwartz, D., & Thompson, M. (1980). Cultural expectations of thinness in women. *Psychological Reports, 47,* 483–491.

Hartmann, A., Herzog, T., & Drinkman, A. (1992). Psychotherapy of bulimia nervosa: What is effective? A meta-analysis. *Journal of Psychosomatic Research, 36,* 159–167.

Head, S. B., & Williamson, D. A. (1990). Association of family environment and personality disturbances in bulimia nervosa. *International Journal of Eating Disorders, 9,* 667–674.

Hsu, L. K. G. (1986). The treatment of anorexia nervosa. *American Journal of Psychiatry, 143,* 573–581.

Johnson, C., Tobin, D., & Enright, A. (1989). Prevalence and clinical characteristics of borderline patients in an eating disordered population. *Journal of Clinical Psychiatry, 50,* 9–15.

Kalucy, R. S., Crisp, A. H., & Harding, B. (1977). A study of 56 families with anorexia nervosa. *British Journal of Medical Psychology, 50,* 381–395.

Kaplan, A. S., & Woodside, D. B. (1987). Biological aspects of anorexia nervosa and bulimia nervosa. *Journal of Consulting and Clinical Psychology, 55,* 645–653.

Kassett, J. A., Gershon, E. S., & Maxwell, M. E. (1989). Psychiatric disorders in the first-degree relatives of probands with bulimia nervosa. *American Journal of Psychiatry, 146,* 1468–1471.

Kaye, W., & Weltzin, T. (1991). Neurochemistry of bulimia nervosa. *Journal of Clinical Psychiatry, 52,* 21–28.

Kendler, K. S., MacLean, C., Neale, M., Kessler, R., Heath, A., & Eaves, L. (1991). The genetic epidemiology of bulimia nervosa. *American Journal of Psychiatry, 148,* 1627–1637.

Klesges, R. C., Mizes, J. S., & Klesges, L. M. (1987). Self-help dieting strategies in college males and females. *International Journal of Eating Disorders, 6,* 409–417.

Kog, E., Vandereycken, W., & Vertommen, H. (1985). Towards a verification of the psychosomatic family model: A pilot study of ten families with an anorexia/bulimia nervosa patient. *International Journal of Eating Disorders, 4,* 525–538.

Mitchell, J. E. (1992). Subtyping of bulimia nervosa. *International Journal of Eating Disorders, 11,* 327–332.

Mitchell, J. E., Pyle, R. L., Hatsukami, D., & Eckert, E. D. (1986). What are atypical eating disorders? *Psychosomatics, 27,* 21–28.

Mitchell, J. E., Specker, S. M., & de Zwaan, M. (1991). Comorbidity and medical complications of bulimia nervosa. *Journal of Clinical Psychiatry, 52* (Suppl. 10), 13–20.

Mizes, J. S. (1985). Bulimia: A review of its symptomatology and treatment. *Advances in Behavior Research and Therapy, 7,* 91–142.

Mizes, J. S. (1988). Personality characteristics of bulimic and non-eating-disordered female controls: A cognitive behavioral perspective. *International Journal of Eating Disorders, 7,* 541–550.

Mizes, J. S. (1992a). The Body Image Detection Device versus subjective measures of weight dissatisfaction: A validity comparison. *Addictive Behaviors, 17,* 125–136.

Mizes, J. S. (1992b). Validity of the Mizes Anorectic Cognitions scale: A comparison between anorectics, bulimics, and psychiatric controls. *Addictive Behaviors, 17,* 283–289.

Mizes, J. S. (1993). Bulimia nervosa. In A. S. Bellack & M. Hersen (Eds.), *Handbook of behavior therapy in the psychiatric setting.* New York: Plenum.

Mizes, J. S. (1994). Eating disorders. In V. B. Van Hasselt & M. Hersen (Eds.), *Advanced Abnormal Psychology.* New York: Plenum.

Mizes, J. S., & Arbitell, M. R. (1991). Bulimics' perceptions of emotional responding during binge–purge episodes. *Psychological Reports, 69,* 527–532.

Patton, G. C. (1988). The spectrum of eating disorder in adolescence. *Journal of Psychosomatic Research, 32,* 579–584.

Polivy, J., & Herman, C. P. (1987). Diagnosis and treatment of normal eating. *Journal of Consulting and Clinical Psychology, 55,* 635–644.

Rodin, J., Silberstein, L., & Striegel-Moore, R. (1984). Women and weight: A normative discontent. In T. B. Sonderegger (Ed.), *Psychology and gender: Nebraska symposium on motivation* (pp. 267–307). Lincoln, NE: University of Nebraska Press.

Rosen, J. C., & Leitenberg, H. (1985). Exposure plus response prevention treatment of bulimia. In D. M. Garner & P. E. Garfinkel (Eds.), *Handbook of psychotherapy for anorexia nervosa and bulimia* (pp. 193–209). New York: Guilford.

Rosen, J. C., Tacy, B., & Howell, D. (1990). Life stress, psychological symptoms and weight reducing behavior in adolescent girls: A prospective analysis. *International Journal of Eating Disorders, 9,* 17–26.

Spitzer, R. L., Devlin, M., Walsh, B. T., Hasin, D., Wing, R., Marcus, M., Stunkard, A., Wadden, T., Yanovski, S., Agras, S., Mitchell, J., & Nonas, C. (1992). Binge eating disorder: A multisite field trial of the diagnostic criteria. *International Journal of Eating Disorders, 11,* 191–204.

Sporkin, E., Wagner, J., & Tomashoff, C. (1992, February). A terrible hunger. *People,* 92–98.

Steiger, H., Liquornik, K., Chapman, J., & Hussain, N. (1991). Personality and family disturbances in eating-disorder patients: Comparison of "Restricters" and "Bingers" to normal controls. *International Journal of Eating Disorders, 10,* 501–512.

Striegel-Moore, R. H., Silberstein, L. R., Frensch, P., & Rodin, J. (1989). A prospective study of disordered eating among college students. *International Journal of Eating Disorders, 8,* 499–509.

Striegel-Moore, R. H., Silberstein, L. R., & Rodin, J. (1986). Toward an understanding of risk factors for bulimia. *American Psychologist, 41,* 246–263.

Strober, M. (1991). Family-genetic studies of eating disorders. *Journal of Clinical Psychiatry, 52* (Suppl. 10), 9–12.

Strober, M., & Humphrey, L. L. (1987). Familial contributions to the etiology and course of anorexia nervosa and bulimia. *Journal of Consulting and Clinical Psychology, 55,* 654–659.

Szmukler, G. I. (1985). The epidemiology of anorexia nervosa and bulimia. *Journal of Psychiatric Research, 19,* 143–153.

Theander, S. (1985). Outcome and prognosis in anorexia nervosa and bulimia: Some results of previous investigations, compared with those of a Swedish long-term study. *Journal of Psychiatric Research*, *19*, 493–508.

Thelen, M., Lawrence, C. M., & Powell, A. (1992). Body image, weight control, and eating disorders among children. In J. H. Crowther, D. L. Tennebaum, S. E. Hobfoll, & M. A. P. Stephens (Eds.), *The etiology of bulimia nervosa: The individual and familial context* (pp. 82–102). Washington, DC: Hemisphere.

Walsh, B. T. (1991). Psychopharmacological treatments of bulimia nervosa. *Journal of Clinical Psychiatry*, *52*, 34–38.

Whitehead, W. E., & Schuster, M. M. (1985). *Gastrointestinal disorders: Behavioral and phsyiological basis for treatment*. Orlando, FL: Academic Press.

Willi, J., Giacometti, G., & Limacher, B. (1990). Update on the epidemiology of anorexia nervosa in a defined region of Switzerland. *American Journal of Psychiatry*, *147*, 1514–1517.

Wonderlich, S. (1992). Relationship of family and personality factors in bulimia. In J. H. Crowther, D. L. Tennenbaum, S. E. Hobfoll, & M. A. P. Stephens (Eds.), *The etiology of bulimia nervosa: The individual and familial context* (pp. 103–126). Washington, DC: Hemisphere.

Wonderlich, S. A., & Swift, W. J. (1990). Borderline versus other personality disorders in the eating disorders: Clinical description. *International Journal of eating Disorders*, *9*, 629–638.

Yager, J., Landsverk, J., & Edelstein, C. K. (1987). A 20-month follow-up study of 628 women with eating disorders, I: Course and severity. *American Journal of Psychiatry*, *144*, 1172–1177.

Yates, A. (1989). Current perspectives on the eating disorders: I. History, psychological and biological aspects. *Journal of the American Academy of Child and Adolescent Psychiatry*, *28*, 813–828.

Yates, A. (1990). Current perspectives on the eating disorders: II. Treatment, outcome, and research directions. *Journal of the American Academy of Child and Adolescent Psychiatry*, *29*, 1–9.

Chapter 21

Psychological Aspects of Pediatric Disorders

Kenneth J. Tarnowski
University of South Florida

Ronald T. Brown
Emory University School of Medicine

Few events are as distressing to parents as a child who is seriously ill or injured. Virtually all children and their parents have experience with common childhood afflictions, such as acute viral infections, stomachaches, headaches, and minor injuries. Unfortunately, many children and their families experience more threatening forms of acute and chronic childhood illness and injury (e.g., cancer, burns). There is significant mortality associated with several of these conditions. In addition, many disorders are associated with marked medical (i.e., residual physical disability) and psychological morbidity (i.e., disruption of normal developmental processes). Not only may children and families experience negative psychological sequelae (e.g., depression) in response to a specific pediatric condition, but behavioral factors have also been demonstrated to be integral in determining the onset, course, and prognosis of many disorders and injuries.

Even children with as benign and common a condition as a headcold may present with behavioral changes (e.g., reduced cognitive efficiency, dysphoric mood), make specific causal attributions (e.g., "I was out in the rain and now I'm sick"), and experience a variety of associated environmental responses (e.g., increased parental attention). It is apparent that psychological variables are relevant to the discussion of any pediatric illness. For our purposes, we exemplify the role and diversity of psychological factors in childhood illness by considering two conditions: pediatric burn injuries and sickle cell disease.

Burn injuries were selected because they represent not a disease, but rather an *acute injury* that can pose serious long-term physical and psychological sequelae. Alternatively, sickle cell disease is a *chronic illness*. Patients with this disorder are frequently without symptoms yet may present with periodic sickling crises that may be of sudden onset and can be fatal. Although there are similarities in the psychosocial challenges both conditions pose for the child and family, there are also important differences that are highlighted in the case descriptions.

By way of background, we now turn to a brief overview of some general considerations in behavioral pediatrics. First, it is important to note that by age 18 approximately 10% to 15% of children and adolescents experience one or more chronic medical conditions. Chronic illnesses are those involving a protracted course that may be fatal or result in compromised mental and/or physical functioning and that often are characterized by acute exacerbations that may result in hospitalization or other forms of intensive treatment. A second point worthy of note is that the importance of psychological variables in understanding health and illness has become well-established in the past two decades (Routh, 1988; Russo & Varni, 1982). As infectious diseases have been eradicated and other serious physical problems of childhood (e.g., acute lymphocytic leukemia) have succumbed to improved medical management, more attention has been devoted to the role of psychosocial factors in health and illness. Currently, there is unequivocal support for behavioral factors as major contributions to disease (and injury) onset and maintenance (e.g., smoking, lack of exercise, diet, treatment nonadherence, substance abuse).

Given the number of children affected and the primacy of behavioral factors in understanding injury and illness, a major focus of recent work has been on increasing knowledge of health-related developmental variables. Such variables are of critical importance in behavioral pediatrics. A child's level of cognitive development influences his or her conceptualization of illness/injury, cooperation with specific care procedures, reaction to and understanding of life-threatening illness, and capacity to comprehend health-related communications. For example, it is apparent that a preschool child's understanding of cancer, death, and chemotherapy differs dramatically from those of an adolescent.

Developmental models of cognitive development, such as those developed by Piaget and Erickson, have been invoked frequently to conceptualize children's understanding of illness and health. Expanding on the work of Piaget, Bibace and Walsh (1980) categorized children's understanding of illness into various stages. The prelogical thinking of children ages 2 to 7 years was characterized by phenomenism and contagion. Phenomenism invokes an external concrete cause of illness that is spatially and/or temporally remote (e.g., How do people get colds? From the trees). Contagion locates the cause of illness in objects or individuals that are proximate to the child (e.g., How do people get colds? When someone gets near them). Concrete logical explanations of illness (ages 7 to 11 years) involve contamination and internalization types of explanation. Contamination involves coming into contact with a contaminant that can be a person, object, or "bad" behavior. Internalization is a more sophisticated explanation that locates illness inside the body even though the cause may be external. Formal logical explanations (after approximately 11 to 12 years of age) involve cause–effect relationships that are physiological (internal malfunction/nonfunctioning with separation of proximal and distal external causative factors). Psychophysiological explanations incorporate psychological causation in addition to physical factors (e.g., heart problem due, in part, to excessive life stress). Children of a given age may differ considerably in their cognitive understanding of illness as a function of a variety of factors including experiential variables. Nonetheless, such models have proven invaluable in guiding communication, psychosocial policy (e.g., parental visitation guidelines), and the design of intervention methods.

Although consideration of cognitive developmental variables is critical, attention must be given to other factors as well (Ferrari, 1990). In many instances, reactions of children to specific illness or injury-related stressors (e.g., medical treatment) are contrasted with those of other children the same age. Although chronological age is a useful marker in outlining possible assessment and treatment endeavors, it should not be used in place of a careful consideration of salient developmental variables (e.g., cognitive developmental status). Mental age and maturation are variables that may be particularly relevant for the subset of patients who present with developmental disabilities (e.g., mental retardation).

Children's socioemotional development deserves special attention. Children who are seriously ill or injured often have to cope with extended hospitalization, separation from parents, siblings, and peers, and frequent painful medical procedures. Children's abilities to cope with the diverse challenges posed by chronic illness or injury may be severely taxed by such stressors. Under these circumstances, children's functioning may be characterized by negative affective responding (e.g., anxiety, overt distress, reduced ability to cope with pain, regressive behaviors, detachment, depression). Adequate family functioning can provide a buffer from the deleterious short- and long-term effects of such stressors. However, child illness can also serve to erode family utilitarian (e.g., finances) and psychological (e.g., coping ability) resources. A dysfunctional family environment serves as an additional risk factor that can function to potentiate socioemotional maladjustment. In general, the socioemotional status of seriously ill and injured children must be carefully assessed and monitored. Of course, the key issues in this domain of functioning are developmentally influenced. For example, for younger children, parental separation can be emotionally devastating. Disrupted peer relationships figure largely for older children as is the case with adolescents who also may be attempting to cope with personal identity issues.

As noted previously, the environmental context of illness or injury is critical. The availability of basic resources (e.g., finances to secure appropriate treatment, medication, transportation) as well as psychological resources (e.g., parental support and caring) are important determinants of how well children function when challenged with compromised health. It is also apparent that the behavioral contingencies that are in effect for an ill or injured child in the hospital, clinic, home, and school environments need careful assessment (Gross & Drabman, 1990; Routh, 1988; Russo & Varni, 1982). For example, pediatric patients evidence behavioral reactions (e.g., crying, flailing, attempts to escape, seeking parental comfort, withdrawal, etc.) in response to certain aversive treatments that may be required as part of their health care (e.g., venipuncture) or in response to a particular disorder-related health symptom (e.g., arthritic pain). Although such responses are a function of biological differences (e.g., pain threshold) as well as developmental factors (e.g., a preschoolers understanding of the need for painful procedure), it is known that the responses of others (parents, staff, peers) to specific child illness-related behavior (e.g., complaints of pain) critically influence and shape the topography (form of the behavior), intensity, and duration of child responding. In brief, although it is imperative that parents and staff create a consistently supportive and caring environment for ill children, it is also important that the behavioral contingencies that are operative in such environments promote developmentally appropriate coping, self-regulation, and self-care skills.

In summary, when considering the psychological aspects of pediatric disorders, it makes considerable sense to start with an assessment of basic developmental parameters. One then should ask how the nature of illness or injury, its cause, treatment, and associated side effects may serve to disrupt child developmental and family processes that are integral to optimal adjustment. The environments (e.g., family, hospital, clinic, school) in which ill children function should be carefully assessed. Utilitarian and psychological resources (e.g., supportive family, coping skills) should be identified. Health-related behavioral contingencies need to be carefully assessed to maximize adjustment and well-being.

We now exemplify the multiple challenges to children's coping and adjustment via discussion of an acute traumatic injury and childhood chronic disease.

PEDIATRIC BURN INJURIES

Clinical Description

Children are a high-risk population for burn injuries. In the United States, approximately 1,000,000 children sustain burn injuries that require medical attention each year. Approximately 50,000 of these injuries result in hospitalization for more intensive treatment. Each year, about 1,000 children die of these injuries. Children less than 15 years of age account for about two thirds of all burn fatalities, with males outnumbering females by a ratio of greater than 2:1. Advances in the medical management of burns have resulted in an increased survival rate for burn victims.

Burns are typically described in terms of burn type (degree) and percentage of body surface area (BSA) affected. A first degree burn involves injury that is restricted to the epidermis. Injuries to the dermis are labeled second degree or partial thickness burns. Extensive injury involving multiple skin layers with possible damage of subcutaneous tissue and peripheral nerve fibers is known as full thickness or third degree burn. Percentage of BSA is calculated using standard charts that display dorsal and ventral views of the body divided into discrete areas of known percentage body surface area. In children, partial thickness burns affecting up to 10% BSA or full thickness burns affecting less than 2% BSA (not including injuries to the face, eyes, ears, or genitals) are classified as minor. Full thickness burns of less than 10% BSA or partial thickness of 10% to 20% are considered moderate injuries. Full thickness burns greater than 10% BSA or partial thickness greater than 20% BSA or inhalation injuries or those affecting the face, eyes, ears, perineum, hands, or feet are considered major, as most burns that are electric or chemical in nature and those complicated by fracture or other major trauma.

Causes of the Problem

The causes of pediatric burn injuries are diverse. Burns typically are categorized as thermal, radiation, chemical, or electrical. Data collected on such injuries reveal that the majority of burn victims are younger children (infants and toddlers). Scalds account for the majority (approximately 50%) of burns and for about 80% of such injuries to younger victims. Most of these injuries involve accidents such as a child pulling down a hot liquid off a table or stove top. Flame burns account for more injuries as a function of increasing age. Such injuries account for approximately 20% of hospitalizations and 80% of burn injury mortality.

Although older children are less at-risk for burn injuries, males are at increased risk at any age. The ratio of male to female injuries is approximately 2:1. Concerning the location of injury, the home is the most dangerous environment. Approximately 80% of children sustain their injuries in the home with kitchens, bathrooms, and living rooms being the most probable sites of injury. It is also known that a subset of such injuries are the result of child abuse. In pediatric burn units, estimates of the incidence of children hospitalized for nonaccidental injuries range from 4% to 39%.

Course of the Disorder

In general, the course of burn patients consists of three overlapping phases: (a) emergency period, (b) acute phase, and (c) rehabilitation. During the emergency period, the major concern is stabilization of the patient. Efforts at this time are directed toward patient stabilization, including maintenance of fluid and electrolyte balance and ensuring cardiovascular and respiratory integrity. In the acute phase, infection (e.g., sepsis) and malnutrition are major concerns. Antibacterial therapy is instituted and total parenteral feedings may be needed. Pain is often severe at this time as damaged peripheral nerve endings regenerate and procedures are implemented to accomplish wound closure and healing. Typical procedures include skin grafting and debridement. Physiological ("live") dressings composed of materials from cadavers, animals, or artificial skin can be used to effect wound coverage. Because such dressings are not permanent and are biologically rejected, autografting procedures are often implemented. This procedure involves harvesting healthy skin from the patient for the purpose of transplanting it to the site of the burn injury. Debridement procedures are initiated at this time as well. This procedure is a major source of patient distress and typically involves daily "tankings" in which the patient is placed in a hydrotherapy tub and devitalized tissue is vigorously removed. Dressing changes, intravenous line placements, application of topical agents, and demands for increased fluid and food intake are routine. Physical therapy is often prescribed to promote function and preclude the development of contractures. During the rehabilitation phase, patients are required to engage in specific self-care practices (e.g., physical therapy, wearing of customized elastic pressure garments). Multiple surgeries over an extended period may be required (e.g., reconstructive cosmetic surgery, release of contractures, etc.).

From a psychological perspective, children hospitalized for such injuries face multiple challenges including separation from family, restricted visitation, extended hospitalization, repeated exposure to painful medical procedures, observation of other seriously ill patients, reduced sensory stimulation in the pediatric burn care unit, compliance with painful physical therapy procedures, and coping with disfigurement (Tarnowski, Rasnake, Linscheid, & Mulick, 1989). A subset of children with severe biological derangement may evidence serious but transitory behavioral reactions such as hallucinations. More common acute behavioral reactions include anxiety and depression. Prolonged crying, clingingness, verbal and physical aggression towards medical treatment staff, sleep disturbances (e.g., nightmares, disrupted sleep–wake cycle), regressive behavior, compromised food intake, disrupted play, denial of the physical consequences of the burn, and suicidal ideation are commonly evidenced during the inpatient portion of treatment. In addition to hospitalization and the attendant medical treatment, a subset of pediatric burn victims also must cope with the loss of their home and belongings. Unfortunately, many children also face the tragic loss of parents and siblings.

Upon hospital discharge, some children experience a tumultuous transition back home, and the return to the school environment can be problem ridden. Problems with self-esteem, dysfunctional peer relations, disrupted body image development, modified school–career trajectories, coping with negative societal reactions to disfigurement, and increased family tensions are often seen in the posthospitalization period.

Children's responses to burn injuries depend, to a large extent, on their developmental status. Younger children may have extreme difficulty coping with separation from parents. Assuredly, they have a limited or incorrect conceptualization of what and why particular events are happening. Young children may view painful treatment procedures as a consequence or type of punishment for some misdeed they believe they may have committed. Older children and adolescents may be devastated by the physical disfigurement and loss of function they currently experience. The coping strategies implemented by pediatric patients and the types of psychological treatments instituted by staff and family vary widely as a function of such developmental variables.

Deleterious long-term psychological sequelae have been reported for pediatric burn survivors. It is quite understandable that many would project poor adjustment for most pediatric burn survivors given the devastating physical and psychological trauma imposed by such injuries. However, a recent review of the empirical literature on this topic provided little support for the contention that the majority of burn victims exhibit severe poor postburn adjustment (Tarnowski, Rasnake, Gavaghan-Jones, & Smith, 1991). It appears that adjustment outcome is a complex function of several variables including patient injury parameters, course of hospitalization, premorbid adjustment, developmental status, family variables, and personal and social demographics (e.g., age, socioeconomic status). Such risk and resource variables may combine in novel ways to produce different outcomes.

Familial Contributions

Family variables are critical in understanding pediatric burns. They are relevant to understanding the context in which children are injured. Familial contributions also are an integral part of the treatment and recovery process.

As previously indicated, most children sustain burn injuries in the home setting. In assessing the circumstances under which children are injured, the interplay between specific setting factors and family variables becomes apparent. For example, the probability of a child sustaining a burn injury increases as one descends in socioeconomic status (SES). Several factors may be operative here. For example, economically disadvantaged families may not be able to afford quality housing. Substandard housing may pose specific risks of injury (e.g., faulty electrical systems). Lack of adequate basic resources also may lead parents to choose unsafe methods to meet their daily living needs (e.g., heating homes with makeshift stoves). Another factor to consider here is that rates of certain psychological disorders are highest in lower SES populations and the symptoms of such disorders may contribute to increased risk of childhood burn injury. For example, parental depression may result in a decreased ability to engage in the child monitoring required to prevent injuries. There is also some evidence that the families of pediatric burn victims experience more geographic moves (Knudson-Cooper & Leuchtag, 1982). A subset of these families may be unstable. Alternatively, the attendant stressors of moving coupled with the natural proclivity of young children to explore their new environments may combine to increase risk.

For all families, the general stressors of daily living may function in the same manner (e.g., multiple stressors can erode psychological resources) such that a child can sustain injury during a momentary lapse of parental supervision. Multiple family stressors may also potentiate the likelihood of child abuse.

Finally, the issue of premorbid (preinjury) psychopathology is of relevance. Essentially, the point here is children may present with specific disturbances in behavior (e.g., excessive risk taking, conduct problems) that increase the likelihood of injury. Certain family factors (e.g., instability, abuse, lack of cohesion, lack of child supervision) contribute to the emergence of specific childhood problems that may increase the risk of injury. It is also the case that poorer psychosocial outcome is associated with children who present with severe premorbid psychopathology and who reside in dysfunctional family environments. Given the severity of the psychological challenges posed by pediatric burn injuries, the family is definitely called on to assist in the treatment and rehabilitation process. The absence of such family support can have devastating consequences for the child.

Psychophysiological and Genetic Influences

Genetic factors do not contribute directly to burn injuries. However, several lines of data (epidemiological, clinical) provide suggestive evidence that children with specific disorders (e.g., Attention-Deficit Hyperactivity Disorder; ADHD) may be disproportionately represented among young burn victims. Data indicate there is, in fact, a genetic component to this disorder (see Chap. 19). Behavioral characteristics such as impulsive responding, high risk taking, and impaired attentional functioning may increase the risk for a variety of injuries including burns. Thus, for a subset of burn injured children, a case can be made for the indirect influence of genetic factors.

Concerning psychophysiological factors, these may be relevant in understanding the circumstances under which the burn injury occurred as well as in conceptualizing pediatric postinjury behavioral distress. As noted previously, high levels of psychophysiological arousal (e.g., stress) can lead to a variety of affective states that may increase the probability of accidental injury.

Psychophysiological variables are also relevant in conceptualizing, assessing, and treating behavioral distress. Pediatric pain is a phenomenon that is a composite of several influences (e.g., sensory, affective, biological, motivational, behavioral). Physiological and biochemical manifestations of pain include increased respiration, muscular tension, diastolic and systolic blood pressure, pulse rate, skin resistance, and endogeneous, opiates. Monitoring of objective and subjective aspects of psychophysiological arousal is an integral component of the assessment and behavioral/pharmacological management of children's pain.

Current Treatments

The empirical literature on the psychological assessment and treatment of the pediatric burn victim is relatively limited. However, recent advances have been reported in the treatment of procedure-related patient distress (e.g., debridement, physical therapy), consummatory behavior (e.g., nutritional intake), sleep-related problems, and self-excoriation (Tarnowski, Rasnake, & Drabman, 1987). Given the numerous challenges facing pediatric burn victims, it is apparent that the clinical child health psychologist has numerous opportunities from the time of initial hospitalization through extended postdischarge follow-up to influence the care of these patients and their families.

Our experience indicates that one of the most frequently encountered consultation requests centers around patient management of distress during debridement and dressing changes. Although analgesic medications are routinely used to mitigate procedure-related patient distress, other nonpharmacologic interventions are often needed. Wound care can require 2 hours to complete and may be conducted twice daily. The following case presentation provides an overview of the approach to assessment and treatment adopted with a severely burned adolescent (Hurt & Tarnowski, 1990).

Keith was a 17-year-old male admitted to the burn unit following an auto accident in which he suffered second and third degree burns over 25% of his body. Psychology was consulted to assess and intervene with Keith's coping with daily burn care treatments. Initial assessment consisted of medical chart review, interviews with shift nurses, and direct behavioral observations of Keith during debridement and dressing changes. A comprehensive review of Keith's developmental, medical, and behavioral history was conducted with his mother and supplemented with an interview with Keith.

Integration of the interview and behavioral assessment data revealed the following:

1. A bright 17-year-old who had not evidenced significant premorbid psychosocial difficulties.
2. Marked procedure-related distress characterized by verbal assaults and physical opposition and attempts to escape the treatment room.
3. Distress inadequately controlled by analgesics.
4. Staff–patient interaction problems related to the fact that most patients on the unit were toddlers and children. Staff were unsure how to respond to Keith's specific questions concerning prognosis and treatment.
5. Keith's physical size made it difficult to manage his oppositional behavior. Physical restraint was not judged to be an option and cooperation was mandated for adequate wound treatment.
6. The inordinate amount of time needed for debridement and antibiotic application left little time for emotional recovery and restricted opportunities to engage in pleasant activities (e.g., television, listening to tapes, visitation, etc.).
7. The amount of time spent in daily wound care reinforced the notion that staff were there only to inflict pain. Medical staff essentially functioned as discriminative stimuli for pain.
8. Keith's affect was deteriorating as he believed he had lost control over any aspect of his current environment.

Staff were informed of our assessment results and made aware of the range of interventions that might prove useful. Keith, his mother, and the medical and nursing staff agreed to our proposal to increase the predictability of his environment and to increase his coping skills via instruction in pain and stress management techniques.

An inservice training session was scheduled with staff to discuss the issues involved in dealing with adolescent burn patients and the modifications of staff–patient interactions needed to promote adjustment. Nurses were advised to facilitate, as much as possible, Keith's participation in his treatment by removing bandages and engaging in self-debridement. This strategy has been shown to be effective in reducing the distress of pediatric burn victims (Tarnowski, McGrath, Calhoun, & Drabman, 1987).

Keith was provided with a variety of pain management strategies tailored to his developmental level. Use of multiple self-control techniques has been found to be useful in controlling procedure-related distress. Patients may use one method for a brief period to obtain relief. Relief may diminish quite rapidly, and patients are prompted to switch to an alternative pain management procedure. The program was modeled after the multicomponent stress inoculation program developed by Wernick (1983). Keith was taught passive relaxation procedures, breathing exercises, guided imagery, and calming self-talk strategies. Attention distraction techniques were presented and included a focus on: (a) aspects of the physical environment (e.g., counting tiles), (b) somatization (e.g., focusing on sensation in nonpainful areas), and (c) imaginative transformation (e.g., transferring pain to a smaller body part like a fingertip). Finally, Keith was taught to use these pain management skills in the context of the four phase stress-inoculation procedure: (a) preparing for pain ("This is going to hurt, but I know how to deal with the pain"), (b) confronting the pain ("Relax, breathe deeply, I have made it through other debridement sessions, I'll make it through this one"), (c) coping with thoughts and feelings at critical moments ("Stay focused, I can switch to another strategy to stay in control"), (d) and positive self-statements ("I made it. Each time I get better at using the strategies. I feel more in control").

To enhance predictability, arrangements were made for debridement and physical therapy to be conducted by the same staff at the same time each day. Medical chart and patient self-report data indicated that this procedure had a marked impact on distress. The power struggle between Keith and the staff was essentially eliminated, and the frequency and severity of observed and self-reported pain was diminished. Brief biweekly sessions were held with Keith's mother to provide support, enhance coping, provide feedback about the efficacy of the interventions, and to provide suggestions on how she could contribute to Keith's recovery (e.g., verbally reinforce his daily accomplishments). Supportive psychological services were provided to address issues related to disfigurement, peer reactions, and physical disabilities. Effectiveness of the intervention package was evaluated on the basis of anecdotal reports of staff, patient, and parent, medical chart progress notes, and via direct behavioral observations of Keith by the psychology staff. These sources of data were consistent and indicated the stress inoculation treatment of procedural distress was marked and immediate. Collateral improvements in general affect were observed. He was followed intermittently on an outpatient basis for a period of 6 months.

Comments

The case presentation outlines the successful management of an adolescent who was exhibiting behavior that was interfering with and compromising the quality of his medical care. The case highlights an approach to assessment and treatment that was developmentally based and targeted multiple aspects of patient functioning. Our experience has impressed on us the importance of verifying via behavioral observations staff reports of problematic behavior. Often, such observations reveal that the optimal target of intervention is not with the patients but rather may be found at the level of the physical environment and/or staff. Specifically, we often have observed children who respond quite appropriately to the circumstance (i.e., normal behavior [crying, flailing)-abnormal circumstance [invasive medical procedure]). Although always worthwhile to determine it self-control control strategies might ameliorate such distress, the goal of such interventions is not suppression of child's responses but rather enhancement of the child's coping skills. This case also illustrates that although providing instruction in self-control skills may be helpful, that one needs to also consider whether simple environmental manipulations (e.g., scheduling to increase predictability) might be helpful. The need to adapt and tailor procedure to the patient's developmental level, cognitive status, and other behavioral characteristics (psychological resources and presenting symptomatology) is stressed. Finally, absence of premorbid psychopathology in this case proved to be a positive factor that was judged to be related to both positive inpatient response to treatment as well as minimization of postinjury psychological sequelae.

SICKLE CELL DISEASE

Clinical Description and Causes of the Disorder

Sickle cell disease (SCD) is a chronic hereditary blood disorder (hemologic) that affects 1 of 400 to 500 African-American babies born in this country. SCD causes normally round red blood cells to assume a rigid crescent or sickle shape. Because of their shape, these cells do not flow readily through the blood vessels but tangle and accumulate in the small blood vessels, blocking circulation and the delivery of adequate levels of oxygen to vital organs, tissues, and aerobic muscles. When adequate levels of oxygen are not delivered to these sites, a person experiences pain, swelling, and fatigue. Frequently, the body attempts to avert this process, referred to as a vasoocclusive phenomenon or sickle cell crisis, by rejecting and removing abnormally shaped cells. Because youth with SCD are unable to produce new red blood cells as fast as the sickle cells are destroyed, anemia may develop. Folic acid, a member of the vitamin B complex, is prescribed to promote red blood cell production; in cases of more severe anemia, transfusions may be indicated. As an iatrogenic effect of these transfusions, frequently these youth develop excess iron, which is stored in the liver; they then require chelation therapy, a chemotherapy procedure for removing excess iron.

The numerous physiologic complications that may accompany SCD include delayed growth, delayed onset of puberty, splenic involvement, gall bladder complications, osteomyelitis, pneumococcal infections, meningitis, cerebral vascular accidents, skin ulcers, necrosis of the femoral head, and priapism. Youth with SCD typically have increased contact with medical personnel and decreased involvement in school and physical activities.

Course of the Disorder

Although advances in the management of chronic complications associated with SCD have resulted in a more favorable prognosis, medical management is typically lifelong and directed at minimizing dehydration, infection, and hypoxia and at treating pain. Symptoms of SCD that may appear as early as the first months of infancy, typically persist throughout life. Although symptoms are variable and often unpredictable, the most common manifestations are episodes of pain in the abdomen, back, extremities, or chest. In infants, the earliest symptom may be painful swelling in the hands and feet (hand and foot syndrome or dactylitis). Pain is the most common reason children and adolescents seek medical attention for SCD. The frequency, intensity, and duration of pain crises vary considerably from person to person. For example, some youth experience pain crises that require frequent medical intervention, including hospitalization; others may report no pain crises for several years. In a study of the natural history of SCD, Platt, Thorington, and Brambilla (1991) prospectively followed more than 3,500 patients, newborn to elderly. The degree of pain varied widely within groups. Moreover, the patients who were more than 20 years of age and had more frequent pain episodes tended to have earlier mortality rates than those with fewer pain episodes, which suggests that pain rate is an important index of clinical severity. Each person's pain history, which is a function of both disease severity and psychosocial factors, influences the choice of pain management techniques: pharmacotherapy (e.g., analgesics); behavioral medicine techniques, including relaxation and imagery; transfusions; and, more recently, bone marrow transplantation.

Psychological factors, including the ability to cope and perceptions of helplessness, are important predictors of pain management in adults with SCD. Those who report less self-control over significant events have benefitted less from internal coping strategies (e.g., relaxation and imagery) when dealing with pain crises (Gil, Abrams, Phillips, & Keefe, 1989). Similar patterns have been seen in pediatric patients and their parents (Gil, Williams, Thompson, & Kinney, 1991). Although these coping strategies were unrelated to intensity or duration of pain, the children who used active problem-solving and coping strategies had fewer emergency room visits; children who used passive-adherent coping had more emergency room visits and participated in fewer household chores and school activities. Psychological distress (internalizing problems of behavior), however, was significantly associated with the frequency of pain episodes.

Familial Contributions

Consistent with other pediatric chronic diseases, SCD produces numerous illness-related stressors that may place these children at-risk for poor psychosocial adjustment (Brown, Doepke, & Kaslow, in press-c). Nonetheless, any pediatric chronic illness involves the interaction between the child and the family system.

Few studies have been devoted to the impact that SCD in a child has on other family members, but the levels of conflict and organization within these families is less adaptive than that reported by control families (Burlew, Evans, & Oler, 1989). The more educated the parents are about SCD and the more stable and available their social network, the better their coping and the higher their children's self-esteem (Burlew et al., 1989). Some evidence suggests less marital satisfaction in parents of SCD children, a finding consistent with that in the general chronic illness literature (Burlew et al., 1989). Further, an association has been found between family variables and the coping of adolescents who have increased family cohesion and organization, which seem to contribute to the resilience or coping competency of boys and of girls; family conflict negatively influenced the coping competency of girls only (Hurtig & Park, 1989).

Recent SCD research has paralleled the pediatric psychology studies conducted from an ecological-systems theory perspective in delineating the adjustment to a chronic illness. Thompson, Gil, Burbach, Keith, and Kinney (in press) assessed the psychological adjustment of mothers of youth with SCD and found support for a transactional stress and coping model in delineating the processes associated with maternal adjustment. Poor maternal adjustment was associated with the use of palliative coping methods or the regulation of emotional states that are associated with, or result from, stress. The maternal cognitive appraisal of stress was specifically important: perceived stress associated with daily hassles, not stress related to SCD illness tasks, was most related to maternal adjustment. The relationship between family supportiveness and maternal adjustment has been found consistently for a number of chronic childhood illnesses, including physical and sensory handicaps and cystic fibrosis. Family functioning characterized by high levels of supportiveness and low levels of control were associated with good maternal adjustment.

Consistent with other studies of the siblings of chronically ill children, the siblings of SCD youth evidence symptoms of psychological distress and seem to have difficulties coping with negative life events (Treiber, Mabe, & Wilson, 1987). Healthy siblings may have more psychological adjustment difficulties and less adaptive responses to life events, and they may evidence greater psychological distress than their diseased siblings (Treiber et al., 1987).

Psychophysiological and Genetic Influences

SCD comprises inherited disorders of hemoglobin (Hb) and reflects a basic deficit in the autosomal beta-globin gene. Healthy people have two A (normal) alleles (the particular copy of the gene inherited from the parent) of the beta-globin gene. Children with SCD trait have one SS mutation allele (S) and one A allele (they inherit an A allele from one parent and an S allele from the other parent). Those with SS trait (AS) are carriers of the disease. Typically, they are healthy and evidence few, if any, symptoms. Only when oxygen is less available (e.g., at high altitudes, pregnancy) does their red blood cells take the form of sickled cells, which may result in pain crises or other complications.

Three main forms of SCD exist: HbSS, HbSC, and HbS beta-thalassemia. HbSS, the homozygous and most severe condition, is caused by two abnormal S alleles of the beta-globin gene. Children with HbSS have inherited one S allele from each parent, both of whom have either the trait or the disease. In Hb SC, a milder form of SCD in which the child has a compound heterozygous condition for hemoglobin S and hemoglobin C, and S allele has been inherited from the other parent. HbS beta-thalassemia, which is more benign, is inherited from one parent who has SCD trait (AS) and a parent who has no evidence of the disease or trait. HbS beta-thalassemia is distinguished from SCD trait only by the structure of the cells. Specifically, each HbS beta-thalassemia cell contains SS hemoglobin, fetal hemoglobin (produced during the prenatal period, it remains in the blood stream in decreasing amounts throughout life and serves as a protective function), and possibly adult hemoglobin; the cells in persons with sickle cell trait contain adult and sickle hemoglobin only. Fetal hemoglobin has an ameliorating effect on pain and may ultimately improve survival (Platt et al., 1991).

Particularly relevant to children with SCD are the frequently encountered physiologically based neurological impairments. SCD occludes blood vessels that may result in infarctions and pain. In the central nervous system (CNS), this may lead to cerebral hemorrhaging (rare in SCD youth), major cerebral accidents (CVAs; strokes), or microvascular infarcts. CVAs, diagnosed in approximately 6% of children with SCD, occur more frequently in youth under the age of 15 than in older adolescents or adults. Incidence of microvascular infarctions is unclear because symptoms are not overt and thus are rarely identified on routine medical examinations. However, recent neuropsychologic research on brain structures that may be affected (Brown et al., in press-b) suggests that a significant percentage of youth with SCD may have experienced microvascular infarctions, particularly in the frontal lobe area. It remains unclear whether these cognitive impairments result from microvascular infarctions at critical developmental periods or from a series of progressive neurologic insults (Brown, Armstrong, & Eckman, in press-a).

In addition to the effects of CVAs or microvascular infarctions, chronic anemia (resulting in oxygen deprivation to the brain), nutritional deficiencies, and ischemia (tissue death) also may account for neurocognitive deficits in SCD youth (Brown et al., in press-a). Further, these cognitive impairments may be the result of significantly altered metabolism, which has been seen in the frontal lobe area on positron emission tomography (PET) scans of adults with SCD. Taken together, these findings underscore the need for comprehensive neuropsychologic examinations to identify these more subtle CNS involvements. In a recent study of the neurocognitive functioning of these youth, Brown et al. (in press-b) compared the cognitive processing and the academic functioning of children with SCD and of nondiseased siblings who were similar in age, socioeconomic status, and gender. Children with SCD scored significantly lower than nondiseased siblings on a reading decoding achievement test and a sustained attention task associated with frontal lobe functioning. More important, hemoglobin was an important predictor of intellectual functioning, fine motor skills, and academic achievement, which suggests that chronic reduced oxygen delivery may be an etiologic factor in the neurological deficits. Should physiologic and cognitive variables be related, children at-risk for later neurologic deficits may be recognized early by cost-effective neuropsychologic assessments. Most important, for children at-risk, appropriate medical (e.g., transfusions, bone marrow transplantation) or educational interventions (e.g., tutoring, special education) may be recommended.

Current Treatments

Although some studies have focused on the management of pain in adults with SCD, few studies have compared effective treatments for children. Although similarities in coping with SCD pain throughout life are likely, demands of SCD probably vary with age, requiring different coping resources at different ages.

In one of the only pediatric interventions with this population, Walco and Dampier (1987) evaluated the efficacy of individual treatment protocols aimed at reducing over reliance on the health care system by adolescent patients (e.g., emergency room visits, hospitalizations, and pain medication). The investigators established a series of behavioral contracts that included fixed schedules for tapering analgesic dosages, maximum days per hospitalization, minimal intervals between hospital admissions, maximum number of emergency room treatments during that interval, and a maximum amount of outpatient analgesics. Each variable was modified over time to approximate successively the norm for matched peers. Although the strategy reduced the frequency and duration of hospitalizations and immediate dependency on the health care system, it did not promote a more adaptive lifestyle (that required significant psychotherapeutic and psychopharmacological interventions).

The limited research on the neurocognitive and psychosocial aspects of SCD provides at best a shaky foundation for practice (Brown et al., in press-a). It has been suggested that only a small segment of the SCD population is at-risk for problems and that these children may be identified early and provided preventive intervention services, such as Head Start for preschool children, appropriate special education placement for school-age children, training in cognitive–behavioral approaches to coping for early adolescents, and education for all parents. However, before global interventions are initiated, we need more research on the incidence and patterns of children's problems.

Individually, however, a markedly more aggressive assessment and intervention strategy needs to be entertained. For some children with SCD, the consequences of the disease can be quite severe. These children need to be identified quickly and provided with intervention services as soon as possible. Clearly, children who have had strokes need repeated, thorough neuropsychologic and academic evaluations, followed by close consultation with the schools to develop an optimal educational program. Similarly, children without a diagnosed stroke but who experience school difficulties should be evaluated and provided appropriate special education services. Children who miss excessive amounts of school because of pain and associated problems should be targeted for help with pain management and coping strategies. Finally, as is true of all pediatric chronic illnesses, children and adolescents who have difficulty with normal developmental transitions (e.g., between adolescence and adulthood) need special attention and programmatic support. The following case presentation provides an overview of a family psychoeducational treatment intervention that we developed for an adolescent with SCD who had frequently sought medical attention for chronic pain.

Tomeka B. is a 13-year-old African-American female who had been admitted to the hospital on several occasions for pain crises. Psychology had been consulted at the last admission as Tomeka appeared to be in some pain, yet overt pain behaviors (i.e., grimacing, guarding, whimpering) were not present. Tomeka reported her pain level to be "very bad" giving a pain rating of 9 on a 1 to 10 scale, yet reported her mood to be "happy," which was inconsistent with Tomeka's stated level of pain. Tomeka attempted various coping strategies prior to coming to the hospital, for example, "trying to think of other things," "trying to get busy/go out and do things," none of which was helpful in alleviating her pain.

Mrs. B., Tomeka's mother, reported that her daughter had a difficult time in school this past year, after the family recently had moved. Tomeka admitted that she intensely disliked the new school, did not inform the school or her classmates of her SCD, and encountered difficulty in making new friends. Psychological testing revealed specific learning disabilities in the areas of mathematics and reading comprehension, although no special education placement had yet been made due to Tomeka's frequent absences from school.

Initially, Mrs. B. appeared very defensive and did not want to discuss Tomeka's difficulties stating that she was "tired of talking to psychologists, psychiatrists, and all of that." Mrs. B. reported that she did not wish to bring Tomeka to the hospital each time that she experienced pain and that she well understood the repercussions of her daughter's reliance on the medical system and her inability to develop adaptive coping strategies. However, she indicated that Tomeka's pain could be managed "if I had the right prescription." Mrs. B. indicated that Tomeka received positive and special attention when she was hurting, especially from her grandmother and older sister. Mrs. B. stated further that it is difficult for her to manage Tomeka's pain when she is continually informed by her family that she is a "bad mom." Moreover, Mrs. B. noted that Tomeka feels "safe" when she is in the hospital, as Tomeka continues to fear death and dying. Mrs. B. and Tomeka resided with her maternal grandmother, with Tomeka's father coming in and out of her life but presenting no stable paternal influence.

Factors that appeared to be promoting Tomeka's pain cycles were: (a) increased positive attention from her parents and family when she is in pain, (b) reprieve from a difficult school environment while she is in the hospital or in pain, (c) increased feelings of well-being and safety while she is in the hospital due to her fears of death, (d) increased attention from hospital staff, (d) increased opportunity for socialization while in the hospital, and (e) reprieve from negative home stressors.

Tomeka and her entire family were enrolled in a 2-month treatment program for youth with SCD and their families. The first session incorporated basic education about SCD and prevention of pain episodes. Tomeka's family was educated about the facts of SCD and information was provided about preventative health care strategies including eating healthy foods rich in iron, taking sufficient breaks when breathing hard from exercise, getting sufficient sleep, reducing stress, and avoiding extremes in temperature. The second session included application of preventative measures when Tomeka had early warning signs that a pain crisis might occur. Pain management techniques, including breathing, relaxation, and imagery also were taught during this session. The third session involved assisting Tomeka and her family to articulate their feelings about the disease. Active listening techniques were taught to Tomeka and her parents to promote parent–child communication. The primary goals of the fourth session were to enhance a mutual understanding among Tomeka's family members that good family relationships facilitate effective coping with SCD and to motivate family members to develop problem-solving strategies to handle difficulties pertaining to SCD. Mr. and Mrs. B. also were assisted in finding a balance between being too restrictive and too permissive regarding family rules and structure. The fifth session dealt with peer relationships, including assisting Tomeka and family to explore the ways in which the peer relations of children with SCD may be both similar and different from the peer relations of children without this disease. An examination of friendship patterns of children with SCD was discussed that included an analysis of involvement in peer activities, degree of isolation, and kind of peers chosen. Helping Tomeka develop more adaptive ways of explaining the causes of both good and bad events (e.g., "I am feeling some pain now and it is probably because I stayed in the cold too long") and helping family members develop adaptive ways of explaining the causes of both good and bad events in her life and in her family (e.g., "SCD runs in my family and here is how we can help her") were the goals of the sixth session. The final session revolved around goal setting in which Tomeka was encouraged to set realistic, attainable, and flexible short- and long-term goals. Her family was encouraged to identify rewards for Tomeka's goal attainment. Finally, family members were encouraged to express their expectations and concerns about Tomeka and her future.

Following this intervention, emergency room visits and number of hospitalizations decreased and school attendance increased. Although Tomeka still experiences some pain episodes, albeit at a reduced frequency, these are managed well at home, with lower doses of analgesic pain medication than prior to the intervention. Tomeka and her family still attend "booster" sessions on an as-needed basis.

Comments

The mortality associated with SCD has been significantly reduced. Unfortunately, many other aspects of the disease have been ignored. This is particularly surprising, given its significant incidence compared with that of other genetic diseases. In our clinical experience with SCD children, the absence of identified problems in the literature, particularly from a behavioral perspective, seems to reflect researchers' failure to ask the questions, not the absence of problems. The impact of the disease does not seem to be universally negative; many children do well in school, are well adjusted, and by many standards, stand out as "superstars" in the normal population. Thus, future research will need to focus both on the problems associated with the disease and the factors that mediate these problems. As is true of other pediatric chronic illnesses, the greatest clinical impact for children with SCD who have adjustment difficulties will come from what we learn from the children and families who develop adaptive strategies for coping.

SUMMARY

As the case examples presented previously illustrate, children, their families, and health care providers are all challenged by the multiple stressors associated with serious injury and chronic illness. The reactions of children, families, staff, and society to such health problems are diverse and a complex function of many interacting variables including children's developmental level, socioeconomic status, family utilitarian and personal resources, and operative environmental contingencies. Due to space limitations, we only were able to describe two disorders in detail. In the interest of expanding the scope of our discussion, Table 21.1 provides examples of some of common psychological variables that are often relevant to specific pediatric health disorders.

We have learned that there is no one pattern of psychological response to a specific pediatric illness or injury. Children with the same health problem present with unique patterns of psychological strength and vulnerability. Alternatively, children with vastly different illnesses may evidence marked similarity in their behavioral responding (e.g., withdrawal, disrupted peer relations). Early research in the area of psychological aspects of pediatric disorders attempted to identify "personality" profiles or typical pattern of responding that would characterize children with specific disorders (e.g., asthmatic personality). These attempts were not fruitful. Subsequent research has also taught us that although specific illness and injury variables are important in understanding and conceptualizing a particular case, such variables by themselves often are of little predictive value. That is, although knowledge of specific illness parameters (e.g., severity, duration, age of onset) provides some guidance in predicting acute reaction and possible long-term sequelae, other variables (e.g., level of pre-morbid psychosocial functioning, family coping resources) often are of more clinical predictive value. Of course, it is often the interaction of health variables with other contextual (e.g., family), developmental, and environmental factors that are of central importance. For example, under typical circumstances a small injury or time-limited

TABLE 21.1
Subset of Pediatric Disorders from Major Pediatric Subspecialty Populations With Examples of Relevant
Psychological Aspects

Subspeciality	Condition	Representative Psychological Aspects
Trauma (Surgery)	orthopedic trauma, burns	coping with intense postinjury pain, adjustment to disfigurement, disability
	head injury	cognitive deficits
Cardiology	congenital heart defects	impaired cognitive function secondary to hypoxia, parental guilt about responsibility for anomaly
	acquired heart defects	restriction of activity secondary to blood trimer used in valve replacement
	hypertension	cognitive/mood effects of antihypertensive medication
Endocrinology	diabetes melitus	nonadherence with complex self-care regimen
	short stature	self-concept, peer relations
Gastroenterology	encopresis	coercive parent–child interactions around toileting, impaired child self-esteem
	nonorganic recurrent abdominal pain	reinforcement of child "sick" behavior, family dysfunction
	ileitis (Crohn's disease)	impaired self-esteem
Hematology	sickle cell	recurrent pain, cognitive changes
	hemophilia	chronic arthritic pain
Infectious Disease	AIDS	cognitive deterioration, depression
	meningitis	cognitive changes
Neonatology	brochopulmonary dysplasia	feeding disorders, developmental delays
	apnea	sleep regulation
Nephrology	renal failure	treatment nonadherence, cognitive symptoms
	Cushing's syndrome	muscle weakness, body composition changes
Neurology	headaches	stress
	seizures	medication-induced changes in cognitive functioning
Oncology	leukemia	coping with aversive medical diagnostic and treatment procedures
	solid tumors	pain, treatment-related cognitive changes, death and dying issues
Pulmononology	asthma	activity restrictions
	cystic fibrosis	repeated rehospitalization, decreased life expectancy

illness may not pose serious threats to a child's adjustment or well-being. However, in the context of a family environment that fails to provide adequate health care and monitoring or alternatively functions to promote inappropriate responding, extent of injury or illness severity provides limited guidance concerning management, course, and outcome.

Assisting children and their families in coping with the stressors induced by injury and chronic disease has necessitated the joint working efforts of pediatric psychologists and pediatricians. Although this has been a relatively new collaboration that has emerged strongly over the past two decades, the result has been a very productive and exciting working relationship that has spawned many innovative clinical and research programs designed to assist children in coping with the ongoing stressors of injury and disease and associated treatments. Moreover, this collaboration also has resulted in successful programs of prevention of injury and disease including school-based programs (e.g., skin cancer prevention via reduced sun exposure, prevention of tobacco use). Furthermore, through family involvement and emphasis on patient education, the physical and psychosocial morbidity associated with serious illness have been reduced significantly by enhancing compliance to treatment regimens. As medical science continues to advance the management of various pediatric injuries and illnesses, it is anticipated that child health psychology will experience concomitant growth and progress requiring the additional training of pediatic psychologists for particular pediatric health subspecialities.

REFERENCES

Bibace, R., & Walsh, M. E. (1980). Development of children's concepts of illness. *Pediatrics, 66,* 912–917.

Brown, R. T., Armstrong, F. D., & Eckman, J. (in press-a). Neurocognitive aspects of pediatric sickle cell disease. *Journal of Learning Disabilities.*

Brown, R. T., Buchanan, I., Doepke, K. J., Eckman, J. R., Baldwin, K., Goonan, B., & Schoenherr, S. (in press-b). Cognitive and academic functioning in children with sickle cell disease. *Journal of Clinical Child Psychology.*

Brown, R. T., Doepke, K. J., & Kaslow, N. J. (in press-c). Risk-resistance-adaptation model for pediatric chronic illness: Sickle cell syndrome as an example. *Clinical Psychology Review.*

Burlew, A. K., Evans, R., & Oler, C. (1989). The impact of a child with sickle cell disease on family dynamics. *Annals of the New York Academy of Sciences, 565,* 161–171.

Ferrari, M. (1990). Developmental issues in behavioral pediatrics. In A. M. Gross & R. S. Drabman (Eds.), *Handbook of clinical behavioral pediatrics* (pp. 29–47). New York: Plenum.

Gil, K. M., Abrams, M. R., Phillips, G., & Keefe, F. J. (1989). Sickle cell disease pain: Relation of coping strategies to adjustment. *Journal of Consulting and Clinical Psychology, 57,* 725–731.

Gil, K. M., Williams, D. A., Thompson, R. J., & Kinney, T. R. (1991). Sickle cell disease in children and adolescents: The relation of parent and child pain coping strategies to adjustment. *Journal of Pediatric Psychology, 16,* 643–663.

Gross, A. M., & Drabman, R. S. (Eds.). (1990). *Handbook of clinical behavioral pediatrics.* New York: Plenum.

Hurt, F. J., & Tarnowski, K. J. (1990). Behavioral consultation in the management of pediatric burns. *Medical Psychotherapy, 3,* 117–124.

Hurtig, A. L., & Park, K. B. (1989). Adjustment and coping in adolescents with sickle cell disease. *Annals of the New York Academy of Sciences, 565,* 172–182.

Knudson-Cooper, M. S., & Leuchtag, A. K. (1982). The stress of a family move as a precipitating factor in children's burn accidents. *Journal of Human Stress, 8,* 32–38.

Platt, O. S., Thorington, B. D., & Brambilla, D. J. (1991). Pain in sickle cell disease: Rates and risk factors. *New England Journal of Medicine, 325,* 11–16.

Routh, D. K. (Ed.). (1988). *Handbook of pediatric psychology.* New York: Guilford.

Russo, D. C., & Varni, J. W. (Eds.). (1982). *Behavioral pediatrics: Research and practice.* New York: Plenum.

Tarnowski, K. J., McGrath, M. L., Calhoun, M. B., & Drabman, R. S. (1987). Pediatric burn injury: Self-versus therapist-mediated debridement. *Journal of Pediatric Psychology, 12,* 567–579.

Tarnowski, K. J., Rasnake, L. K., & Drabman, R. S. (1987). Behavioral assessment and treatment of pediatric burn injuries: A review. *Behavior Therapy, 18,* 417–441.

Tarnowski, K. J., Rasnake, L. K., Gavaghan-Jones, M. P., & Smith, L. (1991). Psychosocial sequelae of pediatric burn injuries: A review. *Clinical Psychology Review, 11,* 371–398.

Tarnowski, K. J., Rasnake, L. K., Linscheid, T. R., & Mulick, J. A. (1989). Ecobehavioral characteristics of a pediatric burn injury unit. *Journal of Applied Behavior Analysis, 22,* 101–109.

Thompson, R. J., Jr., Gil, K. M., Burbach, D. J., Keith, B. R., & Kinney, T. R. (in press). The role of child and maternal processes in the psychological adjustment of children with sickle cell disease. *Journal of Consulting and Clinical Psychology.*

Treiber, F., Mabe, A., & Wilson, G. (1987). Psychological adjustment of sickle cell children and their siblings. *Children's Health Care, 16,* 82–88.

Walco, G. A., & Dampier, C. D. (1987). Chronic pain in adolescent patients. *Journal of Pediatric Psychology, 12,* 215–225.

Wernick, R. L. (1983). Stress inoculation in the management of clinical pain: Application to burn pain. In M. Meichenbaum & M. Jaremko (Eds.), *Stress reduction and prevention* (pp. 191–217). New York: Plenum.

Chapter 22

Substance Use Disorders

Michael D. Newcomb
University of Southern California

Mark A. Richardson
Charles R. Drew University of Medicine and Science

CLINICAL DESCRIPTION

Substance use disorders are unlike most other mental disorders in at least two ways. First, drug abuse and dependence are pathoplastic disorders; their existence and prevalence are dependent on an external agent (the drug) and vary depending on the availability of drugs. Second, drug abuse disorders always involve a willing host (the abuser), who is an active instigator and participant in creating the disorder. If children and adolescents did not choose to ingest these substances and the drugs were not available, there would be no disorder. Nevertheless, many types of drugs are widely available, and there are many individuals willing to use them.

The leading cause of death among teenagers in the United States is drunk driving, accounting for more than 20% of all mortalities (Julien, 1992). Tobacco smoking is the leading cause of death among people in the United States, accounting for nearly 400,000 lost lives each year and will probably be responsible for killing more current children and teenagers later in their lives than any other single cause (Julien, 1992). There are clearly substantial reasons for concern regarding the abuse of nicotine and alcohol among children and teenagers, although clear focus on these drugs is conspicuously missing in the current "war on drugs," with primary attention devoted to the youthful use of illicit drugs, such as marijuana and cocaine (Newcomb, 1992a).

From the outset, we must emphasize the controversies surrounding definitions of drug use, misuse, abuse, and disorders among children and teenagers. There is no one accepted criterion for deciding whether the use of a drug by a youngster represents benign experimentation with proscribed behaviors that is viewed by some as a defining feature of adolescence (e.g., Peele, 1987) or whether this drug involvement constitutes abuse, dependence, or a disorder that may be destructive to all aspects of this person's life. Further, systematic research on adolescent abuse is limited, likely a function of the

411

relatively low prevalence of substance abuse among adolescents (estimated at 6% to 10% of those adolescents currently using alcohol or illicit drugs at any given time).

Several critical issues must be kept in mind when trying to study, understand, or intervene on the use of drugs by children and teenagers. These include: (a) what should be considered a substance use disorder of children and teenagers, (b) the ramifications of treating such a disorder (however defined), and (c) an appreciation of the larger context of attitudes and behaviors within which youthful drug use occurs. The first and second issues are addressed in the Clinical Description and Current Treatments sections of this chapter (respectively), and the third must be confronted from the outset.

Attempts to describe substance use disorders among children and teenagers are fraught with disagreement and controversy. For instance, addiction to tobacco may not be considered a disorder. Alcohol abuse (high quantities ingested per occasion) is probably the most prevalent but often overlooked, drug disorder among teenagers, and political mandates have defined illicit drug use by a teenager, even if only one experimental episode, as abuse. In this chapter, we focus on drug disorders that create problems for youths that may be demonstrated in physically, psychologically, or socially adverse consequences or reactions (e.g., Winters, 1992).

Extent and Patterns of Teenage Drug Use

The most extensive surveys of drug use among U.S. children and teenagers are annual assessments. Monitoring the Future (Johnston, O'Malley, & Bachman, 1991) summarizes high school seniors' reports of their prior and recent alcohol and drug, whereas the National Household Survey of Drug Use (National Institute on Drug Abuse, 1991) assesses drug use among respondents that range from 12 to 17 years old. These national and other local studies yield a fairly clear understanding of drug use patterns among children and teenagers. Although these data are illuminating, several problems cloud their descriptive clarity, including (a) the exclusion of high school dropouts, who are expected to be heavier drug users; (b) limitations on the ability to identify and include adolescents considered at particularly high risk for substance abuse (e.g., inner-city gang members); and (c) the absence of generally recognized measures of drug abuse or dependence. Concern over these surveys' reliance on self-report of drug use (an illegal behavior among children and teenagers) has been addressed. The scales have demonstrated validity and reliability, particularly for recent drug use, when they are utilized under anonymous reporting conditions (e.g., Oetting & Beauvais, 1990).

There is irrefutable evidence attesting to the widespread use of tobacco (64% lifetime prevalence in 1990) and alcohol (90%) among high school seniors (Johnston et al., 1991) and evidence that *abuse* of these substances is relatively common. For instance, nearly one third of U.S. high school seniors reported having five or more drinks on at least one occasion in the past 2 weeks, and over 11% of this same group leave high school addicted to cigarettes, smoking a half-pack or more per day.

The use and abuse of all other drugs currently lags far behind these socially approved drugs. Marijuana is by far the most commonly used illicit substance, with a 40% lifetime prevalence rate among high school seniors in 1990; one quarter (27%) reported marijuana use within 12 months, and 14% reported use within 30 days of the survey. In turn, one tenth of high school seniors also reported that they had tried inhalants, stimulants, cocaine (powder or crack), or hallucinogens at some time in their lives (Johnston et al., 1991; Oetting & Beauvais, 1990).

National survey data suggest that a fairly steady decrease in lifetime, annual, and 30-day prevalence rates have been realized for most types of illicit drugs since the early to mid-1980s (including marijuana, cocaine, stimulants, and sedatives), with limited change in cigarette and alcohol prevalence trends (Johnston et al., 1991). At the same time, though, the use of inhalants and hallucinogens has leveled off or shown a modest increase since the mid-1980s among older adolescents. Further, an alarmingly high number of young people continue to experiment with both "legal" and illicit drugs at very early ages, many of whom progress to drug abuse.

The prevalence and incidence of a significant amount of drug use during the first decade of life is not documented to the degree to which it has been among teenagers. Nonetheless, both retrospective and cross-sectional (small-scale) surveys report very little use (at any level) of illicit drugs (4% to 10% lifetime prevalence rates by Grade 6). At least one third of the same respondents indicate that they have at least *tried* cigarettes or alcohol by the sixth grade; three quarters of the respondents had tried alcohol, and 50% had tried cigarettes by the eighth grade (Johnston et al., 1991; Oetting & Beauvais, 1990). These reports attest to appreciable risk for significant involvement with addictive substance early in life.

Reports also suggest interesting trends in substance use related to demographic characteristics. Roughly equivalent rates of use are reported across all social classes in many surveys (e.g., Brook, Whiteman, & Gordon, 1983; Johnston et al., 1991). Nonetheless, socioeconomic status (SES) is thought to function as a mediating variable, such that lower SES adolescents are at greater risk because lower SES increases the impact of other negative influences (Tolan, 1988). Available evidence regarding the impact of family structure (e.g., intact vs. broken families), however, is more equivocal; still, most investigators argue that greater adolescent drug use is observed within the context of family disruption (e.g., Needle, Su, & Doherty, 1990; Newcomb & Bentler, 1988c). National surveys suggest some reduction in regional differences in drug use in the mid-1980s (still greater use in the West and Northeast, compared with the North Central and Southern United States) and only marginal differences in reported rates of drug use in rural compared to urban settings, though drugs of choice may differ dramatically in rural and urban contexts (Johnston et al., 1991).

Gender differences in rates of use are typically found in these surveys. Except for cigarettes, boys tend to initiate drug use before girls and to use slightly greater quantities, a differential that is maintained throughout high school (Johnston et al., 1991; Newcomb, Maddahian, Skager, & Bentler, 1987). Girls, however, tend to surpass the boys' use of pills with age.

Finally, although African Americans and Hispanics are reportedly overrepresented among adult drug-abusing populations (e.g., Medina, Wallace, Ralph, & Goldstein, 1982), this may represent an artifact of the type of patients and public health service facilities studied, and no similar data are readily available for children or teenagers. Most recent local and national surveys adolescents suggest moderately higher rates of illicit drug use among White and Hispanic, when compared to African-American and Asian, adolescent respondents (e.g., Johnston et al., 1991; Maddahian, Newcomb, & Bentler, 1986). These trends may, however, reflect differential school dropout rates as a function of ethnicity. Students enrolled in regular classroom settings generally report less drug use than same-age peers in alternative education programs, wherein ethnic minority groups are overrepresented (Johnston et al., 1991; Oetting & Beauvais, 1990). We may wish to conclude that, nationwide, there are no real differences in overall patterns of use as a function of ethnicity. Nonetheless, ethnic minorities (particularly African Americans and Hispanics) are currently far *more* likely than other adolescent groups to be targeted for attention from law enforcement officials as a function of drug involvement.

Assessment of Drug Use Disorders

The most widely used, though problematic, clinical description of substance use disorders is provided in the *Diagnostic and Statistical Manual of Mental Disorder-Revised: Third Edition* (*DSM-III-R*), American Psychiatric Association, 1987). There are no specific criteria for describing substance use disorders among children and teenagers within this system. Therefore, the only commonly used criteria for describing and assessing substance use disorders among children and teenagers are based on descriptions of adult mental disorders related to drug use and may be less appropriate or irrelevant for younger aged individuals.

Drug use disorders in the *DSM-III-R* are grouped into two general categories. First are those defined as organic mental syndromes and disorders that are substance induced. These typically involve acute intoxication states and withdrawal syndromes and are not addressed in this chapter. The second grouping involves psychoactive substance use disorders. Although diagnostic categories are provided for 10 drugs (including nicotine and alcohol), most classifications distinguish between two levels of disorder: abuse (the lesser form) and dependence (the more serious form).

Newcomb and Bentler (1989) noted that typical descriptions of drug abuse may be too narrow and adult oriented to capture problems related to drug abuse among children and teenagers. They suggest that additional criteria be considered for young age groups. For instance, ingestion of drugs in inappropriate settings such as the workplace, classroom, driver's seat, or in isolation may be considered abuse, even though potential adverse consequences may not yet have occurred (e.g., a crash after drinking and driving). For every drug, consuming large quantities on any one occasion or moderate amounts regularly over prolonged time periods may be abuse, again because of the potential for psychological or physiological harm. Regular use of drugs at developmentally critical age periods, such as very young or prior to puberty, can be considered abuse because of the potential for interfering with crucial growth and adjustment tasks.

Examples of questionnaires designed to identify potentially problematic drug use among children and adolescents include the Problem Oriented Screening Instrument for Teenagers (POSIT), the Addiction Severity Index for Teenagers (T-ASI), the Adolescent Drug Abuse Diagnosis (ADAD) instrument, the Personal Experience Screen Questionnaire (PESQ), and the Personal Experience Inventory (PEI). The POSIT is a 139-item, self-administered questionnaire designed to identify teens who need more focused assessment in any of 10 domains (Rahdert, 1991), including: substance use/abuse, physical health status, mental health status, family relations, educational status, vocational status, social skills, leisure and recreation, and aggressive behaviors/delinquency. An important aspect of the POSIT is that is is imbedded in a comprehensive assessment and referral system designed specifically for adolescents. The T-ASI is a structured interview designed to assess seven domains (Kaminer, Bukstein, & Tarter, 1991): chemical use, school status, employment-support status, family relationships, peer-social relationships, legal status, and psychiatric status. The T–ASI was modeled after the adult Addiction Severity Index as was the ADAD (Friedman & Utada, 1989). The ADAD is a 150-item instrument with a structured interview format that captures nine life-problem areas (medical, school, employment, social, family, psychological, legal, alcohol, and drug). The PESQ is a 38-item tool designed to screen for the severity of adolescents' drug involvement (see Chatlos, 1991a). The PEI is a 300-item questionnaire designed to provide a more thorough assessment of teenagers' substance use history, patterns, and consequences (Winters, 1992). Alternatively, Anglin (1987) offered excellent recommendations for clinical interview strategies specifically tailored to teens that include a thorough exploration of home and family relationships, peer relationships, school functioning, leisure activity and employment history (with older adolescents), self-perception, *stage* of drug use (experimental, sensation seeking, preoccupation, or abuse), and a detailed drug use history (particularly to describe initial use, past, and present drug use settings and circumstances and functional and emotional consequences of use). In addition, the Adolescent Diagnostic Interview (ADI) is an example of a *DSM–III–R*-based, structured diagnostic interview designed to assess six classes of Axis I disorders, as well as chemical abuse (see Chatlos, 1991a).

Drug Use and Other Problem Behaviors

Drug use and abuse do not occur as isolated events nor as distinct aspects of an individual's behavior. They are typically only components of a cluster of behaviors and attitudes that form a syndrome or lifestyle of Problem Behavior or General Deviance. Problem Behavior theory (Jessor & Jessor, 1977) provided a valuable conceptualization to understand how teenage drug use is only one aspect of a deviance-prone lifestyle of children and teenagers. Adolescent substance use is considered only one facet of a constellation of attitudes and behavior that are considered problematic, unconventional, or nontraditional for a specific developmental stage, ". . . behavior that is socially defined as a problem, a source of concern, or as undesirable by the norms of conventional society . . . and its occurrence usually elicits some kind of social control response" (Jessor & Jessor, 1977, p. 33). For adolescents, these deviant behaviors include alcohol abuse, illicit drug use, academic problems, precocious sexual involvement, frequency of various sexual activities, deviant attitudes, and delinquent behavior.

Problem Behavior theory has been tested in several confirmatory factor analysis studies (Donovan & Jessor, 1985; McGee & Newcomb, 1992; Newcomb, & Bentler, 1988a; Newcomb & McGee, 1991). These studies have identified a syndrome of problem behaviors among adolescents and young adults and revealed that either one common latent factor accounted for the correlations among the several indicators of problem behavior or that all of these constructs were highly correlated. For instance, Newcomb and Bentler (1988a) found that teenage polydrug use was highly correlated with low social conformity, criminal activities, deviant friendship network, early sexual involvement, and low academic potential. McGee and Newcomb (1992) used higher-order confirmatory factor analyses to examine the construct of general deviance at four ages from early adolescence to adulthood and found that the construct was highly reliable at early and late adolescence. In short, the concept of Problem Behavior appears to adequately describe factors that encourage and correlate with adolescent drug use. Nonetheless, these strong relationships may weaken or disappear in adulthood.

CAUSES OF THE DISORDER

Factors that influence drug use and abuse are many, varied, and far from clearly understood. Although most drug use initiation occurs with friends or peers also using drugs, the stage for this event has been set much earlier by parents, the community, and society. We need to examine more closely how earlier childhood experiences, parenting practices, and general attitudes of this society contribute to the choice of using drugs or not.

Hundreds of variables have been studied for their ability to predict youthful drug involvement. These can be conceptualized as reflecting several areas (see Lettieri, 1985): (a) cultural/societal environment, (b) interpersonal forces (e.g., school, peers, and family), (c) psychobehavioral factors (these may take several forms including personality, attitudes, and activities), and (d) biogenetic influences. An individual can be considered at-risk because of factors or forces within each of these areas. A great deal of attention has been devoted to each of these possible influences and can be reviewed from both theoretical and empirical perspectives in several sources (e.g., Hawkins, Catalano, & Miller, 1992; Lettieri, 1985).

Hawkins et al. (1992) reviewed possible risk factors for youthful drug use and identified 17 potential causes that reflect the four general areas listed previously. Included among cultural/societal factors are laws and norms favorable toward drug use, availability of drugs, extreme economic deprivation, and neighborhood disorganization. Interpersonal forces include family alcohol and drug behavior and attitudes, poor and inconsistent family management practices, family conflict (see Familial Contributions section later), peer rejection in elementary grades, and association with drug-using peers. Psychobehavioral influences include early and persistent problem behaviors, academic failure, low degree of commitment to school, alienation and rebelliousness, attitudes favorable to drug use, and early onset of drug use. Finally, biogenetic factors include potential heritability of drug abuse and psychophysiological susceptibility to the effects of drugs (see Psychophysiological and Genetic Influences section). Additional influences not directly addressed in their review include psychological and emotional factors such as anxiety, need for excitement, depression or antisocial personality, and contextual factors such as physical or sexual abuse or stressful life events (e.g, Harrison, Hoffmann, & Edwall, 1989; Newcomb & Harlow, 1986; Newcomb & McGee, 1991; Zucker & Gomberg, 1986).

Although not specifically mentioned by Hawkins et al. (1992), certainly the *best* predictor of future behavior is past behavior; this is no less true for drug use and abuse. Therefore, the strongest predictor of current drug use is past drug use. Peer influences, such as modeling drug use, provision of drugs, and attitudes and behavior that encourages drug use, are generally viewed as secondary only to prior experience with drugs. All other potential psychosocial predictors must exhibit a unique influence on altering drug use or abuse beyond that accounted for by prior involvement with drugs and peer influences.

Another obvious factor related to drug use initiation is age of the youngster. The risk for initiating drug use increases for most drugs to a peak during mid-to-late adolescence and decreases thereafter (Kandel & Logan, 1984). Tobacco has the youngest age of peak vulnerability at about age 16 years. Increased likelihood for beginning use of alcohol, marijuana, and psychedelics occur during the next 2 years of life. Whereas initial cocaine use typically occurs in young adulthood, this pattern may be changing due to the insurgence of crack, the inexpensive and smokable form of cocaine, which may be more alluring and available to teenagers.

Some types of alcohol and drug abuse may have a genetic component (see Psychophysiological and Genetic Influences section). However, for initiation of drug use and progression to drug abuse, environmental, social, and psychological factors have received the most attention. Although biogenetic influences certainly affect the potential emergence of drug use disorders, they are clearly shaped and modified by other personal attributes and environmental conditions (e.g., Marlatt, Baer, Donovan, & Kivlahan, 1988).

Establishing correlates of substance use has been the primary basis for inferring etiological variables, although this approach is seriously flawed for inferring causal effects (Newcomb, 1990). Despite the compelling idea that the causes of drug use may be different from the causes of abuse, little systematic research exists to support such a notion (Glantz & Pickens, 1992). Nevertheless, several investigators have found that most drug use occurs due to social influences, whereas the abuse of drugs is more strongly tied to psychological factors and processes, such as self-medication against emotional distress (Carman, 1979; Newcomb & Bentler, 1990; Paton, Kessler & Kandel, 1977).

Indeed, contemporary biopsychosocial characterizations of alcohol and drug abuse (addiction) generally emphasize both the strong psychological *and* physical dependence, resulting in a withdrawal syndrome when use of the drug is halted. These dependencies are reflected in the driving forces behind addiction, the reinforcing properties of drugs. Of particular import is the biopsychosocial habit model (Marlatt, 1992), which posits that addiction reflects a learned, maladaptive habit pattern, maladaptive to the extent to which it becomes a central means of coping with distressing physical or mood states. Most excessive behaviors are those that are reinforced by immediate consequences. This model holds that two reinforcing principals are critical to addiction: *positive reinforcement* is produced by a stimulus that brings pleasure (e.g., the euphoric rush or "high" when a substance is used) to an individual who is in a "normal" mood state; *negative reinforcement* is produced by a stimulus that provides relief from negative mood states or from physical distress (e.g., withdrawal syndrome), returning the individual to a "normal" mood state.

Four alternative models of addiction remain influential within both conceptualizations of the addictive process and intervention (Hughes, 1989; Marlatt, 1992). Moral models view substance abuse as a sign of character weakness, a reflection of one's personal shortcomings and lack of willpower. The disease model is popular within various circles and holds that drug addiction is caused by an underlying pathology or disease process, such as metabolic or genetic abnormality, or an expression of an elevated biological vulnerability, triggered by critical exposure to addictive substances. Spiritually oriented models favored by self-help organizations such as Alcoholics Anonymous appear to be a combination of the moralistic and disease models, in that drug addiction is conceptualized as a disease from which an individual can never be "cured." However, recovery from such addiction is viewed as possible upon admitting one's lack of personal power over the allure and influence of drugs and turning his or her life over to a higher power for help. Psychological models, such as those that describe substance abusers as having an addictive personality, characterize drug abuse as but one example of a range of behavior patterns to which such an individual is susceptible as a means of coping with unmet psychological needs. These conceptualizations are based on research and clinical evidence from animal and human adult subjects but expect that they apply to adolescent drug addiction as well, although such confirmation is currently lacking. Further discussion of the myriad sociopolitical influences on these definitions of drug abuse and addiction may be found in the section on Course of the Disorder.

At younger ages, the major correlates of use are also the correlates of heavy use, and, by implication, of abuse. Because of the inevitable correlation of other problem behaviors with drug use, many predictors of drug involvement are similar to predictors of general problem behavior or deviance (Jessor & Jessor, 1977). The main mechanism for establishing these etiological factors has been the use of longitudinal studies with statistical controls substituted for the more desirable experimental control, such as is represented by structural equation modeling methods (e.g., Bentler, 1980; Newcomb, 1990).

Many and more of these varied influences have been related to involvement with drug use or abuse, but none has ever been found to be *the* primary factor that causes drug use or abuse. Because the range of variables leading to initial involvement in drug use is so large, recent views of this phenomenon have emphasized the risk factor notion that is often used in medical epidemiology (Bry, McKeon, & Pandina, 1982; Newcomb, Maddahian, & Bentler, 1986; Newcomb et al., 1987; Scheier & Newcomb, 1991). As might be expected, these risk factors include environmental, behavioral, psychological, and social attributes. Still, at this time, it seems highly unlikely that any one factor or even a few factors will ever be found that account fully and totally for all variations of drug involvement. Rather, adolescent drug involvement is multidetermined. This approach suggests that the more risk factors someone is exposed to that encourage drug use, the more likely he or she will use or abuse drugs. Exposure to more risk factors is not only a reliable correlate of drug use but predicts increases in drug use over time as well, implying a true etiological role for these influences (Newcomb et al., 1986; Scheier & Newcomb, 1991). This approach implies that drug use is but one of many coping responses for when the individual is exposed to an increasing number of vulnerability conditions. The particular risk factors appear less important than the accumulation of vulnerability factors in the person's life.

The flip side of risk factor modeling for drug use is that set of protective factors that reduce the likelihood and level of drug use and abuse. Protective factors are those psychosocial influences that have a direct effect on limiting or reducing drug involvement (Newcomb, 1992b). Very recently, the risk factors approach to the study of drug use and abuse has been expanded to test for multiple protective factors as well (Newcomb, 1992b; Newcomb & Feliz-Ortiz, 1992).

Protective factors may operate in a different manner or process than simply a direct effect on reducing drug involvement. Protective factors may, in fact, buffer or moderate the association between risk factors and drug use and abuse (Brook, Cohen, Whiteman, & Gordon, 1992; Newcomb & Felix-Ortiz, 1992; Stacy, Newcomb, & Bentler, 1992). Protective factors that moderate the relationship between risk for drug use and drug use or abuse can involve aspects of the environment (e.g., maternal affection) or the individual (e.g., introversion or self-acceptance). For instance, Stacy et al. (1992) found a high degree of self-acceptance moderated the relationship between peer use of hard drugs and self use of hard drugs; a strong relationship between these variables existed for those low in self-acceptance, and little association was found between these variables for those with high self-acceptance. Newcomb and Felix-Ortiz (1992) also tested the buffering effects of multiple protective factors on the relationship between multiple risk factors and drug use and abuse. Several significant effects were noted, primarily for illicit drugs.

COURSE OF THE DISORDER

We now turn our attention to the course of drug involvement, once drug use has been initiated by children or teenagers. Nonetheless, the particular cause of drug use may directly influence or shape the course of drug use disorders, in that specific reasons for drug involvement may differentially outcomes related to the drug use.

Many who believe that drug abuse and dependence are biogenetically determined, also prefer to consider such disorders as diseases (e.g., Vaillant, 1983), despite significant opposition (e.g., Fingarette, 1988). Such a perspective conforms to the overarching tenet of many antidrug use, self-help support groups (e.g., Alcoholics Anonymous) that *any* abuse of mood-altering substances represents a chronic, progressive, degenerative disease that can never be cured and at best can be controlled through abstinence, in a state of recovery (O'Neill & Barnes, 1987).

Such a strong position obviously creates problems for how to characterize drug use and even abuse among children and teenagers. There is also a major sociopolitical aspect to this dilemma. For instance, under President and Mrs. Reagan's leadership of this country, *any* use of a drug by a teenager had to be defined as abuse, requiring severe and intrusive intervention. Little distinction was allowed between those who may have had a beer at a party or tried marijuana once from those children and teenagers who drink alcohol or use illicit drugs daily, may be dependent on these drugs, and who fail to function adequately in their lives as a result of their use. Conspicuously missing from such clearly biased categorizations of drug users and drug abusers have been those addicted to tobacco, who ultimately experience quite severe, direct long-term consequences of their use in the form of disease and premature mortality.

These philosophical positions are clearly at odds with, if not diametrically opposed to, empirical evidence of the course of adolescent drug use. At one extreme, those youngsters who abstain or who limit themselves to experimentation with various drugs typically do not develop a lifelong addiction, nor do they suffer severe adverse consequences due to this use later in life (e.g., Kandel, Davies, Karus, & Yamaguchi, 1986; Newcomb & Bentler, 1988a, 1988b). In fact, Shedler and Block (1990) showed in a small sample of adolescents with varying histories of substance use that the well-adjusted teenagers were those who experimented with drugs. Abstainers were found to have worse life outcomes, and heavy drug users suffered the most negative consequences. These results support the position that drug use by teenagers is a typical and largely benign manifestation of adolescent growth experiences and quest for experimentation (Peele, 1987). They also suggest that youngsters who refrain from such experimentation may be overly restrained, inflexible, and unable to cope with challenges of later life. This is certainly a controversial position that is blatantly at odds with the sociopolitical reality of the recent Reagan and Bush presidencies (and their associated domestic policies) but also suggests a considered and restrained emphasis on intervention with drug use among children and teenagers.

Consistent across most studies of the course of youthful drug use is the finding that those children and adolescents who develop a lifestyle involving regular and heavy drug use experience severe and even tragic outcomes attributable to this abuse, immediately or later in life. Newcomb and Bentler (1987, 1988a, 1988b) demonstrated direct linear relationships between the level of teenage drug use and later negative consequences. In other words, the more seriously teenagers are involved with drugs, the more adverse are the consequences they experience in later life across several domains, including educational pursuits, work and job conditions, emotional health, social integration, criminal activities, and family establishment and stability. The only exception to this general pattern was that early use of alcohol to the exclusion of all other drugs had a few positive affects on later life that were limited to social relationships and self-feelings, a finding corroborated in other research (e.g., Kandel et al., 1986).

Overwhelming empirical evidence indicates that most teenage users of alcohol or other substances do not become addicted or abusers (Johnston et al., 1991; Kandel & Logan, 1984). Even most of those who indulge heavily as teenagers do not develop substance use disorders later in life. In one study, the magnitude of association between level of consumption and amount of abuse (negative consequences) was examined for alcohol, marijuana, and cocaine (Newcomb, 1992b). There was a substantial association between amount of consumption and abuse consequences for alcohol, a higher degree of association for marijuana, and a perfect association for cocaine. Although no similar study has been conducted for tobacco, it may also rank quite high for addictive, if not abuse, potential.

In their review of adolescent drug use studies, Clayton and Ritter (1985) found that "more often than not, the persons who are using drugs frequently, are multiple drug users" (p. 83). For instance, cocaine users reported significantly higher prevalence rates for all other types of drugs including cigarettes, alcohol, cannabis, over-the-counter medications, hypnotics, stimulants, psychedelics, inhalants, narcotics, and PCP, compared with those who had not used cocaine (Newcomb & Bentler, 1986a). These large differences were found for both females and males and were evident during adolescence as well as young adulthood (Newcomb & Bentler, 1986b). The association between various types of drug use is so high that latent constructs of general polydrug use (Bentler & Newcomb, 1986) and polydrug use in the workplace (Newcomb, 1988) have been identified distinctly and reliably.

Another way to understand drug involvement has been with the progression or stage theory. Kandel (1975) was one of the first researchers to investigate this hypothesis. In general, she found that teenagers initiate use with beer, wine, or cigarettes, progress to the use of hard liquor, may then transition to marijuana, and finally may proceed to the use of other illicit drugs. Of course, these shifts from a lower stage to a higher stage are not guaranteed but are probabalistic (Newcomb & Bentler, 1989). Involvement at one stage does not necessarily lead to involvement at the next stage, but rather, involvement at the next stage is unlikely without prior involvement at the previous stage. This notion has been tested in various cross-sectional and longitudinal studies (Donovan & Jessor, 1983; Newcomb & Bentler, 1986a), with results that generally confirm Kandel's hypotheses, despite some important variations.

Donovan and Jessor (1983) found that problem drinking occurred higher in the progression than general alcohol use. On the other hand, Newcomb and Bentler (1986c) found that several minisequences accounted for drug involvement from early adolescence to young adulthood, when the role of cigarettes and nonprescription medications were included. The mechanism that drives such staging, such as availability, anxiety reduction, peer groups norms, or physiological vulnerability perhaps associated with learning to appreciate the positive effects of a drug, are not known, although there are some hints that these factors may not be the same at all stages. For example, psychopathology has been implicated primarily at later stages or higher levels of drug involvement and not at initiation.

We must conclude, nonetheless, that the course of youthful drug use is varied, unclear, and largely unknown, due to the different type of drugs, drug use pattern, biological vulnerability, and exposure to psychosocial risk and protective factors. It seems prudent that we directly confront the use of drugs by youths but perhaps not overreact to what may be a normal and benign experimentation with experiences that characterizes adolescence. We must not forget that most adult alcoholics and drug abusers began their patterns of abuse in their youth, whereas most youths who try drugs do not progress to abuse nor suffer severe consequences of their ingestion.

FAMILIAL CONTRIBUTIONS

Although biogenetic factors (discussed in the next section) certainly represent parental influences on the drug abuse susceptibility of their children, parents and other family members affect drug use patterns in other important ways. These factors typically represent socialization processes related to parental modeling of drug using behaviors, youths' imitation of parents' behaviors, social reinforcement related to internalization of values and behaviors within the family, and social control aspects of parenting and disciplinary activities of parents. Considerable attention has been given to the important factors of family disruption, quality of parent–child relationships, parental support, parents as socialization agents and value inculcators, and parent use of and attitudes towards drugs (e.g., Johnson & Pandina, 1991; Needle et al., 1990; Newcomb & Bentler, 1988b, 1988c).

In general, family factors have a greater influence on drug-using behavior during preadolescence; in adolescence, peer and friendship networks become more prominent factors (Huba & Bentler, 1980). However, many suggest that parental influences contribute in a substantial manner even at later ages, because they create the basis on which the child constructs his or her social life. Therefore, even though parents may lose their direct effect on their child's drug use as he or she matures through adolescence, they in fact have established the trajectory of their child's evolution and can be considered to have an indirect influence on nearly all later outcomes of the child's development.

This can be seen in the process of parents as models of drug using behavior. For instance, parental alcohol and tobacco use seem to have an indirect effect on their child's use of these drugs as medicated by the child's perception of adult alcohol use (Newcomb, Huba, & Bentler, 1983) and of their peers' use of cigarettes (Hansen et al., 1987). However, during early adolescence, parental use of *illicit* substances may have indirect or direct effects on their child's use of these drugs. For example, Newcomb and

Bentler (1988c) found that more maternal drug use was associated with more socially deviant attitudes and drug use in their children. In addition to actual drug use behavior in the parents, parents' attitudes and restrictions regarding drug use can also affect drug use in their children.

Nondrug aspects of parent and family behavior and functioning may also affect the likelihood of child drug use. Hawkins et al. (1992) categorized these more general family conditions into three groups: (a) poor and inconsistent family management practices, (b) family conflict, and (c) low bonding to family. Numerous factors related to inconsistent disciplinary and authoritarian parenting practices, low and poor quality of parent interaction and involvement with their children, and low aspirations and expectations for their children all reflect poor family management qualities that increase the chances of adolescent involvement with drugs. Family conflict as reflected in marital discord, divorce and separation, and general family conflict also increase the likelihood that children may turn to drugs in attempts to cope with such stress and unreliability (Newcomb & Harlow, 1986; Richardson, 1993). These family characteristics often prevent secure bonding of the child to the family and as a result may also contribute to youthful drug use, as evidence by higher drug use among those families that lack closeness, maternal involvement, and positive parent–child relationships (Jessor & Jessor, 1977; Kandel, 1980). Conversely, close, supportive, involved, but not overly intrusive family relationships may protect children from the allure of drug use.

It is clear that many factors associated with family functioning and behaviors affect children's risk of drug use; other factors serve to protect youth from influences that serve to encourage drug use. Although the child's first use of drugs typically occurs in peer or social settings, the emergence of this event has been established many years earlier in the interactions and connections with parents and other family members (Newcomb, 1992a).

PSYCHOPHYSIOLOGICAL AND GENETIC INFLUENCES

Although literature exists regarding genetic factors related to substance use, the focus of this work is decidedly on the heritability of alcoholism. Our overview certainly reflects that bias. Psychophysiological influences, in turn, relate particularly to the hedonic effects of drug use that encourage continued and accelerated use.

Wise (1988) presented a comprehensive review of psychomotor stimulant theory, arguing that drug-induced stimulant effects are common to a wide array of popular drugs of addiction, including amphetamine, opiates, cannabis, alcohol, barbiturates, and phencyclidine (PCP). Psychomotor effects are distinguished from simple motoric responses in that environmental cues shape both the behavior and affective response to the ingestion of addictive substances. The common physiologic mechanism of addiction for all of these is positive reinforcement (as described previously in Causes of the Disorder), and extant evidence suggests that the same mechanism mediates the positive reinforcing effects of these drugs. Positive reinforcement refers to the activation of brain dopamine systems such that the metabolism or reuptake of dopamine within the medial forebrain bundle is inhibited, producing a magnification of the intensity of most pleasurable sensations. Such effects may be of varying duration but are generally remembered for a long time and highly rewarding.

Negative reinforcing effects, in turn, depend on the aftereffects of stimulation but appear to be of relatively brief duration and may not depend on dopaminergic activation, but rather depletion. Further, negative reinforcement may result from a wider array of drug actions (e.g., anxiolytic, analgesic, sedative) not necessarily linked to physical dependence and independent of positive reinforcement.

There is substantial evidence that certain patterns of alcohol abuse are influenced by genetic or biophysiological substrates (e.g., Goodwin, 1976; Vaillant, 1983). However, the magnitude and mechanism of such factors have not been clearly established. A growing body of literature has also shown that biogenetic factors play an important role in the use and abuse of drugs other than alcohol, in both animal (e.g., Crabbe, McSwigan, & Belknap, 1985) and human studies (e.g., Cadoret, 1992; Merikangas, Rounsaville, & Prusoff, 1992).

Genetic influences clearly play an important, but not exclusive, role in the etiology of alcoholism (Crabbe et al., 1985; Zucker & Gomberg, 1986). Among the best known is the work of Goodwin (1976, 1985). Using adoptees from alcoholic and nonalcoholic fathers in Denmark, he determined that sons of alcoholics were at four times greater risk for developing alcoholism than their peers with a nonalcoholic father. Twin and animal studies have also demonstrated a genetic factor for alcoholism. Nevertheless, even monozygotic twins exhibit far from 100% concordance for alcoholism (Crabbe et al., 1985), establishing that alcoholism is not totally genetic and that other personal, environmental, and societal factors play important roles (Newcomb, in press).

Two patterns of genetic transmission of alcoholism are described (Bohman, Sigvardsson, & Cloninger, 1981; Cloninger, Bohman, & Sigvardsson, 1981). Type I is called *milieu limited* and involves both genetic and environmental factors, affects both men and women, has a late onset, and is associated with few or no alcohol or criminal problems in the parents. Type II is called *male limited* and is affected little by the environment, is restricted to male transmission and early onset, is associated with criminal behavior, and is related to fathers with severe alcoholism, extensive treatment, and extensive criminality. Although these heritability patterns are interesting and informative, they have received substantial criticism on methodological bases (e.g., Searles, 1988) and must be considered with caution. They also tell us little about biogenetic causes of women's drug abuse (Lex, 1991).

An important question concerns what precisely is inherited if there is a genetic influence for alcoholism or other drug abuse. Research evidence, primarily but not exclusively based on animal models, suggests at least two mechanisms (e.g., Bardo & Risner, 1985). Those at genetic risk for drug abuse may inherit a biological vulnerability to the hedonic affects of the drug, so for them the drug effect is more attractive then for others. On the other hand, those at genetic risk for drug abuse may not experience withdrawal effects as severely as those not at-risk (e.g., less likelihood of hangover). However, these and other proposed mechanisms must be evaluated more conclusively in further research.

CURRENT TREATMENTS

Primary Prevention

Prevention programs are aimed at discouraging teens from initiating drug use, at expectations for abstinence, and at halting the progression from experimental to more frequent use or from regular to abusive patterns of drug use. Hawkins et al. (1992) reviewed an extensive range of contemporary programs. Strategies aimed at affecting the availability of illicit drugs and (legal) consequences for their use generally have only a modest impact on adolescent use patterns. In contrast, programs designed to change social norms are fairly successful, particularly media saturation designed to increase the development of antidrug/alcohol attitudes among high-risk (13-to 17-year-old) teens. Social influence resistance programs are generally peer-led efforts to teach teens ways to resist peer pressure to use drugs, particularly refusal skills and social/life skills among children and preadolescents (e.g., Botvin, 1986). Programs designed to target early (family-based) risk factors include parenting skills training, early childhood, and family support programs (e.g., DeMarsh & Kumpfer, 1986) and are increasingly designed to address community-specific needs or risks for youthful drug use (e.g., Myers et al., 1992; Schinke et al., 1988).

In their independent meta-analyses of prevention programs in the United States and Canada, Bangert-Drowns (1988) and Tobler (1986) concluded that peer-directed prevention programs appear to have the greatest impact on teenagers' attitudes and knowledge about drug use. Tobler (1986) argued that programs designed to provide teens with alternative, prosocial activities (e.g., community service) that may be more appealing than drug use and activities designed to increase personal competence (in such areas as reading and job and physical skills) have demonstrated utility in changing attitudes and behavior among high-risk adolescents, such as delinquents and those experiencing significant academic problems (e.g., Bry, 1982; Swisher & Hu, 1983). Nonetheless, changes in attitudes and knowledge do *not* necessarily lead to behavioral changes. Rather, Bangert-Drowns (1988) concluded that shifts in patterns of drug use, particularly among former heavy drug users, were primarily a function of voluntary participation in a drug resistance education program and largely associated with tobacco only.

Outpatient Treatment

Many feel that some form of outpatient therapy be considered for all adolescents for whom regular drug use or early signs of abuse are evident. Some form of family-based psychotherapy is viewed as optimal, given the prominence of the family in shaping adolescents' attitudes and behavior. Such candidates should have no (a) *acute* medical or psychiatric problems that may require intensive, inpatient treatment; (b) chronic medical problems that would preclude outpatient therapy; and (c) prior outpatient treatment failures. Nonetheless, "outpatient therapy is noted to be fraught with denial of the problem by the client and/or family, basic adolescent mistrust of adult authority, continued association with addicts peer groups, unwillingness to abstain, and lack of motivation. These *must* be considered in the treatment choice" (Chatlos, 1991b, p. 236). Both the adolescent and family need to have appropriate motivation to engage with the treatment process. In addition, both target teens and family members are *strongly* encouraged or required to attend 12-step support group meetings (e.g., Alcoholics Anonymous, Alanon, or related groups).

Inpatient Treatment

Inpatient treatment of adolescent substance users is best limited to hard-core abusers, the approximately 6% to 10% of chemical-using teens who meet criteria for dependence. Such an adolescent is described in the following case history from Chatlos (1991b, pp. 240–241):

> A fifteen-year-old female with a history of parental divorce at age 7 followed by multiple geographic moves was admitted with extensive cocaine, marijuana, and alcohol abuse. She was diagnosed as having conduct disorder with a history since junior high school of progressively increasing antisocial behaviors, poor school motivation, truancy, shoplifting, stealing, runaway episodes, and physical fights with involvement with knives. She also had a history of being raped at age 13, and since then had made a serious suicide attempt. She has also been involved for 2 years with satanism, including daily rituals and prior animal sacrifice.
>
> She expressed motivation in treatment, but as she dealt with her involvement in satanism she developed extreme anxiety with sweating, restlessness, and palpitations. During some group sessions this would occur and panic attacks would necessitate removal from groups. Since this appeared to have a separation anxiety component, she was started on imipramine, which was increased to 100 mg/day. During the next 5 days, her mood fluctuated with increasingly frightening dreams and thoughts about attacking a patient with a knife. As she was less overwhelmed by her panic while on medications, issues were worked through regarding rage at her father, the desire for power and revenge associated with satanism, and the guilt and fear of dying associated with betrayal of satan. Breakthroughs into feelings of loneliness and self-hatred were sufficient to continue treatment without further panic attacks.

Most adolescent inpatient drug programs build on the experience of the Minnesota model of adult drug treatment programs, that emphasizes:

1. structured, residential stays (generally 21 to 60 days);
2. the understanding of dependency as a disease based on the idiosyncratic response of the adolescent rather than on the extent of his or her use;
3. an ongoing commitment to an Alcoholics Anonymous-like 12-step recovery support and treatment system (with lectures and group sessions as primary components) and abstinence from *all* mood-altering substances (with the conspicuous exclusion of tobacco and caffeine) and appropriately prescribed medications;
4. parent or family participation (parent education, family therapy, multi-family therapy, or support groups and attendance at Alanon or similar self-help support groups); and
5. extensive (typically 6 months or longer) participation in affiliated outpatient treatment immediately following discharge.

In addition to these relatively "traditional" inpatient treatment modes are a range of structured, long-term drug treatment options that range from highly structured inpatient treatment to therapeutic communities such as Synanon (which may not, in fact, be limited to chemically addicted adolescents). The latter are often used as halfway homes between inpatient treatment and return to the family home or to the community (see Wheeler & Malmquist, 1987).

The family's prominent position at each level of intervention described previously owes to its impact on child and adolescent development. An overarching premise within most models for family therapy is that disruptive behavior (as adolescent drug abuse is viewed) serves as a sign or symptom of more significant disturbance within the functional or structural composition of the family. Corrective intervention requires direct involvement of all prominent family members and serves to address both the *identified* problem (teen's drug use/abuse) and the underlying family-based disturbance.

Criticism.   Many challenges to contemporary inpatient drug treatment programs for adolescents have been offered, charging that more harm than good may result from the diagnosis and treatment of the chemically addicted teen (Peele, 1987). The former gains support from evidence that drug use typically declines during the late teens and early 20s, at least among achievement-oriented samples (e.g., Johnston et al., 1991; Newcomb & Bentler, 1986a). Further, Minnesota-model drug treatment programs emphasize powerlessness and interdependence that are not well matched to the social and emotional development of adolescents. A preoccupation with lifelong drug abstinence is not likely a realistic goal for adolescents and may detract from the development of coping skills that would improve their relationships within their primary social environments. Peele (1987) argued instead for a focus on the reduction of children and adolescents' exposure to factors that increase the risk for later drug use.

Treatment Efficacy.   Few systematic reviews of treatment outcomes among young drug abusers are available. Extant reviews, however, suggest that patient characteristics predictive of favorable short-term (within 2 years after discharge) outcomes are being female, having fewer pretreatment legal difficulties, a lower general delinquency history, less pathological scores on standard personality inventories (e.g., MMPI), and a higher verbal intelligence (Knapp, Templer, Cannon, & Dobson, 1991). Feigelman, Hyman, Amann, and Feigelman (1990) reported that among male young adults 6 years postdischarge from day treatment, poorer outcomes were associated with prior polydrug use, a poor work history, low educational attainment, and poorer psychological health. High-volume posttreatment drug use was also associated with living in their parents' home. Although it is clear that further research in this area is needed to understand more completely the impact of treatment on adolescent patients, these outcomes are generally consistent with previous descriptions of long-term consequences of adolescent drug use (Newcomb & Bentler, 1989).

SUMMARY

The use and abuse of mood-altering drugs by children and adolescents are related to a wide array of various risk factors. Even though very few children experiment to any extent with abusable substances prior to the sixth grade, such drug involvement by these children and older teenagers is of grave concern given the serious risks that such behaviors represent. Most adolescents experiment with alcohol prior to age 18; nearly half also experiment with at least one illicit drug by this age. However, despite common lore and differential media coverage, there are no unequivocal ethnic differences in rates of use, though drug of choice may vary as a function of SES, gender, ethnicity, regional setting, and population density. National surveys indicate that most types of drug use have decreased since the early 1980s, and even rates of cocaine use have consistently decreased since the mid-1980s, although there is significant concern that these patterns may not reflect all segments of the population (inner-city youth, school dropouts, gang members).

Considerable controversy rages regarding the definition of the *use* and *abuse* of licit and illicit drugs among children and adolescents, fueled by contemporary politics. The diagnostic criteria outlined in the *DSM–III–R* describe adult drug using behavior and consequences, yet these are typically used to define drug abuse among adolescents as well.

Drug-using behavior is clearly a multidetermined set of behaviors. Certainly previous experience with drugs is the best predictor of later drug use. Peer influences (such as modeling of attitudes favorable to drug use) are consistently described as the second most powerful psychosocial predictor of adolescent use. Other factors are clearly important, are certainly interrelated, and may be specific predictors of drug use, other problem behaviors, or both as reflected in a syndrome of general deviance.

Family influences primarily affect the emergence of drug abuse and occur most directly at younger ages (i.e., children) in the form of biogenetic vulnerability, modeling of drug use, and socialization experiences. At older ages, family influences continue to affect drug use of adolescents but primarily indirectly via personality, attitudes, and behavior of the teenager and their perceptions of and response to their larger social environment, particularly peers.

Research supports stage theories that generally suggest that youthful drug use progress from experimental use of licit substances (beer, wine, or cigarettes), through hard liquor, to marijuana, to illicit drugs other than marijuana, and to polydrug use. Such a pattern is neither rigidly defined nor linear in nature; further, many who are fairly regular or heavy users in adolescence *discontinue* that use early in adulthood. Nonetheless, as indicated previously prior behavior is the best predictor of later drug using behavior.

Intervention occurs at many levels or stages in the course of an adolescent's history of drug use. Prevention strategies are aimed both at the nonusers at-risk for later exposure to drugs at some level and those who have already been exposed to drug use at some level and who could benefit from additional information and or skills development. Peer-directed approaches appear to be the most promising of these strategies. Both outpatient and inpatient treatment strategies are limited both by the degree to which parents or primary guardians become active (and supportive) participants in the process and by the degree to which the adolescent patient is able and willing to accept the concept of himself or herself as helpless over the influence of a mood-altering substance (a critical underlying assumption of all 12-step based treatment and support programs). An additional and consistent criticism of adolescent drug treatment regards the fact that many who are subjected to treatment and coercive interventions may not, in fact, be in need of this attention. As a result, they may suffer long-term consequences of inappropriate manipulation and exposure to true drug abusers and general adolescent deviants. Such intrusive interventions may be drastically more harmful than the presumed cause or need for treatment (Peele, 1987).

In short, despite evidence suggestive of a consistent decline in adolescent drug use since the early to mid-1980's, most continue to experiment with and use both licit and illicit drugs at some time before their 19th birthday. Future directions in research and intervention need to include: (a) clear delineation of protective factors; (b) precise identification of *at-risk* populations; (c) descriptive/diagnostic criteria tailored specifically to adolescent populations (such that behavioral norms and political/economic realities are considered); (d) tailoring of prevention and treatment strategies to specific populations (as a function of ethnicity, age, gender, regional factors); and (e) gauged to the true *need* for intervention.

REFERENCES

American Psychiatric Association. (1987). *Diagnostic and statistical manual of mental disorders (3rd rev. ed.* Washington, DC: Author.

American Psychiatric Association. (1993).*Diagnostic and statistical manual of mental disorders: Draft criteria*. Washington, DC: Author.

Anglin, T. M. (1987). Interviewing guidelines for the clinical evaluation of adolescent substance abuse. *Pediatric Clinics of North America, 34*, 381-397.

Bangert-Drowns, R. L. (1988). The effects of school-based substance abuse education—a meta-analysis. *Journal of Drug Education, 18*, 243-264.

Bardo, M. T., & Risner, M. E. (1985). Biochemical substrates of drug abuse. In M. Galizio & S. A. Maisto (Eds.), *Determinants of substance abuse: Biological, psychological, and environmental factors* (pp. 65-99). New York: Plenum.

Bentler, P. M. (1980). Multivariate analysis with latent variables: Causal modeling. *Annual Review of Psychology, 31*, 419-456.

Bentler, P. M., & Newcomb, M. D. (1986). Personality, sexual behavior, and drug use revealed through latent variable methods. *Clinical Psychology Review, 6*, 363-385.

Bohman, M., Sigvardsson, S., & Cloninger, C. R. (1981). Maternal inheritance of alcohol abuse: Cross fostering analysis of adopted women. *Archives of General Psychiatry, 38*, 965-969.

Botvin, G. J. (1986). Substance abuse prevention research: Recent developments and future directions. *Journal of School Health, 56*, 369-374.

Brook, J. S., Cohen, P., Whiteman, M., & Gordon, A. S. (1992). Psychosocial risk factors in the transition from moderate to heavy use or abuse of drugs. In M. D. Glantz and R. Pickens (Eds.), *Vulnerability to drug abuse* (pp. 359-388). Washington, DC: American Psychological Association.

Brook, J. S., Whiteman, M., & Gordon, A. S. (1983). Stages of drug use in adolescence: Personality, peer, and family correlates. *Developmental Psychology, 19*, 269-277.

Bry, B. (1982). Reducing the incidence of adolescent problems through preventive intervention: One and five-year follow-up. *American Journal of Community Psychology, 10*, 265-275.

Bry, B. H., McKeon, P., & Pandina, R. (1982). Extent of drug use as a function of number of risk factors. *Journal of Abnormal Psychology, 91*, 273-279.

Cadoret, R. J. (1992). Genetic and environmental factors in initiation of drug use and the transition to abuse. In M. D. Glantz & R. Pickens (Eds.), *Vulnerability to drug abuse* (pp. 99-114). Washington, DC: American Psychological Association.

Carman, R. S. (1979). Motivations for drug use and problematic outcomes among rural junior high school students. *Addictive Behaviors, 4*, 91-93.

Chatlos, J. C. (1991a). Adolescent drug and alcohol addiction: Diagnosis and assessment. In N. S. Miller (Ed.), *Comprehensive handbook of drug and alcohol addiction* (pp. 211-233). New York: Marcel Dekker.

Chatlos, J. C. (1991b). Adolescent drug and alcohol addiction: Intervention and treatment. In N. S. Miller (Ed.), *Comprehensive handbook of drug and alcohol addiction* (pp. 235-253). New York: Marcel Dekker.

Clayton, R. R., & Ritter, C. (1985). The epidemiology of alcohol and drug abuse among adolescents. *Advances in Alcohol and Substance Abuse, 4*, 69-97.

Cloninger, C. R., Bohman, M., & Sigvardsson, S. (1981). Inheritance of alcohol abuse: Cross fostering analysis of adopted men. *Archives of General Psychiatry, 38*, 861-868.

Crabbe, J. C., McSwigan, J. D., & Belknap, J. K. (1985). The role of genetics in substance abuse. In M. Galizio & S. A. Maisto (Eds.), *Determinants of substance abuse: Biological, psychological, and environmental factors* (pp. 13-64). New York: Plenum.

DeMarsh, J., & Kumpfer, K. L. (1986). Family-oriented interventions for the prevention of chemical dependency in children and adolescents. In S. Griswold-Ezekoye, K. L. Kumpfer, & W. J. Bukoski (Eds.), *Childhood and chemical abuse: Prevention and intervention* (pp. 117-151). New York: Haworth.

Donovan, J. E., & Jessor, R. (1983). Problem drinking and the dimensions of involvement with drugs: A Guttman scalogram analysis of adolescent drug use. *American Journal of Public Health*, *73*, 543–552.

Donovan, J. E., & Jessor, R. (1985). Structure of problem behavior in adolescence and young adulthood. *Journal of Consulting and Clinical Psychology*, *53*, 890–904.

Feigelman, W., Hyman, M. M., Amann, K., & Feigelman, B. (1990). Correlates of persisting drug use among former youth multiple drug abuse patients. *Journal of Psychoactive Drugs*, *22*, 63–75.

Fingarette, H. (1988). *Heavy drinking: he myth of alcoholism as a disease*. Berkeley: University of California Press.

Friedman, A. S., & Utada, A. (1989). A method for diagnosing and planning the treatment of adolescent drug abusers (the Adolescent Drug Abuse Diagnosis [ADAD] instrument). *Journal of Drug Education*, *19*, 285–312.

Glantz, M., & Pickens, R. (Eds.). (1992). *Vulnerability to drug abuse*. Washington, DC: American Psychological Association.

Goodwin, D. W. (1976). *Is alcoholism hereditary?* New York: Oxford University Press.

Goodwin, D. W. (1985). Alcoholism and genetics: The sins of the fathers. *Archives of General Psychiatry*, *42*, 171–174.

Hansen, W. B., Graham, J. W., Sobel, J. L., Shelton, D. R., Flay, B. R., & Johnson, C. A. (1987). The consistency of peer and parent influences on tobacco, alcohol, and marijuana use among young adolescents. *Journal of Behavioral Medicine*, *10*, 559–579.

Harrison, P., Hoffmann, N. G., & Edwall, G. E. (1989). Sexual abuse correlates: Similarities between male and female adolescents in chemical dependency treatment. *Journal of Adolescent Research*, *4*, 385–399.

Hawkins, J. D., Catalano, R. F., & Miller, J. Y. (1992). Risk and protective factors for alcohol and other drug problems in adolescence and early adulthood: Implications for substance abuse problems. *Psychological Bulletin*, *112*, 64–105.

Huba, G. J., & Bentler, P. M. (1980). The role of peer and adult models for drug taking at different stages in adolescence. *Journal of Youth and Adolescence, 9*, 449–465.

Hughes, T. L. (1989). Models and perspectives of addiction: Implications for treatment. *Nursing Clinics of North America*, *24*, 1–12.

Jessor, R., & Jessor, S. L. (1977). *Problem behavior and psychosocial development*. New York: Academic Press.

Johnson, V., & Pandina, R. J. (1991). Effects of the family environment on adolescent substance use, delinquency, and coping styles. *American Journal of Drug and Alcohol Abuse*, *17*, 71–88.

Johnson, L. D., O'Malley, P. M., & Bachman, J. G. (1991). *Drug use among American high school seniors, college students and young adults, 1975–1990*. Rockville, MD: National Institute on Drug Abuse.

Julien, R. M. (1992). *A primer of drug action* (6th ed.) New York: Freeman.

Kaminer, Y., Bukstein, O., & Tarter, R. E. (1991). The Teen-Addiction Severity Index: Rationale and reliability. *International Journal of the Addictions*, *26*, 219–226.

Kandel, D. B. (1975). Stages in adolescent involvement in drug use. *Science*, *190*, 912–914.

Kandel, D. B. (1980). Drug and drinking behavior among youth. *Annual Review of Sociology*, *6*, 235–285.

Kandel, D. B., Davies, M., Karus, D., & Yamaguchi, K. (1986). The consequences in young adulthood of adolescent drug involvement. *Archives of General Psychiatry*, *43*, 746–754.

Kandel, D. B., & Logan, J. A. (1984). Patterns of drug use from adolescence to young adulthood: I: Periods of risk for initiation, continued use, and discontinuation. *American Journal of Public Health*, *74*, 660–666.

Knapp, J. E., Templer, D. I., Cannon, W. G., & Dobson, S. (1991). Variables associated with success in an adolescent drug treatment program. *Adolescence*, *26*, 305–317.

Lettieri, D. J. (1985). Drug abuse: A review of explanations and models of explanation. *Advances in Alcohol and Substance Abuse*, *4*, 9–40.

Lex, B. W., (1991). Some gender differences in alcohol and polysubstance users. *Health Psychology*, *10*, 121–132.

Maddahian, E., Newcomb, M. D., & Bentler, P. M. (1986). Adolescent's substance use: Impact of ethnicity, income, and availability. *Advances in Alcohol and Substance Abuse*, *5*, 63–78.

Marlatt, G. A. (1992). Substance abuse: Implications of a biopsychosocial model for prevention, treatment, and relapse prevention. In J. Grabowski & G. R. VandenBos (Eds.), *Psychopharmacology: Basic mechanisms and applied interventions* (pp. 127–162). Washington, DC: American Psychological Association.

Marlatt, G. A., Baer, J. S., Donovan, D. M., & Kivlahan, D. R. (1988). Addictive behaviors: Etiology and treatment. *Annual Review of Psychology, 39*, 223–252.

McGee, L., & Newcomb, M. D. (1992). General deviance syndrome: Expanded hierarchical evaluations at four ages from early adolescence to adulthood. *Journal of Consulting and Clinical Psychology, 60*, 766–776.

Medina, A. S., Wallace, H. M., Ralph, N. R. & Goldstein, H. (1982). Adolescent health in Alameda county. *Journal of Adolescent Health Care, 2*, 175–182.

Merikangas, K. R., Rounsaville, B. J., & Prusoff, B. A. (1992). Familial factors in vulnerability to substance abuse. In M.D. Glantz & R. Pickens (Eds.), *Vulnerability to drug abuse* (pp. 75–98). Washington, DC: American Psychological Association.

Myers, H. F., Alvy, K. T., Arrington, A., Richardson, M. A., Marigna, M., Robbin, H., Main, M., & Newcomb, M. D. (1992). The impact of a parent training program on inner-city African-American families. *Journal of Community Psychology, 20*, 132–147.

National Institute on Drug Abuse (1991). *National household survey on drug abuse: Main findings*. Rockville, MD: Author.

Needle, R. H., Su, S. S., & Doherty, W. J. (1990). Divorce, remarriage, and adolescent substance use: A prospective longitudinal study. *Journal of Marriage and the Family, 52*, 157–169.

Newcomb, M. D. (1988). *Drug use in the workplace: Risk factors for disruptive substance use among young adults*. Dover, MA: Auburn House.

Newcomb, M. D. (1990). What structural equation modeling can tell us about social support. In B. R. Sarason, I. G. Sarason, & G. R. Pierce (Eds.), *Social support: An interactional view* (pp. 26–63). New York: Wiley.

Newcomb, M. D. (1992a). Substance abuse and control in the United States: Ethical and legal issues. *Social Science and Medicine, 35*, 471–479.

Newcomb, M. D. (1992b). Understanding the multidimensional nature of drug use and abuse: The role of consumption, risk factors, and protective factors. In M. D. Glantz & R. Pickens (Eds.), *Vulnerability to drug abuse* (pp. 255–297). Washington, DC: American Psychological Association.

Newcomb, M.D. (in press). Families, peers, and adolescent alcohol abuse: A paradigm to study multiple causes, mechanisms, and outcomes. In R. Zucker, G. Boyd, & J. Howard (Eds.), *Development of alcohol problems: Exploring the biopsychosocial matrix of risk*. Rockville, MD: National Institute of Alcoholism and Alcohol Abuse.

Newcomb, M. D., & Bentler, P. M. (1986a). Cocaine use among adolescents: Longitudinal associations with social context, psychopathology, and use of other substances. *Addictive Behaviors, 11*, 263–273.

Newcomb, M. D., & Bentler, P. M. (1986b). Cocaine use among young adults. *Advances in Alcohol and Substance Abuse, 6*, 73–96.

Newcomb, M. D., & Bentler, P. M. (1986c). Frequency and sequence of drug use: A longitudinal study from early adolescence to young adulthood. *Journal of Drug Education, 16*, 101–120.

Newcomb, M. D., & Bentler, P. M. (1987). The impact of late adolescent substance use on young adult health status and utilization of health services: A structural equation model over four years. *Social Science and Medicine, 24*, 71–82.

Newcomb, M. D., & Bentler, P. M. (1988a). *Consequences of adolescent drug use: Impact on the lives of young adults*. Beverly Hills, CA: Sage.

Newcomb, M. D., & Bentler, P. M. (1988b). Impact of adolescent drug use and social support on problems of young adults: A longitudinal study. *Journal of Abnormal Psychology, 97*, 64–75.

Newcomb, M. D., & Bentler, P. M. (1988c). The impact of family context, deviant attitudes, and emotional distress on adolescent drug use: Longitudinal latent variable analyses of mothers and their children. *Journal of Research in Personality, 22*, 154–176.

Newcomb, M. D., & Bentler, P. M. (1989). Substance use and abuse among children and teenagers. *American Psychologist, 44*, 242–248.

Newcomb, M. D., & Bentler, P. M. (1990). Antecedents and consequences of cocaine use: An eight-year study from early adolescence to young adulthood. In L. Robins (Ed.), *Straight and devious pathways from childhood to adulthood* (pp. 158–181). New York: Cambridge Press.

Newcomb, M. D., & Felix-Ortiz, M. (1992). Multiple protective and risk factors for drug use and abuse: Cross-sectional and prospective findings. *Journal of Personality and Social Psychology, 63*, 280–296.

Newcomb, M. D., & Harlow, L. L. (1986). Life events and substance use among adolescents: Mediating effects of perceived loss of control and meaninglessness in life. *Journal of Personality and Social Psychology, 51*, 564–577.

Newcomb, M. D., Huba, G. J., & Bentler, P. M. (1983). Mother's influence on the drug use of their children:

Confirmatory tests of direct modeling and mediational theories. *Developmental Psychology, 19*, 714–726.

Newcomb, M. D., Maddahian, E., & Bentler, P. M. (1986). Risk factor for drug use among adolescents: Concurrent and longitudinal analyses. *American Journal of Public Health, 76*, 525–531.

Newcomb, M. D., Maddahian, E., Skager, R., & Bentler, P. M. (1987). Substance abuse and psychosocial risk factors among teenagers: Associations with sex, age, ethnicity, and type of school. *American Journal of Drug and Alcohol Abuse, 13*, 413–433.

Newcomb, M. D., & McGee, L. (1991). The influence of sensation seeking on general deviance and specific problem behaviors from adolescence to young adulthood. *Journal of Personality and Social Psychology, 61*, 614–628.

Oetting, E. R., & Beauvais, F. (1990). Adolescent drug use: Findings of national and local surveys. *Journal of Consulting and Clinical Psychology, 58*, 385–394.

O'Neill, S. F., & Barnes, H. N. (1987). Alcoholics Anonymous. In H. N. Barnes, M. D. Aronaon, & T. L. Delbanco (Eds.), *Alcoholism: A guide to the primary care physician* (pp. 93–101). New York: Springer-Verlag.

Paton, S., Kessler, R. C., & Kandel, D. B. (1977). Depressive mood and illegal drug use: A longitudinal analysis. *Journal of Genetic Psychology, 131*, 267–289.

Peele, S. (1987). What can we expect from treatment of adolescent drug and alcohol abuse? *Pediatrician, 14*, 62–69.

Rahdert, E. R. (1991). *The adolescent assessment/referral system: Manual.* Rockville, MD: National Institute on Drug Abuse.

Richardson, M. A. (1993). *Psychosocial predictors and consequences of recent drug use among Anglo and Hispanic children and adolescents: An evaluation of social development theory.* Unpublished doctoral dissertation, University of California, Los Angeles.

Scheier, L. M., & Newcomb, M. D. (1991). Psychosocial predictors of drug use initiation and escalation: An expansion of the multiple risk factors hypothesis using longitudinal data. *Contemporary Drug Problems, 18*, 31–73.

Schinke, S. P., Botvin, G. J., Trimble, J. E., Orlandi, M. A., Gilchrist, L. D., & Locklear, V. S. (1988). Preventing substance abuse among American-Indian adolescents: A bicultural competence skills approach. *Journal of Counseling Psychology, 35*, 87–90.

Searles, J. S. (1988). The role of genetics in the pathogenesis of alcoholism. *Journal of Abnormal Psychology, 97*, 153–167.

Shedler, J., & Block, J. (1990). Adolescent drug use and psychological health: A longitudinal inquiry. *American Psychologist, 45*, 612–630.

Stacy, A. W., Newcomb, M. D., & Bentler, P. M. (1992). Interactive and higher-order effects on social influences on drug use. *Journal of Health and Social Behavior, 33*, 226–241.

Swisher, J., & Hu, T. (1983). Alternatives to drug abuse: Some are and some are not. In T. Glynn, C. Leudefeld, & J. Ludford (Eds.), *Preventing adolescent drug abuse: Intervention strategies* (pp. 141–153). Washington, DC: U. S. Government Printing Office.

Tobler, N. (1986). Meta-analysis of 143 adolescent drug prevention programs: Quantitative outcome results of program participants compared to control or comparison group. *Journal of Drug Issues, 4*, 537–567.

Tolan, P. (1988). Socioeconomic, family, and social stress correlates of adolescent antisocial and delinquent behavior. *Journal of Abnormal Child Psychology, 16*, 317–331.

Vaillant, G. E. (1983). *The natural history of alcoholism: Causes, patterns, and paths to recovery.* Cambridge, MA: Harvard University Press.

Wheeler, K., & Malmquist, J. (1987). Treatment approaches in adolescent chemical dependency. *Pediatric Clinics of North America, 34*, 437–447.

Winters, K. C. (1992). Development of an adolescent alcohol and other drug abuse screening scale: Personal Experience Screening Questionnaire. *Addictive Behavior, 17*, 479–490.

Wise, R. A. (1988). The neurobiology of cracing: Implications for the understanding and treatment of addiction. *Journal of Abnormal Psychology, 97*, 118–132.

Zucker, R. A., & Gomberg, E. S. L. (1986). Etiology of alcoholism reconsidered: Biopsychosocial approach. *American Psychologist, 41*, 783–793.

Author Index

A

Aaronson, C., 244, 250
Abate, F., 69, 85
Abichandani, C., 202, 211
Abidin, R., 123, 130
Abikoff, H., 194, 210
Aboitiz, F., 323, 332
Abrams, A. R., 403, 410
Abramson, L. Y., 260, 278
Achenbach, T. M., 7, 18, 30, 31, 35, 44, 46, 106, 107, 110–113, 115, 118, 130, 132, 166, 169
Ackerman, P. T., 69, 72, 75, 83
Adams, D., 197, 207, 212
Adams, P., 202, 205, 207–209, 211
Adan, A., 345, 349
Addonizio, G., 205, 208
Adrian, C., 97, 102
Agar, M., 221, 227
Agras, W. S., 243, 249, 385, 386, 389, 390
Ainsworth, M. D. S., 53, 56
Albee, G. W., 213, 227
Alder, R. J., 222, 230
Alessandri, M., 313, 316
Alessi, N. E., 197, 212
Alexander, J., 343, 349
Alicke, M. D., 109, 126, 133
Allen, A., 158, 169
Allen, M. H., 141, 145–148, 154, 155
Allen, R., 335, 351
Allison, P. D., 96, 102
Allred, E., 323, 332

Alvy, K. T., 424, 430
Amado, H., 23, 36
Aman, M. G., 196, 197, 201, 207, 208, 212, 329, 330, 331
Amanat, E., 263, 278
Amann, K., 426, 428
Ambrosini, P. J., 198, 208, 211
Ambronisi, R., 271, 276, 281
American Association for the Study of the Feeble-minded, 297, 302
American Psychiatric Association, 15, 16, 18, 22, 23, 24, 25, 28, 35, 44, 46, 88, 101, 117, 130, 138, 153, 154, 190, 204, 206, 208, 222, 227, 235, 236, 238, 239, 242, 250, 255–257, 278, 305, 309, 316, 319, 321, 324, 326, 331, 334, 335, 349, 354, 356, 358, 359, 374, 377–379, 381, 389, 414, 428
Ammerman, R. T., 325, 331
Anastopoulos, A. D., 110, 130
Anderson, J. C., 271, 278, 338, 352
Anderson, L. T., 209
Andreasen, N. C., 28, 35
Andrews, J., 273, 275, 280
Angel, I., 196, 204, 210
Anglin, T. M., 415, 428
Anker, J. M., 96, 104
Anllo-Vento, L., 70, 83
Anthony, J. C., 215, 228
Appelbaum, M., 126, 130
Arana, G. W., 32, 35, 197, 200, 201, 207, 208
Arbitell, M. R., 377, 390
Arend, R., 53, 54, 56, 57

433

Subject Index

451